IT

6

/ES

POLITICAL DEVELOPMENT
IN MODERN JAPAN

This is the fourth in a series of six volumes published by Princeton University Press for the Conference on Modern Japan of the Association for Asian Studies, Inc. The others in the series are:

Changing Japanese Attitudes Toward Modernization, edited by Marius B. Jansen (1965)

The State and Economic Enterprise in Japan, edited by William W. Lockwood (1965)

Aspects of Social Change in Modern Japan, edited by R. P. Dore (1967)

Tradition and Modernization in Japanese Culture, edited by Donald Shively

Dilemmas of Growth in Prewar Japan, edited by James Morley

Political Development in Modern Japan

Edited by Robert E. Ward

CONTRIBUTORS

ARDATH W. BURKS

ALBERT M. CRAIG

ROGER F. HACKETT

JOHN WHITNEY HALL

DAN FENNO HENDERSON

NOBUTAKA IKE

TAKESHI ISHIDA

MARIUS B. JANSEN

ROBERT A. SCALAPINO

BERNARD S. SILBERMAN

KURT STEINER

KIYOAKI TSUJI

ROBERT E. WARD

PRINCETON UNIVERSITY PRESS

PRINCETON, NEW JERSEY

Foreword

SCHOLARLY STUDIES of Japan have had a remarkable growth in the United States and other English-speaking countries since the end of World War II. To some extent this has been the natural result of the popular boom of interest in Japan stimulated by the war and its aftermath and by the increased opportunities which Westerners had to associate with the Japanese people. But it is more directly the result of the spread of academic programs devoted to Japan and particularly the growing number of specialists trained to handle the Japanese language.

In the fall of 1958 a group of scholars gathered at the University of Michigan to seek some means of bringing together in more systematic fashion the results of the widely scattered studies of Japan which had appeared in the years since the end of the war. The Conference on Modern Japan which resulted from this meeting was dedicated both to the pooling of recent scholarly findings and to the possibility of stimulating new ideas and approaches to the study of modern Japan. Subsequently the Conference received a generous grant from the Ford Foundation for the support of a series of five annual seminars devoted to as many aspects of the history of Japan's modern development. Recently the number of seminars planned by the Conference was expanded to six.

The Conference on Modern Japan exists as a special project of the Association for Asian Studies. The Conference is guided by an executive committee consisting of Ronald P. Dore, Marius B. Jansen, William W. Lockwood, Donald H. Shively, Robert E. Ward, and John W. Hall (chairman). James W. Morley subsequently joined this group as the leader of the sixth seminar. Each member of the executive committee has been responsible for the organization of a separate seminar devoted to his particular field of specialization and for the publication of the proceedings of his seminar.

Although the subject of modernization *in the abstract* is not of primary concern to the Conference, conceptual problems are inevitably of interest to the entire series of seminars. Because of this, two less formal discussions on the theory of modernization have also been planned as part of the Conference's program. The first of these was held in Japan during the summer of 1960 and has been reported on as part of the first volume of published proceedings. The second will seek at the conclusion of our series to review whatever contributions to the realm of theory the six annual seminars may have made.

The present volume edited by Robert E. Ward is the fourth in a series of six to be published by the Princeton University Press for the Conference on Modern Japan. The other volumes, of which the first three have already appeared, are: *Changing Japanese Attitudes toward Modernization*, edited by Marius B. Jansen; *The State and Economic Enterprise in Japan*, edited by William W. Lockwood; *Aspects of Social Change in Modern Japan*, edited by Ronald P. Dore; *Tradition and Modernization in Japanese Culture,* edited by Donald H. Shively; *Dilemmas of Growth in Prewar Japan*, edited by James W. Morley.

As their titles suggest, the annual seminars have adopted broad themes so as to cast a wide net about a variety of scholars working within each of several major fields. Within these broad fields, however, the seminar chairmen have focused upon specific problems recommended either because they have received the greatest attention of Japanese specialists or because they seem most likely to contribute to a fuller understanding of the modernization of Japan. We trust, as a consequence, that the six volumes taken together will prove both representative of the current scholarship on Japan and comprehensive in their coverage of one of the most fascinating stories of national development in modern history.

The fourth meeting of the Conference on Modern Japan assembled in Bermuda in January 1965 under the chairmanship of Professor Robert E. Ward. The subject of discussion was the political development of Japan. In all twenty-four American, Japanese, and English scholars participated in the conference. In addition to the writers of the papers presented in the body of the following text (who are identified in greater detail on pp. 605 to 606), the following individuals were present: Professors Hans Baerwald, University of California (Los Angeles); Ronald P. Dore, London School of Economics and Political Science; Yoshinori Ide, Institute for Social Science Research, Tokyo University; Hyman Kublin, Brooklyn College; William W. Lockwood, Princeton University; John M. Maki, University of Washington; Douglas H. Mendel, Jr., University of Wisconsin; James W. Morley, Columbia University; Lucian W. Pye, Massachusetts Institute of Technology; William E. Steslicke, University of Illinois; and Chitoshi Yanaga, Yale University. All contributed most usefully to the discussion, and the editor and authors would like to express their gratitude to them.

The purpose of the conference was to analyze the political aspects of the developmental process in Japan with a view to identifying the major agencies of developmental political change, describing their roles and interactions, and determining whether the Japanese experience might not suggest certain generalizations or hypotheses in this area that might then be subjected to comparative analysis and verification in other cultural and political settings. These goals involved certain initial assumptions about the nature and functioning of the process of political development that will be explained more fully in the Introduction. These initial assumptions are responsible for the structure of the book that has emerged from an extensive revision of the papers originally presented to the Conference. Given the present rather elementary state of our knowledge in this field, one cannot, of course, be certain as to even the identity of all the determinants of political development. It seemed reasonable to assume, however, that we can identify at least some of the major variables concerned with a reasonable degree of certainty. Acting on this assumption, such a list of variables was constructed, and a total of thirteen papers were commissioned on the basis of this list. Revised versions of these constitute the heart of the following text.

Leadership, both symbolic and actual, was considered to be such a variable. Accordingly Professor John W. Hall of Yale University was asked to prepare a paper on the role of the emperor and its relationship to the process of political development in Japan, while Professor Roger F. Hackett of the University of Michigan was invited to write a comparable paper on the role of the *genrō*. Nationalism was the second variable selected, and Professor Albert M. Craig of Harvard University was asked to write on this subject. He elected to do so in case study fashion, and the chapter on Fukuzawa Yukichi is the result. The linked influences of foreign relations and war upon political development were also seen as significant, and Professors Marius B. Jansen of Princeton University and Nobutaka Ike of Stanford University were invited to submit papers on these topics. Another characteristic of modern political systems seemed to be a high degree of popular political participation. Professor Kurt Steiner of Stanford University was, therefore, asked to treat this at the rural and less formal level of political organization and practice, while Professor Robert A. Scalapino of the University of California (Berkeley) prepared a corresponding paper on electoral participation at the national level and its relation to political development in Japan. The modern polity was also perceived as one characterized by a high degree of functional and structural differentiation. The paper by Professor Takeshi Ishida of Tokyo University's Institute for Social Science Research on the development of Japanese interest groups treats one aspect of functional differentiation in political representation and decisionmaking, while that by Professor Bernard S. Silberman of the University of Arizona seeks to explore the possibility of devising quantitative means of measuring the progress of structural and functional differentiation within a modernizing political system. Similarly the rationality, secularity, and impersonality of legal and decision-making systems were also viewed as defining characteristics of politically developed societies. This assumption resulted in Professor Dan F. Henderson's (University of Washington) study of law and political modernization in Japan, and Professor Kiyoaki Tsuji's (Tokyo University) paper on decision-making in the Japanese government.

The last two papers represent attempts to deal with special problems in the study of political development. Professor Robert E. Ward of the University of Michigan treats the general problem of the amenability of the developmental process to external control and manipulation. He does this through a case study of the Allied Occupation of Japan viewed as an experiment in planned political change. Professor Ardath W. Burks of Rutgers, the State University of New Jersey, has provided a study of perhaps the most fundamental and difficult problem of all, the degrees of freedom or determinism that are implicit in the process of political decision-making and political change. He does this in the context of the political modernization of Japan.

Professor Ward has added to these papers a brief introduction setting the scene for the chapters that follow and giving his own version of what is meant by the key terms "political development" and "political modernization." He has also provided an epilogue that represents an attempt to sketch the sorts of general propositions and findings about the process of political development that the Conference discussions and papers have suggested to him. He has asked that it be made clear that he alone is responsible for the contents of both the introduction and the epilogue. While gratefully acknowledging his indebtedness to the paper writers and discussants, the claims advanced in these chapters are not intended to represent a viewpoint shared by any or most of the other participants in the Conference. In fact they are in basic disagreement with the known views of some participants. Professor Ward in his capacity as editor would also like to thank both the Ford Foundation and the Carnegie Corporation of New York for their support respectively of the Conference and of the research underlying several of the papers.

JOHN WHITNEY HALL

Contents

xi

POLITICAL DEVELOPMENT
IN MODERN JAPAN

CHAPTER I

Introduction

ROBERT E. WARD

IT IS FREQUENTLY claimed that when historians of the future look back on the twentieth century they will identify it in terms of what we can now only hope will prove to have been its most prominent and meaningful manifestation as "the age of new states" or "the age of emerging nations." There is justification for such speculation about the role of our times in historical perspective. In 1900 there were only about fifty-four states that were commonly recognized as independent. Today this number has risen to over one hundred and eighteen, more than double the 1900 figure. The majority of these newer states fall in the category that, with varying degrees of euphemism, we describe as "underdeveloped," "emerging," or "developing." It seems appropriate, therefore, that in the mid-twentieth century social scientists should display a substantial interest in new states and their development. Economists have engaged in this sort of study for the last ten to fifteen years under the rubric of economic development. Political scientists have acquired a comparable and complementary interest only more recently, however.

"Political development" or "political modernization"—the terms are here used synonymously—is one of the newer and more fashionable organizing concepts under consideration by political scientists and social scientists in general. Although it has been widely discussed within the profession only since about 1960, the basic idea is, of course, not new. It is related to a vast variety and depth of earlier writings about general or specialized theories of social, economic, and historical change, evolution, or progress. Perhaps the only novelties that can be claimed for current speculation and scholarship in this field are

3

the tentative, experimental, and hopefully scientific nature of most of the approaches and the sheer scope and complexity of the data under examination. The actual results in terms of established and demonstrated theories of political development or even of particular typologies or stages of political modernization are not as yet impressive. Most of us who have been involved in the inquiry, however, regard it as promising and console ourselves with the reminder that, after all, the child is only six years old, scarcely out of kindergarten.

Curiously enough, this particular type of inquiry into the dynamics and phasing of the process of political development may well have been conducted more systematically and pressed further in the case of Japan than in that of any other modern society or group of societies. The reasons for this are complex and need not be recounted at length. Suffice it to say that they relate in general to the intensive and relatively planned way in which the entire field of Japanese studies has been developed since World War II and, more specifically, to the initiatives and work of two committees: the Conference on Modern Japan under the chairmanship of Professor John Whitney Hall, and the Social Science Research Council's Committee on Comparative Politics under the successive chairmanships of Professors Gabriel A. Almond and Lucian W. Pye.

The present inquiry into political development in modern Japan—in addition to a number of specific questions and problems to which the following chapters are addressed—poses two more general questions:

1. What is meant by the terms "political development" and "political modernization"?
2. What does the particular case of Japan suggest with respect to the process of political development in general?

The first of these will be considered in the paragraphs that follow. The latter will be treated in the epilogue.

Let us turn first then to the definitional problem: What is meant by the terms "political development" and "political modernization"? In an historical sense, the Oxford English Dictionary has, as usual, relevant and interesting things to say.

"Modernization" in its root form of *modernus* has a far longer etymology than does "development" in its elemental form of *developper* or *disvelopper*—sixth century Latin as against twelfth or thirteenth century Old French. In English, however, "modern" is not used in a sense other than "now existing" or "being at this time" until about 1585. In the early sixteenth century its most common synonym was "hodiern" (from *hodie,* "today"). By the late sixteenth century "modern" had acquired the further meaning of "pertaining to the present and recent times as distinguished from the remote past." A favorite example is a prescient passage from the English translation of *Advertisements from Parnassus* in 1656: said Boccalini, "The women of this Modern Age had need of amendment." Oliver Goldsmith in 1774 produced a doomful variant on the root that also should not be allowed to pass unnoticed, especially by those of us most closely identified with "modernization" as a subject of academic study. A character in his *Visit to Elysium* declaims: "I should certainly have fallen beneath the hands of this company of men, who gloried in the title of Modernicides." One suspects that Goldsmith's "Modernicides" have surviving lineal descendants who may well present similar perils to the unwary.

The root word "modern" in our sense of the term is not encountered, therefore, until the late sixteenth century. Together with its variants "modernize" and "modernization," it seems not to have been commonly used until the eighteenth century. "Develop" and "development" used in an analogous sense appear even later in the mid-nineteenth century. Such a chronology seems appropriate. It suggests that the need for specific terminology to demarcate clearly present and recent times as something qualitatively different from the stream of earlier history and to depict the present as evolving from earlier and more elemental social forms was not widely felt in English till at least the seventeenth century. This is perhaps

5

the period when a new dimension of self-consciousness was added to the study of social change.

While of definite historical interest, these etymologies still do not really tell us how the term "political development" is interpreted in current social science usage. In fact, there are at present so many and such variant attempts at definition that this is not easy to do. Permit me, therefore, to concentrate on what the term means to me.

Fundamentally, I find the concept of political development too complex to be encompassed by a dictionary-type definition. It takes instead a trait-list approach to convey its meaning adequately. In setting forth such a list, it is also helpful to distinguish traits or aspects that are both prerequisite to and defining of political modernity from those that are simply definitive products or effects of the development process. The distinction is one of degree in the sense that the four traits that are here viewed as prerequisites do not necessarily lose force or status once the threshold of modernity has been crossed; they remain valid and defining thereafter as well. The four traits that are viewed as products or effects of the political development process on the other hand seem to be somewhat less prime or elemental when viewed from the standpoint of their role in generating the transition from premodern to modern political circumstances; their role as basic effects of the process is more salient than their role as causes.

The four traits that are prerequisite for a modern political system are:

1. A sense of nationalism widely shared among at least the society's ruling political elite.
2. Enough stability and security vis-à-vis internal or external political threats to permit sustained governmental planning and action.
3. A system of allocating and terminating roles of political leadership that on balance evaluates achievement more highly than status.

6

4. A ruling political elite that on balance regards political, economic, and social change as either desirable or necessary and looks upon government as an appropriate agency for achieving such change.

These four traits are viewed as the prime characteristics of a politically modern society. In this sense all four must be acquired in some minimal quantity and combination that we are as yet unable to define with much specificity. Only then— to employ an atomic analogy—is the process of political modernization capable of "going critical" and of acquiring the capacity for sustained and self-generating political change or development that is so characteristic of all modern societies. Such an analogy, while apt in some respects, evokes, however, an imagery that is both too precise and too elegant for the relatively amorphous sociopolitical forces and processes with which we are concerned. The speed and timing with which a given political system acquires an adequate amount of each of these four prime traits may vary widely from characteristic to characteristic, and the entire process of "going critical" may, therefore, be prolonged for very appreciable periods of time. It is also conceivable that under certain circumstances some societies may simply remain incapable of passing this threshold at all or, at least, that they may not be able to go far beyond it.

The other four defining characteristics of a politically modern society are closely interrelated; indeed in a sense all are aspects of what is sometimes referred to as "the administrative state":

5. A sphere of governmental involvement and action that in a long term sense is expanding, usually by means of progressive encroachments on spheres of decision or action traditionally regarded as private or at least nongovernmental.
6. Increasing popular involvement with the political system, though not necessarily with its decision-making aspects.
7. A governmental structure characterized by a high and

increasing degree of functional differentiation (together with the integrating mechanisms that this makes necessary).

8. An increasingly secular, impersonal and rationalized system of governmental decision-making.

These eight traits then are seen as constituting the essential elements of politically developed societies. Several general comments and qualifications are in order.

First, despite the partial segregation of the first four as prerequisites, all eight are regarded as essential to the modern condition. Politically developed societies possess all of them, although some will doubtless be present in greater measure than others.

Second, each trait represents a broad range rather than a precise state of being. This in fact is one of the principal problems besetting this field of investigation at the moment—just what are the lower limits of the modern condition? In what quantity or degree must this combination of traits be present before it can be said that the threshold of political development has been crossed? The only quantifiable measures currently available are unfortunately both crude and derived from fields other than politics.

Third, the traits are products of historical analysis and are not conceived of as possessing indefinite future validity as well. The role of nationalism, for example, may well diminish with the passage of time. All that is claimed here is that our historic experience thus far has not produced its functional equivalent as a modernizing force.

Fourth, the trait list has been deliberately phrased in value-free terms that lack direct relevance to the classic normative issues of the democratic society. What is sought is a dispassionate and objective instrument of comparative political analysis, not a canon of moral judgment. For maximum utility this instrument of analysis should be applicable to all types of political systems, totalitarian as well as democratic. This is not intended to derogate the importance of democratic values or the classic political issues. The purpose of the inquiry is simply different.

Finally, the trait list does not assume the real existence of "any perfectly modern political system." Such a society would obviously be an intolerable monstrosity by any humane standards. All contemporary societies are mixtures of traditional and modern traits in varying balances ranging from the barely modern to the most modern.

CHAPTER II

A Monarch for Modern Japan

JOHN WHITNEY HALL[1]

AMONG the varied examples of modern nation building,
Japan has come to occupy a distinctive position, for Japan has proved the exception to most of the assumptions
which we have commonly held about Oriental peoples or underdeveloped societies in their struggle for political modernization. Defying the obvious comparisons with her neighbors on
the continent of Asia, Japan has not only emulated the most
advanced countries of Europe but has increasingly forced historical comparisons with them. The simple circumstance that
Japan exists today under the second of her modern constitutions reveals two remarkable political facts: first that during
the nineteenth and twentieth centuries Japan was able to maintain an unusual degree of political stability, and second that
along with this stability the country has undergone two revolutionary changes of political complexion within the context
of a constitutional monarchy.

Central to Japan's history of political modernization has
been the role of the monarch—the *tennō*—and the institutions
and ideas adhering to the imperial tradition. No aspect of the
Japanese political system has proved so controversial and so
little understood, for as with the English monarch, constitutional definitions of powers and functions reveal but a narrow
range of the manifold sensibilities which the emperor was able

[1] I wish to thank the many persons, particularly Ishida Takeshi,
William Lockwood, Herschel Webb, and James Crowley, whose suggestions at the time this paper was first read or at some later time
proved helpful in my final revision. I would also like to express my
gratitude to the Carnegie Corporation of New York for financial
support received in connection with the preparation of this paper.

to touch in the lives and minds of his subjects. The very diffuseness and mysteriousness of the imperial presence has frustrated systematic or objective analysis. The emperor has been many things to many people. In fact he has often seemed to hold contradictory meanings for the same individual who might rationally disapprove of, yet emotionally admire, the deep feelings of national pride which the monarchy stirred within him. The Emperor Meiji has been extolled as the father of progress in modern Japan, and yet his memory has at the same time been maligned as the ultimate source of the destructive forces of imperialism and militarism which nearly destroyed his country.

After the end of World War II, when the taboos against criticism of the monarchy were lifted in Japan, the emperor was subjected to a deluge of disparaging literature which heaped upon the "*tennō* system" blame for centuries of suffering by the Japanese people, for the recent failure of democracy, and for the drift toward disastrous war in the Pacific. In much of this literature of disenchantment and resentment, Japanese writers took refuge in the unhappy though self-comforting claim that they had faced unique handicaps as a nation because of the unmatched virility of reactionary forces which oppressed their country through the agency of the emperor system. Modern Japan, they have implied, was a victim of its monarchy.

Granted that from the point of view of its history and cultural context the Japanese monarchy has had features quite distinct from the monarchies of the Western world, yet taken in broad perspective, in terms of the many interrelated processes of political change out of which modern nation states have evolved, the relationship of the Japanese emperor to the problem of nation building has not been so unique as some have claimed. The fact that Japan, unlike China or Indonesia, carried its monarch into modern times is an index to one of the most obvious and significant differences separating Japan's political history from that of other Asian states, making it in reality more nearly comparable to those of the Western democracies today. "The stability of any given democracy," Martin Lipset has observed, has depended "not only on economic development but also upon the effectiveness and the legitimacy of its political system." And monarchies have proved sufficiently useful as legitimizing devices that today "we have the absurd fact that ten out of twelve stable European and English-speaking democracies are monarchies."[2]

Of course these Western monarchies are not the only "modern" states in the world today, and many a Japanese will opt for the greater openness of an America or the social policies of a Russia. But if we are inclined to place value upon the factor of stability during the process of political modernization, monarchy has been able to play a crucial and not altogether negative role. If Japan has achieved in outcome a condition comparable to the "stable democracies," she also shared at the outset many of the problems which confront the late modernizers in the world today. And though the Japanese may look back upon the last hundred years of their history to decry the burden of state authoritarianism which weighed upon them, one wonders whether they are prepared to exchange those conditions for the prospect of national disintegration which could have resulted from a society warring upon itself or under a headless political anarchy. It is possible, then, that the monarchy helped carry Japan through certain phases of modernization that would have proved difficult under a less controlled political system.

In their study of the challenges faced by Japan and Turkey in achieving the transition between traditional and modern national organization, Ward and Rustow have observed a typology of crises and necessary responses. These nations—and they suggest others fit the pattern as well—were faced first with the crises of national identity, then with the critical need of self-defense against external enemies, then with the need for adequate development (chiefly economic), and ultimately with the

[2] Seymour Martin Lipset, *Political Man, The Social Basis of Politics* (New York, Anchor Books, ed., 1963), pp. 64, 65.

13

need to achieve a satisfying internal political adjustment—the problem of popular relationship to the political process.[3] Unquestionably in the case of Japan the emperor played a decisive role in getting Japan through the first several crises on the path toward modernization. As an embodiment of Japan's sense of national identity, as the bridge linking traditional sources of legitimacy to the new state authority, as the father figure which justified his subjects' self-discipline and sacrifice, the monarch became both a rallying point for his people and a means of concentrating authority behind the emerging national leadership. In the first decades after 1868 the emperor came to symbolize all the forces of self-control and enforced stability which combined to channel the prime energies of the Japanese toward meeting the foreign challenge and toward adopting essential social and economic reforms.

Yet if the emperor served the Japanese people well in the initial stages of the forced march toward modernization, the same cannot be said for all that followed. No thinking Japanese who lived through the 1930's and 1940's can easily forget the extremes to which the Japanese people were driven in the name of the emperor. (And the fact that the same individual continues on the Japanese throne perpetuates to this day a lingering fear that the spirit which once made him the agent for nationalist excesses may still lie latent beneath the benign exterior of the postwar polity.) It is understandable too that thinking Japanese, who had been obliged to make their settlement with the dogmas of the imperial polity (*kokutai*) and the public ritualism of emperor veneration during the prewar decades should live in horror of a repetition of that experience. Outsiders who have come upon Japan in her second modern incarnation, reborn out of the ashes of war and defeat, have sometimes dismissed too casually those black years. Yet they need only refresh their memory of the literature of hatred

[3] Robert E. Ward and Dankwart A. Rustow, eds., *Political Modernization in Japan and Turkey* (Princeton, 1964), ch. 10, particularly pp. 465–66.

and denunciation in the West which accused Japan so vehemently of a "crime against herself and against civilization."[4]

What went wrong? Why was it that an institution which seemed so appropriate to the problems of Meiji Japan should have failed so disastrously in the age of Shōwa? Our typology of political modernization suggests that the answer lay in the area of adjustment between the mass needs of the modern state and the political process as a whole. With respect to the monarchy this involved essentially the related problems of the transfer of sovereignty from out of the hands of the emperor into those of the people and of relinquishing the mythological beliefs surrounding the throne. The conversion of transcendental monarchy into a modern representative government, of whatever political orientation, has never been smooth, and it may well be that it has never been achieved without violence or at least the generation of a great deal of social heat. Nonetheless, the eventual change from monarchal to popular sovereignty has been a necessary prelude to the formation of the modern state, and the alternative routes which Japan might have used to achieve a government responsible to the people were perhaps more limited than we care to admit. The question even suggests itself whether, if the transfer of sovereignty had been accomplished without the experience of the totalitarian 1940's, it could have been done without an equal and compensating trauma of another sort. Was Japan's recent war simply the direction outward of the violence of the social and ideological revolutions which Japan had avoided by its conservative resolution of its first steps in the modernization process? Or was there a more moderate alternative?

It would be hard to deny that the initial form that the modern Japanese monarchy took proved resistant to the changes which might have permitted an easy transition to popular sovereignty. The present status of the emperor, though perhaps anticipated in the hidden desires of the Japanese dur-

---

[4] The phrase is taken from Willis Lamott, *Nippon: The Crime and Punishment of Japan* (New York, 1944), p. 1.

ing the tragic years of wartime suffering, was brought about only as a result of defeat and occupation directive. The constitution of 1946, in giving legal form to a government "of the people with whom resides sovereign power" and in which the emperor assumed the position of a "symbol of the state and of the unity of the people," has completed the long transition of the monarchy from absolute sovereign to popular symbol. Has Japan, then, at last entered the ranks of the "stable democracies"? Have the Japanese attained a state of affairs in which they feel secure in their own sense of achievement and control over their political destinies and sufficiently affluent that they can support without begrudging it a family-man monarch and a tennis-playing crown prince? Or is the emperor still a lingering threat to popular sovereignty and democratic life in Japan? The masses, who are so often evoked in regard to questions of this kind, seem to forget the past more readily than do their interrogators. The recent acts of right-wing violence which have struck terror into the hearts of the intellectual keepers of the Japanese conscience have not stirred many to demand the total eradication of the "emperor system."[5] And certainly the framers of the new constitution have made it most difficult to return the emperor to the center of a virile ultranationalist movement without the most obvious tampering with the legal foundations of the state. Time may indeed have fashioned a safe monarch for modern Japan.

But among the Japanese people some are apt to be skeptical. After having succumbed to the myth of imperial omnipotence during the years of wartime hysteria, they find it hard to believe that the imperial institution can be easily restructured. And although the literature of polemic criticism of the "emperor system" has begun to subside, Japanese writers are still inclined to question whether the emperor has been safely democratized and whether on historical grounds the monarchy can justly be admired. To follow this critical literature too closely would

[5] Ishida Takeshi, "Popular Attitudes towards the Japanese Emperor," *Asian Survey*, II (1962), 29–39.

distract us unduly from the effort to bring impartial judgment to bear on the problem of the emperor's role in the modernization of Japanese politics, yet it is of some use to put it on the record so as to identify one extreme in the range of interpretations to which serious scholars subscribe. It is hard, furthermore, to attempt any discourse on the Japanese monarchy without implicit engagement with this literature because of its continued prevalence.

Let us take for example the works of Inoue Kiyoshi, not because he is necessarily a representative writer, but because he is respected as an historian, and is in fact rather moderate among those who have written to "expose the *tennō* myth" since the war. His 1953 paperback publication entitled *The Emperor System* (*Tennōsei*) brings together articles published by him from 1946 to 1952, and features his "History of the Emperor System" which had served as the lead article in the important volume edited by the Rekishigaku Kenkyūkai in 1946 entitled *How Do Historians Look at the Emperor System?*[6] Inoue's history of the emperor in Japan has little good to say for the monarchy. "The line of emperors, unbroken for ages eternal," he begins, "was able to perpetuate itself only because it served as the apex of an unbroken condition of suffering for the people." There was, of course, a prior condition, before the appearance of the emperor, "when the Japanese people inhabited the islands enjoying a democratic society in perfect peace and freedom. All land was owned communally and there was neither ruler nor subject." But thereafter, with the appearance of social class distinctions, the *tennō* emerged to serve as the legitimizing element behind an elite power hierarchy. The climax to the long line of exploitation of the people perpetrated in the name of the emperor came with the Meiji Restoration. By the middle of the nineteenth century, Inoue claims, evidence of a popular desire for a "people's state" had begun to manifest itself, but before

[6] *Rekishika wa tennōsei wo dō miru ka* (Tokyo, 3rd ed., 1949), pp. 1–113.

this could be achieved, the samurai leadership, utilizing the revolutionary energies of the people, had carried out a counterrevolutionary movement.

The people, betrayed by their leaders, traded the domination of feudal rulers for a modern absolutism. And so, "Japan put into practice an absolute monarchy of the kind that France had discarded a hundred years before, an absolutism much more colored by pure feudalism than that which had prevailed in France, in other words a 'Japanese variety' of absolutism." With the promulgation of the Meiji constitution this system was legitimized and the modern emperor system was created. "What this *tennō* system represented was a feudalistic control mechanism in which the bureaucracy and military using the police and the armed forces and in complete accord with the *zaibatsu* capitalists and landlords carried out a policy of domination over the workers at home and of militarism abroad. The emperor stood at the head of this state, at the point at which the bureaucracy, military, *zaibatsu*, and landlords came together, serving as their pivot. He himself was the greatest of the feudal landlords, the greatest of the *zaibatsu*, the highest bureaucrat, and the highest military officer."[7]

There are many variations on this line of interpretation, differing chiefly in the manner in which the Meiji Restoration is handled. But it is not the bias which needs to concern us so much as certain viewpoints of a more general nature which these and other writings take for granted. Inoue has in fact made four basic assumptions which take him beyond pure polemic or historical dogma and serve to define a recurring set of questions which appear in nearly every treatment of the emperor in Japan today. These are, first, that the emperor system in premodern times had a notoriously bad influence on Japan's historical development and should be evaluated chiefly as a force for political conservatism in Japan. Second, that the

[7] *Ibid.*, pp. 111–12.

emperor system of Meiji times was not a direct legacy from (2)
this earlier tradition but was an entirely new and reactionary
creation. Third, that the modern monarchy was essentially (3)
antidemocractic and bears the responsibility for bringing the
era of fascism and war into being. And fourth, that the present (4)
emperor represents a continuation of the prewar system. These
four assumptions which characterize what might be called the
"antiestablishment" approach to the imperial institution are
not necessarily new with the present generation of Japanese
scholars. They have commonly been voiced by critical writers
outside of Japan who had no reason to be bound by the taboos which hampered free discussion of the emperor within
Japan. But from whatever source they come, they pose for us
four important lines of inquiry which this paper proposes to
probe, namely:

1. What is the historic nature of the imperial institution?
2. What was the role of the emperor in the critical period
   of transition from traditional to modern government?
3. What link was there between the modern institutions of
   monarchy and Japan's course of development as a
   modern state?
4. What is the significance of the monarchy today?

The Historic Nature of the Japanese Monarchy

Let us begin with our first question concerning the historic
nature of the Japanese monarchy and, by extension, its relevance to the present. The history of an institution does not
necessarily explain or justify its later manifestations. But where
continuities exist, history can provide revealing insights. Like
monarchs in general, the Japanese emperor has functioned
historically at three levels. As an actual holder of *power*, he has (1)
served as a supreme ruler or at least a participant in the competition for power within Japan. As the repository of *sovereignty*, he has served as the ultimate source of authority within (2)

the Japanese state, exercising such authority if only to provide legitimacy for successive de facto hegemonies.[8] Finally, as an ultimate *symbol* of the moral order and identity of the Japanese people, he has served as the sanctifying element in a variety of theories of government and national organization. Historically the imperial institution has been many things at many times as it has undergone changes within these three functional levels; for although a single imperial lineage was able to perpetuate itself in Japan, the relationship between the dynasty, the government, and the people of Japan has changed frequently in the course of events.

The head of the Japanese imperial family did not often exercise political power. At the outset the dynasty was obliged to establish itself through forceful leadership, military prowess, and direct sacerdotal influence.[9] But it was the nature of the Japanese authority system that the ultimate holder of authority was quickly raised above the realm of personal influence, freely exercised, to serve as ritual head of the corporate power body. What we can surmise about the emperor prior to the Taika Reform of 645 is that his position was largely ritualistic, while the decision-making functions of government were exercised at a level where they were responsive to the competitive interests of the group of families which constituted a ruling oligarchy. This might always have remained the norm if it had not been for the influence of Chinese political theory and institutions. The Chinese model, having been impressed upon Japan fairly early in the develop-

[8] The practice of sovereignty obviously has different manifestations and usages between Japanese and European society. As a general concept I use this term here in the broad sense as defined by Lasswell and Kaplan to be "the highest degree of authority." Harold D. Lasswell and Abraham Kaplan, *Power and Society, A Framework for Political Inquiry* (New Haven, Yale paperbound ed., 1963), pp. 177–81.

[9] Herschel Webb has suggested that the Japanese emperors never served as military leaders as the myths of Jimmu or Jingō imply. No doubt our picture of the early Yamato chiefs is confused, and the tradition of ritual leadership appears to predominate from the outset.

ment of the Japanese monarchy, tended to overlay native
practices of rulership so that the latter were placed on the
defensive. Japanese tended to accept the Chinese concept of
emperor as both sovereign and ruler, and for this reason the
constant tendency of "political heads" in Japan to retire into
ritual seclusion has been considered undesirable. The historical records, written under Chinese influence, depict the emperor as constantly struggling to retain elements of power
which he should be exercising by virtue of the very idea of
monarchy. Yet the Japanese tradition of power-holding has
never really supported the possibility that the monarch might
rule as well as reign.

Surely the model to which the Japanese returned time after
time was not the Chinese style of monarchy but rather the
kin-based system of ritual headship or legitimizing symbol.
The Yamato sovereign, for instance, served in two capacities,
as head of the imperial house and head of a power coalition
made up of other family heads. In neither situation was he
expected to function as a real power but rather as the legitimizer of group consensus. An obvious result of this has been
that the machinery for the direct exercise of power by the
monarch has normally been neglected, while the apparatus
of ritualism which placed the monarch in a position of veneration but political powerlessness has constantly proliferated.
For all the respect paid by Japanese writers toward the men
of action in Japanese history, and especially the decisive
monarchs, the actual system of government has not encouraged
such decisiveness.

It is informative to look at Japanese monarchs who have
shown administrative vigor. First of all it is evident that most
of them reigned during the period of heaviest Chinese influence. In addition, in almost every instance these rulers found
sources of influence outside of the institution of monarchy
itself, outside the monarch's normal channels of action. Tenchi (668–671) remained behind the scenes for sixteen years
while Emperor Kōtoku and Empress Saimei fronted for him.

Temmu gained the throne in 672 after leading the successful side in a succession war. Kammu came to the throne after a plot in which he had joined forces with the Fujiwara and Wake families against the priest Dōkyō. Shirakawa and his successors exercised power through the office of the cloister. Godaigo plotted for power as a result of the division of the imperial house into two branches, and to gain a direct voice in government he had to create an entirely new machinery of rule.[10]

A complicating factor which makes this point seem less clear-cut stems from the history of the imperial house itself. To say that the monarch normally was cut off from sources of real power does not mean that the imperial family was necessarily devoid of influence. What distinguishes the Nara and early Heian periods in particular is not so much the fact that an occasional monarch actually ruled as well as reigned but rather that the imperial house was successful in its control of both the sovereign and the organs of government. Thus with the rise of the Fujiwara at court, the imperial *family* was obliged to become a competitor for power along with the rest of the court nobility, and it is in this context that the headquarters of the cloister came into being. So long as the game of court politics was played for real political or economic stakes, the imperial family competed quite successfully along with the rest. But we know the result. Godaigo's ill-fated attempt to realize the myth of imperial rule did as much as anything to throw away the assets behind those stakes.

Historically, then, it has been in the role of sacred legitimizer that the emperor has most typically been cast. As the ritual monarch—the supreme repository of sovereign authority—the head of the imperial family has been an essential part of the Japanese polity from its inception. And this continuity of the imperial institution (and the imperial house) constitutes one of the undeniable and remarkable *facts* of Japanese political

[10] For details note my *Government and Local Power in Japan, 500 to 1700, A Study Based on Bizen Province* (Princeton, 1965), chs. 1–7.

history. The fact of continuity (and the reasons for it) cannot be shrugged off as myth or hoax, for it relates to some of the deepest realities of the Japanese political tradition. First of all, continuity of the emperor, whether as a ruler or merely as a symbol, reveals as nothing else the enduring homogeneity of the Japanese political corpus. Japan has literally been a "single country" from the beginning of its political history. While there were civil wars in Japan, the political fabric was never torn so far that such wars became a contest of sovereignties. (The so-called dynastic wars from 1336 to 1392 represented only a momentary factionalism between claimants to the same throne.) Protected from conquest by foreign powers because of their isolation, the Japanese islands themselves never seemed to afford a geographic base of sufficient size so that a rival indigenous dynasty might gain sufficient power to challenge the established order. Even the shocking assertions of sovereign ambition made by Taira-no-masakado in 939 were only that he was a rightful claimant to the existing throne.

This continuity of dynasty then suggests the continuity of a political order in Japan of unusual homogeneity and constancy. While the pyramid of power in Japan has frequently changed in composition, its structure—namely a federated hierarchy of aristocratic houses presided over by the emperor—did not change its fundamental characteristics from the time of its first appearance. And this structure was the result of a recurring pattern in the manner in which the power hierarchy was formed and reformed as the result of internal factional wars rather than massive and unilateral conquest. Even the initial conquest of the islands by the sovereign family, as it is recorded in the earliest histories, did not rest on an absolute victory over all the country. The imperial group (*tenson*) did not obliterate its rivals but conquered when necessary and compromised where possible, constantly exalting the powers of its chief as a religious as well as political leader. From the beginning, the head of the imperial family played the role of a sacred peacemaker exercising hegemony over a constantly expanding federation of elite families. His position was gained through incomplete civil war in which compromise and conciliation had been extensively used, and in which the competitors were frequently not eliminated but rather incorporated into the balance of power but in a reduced capacity.[11]

Once the head of the sovereign family was established as the symbol of elite unity, he continued to serve this function without serious lapse into modern times. The failure to exercise real political influence probably served in the long run to protect the head of the dynasty from destruction. Conversely the strongly oligarchic nature of Japanese power politics that served to make political authority and social position synonymous had much to do with perpetuating a condition in which a peacemaker possessed of only residual sovereignty continued to be useful. In premodern times struggles for national hegemony tended to take the form of factional intrigues or of restricted military action which repeated almost exactly the pattern of incomplete victory and compromise which had brought the imperial house to its original position. And in these struggles each leader of a winning coalition eventually sought legitimacy for his de facto hegemony by acquiring imperial backing, just as the emperor had justified his own position of sovereignty through his claims to sacerdotal legitimacy. Even the Emperor Meiji was similarly relied on as the symbol of legitimacy for the real leaders of the Restoration.

All of this helps to explain why, even after the decline of the court nobility, the whole set of attitudes toward court ranks, the traditionally "noble" genealogies, and certain ancestral or guardian Shinto shrines retained their importance. Despite the loss of power by the emperor and later the court nobility, the social hierarchy remained, so that in each age the politically ambitious families were obliged to climb the same ladder of social prestige as they gained political power. Even those

---

[11] The disposition of the chieftain of Izumo by the Yamato group is the best early example.

leaders who came to the fore by military force were no exception. Since the power of each military hegemon rested upon a coalition rather than absolute force, legitimacy secured through the imperial system was always a necessity. One of the first acts of a newly risen military leader was to adjust his genealogy so as to place his family comfortably high in the social hierarchy. Along with a military title, such as shogun, went court ranks and honorary posts which gave its bearer the requisite prestige to assume leadership over a sometimes reluctant following.[12]

This functional explanation of the continuous role of the emperor in Japanese politics is to some extent an explanation after the fact. The ultimate source of the emperor's peacemaking or legitimizing authority came from his exercise of what we have called sovereignty. If such a term is justified it needs explanation, for the concepts of legitimization and of ultimate authority which are meant by it were decidedly original to the Japanese system.[13] What was it that the imperial family retained throughout its long descent through Japanese history? Essentially, it was the fact of its own existence through direct succession together with the special charisma derived through religious sanctification. Both these practices of succession and sanctification were common to the larger body of socioreligious practices to which we give the generic name Shinto. Succession was not strictly biological but ritualistic, following the rules which sociologists have made familiar in their studies of the Japanese system of family (*ie*) succession. In other words, perpetuation of the lineage was maintained in

[12] For a modern example of this practice we have the reconstitution of a nobility in 1885 by which the new political power structure was set by reference to a hierarchy of social ranks.

[13] Sir George Sansom's observation is particularly apt at this point. European rulers, he wrote, "might call themselves sovereign 'by the grace of God,' but the emperors of Japan described themselves as 'manifest gods.'" *A History of Japan to 1334* (Stanford, 1958), p. 45. Differences with the Chinese concept of "mandate of heaven" have received frequent attention.

the abstract by the family acting as a corporate body, so that fictionalization of the actual kinship lines was liberally permitted. Once succession was determined, however, the designated head of the lineage received all the authority vested in the position as though he were a direct blood successor. And it was this authority which was sanctified through Shinto practices directed toward the deified ancestor (uji-gami).

The relationship between "lineage deity" (uji-gami) and "lineage head" (uji-no kami) upon which the charismatic leadership of the ancient chieftains of Japan was based is well known. The ritual symbolism of this relationship as it pertained to the imperial house became institutionalized as the fundamental rituals of accession for the Japanese monarchy. In theory, each successive head of the lineage is conceived of as having renewed the tie between the sun goddess Amaterasu (the lineage deity) and himself (the lineage head) through ceremonies performed before the earthly "deity body" (shintai, most importantly the mirror) of the sun goddess. The powers of the ancestral deity are considered available to the living head through the power of "linkage" by which the worshiper is literally possessed by the power of the deity, becoming a kami (hence the concept of kannagara or living deity). Symbolic of this successive identity between emperor and ancestral deity was the sacred necklace (mikubi-dama), the soul spirit (tama) of which held the power to evoke the deities and assure spiritual linkage.[14]

Probably the most significant feature of this entire ritualism of succession is that the religious concepts were particular rather than universal. Succession was genealogical, and "divine right" came as a private bond between the sun god-

[14] Religious Affairs Section, Research Bureau Ministry of Education, Government of Japan, Religions of Japan (Tokyo, 1959), pp. 9–24. See the appearance of these concepts in the coronation of the Shōwa Emperor, Asahi Shimbunsha, Gotairei gahō (Osaka, 1928).

dess and the emperor.[15] No person could substitute in this relationship. There was no superior priesthood. Or to put it another way, without the continuity of the imperial family, the powers of the sun goddess could not have been properly evoked. No other person could have accepted the necklace and obtained "linkage" with the imperial ancestor. And it is this fact which gave to the imperial family its ultimately unassailable status and made usurpation an impossibility. In its final residual form, then, sovereignty was simply the fact that within the Japanese political order no higher authority could be evoked. Political power could be exercised legitimately only "in the name of" this authority.

Another reason that the emperor retained his powerless though exalted role can be explained in terms of the distinctive decision-making process which the Japanese clung to throughout their history. For at all levels of the society, power groups normally resorted to the pattern of consensus decision behind *the name of* a legitimizing authority. The "family council" served as a model not only for family affairs but also for the highest level of state deliberation. And while at the more intimate levels the leader might well play the role of an autocrat, at higher levels the leader was most often assigned a passive role of merely adding his presence to the debate of policy, legitimizing by his presence the ultimate consensus. Unlike the medieval kings of Europe, who heard the counsel of their courts but then retired in private to make their own "absolute though not arbitrary" decisions, the Japanese sovereign remained above responsibility.[16] This function gave to the sovereign an unusual duality, for though the emperor was absolute and in theory could rule arbitrarily, he nonetheless was little more than the repository of the will to

[15] The emperor in essence "announced" his own succession before the spirit of the sun goddess.

[16] See Paul L. Ward, "On the King's Taking Counsel," paper read at Annual Meeting of American Historical Association, Dec. 1960.

27

achieve agreement and maintain order among the various interests which competed for power under him. His sovereignty was to this extent a reflection of the continuing sense of responsibility among the Japanese political elite to maintain order within the power coalition.[17]

Beyond these aspects of the emperor's actual performance of the functions of sovereignty, we enter the realm of the ideological and religious extension of the sovereign's position in the culture. To the Japanese the emperor served not only as sovereign but also as pope, except that in Japan the emperor's rulership was idealized from the point of view of two religious systems, Shinto and Confucism (Buddhism exerted a less sustained influence). The first conceived of the emperor essentially as high priest in the worship of the sun goddess and other national deities. And although strictly speaking Amaterasu was related to the imperial family in a genealogical, and hence private, capacity, yet since she was considered the most exalted of the heavenly *kami*, it was believed that her powers extended to the ultimate protection of the entire Japanese homeland. If we reverse this set of beliefs, we have the ingredients—historically quite variable in intensity to be sure—of a national sentiment directed toward the emperor as supreme guardian of the nation. As a Shinto monarch, then, the emperor was expected to serve as the agency through which the national *kami* could be evoked for the protection of the land. And he himself was venerated as the embodiment of the genius of the Japanese people. Characteristically this placed no moral obligation or responsibility for ultimate performance on the emperor. But it is also significant that not until the last war did the emperor face the possibility of being held responsible for national disaster. And it is perhaps even more sig-

[17] For discussions of this fundamental function of the emperor in modern context, see Warren M. Tsuneishi, "The Japanese Emperor, A Study in Constitutional and Political Change," unpublished Ph.D. dissertation, Yale, 1960, particularly pp. 21–29; also T. A. Bisson, "Japan as a Political Organism," *Pacific Affairs*, XVII (1944), 392–420.

nificant that in this recent instance the emperor acted in the capacity of a "savior" who intervened to save the Japanese from ultimate extinction and not as the one who took onto himself the ultimate responsibility for the war.[18]

Confucian theory called for a more positive assertion of imperial responsibility for the well-being of the state, but even here the ultimate necessity to prove possession of a mandate from heaven was never acknowledged in Japan. By contrast to China, which was governed by a succession of upstart emperors who were obliged to prove their legitimacy by demonstration of the possession of the Mandate of Heaven, the Japanese emperor conceived of himself as having received the mandate by virtue of succession. Thus there was no recognized separation of the moral order from the actual, or of a divine law to which the sovereign was accountable.[19] What the Confucian scriptures added to the Japanese practice of monarchy was the conception of a moral society presided over by a benevolent authority. The emperor, in other words, was "concerned" for the well-being of the people. In return he expected to be served by loyal and responsible officials and submissive subjects. It was difficult to give such principles meaning in actual performance, of course, unless a fairly extensive and unified system of administration was in existence. And since for so many centuries after the decline of the Nara administration Japanese government remained decentralized, these ideas remained largely disembodied until the Tokugawa period, voiced only in isolation by such writers as Nichiren or Kitabatake Chikafusa.[20]

The Tokugawa period deserves special attention not simply because it provided the immediate background out of

[18] Tsuneishi, *op.cit.*, pp. 120–31.

[19] The point is brought out by Reinhard Bendix in his paper "Preconditions of Development: A Comparison of Japan and Germany," in R. P. Dore, ed., *Aspects of Social Change in Modern Japan* (Princeton, 1967).

[20] Bitō Masahide, "Nihon ni okeru rekishi ishiki no hatten," *Iwanami kōza, Nihon rekishi* (Tokyo, 1963), XXII, 30–43, for Nichiren's views.

29

which the emperor emerged to assume his modern guise, but because of the significant additions it brought to his institutional and symbolic status. The "mikado," whom the nineteenth century Westerners found secluded in Kyoto, is commonly depicted as having reached the lowest ebb of significance, a condition from which only the Mito loyalist movement succeeded in rescuing him. But the judgment stems from a too narrow concern over the emperor's exclusion from political power. It overlooks the many important institutional and ideological functions which the emperor played in the Tokugawa political system and in the political attitudes of the day.

Admittedly as a ruler the emperor had reached a point of negligible influence. The emperor and his court had been relegated to the city of Kyoto, placed under restrictions imposed by the shogunate, and even under the surveillance of shogunal ministers. But the emperor was not deprived of sovereignty nor of his position in the ideal Shinto and Confucian worlds. Ishii Ryōsuke in discussing the status of the emperor makes the point that the shogun exercised "sovereign political rights" by seizure and not by delegation.[21] Yet he also admits that the residual functions of the emperor as "titular sovereign" (*meimokuteki tōjisha*), namely to grant titles and award ranks, to adjust the calendar, and to announce era names, were of high symbolic significance for the entire country. Since even constitutional historians like Minobe appear to share the opinion that the shogun exercised sovereignty (disputing only whether there was delegation or not), it may seem presumptuous to suggest that these writers are missing an obvious and important point.[22] If we draw a distinction between the seat of political *power* and of legitimizing *authority*, it seems clear enough that the shoguns, though they

[21] Ishii Ryōsuke, *Tennō* (Tokyo, 1950), pp. 152ff. Also Tsuda Sōkichi, *Nihon no kōshitsu* (Tokyo, 1952), pp. 7–9.

[22] Ishii Ryōsuke, *Meiji bunkashi, Hōsei hen* (Tokyo, 1954), pp. 46–47.

exercised power to the fullest, were obliged to recognize the emperor as the source of legitimacy (in other words, as the ultimate sovereign).[23] Granted that historically the Tokugawa house first grasped power and then set to work to exalt the prestige of the emperor, the fact remains that the shogun subordinated himself to the emperor. And such subordination was no less real, even though the emperor was powerless and the act of submission was voluntary. The legitimization provided by the emperor through the title of shogun was no less valuable to the Tokugawa house in its effort to assert its mastery over the country.

The claim that the shogun did not receive a specific delegation of powers from the emperor (in other words, that the shogunate was a usurpation) is really beside the point. The emperor in 1603 had no real powers to delegate, and furthermore Japanese politics had never resorted to comprehensive and public clarification of the distribution of authority. The exercise of political powers and responsibilities, since there had been no real break in the continuity of Japanese political development, was commonly publicized ceremonially and assumed by reference to the precedents which adhered to certain titles or posts. The title of shogun awarded no powers that the shogun could not personally command but justified the exercise of nearly every function of governance save only that final residual element of sovereignty, which was retained by the emperor.

Again it is claimed that the shogun did not actually rule "in the name of" the emperor. The closing of the country to foreign travel, minting, negotiations with foreign powers, all these were carried out by the shogun without even a passing reference to imperial authorization. To the early Westerners,

[23] European observers commonly referred to the shogun as the temporal king or emperor and the mikado as the spiritual monarch. See Sir Ernest Satow, *A Diplomat in Japan* (London, 1921), p. 33. Lasswell has no difficulty in separating "sovereignty" and "rule" as differences between formal and effective power. *Op.cit.*, p. 188.

the shogun was king. But his actions were covered by powers which had gradually accrued to the military hegemon in Japan and could presumably have been explained as having been delegated sometime in the past. Shogunal control of the channels of imperial audience was such that it could be assumed that imperial sanction would be received whenever it was needed. And near automatic sanction was constantly being given throughout the Tokugawa period, as the emperor "granted" court ranks and "approved" successions. It was certainly expected between 1853 and 1858, when the shogunate sent to Kyoto for the ratification of the treaties with foreign countries. The very fact that a situation arose in which the denial of ratification could be used to embarrass the shogun illustrated the importance of the emperor's expected support.

But what the emperor lost in real power he gained in the ideological stature assigned him in the several theories of government which blossomed during the Tokugawa period. The point is often overlooked because of our more consuming interest in the theme of "restoration." The attention given to the loyalist element in the Mito school of thought, for example, obscures the more obvious and more important point that the Tokugawa period contained the beginnings of a change in theory of government which greatly enhanced the significance of the Japanese monarch. At the root of this change was the fact that society had begun to transform itself from one of rule by custom to one of rule by law—or should we say principle.[24] Specifically the Japanese of the Tokugawa period were in many important respects moving away from conditions in which the individual's life was determined solely by his private relationships with superior authority as personified in the head of his house, the land steward, or the military or proprietary lord. Instead, with the formation of villages, towns, bands of retainers, and other such administratively de-

[24] The concept of "rule by status" as applied to Tokugawa law by Dan Henderson is a useful one. See p. 392 below.

fined bodies, the individual was coming increasingly under legal codes enforced by a generalized higher authority, through impersonal administrative devices.[25] It was this which began to instill in the Japanese a new consciousness of authority in the abstract, and of their being "subjects" rather than simply personal lieges, serfs, or bondsmen. For the first time in Japanese history, government was becoming an object of contemplation as an external order which could be manipulated and in any case should be made to justify itself.

If, then, we read the great outpouring of philosophical writings after the middle of the seventeenth century not for signs of the technical differences between schools of thought, of whether writers showed more or less reliance on Chinese precedents, or of whether they were proshogun or proemperor, but instead look upon them for what they reveal of a new conception of man and state, we find in them a remarkable consistency of purpose and ultimate design. From Hayashi Razan to Yoshida Shōin the common theme that runs through the writings of both supporters and critics of the Tokugawa regime is the effort to define a theory of social order and political action which would fit the realities of the time. If Hayashi sought to discover a way of explaining an ideal society in which emperor, shogun, and the four classes could take their proper stations, Yoshida groped for a more concrete conception of the nation and of a theory of personal action in defense of the nation.

This does not mean that all Tokugawa thinkers wove identical theories about the ideal nature of government or the political values by which the individual should live. Confucianists and Shinto revivalists inhabited quite different

[25] The point has been made in as early a work as Kan-ichi Asakawa, *The Documents of Iriki* (New Haven, 1929), p. 46. It is also the burden of Thomas C. Smith's *The Agrarian Origins of Modern Japan* (Stanford, 1959) and chs. 12 and 13 of my *Government and Local Power in Japan*.

worlds. The humorless Confucianist still dreamed of a rational universe in which rulers justified themselves by their benevolent concern for the people. He sometimes extolled the fact of Japan's "political uniqueness"—comparing Japan's divinely descended emperor with China's changeable dynasties—but he was most comfortable when he could conceive of the emperor as a moral monarch and assign symbolic rather than actual significance to the myths of succession and sanctification. Hayashi Razan, by rationalizing the "three sacred treasures" as benevolence, wisdom, and courage, hoped to magnify the emperor's distinction by virtue of his possession of these supreme virtues. Shintoists, on the other hand, would have none of such rationalization, for to them the *fact* of being was its own justification. The eighteenth century scholars who began the revival of interest in Japanese literature and history (the Kokugakusha) called for a return of the actual state of innocence which Japan had enjoyed before contamination from China. To them the emperor and the elements of the imperial myth continued to exist as facts which had power by virtue of their existential being. Their approach was irrational, perhaps, but emotionally verifiable.

Yet once we grant these differences, we see that both schools of political thought shared important areas of commonality—shared them in fact with parallel developments in the real world of administrative technology—namely that they both contributed to the intellectual rationale supporting what can be described as the shift in government from private to public authority and from custom to law. We have tended to neglect these common elements in Tokugawa political theory because they remained strictly within the confines of traditional philosophical schools and hence seemed irrelevant to Japan's later political development. Yet surely the measure of increased political sophistication is not to be looked for simply in the increase of "predemocratic" aspirations or of social "class consciousness." If after years of combing the sources only one

34

maverick, Andō Shōeki, can be found to have voiced an alienated attack on Tokugawa feudalism, it is quite obvious that the entire discourse remained within the establishment.[26] But this need not be discovered with disappointment, for we know full well that there was nothing in either the Confucian or Shinto traditions that might have suggested the desirability of an egalitarian society or could have supported the possibility of popular sovereignty.

What was happening was that an increasingly rational approach to political ideas as bodies of general principles was gaining momentum during the Tokugawa period along lines quite independent of the West, but the implications for Japan's political modernization were no less significant because of this independence. We can see this exemplified in at least three related developments in late Tokugawa thought and political practice, to which we should turn our attention. We notice first of all a trend toward what was clearly an idealization of the concepts of authority and loyalty. Since both Confucian and Shinto theorists conceived of the political world abstractly as a general order in which monarch and subject related according to ideal principles, they gave rise to concepts of "rulership" and of the "way of the subject" which applied broadly and not simply to particularistic conditions. The principles of loyalty expounded by the Confucianists made everyone within a status equally responsible for the achievement of good government. Conversely, the loyalist writings of the late Tokugawa period made the emperor "available" as an inspiration to all Japanese. These attitudes were not necessarily new, of course, to the Japanese of the late Tokugawa period. What is new was that they for the first time gained wide currency and even application in the behavior of whole groups and classes.

[26] E. Herbert Norman, "Andō Shōeki and the Anatomy of Japanese Feudalism," *Transactions of the Asiatic Society of Japan*, 3d ser., II (1949).

Second, the Japanese by the end of the Tokugawa period were beginning to acquire a sense of nation.[27] The sentiment was still vague, to be sure, and gained expression in the writings of only a few scholars; nor could its spread be separated completely from the new awareness of the encroachment of the West. If the accent on Japan's uniqueness which colored the writings of Motoori Norinaga came from a rejection of the central position which the Confucianists gave to China, the discovery by the late Mito scholars of Japan's "unique position" among nations of the world—"a divine land where the sun rises and where the primordial energy originates"—came from an unsought-for familiarity with world geography.[28] The first steps in the search for a national identity, therefore, took the Tokugawa Japanese back into the familiar realm of Shinto beliefs to the secure landmarks of an "unparalleled" polity (*kokutai*) and a "divine" emperor. Yoshida Shōin for all his obscurantism and his emotionalism was struggling for a more inclusive conception of the Japanese political order and of the individual's place in it. He saw, if only dimly, the outlines of a nation personified by the emperor. And he saw himself and others being called to act on behalf of a greater national loyalty, even to "die" loyally for the sake of their country.[29] The coalescence of Shinto revivalism and emperor-centered loyalism was a natural development leading toward a new national consciousness. That it was to join the myth of Japan's uniqueness to the ideas of nation and nationalism as these began to take shape in the mid-nineteenth century was perhaps an inevitable by-product of this Tokugawa background.

The third area of development is rather more difficult to

[27] R. P. Dore, in his *Education in Tokugawa Japan* (Berkeley, 1965), pp. 295–301, makes a major point of the sense of nation as a legacy of Tokugawa education.

[28] Tsunoda, de Bary, and Keene, *Sources of the Japanese Tradition* (New York, 1958), p. 595 (quoting Aizawa Seishisai's *Shinron*).

[29] David Magarey Earl, *Emperor and Nation in Japan* (Seattle, 1964), p. 170.

demonstrate, yet there is evidence that acceptance of the principle of "responsible rule" had begun to call forth a rudimentary concern for a sort of representation in the exercise of government which was to have important repercussions during the Restoration era. A growing emphasis on government by merit and according to group discussion (*kaigi*) or representation was finding its way into the political writings of the day. The argument that if government was to be truly solicitous of the well-being of the people, administrators should be selected on the basis of merit rather than heredity, and decisions should be based on counsel widely solicited, was essentially an attack upon an overly closed political system.[30] Both these principles called for the exercise of authority on a more "responsible" basis. And though the Japanese remained indifferent to concepts of a divine law superior to government or of the sovereignty of the people, they nonetheless, without breaking with the elite premises of their theories of government, managed to justify demands for wider involvement of individuals in the political process.

Our views of Tokugawa Japan as a "traditional base" from which to measure Japan's political development have changed sufficiently to allow us to absorb the evidence that important structural and attitudinal changes had taken place, especially after the middle of the eighteenth century. The emperor in his personal life and his daily round of activities in the Kyoto *gosho* may seem not to have shared in these changes. Yet the emperor as *institution* and as *belief* was certainly far different in the 1850's from what he had been in 1600, and it is worth reflecting on precisely what the emperor stood for among *the politically significant and articulate* segments of the Japanese populace in the years prior to the breaking of the foreign crisis. In 1850 the emperor was no forgotten relic destined to be discarded at the first sign of weakness in the Tokugawa regime. The Tokugawa shogunate had enhanced

[30] See T. C. Smith's treatment of this point in R. P. Dore, ed., *Aspects of Social Change.*

so ideological formalization of emperor's role

and institutionalized the emperor's status as legitimizer. More-over, in the efforts of the shogunate and the political theorists to evolve a rationale for a government which was touching the people in an increasingly pervasive and impersonal manner, the emperor was placed at the center of political ideologies of both Confucian and Shinto persuasion. The emperor had entered the Tokugawa period as a private legitimizer for the Tokugawa shogun; he came out of it a symbol of national consciousness and unity—the natural rallying point for the nation once it felt the threat and the challenge of the West upon it.

(2) *The Emperor and the Meiji Restoration*

We have now reached the threshold of the period of crisis precipitated by Perry's arrival during which the shogunate was swept away and the emperor was projected into his po-sition as monarch of the new Meiji state. The momentum of our argument up to now should not lead to an expectation that these changes took place easily, or above all that they might have been foreordained. The years between 1853 and 1871, into which Japan squeezed a political revolution and the be- *foundation of Meiji* ginnings of a cultural transformation of revolutionary pro-portions are the despair of the historical generalizer. The com-plex interaction between interests and ideas which caught the emperor up from his world of ancient rituals behind the plastered walls of the Kyoto palace created the most baffling problems of interpretation.

What role did the emperor play in these dramatic events which led to his "restoration"? For all the importance of the emperor in the Restoration movement and in the resulting Meiji polity, the question has not received a great deal of direct attention. The vast literature on the Restoration and on the origin of the "emperor system" consists by and large of broader political and social histories which deal mainly with what was done by "using" the emperor or in the name of loyalism. The kind of history by formula that this has produced is all too familiar. On the one hand, by the 1940's the official version which claimed that the emperor had been the recipient of a spontaneous surge of loyal support from the nation had given form to the most grotesque distortions. "The great Emperor Meiji," a *Japan Times* publication told its foreign readers, "purged all the evils of feudalism from the national structure and assumed charge of the nation and race. The people reverently began to sing the 'Kimi Ga Yo' and the whole nation cooperated with the Emperor and his officers to bring the Island Empire up to the level of other modern nations."[31] That a whole generation or more of Japanese youth was forced to accept such propaganda explains much of the vehemence of the postwar reaction which has proclaimed that the whole Restoration movement was a betrayal of the people. Inoue's exposé is quite restrained by comparison to many. "The modern *tennōsei*," he claims, "did not evolve through the gradual modification and improvement of something which Japan had possessed for ages in unbroken succession from the beginning of the country. It was created only very recently at the time of the so-called Imperial Restoration. . . . At the same time among the people there was a desire to create a nation in which sovereignty would reside in the people, not the emperor. And among the most advanced groups there was even a movement to create a people's republic. But Meiji Tennō, the bureaucracy, and the military used every device, heaping pressure upon pressure, to combat this movement . . . and so establish the emperor system."[32]

Interpretations of this sort suffer from the all too common habit of historians to see what they want in history by looking back on past events from the vantage point of a particular age or a particular political belief. But it would surely have taken the mass-indoctrinated fervor of the 1930's to have aroused the Japanese of the 1860's to "rally spontaneously" around the Emperor Meiji. And similarly it would have taken

[31] Amar Lahiri, *Mikado's Mission* (Tokyo, 1940), pp. 11–12.
[32] Inoue Kiyoshi, *Tennōsei* (Tokyo, 1953), p. 1.

a heavy seeding of the political leadership in the 1870's with men brought up on the social welfare ideas of the mid-twentieth century and trained in party techniques to have brought Inoue's "people's republic" into being.

But between the "must have happened" claims of the official historians and the "should have happened" regrets of the historian critics, we have the task of comprehending in terms of the Restoration age itself the significance of the [historicism] irreducible political facts behind the Restoration. We can begin with at least two givens: that between 1853 and 1871 the Japanese abolished the shogunate while retaining the (1) sovereign position of the emperor, and that they tore down the Tokugawa political order while creating a new one that pre- (2) sided over the rapid modernization of Japanese society. The bare statements in themselves are startling enough, for Japan not only carried its monarchy into modern times, but actually strengthened the institution while undergoing its initial effort ✳ at creating a modern state.

While monarchies have preserved themselves in many of the most stable democracies of Europe, the emergence of modern states in Asia have more often been accompanied by a rejection of monarchy and bitter attack on the traditional aristocracy. But Japan produced no Nasser or antidynastic T'ung-meng Hui and left no Farouk or Pu Yi in the wake of its revolution. The simple fact of monarchial continuity therefore is doubly significant in Japan's case. Was it due to the irre-explanations sistible loyalties of the Japanese people? Even the loyalists (1) (*shishi*) discovered the emperor late in their active careers. Was there a conscious fear of social revolution on the part of (2) the ruling interests? Mito Nariaki pointed to the specter of urban riots of the Ōshio variety, but he did so as much to startle the shogunate as out of conviction that his society was on the edge of upheaval. Was it alarm over the approach of the West which sent the Japanese searching for a new rallying (3) point? This certainly brings us closer to the heart of things, for without the foreign crises there was certainly no real likelihood that the shogunate would have collapsed as it did. It was the foreign crisis which revealed to those in a position to dispute the shogun's authority that Edo had proved inadequate to its mission. Without denying the many real social and economic problems which complicated the power struggle of the 1850's and 1860's, the chief actors in that struggle behaved as if their main concerns, other than self-interest or local interest, were for the identity and inviolability of their country. And it was surely significant to the outcome of that struggle that the emperor had been institutionalized by the Tokugawa as a secluded, but ultimately "concerned," sovereign of the entire nation. The mikado of Kyoto had been neither a scourge nor a burden to his people. Thus in the search for a new symbol of unity, the emperor could be raised aloft, uncontaminated by responsibility for the Tokugawa policies. The old order could be attacked in the name of a still higher and more venerable one.

How was the monarchy carried into modern times? Was it simply as a sacred ark of tradition, an inanimate symbol manipulated by whatever hands could reach it? To large degree the tradition of the "passive emperor" remained undisturbed. But also, as at various times in the past, political instability provided the opportunity for involvement. The emperor played a role in his own "restoration." This was not as a full-fledged ruler, to be sure, for admittedly if the emperor and his immediate advisors had been able to gain control of the government during the crisis years, they would have handled things differently from the way they eventually turned out. But it is also true that the Kyoto court and the emperor became (if only for a moment) an active element in late Tokugawa politics. First of all, the existence of a community of courtiers in Kyoto and of an imperial establishment of palaces, shrines and rituals provided, if nothing else, a dead weight of institutional inertia. The court possessed sufficient resources and vitality (especially among some of its younger members) to allow it to work for its own perpetuation

41

and even enhancement. Moreover, once the slightest opportunity was given for emperor and courtiers to engage in political affairs, they quickly exploited it. Emperor Kōmei and courtiers such as Iwakura and Sanjō were deeply enmeshed in the intrigues which first challenged the shogunate to adhere to its seclusion policy and later connived to put the emperor into the hands of Satsuma and Chōshū. In fact the first breaks in the monopoly power enjoyed by the shogun came with Kōmei's expression of "imperial concern" in his letter of 1846 over the state of Japan's coastal defenses and in 1858 when he refused to ratify the treaty of commerce with the United States.[33] Emperor and court thus found ways to carry on the kind of intrigue which became possible in those transition periods when the power structure was being shaken. But the possibility of interference in political affairs was short-lived and the range of influence limited largely to the realm of factional intrigue. And above all the emperor did not represent a powerful vested interest capable of obstructing political and institutional change.

For the most part it was in the two familiar roles of legitimizer and symbol of national consciousness that the emperor was cast during the transition years. And it was part of the nature of the first of these roles that the emperor should serve two purposes: one as peacemaker and the other as ultimate source of authority. Throughout most of the transition period the peacemaker function predominated, the emperor providing a sort of umbrella under which a revolution in the locus of power was carried out while keeping intact certain fundamental features of the Japanese political structure (the *kokutai*). To this extent critics such as Inoue are justified in linking the continuity of the emperor with the perpetuation of a conservative social and political order. But this was not the only motivation behind the preservation of the imperial

[33] Sakata Yoshiō's works are useful at this point. Among them "Meiji dōtoku shi" in *Meiji bunka shi* (Tokyo, 1955), pp. 439ff. Also "Changes in the Concept of the Emperor," *Zinbun*, II (1956), 1–22.

authority. There was the influence of the foreign threat as well.

The foreign crisis had two immediate effects on the Japanese political scene. It shocked responsible leaders into a realization of national danger, and it placed new and difficult responsibilities on the shogunate. Once the shogunate lost its ability to act decisively as though its decisions carried sovereign authority, the structure of assumed delegation which had been carefully exploited by the shogunate fell apart. From the instant that Abe Masahiro made inquiry to the court and daimyo on how to deal with Perry, the process of deterioration set in. At that moment the emperor suddenly took on renewed importance. The rapid shift of the political center of gravity to Kyoto, once the "automatic" legitimacy which the shogunate had held broke down, indicates how much the shogun had relied on his ability to act "as if" he possessed a national mandate. Mito Nariaki's attack on the shogunate, couched in terms of the failure of the shogun to look to the defense and well-being of the country, opened a new competition for that mandate but in terms of a new context created by the foreign menace and by the new expectations for government performance which were being formulated by the late Tokugawa political theorists. Increasingly in the years of crisis the emperor was brought into the political process, first as the shogunate tried to regain his public backing, then as referee in the efforts to balance the interests of the daimyo and the shogunate (the so-called *kōbu-gattai* policy), and finally as the authority through which the anti-Tokugawa coalition legitimized itself. The final stages of the struggle were played out in familiar fashion until among the contending political interests the activist agents chiefly of Satsuma and Chōshū, holding on to a precarious balance of military power, managed to "gain possession" of the emperor and by speaking through his person carried out a "conquest" of the country in the name of a new mandate.[34]

[34] *Ibid.*, pp. 16–17.

In the history of Japanese factional politics possession of the emperor was nine tenths of the game. Once the Sat-chō group obtained control of the young Emperor Meiji, it could invoke his authority for all subsequent action. With this advantage, between January 3, 1868, and August 29, 1871, the new group executed a series of measures in the name of the emperor which brought the entire country firmly under its command. From the declaration which named the Tokugawa rebels and led to the prosecution of military operations against Edo, to the demand that the daimyo turn in their land registers and submit to the direct authority of the central government, to the final abolition of the daimyo territories (*han*) and the unification of the country under a prefectural system, each step was carried out through a combination of military power in hand (though often barely sufficient to gain the initiative) and the assertion of imperial authority. Certainly at no time did the Sat-chō group have the capacity to win an outright military victory over the country had a substantial portion of the daimyo decided to challenge its authority. And granted that much of the country was immobilized by weakness or confusion, it was still a major factor in favor of the precarious Sat-chō coalition that it could act in the name of the emperor. Thus the emperor was retained as the ultimate symbol of unity, serving, as it were, to remind the competing political factions of their primary responsibility to the corporate interests of the nation.

To the extent that the new government returned to a direct public reliance on the supreme authority of the emperor it affected a restoration. There was, of course, no literal "return to imperial rule" as the words *ōsei-fukko* implied. Yet it was as much a restoration as Japanese tradition would have permitted. The confusion over the meaning of *ōsei-fukko* comes both from the tendency to claim too much for the Meiji emperor and from failing to recognize the importance of the less dramatic changes which actually took place in the status of the monarchy. The coup d'état of 1868 returned no more real

44

power to the emperor than he had possessed under the Tokugawa system. (He remained isolated, idealized, and passive.) But by wiping out the distance between shogunate and court it again placed government directly under his symbolic leadership and returned to the idea of government "in the name of" the emperor. Under such a system it was to the interest of the government to enhance in every way possible the degree to which the imperial authority was recognized and respected in the country.

The techniques used by the new power faction to extend the emperor's prestige and visibility went far beyond anything employed by the Tokugawa. The shift of the imperial court to Tokyo renewed the unity of imperial ritualism and administrative affairs which had been separated under the shogunal system. By making the emperor party to the deliberations of state (though he had no voice) and by making all government decisions "imperial decisions," the possible discrepancy between the imperial will and the actions of the government was eliminated. Meanwhile the decision to assign private wealth to the imperial house soon made the emperor independent of political vicissitudes and permitted the elaboration of an imperial ceremonial capable of dazzling the eyes of the populace. On a more immediate level, "imperial agents" were sent out across the country to instruct the local administrators on the nature of the "imperial rights."[35] Simultaneously the forces which ultimately linked the emperor to the vast network of Shinto shrine worship and which placed the emperor at the center of instruction in national history were also released. The secluded rituals and the esoteric philosophies which had made the imperial institution such a potent element of elite political affairs under the shogun were now applied to the entire nation.

Historians who describe all of this as either a sleight of hand trick which denied the fundamental desire for freedom

[35] Mombusho, *Ishin shi* (Tokyo, 1942), v, 482. The agents were known as *senkyōshi*.

So Meiji oligarchy further institutionalizes and formalizes the emperor's pol + symbolic role

of the Japanese people or as a literal return to a long neglected ideal of direct imperial rule miss the essential dynamics of the role of the emperor during the early phase of the Restoration era. In becoming the revitalized symbol of national unity and the new rationale for the exercise of government, the emperor in many ways was actually fulfilling the new expectations which had grown up around the conceptions of monarch and government during the late Tokugawa period. On the one hand the emperor by amplifying the traditional myths of sanctification that made him a transcendental monarch reaffirmed the principles upon which the Shinto nationalists built their theory of Japan's national uniqueness against the threat of foreign encroachment. And by making his person visible to the entire populace, the emperor became the very embodiment of the nation in the Shinto sense. At the same time the new government, in the name of the young emperor, accepted the obligation to provide for good government and the national welfare as these aims had been understood by the Confucianists. If the imperial rule was to be in the best interests of all, it would have to rest upon responsibility in the execution of government and the formation of policy. And this evoked the principles of "government by agreement" (kōron) and the willingness to adopt policies of political and social reform, in other words the vision of modernization. Finally, the emperor's government took over the defaulted political debts of the shogunate, namely the responsibility to unify the country and to defend it against its external enemies, particularly the West. Thus the Restoration, for all the private and sectional interests which lay behind it, contained an element of response to public aspiration which cannot be discounted.

We need go no further than the Charter Oath of January 1868 to find a clear statement of the broader ideological foundations adopted by the new monarchy and the government taken in its name. Among its five articles the first advocated the idea of wide discussion; the second called for the common effort of the people to enhance the national good; the third promised social reforms to eliminate popular discontent; the fourth and fifth foresaw the modernization of the culture so as to bring justice to the people and strength to the imperial polity. These were the principles upon which the Meiji government proposed to rest its appeal for its mandate to rule the country, but they were principles taken in the name of the emperor and presumably issued by him. They became, as a consequence, part of the theoretical justification for the exercise of imperial authority. The ideas behind the Japanese monarchy to this extent went beyond either a pure "restoration" or a maneuver to justify the ascendancy of a new power oligarchy.

By 1871 the first stage in the transformation of the Japanese monarchy was essentially complete. Four years after the Restoration and eighteeen years before the promulgation of the Meiji constitution the basic foundations of the modern Japanese monarchy had been laid, and this largely out of building stones taken from Japan's own institutional and ideological traditions. (The influence of the West up to this point had been minimal.) The emperor continued as a transcendental and passive sovereign with authority which was theoretically absolute but which was actually exercised by ministers who governed in his name. A department of religion (Jingishō) supported the ceremonial and sacerdotal features of the monarchy. The imperial ministry (Kunaishō) provided for an independent monarchal establishment, and the continuation of the imperial court system kept alive a social elite surrounding the monarch. Sovereignty and the locus of "accountability" remained with the emperor, but political influence remained in the hands of an oligarchy which could be entered only by simultaneous ascension of the social and bureaucratic ladders. And so the new monarchy perpetuated that peculiar feature of the Japanese imperial tradition in which the elite both controlled and were controlled by the emperor, in which the high bureaucracy both governed and was governed by the "imperial will." It continued, also, the particular style of

47

decision-making by consensus that had proved congenial to the Japanese power elite throughout the ages. Government remained "unrepresentative." Yet the reluctance of the new leaders to share their political influence was balanced by an extreme sensitivity to the mission of domestic reform and the need to satisfy a wide range of the popular desires. They may have been politically conservative, but they were remarkably progressive in their social and economic policies.[36]

But was this remarkable combination of political conservatism and technological progressivism enough? Did the monarchy serve simply as an instrument for preserving a political absolutism in the face of an incipient social revolution so as to put off indefinitely the achievement of popular representative government? This is the frequent criticism laid against the Restoration by antiestablishment historians. And this assumption that things might have been different, and presumably better, is one that cannot be ignored. Were there alternatives to what happened in Japan between 1853 and 1871? And did the alternatives lie in the direction of greater or lesser social change? Was Japan prevented from following the models of France or England or was she saved from going the way of China or the Congo? Alternatives, if they are to be more than wishful projections of theory into history, must be treated realistically and must be followed through to their real consequences.

If we are to think of alternatives we need to start with the obvious. To begin with, what were the alternatives facing Japan as a nation in the years between 1853 and 1871? During these years Japan certainly confronted the very real danger of falling apart into competing (and possibly warring) fragments. The fact that the Japanese avoided civil war, deepened their sense of national identity, and protected their independence as a nation was not accidental. It was the purposeful achieve-

[36] The concept of "reinforcing dualism" as applied by Ward and Rustow in their study of Japan and Turkey has suggestive possibilities at this point. *Op.cit.*, pp. 445-47.

ment of leaders, on both sides of the late Tokugawa struggle
for power, to whom unity in the face of the foreign threat was
an obsession and for whom the idea of national breakdown
was deeply abhorrent. But what if this had not been so, or
supposing the leadership had been unable to maintain unity,
would the possibilities of social revolution have been enhanced? Had Japan in 1853 been dragged into an era of
civil war or perhaps colonization, would not this have pro-
foundly altered the calendar of political and social reform
and wiped out for an equally long time the possibility of attaining a popular sovereignty? Present-day historians seem
more willing to take a chance with this alternative, especially
since it would have pushed back to their fathers' and grand-
fathers' times the problems of dealing simultaneously with
the tasks of nation-building, social revolution, and cultural
transformation.

Let us assume, then, that social revolution achieved under
fairly stable political conditions was more desirable for Japan
than the sort of progress through chaos which China was to
exemplify. If national unity and independence were essential,
then what alternatives were left? There was, of course, the
possibility that the shogunate might have gathered strength
and assumed dictatorial rule, abolishing the daimyo. Or an
anti-Tokugawa coalition of daimyo might have seized the
government. But neither of these alternatives is likely to
have made much difference in the status of the monarchy or
to have led to more generous social policies.[37] What then of
the alternatives on the other side; was there any real likelihood that a successful social revolution could have thrown up
a leadership between 1853 and 1871 capable of unifying the

[37] A contrary speculation is made by Marius B. Jansen in his "Changing Japanese Attitudes toward Modernization." If there had been no
downfall of the shogunate, he believes, "Tokugawa hegemony would
probably, for instance, have spared Japan the Emperor system."
Marius B. Jansen, ed., *Changing Japanese Attitudes toward Modernization* (Princeton, 1965), p. 44.

country and devising a new and more popular form of government? Where were such leaders to be found—some Tosa *gōshi*, a few disgruntled lower shogunal officials, a Shibusawa here and a Emori there? The possibility seems fantastic because not only was the very idea of social revolution alien to most Japanese at that time, but also there was so little organizational base upon which a revolutionary group might have built a national following.

If, then, we accept the rise of the Restoration leadership as a fortunate alternative to national chaos, it is still conceivable that these men could have espoused very different policies once they had gained power. What if they should have persisted in an anti-Western policy, inviting perhaps a disastrous conflict with the Western powers? What if the samurai aristocracy had clung to their hereditary political and economic privileges? This, in fact, was the more common reaction in other parts of Asia. Or is it possible to expect that the Meiji leaders might have moved to the other extreme, adopting by 1871 even more revolutionary policies than the ones they actually undertook? Inoue Kiyoshi suggests that 1871 was the appropriate time to have abolished all social distinctions and to have established a popular sovereignty.[38] But how much can we ask of leaders who already were pushing reforms in the face of considerable opposition? And at any rate could a further leveling of the center of political influence have been achieved without even greater reliance on imperial authority? Certainly it is inconceivable that both the shogun and emperor could have been eliminated without disastrous consequences to the Japanese ability to maintain political cohesion as a nation. And it is hard to imagine how, once the Sat-chō leaders were in control of the government, they could have unified the

---

[38] A novel twist to the idea that the people should have been "led into democracy" during the early Meiji years is suggested by analogy by Nakamura Kichisaburo. Given democracy by the Allied Occupation "the people realized that democracy was quite acceptable." *The Formation of Modern Japan* (Tokyo and Honolulu, 1962), p. 126.

country and urged the adoption of modernizing policies had they not been able to dramatize the conception of the national unity and destiny in the person of the emperor, gaining through him the commitment to group discipline and private sacrifice which so distinguished the Japanese of the time.

But of all the obstacles to the successful ascendancy of the social revolution, it seems likely that the administrative decentralization of the country would have made the seizure of power from outside of the establishment most difficult. The activist leaders (*shishi*), having first joined in common cause in the fencing schools of Edo, remained in a position to work through their respective domain administrations until the new government had taken form. What kind of political apparatus could nonsamurai leaders have taken over? Would it not have required simultaneous uprisings in the several domains each successful in putting a locality under revolutionary control? And how then could these separate revolutions have been unified without resort to warfare or reliance on a transcendental imperial will? In essence it is hard to conceive that there was a reasonable alternative to the kind of samurai leadership which arose at the end of the Tokugawa period and the kind of "enlightened absolutism" which they had established by 1871. All of this is not to say that the Restoration led to the only and best possible resolution of the crisis which Japan faced after 1853, but it does suggest that the realistic alternatives to what happened were less along the lines of further social change than in other and less desirable directions of national disintegration, terror perhaps, or some sort of traditionalist reaction.

The Emperor and Japan's Development as a Modern State

But if the imperial institution and the leadership behind it may have been right for Japan in 1871, this does not mean that it remained so. And while the fundamental elements of the monarchy remained unchanged until 1946, it is equally clear

51

that the form of the monarchy and its relationship to the needs of the country underwent considerable change. As for the monarchy, there was a constant intensification of its involvement in national affairs reflected in a broadening institutionalization of its political and cultural role and a deepening ideological penetration of the popular mind. Even before the adoption of the constitution of 1889 the Japanese emperor had begun to adopt the guise of a European monarch, appearing resplendent in Western-style uniform, acting the part both of head of state and commander in chief. At the same time the indigenous instruments of monarchal prestige and influence were expanded with the augmentation of state support to the Shinto establishment and the insertion of nationalist themes in the school curriculum. It was the document in 1889, of course, which fully clothed the monarch in the role of constitutional legality, putting into terminology consistent with Western practice the particular institutions which had been carried out of the Japanese past. All of this was, however, essentially an intensification of the patterns which had been set in 1871, so that Japan was to retain for the next seventy-five years a polity headed by a transcendental monarch, dominated by aristocratic groups, and strongly dedicated to the retention of traditional values. Since Japan was not a Western nation, it is somewhat beside the point to accuse Japan of failing to "continue in what many have thought to be the main line of the evolution of Western society."[39] But did Japan continue along the main line of evolution to which she herself may properly have aspired?

Admittedly once we enter the course of history which leads from 1871 beyond the Meiji constitution and into the twentieth century we find it difficult to keep our eyes from the disastrous party struggles of the 1920's and the fanatical ultranationalist excesses of the 1930's and 1940's. It is hard to avoid the conviction that some fatal flaw of original sin was lodged

[39] Bendix, op.cit., takes this phrase from Talcott Parsons, Essays in Sociological Theory (Glencoe, 1954), pp. 116, 287.

in the Meiji settlement, and that the emperor himself was its foremost embodiment. "When the leaders of the Meiji clan clique," writes Maruyama Masao, "using every means in their power to suppress the movement for democratic rights, set about constructing an absolutist regime (discreetly covering it with a figleaf of a constitution patterned after that of Prussia), they were in fact laying the foundations for the country's bankruptcy."[40] The chain of causation argued by Maruyama has seemed irresistible to a whole generation of historians and political scientists. And with it we hear the repeated recrimination: if only the "clan clique" had listened to the voice of the people or of their "proper leaders."

Maruyama does not argue, of course, that Meiji Tennō astride his white charger or dressed in white robes before the Kashiko-dokoro was the unassisted cause of "Japanese Fascism," but rather that he became the ultimate incarnation of the ideology of the fascist state. This surely was true. The New National Structure of 1940 placed the emperor at the center of its conception of the "family state." And it is also true that as of 1871 all the elements which went into the later Shōwa manifestation of the Japanese monarchy were at hand. Nothing new had to be invented, merely amplified or distorted. But the question of whether these elements, particularly as given legal form in the constitution, necessarily led to the national bankruptcy of the 1940's can hardly be answered categorically; for it raises problems of alternatives both with respect to what might have happened and to explanations of how that bankruptcy came about.

How, for instance, are we to account for the changes in the imperial institution which took place after 1871 either with respect to the attitudes of the Japanese people toward the imperial myth or the manner in which it touched their lives? Some changes stemmed from Meiji Tennō's own increase in stature, his putting on of the beard and his filling out of the

[40] Maruyama Masao, *Thought and Behavior in Modern Japanese Politics* (London, 1963), p. 126.

father figure. Some resulted from the deliberate work of men such as Motoda Eifu behind the throne and in the Shinto establishment. But what of the pressures from the people themselves who clothed the emperor in new uniforms or old myths and pinned on him their hopes for national preeminence in an imperialistic world? The increasing intensity with which the Japanese identified with their emperor their deepest feelings of national pride and aspiration and their willingness to submerge in him their political and private interests were as much their making as his. Was all this imposed upon the mass of the Japanese against their better conscience? Or was it a product of their own feeling of discrepancy between national achievement and aspiration? Did belief in a "uniquely Japanese emperor" provide a psychic substitute perhaps for the failure to match the West in the arts of civilization and the products of industry? Is it not quite possible to conceive of the modern Japanese monarch, not so much as a device by which the vested interests managed to suppress the will of the majority but rather as a reflection, in part at least, of the irrational and contradictory aspirations of a Japanese people, bewildered by the changes which the modern world was forcing upon them, exhilarated by new challenges and opportunities, and above all unwilling to take a second place among the people of the world?

Surely the emperor-centered totalitarian regime of the 1940's was neither the inevitable outcome of the form which the monarchy had taken in 1871 nor the intent of even the most unenlightened of the Meiji leaders. Why then did not Japan avoid the disastrous turn to war and political regimentation after 1930? Was it, as the answer is so often given, a result of the failure to move in due course toward democratic government and popular sovereignty? History offers no assurance that the voice of the people is less apt to call for nationalist extremes than that of a leading minority, yet there was undoubtedly in Japan's case a close connection between the continuing transcendental position of the emperor and the buildup of popular pressures which ultimately found their release in the restless drive for expansion and the fanatical dedication to conformity at home.

But if the monarchy was unquestionably involved in the spread of militarism and totalitarianism in Japan, it still does not follow that the "emperor system" was the driving force in this relationship. If there was a failure to liberalize the powers of the monarchy or to curtail its prerogatives, where did the responsibility lie? There were at least three major points along the road toward the New National Structure at which important choices affecting the meaning of the monarchy were offered to the Japanese. The first of these came at the time of the framing of the Meiji constitution when alternatives in the legal definition of the emperor's powers were debated. The second came during the period from 1890 to 1910 when the meaning of the imperial institution as defined in the constitution was interpreted by the highest legal minds in the country. And the third came with the effort to modify the interpretation of the "absolute and irresponsible" monarch *in practice* by the adoption of responsible party cabinets. In each of these instances, presumably, the course of political development (and with it the interpretation of the powers of the monarchy) could have taken a turn toward greater popular representation or toward abandonment of the mystical traditions surrounding the throne. But the turn was not taken, and we need to know why.

For those who see in the emperor system the shadow of original sin, it has become axiomatic to claim that the Meiji constitution merely gave legal form to the effort of the oligarchy to suppress the movement for "democratic rights." But the crux of this accusation lies in whether the movement, even though it bore the high-sounding slogan of "liberalism and popular rights" (*jiyū-minken*), was as sincere a people's cause as it purported to be. Recent studies have probed the movement in terms of actual rather than idealized objectives, asking the hardheaded question whether Itagaki and

Ōkuma offered genuine alternatives to the leadership of Itō and Yamagata. Can the words "liberal" and "democratic" be used to characterize the opposition leaders? If so, then, how is one to explain the ease with which they changed their political objectives or became chauvinistic nationalists? One suspects that as far as the institution of the monarchy was concerned they represented no great choice.[41] For in the final analysis even men like Fukuzawa found themselves more concerned with Japan's competitive powers as a nation than over whether the people were given adequate political voice.

We too often fail to appreciate how unusual it would have been in the decades of the 1870's and 1880's to have found political figures of any consequence who would have denied the special symbolism of the emperor and have advocated the establishment of a popular sovereignty. Real issues were publicly and officially debated, and these included questions of how much power should be given an elective assembly and where the locus of responsibility in government should rest. But one looks in vain in this debate for a clear and articulate demand for the establishment of a government responsible to an elective process. Even Ōkuma, who startled the government in 1881 by openly coming out in favor of the British form of parliamentary government, proved unspecific on the point of the locus of sovereignty.[42] Beyond this we must also realize that the choice offered the Japanese people at this time was not simply one between greater and lesser repre-

[41] This point requires considerable substantiation which is only recently appearing in English. Joseph Pittau's "Ideology of a New Nation" (Ph.D. dissertation, Harvard, 1962), pp. 150–53, is a recent treatment. Maruyama Masao's "Meiji kokka no shisō" is probably one of the most balanced Japanese treatments. But Inoue Kiyoshi has written a whole article on the historiography of the thesis that the movement was democratic. "A Historical Outline of Studies in the 'Ziyu Minken' Movement," *Zinbun*, II (1958), 23–50. Nakamura, *op.cit.*, p. 89, has it both ways by claiming a division between "sincere democrats" and the "opportunists."

[42] See the translation of Ōkuma's opinion in George M. Beckmann, *The Making of the Meiji Constitution* (Kansas, 1957), pp. 136–43.

sentation, it was in fact between some representation and none at all. The final inclusion of the Diet in the constitution of 1889 was no mere concession tossed to a noisy opposition. Itō worked hard against heavy resistance within the government to gain its acceptance, and he himself believed that he had provided the apparatus for a true sounding of public opinion and the eventual expansion of popular participation in the decisions of government.[43] The constitution was carefully devised to maintain the political status quo, but it proved far less authoritarian than some members of the high bureaucracy would have wanted. And once it was promulgated, it had the hearty approval of the Japanese press as well as constitutional lawyers and scholars the world over, from Herbert Spencer to Oliver Wendell Holmes.[44]

As it turned out, the Meiji constitution had its defects. Not only did it institutionalize sovereignty in the person of a divine emperor, it gave a cloak of credibility to the myths and dogmas of sanctification which had historically supported the Japanese monarchy. It added to the Japanese monarchal tradition, in other words, the legal magic and imperial ritualism of the modern Prussian system. But were there voices which might have been raised against this in the days before the principles of popular rule were fully understood or before the doctrine of socialism had touched many minds? Figuratively and emotionally the emperor remained the most cherished symbol of national identity to Japanese from Iwakura to Uchimura Kanzō. However clearly the issues may have been drawn over the question of monopoly of power by the "clan clique," there were certainly few who foresaw in 1889 the problems created by carrying "Japan's particular form of monarchy" into modern times.[45] The constitution also perpetuated

[43] Pittau, *op.cit.*, ch. 6.

[44] Takayanagi Kenzo, "A Century of Innovation: The Development of Japanese Law, 1868–1961," in Arthur T. von Mehren, ed., *Law in Japan* (Cambridge, Mass., 1963), pp. 6–9.

[45] Takeda Kiyoko, "Tennōsei shisō no keisei," *Iwanami kōza, Nihon rekishi* (Tokyo, 1962), xvi, 281–98.

that particular form of Japanese political decision-making which obscured the locus of responsibility behind an "irresponsible" sovereign who spoke for the consensus of his political advisors. The combination of imperial absolutism and undefined responsibility continued a practice of government which was second nature to the Japanese leadership. That it passed so easily into the clauses of the Meiji constitution is to some extent the result of the failure of the German advisors to the Japanese drafters of the constitution to appreciate fully the practical differences between the Prussian and Japanese monarchies.[46]

If, then, the constitution was a relatively progressive document for its day and in its context, why did its defects loom larger and larger in the years which followed? Why was the document never really liberalized through interpretation, but on the contrary came to be applied more narrowly and rigidly, and the emperor made the object of an increasingly irrational devotion? Was it simply that the constitution had so protected its "authoritarian and antipopular bias" as to make it unassailable, particularly for a people who had no tradition of orderly process of political change? Somehow the answer seems too easy. Why, for instance, did not a responsible opposition to the government come into being with the creation of the Diet? What brought on the change of national mood which made nationalists of Fukuzawa Yūkichi and Tokutomi Sohō and drew crowds to Ueno Park to imbibe the emotions of national indignation? Why was there no real opposition to the Hozumi interpretation of the "emperor as state" and the variations of the imperial myth which were fed into the educational system? Why did Yoshino Sakuzō have so little success in his effort to create a theoretical basis for party government?

[46] Pittau, op.cit., pp. 249–51. The German expectation that the emperor would play a positive role in political decision-making was thwarted both by the traditional relationship of the "sacred emperor" to government and by the personalities of the Taishō and Shōwa emperors.

We have too often interpreted these "failures" as part of a continuing fall from grace in which popular political aspirations lost out against the entrenched forces of authority and chauvinism. But surely there was a more fundamental key to this behavior, the possibility that the drift toward totalitarianism was eased by something which the Japanese desired even more than the conversion of their emperor to a symbol of their own self-government. For such a key we would need to probe the inner psychology of a people struggling for preeminence in a hostile world. For once on the defensive, where were the Japanese to find comfort but in the dream world of the imperial myth and the warmth of a family-state togetherness? And certainly once the retreat to unreality was begun, the very sacredness of the emperor and self-deceptions embodied in the revived concepts of national uniqueness precluded the possibility of self-awakening. In all of this the web of responsibility between leadership and followers, between system and masses is not easily untangled.[47]

4 *The Emperor Today*

In the end it took defeat in war and the intercession of an occupation force to explode the imperial myth and to wrest sovereignty from the inviolable emperor and grant it to the people. The new constitution not only limited the emperor to the status of national symbol but drastically stripped from him the means of maintaining himself independently of the peoples' representatives. The emperor's disavowal of his divinity, the discrediting of nationalist myths, the withdrawal of state support from Shinto, the abolition of a separate imperial military command, the elimination of the emperor's private wealth were all significant subtractions, each devised to remedy a major source of danger in the prewar system and to prevent the emperor from again being used either by an

[47] See the excellent treatment of this period by Marius Jansen, *op.cit.*, pp. 65–81.

irresponsible leadership or an irrepressible people for ultra-nationalist purposes.

But if the institutionalization of the Meiji monarch had the full force of Japanese historical tradition behind it, the postwar establishment of a shadowy symbol devoid of power had a ring of artificiality about it. The logical result of military defeat for a Japan which had gone to war behind its sacred emperor would have been the destruction of the imperial system. Not only was it clear to the Japanese that the victorious forces after World War II could just as well have abolished the emperor, but they also took into the postwar period their own private aversion to the institution for which they had so recently been ready to give their all. For once the war was lost, the emperor inevitably became a victim in the effort of the Japanese to fix the blame for their wartime experience. And despite the spread of the word that the emperor had been opposed to the war and the confirming judgment of the Tokyo Trials absolving the emperor of war guilt, the thought was to persist that he should have abdicated, or even committed suicide, in 1945 and that the new constitution should have abolished the institution once and for all. The knowledge that prior to the Japanese surrender there were strong voices raised in the Allied councils which demanded the elimination of the emperor as a necessary corollary to "unconditional surrender" served as a reminder that the institution was saved only by the decision of a conquering enemy. The pre-surrender disagreement among the Allies on what to do with the emperor had brought out all of the questions which still remain unresolved in the minds of the Japanese: the questions of the necessary relationship between emperor and emperor system, between emperor and aggressive militarism, and between emperor and the capacity of the Japanese to achieve political democracy. And many Japanese were unconvinced of the wisdom of the ultimate American decision and refused to believe that the emperor could be "democratized," that a knife could be inserted between the emperor as symbol of national unity and his rampant other being, the emperor as champion of conservatism and ultranationalism. For such sceptics it was no comfort to know that retention of the emperor was in part agreed upon as an occupation expediency.

The early years of the Occupation during which the Japanese awoke to their first freedom to attack the emperor produced a flood of critical literature which questioned the intentions of the Americans in retaining the emperor and refuted the possibility that the "emperor system" had been destroyed.[48] Inoue Kiyoshi, for instance, put the entire subject into the context of America's desire to use Japan as a base of operations against Soviet Russia. "In keeping with this ultimate objective," he wrote "America, making superficial concessions to the forces of international democracy and to democratic forces in Japan, carried out 'a colonization of Japan in the name of democratization.' The emperor and the emperor system were part of this same design. And so, enacting a phony land reform and *zaibatsu* dissolution, they laid the economic foundations for a continuation of the *tennō* system."[49]

But as Ishida Takeshi has shown in his study of postwar Japanese opinion toward the emperor, this hypercritical attitude ultimately faded.[50] The relative stability of postwar politics, the growing economic prosperity, and the new public image of the imperial family all contributed to the acceptance of the new constitutional formula and a return of the monarch to a position of popularity of a vastly different sort from the prewar style. The new popularity retained little of the fanatic nationalist fervor of prewar days but took delight in a sense of familiarity and intimacy. The great outpouring of interest in the wedding of the crown prince, the new ease with which the Japanese have turned back to the prewar years without rancor, taking pride in the "great men of Meiji" or in the

[48] Ishida Takeshi, *Sengo Nihon no seiji taisei* (Tokyo, 1961), pp. 7–25.
[49] Inoue, *op.cit.*, p. 3.
[50] Ishida, *Sengo Nihon*, pp. 40–47.

figure of Emperor Meiji, the ability to look with clinical objectivity at movies depicting the patriotic excesses of Japanese wartime behavior, all indicate a new maturity of the popular mind.[51] And although there are still cynics who warn of the danger inherent in the emperor's continued existence, the behavior of the Japanese in recent years would seem to indicate otherwise. The emperor today stands as symbol, not of some irrational "superiority" of the Japanese race, but rather as a projection of their own pride in their own achievements as a modern people; not as a reminder of the terrors of war and humiliation of defeat but rather as symbol of Japan's purity of intent to lead the world in working for peace.

Perhaps it was in the ceremonies attending the 1964 Olympics that the new popular sovereignty and the status of the emperor were most clearly displayed to the rest of the world. For amid the frenzied efforts to bring order out of the chaos which was Tokyo and in the excitement of the opening-day pageantry, the mild-mannered Shōwa Tennō belied the fact that he had once served as the mystical center of every national ritual and the rationale for every major national effort. As he stood before his countrymen in the great Olympic Stadium, it seemed no longer that it was simply through him that the fiercest feelings of pride were drawn from the hearts of the Japanese. Rather it was in the physical surroundings themselves, in the bold sweep of prestressed concrete, in the visions of superhighways arched over central Tokyo, and in the thought that the athletes of the world had been assembled with unprecedented efficiency and hospitality that the majority seemed to find their deepest satisfaction.[52] To an observer of that moment it appeared that for the Japanese their knowledge of what they had wrought was sufficient to the occasion; through their own works they

[51] Note the recent issue of *Bungei shunjū* containing a special series on Emperor Meiji (XLIII, Jan. 1965). Ishida cites the examples of the films *Meiji Tenno to Nichi-ro daisenso* and *Nippon horobarezu*.

[52] On the "Japanese features" of the Olympic architecture, see Kōjirō Yuichirō, "Building for the Olympics," *Japan Quarterly*, IX:iv (1964), 437–55.

were speaking to the world in a language more direct and universal than that which could have been expressed symbolically through a sacred emperor. Clearly, a basic change in the relationship between monarch and people was being ritualized.

FOR THE HISTORIAN, the Japanese monarch today stands as both a symbol of national unity and a reminder of the vicissitudes through which the institutions of national sovereignty have passed in modern times. Few Asian nations entered the modern world by strengthening a monarchal system rather than destroying it. For Japan in its period of crisis between 1853 and 1871 the monarchy served the essential functions of assuring national unity and impressing a sense of responsibility upon the nation's leaders. Thereafter the emperor became a symbol of Japan's determination to modernize and to gain a place among the nations of the world. Japan's modern monarchy was a direct institutional and functional inheritance from the Japanese past, yet it served as a receptacle for new national aims. As the sovereign who presided over Japan's early steps toward modernization, Meiji Tennō became an inspiration to his people in their struggle to create a strong independent state. The person of the emperor linked both past and future, giving the Japanese a sense of security and identity while encouraging their dedication to the difficult tasks of reforming their social and economic institutions. But the government he stood for remained shrouded from public view by its transcendental nature and remained resistant to the kinds of modern change which were affecting the rest of the culture. If history could ask more of the Meiji leaders, it would be that they might have built into their constitution a broader vision of political tutelage which would have looked forward to both the material development of the country and to its political evolution toward fuller representation. For without such enlightened guidance the Japanese people as a whole, overwhelmed perhaps by manifold domestic and international problems, found the further reform of their government beyond their capacity. Increasingly they heaped upon their emperor the burden of their frustrated aims until they found themselves caught in the mythology of the most traditional and irrational inheritances which the emperor had brought with him out of the Japanese past.

Reborn out of the ashes of military defeat and wartime disillusionment, the Shōwa Emperor, by virtue of retaining the same body under a new constitutional system, has again become the symbol of continuity despite drastic change. And by virtue of the new myth which depicts the emperor as the symbol of Japan's good conscience which suffered silently during the war, he has literally come to embody the new determination of the Japanese to remain a peaceful democracy. Thus in its second modern transmutation the monarchy has passed still further into the realm of symbolic meaning, hopefully leaving behind those many irrational inheritances from the past which proved so dangerous when taken literally by the modern nationalist. Stripped today of power and sovereignty, the emperor serves only in the most disembodied of the manifestations with which he was historically endowed, as symbol of his country's moral consciousness. Yet behind this symbol there burns as fierce a fire of determination that Japan shall be first—this time in peace, not in war.[53]

[53] Eto Jun has put this into critical context. "Before the war Japanese intellectuals wished to make Japan rank first among all nations by force of arms. These same intellectuals are still out to make Japan first among all nations, but this time by merely chanting, 'Absolute peace!' " "The Bankruptcy of Our Idealistic Intellectuals," in *Journal of Social and Political Ideas in Japan*, ii:ii (April 1964), 105.

CHAPTER III

Political Modernization and the Meiji *Genrō*

ROGER F. HACKETT[1]

T WICE in her history Japan has responded with remarkable success and speed to the urgent demands of an encounter with more advanced civilizations. In the seventh century Japan was transformed by policies stimulated by the unification of China under the Sui and T'ang dynasties; in the nineteenth century she was transmogrified by reforms that met the irresistible challenge of an industrialized Western civilization. In both instances sweeping changes in the political administration, in the tax system, in national defense, and in many other aspects of her society ushered in prosperous and brilliant periods in Japanese history. The achievements of both of these pivotal experiences have frequently been credited to enlightened leadership. One eminent historian goes so far as to assert that "It was entirely because of the foresight, diligence and self-devotion of these eminent statesmen that Japan was successful in reforming her country in the 7th and 19th centuries."[2] In neither case are the transforming changes attributed to the role of one dominant political leader. Indeed, compared to the history of other nations, "The tendency throughout Japanese history toward group leadership rather than the leadership of some dominant personalities"[3] is

[1] The author would like to express his appreciation to the Carnegie Corporation of New York City for assistance received in connection with the preparation of this essay.
[2] K. Enoki, "Japan in World History," *India Quarterly*, XII (Oct.–Dec. 1956), 422.
[3] E. O. Reischauer, "Special Features in the History of Japan," *Japan-American Forum* x (Nov. 1964), 4.

commonly identified as a special characteristic of the Japanese experience.

Certainly leadership in the nineteenth century political modernization of Japan is ascribed to a group rather than to any single individual, unlike the thrust toward modernity in the less developed countries of the twentieth century, which seems to require national discipline of a sort stimulated and enforced by a single powerful personality who succeeds in curbing divisive conflict and averting social disintegration. There is no agreement on the size of this collective leadership, although it is acknowledged that each challenge to central power, such as the open resistance to reforms and discussion over the political system that was to be established, narrowed the ruling group. In each instance where there was a contest for power it was the minority forces which were galvanized by individual leaders while those retaining government authority held it as a group. This is dramatized by the civil war of 1877, when the unsuccessful rebels were led by the heroic Saigō Takamori while a number of leaders of the victorious government forces shared the honor of victory. The absence of a single hero-type leader in the nineteenth century is often explained by the fact that changes were carried out in the name of an emperor imbued with absolute virtue and total wisdom. This prevented the emergence of charismatic leadership because institutional charisma already existed in the form of an emperor cult.[4] It is also ascribed to the tenacity of traditional social forms that favored a group orientation and a pattern of decision-making that was consensual rather than personal, so that collective leadership in the modern period is viewed as evolving naturally in a system run by collegial rule.

The absence of a single "great man" leading the vital transformation of Japan in the nineteenth century is underlined by the use of such popular labels as "triumvirate" to designate

[4] Nobutaka Ike, "Political Leadership and Political Parties," in D. Rustow and R. E. Ward, eds., *Political Modernization in Japan and Turkey* (1964), p. 402.

the first group of leaders (usually meaning Saigō Takamori, Ōkubo Toshimichi, and Kido Kōin) who guided the nation during the first years following the Restoration, and "oligarchy," "*han* clique," or "*genrō*" (elder statesmen) to describe the second generation of leaders who held dominant political power well into the twentieth century. In the 1930's and 1940's the term *jūshin* (senior statesmen) was used to refer to court officials and former prime ministers who were called on to advise the emperor on the selection of new prime ministers and on other important matters. These labels were applied to informal groups of leaders who by virtue of political experience and achievement were regarded as the highest advisory body which the emperor could turn to in solving the most critical internal and external problems facing the nation. The most important such group in the political modernization of Japan was the Meiji *genrō*, and it is with the genesis, composition, and role of the *genrō* in the modernizing process that this inquiry is concerned.

The key role of the Meiji *genrō* in leading the modern development of Japan is emphasized by all commentators. In most studies of the anatomy of political power in Japan they have been included at the vital center and identified with such phrases as "the power behind the throne," "commanders of the inner circle," or "the real rulers of Japan." Most students have assessed their role in negative terms, stressing their unscrupulous manipulation of power and their hostility to the growth of genuine representative government. A few have indicated their stabilizing influence, which was an essential contribution to a period of rapid change. Whatever the assessment, for a group which operated at the summit of the political pyramid during the first half of Japan's modern century there are some basic questions, such as who the *genrō* included and how they operated, which have received only limited attention.

The absence of any systematic study of the *genrō* as a political body is understandable. In the first place as an informal, nonlegal body no records of their meetings and deliberations were kept. In the examination of their activities reliance has been placed on the biographies and studies of the individual *genrō* (the term being used to refer to both the collectivity and to its members). Dependence on separate studies of the individuals involved leads to a second problem: it accentuates the differences between the members, rather than viewing the *genrō* as a political group. Still another cause for difficulty is the problem of segregating the activities of each as an important official fulfilling quite specific functions from his larger responsibility as a *genrō* of guiding the course of the nation. Indeed it is quite impossible to separate their roles, for their individual accomplishments in the construction of the new state determined in some measure their forcefulness as *genrō*, and, conversely, *genrō* status added authority to their many other activities.

The Genesis of the Genrō System

Our first task is to establish who the *genrō* were and when they can be identified as a political body. And the frustration as well as the fascination in studying this important group begins with these simple questions. The failure to distinguish between the *Genrō-in*, a legally constituted council of elders (a senate) established in 1875 "to enact laws for the Empire"[5] and abolished in 1890 without ever achieving real legislative power, and the *genrō* has almost disappeared in Western writings.[6] Yet there is not complete agreement on who to designate as the *genrō*, even in Japanese scholarship, though the lists do not vary widely.[7] Most authoritative sources include

[5] W. McLaren, *Japanese Government Documents* (1914), p. 41.

[6] The error reappears, however, in the glossary of Allan B. Cole, *Japanese Society and Politics* (1956), p. 146.

[7] For example, see Hayashi Shigeru's entry under "*genrō*" in *Hyakka jiten* (Heibonsha, 1956), x, 38, or Umetani Noboru's chart in *Nihon kindai shi jiten* (1961), p. 161. Professor Oka Yoshitake omits Kuroda from his list in *Kindai Nihon seiji shi* (1962), p. 254.

seven original *genrō* (by order of birth): Matsukata Masayoshi (1835–1924), Inoue Kaoru (1836–1915), Yamagata Aritomo (1838–1922), Kuroda Kiyotaka (1840–1900), Itō Hirobumi (1841–1909), Ōyama Iwao (1842–1916), and Saigō Tsugumichi (1843–1902). Later additions to the list always include Saionji Kimmochi (1849–1940) and, more often than not, Katsura Tarō (1848–1913).

What was the selection process that determined this original group of seven senior advisers? If, for the moment, we arbitrarily date the origins of the Meiji *genrō* institution at 1890, we discover certain common features. All were from Satsuma (Matsukata, Kuroda, Ōyama, Saigō) or Chōshū (Inoue, Yamagata, Itō). Each was the son of a samurai family of moderate or low status born between the years 1835 and 1843. All had been active in the Restoration movement. Kuroda was influential in the formation of the Satsuma-Chōshū military alliance and achieved recognition and rewards for his part in the campaign to subdue stubborn Aizu forces defending the shogunate. Matsukata played a part in wresting control of Nagasaki from Tokugawa administration, while Saigō Tsugumichi, the younger brother of Takamori, and Ōyama fought in the Restoration battles after some years as extremist activists. Inoue, Itō, and Yamagata were Chōshū *shishi* (loyalist extremists) who had led militia units in the conflict against the conservative forces within Chōshū, had participated in antiforeign incidents, and had shared in the brief but decisive final encounters with the *bakufu*. They had all risen to power through the hurly-burly of Restoration politics as participants in the political and military actions leading to the triumph of extremist forces within their *han*, and to the formation of the Satsuma-Chōshū alliance which was decisive in the defeat of Tokugawa authority. Except that they were from two different *han*, there was, therefore, no great diversity in their backgrounds. It is not surprising to read Katsura's statement, in his autobiography in 1898, that it was only natural for Satsuma

69

and Chōshū leaders to lead the government since it was common knowledge that the contribution of the two *han* was decisive in the Restoration.[8]

In the early years of the Meiji government all those who were to achieve the status of *genrō* were assigned to lower bureaucratic posts, but they moved up rapidly as the leadership narrowed. Only the names of Inoue and Itō appear among the 106 councillors (*sanyo*) who were appointed in the first post-Restoration government, and this undoubtedly was due in part to the foreign experience which they had gained illicitly in 1864. The selection of these councillors from so many *han* (they came from nineteen) was an effort to include a wide representation of high-ranking retainers or of those who had gained a position of control of all the major *han* allied to the imperial cause. When the government was reorganized in June 1868 and such a broad base was no longer felt essential, the number of *sanyo* was reduced to twenty-two, representing only seven *han*. When the Council of State (*Dajōkan*) system was instituted in 1869 and the title *sangi* was substituted for *sanyo*, the councillors numbered only twenty-six (nine from Satsuma, seven from Chōshū, four from Hizen, and five from Tosa) plus a single representative, Katsu Rintarō, from the ranks of the bureaucracy, but more significantly they represented only the four *han* that formed the core of the Restoration forces. But, as W. G. Beasley analyzes it, even more significant in this shift was that rank was less important in advancement than able performance and service to the state. "Political authority," as he puts it, "was becoming more and more linked with the possession of non-traditional knowledge and experience."[9] For our purposes the most significant fact is that all of the Meiji *genrō* were *sangi*. In each crisis confronting the government from 1873 on, a number

[8] Quoted in Otsu Jun'ichirō, *Dai Nihon kenseishi* (1927), IV, 742.

[9] W. G. Beasley, "Councillors of Samurai Origin in the Meiji Government, 1868-69," *Bulletin of the School of Oriental and African Studies*, XXX (1957), 101.

of *sangi* withdrew from office and others retired or died, so that when the title of *sangi* was abolished in 1885, to make way for the cabinet system, the surviving Satsuma and Chōshū leaders were the seven to gain the designation of *genrō*. Thus we observe almost a natural selection process in operation whereby the surviving members of the coalition which provided the major military force in the defeat of the *bakufu* gained the designation *genrō* and consequently represented a narrow regional base.

From the beginning of the Meiji period all the future *genrō* became involved in the formulation and implementation of the plans adopted to accomplish the goal of building sufficient national strength to prevent domination by the Western powers. Each rose through one of three channels of the new bureaucracy: departments concerned either with economic developments, such as the Ministries of Finance, Public Works, or Hokkaido Development; with military modernization; or with foreign affairs. In striving for prosperity and strength (*fukoku kyōhei*) for the purpose of preserving the nation's independence, these were the critical government agencies which introduced institutional reforms. In the early Meiji years Itō, Inoue, and Matsukata served in the Finance Ministry, and Kuroda was assigned to the Hokkaido Development Bureau. Yamagata, Saigō, and Ōyama participated in the organization of the new army and served as war minister in 1873–1878, 1878–1880, and 1880–1885, respectively. In the field of foreign affairs Kuroda and Inoue served as the chief negotiators in the signing of a treaty with Korea in 1876. In 1879 Inoue began his eight-year tenure as foreign minister.

After the inauguration of the cabinet system they occupied the posts given in the table on page 72.

These data show that the *genrō* were those who dominated the ministries of the government in the middle decades of the Meiji period. But their influence extended beyond the central bureaucracy. For example, Matsukata's long tenure in the Finance Ministry suggests his controlling position in the

Cabinets	ITŌ	YAMAGATA	KURODA	MATSUKATA	INOUE	ŌYAMA	SAIGŌ
1. 1885–1888	Prime Minister	Home	Agriculture and Commerce (1887–1888)	Finance	Foreign	Army	Navy
2. 1888–1889		Home (to 1888)	Prime Minister	Finance Home (to 1889)	Agriculture and Commerce	Army	Navy
3. 1889–1891		Prime and Home Minister (to May 1890)		Finance		Army	Navy (to 1890) Home (1890–1891)
4. 1891–1892				Prime Minister and Finance			Home (to June 1891)
5. 1892–1896	Prime Minister	Justice (1892–1893)	Communications (1892–1895)		Foreign (1892–1894)	Army	Navy (1893–1898)
6. 1896–1898				Prime Minister and Finance			Navy
7. 1898	Prime Minister				Finance		Navy
8. 1898							Navy
9. 1898–1900		Prime Minister		Finance			Home

financial affairs of the government[10] but does not disclose his
vast influence in the business world through marriage connections and other associations. Similarly, Inoue's role as an
adviser to the Mitsui Company extended his sway far into
the commercial and industrial world. Ōyama's long service as
war minister does not properly underline his eminence as a
field commander and war hero. What this and other official
career data confirm, however, is that those who became *genrō*
were intimately connected with the birth and early growth
of the modern bureaucracy and that as ministers during the
period of radical political innovation they had accumulated
years of experience at the highest level of the government.
They were a talented elite, conscious of their role as leaders,
with the capacity to meet the requirements national survival
seemed to them to demand.

In addition to similar careers as Restoration activists and
modernizing bureaucrats, there were marriage alliances which
gave the *genrō* greater cohesiveness as a political body. Indeed
the complicated maze of marriage connections among the
leaders of government, business, education, and the military
seemed to interlock the top levels of Meiji society.[11] For example, Inoue, Itō, and Katsura were related through family
marriages. Inoue adopted as heir his older brother Gorosaburō's eldest son, Katsunosuke, while Gorosaburō's fourth son,
Hirokuni, became the adopted heir to Itō. Thus the heirs of
Itō and Inoue were blood brothers. Inoue Katsunosuke entered
the Finance Ministry, moved to the Foreign Office, and then
became an official in the Imperial Household Ministry, joining the Privy Council late in life. Itō Hirobumi spent thirty-

[10] One writer could not resist the temptation to compare him with
Alexander Hamilton and wrap up Meiji history by concluding that
"Itō made the constitution; Yamagata made the army; Matsukata made
the maintenance of both possible by fashioning a solvent state." Marvin
George, "The Alexander Hamilton of Japan," *Asia*, xxv (Jan. 1925),
54–57.

[11] On these marriage connections I have followed Fukuchi Shigetaka,
"Meiji shakai ni okeru 'batsu' ni tsuite," *Shichō*, xL (June 1952), 28-41,

nine years in the Imperial Household Ministry. One of
Inoue's daughters married Tsuzuki Keiroku, who was Inoue's
private secretary when he was foreign minister, diplomatic
assistant to Itō during the latter's foreign journeys, and later
a privy councillor. Inoue's connections with Katsura were
through his adopted daughter, Kanako, who became Katsura's
second wife in a marriage arranged by Itō and held in 1898
at the War Ministry, and through his niece who married Katsura's heir and son Yōichi by his first marriage. Katsura Yōichi entered the Fujita Company in Osaka and became very
prosperous. In addition, Inoue Katsunosuke adopted Saburō,
son of Katsura and blood brother of Yōichi. Inoue's marriage
connections with the political party world came through the
marriage of his wife's daughter, by her first marriage, to
Hara Takashi. Itō also was related to Katsura, although post-
humously, through the marriage of his son Bunkichi, born of a
concubine, to one of Katsura's daughters.

Ōyama and Saigō were related through Ōyama's wife,
who was Saigō's cousin. Ōyama's older brother was married
to Saigō's younger sister and his younger brother to Saigō's
older brother Takamori's illegitimate daughter. It might be
added that Ōyama's wife's elder brother was Yamakawa
Kenjiro, a samurai of Aizu who became president of Tokyo
University, member of the House of Peers and a privy
councillor. Matsukata's numerous progeny tended to marry
into banking and business (his second son married an Iwasaki
daughter) or navy families (his fourth and fifth sons married
daughters of admirals).

Although *genrō* was neither a formal rank nor an office title,
a quasi-legal basis for the institution is sometimes attributed to
a specific type of imperial message which most of them received. However, in these proclamations (*chokujo*) or letters
(*shochoku*) the designating term was *genkun* rather than
genrō. The former, meaning "meritorious elder," was often
applied, in a general sense, to those who had made important
contributions to the success of the Restoration (*ishin no*

genkun). Genkun is a term which appears in the Chinese classics and was applied to ministers who helped a monarch in the founding of a new dynasty. Emperor T'ai Tsung erected a special temple to celebrate the genkun who had contributed to the founding of the T'ang dynasty. The bestowal of such a title gave great honor and prestige to the receiver.

Kuroda and Itō were the first to receive this type of imperial proclamation. On November 1, 1889, when the former resigned as prime minister and the latter left the presidency of the Privy Council, they received identical messages in which the emperor expressed his wish to continue to regard them as his ministers and accord them status as meritorious elders (daijin no rei o motteshi koko ni genkun yūgū no i o akiraka ni su).[12] When Yamagata resigned from his first cabinet (May 6, 1891) and Matsukata completed his second term as prime minister (January 12, 1898), they received the same type of proclamation. Inoue received a similar message, asking him to render advice on important matters of state, in February 1904. In 1911 and 1912 Ōyama, Katsura, and Saionji each received imperial messages requesting them to serve as advisers to the throne. There is, however, no record of Saigō having received this type of message.[13] On the morning of August 13, 1912, just two weeks after the death of the Emperor Meiji, the new emperor invited Yamagata, Inoue, Matsukata, Ōyama, and Katsura to court to receive an imperial message (chokugo) which thanked them for the services they had rendered his father and requested their continued counsel and help.[14] The inclusion of Katsura in this invitation has often been used to include him among the genrō.[15]

While the "genkun messages" received by all the genrō save Saigō are used as a way of establishing the composition of

[12] Kaneko Kentarō, Itō Hirobumi den (1943), II, 699.

[13] Nihon kindai shi jiten (1958), p. 679.

[14] Otsu Jun'ichirō, Dai Nihon kensei shi (1927), VI, 723.

[15] Although in a letter to Yamagata, dated August 30, 1911, Katsura indicates that he had received a message from the emperor in which he was referred to as a genkun. Letter reprinted in ibid., VI, 666.

the group, its utility as a defining characteristic is open to question, since many of them were consulted in their capacity as elder statesmen long before receiving such an imperial message. Furthermore, the actual word *genrō* does not appear in these messages. We must therefore seek other explanations for the emergence of the term, and for this we turn to the popular usage of the label as it appeared in the press.

The press originally referred to the ministers participating in the selection of a prime minister as *genkun*. When many of those who had been consulted in the selection of Kuroda in 1888 were to serve in his cabinet, it was dubbed by the press as the "*genkun* dominated cabinet."[16] When Kuroda resigned, readers of the *Tokyo Nichi Nichi* were told that secret meetings were being held among various ministers to determine his successor, but these gatherings were not referred to as *genrō* meetings.[17] When Itō formed his second cabinet in 1892 there were references in the newspapers to *kuromaku kai* (behind the scenes meetings), *genkun kai*, and *Satchō genkun kai*. The August 7 *Tokyo Nichi Nichi* reported a *genkun kai* at Kuroda's Mita residence after which Kuroda and Yamagata went to the palace to recommend that Itō form the next cabinet.[18] However, the first appearance of the term *genrō* may well be in an article in the *Choya Shimbun* of August 8, 1892, which reported the appointment of Watanabe Kunitake as finance minister in Itō's cabinet and noted that he was not of the dominant Satchō faction and that he was joining various "*genrō*" in its formation.[19] From 1892 on the use of the terms *genrō* and *genrō kai* became more frequent in the press. After the Sino-Japanese war, for example, Itō's resignation as prime minister was followed by a long series of meetings to decide on a successor. "After three weeks of inner conferences," said the *Tokyo Nichi Nichi* on September 19,

[16] *Ibid.*, III, 69.
[17] Yamada Shikazō, *Seiji kenkyū* (1926), p. 35.
[18] *Ibid.*, pp. 40–41.
[19] *Shimbun shūsei Meiji hennenshi*, VIII, 287.

1896, "there were signs in the past two or three days that the situation was changing with regard to the Matsukuma [i.e. Matsukata-Ōkuma] cabinet—with the emperor's inquiries and the influence of the mediation of the *genrō*. Finally this morning agreement was reached."[20] By 1898 the term had become common coin, although doubts lingered as to whom it should apply. On November 5, 1898, the editorial writer of the *Tokyo Nichi Nichi* attempted a clarification:

> There is no sound basis for determining who should be and who should not be considered the *genrō*. Are they those who are treated as ministers because the emperor wishes to recognize them as veteran statesmen (*genkun*)? If so, only Itō and Yamagata fit that category. Are they those ex-ministers who are treated with the same honors as when they occupied official office? If so, Count Ōkuma, Count Itagaki, and Count Hijikata and others would be included.
>
> In point of fact, the term *genrō* is limited to Marquises Itō, Yamagata, Ōyama, and Saigō and Counts Kuroda, Matsukata, and Inoue—all senior Satchō clansmen and previously appointed *sangi*. They did not adopt the term *genrō* themselves. The public applied it to these seven selected by the emperor as advisers, who function as a special body to advise on the major tasks facing the nation as a separate but extraconstitutional body supplementing the highest political organs of the state.[21]

Thus it would appear that the press played a role in the popular designation of those whom the emperor consulted on the problems of cabinet succession as *genrō*. But at what point the senior Satchō statesmen who were consulted can be thought of as an informal advisory body it is difficult to say. Some contend that the appearance of the *genrō* in this sense dates from when Itō resigned in 1888 after serving as the first prime minister under the cabinet system and persuaded Kuroda to suc-

[20] Quoted in Yamada, *op.cit.*, p. 42.
[21] Quoted in *ibid.*, pp. 49–50.

ceed him.[22] Others claim that the term is more applicable to the selection of Matsukata as prime minister in 1891.[23] The *Tokyo Nichi Nichi* described the process: "After the firm refusal of Counts Itō and Saigō, it was decided two nights ago to persuade Matsukata to accept the prime ministership. After several ministers implored him to agree, and after he declined once or twice out of a sense of modesty, he then said yes, yes." The same account includes the observation that "The new minister was decided upon as a result of Count Itō's mediation."[24] But most frequently the origin of the *genrō* as an advisory group is identified with the formation of the Itō cabinet of 1892. By that date the emperor had issued a number of "*genkun* messages" to specific ministers as they left office requesting them to serve as personal advisers. Furthermore, it is associated with this event because it is known that the emperor called Itō, Kuroda, Inoue, and Yamagata to the palace to decide who should succeed the resigning Matsukata.

Whatever the precise date may be for the emergence of the *genrō*, it is noteworthy that the institution took shape at the very time that the new political structure had been completed. The cabinet system and the office of lord keeper of the privy seal had been created in 1885, in 1886 the Imperial Household Ministry with its councillors was established, and in 1888 the Privy Council was organized as "the supreme advisory body to the emperor."[25] All of these legal bodies were incorporated into the new political framework through articles in the constitution of 1889. But in the early 1890's these institutions were still relatively untried, and under these circumstances it is understandable how the practice evolved of relying informally on the advice and guidance of the most influential Satchō ministers. This reliance on an oligarchy of distinguished political entrepreneurs who now managed the institutions they

[22] Hirota Naoe, *Naikaku kotetsu gojunenshi* (1930), p. 248.
[23] Fukaya Hiroji, *Shoki gikai: jōyaku kaisei* (1940), p. 241.
[24] Quoted in Yamada, *op.cit.*, pp. 35–36.
[25] *Tokyo Nichi Nichi*, quoted in Yamada, *op.cit.*, pp. 35–36.

had helped to create was probably well suited to the needs of
the political capacities of Japan at the time. Whether the less
flattering term *kuromaku* or the more complimentary designation of *genkun* or *genrō* was used for this group, in the
popular mind of the day it became associated with the real
leadership of the nation. *Genkun* and *genrō* were terms laden
with historical connotations which carried prestige and honor
for those so designated, and the popular knowledge that the
eminent men of the realm were called on at critical times to
guide the nation may have well contributed to a general feeling
of national confidence. The *genrō* became a symbol with wide
appeal that gave a sense of stability during periods of great
strain. Even in 1911, Katsura is alleged to have told the Emperor Meiji that one of the reasons he contemplated the formation of a "model party" was his fear that the great popular
confidence enjoyed by the *genrō* was fading.[26] In 1915 we discover Miura Gorō, a conservative in the House of Peers who
had distinguished himself in the Restoration but who frequently opposed the *genrō*, proposing to the party leaders that
the surviving *genrō* join the Ōkuma cabinet to strengthen the
feeling of national unity.[27]

Genrō Politics and the Political System

As we have seen, by the early 1890's a group of men, by
virtue of requests from the emperor that they advise on the selection of a prime minister, and by virtue of their positions in
the dominant Satchō coalition and within the political bureaucracy, came to be known popularly, both individually and collectively, as the *genrō*. As a group their main function was to
resolve the leadership crisis brought on by the resignation of a
prime minister and, later, to participate in the vital decisions
affecting war and peace. But as individuals, carrying the prestige of a *genrō*, they became involved in most of the domestic

[26] Otsu reports hearing of this conversation in *Dai Nihon kenseishi*,
VII, 12–13.

[27] *Ibid.*, VII, 12–13.

and foreign policies affecting the national condition. In approaching problems they were in a position to initiate action as well as to approve it, to reconcile conflicting policies as well as to moderate policies.

The *genrō* exerted influence in a number of ways. First, two or three of them might meet quite casually at one or another's home to discuss a whole spectrum of issues. The results of these conversations, the area of agreement or any conspicuous disagreements, would filter out to government leaders. Second, they would gather in response to a specific request, from one of their number, the prime minister, or from the court, to attend to a more specific problem. The term *genrō kaigi* was frequently applied to these meetings, and they would often take place at an official residence or perhaps at the palace. The third type of meeting was a more formal gathering that would include the *genrō* and major cabinet ministers and therefore was known as a *genrō-daijin kaigi*. The fourth and most formal meeting which the *genrō* attended was the Conference in the Imperial Presence (*gozen kaigi*).[28] These imperial conferences were generally convoked by the court, through the grand chamberlain, or by the prime minister to consider, but more usually to approve, major foreign policy decisions and would include the *genrō*, cabinet ministers, and chief of the armed forces.

It is doubtful that the number of times the *genrō* (and exactly which *genrō*, when they were not all present) met in these various gatherings can be determined. Because of the informal character of the meetings, the fact that some went on for a number of sessions (for example, the ten separate meetings they held between December 6 and 17, 1912, during the "Taisho Crisis"), and the difficulty of giving precise definition to these various types of meetings, it is virtually impossible to arrive at

[28] *Gozen kaigi* might refer to any meeting before the throne, such as the *genrō* themselves sometimes held, and it applied to meetings held before the *genrō* emerged, but it is frequently reserved for the more formal type of meeting described.

a meaningful figure.[29] Meetings increased in frequency as major issues arose, but there was a continuous exchange of views between the *genrō*, through correspondence, through secretaries and confidants, and through casual visits. It is likewise difficult to pin down the origins of many of these meetings, though the initiative for more formal meetings, such as the *gozen kaigi* or *gozen-daijin kaigi*, can be identified. However, some of the *genrō kaigi* were in response to an imperial request, such, as already noted, the emperor's request in August 1892 that Itō, Kuroda, Inoue, and Yamagata meet in order to recommend a successor to Matsukata. Frequently the initiative seemed to be in the hands of the individual *genrō* most vitally concerned with an issue, and after correspondence or visits with one or more of his colleagues these consultations would evolve into a meeting of the *genrō* as a whole, and perhaps beyond that to meetings with cabinet members. An example of this is seen in the evolution of the treaty with Russia in 1916, which began with Yamagata's proposal, gained support of the other *genrō* through correspondence and consultation, moved to *genrō* conferences with cabinet ministers, and finally became government policy.

In any case, the *genrō* carried out their "advisory" role in different ways and through a variety of channels. Through their meetings they confronted the ordinary and extraordinary problems facing the nation from the mid-Meiji period on. But this should not imply that they faced issues with one mind. The ready use of terms such as *genrō*, *hambatsu*, and oligarchy tends to obscure their differences in attitude and style. Without denying the high degree of unity they expressed in a common commitment to transforming Japan into a strong, united nation, the individual *genrō* were strikingly different in approach to problems and often bitterly in disagreement.

The Satsuma or Chōshū origins did not seem divisive at the *genrō* level, for there were greater contrasts among than be-

[29] The *Sakuin seiji keizai dainempyō* (1943) lists, between 1898 and 1921, fourteen *genrō kaigi*, seven *genrō-daijin*, and eight *gozen kaigi*.

tween the four from Satsuma and three from Chōshū. On the other hand, to the extent that they were interested in preventing the Satchō balance within the government as a whole from being radically altered each was doubtless drawn to favor his own region to maintain the equilibrium. It is true that with the exception of Ōyama each had been minister of at least two departments, and this would support the thesis of the generalized character of the early Meiji leadership, yet their roots extended into different parts of the bureaucracy. Itō's base was the civil bureaucracy while Yamagata, Saigō, and Ōyama were military professionals. Matsukata and Inoue built their followings in special segments of the bureaucracy and in the business and financial world. Kuroda was a general but his activity in the development of Hokkaido gave him a quite different base.

Differences were as much a product of differing political styles as anything. The two strongest *genrō*, Itō and Yamagata, had contrasting personalities. Itō was more open and frank, confident of his abilities, less dependent on the judgment of others though a "court politician"[30] relying on connections at the palace. Yamagata was a more complicated figure, cold, guarded, almost secretive, yet "thinking of himself and his function as the central focus";[31] he was slow in changing, a martinet with broad political power through a numerous following. The perceptive Meiji journalist Toyabe Shuntei depicts Inoue as more concerned with his own feelings than the other *genrō*, a skillful collector of followers but few political adherents, a realist capable of composing differences.[32] Saigō is viewed as unassertive, effective at harmonizing the views of other *genrō*, more successful in this than Inoue's purposeful efforts because they were almost unconscious.[33] Kuroda is portrayed as single-minded, brusque, a bitter opponent of Itō, with a predilection for *sake* that prompted criticism from

---

[30] This is Toyabe Shuntei's characterization, *Shuntei zenshū*, p. 53.
[31] *Ibid.*, p. 232.   [32] *Ibid.*, pp. 312–16.
[33] *Ibid.*, pp. 202–04.

the emperor.[34] Matsukata was staunchly conservative, an efficient bureaucrat and shrewd businessman but considered a weak leader. Ōyama is characterized as an affable, good-natured soldier who preferred to stay aloof from politics. Although presumably they were equals in their role as *genrō*, these marked personality differences, as well as the contrast in their political ambitions and personal influence in the government, affected their relative importance as *genrō*. Itō, Yamagata, Matsukata, and Inoue were the most influential, while Ōyama, who often chose not to attend *genrō* conferences, and Kuroda and Saigō, who died in 1900 and 1902 respectively, must be considered of second rank.

Another characteristic of the *genrō* was the shifting alignments and the disagreements that took place within the group. In 1889, for example, Kuroda's strong support of Foreign Minister Ōkuma's treaty revision scheme was opposed by the other *genrō*. Itō, with support from Inoue, was displeased with Yamagata's handling of the first Diet in 1890, and the government's interference in the elections of 1892 when Matsukata was prime minister split the *genrō*. Inoue, on the other hand, opposed Itō's use of an imperial rescript against the intractable Diet in 1891. Again, in 1892 Matsukata, Kuroda, and Yamagata strongly opposed Itō's suggestion that he might establish ties with a political party, and a major crisis within the *genrō* was precipitated. This ran counter to the conviction shared by the *genrō* that the government should be run by the leaders of the bureaucracy who represented national interests rather than by party leaders, who, as they saw it, represented the narrow interests of a political party. While there were sharp divisions on these and other issues, there was a certain self-regulative device which enabled the *genrō* as an institution to carry out its function. The need to establish a consensus in order to advise the emperor helped to regulate the tendency of any member to take too independent a position.

From 1890 to the death of Matsukata in 1924, the role and

[34] Maeda Renzan, *Rekidai naikaku monogatari*, 1, 19–22.

influence of the original *genrō* moved through three phases. The first phase, which runs down to the turn of the century, centers on the rise and fall of the *genrō*'s own cabinets. This can be called the "seven *genrō* stage" during which each was a player as well as a referee, combining advisory with executive functions. It is the stage where these "founding fathers" formed an oligarchy which presided over the new political framework that was developed in the 1880's. While the seven *genrō* were by no means the only contributors to the new synthesis, they were all involved in the process of developing a more modern political system. At the same time, as administrators, as ministers running the key departments of the government, and as advisers to the emperor on who should be the prime minister, their role was to conserve and consolidate the changes they had helped to bring about, to give thereby as much stability as possible to the new political system.

Four of the seven *genrō* took turns as prime minister. During the period between the resignation of one cabinet and the inauguration of the next the "succession drama" was enacted with one after another of the circle being asked to form a government. The resigning *genrō* would suggest a successor after exchanging views with the colleagues whose support he felt he could get. The nominee would usually reject the offer, suggesting one or more others as possible successors to the resigning premier. Meanwhile court officials entered the act to attempt to expedite the procedure, sounding out and encouraging one *genrō* after another to accept the post. It was only a question of enough of the small circle agreeing on a single person who would be willing to shoulder the burden of the premiership. For example, when Yamagata resigned in 1891 he encouraged Inoue to get Itō to accept the nomination. Itō declined and nominated Saigō and Matsukata, neither of whom was anxious to accept it, but the latter finally acceded when the others agreed that his services were needed. The pattern of alternation between Satsuma and Chōshū members was not rigidly set, but it was commonly adhered to, one suspects,

84

because in addition to providing a balance wheel, it also was a useful rule in the game of selecting a successor. In any case, in the first phase of *genrō* politics leadership crises were met by the *genrō* themselves assuming responsibility for the government. In this way a measure of stability was insured by avoiding an abrupt shift in government power. Despite some disagreement on political tactics, the fact that those designated to recommend the prime minister selected only from among themselves meant that consensus had to be reached if their advisory role was not to be meaningless.

The major challenge to this state of affairs, of course, was Itō's proposal in 1898 that he form a government party. With the exception of Inoue, the other *genrō* were opposed. Yamagata charged this to be a violation of the spirit of the constitution and conjured up for Japan "the same fate as Spain and Greece."[35] In the well-known *genrō* meeting of June 1898, following Itō's proposal, Yamagata strongly opposed the plan by saying "You are a *genrō* and *genrō* always bear the responsibility of passing judgment on the gravest issues confronting the nation. If a *genrō* becomes the leader of a party he loses his independent position."[36] Itō was blocked by a united stand against him, but none of the other *genrō* felt able to step forth to retain government power in their hands. While the party of Ōkuma and Itagaki, which took over, had a short life and the *genrō* retrieved their power, the principle of having only nonparty cabinets had been violated, and it presaged Itō's defection from the concept of bureaucratic cabinets.

The second phase of *genrō* politics dates from the appointment of Katsura Tarō as prime minister in 1901 and extends to the end of the Meiji period in 1912. Katsura's ascendency to power is taken as a turning point in Meiji history because for the first time the *genrō*, reduced to five by 1902, withdrew from all administrative posts and a new leadership took over. Throughout this "five *genrō* stage" Katsura and Saionji,

[35] *Yamagata den*, III, p. 310.
[36] *Itō Hirobumi den*, III, p. 378.

as inheritors of the political mantles, respectively, of Yamagata and Itō, alternated in control of the government much as the Satsuma and Chōshū leaders had during the previous fifteen years. Conspicuously, none of the *genrō* produced an outstanding son, and there was no attempt to create a hereditary political aristocracy. In one sense the patronage of political heirs by Itō and Yamagata compensated for the encouragement of natural sons. But in the last analysis the political roles of Katsura and Saionji were determined more by their ability and achievements than by other standards. This in itself was a symptom of modernity. The absence of successors also suggests that the "seven *genrō* stage" was a transitional phenomena, one in which the perils of manipulating untested institutions were most effectively met by an oligarchy which combined administrative power with final advisory authority. After political institutions were stabilized, however, and after the nation had triumphed in a war with China and had succeeded in revising the unequal treaties, a new measure of confidence was achieved. Under these circumstances it is not surprising that the "founding fathers" were willing to pass on the active control of government to a new generation of leaders.

Of course, the *genrō* retained their advisory authority and in some instances showed that they exercised out of office almost as much influence over routine political matters as they did when they were in. Their role was still of the highest importance to the success of the system as a whole. Nevertheless, there were visible changes in their relationship to the political process. For one thing, there was growing restiveness among the second-rank bureaucrats who had labored in the shadow of the great men. This is revealed in the fewer number of *genrō* meetings. For another, as the *genrō* grew older they acquired the role of spokesmen for their own political following and, being less directly involved in the day-to-day issues, were forced to rely more on their followers to assert their influence. The shift in the role of the *genrō* is revealed by the obser-

86

vations of Itō Miyoji, the able political lieutenant of Itō Hirobumi at the time of Katsura's ascendency to power. When Itō
Hirobumi resigned in 1901 he fully expected to succeed himself
with a reorganized cabinet. But the four *genrō* (Yamagata,
Inoue, Matsukata, and Saigō) who met to perform their
duty of nominating a successor refused to recommend Itō, and
after Inoue failed in an effort to form a cabinet they nominated
Katsura. Itō Miyoji attempted to persuade Katsura not to
accept because he feared he would fail in forming a cabinet and
thereby injure the second-rank bureaucrats (such as Saionji,
Katsura and himself). Itō Miyoji wrote in hs diary:

> Although the *genrō* have controlled national politics since
> 1881, their strength today is not what it was. Nevertheless
> the afterglow of their brilliant achievements lingers on so
> that they are quickly summoned whenever a problem arises.
> This practice was not questioned in the past but now people
> are tired of these *genrō* activities. Besides, without the aid of
> others the efforts of the *genrō* are fruitless and they get no-
> where. It must be said that the political life of the *genrō* is
> about to expire. Whenever things go well they are arrogant
> and ignore those of the second level and below. Haven't
> you and others experienced such treatment for all these
> many years? ... This moment is truly the Sekigahara of the
> *genrō* and the younger men. ... While we must always re-
> spect the *genrō* we should let them use their own methods
> and thereby reveal their incompetence to the nation. Popu-
> lar support will then desert the *genrō* and public opinion
> will demand that the second-rank statesmen step forth.[37]

The hopes of the second-level statesmen to some extent were
fulfilled. There was no *genrō kaigi* when Katsura passed on the

[37] Itō Miyoji's diary quoted in Kurihara Hirota, *Hakushaku Itō
Miyoji*, p. 353. For this lead and analysis I am indebted to George
Akita's essay "Itō, Yamagata and Katsura: The Changing of the
Guards, 1901" presented to the International Conference on Asian
History, 1964.

reins of government to Saionji in 1906[38] and little consultation with them when Katsura resumed government leadership in 1908. So long as power rested between Katsura and Saionji, and the practice grew of the resigning prime minister yielding to his political opponent, the *genrō* were not called upon to make the selection. Each of these shifts, to be sure, were preceded by deferential consultations with the *genrō* to make sure there were no strong objections. But it was a matter of approving rather than nominating prime ministers.

Another characteristic of the *genrō* during this period was the rift between Itō and his colleagues. Disagreements among the *genrō* were not new, but the division became more marked after Itō assumed the presidency of the Seiyūkai in 1900, for this action clashed with long-held views of the *genrō* that the government should be run by those whose loyalty and interests transcended those of a political party leader. Above all, the *genrō* were irritated by Itō's dual role as party president and as *genrō*, letting a party leader share with the other *genrō* the confidence of the emperor and, second, the Seiyūkai's opposition to increasing taxes to pay for military expansion in 1903. Katsura resolved to overcome Itō's opposition by asking him, as a *genrō*, to yield his position as leader of the Seiyūkai. When Itō refused, Katsura resigned. But Yamagata made it unnecessary to accept Katsura's resignation by securing the support of the other *genrō* in requesting the emperor to ask Itō to relinquish his party position and lead the Privy Council. With the other *genrō* united against him, Itō was enraged at this trick but nonetheless was forced to give way and leave the party.[39]

It was also during this period that the *genrō* turned their attention more toward the critical foreign issues of the day. This was partly because of the relative stability of the political system during the "Katsura-Saionji era," which resulted in

[38] Yamada, *Seiji Kenkyū*, p. 57.

[39] I have followed Watanabe Ikujirō's reconstruction of this incident in *Meiji tennō to hohitsu no hitobito*, p. 282.

more limited consultations with the *genrō* on the formation of new governments. It was also because of the changing external situation following the new international position Japan had achieved after the Sino-Japanese war. The most important decisions in foreign affairs—wars and their settlement, treaty revision, the commitment of troops overseas in international ventures, and the negotiation of major treaties and agreements—all received the attention of the *genrō*.

There was no single *genrō* view on major external issues during the first decade of the twentieth century. Indeed there was sharp division on the question of an alliance with Britain. For the most part, however, the *genrō* advocated a balance between expanding Japan's power on the Asian continent and international cooperation. They participated in molding and endorsing policies which led to the decision to go to war with Russia, to sign the Treaty of Portsmouth, and to annex Korea. In other words, the *genrō* consensus was an important link in the government's process of deciding policy on the most vital external issues.

The third phase in the activities of the Meiji *genrō* may be dated from 1912 to Matsukata's death in 1924. Four *genrō*, all of them in their seventies, survived into this period, and by 1916, by which time Ōyama and Inoue had died, only Yamagata and Matsukata remained. However, in 1913 Saionji retired as leader of the Seiyūkai and joined the *genrō* ranks and endeavored to carry on the traditional *genrō* function until his death in 1940. One feature of this phase was the increasing resentment voiced against the actions of the *genrō*. With the advance of modernization, new groups developed with special interests and competed for national power. In this growing contest the privileged position of the *genrō* was more frequently challenged. Accusations of meddling in government business and arbitrary use of their power were more openly expressed. It was a symptom of the decline in the authority of the *genrō*. Even Katsura, after the failure of his government to survive the unified opposition of the political parties in 1912 and early

1913, tried to detach himself. "The *genrō* will have nothing to say about my future proceedings," he told a reporter in the midst of the Taisho Crisis in December 1912, "I am now on a footing of absolute independence."[40]

Despite their declining numbers, advancing age, and growing hostility they suffered, the *genrō* were still an influential body, both in selecting a prime minister and in guiding government policy. Greater age and long experience gave them perhaps a sense of stewardship over the nation's welfare. In recommending a candidate to the emperor the *genrō* were forced to consider the various factors that would contribute to stable government under a given candidate's ministry. The growing vigor of the political parties and the declining power of the aging oligarchs made the selection of a prime minister a trial of strength. But challenges to the government-appointing role were surmounted.

The selection of a successor to Ōkuma Shigemobu in 1916 proved to be such a challenge. Ōkuma was determined to propose Katō Kōmei as his successor. He quickly discovered that the *genrō* were opposed to Katō, and while still occupying the office of prime minister, he approached the emperor directly on the question. It was unprecedented for a prime minister to try to arrange for his successor while remaining in office, and it was a clear challenge to the role of the *genrō*. When Ōkuma maneuvered to persuade General Terauchi to join Katō in a coalition government, the former refused and reminded him that it was the emperor's prerogative to appoint the head of the government.[41] Upon submitting his resignation to the emperor, Ōkuma tried to bypass the *genrō* by including in his letter the statement, "Katō Kōmei is a man of great competence and skill . . . so I should like to select Katō as my successor."[42]

[40] Interview with *Jiji Shimpō*, translated in *Japan Weekly Mail*, Jan. 15, 1913, pp. 54–55.

[41] Kuroda Koshirō, comp., *Gensui Terauchi hakushaku den* (Tokyo, 1920), p. 814.

[42] Shinabu Seisaburō, *Taishō seiji shi* (Tokyo, 1955), I, 284.

Discovering what Ōkuma had done, the *genrō* (Ōyama, Yamagata, Matsukata, and Saionji) quickly came together and met before the emperor to recommend General Terauchi as the next prime minister. Terauchi was designated to form the next government and Ōkuma's challenge to the *genrō* was defeated.

In the field of foreign relations during this same period we find convincing illustration of the vigor and continued influence of the *genrō*. During the Ōkuma government (1914–1916) the prime minister, who was himself a distinguished elder statesman but by choice had declined *genrō* status, retained good relations with the *genrō*. Foreign Minister Katō, on the other hand, scarcely bothered to disguise his opposition to *genrō* influence in the government's policies. As a party politician and as an experienced diplomat with previous service as foreign minister, he particularly disliked outside interference in the development of foreign policy.

For their part, the *genrō*, led by Inoue and Yamagata, expressed little confidence in Katō's foreign policy, especially his China policy. They advocated adopting more positive measures to improve Sino-Japanese relations and to conclude an agreement with Russia. In August 1914 Yamagata proposed that the cabinet reexamine the nation's general foreign policy,[43] and specific suggestions were drafted and submitted to Ōkuma and to Katō.

These suggestions were received in the foreign office with cool courtesy. Katō felt no obligation to keep the *genrō* abreast of all diplomatic negotiations, and he studiedly refrained from more than a perfunctory response to their proposals. Moreover, on grounds of wartime security, he limited the practice of sending the *genrō* copies of secret documents relating to foreign affairs. This slight stirred the *genrō* to action.

[43] On this decision the Tokyo *Asahi* editorialized, "more than ever we realize the great influence of the *genrō* in our political life and, at the same time, are aware of their very great responsibility." Quoted in Yamada, *Seiji kenkyū*, p. 70.

On September 29, 1914, Prime Minister Ōkuma came together with the *genrō*, Yamagata, Inoue, Matsukata and Ōyama, in a most extraordinary meeting,[44] to reach an accord regarding the role of the *genrō* in the formation of foreign policy. Inoue's secretary recorded the agreements reached, which included such general points as the understanding that the prime minister and the *genrō* would confer closely and exchange views on the long-range goals of the nation, and that the foreign minister would "faithfully carry out the unanimous foreign policy views agreed upon by the prime minister and the *genrō*," and such specific points that "henceforth all diplomatic correspondence, both original copies and translation, shall be shown the *genrō* and consultation shall be conducted prior to any important negotiations relating to foreign nations."[45]

This was indeed a remarkable meeting. That the prestigious elder statesmen were called on to compel the prime minister to recognize their influence was a new development. To be sure it was caused by the independent attitude of Katō, who felt no obligation to filter each decision through the elderly and often ill-informed *genrō*. But that the *genrō* felt forced to negotiate for what had been accepted practice was a measure of their loss of power. On the other hand, the strength of their position was acknowledged by the nature of the agreement. In principle, then, their power was reaffirmed, their influence was to be preserved.

Following this agreement the four *genrō* signed a policy memorandum to Ōkuma covering their recommendations on foreign policy issues.[46] It advocated, among other things, better relations with China through economic assistance to Yüan Shih-kai and an agreement on the return of Kiaochow Bay, an alliance with Russia, and friendlier Japanese-American relations. These recommendations served as a gauge with which the elder statesmen could judge their influence.

---

[44] *Yamagata den*, III, 919–20.   [45] *Ibid.*, III, 912–13.
[46] *Ibid.*, III, 916–17.

In two particular instances—the "twenty-one demands" on China in 1915 and the secret alliance with Russia in 1916—it is possible to measure the role of the *genrō* in foreign affairs. In both instances the policies and procedures advocated by the government and the attitude of the *genrō* varied, and in both the *genrō* were to modify government policy. The *genrō* agreed with Katō Kōmei's belief that Japan's participation in World War I presented an opportunity for concluding a settlement with China regarding Japan's position in Manchuria and Shantung. But the extent of the demands made on China in the twenty-one demands and the manner in which they were presented and negotiated were not acceptable to the *genrō*. Katō did not keep them abreast of the negotiations with China. Angered, they refused to approve the most extreme demands and the initial plan to issue an ultimatum that carried the threat of military force. They also refused to endorse cabinet policy, arguing that it would jeopardize the chances for friendly relations with China and arouse the hostility of all the major powers. In the end the *genrō* succeeded in curbing the demands and modifying the conduct of negotiations.

In the negotiations leading to an alliance with Russia the *genrō* played a more important role. Although support was initiated by Inoue and Yamagata, unanimous *genrō* support for the alliance was expressed in a joint memorandum to the cabinet dated February 20, 1915. The government hardly reacted to the proposal. It was three months later when Yamagata queried Katō: "What consideration has been given the memorandum advocating a Russo-Japanese alliance which I signed jointly with Matsukata, Inoue, and Ōyama and sent to you some time ago?"[47] Katō had actually opposed it, because he feared that it would weaken the existing alliance with England. It would be, he said, like "adding too much water to whiskey."[48] This resistance to their scheme irritated the *genrō* and led them to encourage Ōkuma to drop Katō from

[47] Quoted in Shinobu, *Taishō seiji shi*, I, 257.
[48] Quoted by Itō Masanori, *Katō Kōmei den* (Tokyo, 1929), II, 49.

his cabinet. Inoue told Ōkuma to "choose between changing the foreign minister and severing all connections with me."[49]

By July 1915 Katō had left the cabinet, although primarily for reasons other than his strained relations with the *genrō*, and a new effort was made by the *genrō* to encourage the alliance. The visit of Grand Duke Georgi, uncle of Czar Nicholas II, in January 1916 presented an opportunity to further their objective. Although the precise way in which the *genrō* influence was brought to bear in the negotiations cannot be completely reconstructed from the available documents, it is known that the grand duke visited Yamagata and solicited the aid of the *genrō* in concluding a mutually satisfactory alliance. It is also known that the foreign office, now under Ishii Kikujirō, still favored delaying negotiation but a few weeks later reversed its position. The logic of the situation and the available information compel one to conclude that the shift was the consequence of the *genrō*'s activity on behalf of the alliance. The treaty was signed on July 3, 1916.

These two episodes in Japan's foreign relations demonstrate how the Meiji *genrō* were, in this last phase, able to modify some policies and to initiate others. It reflects their inclination and capacity to intrude somewhat arbitrarily but no less effectively into the decision-making process outside of their participation in the selection of prime ministers.

Conclusion

This study of the *genrō* institution is an inquiry into one aspect of the problem of leadership in Japan's modernization. In the political development of modern Japan this institution served as the link between the formal government and the emperor. It operated at the penumbra of Japanese politics, where it was difficult to distinguish between the political system, subject to rational development, and the sacred traditions symbolized by the emperor which legitimized that system. As

[49] Shinobu, *Taishō seiji shi*, I, 259.

an adjunct of the imperial institution, the *genrō* operated both in the area transcending the political process, where the political system and the religious system began to fuse, and within the political system through their personal ties to the newly formed institutions in the creation of which they presided. It thus had a double aspect: it functioned as a free-floating decision-making body, informal, independent, and nonpartisan, attempting to determine issues in a detached manner from the perspective of long-range goals; on the other hand, it was a structural unit at the top of the political hierarchy dependent on the whole system, which was manipulated by the senior leaders of the Satchō coalition to preserve their dominance. Facing upward it was a dependent part of the whole imperial system; facing downward it behaved independently and autonomously. This dual nature could not be reproduced, and the *genrō* were not able to recreate a political aristocracy which combine similar ties to the past and to the founding of the modern institutions.

Yet the role of the *genrō* was decisive in the overall modernization process. In the first place, it contributed to the relative stability of the political system during a period when political institutions were undergoing enormous changes and strains. In each of the three phases we have sketched, the *genrō* institution carried out its primary role, for which it had been brought into existence, of resolving the frequent leadership crises caused by the resignation of a prime minister. In effect, this meant that when the authority represented by the cabinet was destroyed by its resignation, power was transferred to the *genrō*, which, after arriving at a decision on the next prime minister, transferred power back again to the next cabinet. Beyond this cabinet-making role, the *genrō*, consulted and involved as a body in all the major state decisions, served the function of custodian and protector of the national welfare. In its capacity to restrain or mediate policy, as well as to guide or initiate government action, it functioned as a supreme coordinating body that helped to preserve political equilibrium.

Second, the *genrō* contributed to the unity of Japan and the centralizing power of the state. As individuals they represented different segments of the bureaucracy, but as an institution the *genrō* was a mechanism for adjusting differences between the major divisions of the power structure, most notably between the civil and military sectors, and thereby helped to maintain centralized control. When the *genrō* came together as a group charged to act in the interest of all, the chances for mediating and controlling disruptive conflict were good. As the highest coordinating organ of the state, it was a balancing force which provided a unifying element assuring sufficient order to permit rapid change. As strong-minded men of dissimilar temperaments, the *genrō* differed in their views and divided sharply on many issues. But far more impressive was their sense of group solidarity and the adjustment of their differences which produced a high degree of harmony at the top of the political system. Furthermore, by being responsible for all important decisions the *genrō* protected the theoretically absolute power of the emperor, which served as the ultimate source of national unity.

Third, by their durability as well as their unity the *genrō* contributed an element of continuity to the period of modernization. As they grew older they were increasingly resented, but they were no less respected for their accumulated experience and their closeness to a past that sanctified tradition. Their long and eminent service gave almost a Confucian quality to their influence in mobilizing support for the government. This may have helped to provide an integrating, cohesive element that assisted in holding the order together during an era of astounding change and stress. Furthermore, while other official advisory bodies to the emperor, such as the office of the lord keeper of the privy seal and the Privy Council, had foreign models, this unofficial group of personal advisers preserved a distinctly Japanese ingredient in the political system. The *genrō* institution was a political collectivity based upon consensus or conformity that accorded with the character-

96

istics of traditional Japanese collectivities. The result was an oligarchic system of rule, but a leadership system well known in the past and perhaps the one best suited to the leadership needs and capacities of Japan during the process of political modernization.

Thus the role of the collective leadership of the *genrō* contributed to the high degree of stability, unity, and continuity during Japan's political transformation. This affected the speed and degree of modernization, but there were flaws in the *genrō* system. The deliberate imposition of order, to which the *genrō* were dedicated, had what might be called counter-modernizing influences. For one thing, their rigid conservatism *(a)* and authoritarianism curbed dissent and stifled opposition. The marked imbalance of power between the bureaucracy, with *(b)* the *genrō* at its inner circle, and the political parties produced the frustrations, rancour, and bitterness which set the climate of Meiji political life. For another, the unbridled and arbitrary power of the *genrō* contributed a legacy of irresponsi- *(c)* bility in the political process. The intriguing and behind the scenes activity of the *genrō* caused frequent clashes, and indeed was often the cause of a change in government. But since there was no public accounting of their decisions, rumors and gossip were the usual source of information, and the opposition was frequently hobbled because it was difficult to be sure what the view of a single *genrō* was. Relays of visitors to the homes of the *genrō* would produce conflicting accounts. In this way, a political tradition was nurtured in which the most important decisions of state were made outside the formal channels of government, through an arbitrary and even irrational procedure. One might even argue that the *genrō* leadership institutionalized a "system of irresponsibility," which obstructed the development of a more rational decision-making process and retarded the political modernization of Japan.

CHAPTER IV

Fukuzawa Yukichi: The Philosophical Foundations of Meiji Nationalism

ALBERT M. CRAIG

THE most popular and influential thinker in Meiji Japan was undoubtedly Fukuzawa Yukichi. His early writings were the backbone of the civilization and enlightenment movement of the 1870's, and thousands of copies were sold in legal and pirated editions. During these years Fukuzawa possessed a liberal, utopian vision of what the Japanese nation ought to become and what its proper relations with other nations in the world ought to be. But by the beginning of the 1880's this ideal was scrapped. Fukuzawa had come to see the world as a jungle in which the strong were ravening predators and the weak their hapless victims. The objects of this paper are: (1) to investigate the changing philosophic assumptions underlying his views of the world, (2) to probe the relations between these world views and the content of Fukuzawa's nationalism, and (3) to relate the development of nationalism in Japan to the early phase of its modernization.

The Background of Nationalism

One advantage enjoyed by Japan at the start of its modernization was a genus of indigenous nationalism. Many Japanese were aware of Japan as a political entity, standing in contrast to other, non-Japanese states. They saw themselves as Japanese and viewed non-Japanese as foreigners, as interlopers, whose presence in Japan threatened its integrity. They were concerned about the preservation of Japanese independence by making Japan rich and strong. Still others, while only passive onlook-

99

ers, recognize as legitimate the demand that Japan be made rich and strong.

But the degree to which the Japanese were nationalistic at the start of the Meiji period is often overstated. Some writers have confused the ingredients of later Japanese nationalism with its actuality. Ethnically a single people, linguistically united, socially homogeneous, undivided by religious antagonisms or widely divergent political creeds, the Japanese of the late Tokugawa period had few obstacles to the development of a strong national awareness. But for most Japanese in 1853 that awareness did not yet exist.

The content of political awareness in the Tokugawa period was largely Confucian, Confucianism adapted to fit Japanese institutions and the Japanese imperial tradition. Confucianism defined the samurai as a political class in this late feudal society. The sphere of governance was universal; it included everywhere under heaven. But for the samurai the sphere of political action was delimited by the time-hallowed policy of seclusion that made Japan the world and the domains of the daimyo the states within it. For most, foreign relations were relations with other domains (*han*). As Itō Hirobumi expressed it: "Patriotism during the feudal period was usually confined to the domain."[1]

Of course the bamboo curtain of Tokugawa seclusion was never completely impenetrable. Scholarly writers constantly grappled with the problem of how to be Chinese in culture without losing their Japanese identity. (Their solutions were to partially set the patterns for Meiji thinkers who wanted to stay Japanese while becoming Western.) And from the 1790's a political-military dimension was added as Western ships appeared ever more frequently off the Japanese littoral. Japanese leaders were further alarmed by reports of the Opium War. But changes in the outer world had little direct effect on the majority of samurai; little scope was offered for new ways of acting.

[1] *Itō-kō zenshū* (Tokyo, 1928), iii:ii, 43.

More important to later developments in Japanese nationalism were the internal changes in the nature of feudal relations. As the daimyo domains, with the exception of smaller "hereditary" domains (*fudai han*), became stable territorial units, and as personal government by feudal lords became routine and bureaucratic, the daimyo became figureheads. What had been vital to the military fief became less critical to the peacetime domain. Loyalty that had been given to the daimyo as a person now came to focus on the person of the daimyo as a symbol of the domain. This more abstract loyalty was potentially transferable from one symbol to another in a way that would have been impossible in the case of the personal loyalty of 1600. I have termed this more abstract loyalty domain nationalism.[2]

The first shock to the parochialism of the average samurai was Perry's visits to Japan. This occasioned a major change in political consciousness, forcing the samurai to see Japan—symbolized by the emperor—as their nation and the domains only as subnational units within it. Compelled to accept a treaty of friendship, the natural enmity that had been directed toward samurai of other domains was extended to foreigners. All Western observers of Japan at this time agreed with Alcock that commoners were apolitical and friendly and that only the "yaconin or samourai" were not: "I can see no sign of popular ill-feeling or hostility toward foreigners. If insult or menace is offered, it comes from the bearers of two swords, and this class alone."[3] Such hostility was the measure of late Tokugawa protonationalism.[4]

---

[2] I have gone into the problem of domain nationalism more extensively in *Chōshū in the Meiji Restoration* (Cambridge, Mass., 1961), pp. 143–64, 299–300, 358–59.

[3] Rutherford Alcock, *The Capital of the Tycoon* (New York, 1863), p. 39.

[4] Whether the provenance of this hostility is Confucian or samurai is a tangled question. Some peasant village officials were more a part of the official hierarchy and as educated as many samurai. Shibuzawa is a splendid example of the potentials of this class. Some merchants were

The second shock came in 1858 when the shogun agreed to a commercial treaty without the emperor's approval. This opened the way for action on behalf of emperor and nation, but only a few domains acted; the majority remained bound to their particular interests even during the 1860's. Ernest Satow wrote of "the great satisfaction" expressed by Ogasawara samurai when they learned of "the complete thrashing" given Chōshū by the four-nation Western expedition of 1864.[5] Foreigners were still "out there" somewhere and were regarded with less hostility than internal enemies. In 1867, however, the *bakufu*, the government of a divided Japan, was abolished, and the Meiji government established. And in 1871 the process of moral centralization was brought to completion by the abolition of the domains and the formal transfer of samurai loyalty from daimyo to emperor.

Only 5 or 6 percent of Japan's population at the time of the Restoration were samurai. Many soon became impoverished and some even rose up against the new government. Yet however unreliable the habit of samurai loyalty may have seemed at times, it was critical in the early Meiji decades. Samurai staffed both central and prefectural government; they were the teachers in the new schools, the officers in the new army. Their values both inspired the government and provided the articulate response to government directives and reforms. Samurai loyalty played a stopgap role, giving cohesion and direction to Japan at a time when a more modern nationalism was unavailable. By 1900 it had been succeeded by a newer and more widespread patriotism—incubated in the new schools, in the Meiji draft army, and in an ever more centralized political system. But even this new patriotism was substantially shaped by the old loyalty.

---

also educated in the Confucian classics. For the purposes of a discussion of nationalism many of these may be regarded as honorary samurai.

[5] Ernest Satow, *A Diplomat in Japan* (London, 1921), p. 114.

The Early Fukuzawa

THE SAMURAI SCHOLAR

In the *bakumatsu* period (1853–1868) Fukuzawa Yukichi was very much a man of his class. He was politically aware, he was concerned for Japan and its place in the world. Like other samurai he expressed this concern from his particular position in the Tokugawa political structure. While born a samurai in the Nakatsu domain, Fukuzawa became a retainer of the shogun as well, with a stipend equivalent to that of a *hatamoto*. Consequently Fukuzawa was a staunch supporter of the *bakufu*, making its interests and enemies his own. He supported the early *bakufu* plan for an alliance of daimyo under the shogun. He opposed a later Satsuma plan for an alliance of daimyo guided by Satsuma. He was violently antagonistic toward the "rebel Chōshū" and to the "perverted theory of *sonnō jōi*" put forth as a "subterfuge" to conceal a "vicious plot" by ambitious men.[6] So violent was his antipathy to Chōshū that at the time of the 1866 *bakufu* expedition he even advocated the use of foreign funds and troops to crush that domain.[7]

[6] For Fukuzawa's views during the *bakumatsu* period, see Konno Washichi, "Jiyū minken undō ni kansuru ichi kōsatsu 1," in *Shigaku*, XXIV:ii, iii (1950), 189–94.

[7] In his *Autobiography* Fukuzawa describes himself as having been a strict neutralist during the disturbances of the *bakumatsu* period, and of his general attitude he writes: "It was as if my mind were washed clean of what people call the 'yearning for honor.'" But the real Fukuzawa bears little resemblance to the Fukuzawa described in the *Autobiography*. At least in political matters, the latter is an old man's imagining, years later at the turn of the century, of what he ought to have thought and felt as a youth. It masks Fukuzawa's misjudgment of the political forces involved in the Restoration movement. After the Restoration Fukuzawa's ardor for the *bakufu* cause apparently turned to philosophical resignation. He criticized the "shifty faintheartedness" of those who went over to serve the new government, and he himself refused to take government office; he rationalized his position outside the government in terms of the importance of nongovernmental roles in a laissez-faire society.

Yet there are two characteristics that bring Fukuzawa out of the ruck of ordinary samurai protonationalism. One was an awareness of a wider world gained through study of the West and travel to the United States and Europe. Like other students of Dutch learning, he saw Japan as a total unit earlier than most samurai. Dependent for his livelihood on his "professional" skills, and not on simple, unflagging, hereditary loyalty, he could in 1866 express his concern for Japan in more general terms than most: "Our vassals with feudal stipends know only how to devote their loyalty to the single person of their lord, but their sense of patriotism (*hōkoku*) is weak. Had the Japanese a true sense of patriotism, then, without vain chatter about the merits of opening the country or seclusion, Japan would become an open country, rich and strong. ... Japan's samurai must establish the national honor, vowing not to be bested by foreign countries. If foreign countries have an advantage due to battleships, then our country, too, must build them. If foreign countries enrich themselves with trade, then we must imitate them. True patriotism lies in not falling one pace behind others." In Fukuzawa's eyes Western studies were thus a better means for the attainment of indigenous, "Confucian" political ends.[8]

The second characteristic of Fukuzawa was that even in *bakumatsu* times he saw Western studies as offering a truth superior to those current in Japan. His support of the *bakufu* rose partly from his belief that it was the most enlightened political force in Japan. Fukuzawa wrote in 1866: "Buddhism is a cult. Confucianism is also a cult. ... In Japan there is another cult called something like the spirit of Yamato." Observing that these cults wrangled incessantly, he continued: "But if we would be civilized gentlemen, we must first broaden our knowledge and familiarize ourselves with conditions in all of the countries in the world. Let universal ethical principles (*sekai no dōri*) be determined by competitive bidding (*nyū-*

[8] Koizumi Shinzō, ed., *Fukuzawa Yukichi no hito to shokan* (Tokyo, 1950), pp. 78–79.

satsu); if that which the millions in the world say is true should be contrary to our cult, then we should resolutely change our religion and enter the gate of the cult called international law."[9] The openness of these views provided the foundation for the development of his thought in the early Meiji period.

NATURE AND ETHICS

During the 1870's men educated in the Tokugawa tradition of Dutch learning introduced almost the full sweep of the thought of the European Enlightenment into Japan. In some instances the works of eighteenth century writers were translated first. But in many cases nineteenth century writings became available before their eighteenth century antecedents. Thus Nakamura Masanao's translation of J. S. Mill's *On Liberty* was published in 1871, eleven years before Nakae Chōmin's translation of Rousseau's *Social Contract*. And Fukuzawa translated a mid-nineteenth century popular work on political economy before going on to translate a section of Blackstone's mid-eighteenth century *Commentaries on the Laws of England*. These disjunctions led at times to intellectual confusion. But in general the basic notions of European natural rights were simplified and taken in as a single system. In the late 1870's and early 1880's these ideas gradually gave way to the more diverse tendencies of the later nineteenth century in which theories of natural rights were either repudiated or drastically modified.

In such a setting the career of Fukuzawa was in many ways typical. After studying in a school of Dutch learning, working at the *bakufu* Institute for the Study of Barbarian Books, and traveling in the United States and Europe, he began his scholarly career as a translator. Translation was not a neutral task: it involved transposing from one cultural milieu to another. The structure of ideas in his *Seiyō jijō gaihen* (*Conditions in the West*, Volume 2), for example, is derived from the original Western work, but the translation reveals commitments in

[9] *Ibid.*, p. 78.

Fukuzawa's thought. The concepts expressed in it form a bridge between the Dutch science tradition of the Tokugawa and the ideas in Fukuzawa's original writings in 1872 and after. There is no sharp break, only differences of shading, between his "Confucianized" translation in the *Seiyō jijō gaihen* and the "Westernized" Fukuzawa of *Gakumon no susume* (*An Invitation to Learning*).

Fukuzawa wrote of science from time to time, but his primary concern was with Western societies, with their forms of government, their economies, their customs, and the spirit of their intellectual life. The most fundamental assumption in his early writing was that there is an order in the universe, that all things function according to natural laws, and that these apply both to the natural world and to human society.

Economics is a prime example of the workings of this law: "Economics is in its essentials clearly not a man-made law. Since the purpose of economics is to explain natural laws (*tennen no teisoku*) that arise spontaneously in the world, the explanation of its principles is [to trade or commerce] like making clear the relation of geology to descriptive physical geography or of pathology to medicine."[10] Private property is also a condition of nature. It is not only inherent in man but "is a characteristic which all living things possess naturally (*tennen ni*)." Thus: "The bird's private ownership of its nest is like a man's of his house: a nest is built by a bird's labor, a house by that of man. Gains and losses all follow from basic principles (*dōri*). In the case of human property there are manifold conditions and complications. But there are none that do not stem from nature."[11]

[10] *Fukuzawa zenshū* (Tokyo, 1926), I, 516. Hereafter cited as *F.Z.* The original work on which this "translation" is based reads: "From these few examples, it is perceived that political economy is not an artificial system, but an explanation of the operation of certain natural laws. In explaining this system, the teacher is not more infallible than the teacher of geology or medicine." See William and Robert Chambers, pub., *Political Economy for Use in Schools, and for Private Instruction* (Edinburgh, 1852), pp. 53–54.

[11] *F.Z.*, I, 517. The first sentence in this passage is similar to the

Even rent is but a consequence of the subtle forces of the natural universe: "Therefore, after buying land and improving its quality, interest on the investment must be obtained. This is what is called rent. The profit from rent is not determined by man-made state laws. Rather it is determined by nature, just like the downward flow of water."[12]

Based on natural law as it applies to man are certain inalienable natural rights. The most important right in Fukuzawa's early writings was freedom. Paraphrasing an English work, he wrote in 1867: "heaven bestows life and along with it the ability and strength needed to preserve it. But though man might attempt to use his natural powers, if he lacked freedom his abilities and strength would be of no use. Therefore, throughout the world, in all countries and among all peoples, self-determined free action is a law of nature (*tendō no hōsoku*). In other words, each individual is independent and society is for the good of all. Man is born free. The right to freedom and independence which he receives from heaven cannot be bought or sold."[13]

Perhaps the most interesting line in this quotation is the phrase "society is for the good of all" (*tenka wa tenka no tenka nari*), which is not found in the English original. Earlier in the Confucian tradition this meant that the ruler must be moral and should not use the empire for his own personal ends. Now, by emphasizing individual freedom, the same expression is used to suggest that a society made up of autonomous individuals must be directed to their welfare. It suggests that society for the good of all derives from the nature of men as individuals, and not from the moral relation of the ruler to heaven. But in both cases the ethical principle is cosmologically grounded.

In *Gakumon no susume* Fukuzawa elaborates on the universality of the right of freedom by comparing it to the sense

---

English original; the second sentence is not present in the original; and the last sentence sums up several sentences of the original.

[12] *F.Z.*, I, 538. [13] *F.Z.*, I, 426.

of taste that all men possess: "Landlord and peasant are different in their condition of life, but are no different in regard to rights. What is painful to the body of a peasant is painful to a landlord, what tastes sweet to a landlord also tastes sweet to a peasant. To take the sweet and shun the bitter is human nature. While not interfering with others, to pursue pleasure is a human right. In respect to this right there is not the slightest difference between landlord and peasant."[14] These rights are in man as he is "born from nature."

The ideal society is one that conforms to man's true nature, one that permits the full development and exercise of man's natural rights. The history of social evolution is thus a tableau of ethical progress.

> Observing history, man is unenlightened in the beginning and gradually advances toward civilization and enlightenment (*bummei kaika*). In the age of illiteracy and unenlightenment there are no standards of morality (*reigi no michi*), people are unable to restrain their animal spirits and passions, those who are large violate those who are small, the strong torment the weak. . . . As progress is made toward civilization, these ways gradually decline. Moral codes are honored, passions are restrained, the large help the small, the weak are protected by the strong . . . and the numbers of those who think of the good of society in general and not just of their own selfish good increase.[15]

In terms of existing societies the stages from the barbarism of Africa to the half-civilized states of East Asia to civilized Europe represent a development from a less natural to a more natural state of man. Europe was not perfect, but was the most advanced and could be taken as a model for Japan.

One might query whether the unrestrained exercise of the passions is not more "natural" than restraint? Fukuzawa replies:

[14] *F.Z.*, III, 11.   [15] *F.Z.*, I, 430.

"There are some who say that barbarism is in accord with nature (*tennen*) and that civilization is man-made (*jin'i*). Yet this position misinterprets the proper meaning of the terms. Of all that occurs in civilized society, there is nothing that does not arise from nature. As society becomes enlightened, laws (*hōsoku*) are established, and though they are lenient no one violates them. It is characteristic of civilization that people are not restrained by force but by their hearts. Human nature most fully embodies the character of nature (*tennen no shisei*) and must not be called man-made."[16]

As proof of this thesis Fukuzawa notes that though primitive man lived amid filth the enlightened man is clean. And since man's true nature (*tensei*) evidently prefers cleanliness, it is clear that primitive man has not yet realized his true nature; he is like a child who has not yet developed his inherent abilities. As further evidence that primitive man is not natural man Fukuzawa cites the example of natives of a certain country who shape the heads of infants by binding them to a board, and of the half-civilized Chinese who bind the feet of girls and see beauty in their crumpled, unnatural shapes. Unenlightened human action may injure nature; enlightened civilized action accords with it.

Fukuzawa's key term for describing an ideal social order in accord with natural law (or an advanced stage of society progressing in that direction) was *bummei*, or civilization. To illustrate the all-encompassing character of *bummei* he resorted to metaphor:

Civilization is like a great theater with political institutions, literature, commerce, etc., as the actors. Each actor performs his special skill and works at his part in the production. An actor is called skillful who is in harmony with the dramatic intent of the play, who displays true emotion, and who pleases the spectators. One who misses his cues, forgets his lines, one whose laughter rings false and whose sobs are

[16] *F.Z.*, I, 431.

without feeling, who thereby causes the play to lose its significance, is called awkward. . . . Civilization is like a sea;
institutions, literature, etc., are like rivers. . . . Civilization is
like a storehouse in which man's clothing and food, the
money and goods he uses in earning a living, and his life
energies are stored.[17]

This civilization was to Fukuzawa what culture is to the
anthropologist, the highest-level generalization expressing the
totality of systems, sciences, ideas, and feelings of a people or
state. The motive force for the progress of civilization, however, was more narrowly defined: "Civilization does not arise
by the action of government from above, nor is it born from
the lower classes. Without fail it is a product of the middle
classes, it expresses the tendency of the people [not the govern-
ment], and it can expect to progress only as the people
stand independent and parallel to the government. Viewing
the histories of Western countries, there is not one example of
commerce and industry begun by government. Their bases in
every case stemmed from the inventiveness of middle-class
scholars. The great men responsible for the steam engine . . .
the railroad . . . the laws of economics . . . were from the
middle class, not politicians or laborers."[18]

Within this scheme government is reduced almost to an epi-
phenomenon. What is basic is "natural man": "man in the
condition in which he is born from nature," "man as unrelated to other men." Individuals in this state of nature
originally punished those that inflicted injury on them. But
since some were weak and others strong, this was unsatisfactory. Therefore as civilization advanced individuals joined
together, formed a government, and delegated to it the right
of punishment. The proper functions of government are
limited; they are, in short, those of the watchdog state of early
liberalism.

Government is posterior to the law that informs man's

[17] *F.Z.*, I, 39.   [18] *F.Z.*, III, 39.

nature; yet it must be obeyed, for it "is the representative of the people, it acts in accordance with the will of the people." Fukuzawa continues: "Since the government has the right, as the representative of the people, to do things, actions by the government are in effect actions by the people. That the people must obey the laws of government ... is not obedience to laws made by the government, but to laws made by themselves. ... Those punished after breaking a law are not punished by government, but punished by a law which they themselves made."[19]

But what should an individual do in the face of an oppressive government that acts contrary to nature's dictates? Fukuzawa answers: "To simply obey it will not do. It is man's duty to follow the virtuous way of heaven (*ten no seidō*). Therefore, to compromise one's virtue and follow the man-made, evil laws of government (*seifu jinzō no akuhō*) is not to fulfill one's duty. Moreover, to compromise one's virtue and obey an immoral law sets a bad example for later generations."[20] The solution given in *Gakumon no susume* in 1872 was not violent opposition that could "lead to civil war," but "moral action and self-sacrifice" based on belief in "the principles of heaven" (*ten no dōri*).[21] Though influenced by Francis Wayland's *Elements of Moral Science*, this sounds not unlike the proper Confucian response of a loyal vassal to a wicked lord. Another interesting aspect of the quotation above is the almost Rousseauan contrast of what is natural and good with what is man-made, unnatural, and bad.

On the whole, however, bad government was not a serious problem for Fukuzawa. The lines of force in society were overwhelmingly from the people to the government: the government merely follows. Time and time again Fukuzawa states that people get the government they deserve:

"To control an ignorant people there is no reasonable method except the use of force to cause them to fear. Thus in the

[19] *F.Z.*, III, 43.   [20] *F.Z.*, III, 57.   [21] *F.Z.*, III, 58.

West there is the proverb 'An oppressive government above an ignorant populace.' The point is not that the government is harsh, but that an ignorant people naturally invites troubles. If harsh government is to be found over an ignorant people, then good people will have a good government. Therefore, today in Japan we have this kind of people and so we have this kind of government. If, hypothetically, the virtue of the people should decline, if they should sink into ignorance and illiteracy, then laws would naturally become harsher. But, on the other hand, if the people all devote themselves to learning, studying the principles of things (*monogoto no ri*), and acquiring the habits of civilization, then the government's laws will become more lenient and more in accord with virtue. The harshness or permissiveness of laws varies naturally according to the virtue of the people."[22]

Government does have a small scope for action; within this scope it may be judged according to its contribution to progress. "A government that does much to promote civilization is called good; one that does little to promote it, or one that injures it, is called bad. Therefore, in appraising the merits of a government, one must measure the degree to which its populace has attained to civilization (*bummei*) and then judge it. As there has not yet appeared in the world a country of the highest culture and enlightenment, it follows that there does not yet exist the best and most beautiful government. If the highest degree of civilization were attained, then *any government at all would be a completely useless thing*."[23] The last line of the quotation makes explicit Fukuzawa's ideal of a civilization wholly in accordance with natural law in which the purity of men's hearts would suffice to police their actions and government would wither away. Here in a Japanese context is the "moving hand" of Adam

[22] *F.Z.*, III, 6–7.
[23] *F.Z.*, IV, 52. (Emphasis added.)

Smith, here is a bold statement of the eighteenth century Lockian ideal of a natural social order that in early nineteenth century Europe undergirded the writings of economic liberals, utopian socialists, and anarchists alike.

Does Fukuzawa's world view during the 1870's represent a clean break with the past, or do the assumptions of the Confucian, Dutch-learning tradition continue in some form? This question must be posed both in regard to Fukuzawa's conceptual framework and to his values.

In its Tokugawa conceptual setting Dutch learning was more than just a means. The ideas of Western science were taken in, put in a Neo-Confucian setting, and viewed as a portion of universal truth. The Neo-Confucian principle of ultimate being was *ri*: this was intuitable as the ground of moral being and present in all things as the ordering principle for their particular existences. In the late eighteenth century Confucian Dutch-learning tradition the laws of nature discovered by European science were recognized as having uncovered a hitherto neglected portion of the *ri*. From the perspective of science the students of Dutch learning became totally concerned with the *ri* of objective nature. They lost interest in the *ri* as an essence or noumenon that could be contemplated within man.

By the 1850's so much new content had been read into the *ri* (or *kyūri*) of Western studies that it was stretched out of shape, no longer resembling the *ri* of Chu Hsi. But the differentiation between two kinds of *ri* was never made. Most students of Dutch learning remained followers of Chu Hsi in their assumptions. Their *ri* still had explicitly ethical implications. The principles governing the physical universe were still seen as essentially identical with the Confucian ethical principles of government and morality.[24]

[24] See Albert Craig, "Science and Confucianism in Tokugawa Japan," in Marius Jansen, ed., *Changing Japanese Attitudes toward Modernization* (Princeton, 1965), pp. 133–60. My perspectives on the intellectual transition to Meiji Japan have changed somewhat since writing this

As Western social theories were introduced into Japan during the 1860's, they were fitted within the conceptual framework of Confucian Dutch learning. The *ri* of Chu Hsi that had been stretched to encompass natural science was now further stretched and distorted to cope with the "natural laws" of society. As a consequence the metaphysical status that earlier had been ascribed to scientific laws was now assumed to inhere in the Enlightenment natural rights as well. An early form of the juncture of ideas from the two traditions can be seen in the phrase "universal ethical principles" (*sekai fūtsū no dōri*) used by Fukuzawa in an 1866 letter to a friend. Or, in his earliest translations, Fukuzawa frequently takes statements that stress the empirical discovery of the God-given, natural laws of society and transforms them into statements about the metaphysical nature of man. He translates from a deistic framework into one that is tinged with Confucianism.

By 1869 Fukuzawa could detach the *kyūri* of science from the *ri* of Neo-Confucianism, explicitly rejecting the latter. He wrote: "Science (*kyūri*) is not the pursuit of a formless *ri* or the discussion of unreal matters. It is rather the pursuit of knowledge about the nature and functions of the universe (the 10,000 things). The movements of heavenly bodies, the changes of wind, rain, snow, and frost, the reason why fire is hot and ice cold. . . . Science is the observation of phenomena and the explanation of their causes."[25]

This broke with one element in the framework of earlier Confucian Dutch learning. But there still remained a number of assumptions common to both the Dutch-learning tradition

---

earlier piece. I previously felt that the philosophical breakdown of *ri* into science and ethics reached its endpoint in the distinctions made by Nishi Amane. In one sense this is true. Nishi analytically separated the *ri* of science from the *ri* of ethics. But most early Meiji thinkers could not equal Nishi's technical grasp of Western philosophy. Most went from *ri* to an ethical natural law. For these thinkers the breakdown of a *ri*-like natural law, the differentiation of science and ethics, did not occur until the early 1880's.

[25] *F.Z.*, II, 826.

and Enlightenment thought. Fukuzawa could reject *ri* as an intuitive category and go on to European thought without questioning a number of his earlier postulates. It is useful to bear these earlier postulates in mind when considering the rapidity of Fukuzawa's emergence as an enlightener.

1. There is a natural order in the universe.
2. The natural laws of science inhere in this order.
3. Ethical norms are also grounded in this order; ethics are objective or natural.
4. Man is a part of this order and is thus moral in character.
5. The ideal social order is one that completely conforms to the natural ethic.

Fukuzawa's vocabulary during the early 1870's is a mixture of the old and the new. On occasion, as in the following passage written in 1871, his writing is redolent of Confucianism: "Man is chief among the 10,000 things. That his nature is good is beyond discussion. Moral education, based on this principle, distinguishes between good and bad, and emphasizes morality (*reigi*) and purity (*rensetsu*); externally it concerns the relation between government and people, internally it defines the rights and duties of parent and child, husband and wife. Following the laws of nature (*tenri*) it clarifies the way of proper social intercourse."[26]

Fukuzawa's interpretation of natural law was closer to tradition than Fukuzawa realized in the early 1870's.[27] Yet the

[26] *F.Z.*, II, 827.
[27] Fukuzawa lived half of his life before the Meiji Restoration. He never traveled abroad after the Restoration. Though a constant target for satirists during the *bummei kaika* period, he was not a faddist; his habits were less flexible and less up to date than his thought. Fukuzawa liked to live in Japanese style, wearing Japanese dress and eating Japanese food. He pounded his own *mochi*. He was extremely fond of *sake* and only with great reluctance gave it up for reasons of health in his later years. He liked walking and horseback riding. He was proud of his quick draw with a sword and would demonstrate his prowess by flipping a copper coin into the air, drawing, and cleaving

implications of the traditional assumptions, if considerable in some spheres, were not so important in his ethics. In spite of the fact that he continued to maintain a "natural" ethic, the relation of the new ethic to the social order was diametrically opposite to that of the Confucian ethic. The Confucian ethic was conservative because of its content and because the existing Tokugawa society was seen as the embodiment of the natural order. Fukuzawa's new ethic was dynamic because it supported an ideal that while largely realized in the advanced countries of the West differed fundamentally from Japanese society. In Fukuzawa's ethic the ideal (*ten no seidō*) was real and Japanese society was seen as man-made (*jinzō*) or artificial (*jin'i*). It was the authority of the new, ideal, natural ethic and the tension between it and the Japanese sociocultural patterns that provided the dynamism in Fukuzawa's philosophy of human progress.

FREEDOM AND THE KOKUTAI

During the early 1870's Fukuzawa tended to avoid the Mito term *kokutai* (national polity), using instead the neutral term *seitai* (form of government). In 1875 he began to talk of Japan's *kokutai,* but his discussion of the term mirrored the liberalism, openness, and idealism of his early political thought. He did not attack the Mito synthesis head-on: in his eyes such antique notions were not worthy of mention. But obliquely he attacked the old ideas by redefining their key concept.

The essential characteristic of Fukuzawa's *kokutai* is autonomy. If a country loses its independence, it thereby loses its

---

the coin before it struck the ground. A tireless partisan of women's rights, he was quite traditional in the education of his own daughters and conservative in most respects in his own home. Similarly, though he taught the innate equality of all men, he liked to be thought a samurai and felt great displeasure when mistaken for a *chōnin*. See Fukuzawa Taishirō, *Chichi, Fukuzawa Yukichi* (Tokyo, 1959), pp. 145-46.

kokutai. For the rest the *kokutai* of any nation is its form of independent government, and all independent nations have a *kokutai*. There is nothing special about Japan's *kokutai*, and all *kokutai* are constantly changing. The changes are the result of changes in language, education, customs, the economy, and political thought, which reflect the progress of civilization. And such changes are good.

Japan has never lost its independence, writes Fukuzawa, so its *kokutai* has never been lost. And Japan's imperial house is a single, unchanging blood line. But the continuity of Japan's *kokutai* is in no sense derivative from its line of emperors. Rather, the continuity of emperors is a "symbol" of its *kokutai* that has never fallen into foreign hands. Fukuzawa compares the imperial house to the eye in a human body: by the glint of the eye we know the body is alive, but for the sake of health we must be concerned with the total organism, not just a part. Too great a concern for the part can lead to the destruction of the whole.[28] Fukuzawa concludes:

> At this time the duty of the Japanese is solely the preservation of their national polity. By the preservation of their national polity I mean not losing their political independence. In order not to lose political independence, the intellectual powers of the people must be advanced. This includes a great many items. But for intellectual development the first step that must be taken is to sweep away attachments to old customs and take in the spirit of civilization current in the West. If the attachment to yin, yang, and the five elements is not swept away, science cannot be adopted. . . . Western civilization will enable us to consolidate our polity and at the same time increase the luster of our imperial line.[29]

Such infrequent references as there are to the imperial line at this stage in Fukuzawa's thought merely show an aspect of his concern for the nation. He sees Japan's *kokutai* in a

[28] *F.Z.*, IV, 28–29.   [29] *F.Z.*, IV, 30–31.

purely rational light. The *kokutai* of some nations with more advanced civilizations than Japan obviously did not require emperors and did not suffer from their absence.

Just as men are by nature free and independent, so are nations. Just as a *sumo* wrestler must not use his strength against an invalid, so stronger nations must respect the rights of the weak.[30] Thus in *Gakumon no susume*, a section titled "Men Are Equal" is followed by "Countries Are Equal." Fukuzawa argues: "A country is a gathering of people. Japan is a gathering of Japanese and England a gathering of Englishmen. Japanese and Englishmen alike are members of a common humanity (*hitoshiku tenchi no aida no hito*); they must respect each others' rights. If one individual may not injure another, then two may not join to injure two others. And the same logic applies to one million or ten million: the principles of things do not change according to the numbers involved."[31]

But some countries were so blighted by xenophobic prejudice as to be unworthy of respect. These, wrote Fukuzawa in 1872, are in danger of losing their independence to the very barbarians they despise: "If like the Chinese and others we say that there is no other country but our own, if we call all foreigners barbarians and despise them as animals that walk on all fours . . . if without measuring our strength we try to expel them, then on the contrary we shall be punished by these barbarians. This would truly be a case of not knowing the proper limits of national action. Likening this to the case of the individual, it would be as if, without realizing his natural freedom (*tennen no jiyū*), one fell into selfish dissipation."[32]

What was Japan's condition? In the early 1870's Fukuzawa spoke very little of the advantages of nationalism; he was concerned with other virtues. By 1875 he began to talk of nationalism and to wish that the Japanese had more of it: "Suppose that the entire country had to stand against a foreign enemy. Suppose further that we were to divide the Japanese into those who would stand by as spectators and those who would

[30] *F.Z.*, III, 17–18. [31] *F.Z.*, III, 17. [32] *F.Z.*, III, 4.

fight—including those not armed but fighting in spirit. Which would be more numerous? The result is not hard to guess. Thus I say that though there is a government in Japan, there is no nation."[33]

Behind this criticism is Fukuzawa's understanding of the gulf between Japan and his ideal of civilization. In Fukuzawa's mind only a people who were independent in character and intellectually advanced could be truly nationalistic. Only after a man could take care of himself could he help with the affairs of the nation. His reasoning is interesting partly because it focuses on the psychological dimension of modernization of which Japanese scholars today continue to be intensely aware. One of the shortcomings of the Japanese was a lack of independence. It is not enough for the government to be active and the people passive.

Those who lack an independent spirit cannot care deeply about their country. . . . If the entire populace is dependent, then there will be no one to take on its care: it is like a parade of the blind without a guide. . . . In facing foreign countries, for our own protection, we must develop a free and independent spirit throughout the entire country. Without regard for status, the entire populace must take on themselves the cares of the nation. . . . Each must fulfill his duty as a citizen. . . . The Japanese . . . cares for his country as for his family. For his country he should not only be willing to lose his possessions, but should not regret giving up his life. This is the great virtue of repaying one's debt to the country (*hōkoku no taigi*). Of course, those who act for the nation in politics are the government and those who are supervised by them are the people, yet it is merely for convenience that the responsibilities of the two are divided. In matters which affect the honor (*memboku*) of the entire country, can it be that it is the duty of the people to entrust the country to the government alone and watch from the sidelines?[34]

[33] *F.Z.*, IV, 186–87.   [34] *F.Z.*, III, 18–20.

Passivity in a people will also lead them to be ineffective in their relations with foreigners. Foreign relations are not simply relations between governments. Fukuzawa continued:

> Those who have no independence within the nation will be unable to maintain their independent rights in dealings with foreigners. Those without a spirit of independence will inevitably depend on others. Those who depend on others will fear them. Those who fear others will flatter them. Those who always fear and flatter others will gradually become accustomed to this; they will become brazen-faced, feeling no shame when they should feel shame, not speaking out when they should speak out, always bowing and scraping . . . and once accustomed to this it is not easy to change. Thus at present in Japan the commoners are permitted to have names and ride on horses; the judicial system has also changed so that in the eyes of the law they are the equals of the former samurai. Yet their attitudes do not immediately change. In character they are no different from the commoners of old. . . . Now that we have entered into relations with foreign countries this is a great failing. If a country merchant came trembling . . . to trade in Yokohama . . . he would be astonished at the girth and strength of the foreigner, at his wealth, at his enormous commercial buildings . . . at the sharpness of his trading practices . . . and he would suffer a great loss and feel intense shame. This is not just an injury to one person, it is a national loss. It is not an individual disgrace, but a national disgrace.[35]

A second shortcoming in Japanese national character was intellectual backwardness. Comparing Japan to the West, Fukuzawa observed that social stability was not a major problem. Quite possibly the Japanese were even more orderly than citizens of Western nations.

But when it comes to knowledge the situation is completely different. If we compare the knowledge of the Japanese and

[35] *F.Z.*, III, 21–23.

Westerners, in letters, in techniques, in commerce, or in industry, from the largest to the smallest matter . . . there is not
one thing in which we excel. . . . Outside of the most stupid
person in the world, no one would say that our learning
or business is on a par with those of the Western countries.
Who would compare our carts with their locomotives, or
our swords with their pistols? We speak of the yin and yang
and the five elements; they have discovered 60 elements.
. . . We think we dwell on an immovable plain; they know
that the earth is round and moves. We think that our country is the most sacred, divine land; they travel about the
world, opening lands and establishing countries. . . . In
Japan's present condition there is nothing in which we may
take pride vis-à-vis the West. All that Japan has to be proud
of . . . is its scenery.[36]

To become strong Japan must emulate the West.

The Middle Span

In the early years after the Restoration Japanese thinkers
made the leap from Confucian Dutch learning to natural
rights. Virtually all of the early Meiji enlighteners held
some version of this thought. Then, from the middle of the
1870's new currents of thought gained in importance. Under
the influence of positivism, materialism, utilitarianism, and
particularly Spencer's Social Darwinism, Japanese intellectuals
followed lines of development from early nineteenth century
positions on to more diverse positions within the spectrum of
late nineteenth century thought.

Fukuzawa was one of the leaders of this advance. The evolution of his thought lacks the stark switch from metaphysical natural rights to "scientific" evolutionary materialism that can be found in Katō Hiroyuki. Fukuzawa never
put advertisements in the newspaper repudiating earlier stages
of his thought. Yet the same change from his earlier thought

[36] *F.Z.*, IV, 125–26.

is clearly visible in Fukuzawa's writings. At the start of this new phase we see in his writings a growing awareness of the difficulties inherent in a philosophy of natural law and natural rights. Within a few years he is willing to dispense with the idea entirely. In place of a Confucian-tinged, metaphysical natural order he posits an amoral universe, to be understood by science and exploited by utilitarian and nationalistic principles.

In *Bummeiron no gairyaku,* published in 1875, Fukuzawa underlined the crucial importance of the metaphysical question by raising in the first paragraph of the introduction the problem of what is natural (*tennen*) and what is man-made (*jin'i*). What earlier had been accepted as a fixed verity was now a matter of perplexity: "In the case of long-standing customs it is almost impossible to distinguish between what is natural and what is man-made. Among those principles that are considered natural there are some that are merely customary. And, among those recognized as customs, there are not a few that are natural. Searching for fixed principles amid this confusion one must say that a discussion of [the nature of advanced] civilization is indeed difficult."[37]

In the same essay Fukuzawa also wrote: "First there are things and only afterward ethical principles (*rin*); it is not that principles come first and that things emerge afterward."[38] Some scholars have interpreted this sentence to signify that values are *a posteriori* and not grounded in nature. But, I do not believe that Fukuzawa meant to say this in 1875. What he meant was that even though human relations stood in a secondary relation to nature, some relations were still grounded

[37] *F.Z.,* IV, Foreword, I.

[38] *F.Z.,* IV, 46. To say that *rin* came after things resembles the position of those Tokugawa thinkers who held that *ri* is found in *ki*. This was a denial of the more idealistic Chu Hsi position in which *ri* is the supreme ultimate and *ki*, while an independent force, is of lesser stature. But even postulating the primacy of things, the real question is whether values are to be found in the natural order at all. Fukuzawa felt that some values are.

in nature and some were not; and that the boundary confusion regarding which relations were natural and which not could only be clarified by thorough empirical study.

Fukuzawa thus affirmed that four of the five Confucian relationships (*rin*) were universal and a part of what man received from heaven. In his eyes only the "ruler-subject relationship that in Japan and China had been viewed as inherent in man's nature" did not stand up under empirical scrutiny. He wrote:

> Do not violate the true principles of things by overly hasty hypothesizing. The matter of the ruler-subject relationship is an example of this practice. The relation between a ruler and subject is one between man and man. Now a principle (*jōri*) may be discerned in this relationship. But this principle is derived from the occasional existence of rulers and subjects in the world. One may not say on the basis of this principle that to be in a ruler-subject relationship is the nature of man. To say that this was man's nature, one would have to show that it existed in every country of the world where man is found. But in fact this is not the case. Thus we may say that in all human societies there are parents and children, husbands and wives, old and young, and friends: these four [of the five Confucian] relations are what man receives from heaven and are part of his nature. But the ruler-subject relationship alone is not to be found in certain countries such as in republics with representative governments.[39]

It is not, therefore, a necessary part of nature.

A second change in his thought is in the concept of civilization (*bummei*). Earlier it was concrete and embodied to a great extent in European society. It was close at hand, almost there for the taking. Now, however, the very notion of civilization becomes relative. "When we say that things are heavy or light, or right or wrong, we are speaking relatively. The concept of civilization and enlightenment is also a relative one.

[39] *F.Z.*, IV, 46.

Discussing civilization in the world today, the countries of Europe and the Republic of North America are the most civilized, Turkey, China, Japan, and the other countries of Asia may be termed half-enlightened, while Africa and Australia are primitive."[40]

But China is civilization to Africa. And even the West, which must be taken as Japan's model at present, is no longer seen as perfect, is no longer seen as the embodiment of a most natural order. Japan ought not to imitate its imperfections. "Though we say that the countries of the West have attained to civilizations, it is only in relation to the present world that this is so. Strictly speaking, they are deficient in many respects. There is no greater evil in the world than war, yet the countries of the West are constantly at war. . . . Within [the Western nations] factions are formed to struggle for power, and others, losing power, spread dissatisfaction. . . . If several thousands of years hence the knowledge and virtues of mankind have advanced and an order of complete peace and security attained, then the present state of the West will seem that of an unfortunate, backward society. Civilization is unlimited; we must not be satisfied with the West of the present."[41]

The year 1875 is a transitional point in Fukuzawa's thought. He has become uncertain. He has become a moderate relativist. Utopian civilization has receded several thousand years into the future. But he has still not come to the point where he is willing to deny nature outright. Fukuzawa writes: "There can be no limit to man's faculties. His body has certain functions, his mind has others: their reaches are extremely broad, their needs are exceedingly numerous. Man's nature (*tensei*) is intrinsically fitted for civilization. As long as he does not go against this nature all will be well. The essence of civilization is in the full exercise of the faculties which man has received from nature (*tennen*)."[42] Fukuzawa continues to argue that civilization is more natural than primitive so-

[40] *F.Z.*, IV, 10. [41] *F.Z.*, IV, 12.
[42] *F.Z.*, IV, 18.

ciety since the latter is based on brute force alone, on only one
among man's many potentials, whereas civilization develops
them all.

In 1875 Fukuzawa was still struggling with the idea of
nature. He was growing disillusioned, but had not given it up
entirely. By 1878 the break was complete:

The Boddhisattva of Asakusa . . . is said to have miraculous
powers and many make pilgrimages to her. But few believe
in the Buddha statues of lonely villages and out of the way
places. . . . It is not the statues in which believers believe.
They believe other believers and make their pilgrimages to
temples accordingly. Writers are apt to speak of what is
natural (*tenri jindō*). They say that such and such is based
on the principles of nature (*tenri*) or that such and such goes
against the nature of man (*jindō*)—as if these were fixed,
unchanging, immovable principles true for all time. . . . Putting aside the distant past, even at present what is viewed as
natural varies from country to country. Or it may change
within a few years. In Chinese and Japanese families it is
natural for the husband to be pompous and domineering.
In the West it is natural for the wife to be arrogant. A few
years back during the feudal period it was natural for the
vassal to give up his life for his daimyo; today it is natural
for him to treat his [former] daimyo as an equal. . . . What
some writers refer to as natural is not a careful explication
of the principles underlying their own thought, but merely
consists of the ideas in the prevailing opinion of their society
by which they have been carried along. If public opinion
holds that something is a true principle, they believe it. If
opinion holds that it is false, they doubt it. . . . They do not
seek that which is truly natural (*tenri jindō no hontai*). . . .
They are not a whit different from those who believe in the
Boddhisattva of Asakusa.[43]

Fukuzawa then delivered his conclusion: "Scholars of my

[43] *F.Z.*, IV, 541-43.

persuasion do not believe in what has been called a natural social order (*tenri jindō*) in the past or present. We seek a realistic intellectual position. Our aim is to bring peace to the world and security to the units of society so that mankind may receive the greatest happiness."[44]

By 1881 Fukuzawa's disillusionment with the morality of natural law had become even more profound. He retained the ideal of civilization as a noble concept, but he denied it any real grounding in nature. And he advocated that action be based on the world as it was, not on empty constructs about an unreal "nature."

> In human society good and evil are mixed just as sick and healthy individuals are mixed. Originally it was not man's nature to become sick. That he becomes so is due to malnutrition, the spread of infectious disease, or to his heredity. Yet under prevailing conditions it would not be a wise policy to abolish medicine as a useless art on the grounds that man is naturally without disease. It would be better to wait until that time in the distant future when disease has actually disappeared. We *cannot guarantee that such a time will come.* Thus, not realizing that good and bad are mixed in the present human society, to advocate the abolition of governmental laws as useless is to lean too much to one side. To speak of what is natural is like wanting to abolish medicine while forgetting the sick. Laws are made for evil men as medicine is for the diseased. *Millions* of years hereafter, when disease has vanished and all men are good, laws and medicine may be abandoned. In the meantime it is useless to speak of popular rights based on nature (*tennen no minkenron*); they are not worth discussing.[45]

Thus in the early 1870's utopia was near at hand. Like the *philosophe* whose vision of a perfected social order was so real that he could almost reach out and touch it, Fukuzawa

[44] *F.Z.*, IV, 543.
[45] *F.Z.*, V, 252. (Emphasis added.)

was very optimistic. By 1875 Fukuzawa's ideal had receded several thousand years into the future, and by 1881 it was millions of years off and perhaps would never come. Fukuzawa now felt that an ideal nature was not to be found in nature; it was but a chimera in the mind of men. All that can be found in nature are the laws of science, and these are devoid of any ethical content.

Such ideas contributed to a new view of international politics. In the turbulent years immediately following the Restoration, Japan's overriding concerns were internal. Fukuzawa was exceptional in not being directly involved in a government office or economic projects, but even he contributed to modern institutional structure as the founder of Keiō University. From the late 1870's, after the Satsuma rebellion, the domestic situation became stable and Japan became more deeply concerned with the international scene. The years of relative quiet following the Iwakura mission gave way to renewed concern for treaty revision. Years of party strife culminated in Itō's journey to Europe in search of a constitution. From 1876 into the early 1880's Japan was increasingly involved in Korea. The 1880's saw the rising of a more demanding European imperialism in other parts of Asia. Whether the objective threat to Japan was greater than during the earlier period of internal strife and political consolidation may be questioned. But Japanese thinkers now looked out on the world through the lens of new doctrines and were greatly disturbed by what they saw.

As long as Fukuzawa believed in an ideal order of nature underlying the less than perfect reality of the world, he could work with confidence at his vision of an ideal, free civilization and take independence almost for granted. Man on occasion may falter, foreign powers may threaten, but the immanent, beneficent laws of nature would prevail in the long run. But as his view of nature changed from normative to amoral, his perceptions of the short-term dangers in international politics became magnified. Note the scorn that Fukuzawa heaps on ideas that he himself had maintained only a few years earlier in the following passage written in 1881.

Inquiring into the nature of relations between the countries of the world there are the two perspectives of theory and fact. According to theory all of the peoples of the world . . . though different in their degree of civilization and enlightenment . . . are created equal and are brothers before God (*jōtei*). . . . At times, bearing fearful weapons, they kill their fellow men . . . yet as universal love advances, as the regulations of international law [are put into practice], the day will soon arrive when the entire world will be at peace and war will have disappeared. . . . This theory at the present time is espoused mainly by Western Christian ministers or by persons who are enamored of that religion, and by and large it coincides with the theory of natural freedom (*tennen no jiyūron*). . . . When we hear of this we cannot help exclaiming that it is just and beautiful in its virtue. However, when we leave this fiction and look at the facts regarding international relations today, we find them shockingly different. Do nations . . . honor treaties? We can find not the slightest evidence that they do. . . . When countries break treaties . . . there are no courts to judge them. Therefore, whether a treaty is honored or not . . . depends solely on the financial and military powers of the countries involved. . . . *Money and soldiers are not for the protection of existing principles they are the instruments for the creation of principles where none exist.* There are those moralists who would sit and wait for the day when wars will end. Yet in my opinion the Western nations . . . are growing ever stronger in the skills of war. In recent years every country devises strange new weapons. Day by day they increase their standing armies. This is truly useless, truly stupid. Yet if others work at being stupid, then I must respond in kind. If others are violent, then I must become violent. . . . At the beginning of this chapter I referred to the man-made theory of state right (*kokken*) as the way of force (*kendō*) [in contrast to the way of virtue (*seidō*)]. Those of my persuasion follow the way of force.[46]

In a brutal world where principles are created only by money and guns, it is necessary to rely on one's own strength. This view of the world led Fukuzawa away from general theories about civilization to a more specific concern for Japan's immediate national needs. It was almost as if the urgent crisis nationalism of the late *bakumatsu* period had been revived in his 1880 writings. In the process of this revival much of the liberal content of his earlier thought slowly seeped away. Fukuzawa continued to see the individual as the end of the political process—although even this is lost sight of at times—and government as a means (*hōben*). But what an individual enjoys depends on whether his country is weak or strong. Fukuzawa wrote: "The English export opium, a poisonous drug, to China. The Chinese lose money, injure their health, and

[46] *F.Z.*, v, 254–56. (Emphasis added.) Carmen Blacker has a number of nice quotations further illustrating Fukuzawa's changing view of international relations in *The Japanese Enlightenment, A Study of the Writings of Fukuzawa Yukichi* (Cambridge, G.B., 1964), pp. 129–33. Miss Blacker believes that Fukuzawa remained committed to a natural moral order throughout the 1880's and that his stress on state power was a temporary political expedient. I think that Fukuzawa gave up his belief in such an order during those years, though he did so with great reluctance and continued to feel the fascination of his former ideals. Miss Blacker's book is one of the best studies in English of a Japanese thinker. Considering this, and considering that so many Meiji thinkers remain unstudied, I hesitated for some time before beginning on Fukuzawa. One justification is that he does exemplify many aspects of Meiji nationalism. Another is that my perspective on the transition to Meiji differs somewhat from that of Miss Blacker. While pointing out the Confucian overtones in Fukuzawa's vocabulary, Miss Blacker follows his *Autobiography* and stresses the areas of conflict between Neo-Confucianism and the Dutch learning tradition. I would agree that science and Confucianism are largely incompatible in theory, but I am inclined to see Dutch learning (*rangaku*) as an historical combination of the two that greatly facilitated the introduction of Western thought in Meiji Japan.

year by year their national strength is sapped. And no one criticizes this." But what would happen, Fukuzawa asked, if the Chinese treated Englishmen or Americans in the same way? "Although there are those who give one or another specious explanation as to why things are so, penetrating to the bottom of the matter, I must clearly state that this depends solely on the fact that one country is stronger and one weaker."[47]

The new significance attributed to the nation caused Fukuzawa to turn away from his earlier exclusive preoccupation with an ideal civilization (*bummei*). The logic of science found in modern civilization was necessary to Japan. But morality and national spirit were also necessary to strengthen Japan internally. The sources of these cathectic elements (*jō*) were to be found not in *bummei* but in tradition. Fukuzawa argues: "As scholarship progresses, ethical doctrines may change completely. Yet these changes are but the introspections of scholars and will not fit the realities of the present day. Evolutionism and utilitarianism, for example, are kinds of theory that affect only the scholar in his pursuit of truth. Seeking a teaching that can be made the ethical standard for our Japanese samurai, I find that the most appropriate is 'repaying the country with loyalty' (*hōkoku jinchū*)."[48]

What is this *hōkoku jinchū*? Why will it work? What is its basis in history? Fukuzawa continues: "It is extremely difficult to maintain morality without religion. The great scholars of the West constantly struggle with this problem. Yet, accidentally, in Japan during the hundreds of years since medieval times our samurai have been able to maintain a high personal morality while ignoring religion. . . . One reason why they were able to maintain high standards of virtue apart from religion was that they were aided by Confucianism. But a still more potent factor was the feudal system itself: from the government of the Tokugawa down to the smallest *han*, each

[47] *F.Z.*, v, 259–60.　　　　　　　[48] *F.Z.*, ix, 378.

had his place as lord or vassal, as superior or inferior, and a clear social order was formed."[49]

The feudal system was based on an ethic of loyalty. Fukuzawa observed that the strength of this loyalty was akin to the fervent belief of a religious devotee. Seeking a simile to explain the ubiquity of loyalty in Tokugawa (and Meiji) Japan, he compared the institutional norms in which the broader cultural value was specified to the multiple applications of a single industrial principle: "The spiritual character of samurai raised in our country's feudal period derives fundamentally from the single fact of their unswerving loyalty to their lord. Yet in the course of its development loyalty is not limited solely to the lord-vassal, superior-inferior relationship; its functions extend to the most minute, most distant aspects of [all] human relationships. To depict its significance we may liken it to an engineer who first learns the operation of a steam engine at a steel mill; then, as his skill gradually develops, he becomes able to run a steamship or manage a locomotive: even if he encounters one hundred other varieties of steam engine . . . their operation will not trouble him."[50]

The distinction between institutional norms and cultural values enables Fukuzawa to explain the differences between Japan and China or Korea. These countries have the same letters, but have different institutions and consequently different interpretations of the same thought. Thus, "when Chinese or Koreans read Confucian texts they understand them in a Chinese or Korean sense; when Japanese samurai read the same books they comprehend them in a feudal sense."[51]

The distinction between institutional norms and cultural values also makes it possible for loyalty to outlive the Tokugawa system. Fukuzawa views loyalty as having developed during Japan's early feudal history. By Tokugawa times it was deeply entrenched. It had become an "independent virtue" (*dokuritsu no dōtoku*) which continued whether lords were

[49] *F.Z.*, IX, 378.   [50] *F.Z.*, IX, 381.   [51] *F.Z.*, IX, 387.

good or bad. So it was not unexpected that even after feudalism was abolished the ex-samurai continued to be "followers of the religion of loyalty." They continued to be receptive to demands couched in terms of "repaying the country with loyalty."[52]

This did not mean, however, that Confucianism was also to be continued. "Its advantages are not worth the efforts required to master it," it is an impediment to civilization and enlightenment, and one "can only pity the minds that are intoxicated by its doctrines."[53] It no longer "fits reality." Fukuzawa argued that Confucianism must be replaced by a new moral education based on loyalty.

What will work with samurai, the "upper stratum" of Japanese society, will not work with the lower classes, who lack an education in loyalty and who are religiously inclined. Some of Fukuzawa's contemporaries proposed the Confucianization of the masses as a halfway step in the direction of reason. Fukuzawa, however, thought it would be better to use "religion that is completely distinct from the logic of science (*suri*)" than Confucianism, which possesses a logic that conflicts with the logic of science. He therefore advocated the "implantation of religion" as the best means of upholding general morality.[54] As the level of education rose the masses would gradually shuck off their superstitions and join in the purer morality of the "samurai."

The capstone of Fukuzawa's doctrine of loyalty was his startling new appraisal of Japan's imperial institution. His first treatise, *On the Imperial House* (*Teishitsuron*), was published in 1881, the second, *On Honoring the Emperor* (*Sonnōron*), in 1888. The two are virtually identical in content. Fukuzawa's argument begins with a definition of the political position and historical character of the imperial house: "The imperial house is outside of political society. Moreover, I have long maintained that those who discuss politics or are active in political affairs ought not to make improper use in their doc-

[52] *F.Z.*, ix, 382, 387.   [53] *F.Z.*, ix, 387.   [54] *F.Z.*, ix, 394.

trines of the majesty and sacredness of the imperial house.
. . . The Japanese people are the subject-children of the imperial house. . . ." It may appear that at times some have fought
against the court. But, "in our Japan from ancient times to
the present there has never in fact been a rebellious subject.
Nor will there be one in the future."[55]

Fukuzawa goes on to relate past history to the promised
Diet, and to discuss the role of the imperial house in Japan's
future constitutional state. "At this moment we are most anxious about the imperial house. The groups called political
parties each have different doctrines; some are termed liberal or
progressive and some conservative. Although we say that these
are struggling over issues, in truth they are struggling for
power: each is trying to seize the handle of power for itself.
Although force and weapons are not used in these struggles,
in fact they are like those between the Minamoto and the
Taira. . . . If each time power changes hands one party moves
toward the emperor and the other turns away, then the imperial house will be sullied by the dust of political society: its
peerless majesty will be injured, its unparalleled sacredness
damaged. For the nation this is a matter of great anxiety. . . ."[56]

At this point Fukuzawa makes a distinction between attending to affairs of state and overseeing them; the latter is the
function of the emperor, and only by keeping it separate from
the former can the emperor be kept clear of politics. But if
the emperor only "oversees" and does not participate in
government, why is he important?

There may be some who, noting that the imperial house is
outside political society, wonder if it is not an empty ves-
sel. . . . The emperor does not attend directly to the affairs
of state, he oversees them. He does not concern himself
with the physical state of the people, but gathers their spirits
to himself. In a despotic form of government the monarch
attends directly to affairs of state and to those of the people.

[55] *F.Z.*, v, 439.   [56] *F.Z.*, v, 440–41.

But in a constitutional government it is only the physical order of the nation that is maintained by the government; a focus for the spirit is lacking and for this it is necessary to depend on the imperial house. Which is more important, human spirit or physical nature? Spirit governs the body. The imperial house controls that which governs and oversees practical matters as well. Can this be called an empty position?[57]

Fukuzawa observes that people like to win and dislike losing. But how can individual desires to win be subordinated to the need for national unity? How can the elites of the proposed constitutional government—the political parties, the bureaucracy, the army and navy—be brought to cooperate? Only through the emperor. Fukuzawa writes: "There are many who fall prey to a nervous disease known as the desire for fame. To ease this, to free them from time to time from its pangs, a strange, nonrational therapy must be used; we especially rely on the majesty and sacredness of the imperial house. . . . There is no other way of satisfying men than by using the light of the imperial house, a limitless means containing limitless significance."[58]

But this is not all. Fukuzawa argues that the role of the emperor in government is but a minor aspect of his importance. Once parliament is established, government will follow its legislation. But the functions of law in society are limited. Morality and customs cannot be controlled by law alone. "In Japan who can fully control the world of human feelings and preserve habits of virtue and righteousness? Only the imperial house. In the countries of the West religion flourishes not only among monks in monasteries but also in secular society . . . and this attracts men's hearts and preserves virtuous ways. But in our Japan religion lacks this efficacy in society at large: it is solely a matter of sermons in temples. It is clear that religion alone will not suffice to uphold morality, and even

[57] *F.Z.*, v, 446–47.   [58] *F.Z.*, vi, 246–47.

clearer is the necessity of depending on the imperial house."[59] Fukuzawa's conclusion is that "one who, thinking of his descendants, prays for the stability of our Japanese society, views the augustness and sacredness of the emperor as our country's greatest treasure."[60]

This view of the imperial house was not wholly reactionary, despite its dependence on irrational sentiment. Fukuzawa continued to advocate progress along lines taken by the West, though he also came to feel that the arts and learning of Japan's tradition should be preserved as well. He favored cultural diversity and political pluralism. But he felt that Japan, at its stage of civilization, could not handle these things without grave internal disturbances. Fukuzawa foresaw that instant constitutional government in a developing nation could lead to violent rifts in the national consensus, which in turn might destroy constitutional government and bring dictatorship. And his concern for Japan's success in competition with foreign powers was such that national disunity could not be tolerated. Therefore he stressed the emperor, who alone could make Japan strong and united while advancing toward full constitutional government.

By the mystique of the emperor Japan was to eat its cake and have it too. But in the process Fukuzawa's earlier emphasis on the independent spirit of a democratic people was to a large measure lost. The older Fukuzawa spoke more of duties and less of rights, more of science and less of freedom. He argued now that the imperial house should become "the center of civilization and enlightenment."[61] But he overlooked the close ties between the imperial house and some of the most backward aspects of the Japanese tradition. The effect was to emasculate much of the liberal content of his earlier views.

After 1895: The Mellow Years

The Sino-Japanese War marked the final turning point in Fukuzawa's thought. Internal reforms had won Japan the

[59] *F.Z.*, v, 464.   [60] *F.Z.*, vi, 264.   [61] *F.Z.*, vi, 267.

approval of the world community, unequal treaties had been revised, and dynastic China had been defeated—Fukuzawa termed this the victory of civilization over barbarism. He exulted over what Japan had accomplished in less than thirty years:

> The Sino-Japanese War is the victory of a united government and people. There are no words that can express my pleasure and thankfulness: to experience such an event is what life is for. How unfortunate are my friends who died earlier! I weep each time wanting to let them know. In truth the Sino-Japanese War does not amount to much; it is but a prelude to Japan's future diplomacy, and is no occasion for such rejoicing. Yet I am so overcome by emotions that I enter a dreamlike state. . . . The strength, wealth, and civilization of the new Japan are all due to the virtues of those who went before. We who are born in this fortunate age have merely received these gifts from our ancestors. . . . As I look back on my own life I have no regrets; there have been only pleasures.[62]

Victory in war removed the load of Japan from Fukuzawa's shoulders. No longer was it necessary for him to talk up the national spirit or warn the people of present perils, although he never got entirely away from Japan. He talked a great deal of the need for higher moral standards and he continued to concern himself with the issues of the day. But the old urgency was gone and he began again to talk of the larger philosophical issues of ethics and cosmology that had occupied his attentions during the early 1870's.

Fukuzawa's vision of the world during the years before his death in 1901 can only be described as mellow. The bleak harshness of the amoral universe of the 1880's was seen, *sub specie eternitatis*, not as the true character of things, but as a consequence of man's presently constricted vision. As science developed and man gained a truer knowledge of things, it

[62] *F.Z.*, VII, 617–18.

would become clear that the universe was favorably inclined toward human beings. From one perspective the universe is neutral, "all heaven does is to strictly maintain its laws."[63] But this neutrality contained a higher goodness that would benefit man.

Where did this higher goodness come from? In part it was an envisioned expansion of science into the spheres of man and society. Once quantitative science discovered the laws of human nature and society—and that they could be discovered was an idea that nineteenth century positivism inherited from eighteenth century utopianism—then an ideal society based on science could be created. Fukuzawa did not return to a theory of natural rights during this last phase of his thought; he continued to regard this theory as metaphysical and pseudo-scientific. But his positivistic vision of human progress was suffused with an optimism that was not unrelated to the assumptions he had held in the 1860's and early 1870's. In some respects this was a revival of Fukuzawa's earlier "enlightenment" belief in a beneficent natural order, for once again he saw progress toward an ideal society as possible within a finite period of time.

Fukuzawa began his *Fukuō hyakuwa* in 1897 with a discussion of the universe and its creativity. He spoke of its fineness, of the intricacy with which it had fashioned the wing of a butterfly, and of the limitless light-years of its breadth. He mentioned the unchanging character of its laws. He described man as the highest creation of its workings, for man can know shame as well as be driven by bodily drives. In the face of this universe man can only marvel and feel awe. Man refers to those parts of the universe which he does not yet understand as heaven (*ten*).[64]

Fukuzawa next asked the "perennial question," whether the laws of nature "are harmful or beneficial to man." He began by dismissing one historicist fallacy: "Ssu-ma Chien questioned whether the will of heaven was good or bad be-

[63] *F.Z.*, VII, 36.　　　　　　　　[64] *F.Z.*, VII, 1–6.

cause of his personal misfortune. . . . The universe is broad and eternal. Just because in a few thousands of years there are some thousands of misfortunes a judgment cannot be made regarding its goodness or evil. The philosophy of the historian, it must be said, had not yet grasped the nature of the universe. This sort of reasoning is shallow, so let us put it aside."[65]

He then turned to the problem of evil. He speaks of innocents who die of childbirth or disease: "Such things appear to us as the unfolding of laws established by a murderer. If nature were good, if it were compassionate, then would it not have been better for the mother not to have borne a child in the first place? Rather than to kill men with disease and capriciously cause them . . . to suffer, would it not have been true goodness not to have caused them to be born? This is the wanton destruction of life."[66] Fukuzawa continued with a discussion of earthquakes, storms at sea, and volcanic eruptions. Why did nature permit these? Why did nature (*tendō*) not make man's heart good? And is not the playful malice of nature matched by the puerile judgments of man? Those who kill other human beings and carry out evil plots are praised as great patriots and statesmen and emulated by others as moral exemplars.[67]

Fukuzawa's answer to the problem of evil is optimistic. In his optimism is a belief in progress and a rekindled belief in history:

> Although there are many who suffer sickness, man's body is not diseased by nature. That it becomes so is due to the insufficient development of human knowledge. Man's passions arise, he breaks the laws of nature (*tensoku*) . . . and thus is guilty of injuring himself. That this is so can be seen by observing animals and birds which, following nature well, are without disease. But parallel to the vigor of man's passions is the development of his intellect. This is considerable and enables him to determine his long term

[65] *F.Z.*, VII, 6.   [66] *F.Z.*, VII, 7.   [67] *F.Z.*, VII, 8.

interests. Therefore a clear mind can hold in check the passions and care for the body. Generation by generation [these characteristics] will be transmitted to his descendants, and it cannot be doubted but that the day will finally come when man will have regained his original diseaseless state. Moreover, that man falls prey to infectious or epidemic diseases is due, in fine, to his own lack of knowledge. As human knowledge advances it will be easy to get rid of the causes of this sort of disease just as one protects oneself from wind and rain by entering a building or donning an overcoat. To say that damage from typhoons, torrential rains, earthquakes, etc., are signs of heaven's malevolence is the extreme of absurdity. These arise spontaneously from nature. He is foolish who, not knowing why they are inevitable, willy nilly fears their consequences. . . . Nature gives notice in advance that such events will occur. . . . Man's understanding is opaque. Even though he receives these notices . . . he does not know how to avoid the disasters. . . . This is like receiving letters from a friend and not being able to read them.[68]

The past history of human progress is brief, "like three years in the life of a man who will live to one hundred." The businessman "who seeks to increase his wealth, the politician who strives for fame, are like greedy children fighting over toys. Or like a child who, on becoming king of the mountain, looks down on his playmates without shame or virtue." But Fukuzawa is willing "to leave [the situation] to nature," and wait for the child to grow up.[69]

We might question his metaphor. For children to grow up is a natural consequence of organism and social life. Are there comparable processes at work in human society as a whole? And is the adult morally better than the child? Fukuzawa's answer to this question is in two parts. The first part concerns science.

[68] *F.Z.*, VII, 8-9.   [69] *F.Z.*, VII, 9-10.

If we seek the vital difference between the learning of the present civilization and the traditional learning of Japan and China, it is simply a matter of whether or not it is based on science (*butsuri*). Clarifying the quantity, form, and nature of things according to the true principles of the natural universe, learning their functions, and using things for the good of mankind is science. . . . However, when we leave the quantitative sciences (*yūkei no butsuri*) and move to the logic of quality (*mukei no ronri*), then truths are not always the same. . . . What the ancients looked up to as virtuous government, the present age views as oppressive rule. . . . As human culture gradually progresses, as the laws of nature gradually become known, then what today are called the formless areas of human affairs (*mukei no jinji*) such as economics and politics will finally be absorbed completely into the sciences.[70]

As this occurs, an ideal society will become a real possibility. Today, therefore:

Man should not be surprised at the malignity of nature. Rather, he must make efforts to discover its secrets and make them his own. Step by step man must increase his dominance [over nature] and increase the sum of his happiness. This is what is known as fighting against nature to extend man's powers (*zōka to sakai o arasou*) . . . and it is just this that is the essence of science. Although the present is spoken of as an age of enlightenment, the power of heaven is immeasurable, its secrets are unlimited. It is the duty of man over the next five hundred or five thousand years to gradually control and restrain this power and, uncovering heaven's secrets, to use them for the good of humanity.[71]

The second reason why Fukuzawa felt that the child of three would grow in virtue was that it was in his nature. Be-

[70] *F.Z.*, VII, 278–80.   [71] *F.Z.*, VII, 37.

cause Fukuzawa believed that man's nature was good, he was optimistic about the future findings of science. "Human society today . . . is a hotbed of ignorance and wickedness. Yet, though everything does not proceed according to our ideal, this is not the will of heaven (*temmei*), but the fault of man. . . . Man's true nature (*honshin*) is to love the good, his mind is for progress and improvement. As this inherent nature (*honrai no soshitsu*) is cultivated, man will reach perfection. This cannot be doubted."[72]

Some argue that to speculate about the distant future and take comfort therein is not the job of the scholar. Fukuzawa insists, however, that his "vision does not lack foundations. The basis for speculation about the future is the record of the past." And the past, for those with the power to perceive it, is the history of human progress from a life that was short and brutish to its present improved state. The progress made to date "proves the thesis that nature (*tendō*) is good to man. We are better off than our ancestors. But we are miserable in comparison to what our descendants will be. That we are better off is a gift (*onshi*) bought by the suffering of our predecessors. To pay back this obligation (*hōon*) we too must suffer and work for the benefit of our descendants. This is man's duty."[73]

In this argument are overtones of the hereditary chain of moral obligation that rested on the Tokugawa samurai: by protecting one's own body and providing descendants for one's family, one repays the debt owed to one's parents and their parents for one's life and body; by working for one's lord one repays the obligations of one's ancestors to the ancestors of one's present lord. Though some of the old logic remains, the ethic is now universalized. In the Tokugawa period the debt to the ages was repaid within the family; in the 1880's Fukuzawa put primary emphasis on repaying the nation; but now Fukuzawa talks of repaying all humanity for the benefits of civilization.

[72] *F.Z.*, VII, 11.   [73] *F.Z.*, VII, 12.

Conclusions

Fukuzawa Yukichi was typical of the politically oriented, Confucian educated, Western inspired generation of Meiji thinkers. If nationalism may be defined as the aggregate of ideas and sentiments that focus on the nation, or, more simply, as in-group feeling that takes the nation as the group, then Fukuzawa was highly nationalistic. Concern for Japan was central in his thinking. At moments of crisis his concern for Japan became intense, as during the late 1860's or the 1880's. At other times it was muted and qualified by more general cultural concerns. Indeed there appears in Fukuzawa's thought a constant tension between universal cultural goals and the more particular needs of Japan. But the two were always joined, cultural goals were always seen as related to Japan's long term welfare.

The contribution of nationalism to the process of modernization is not a matter that can be simply judged. An evaluation based on its content may differ sharply from one based on its function. Some see nationalism as bad: xenophobic, chauvinistic, jingoistic, irrational, and expansionistic. It appears as the antithesis of what is rational, efficient, and modern. Others may evaluate it highly and credit it with developmental virtues: it enables government to tap the energies of the people; it gives to citizens a supralocal identification and a willingness to participate in government. It creates unity and national purpose. It is what backward nations wish they had more of.

Fukuzawa saw nationalism as a good. The advance from *han* to nation was parallel in his mind to the advance from a static tradition to a more enlightened civilization. And both advances, he felt, were the work of samurai. Late in life, looking back on thirty years of Meiji history, he wrote that Japan had succeeded in strengthening itself because of the positive virtues of the samurai spirit. Not that he forgot samurai obscurantism: in 1876 he wrote with exasperation that talking politics with reactionary samurai who could not even decide to change their hairdos "is like discussing arrangements for a debate with a stone Buddha."[74] But on the whole he esteemed the ex-samurai as a nonreligious, politically aware, and enlightened class. Even the imperial house had merely served as the focus for a psychological "set" that was a legacy of feudalism.

Fukuzawa's reasoning on samurai nationalism is not unlike Veblen's later observation that the strength of the Japanese nation derived from the "unique combination of feudalistic fealty and chivalric honor with the material efficiency given by modern technology."[75] It prefigures the findings of Ruth Benedict, who similarly underlined the importance of duties and the fulfillment of obligations. Fukuzawa gives us a not wholly fanciful analysis of how the Meiji government could justify sacrifices, the rewards of which the Meiji Japanese would not themselves enjoy. Fukuzawa's analysis is compelling in part because it was a statement in a historical context of what he himself believed. Speaking of the *shishi* whose slogan was to expel the barbarians, he wrote: "We must truly admire their spirit of love for country. Our position is no different. We only want to change the form of their patriotism and apply it to the present."[76] Fukuzawa's analysis of the samurai ethos helps explain political stability and the high level of energies available to the Meiji government. But if we would explain the full contribution of samurai nationalism to the Meiji success, we must inquire further into its cultural content.

It has been suggested recently that too much Westernization too soon can swamp a country bent on modernizing. It can produce anomie, a rudderless condition in which ordered

[74] *F.Z.*, IV, 339.
[75] Thorstein Veblen, *Essays in Our Changing Order* (New York, 1934), p. 251.
[76] *F.Z.*, V, 267.

priorities are lost, in which values drift out of a set of calculus, compete, and impede the enactment of any program.[77] Similarly, it is obvious that too little Westernization will not open up an adequate number of lines for change. Japan during the early Meiji era steered successfully between these two extremes. The emperor, a small number of values such as loyalty, filial piety, and harmony, and a cluster of slogans stressing wealth, strength, and unity were preserved from tradition. Recombined in suitable patterns, these enabled the state to draw support from diverse segments of the traditional society. That mobilization of this support occurred only slowly was due to the slow development of education, military service, and communications, and to the gradual extension of state authority. The symbol of the emperor also became the focal point for new energies. The slogans defined the overall direction of government programs.

Yet for all of this the cupboard of emperor-particularism was almost bare in the early Meiji years. In contrast to the complex Mito philosophy or the even more involute ratiocinations of the school of national studies, the stripped-down *kokutai* of the early Meiji had little content. Fukuzawa could shrug his shoulders and say that every nation had a *kokutai* and no one minded. Many ignored the *kokutai* altogether; to the extent it was present it was almost no impediment to the program of Westernization supported by both officials and nonofficial enlighteners.

An ideal pattern for modernization might be one in which universal elements from the traditional culture are picked up, emphasized, and then used as a vehicle for the introduction of the universalism of the modern West. When we think of Japanese nationalism—of the attempt to base a value order on the figure of the emperor—it seems far removed from this ideal pattern. Yet this use of the emperor really only began in

[77] Robert N. Bellah, "Epilogue," in Robert N. Bellah, ed., *Religion and Progress in Modern Asia* (New York, 1965), pp. 170-71.

the late 1880's. There was much of the ideal in the early Meiji years. It is extremely important that just when the foundations of the modern system were being established in Japan the particularistic guideposts kept from the earlier tradition were set in new, more universalistic philosophies. In the early Meiji period Fukuzawa clearly saw the emperor and state as means to more universalistic cultural and social ends; his ideal was the formation of a civilization based on science in which the faculties of individuals could be developed to their full capacity.

Where did Fukuzawa's early universalism come from? I am inclined to answer that the source was Chu Hsi Confucianism, or better, the late Tokugawa blend of Neo-Confucianism and Dutch learning. Fukuzawa appears to have moved from a relatively open position within the Tokugawa tradition to that of nineteenth century British liberalism. This pattern may be discerned in his belief in a common moral nature of man, in his Mencius-like emphasis on the welfare of the people as the end of the state, and in his stress on men of ability. As earlier Japanese had universalized *ri* to include Western science, Fukuzawa and others of his generation went one step further to put the social content of the Enlightenment in a framework of *ri*-like natural law. His commitment in 1867 to the universal principles (*sekai no jōri*) of the law of nations is an early example of this. By the early 1870's the transition to a more completely Western position had been made.

The transition was not a simple matter. Intellectually it can be seen as the unfolding of tendencies already begun within Tokugawa Dutch learning. Yet the difficulties in the transition were such that it cannot be adequately explained without taking into account the emphasis on Westernization in the political atmosphere of post-Restoration Japan. Natural law and *ri* have within their respective world views somewhat similar "valences." Yet the move from *ri* to natural law was a leap between positions with vastly different ethical and cog-

145

nitive implications. In the early 1870's Fukuzawa was well aware of the differences, but he did not fully appreciate the extent to which he maintained old assumptions.

There was a considerable variety among the early Meiji thinkers. However, the kind of natural rights expounded by Fukuzawa was perhaps the mainstream among the advanced circles of the day. Katō Hiroyuki, trying in 1870 to explain the idea of natural rights, wrote that "in man's nature (*tensei*) there are various emotions (*jō*) of which the desire for unfettered independence is the most poignant." At the base of each such emotion was a right common to all men, a right that each man should respect in others. Appealing to Confucian notions, Katō went on to compare such rights (*kenri*) with the duties arising from the virtues of *jin, gi, rei,* and so on that also are found in man's heart. He concluded that duties and rights are necessary to each other, that each limit the other, and that both are found in man's original nature.[78] An introduction to Kanda Kōhei's 1871 translation of a European work on natural law stated that natural law was valid for all places and times since it was "based on the true nature of man." The foreword by Kanda then continued: "Though the various laws differ, there is not one that does not have its source, if one but investigates, in natural law." The differences are to be explained by the admixture of local customs and precedents. Where civilization does not prevail laws may not be in accord with natural law, "but as civilization gradually advances the practice of natural law will slowly be realized."[79]

Nor were ideas such as these limited to the 1870's and the thinkers of the Meiji Six Society (Meirokusha). Activists in the popular-rights movement of the 1880's continued to rely on them. Nakae Chōmin's writings were a mixture of Con-

[78] Katō Hiroyuki, "Shinsei taii," in *Meiji bunka zenshū* (Tokyo, 1925), v, 89–90.

[79] Kanda Kōhei, "Seihōryaku," in *Meiji bunka zenshū* (Tokyo, 1957), XIII, 3–4.

fucian ideas and Enlightenment thought. The writers in the movement for popular rights who attacked Katō after his switch to Social Darwinism appealed to the same natural-rights concepts that Katō had propounded earlier.[80] The party movement lost much of its former fire after entering the Diet, but even during the 1890's a fresh sidestream emerged from its left wing that not only continued a variant of natural-law thought but also continued to feel a vague affinity with Confucianism. Sakai Toshihiko wrote in his autobiography that one aspect of advancing in the world (*risshin*) was to act virtuously (*michi o okonau*) and that the will to do this had led him to socialism.[81] Kōtoku Shūsui, a one-time disciple of Nakae, wrote, too simply perhaps: "I entered socialism from Confucianism."[82]

Nevertheless, by the 1880's the most advanced thinkers in Japan no longer wrote of natural rights. Fukuzawa's denial of natural moral laws in 1881 and Katō Hiroyuki's refutation of natural rights in 1882 were archetypal of a far-reaching change that overcame Japanese thought in that decade, a change with drastic ethical implications. When the Confucian *ri* was replaced by Enlightenment natural law in the 1870's a new ethic was introduced, a new ethic was available. But when the kindly natural law of the 1870's was replaced by the amoral, struggle-for-survival natural law of the 1880's, no new source of positive social values was provided.

Under these circumstances there was nothing other to turn to than the spiritual power of the emperor or the residues of irrational samurai morality. Other genuine alternatives in the Japanese tradition had been discredited during the 1870's. Where earlier the emperor had been merely one aspect in a universal civilization, the emperor was now made the source of the political and ethical order.[83] Fukuzawa's statement

---

[80] See *Meiji bunka zenshū* (Tokyo, 1925), v, 389–482.

[81] Nishio Yōtarō, *Kōtoku Shūsui* (Tokyo, 1959), p. 13.

[82] *Ibid.*

[83] See Masao Maruyama, *Thought and Behavior in Modern Japanese Politics* (London, 1963), pp. 1–23.

that Japan must depend on the imperial house to uphold morality, like Itō's report to the Privy Council that only the imperial house could serve as an adequate principle of state, reflects this ethical predicament.[84] That it occurred just as the Meiji constitution was being written gave it a special significance in subsequent Japanese history.

In Fukuzawa's own thought the emperor issue was temporary. Viewing the full sweep of his intellectual evolution, the emperor and religion were utilized only as temporary expedients, as crutches to maintain order in a competitive world, and order itself was but a precondition for progress toward a rational civilization. Fukuzawa's belief in science was never lost. In the 1890's his hopes were rekindled for a world order both rational and ethical that would be based, not on the false imaginings of eighteenth century European metaphysicians, but on truly universal, scientific laws of human society. So distant in the future was this positivistic ideal that it had little appeal for his contemporaries. Yet it was Fukuzawa's sustained belief in this idea that has made him a cultural hero for more recent generations of Japanese. In 1943 Maruyama Masao began an essay on Fukuzawa with the words: "Fukuzawa Yukichi was a Meiji thinker, but at the same time he is a thinker of the present day."[85]

[84] The relevant portion of Itō's report is quoted in Fairbank, Reischauer, and Craig, *East Asia, The Modern Transformation* (Boston, 1965), p. 533.

[85] Maruyama Masao, "Fukuzawa ni okeru chitsujo to ningen," in Hidaka Rokurō, ed., *Kindaishugi* (Tokyo, 1964), p. 55.

CHAPTER V

Modernization and Foreign Policy in Meiji Japan

MARIUS B. JANSEN

IN THE YEARS before World War II the foreign policies of modern Japan were a principal focus of historical studies. The rapid rise of an Asian power to equality and partnership with the Western powers forced dramatic changes in the international order of the nineteenth century, and Japan's growing power was an important factor in the profound readjustment of that relatively stable order in the course of twentieth century wars and revolutions. More recent scholarship has preferred to examine the domestic sources of Japan's transformation in efforts to locate the elements of traditional culture and society that may have been conducive to the changes of Japan's modern century. It now becomes of interest to relate foreign policy to modernity, and to ask what part of that policy may be ascribed to the broader process of Japan's development as nation-state and what to a more narrow setting of contingency and individuality. The consideration of Meiji Japan's foreign policies under the categories of modernization makes it appropriate to begin with the development of a new view of the world order. In recent scholarship, descriptive definitions of modernization include reference to the consciousness of an international society made up of national units, nations which order their relationships through functionaries trained in the practice of foreign relations and to some degree responsive to the interest in public affairs generated among growing numbers of people through the institutions of education, communications, and representation which

149

have everywhere accompanied the development of modern nation states.

The traditional world of East Asia had few precedents for such a world order. Political modernization required the development of attitudes and institutions appropriate to a new kind of world. Struggles over areas of multiple or uncertain national affiliation engaged the attention and energies of governments and statesmen. As foreign affairs became a principal concern of the Japanese state, they gradually became the object of specialist bureaucracies specifically charged with the mastery of relationships between sovereign governments. But specialists were not the only persons interested in foreign policy. Efforts to enlist popular interest and participation by diffusion of the literacy and mass communications that could activate and channel public response soon resulted in the creation of a much more complex setting for consideration of foreign policies. The spectator attitude of the peasants who watched with interest the foreign bombardment of the Shimonoseki batteries in 1864 and who helped dismantle them when stilled gradually gave way to the surging rage of the Tokyo mobs that expressed their dissatisfaction with the Treaty of Portsmouth in 1905. The importance of this change for the conduct of foreign affairs, as limitation on government initiative, and as spur to government action, can hardly be exaggerated.

It is necessary to add to these considerations, which bear on the importance of modernization for foreign policy in all countries, reminders of the special nature of the case of nineteenth century Japan, for in Japan the modernization process was itself to a large degree the product of foreign policy. It was in consequence of Japan's encounter with the West and its leaders' conviction that modernization was prerequisite to independence and equality that the Meiji changes were set in motion. The external challenge and goal meant that national, rather than individual, ends would receive priority, and indeed that individual concerns could best be justified as important to national strength. Nationalism was, from the first, in government service; in Maruyama's words, "Japanese nationalism prematurely abandoned any thought of popular emancipation, popular movements being repressed in the name of national unity."[1] This affected the goals and the pace of the modernization program, and those goals and pace in turn affected its content.

The pages below will take up five aspects of Meiji foreign policy to examine these interrelationships. The location and awareness of the foreign-policy–modernization problem came first. Institutional measures were then needed to deal with it. Determination of the extent of the national unit involved controversy with Japan's East Asian neighbors, while the recovery of sovereignty involved decades of effort for revision of the unequal treaties. Finally, the end of the Meiji period saw the achievement of success in war and empire.

Awareness of the Problem

The foreign policy problems Japan faced at midpoint in the nineteenth century were a consequence of the discovery that Japan's weakness relative to the powers of Europe and America was so great as to invite interference, defeat, and possible control.

The nature of the danger the country faced has been the subject of much debate. But the fear was real, and it constitutes a fact. A country whose world view had been for the most part bounded by the Chinese cultural sphere had seen the center of that world humiliated by the maritime power of the West, and it had no reason to expect to fare differently itself. The real and imagined possibilities of French and, later, English interference in the course of the Meiji Restoration have been convincingly documented by Ishii Takashi. At first it seemed likely that the shogunate would be the chief beneficiary of outside help. The Netherlands began with a

[1] Ivan Morris, ed., *Thought and Behaviour in Modern Japanese Politics* (New York, 1963), p. 143.

naval mission in 1855, and soon France took over with help in building the Yokosuka shipyard and arsenal. Minister Leon Roche's offers of a military aid mission drew the quick response of Harry Parkes' offer of British help in organizing a Tokugawa navy. When in 1863 the Tokugawa councillor Ogasawara proposed that outside assistance be used to establish a stronger, more centralized and modern Tokugawa regime, he illustrated one way in which Western help might have affected Japanese political processes. In 1865 Parkes' interpreter Ernest Satow wrote a pamphlet on British policy suggesting that foreign agreements would have force only if concluded with a council of daimyo sitting for the emperor. He had the effect of encouraging groups in Satsuma and Chōshū to expect outside help in discrediting and overthrowing the shogunate.[2] As things worked out, the European powers remained neutral in the political struggles of the 1860's, although their professions of neutrality had as consequence the denial of military assistance—even the previously purchased American ram *Stonewall*—to the Tokugawa authorities,[3] and their insistence on keeping the ports open despite hostilities embarrassed the regime and helped its enemies. Nevertheless such "interference," especially when it is compared with the role of the powers in China in these same years, was quite insignificant. It is not difficult to understand the lively fears of a generation whose sense of patterned hierarchy in internal and external relationships had been destroyed, but it is equally useful to reflect on the fortunate coincidence of real fear with what turned out to be slight danger for Japan at the time of the Restoration.

Once the ports were opened to trade in 1860, the conscious-

[2] "Rekkyō no tai Nichi seisaku," *Iwanami kōza Nihon rekishi*, XIV (*kindai* I Tokyo, 1962), 224. This article is an updating and summary of Ishii's earlier *Meiji Ishin no kokusaiteki kankyō* (Tokyo, 1957).

[3] Details from the American side, in E. and J. A. Barnes, eds., *Samuel P. Boyer, Naval Surgeon: Revolt in Japan, 1868–1869* (Bloomington: Indiana Univ. Press, 1963).

ness of weakness made efforts to ascertain the sources of Western strength inevitable. This need occupied much of the decade outlined by the great learning missions of 1862 and 1872. The former, ostensibly charged with negotiations to delay further opening of ports in order to prevent antiforeign disorders, was additionally instructed to investigate governmental, educational, and military institutions of the West.[4] Twenty-two in number, with as many more supporting personnel, the 1862 mission was not narrowly "official" but included a sample of regional representatives.[5] Much better known, larger, and more prestigious was the Iwakura Mission, which sailed in 1871 with forty-eight men who studied, in the words of a letter from Ōkubo Toshimichi (from England) to Ōyama Iwao (then in Switzerland), "courts, prisons, schools, trading firms, factories and shipyards, iron foundries, sugar refineries, paper plants, wool and cotton spinning and weaving, silver, cutlery, and glass plants, coal and salt mines, not to speak of old castles and temples—there is nowhere we haven't gone."[6] Some, like Kido, concerned themselves chiefly with institutions of government and returned convinced of the relevance of what they had seen for Japan. It was essential to plan reforms to increase participation and involvement on the part of ordinary citizens. "In enlightened countries," Kido wrote upon his return to Japan, "all who hold office respect the wishes of the whole nation and serve their country under a deep sense of responsibility so that even in extraordinary crises they take no arbitrary step contrary to the people's will. . . . My belief is that although Japan is not yet ready for parliamentary inspection of the affairs of state, in the importance of its laws and the

[4] Ishii, *op.cit.*, p. 220.

[5] Names in Osatake Takeshi, *Iteki no kuni e* (Tokyo, 1929), pp. 222–24, include Fukuzawa, Mitsukuri, Matsuki Kōan (Terajima Munenari), Fukuchi. That experience was still limited is suggested by the discussion about straw sandals (*waraji*), of which one thousand pairs were taken along.

[6] Quoted by Haga Tōru, "Kindai Nihon no sekkei," *Jiyū* (Nov. 1964), p. 17.

magnitude of its affairs it is no different from those countries of Europe and America the conduct of whose governments embodies the will of the people."[7]

From these experiences the Meiji leaders returned with an idea of the institutional and economic structure that Japan would require for survival in the modern world. They learned also that what they had seen in the West was relatively new there as well. There is no discouragement to be found in Kume Kunitake's pointed reminder that "the present wealth of the Europeans is something that has developed since 1800"; at that date, he went on, urban populations had been small and their products few; even when Prince Albert opened an exposition at Hyde Park in 1851 few countries had much to send, "and the Russians had sent only some quite barbarous things"; it was quite recently that France, which had fallen behind England after a lengthy period of cultural preeminence, had been stirred to competitive effort by exhibits in England. "If one compares the Europe of today with the Europe of forty years ago, it can be imagined how great the changes are; on land there were no trains, on sea no steamers; there were no telegraphic communications, small boats were pulled along canals, sails were hoisted at sea, horse drawn carts moved along the roads and people took coaches to stations. Soldiers using used brass cannon and breach-loading muskets fought at close range, wealthy families' finest clothes were of wool, and cotton cloth was a remarkable item of import from overseas. Although they knew about the Far East people saw no reason to seek its goods, and they knew Japan's products only by the things the Netherlands traders brought from Java."[8]

The manner in which the embassy members used their

[7] Quoted in R. Tsunoda, T. deBary, D. Keene, eds., *Sources of the Japanese Tradition* (New York: Columbia Univ. Press, 1958), pp. 650–51.

[8] Kume Kunitake, *Tokumei zenken taishi Bei-Ō kairan jikki* (Tokyo 1876), II, 56–57. Haga, *op.cit.*, p. 19, comments also on the further statement that the Westerners' gains had come by developing what Japanese had considered "foolishness," i.e. science.

European lessons to argue against war with Korea when they returned is well known. It was, they argued, a time for internal reforms to make good the half-century's lead that the West had, and not a time for foreign adventures. The association of recent Western experience with diplomatic caution and united effort in the tasks of modernization became typical. Many of the "experts" who accompanied Iwakura had become such in Tokugawa service earlier, and they were well aware of the difficulties of dealing from weakness.[9] A decade later the opposition leader Itagaki Taisuke returned from Europe less intent on opposition, and more convinced of the need for unity and harmony to prove to the West that the Japanese could make constitutionalism work.[10] Until the fall of imperial Japan, those best versed in the state of the outside world were most chary about affronting or challenging its leaders.

The need, then, was for domestic reforms—expressed in the slogan "rich country, strong army" (*fukoku-kyōhei*)—to catch up with the industrialized West. But factories, schools, uniforms, trains, and guns cost money, and the Meiji leaders found themselves saddled with severe handicaps in the unequal treaties. Humiliating as the provisions for extraterritoriality, most-favored nation, and treaty ports might be, it was the fixed customs rate (5 percent ad valorem) that most inhibited government planners.

The early treaties had five years to run, and the Restoration leaders thought optimistically of an early revision. But the treaties did not all expire at the same time, and the most-favored nation clause made it impossible to renegotiate any single treaty on a basis less favorable than that other countries enjoyed. Far from eliminating the unfavorable aspects of the treaties, the early Restoration government found itself con-

[9] Haga, p. 16, gives the names.

[10] *Segai Inoue Kō den* (Tokyo, 1936), III, 278 ff. Foreign Minister Inoue had secretly promoted the trip to further understanding of the problems Japan faced. Discussed further in Cecil Cody, "A Study of the Career of Itagaki Taisuke (1837–1919)." Unpublished doctoral dissertation, University of Washington, 1955.

strained to grant additional treaties to Sweden, Norway, and Spain in 1868, to Germany and Austria-Hungary in 1869 (this last masterminded by Harry Parkes), to Hawaii in 1871, and to Peru in 1873.[11] Reform was not simplified thereby.

Much of the diplomatic history of the Meiji period is the story of the attempts to overcome these treaty handicaps. The effort was given first importance, and to it most alluring diversions were sacrificed. Success in this enterprise required the good will and approval of the Western treaty powers, and consequently talk of Japan's role in Asia tended to come to the fore more often when the treaty program was temporarily shelved as impracticable. The 1870's, before treaty reform could be begun, and the 1890's, after it had been achieved, heard a good deal more such talk than did the 1880's. That decade, in contrast, featured the most resolute attempts to Westernize Japanese life and carry out treaty reform.

Although it had to take second place to relations with the Western powers as long as they had the upper hand, Japan's Asian dream—a modernized, strengthened Japan leading its neighbors—was a significant element in the view of many Japanese and constituted one of the goals of the leadership. It was a necessary goal, justifying as it did the temporary or tactical abandonment of the traditional East Asian view of nations and of values. It made it possible to be "Eastern" while going to school with the West and to answer nativist critics with arguments of long-range, ultimate victory. One finds Katsu Rintarō using such arguments in persuading anti-foreign zealots of the necessity to open the country in the 1860's. "What we ought to do," he told Kido in 1863, "is to send out ships from our country and impress strongly on the leaders of all Asian countries that their very existence depends on banding together and building a powerful navy, and that if they do not develop the necessary technology they will

[11] Tokinoya Masaru, "Meiji shonen no gaikō," *Iwanami koza Nihon rekishi*, xv (*kindai* ii, Tokyo, 1962), 217.

not be able to escape being trampled underfoot by the West. We should start with Korea, our nearest neighbor, and then go on to include China."[12] This was a hope held by Japanese of many affiliations. In the nature of things, government leaders, who were directing the programs which had Western treaty powers in mind, could talk about it less than could their critics. But the "outs," whether conservative-Japanist or radical-internationalist, found the argument attractive. It received respectable formulation as the "Ōkuma Doctrine" in 1898[13] and foreign approbation in the encouragement for a "Japanese Monroe Doctrine" which Theodore Roosevelt provided in 1905.[14]

A transitional step in Japan's efforts to grasp the nature of the problem that lay ahead was a short burst of enthusiasm among some scholars for international law. Maruyama Masao has pointed out that Japanese conceptions of Confucianism provided a transcendental standard of international life which served as a useful bridge to more serviceable ideas of international relations,[15] and no doubt this helped bridge old and new for a time. Fukuzawa, Carmen Blacker shows, shared this willingness to assume a rational, normative behavior for nations into the 1870's. Optimistic views of the outside world owed much to the way textbooks on international law were translated into the terminology appropriated from Neo-Confucian morality. They also served the short-run needs of the Meiji government, which gladly argued the "universal

[12] Quoted in M. B. Jansen, *Sakamoto Ryōma and the Meiji Restoration* (Princeton: Princeton Univ. Press, 1961), p. 165.

[13] Documentation and details in M. B. Jansen, *The Japanese and Sun Yat-sen* (Cambridge: Harvard Univ. Press, 1954), p. 53. See also Ōkuma's later comment that it was the "heaven-ordained office" of Japan "to introduce the civilization of the Occident to the Orient." *Fifty Years of New Japan* (London, 1909), II, 574.

[14] John A. White, *The Diplomacy of the Russo-Japanese War* (Princeton: Princeton Univ. Press, 1964), p. 163.

[15] Maruyama Masao, "Kaikoku," *Kōza rinri*, XI, *Tenkōki no rinri shisō (Nihon)* (Tokyo, 1959), 95.

principle" whereby Japan should be friendly with foreigners.[16]

But the initial optimism did not long survive the Restoration. On second thought (for Fukuzawa, by 1876) international life was much more predatory and the powers far less rational and disinterested. For some of Fukuzawa's peers, this correction had been borne out several years earlier in the pointed response Bismarck made to questions addressed to him by members of the Iwakura Mission: "although people say that so-called international law safeguards the rights of all countries, the fact is that when large countries pursue their advantage they talk about international law when it suits them, and they use force when it does not . . . small countries try and try to get a favorable decision only to fail sadly; it happens time after time that they can hardly maintain themselves and have to endure insult and aggravation even though they do their best to maintain their sovereignty." The only course, Itō and his colleagues were told, was to develop national strength and to cultivate patriotism among the populace. This was the policy Germany had followed. Advocates of peace, of conciliation, were proved wrong by the German example.[17] Iwakura himself did not need to learn this from Bismarck. A memorandum on foreign affairs he sent to Sanjō in 1869 pointed out that too many people misunderstood the real meaning of Japan's policies of cordial relations with foreign powers. "Although we have no choice in having intercourse with the countries beyond the seas, in the final analysis those countries are our enemies. Why are they our enemies? Day by day those countries develop their arts and their technology with a view to growing in wealth and power. Every foreign country tries to become another country's superior. Country A directs its efforts at country B, country B

[16] Carmen Blacker, *The Japanese Enlightenment: A Study of the Writings of Fukuzawa Yukichi* (Cambridge: Cambridge Univ. Press, 1964), pp. 122 ff.

[17] Kume, *Tokumei zenken . . .* , iii, 371. The official narrative.

at country C—they are all the same. That is why I say, all countries beyond the seas are our enemies."[18]

The Meiji leaders' sense of problem thus developed in conjunction with experience they gained in the new world of international relations. They interpreted what they saw in the light of Japan's own difficulties and handicaps, and these made necessary a prudent assessment of priorities in foreign and domestic policies.

Management of Foreign Affairs

A good deal has been written on the problem of fitting modern international relations into the world and governmental order of Imperial China, but Japan's difficulties in this regard—perhaps because they were successfully overcome—have come in for less attention. Yet they were of somewhat the same order, though probably moderated by the fact that Japan's world view was never as self-sufficient as China's. Nevertheless, foreign affairs had to be fitted into an institutional structure that had been devised with no thought for them.

The Tokugawa political system had no place for specialists in foreign affairs. The Dutch traders at Nagasaki were a part of the city commissioner's responsibility while there, and they became integrated into the daimyo travel system on their trips to Edo. Corps of specialists were developed to deal with the knowledge and the books the Dutch brought, but not to deal with *them*. Indeed, Japan had virtually no experience of dealing with outside countries on a basis of equality. After the first missions to China with their messages from the "emperor of the Land of the Rising Sun" to his counterpart the "emperor of the Land of the Setting Sun," later missions—as in Kamakura and Ashikaga times—had been sent by headquarters of less than imperial dignity in Japan. Even Hide-

[18] Quoted in Oka Yoshitake, "Kokuminteki dokuritsu to kokka risei," in *Kindai Nihon shisōshi kōza* (Tokyo, 1961), VIII, 12.

yoshi, who intended to conquer China, seems to have treated the Ming ambassadors as honored guests from a superior land. Koreans, also representative of the zone of literacy and culture, were treated with honor, however sticky negotiations (as with Arai Hakuseki) might become on matters of terminology for sovereignty.[19]

Westerners, on the other hand, were outside this whole system, untutored in etiquette and illiterate in the languages of civilization. In 1868 the new Meiji government still felt it necessary to call for abandonment of "the ignorant opinion that foreigners are wild barbarians, dogs, and sheep. We must set up new procedures to show that they are to be considered on the same level as Chinese."[20] The greater the uncertainty the Japanese felt in their early negotiations with Perry and Harris, the more tenaciously they retained petty devices of address and ceremony to carry off minor ceremonial triumphs.[21] It was partly at the insistence of the American negotiators, and partly in consequence of the importance of the matters at issue, that the status and honor of the Japanese who dealt with them began to rise.

In 1858 the post of commissioner of foreign affairs (*gaikoku bugyō*, literally commissioner of foreign countries) was set up to deal with foreign envoys.[22] Five to ten men were to serve, as did other commissioners, on the system of monthly alternation. They were paid two thousand *koku* and an allow-

[19] Osatake, *Kokusai hō yori mitaru Bakumatsu gaikō monogatari* (Tokyo, 1926), p. 73.

[20] *Ibid.*

[21] *Ibid.* In discussions between Harry Parkes and the *gaikoku bugyō*, the British interpreter, Alexander Siebold, complained that the *bugyō*'s form of address to him, *omae*, was not sufficiently polite for the representative of the British crown. When the *bugyō* countered that it was the same as *gozen*, Siebold responded that in that case he would prefer *gozen*.

[22] Chronology in *Nihon rekishi daijiten* (Tokyo, 1956), IV; discussed also in Tokinoya Masaru, *op.cit.*, pp. 217 ff.

ance of 300 *ryō*, sat in the Lotus Chamber, and were given Shotaifu rank (which placed them on a par with *ōmetsuke, kamibangashira, jinjā-, kanjō-,* and *machi-bugyō*). Directly under the Council of Elders, they were also allowed a corps of assistants who included translators. In 1867, with the opening of Kobe, a chief commissioner (*gaikoku sōbugyō*) was established with the simulated rank of junior councillor (*wakadoshiyori-nami*); his underlings retained the rank of commissioner. The final Tokugawa administrative rationalization of 1867 found this changed to director of foreign affairs (*gaikoku jimmu sōsai*). The monthly rotation system was now abandoned (as it was also among the senior councillors). As functional specialization advanced, this became one of the highest Tokugawa offices; until the collapse of Tokugawa power it was filled by Ogasawara Nagamichi.[23]

The Meiji reforms were directed by men who realized that foreign affairs could not be conducted as part of the old administrative structure and that effective direction of foreign relations would ultimately require administrative specialization and centralization. Thus the Restoration programs of the Tosa leaders spoke in optimistic terms of an order in which "foreign affairs will be carried on according to appropriate regulations worked out on the basis of general opinion," and the last shogun resigned in response to a memorial from Yamauchi Yōdō proposing that "foreign relations should be carried out at Hyōgo. New treaties based on enlightened reason should be negotiated with the foreigners by imperial ministers after consultation with the *han*. Commercial transactions must

[23] Mikami Terumi, "Dajōkansei ka ni okeru kindai gaisei kikō no keisei," *Chūō Daigaku bungakubu kiyō* (shigakka, 10), Dec. 1964, provides careful coverage for the first years of Meiji rule, but for the late Tokugawa period W. G. Beasley's comment, *Select Documents on Japanese Foreign Policy, 1853–1868* (Oxford: Oxford Univ. Press, 1955), p. 20, still holds good: "The impact of Western trade and diplomacy on the administrative structure of a largely feudal society would make an interesting study, which seems hitherto to have been neglected."

be carried out in all sincerity lest the foreigners lose faith in us."[24]

The first Meiji governmental structure (announced February 25, 1868) established a *gaikoku kan*, or bureau, one of eight that were set up under the "Three Offices" (*san shoku*). Soon this was moved into the Administrative Bureau (*gyōsei kan*) and staffed by, successively, Date Munenari, Sawa Nobuyoshi, and under them by Ōkuma Shigenobu and Terajima Munenari. The following year this structure was retained within the newly established Council of State (*Dajōkan*).

During the first decade of the Meiji government a number of changes of nomenclature and administrative organization affected posts concerned with foreign affairs, but they remained consistently in the hands of members of the leadership group who had personal experience or knowledge of the outside world. More important, major decisions (and even minor decisions that affected foreigners became major as they affected the government's larger purposes) were invariably made by the leaders of the oligarchy of the court—Satsuma and Chōshū men. The Europeans encouraged this. Harry Parkes, for instance, tended to bypass the specialist functionaries and to deal directly with Iwakura Tomomi and Sanjō Sanetomi. During the long tenure of Inoue Kaoru's responsibility in foreign affairs (1879–1887) a major figure of the inner group was at the helm, and in times of crisis men like Ōkubo Toshimichi, Itō Hirobumi, and Inoue himself would travel to trouble spots like China and Korea.

The Meiji leaders' perception of their problem was thus one in which foreign policy considerations bulked very large. On the one hand it was essential that the Western powers should not be provoked into harsh measures or hostile attitudes; their views on even internal situations were of relevance in hopes for treaty revision. Certainly those powers required the attention of the top-level leadership. Major issues with Japan's East Asian

[24] Quoted in Jansen, *Sakamoto Ryōma*, pp. 296, 301.

neighbors also were carried out in part with thoughts of Western approbation or disapproval in mind, in part in the consciousness of the need to consider a growingly articulate Japanese public opinion. Both considerations worked to leave negotiations in the hands of the inner leadership group. There were also other factors. The first generation of leaders were generalists, more or less omnicompetent. Specialist bureaucracies were a phenomenon of special schools and training courses not yet in being in early Meiji Japan. Again, the stimulation and excitement of travel abroad were sufficient to make the Meiji oligarchs anxious to take turns in going. Until specialist careers were the path to eminence, recent and frequent foreign exposure was a help, and not a handicap, in any public career. To the degree that Japan's problems were "external," there could not be too many public servants personally acquainted with the external world. Meanwhile the specialist corps, itself clearly a part of modern international practice, was slowly taking form. It came into its own only toward the end of the Meiji period, gaining both success and confidence. Foreign Office official Hayashi proved more successful in London than did *genrō* Itō in St. Petersburg in 1902, and in 1915 Kato, as foreign minister, first succeeded in challenging the close supervision the *genrō* had always exercised over foreign affairs.[25]

Given the nature of the Western presence and problem, it is not surprising that there was a remarkable continuity in the perception and conduct of foreign policy from late Tokugawa to late nineteenth century Japan. Few problems could be designated as really "new," and this was of decided advantage for the oligarchs. So was the fact that Japanese diplomacy could largely restrict its attention to a few imperialist superpowers. The brief flurry of German interest in Pacific problems after 1895 complicated matters, as the Japanese saw to their regret, but for the most part it was perfectly possible for the leading

[25] Discussed in Oka Yoshitake, *Yamagata Aritomo* (Tokyo, 1958), p. 135.

163

oligarchs to read, follow, and direct the dispatches dealing with Britain and Russia. As a result, during a period when hardly any nation had a fully professional foreign service, Japan's stability and continuity in leadership made for unusually competent and calm direction of foreign policy. Japan's leaders were not under the limitations of terms in office or election deadlines. Until the Trans-Siberian Railroad seemed to be nearing completion, they could afford to bide their time. In the meantime they devoted their attention to what they saw as their most pressing problems.

The National Unit

In the modern world boundaries are clearly drawn. There is little tolerance for divided or partial allegiance. This is a recent development, the product of mass communication, education, and centralized administrative efforts. In Western Europe most borders became clear during the nineteenth century; in Eastern Europe the process began in the twentieth century and accelerated in the years after World War I. In Southeast Asia it is still in process. Since Japan was the first East Asian state to modernize, it was also the first to feel it necessary to make these distinctions. In the process of clearing up its own boundaries it came into contact with each of its neighbors and into conflict with the tributary order of imperial China, which had numerous degrees and varieties of subservience and dependence.

Early modern Japan had had to do the same thing in internal administration. Before the land surveys Hideyoshi set in motion, there were numerous areas of overlap and ambiguity in local administration, as the boundaries of realms and of villages were often unclear. Clarifying this, setting the record straight, often meant forceful assertion of authority and jurisdiction in areas that had previously escaped survey and exaction. A comparable process of rationalization now became inevitable in terms of larger units.

The first area in which this became necessary was the kingdom of the Ryūkyūs. Since 1609, when a military expedition from Satsuma had brought back the Okinawan king, Ryūkyū had been a tributary to Satsuma. Nominal military and political supervision had never been made obvious, so that the Okinawans might maintain their tribute position vis-à-vis China. As a result Ryūkyū became an avenue for foreign trade for a Tokugawa vassal. In the nineteenth century French, British, and American ships were permitted to negotiate trade agreements (with Tokugawa approval), thus maintaining the fiction of Okinawan independence. Yet since this trade, like the trade with China, was carried on with the knowledge and approval of the feudal government in Japan, it was certain that a more powerful and truly central government would bring the system to a close. Inoue Kiyoshi and other historians have found it important to stress the relative autonomy of Ryūkyūan culture and administration, but such considerations, while important, do nothing to clear up the lack of clear-cut distinctions in sovereignty.[26]

In 1872 the early Meiji government's decision to designate the Okinawan king as "king of the Ryūkyū *han*" (*Ryūkyū han Ō*), although it granted him a status higher than those of the feudal lords, also left little doubt that once the *han* were abolished integration into Japan was to be expected.[27] Alternatives were considered. Inoue Kaoru argued for full abandonment of "errors" of the past and formal assertion of sovereignty over Ryūkyū, and his view came to prevail over milder suggestions put forward by Soejima and the early diplomatic officials.[28] It is quite true, as Professor Inoue writes, that this was aggressive (it certainly seemed so to the reluctant Okinawans), and possible that it did not benefit Okinawans eco-

[26] Inoue, "Okinawa," in *Iwanami kōza Nihon rekishi*, XVI (*kindai* III, Tokyo, 1962), 325.

[27] Hyman Kublin, "The Attitude of China during the Liu-ch'iu Controversy, 1871-1881," *Pacific Historical Review*, XVIII, 213-31, remains the most convenient summary.

[28] Inoue Kiyoshi, p. 321; also *Segai Inoue Kō den*, I, 489-90, for text of Inoue Kaoru proposal.

nomically because of Japanese attempts to mollify the previous aristocracy; it is also true that the Japanese action was related to domestic political pressures relieved by the Formosan expedition, itself justified by the need to protect Okinawan mariners. But most of all the decision is to be understood as an aspect of the centralization of political authority that accompanied the abolition of feudalism. And as such it was inevitable. Ryūkyūan boundaries remained sufficiently obscure for the Japanese to propose a compromise settlement in 1880 involving division of the island chain so that China would retain the small islands nearest her in return for further Japanese privileges in China. This was approved by the Tsung-li Yamen, only to have Li Hung-chang persuade the court to veto the proposal. Japan's final show of force in Okinawa in 1879 required the services of only 160 soldiers. As this swept Ryūkyū into the main stream of Japanese political history, so it swept the Ryūkyūans into modern economic history. The survivals of an early land-division (*jiwari*) system were abandoned in the interest of individual responsibility and capitalist relationships when land measures were finally implemented between 1899 and 1903. With individual tax liability, mass education, prefectural government (1909), and elections (1912), further debate about Okinawa's independence became academic.[29]

Premodern boundaries were equally ambiguous to the north. Here the problem was not an antecedent or simultaneous relationship to the mainland, but competition with Russia, whose influence was extending southward. By late Tokugawa times there had been local disputes with Russia. The Shimoda treaty of 1855 provided for division of the Kuriles between Etoroppu (which, with islands south of it, went to Japan) and Uruppu. Of Sakhalin it said only that no boundary was to be established and that current practices should be continued. But when the Russians increased their activity after the Crimean War, and particularly after Russian acquisition of the

[29] Inoue Kiyoshi, *op.cit.*, pp. 330–35.

Maritime Provinces in 1860, the Tokugawa government and its
Meiji successor became alarmed and anxious to extend Japanese influence. Tokugawa efforts to work out a Sakhalin
boundary with Russia were unsuccessful.[30]

Tokugawa rule had made no attempt whatever to administer the Kuriles and Sakhalin. Hokkaido itself had been the
fief of Matsumae, who enjoyed virtual autonomy from Hideyoshi's time. He enfeoffed his principal retainers by giving
them monopoly rights over littoral territories whose marine
products were the chief source of income, and these retainers in
turn leased their rights to contractors from central Japan,
often Ōmi merchants.[31] In 1799 the *bakufu* took over the administration of Hokkaido, only to return it to Matsumae in
1821. With renewed foreign danger it took charge again in
1854, both to prepare for the Russian advance and to have
the profits of Hokkaido's raw materials for the new economic
program.[32]

Both economic and strategic interests were served by the
program that followed. The Meiji government began with ambitious plans for the development of Sakhalin as well as Hokkaido, and set up parallel development bureaus (*kaitakushi*) to
make this possible. But when it proved unable to support both
ventures, and after diplomats like Harry Parkes warned that
Japan could only lose in a confrontation with Russia, the
government removed its settlers from Sakhalin in 1874. Eno-
moto, sent to St. Petersburg to negotiate a border division in
1875, managed to gain the rest of the Kuriles in return for
abandoning Japanese claims to Sakhalin. Japanese noted
with satisfaction that this was the first compromise treaty Japan had made with a Western power.[33]

[30] Tokinoya Masaru, *op.cit.*, p. 237.

[31] For thumbnail sketch of contract system (*basho ukeoinin*), see
Otsuka shigakkai, comp., *Kyōdoshi jiten* (Tokyo, 1955), pp. 586–87.

[32] Below I follow Tokinoya, *op.cit.*, p. 237, and Hatate Isao, "Nihon
shihon shugi to Hokkaidō kaitaku," Iwanami kōza Nihon rekishi, XVI
(*kindai* III), 337ff.

[33] Hatate, *op.cit.*, pp. 338-39.

Hokkaido remained as focus of all the development enthusiasm of the Meiji government. The *kaitakushi* grew in scope and privileges until it was described as a Japanese East India Company. Samurai resettlement (Saigō was among those who advocated a land-division system for samurai), export of capital, and development of extractive raw materials and marine products for fertilizer made the island central to Meiji hopes and deficits.[34] Even after the sale of the industries, the government cooperated by making available convict labor as well as special subsidies and guarantees. Until the victory over Russia in 1905 and the consequent move of the border into Sakhalin, Hokkaido was a main strategic concern. Modernization, with its fixed boundaries, had thus changed the late Tokugawa world in which Hayashi Shihei, in his *Sankoku tsūran*, had written of Hokkaido and Ryūkyū with Korea as three "foreign" countries.

No part of Meiji foreign policy has received more attention than the debate over Korea. It was the first major turning point in national policy after the Restoration, and its resolution was achieved at the cost of a drastic narrowing of the base of political leadership. Without recounting the details of that struggle once more, I would suggest two considerations that have received little attention. The first is that stability of leadership and purpose was well served by the narrowed base. After the oligarchic leadership was reduced in numbers, it became far more united and effective.

Second, and more to the point, is the fact that the Korean issue derived in good measure from the forms and nature of "modern" national, as opposed to traditional and local, address between countries. Traditional courtesies and status relationships, acceptable to semiautonomous or "private" agen-

[34] Hatate, *ibid.*, in charts on pp. 342-43, gives investment in Hokkaido as 7.2% of the national budget at their peak (1880), and shows exports from Honshu to Hokkaido as 40% of total in the 1770's, double those to the U.S. and China and triple those to Great Britain. Imports from Hokkaido were 23% of total.

cies, could not be countenanced by representatives of an imperial Japanese government whose borders were becoming consolidated. In this sense it was the change from East India Company to British crown representation at Canton all over again.

During Tokugawa times the Korean government sent official embassies which numbered (including guards) from three hundred to five hundred men on twelve occasions. These were received with honor by the *bakufu*, and entertained during several months of ceremonial which included a visit to Nikko, where they visited Ieyasu's shrine, before returning to Seoul. The visits involved numerous problems of status in forms of address (as when Arai Hakuseki changed references to the shogun from great minister [*taikun*] to king [*kokuō*]), calendar (ultimately solved by the use of zodiacal terms instead of year periods [*nengō*]), and ceremonial. They were also expensive for *bakufu* and daimyo along the route, and were discontinued after 1811.[35]

Commercial relations were a different matter entirely. These were allocated by the shogun to the daimyo of Tsushima, Sō, who maintained stations at Pusan and also at Nagasaki, Osaka, and Kyoto. This trade was the lifeline of the Tsushima economy. Although it gradually diminished throughout the course of Tokugawa rule as restrictions on export of copper became applicable to Korea (as well as to Deshima, a process better chronicled), it continued into the middle of the nineteenth century. The daimyo found it well worth his while, and not beneath his dignity, to treat Korean officials with terminological deference. The Meiji government, indeed, concluded that Sō had accepted a tributary relationship with Korea in addition to his vassalage in the Tokugawa system.[36]

National unification and central direction of all foreign re-

[35] Numata Jirō, "Edo jidai no bōeki to taigai kankei," *Iwanami kōza Nihon rekishi*, XIII (*kinsei* v, Tokyo, 1962), 69–70.

[36] Hilary Conroy, *The Japanese Seizure of Korea: 1868–1910* (Philadelphia: Univ. of Pennsylvania Press, 1961), p. 25.

lations now meant the incorporation of Tsushima into a "Japan" and transfer of all foreign correspondence into hands of representatives of a sovereign imperial power which would not brook even the *bakufu* compromises in terminology, much less the Tsushima subservience. Since the Koreans, on the other hand, continued to inhabit a world order in which accedence to the Japanese desires constituted rejection of the preeminence of Peking, their recalcitrance was certain.[37] Ritual insult inexorably led to the precipice of war with Korea. Significantly, the decisive turn came with the abolition of the *han* and Hanabusa's effort to convert the Pusan trading station into a modern consulate.[38]

In the debate which followed, victory went to Iwakura and the leaders who opposed war. They derived their arguments from their knowledge of the West, and their authority from their recent experience. Western exposure converted some, like Kido, from bellicosity to moderation,[39] and no leaders with first-hand knowledge of the West favored foreign adventure in Japan's state of unpreparedness. When an expedition to Taiwan was mounted in 1874 as palliative for the dissatisfaction the earlier moderation had aroused (and also to strengthen the claim to the Ryūkyūs), the advice of foreign counsellors was a significant element in the decision to undertake the venture.[40] No better evidence is needed of the

[37] See Mary C. Wright, "The Adaptability of Ch'ing Diplomacy: The Case of Korea," *JAS*, xvii (May 1958), 368 and *passim*.

[38] Tokinoya, *op.cit.*, p. 229.

[39] Kobayashi Katsumi, "Meiji shoki ni okeru tairiku gaikō," *Rekishi hyōron* No. 107 (1959), pp. 68–78, for details of Iwakura and Kido positions.

[40] In addition to LeGendre (documentation and details in Conroy, *op.cit.*, pp. 37 ff.) and the American Minister deLong, mention may be made of E. P. Smith, who affected two swords and *hakama* (Tokinoya, *op.cit.*, p. 228), and who "declared in public" to the shock of his auditors that "not one foreigner in ten in Japan was murdered who ought to have been murdered." F. V. Dickins, *The Life of Sir Harry Parkes* (London, 1894), ii, p. 183, who goes on to say, "To deal with

importance of "Western" power to deter or to incite. At the same time, as recent studies show, there was some hope of finding in aboriginal areas of Taiwan itself a sphere for Japanese colonization, control, and suzerainty.[41]

By 1875 the boundaries had been made clear. Ryūkyū, Hokkaido, the Kuriles, and Tsushima were directly controlled. Modern machinery of foreign intercourse was beginning to take form. Japanese, even commoners, were beginning to feel themselves well ahead of their neighbors. J. R. Black's account of a Korean mission to Tokyo in 1876 describes the spectators' response to the costumes and music of the procession; "Their strains were most distressing, but utterly indescribable. The Japanese crowd were tickled immensely with the music, and laughed immoderately. . . . The whole affair had a very bombastic, farce-like appearance; and the very adjuncts which were probably designed to be the most impressive only provoked the laughter and jeers of the spectators."[42] And Mori Arinori, when asked by Li Hung-chang whether Japan did not find it shameful to abandon so precipitously the customs and values of the past, replied that on the contrary they were laying thereby a basis for the boasts of the future.[43]

Recovery of Sovereignty

Once the borders were defined, the problem was to become master within them. The Meiji leaders saw the restrictions on their freedom to set tariffs as a major barrier to their schemes for modernization. Industrialization could be accelerated if tariff autonomy could be achieved, and this goal, the true basis of national power, was given priority over all others. A succession of foreign ministers—Terajima, Inoue, and Ōkuma

---

a Foreign Office depending on advisers of this kidney was no easy or pleasant task."

[41] Leonard Gordon, "Japan's Abortive Colonial Venture in Taiwan, 1874," *Journal of Modern History*, xxxvii (June 1965), 171–85.

[42] J. R. Black, *Young Japan* (London, 1881), ii, 467.

[43] Kimura Kyō, *Mori sensei den* (Tokyo 1899), p. 101.

—experimented with ways of compromising, by trading prestige and dignity—extraterritoriality of various degrees, unrestricted residence for foreigners—in return for relief from the less visible but more basic inequality of fixed tariffs.[44] Without exception these proposals, however carefully worked out and unpopular in Japan, failed to satisfy the treaty powers and especially Great Britain.

In a setting so affected by problems of equality with the West, the rosy hopes of the 1870's for leadership in a resurgent East Asia had to take a back seat. Except, in fact, for the fringe activists of the political party movement like Ōi Kentarō and the patriotic societies, they seemed virtually forgotten. Europe was too big a problem, and Asia could be too little help. The need was to satisfy Europe, and this was best done by emphasizing the differences between Japan and "Asia." Asia was weak. In 1882 Yamagata could still warn of China's growing strength, but the Franco-Chinese war of 1884 saw this concern diminish, although the Chinese fleet remained a problem until 1894.[45] During the 1880's Japan's Korean policy was also on the whole moderate, even weak. Inoue urged China to accept and implement the authority and power it claimed in Korea. The government was scrupulously correct in its relations with the fugitive Kim Ok-kiun, and it turned a deaf ear to complaints that it was neglecting great opportunities on the continent. The West was the main problem. Familiar problems like Korea would look different only after it could be shown that they were being threatened or affected by a hostile Western power.

In the 1880's there was little doubt among the Meiji leaders that Japan's economy was in for a long period of handicap because of the unequal treaties. It was against this back-

[44] Usui Katsumi, "Jōyaku kaisei to Chōsen mondai," in *Iwanami kōza Nihon rekishi*, XVII (*kindai* IV, Tokyo, 1962), 104.

[45] Oka, *Yamagata*, pp. 25-26. Tanaka Masatoshi, in "Shin-Futsu sensō to Nihonjin no Chūgokukan," *Shisō* (Feb. 1967), pp. 14-34, shows the conflicting emotions the French successes stirred in Japan.

ground that the institutional, social, and cultural modernization of the 1880's was carried out. Inoue's concern for greeting foreign guests properly, which led to the *Rokumeikan* and its elaborate social functions (including a dancing master imported to school the leaders and their wives in social graces), his efforts on behalf of romanization, of modern drama, and of extensive agriculture, were all part of a genuine conviction of need to make Japan over along Western lines. Yamagata's persuasion (by Katsura) of the advantages of remodeling the army administration along German lines with an autonomous general staff, his interest in improved centralization of local administration, and Itō's search of European constitutional history for useful precedents and examples all reflected the same setting and need.

The course, and often the superficiality, of the Westernization programs provoked countercurrents that make the years immediately preceding the implementation of constitutional government one of the most interesting periods in modern Japanese history. A new sense of national consciousness inspired the pages of a periodical like *Nihon*, prompted a greater amount of nationalist teaching in the new school system, encouraged conservatives and reactionaries to break their silence, and resulted in the first large-scale expression of popular dissatisfaction when the details of Inoue's treaty reform proposals became known. We are therefore fortunate in having for these years three views of foreign policy that outline the parameters of thinking in the highest circles of Japan's leadership.

The first of these is a document submitted to his colleagues by Foreign Minister Inoue Kaoru just before his resignation in 1887. Inoue had been harshly criticized for his willingness to retain the services of foreign judges in the more serious categories of mixed-nationality suits and for granting foreigners rights of unrestricted travel and residence within Japan in return for tariff concessions. Conservatives had denounced his diplomatic moves as appeasement and his cultural and social policies as shameful, and he therefore set out at considerable length the rationale behind his policies. Earlier he had summed up his goals in two phrases: popular commitment to patriotism, and achievement of European and American development.[46] This time he structured these conclusions against the background of the world situation; "What kind of position can be established for our country in view of the present state and future course of world trends?"[47]

Inoue began by noting the expansive tendency of Western imperialism. Although this had begun in earnest a century earlier, in the last three or four years a new round of land grabs had begun. European powers were competing ruthlessly for the areas of Asia and Africa still unclaimed. In Asia only China and Japan could be said to retain their independence. Central Asia, the Pacific islands, even Siam and Korea, could scarcely be said to have the capacity of preserving their autonomy. Japan's neighbors, with the exception of China, were to a greater or lesser degree colonies of the Western countries.

European countries were devoting enormous sums to the strengthening of their armed forces and the development of their colonies. Recent returnees spoke with astonishment of the strides the colonial areas were making toward modernization. They were being tied together by communications and administration, their populations were growing rapidly, and they were becoming an ever larger element in the mother countries' power. No one could doubt that this restless expansive force would continue, and that at the proper moment it would threaten the remaining areas of Asia. Even if it was temporarily stilled, the reasons for this were to be sought in timing and convenience, and not in a change of heart in the West. Nor would Japan be able to seek shelter in neutrality when the powers came to blows in Asia. Expansion could be checked only with countermoves, and strength with strength.

[46] *Inoue den*, III, 350.   [47] Document in *Inoue den*, III, 907–37.

The Ryūkyū claim had succeeded only because China had not been disposed to press the issue; for the disputes that lay ahead, preparations had to be made now.

"It is my opinion," Inoue told his colleagues, "that what we must do is to transform our empire and our people, make the empire like the countries of Europe and our people like the peoples of Europe. To put it differently, we have to establish a new, European-style empire on the edge of Asia." Every means at hand should be used to stimulate and speed these changes. Mixed residence and unrestricted travel for foreigners would help serve this purpose by awakening and stimulating Japanese in all parts of the country for the struggle ahead. Communications and techniques of mechanization had already had this effect for some; further extension of the contact that was now restricted to the few would involve all sectors in the competitive struggle that lay ahead. The result could only be activation, alarm, and progress. Foreign capital and foreign industry would come in and help get the job of modernization done. Only the timid and faint-hearted could have so little confidence in Japan as to think the country would end up in foreign hands. To achieve the things that counted, it would be necessary to compromise on others. Extrality would have to go by degrees, as Japan's codes became modern in language and implementation. It was unrealistic to expect to get the job done all at once.

Inoue's goals were still those of the Restoration, still premised upon the backward state of Japan's statutes and institutions. ("After all," he put it in a different context earlier, "would we expect Japanese subjects to subject themselves to Korean law and courts?")[48] His world was still dominated by a West at once attractive and demonic, one which Japan could not expect to equal, much less repulse, for many years to come.

A year or so later, probably on his return from a trip to

[48] Usui, *op.cit.*, p. 108.

Europe, Yamagata Aritomo summed up in a memorandum the problems as he saw them.[49] His paper was understandably concerned more with strategic than with diplomatic problems, but the two intersect at numerous points. As with Inoue, the world Yamagata saw was an unfriendly one dominated by the European powers. But only two really counted. The English were moving much closer to East Asia by the completion of the Canadian Pacific Railroad, the Russians by their work on the Trans-Siberian. Conflict between these giants would come first in Afghanistan, where the Russians would have the advantage, and then in Korea, where the Russians would have to seek a warm-water port as a railroad terminus. Japan could not hope to remain neutral in this struggle. If it sided with Russia, it would alienate England and China; if with England, it would have to face a Russian threat to Korea. In any event, military and naval strength was essential. All the European powers were pouring their resources into arms, and Japan would have to do the same. Even the Belgians, professedly neutral and pacific, were fortifying their frontiers. But Japan was all frontier! "In short," he concluded, "no matter how you look at the present situation in East Asia from the point of our diplomatic strategy, the most critical need we have is to build up our military strength."

A third view, also put on paper in 1887 after a trip to Europe, is often cited as a classic summation of the conservative, "Japanist" position. It is by Tani Kanjō, minister of agriculture in the Cabinet that included Inoue as foreign minister and Yamagata as home minister. His complaint was a fascinating one. On the one hand he criticized the Cabinet from a "modern" perspective, describing it as vacillating, not sufficiently responsible, populated by self-indulgent powerholders who paid themselves enormous salaries ("salaries in Japan are even

[49] Yamagata's state paper was published only recently. Text in Nihon kokusai seiji gakkai, *Nihon gaikōshi kenkyū: Meiji jidai* (Tokyo, 1957), pp. 186–92.

higher than in Europe and America"), required extensive personal protection ("History shows clearly that if there are those who are really bent on assassination, even though there are one or two guards they will be unable to prevent it."), and were unable to agree upon enduring policies or to rationalize the administrative structure. Tani's "Japanism" found expression in his scorn for cultural Westernization ("Ministers encourage the holding of dancing parties, and women are imitating the West completely in their clothing.") and the succession of foreign models finally capped by the preference for imperial Germany.

There was little need of such emulation and anxiety, Tani went on, for "our country . . . stands far off in the Eastern ocean with rocky coasts on all sides. We cannot see anywhere else such a natural fortress. . . . We have not had to worry about conspiracies for the independence of fiefs and colonies. Since there are no enemy countries contiguous to us, there is no danger of alarms and violations of our borders by enemy troops."

One should not exaggerate the divergence between Tani and Yamagata, for Tani too was in favor of "deepening the moats and heightening our fortifications." But in his view the coming war in Europe represented opportunity and safety for Japan rather than danger. "Sooner or later Europe will inevitably fight and break up, and horses will trample the fields. . . . The disturbance will spread to East Asia also. . . . We will not take part, but we will then be able to strike a balance in the East. . . . Therefore our country while doing nothing will achieve power in the Orient and the other countries will respect us."[50] It is clearly wrong to suggest, as some have done, that these words of Tani's should be taken as evidence of long-range artifice and cunning which had as its aim the domination of Asia.

[50] Tr. by Barbara Joan Teters, "The Conservative Opposition in Japanese Politics, 1877–1894," unpublished doctoral dissertation, Univ. of Washington (1955), pp. 208–40.

Actually Tani favored a milder peace with China in 1894, and he was unenthusiastic about the war with Russia.[51] However confident Tani's words, his Japan was still too weak and too discouraged by repeated failure of treaty reform attempts to have more than the fuzziest ideas about future equality and rivalry with the West. All that could have been suggested is that the European rivalries would probably cancel each other out, and that it was not necessary to be obsequious or defiant. Time would take care of it.

As it worked out, each of these men proved partly right. The Western-style institutions and modern military machine developed by civilian and army leaders undoubtedly played their part in persuading the powers, and especially Great Britain, that Japan deserved to be treated as an equal. But Tani was probably closest to the mark, for it was really the competition and rivalries of Europe that presented Japan with the equality it had sought. The Trans-Siberian Railroad Yamagata feared so much made the English ready to talk with Japan, just as England's exclusion from the network of alliances made Japan a desirable partner in 1902. When Salisbury accepted Aoki's proposals for treaty reform in 1894, the Japanese were astonished. They had seen no end to it. "With this treaty," Aoki said, "Japan has entered the ranks of civilized countries."[52]

War and Empire

Wars to achieve and expand continental importance punctuated the stages of Japan's rise and fall, and the historian is forced to consider the relation between Japan's military achievements and its political modernization. Most writers have seen the wars as central to Japan's development. It is striking to see how substantial the areas of agreement can be between "old" and "new" styles of analysis in Japan, however different the moral judgments drawn from them. Thus Watanabe Ikujirō, writing in 1937, explained the Sino-Japa-

[51] See Oka, "Kokuminteki dokuritsu to kokka risei," pp. 39–40.
[52] Usui, *op.cit.*, p. 118.

nese and Russo-Japanese wars as a logical consequence of the
spirit and ideology with which the Japanese race had undertaken the Meiji Restoration. "These wars did not by any means
break out accidentally," he wrote, "but they took place because
they had to. They came in the inevitable process of Japan's historical development and rise to status as a modern nation with
spirit and purpose."[53] Watanabe's postwar successors agree that
the violence was an inevitable consequence of Japan's type of
modernization, but they are less gratified by it. Emperor-
centered ideology and a social order based upon the autocratic
family system, Fujiwara Jun holds, could only be maintained
through the values of militarism. Inoue Kiyoshi's work is an
extended essay, rich in prophetic denunciation, of the evils of
emperor-centered imperialism.[54] Even Watanabe was not un-
aware of "the so-called materialistic view of history" that interpreted Japan's expansion as the consequence of its capitalist
course, but said that he preferred "to see this as result, rather
than the cause," of the modern wars.

On the whole, Fujiwara, Inoue, and the economic determinists state their case in very general terms. When it comes to
the decision process at specific turning points, they are very
vague about identifying the inevitable forces that were at work.
And Japan's is indeed a special case. If, for example, one approaches Japan's imperialist course with Leninist assumptions
of surplus capital in search of foreign outlets, it immediately
becomes apparent that Japan's leaders were mindful chiefly of
their inadequate resources for open competition with the giants
of Western industry, worried about their inability to compete
on equal terms, fearful that "open doors" would mean doors
closed to Japanese entrepreneurs, and intent upon special po-

---

[53] *Ni-Shin, Nichi-Ro sensō shiwa* (Tokyo, 1937), pp. 1–2.

[54] For Fujiwara, *Shisō*, No. 399 (Sept. 1957), pp. 1–2. For this reference and a thoughtful discussion of related problems I am indebted
to an unpublished manuscript of James B. Crowley, "Japanese Military
Foreign Policy, 1868–1941." For Inoue, see particularly *Nihon no
gunkokushugi* (Tokyo, 1954), 2 vols.

litical advantages that would make it possible for them to compensate for their economic inequality.[55]

Attempts to trace war decisions more generally to business influence find historians hard put to isolate and identify those elements. Nakatsuka's recent summary of scholarship on the Sino-Japanese War shows that the claim that textile manufacturers pushed the government into war cannot be supported. It was not, as some had called it, a "textile war." The Korean market did not agitate the Japanese bourgeoisie; the China market was much bigger, and exports to Korea were mostly reexports. Despite the importance of foodstuffs imported from Korea, the Japan-Korea trade balance was favorable, and there were few reasons to call for war.[56] Hilary Conroy's study of the economic aspects of Japan's Korea policy bears out these conclusions.[57] And when it comes to the Russo-Japanese War, when capitalist interests were stronger, Professor Shimomura finds it equally necessary to qualify and deprecate the simple, teleological denunciations of the economic determinists. He tracks down and disproves many references to business pressure, and his most effective refutations show members of the leadership group working hard to get merchant support for their policies. "You men can make or break the war," General Kodama said to Shibusawa Eiichi. This is a different thing from saying that they wanted to.[58] And indeed, one risks distortion by treating figures like Shibusawa and Inoue Kaoru as representative of business interest, for they were neither bourgeoise nor nonbourgeoise, but full members of the power elite on the basis of their goals and experience, men more con-

[55] See, in this connection, M. B. Jansen, "Yawata, Hanyehping and the Twenty-One Demands," *Pacific Historical Review*, XXIII (Feb. 1954).

[56] Nakatsuka Akira, "*Ni-Shin sensō*," *Iwanami kōza Nihon rekishi*, XVII (*kindai* IV, Tokyo 1962), 133.

[57] Conroy, *The Japanese Seizure of Korea*, pp. 442ff.

[58] Shimomura Fujio, "Nicho-Ro sensō no seikaku," *Nihon gaikōshi kenkyū: Meiji jidai*, p. 145.

cerned with bringing interest groups into being than they were with representing groups already formed.

Historians have had better results in their investigation of the military power and decision structure. Matsushita Yoshio's studies show how the principles of independent command, the separation of administrative from command functions, and the separation of the military from political pressures (so that they could return to engage in politics from a secure base) affected the course of national politics.[59] Success naturally reinforced such trends and strengthened the prestige and position of the military. Of the peerage awards handed out after the victory over China, five went to civilians and thirty-three to army and navy men. Even so, institutional advantage would be determinant only when, in the future, functional bureaucracies with special interests came into conflict as autonomous entities. It would not be very helpful, in discussing the first stages of the story, to credit Yamagata's victory over Itō to the fact that he had an army interest "behind" him. It is true that some historians credit the army, and especially Kawakami Soroku, with deceit of Itō in 1894 by sending a "mixed brigade" to Korea considerably more heterogeneous in makeup than the term implied, but logic favors Nakatsuka's rejoinder that Itō was not so easily fooled and that the claim is in all probability the work of vainglorious army men happy to take full credit for things after they had gone well.[60]

In a measure these problems of interpretation derive from attempts to measure Japan's course against a normative pattern of modernization and sequence. But Japan's drive to modernize had a particular quality because it was undertaken out of fear, in reaction to a dangerous and hostile international

[59] *Meiji gunsei shiron* (Tokyo, 1956), 2 vols.

[60] For discussion of the mixed brigade, Ernest P. Young, "A Study of Groups and Personalities in Japan Influencing the Events Leading to the Sino-Japanese War (1894–1895)," *Papers on Japan* (Harvard University, East Asian Research Center), II (1963), 255–56; and Nakatsuka, *op.cit.*, p. 143.

setting. National and cultural survival were interpreted in terms of resistance and strength, and these categories continued to dominate discussions of foreign policy long after the terms of reference could have changed. Instead, definitions of security against the West were revised upward in line with Japan's capacities.

Thus in a document of 1890 Yamagata Aritomo set out his views on national policy by distinguishing between Japan's line of sovereignty (*shukensen*) and line of interest or advantage (*riekisen*). The latter, he argued, was essential to the former if Japan was to become truly independent of reliance on outside help. And Korea was Japan's line of advantage. Its independence was essential to Japan, and that independence was being endangered by the eastward progress of the Trans-Siberian Railroad. It followed that Korea could be entrusted neither to hostile Western hands nor to a power unable, as was China, to preserve it as Japan's sphere of interest.[61] "Independence" for Korea gradually became altered to "dependence" as the Meiji leaders became convinced that Korea's backwardness and weakness made it too inviting a prey for other powers. Similar considerations, as Oka Yoshitake shows, came into play to transform hopes for cooperation with China to hopes for leadership of reform in China, and finally to "protection" and coercion of a China apparently incapable of playing its true role in international politics.[62]

In the case of Korea the beginnings of this shift came in early reports of misgovernment which, the Meiji leaders felt, would require Japanese assistance in charting reforms.[63] For some the turn came slowly. For others it came with dramatic suddenness, as when Yamagata, stirred to exultation by the only real field command of his career (and it a very short

---

[61] Document printed in *Nihon gaikōshi kenkyū: Meiji jidai*, pp. 192–95. See also a similar statement of Yamagata's views quoted by Matsushita Yoshio, *Ni-Shin sensō zengo* (Tokyo, 1939), pp. 8–10.

[62] Oka, "Kokuminteki dokuritsu to kokka risei," pp. 23ff.

[63] Usui, *op.cit.*, p. 89, for Hanabusa report of 1880.

one),[64] wrote his emperor that Korea's weakness stemmed from deficiencies in its national character. A want of will, ambition, and drive lay at the root of the failure to modernize. Consequently, Japan's line of interest could be held only by getting Japanese to move in to modernize the country, and by the construction of a Pusan–Seoul railway, one which could serve as the first link of that "great Asian railroad that can one day lead through China to India."[65]

If Japan's situation was special, its response to the international setting in which the Meiji leaders matured was one that might have been predicted from samurai who had come to manhood in a structured, hierarchic society. The international society they came to know was a world in which rights were defined by guns and in which nationalism had to be encouraged by every aspect of political and cultural policy if a nation was to maintain its independence. There is no need to dismiss the optimistic statements about independence for Korea and respect for China that were standard until the last decade of the nineteenth century in Japan. Those words changed meaning only after international pressures had made it unlikely, in the view of the Meiji Japanese, that Korea or China could maintain its territorial integrity. The successive weakness of Korea, and then of China, next of Russia, and ultimately of the Western powers provided an uncertain setting in which an ever more illusive security was sought through ever greater strength and power. Every element of observation and experience served to underscore the desirability and strategic importance of continental buffer zones for insular security.

Equality and membership in the circle of great powers were not easily gained, and when Meiji Japan thought itself ready to enter international politics, it proved to have more to learn. The diplomacy of the Sino-Japanese War was based upon the

[64] See Matsushita Yoshio, *Meiji gunsei shiron* (Tokyo, 1956), II, 225, for discussion of Yamagata as a "political soldier."

[65] Oka, *Yamagata Aritomo*, p. 61, for sections of letter.

misapprehension that Japan and China would be left alone to settle their differences. The unpleasant consequence, the Triple Intervention, was handled awkwardly and constituted, as Watanabe entitled his chapter, a failure in diplomacy.[66] After assurances that Japan had no territorial aims, Japan demanded Liaotung; although intervention was a possibility, little effort was made to avert it or to enlist support against it; and after retrocession of Liaotung was necessary no effort was made to get Russia, Germany, France, or China to agree not to request or grant the same or similar territorial rights. "It is no exaggeration to say that the retrocession of Liaotung dominated the rest of my life," the journalist Tokutomi later wrote. "After hearing about it I became almost a different man psychologically. Say what you will, it had happened because we weren't strong enough. What it came down to was that sincerity or justice didn't amount to a thing if you weren't strong enough."[67]

The next few years saw these lessons put to good use. During the Boxer Rebellion the Tokyo government never doubted that European assistance was the only thing that could remove the Russians from Manchuria, and it passed up several possibilities for private gain to maintain a correctly cooperative posture.[68] The negotiations leading to the Anglo-Japanese Alliance and to the Russo-Japanese War were handled far more skillfully than those that followed the Sino-Japanese War. Every care was taken to avoid international support for Russia, and Japan made no attempt to align China with the Japanese cause lest it seem, to Europe, to become a war of East against West. Instead it skillfully portrayed itself as defender

---

[66] Watanabe, *op.cit.*, pp. 225ff.

[67] Quoted in Oka, "Kokuminteki dokuritsu to kokka risei," p. 34.

[68] Kawamura Kazuo, "Hokushin jihen to Nihon," *Nihon gaikōshi kenkyū: Meiji jidai*, pp. 93–118; M. B. Jansen, *The Japanese and Sun Yat-sen*, pp. 99ff., the last modified by means of Foreign Office documentation published in 1956–1957 by I. H. Nish, "Japan's Indecision During the Boxer Disturbances," *JAS*, xx (Aug. 1961), 449–61.

of Western interests on the East Asian continent.[69] The Meiji leaders learned these lessons sooner and better than the commoners, as can be seen by the popular fury that followed the release of the terms of the Portsmouth Treaty. If the 1887 movement against treaty revision was the first large-scale expression of participation in foreign policy, the Portsmouth riots brought the first mass participation, a fact of significance for what lay ahead.

In 1890 Yamagata still considered it necessary to emphasize the importance of education in patriotism. In other countries, he wrote, education was the chief vehicle for inculcating love of country and transforming the character of the people. Thanks to education, Europeans were nation-minded. As soldiers they became brave, as officials pure, as sons filial, as neighbors friendly; parties and factions submerged their differences for the good of the country and sought its independence. It was now up to Japan to consolidate its line of sovereignty and to see to its line of interest, and thus assure its independence. It would probably, he thought, take twenty years to accomplish this. But if the plans were well laid and the determination deep, the generation that followed, schooled in love of country, would inherit the sense of purpose his generation had known.[70]

But Yamagata's concern was not, in retrospect, warranted. Meiji Japan was much more than a setting in which impersonal factors of economic and international considerations worked themselves out among an indifferent populace. The cautious apprehension of the leaders was magnified in the fears of those they led, and their gratification was lost in the exuberance with which the masses greeted attainment of Japan's national goals. All this became important precisely to the degree that Japanese society became modernized, multicentered, articulate, and involved. For the first decade participation was limited to a small proportion of the samurai,

---

[69] White, *Diplomacy of the Russo-Japanese War*, p. 120.

[70] Document in *Nihon gaikōshi kenkyū: Meiji jidai*, p. 195.

mostly from the southwestern regions that had sparked the Restoration, whose heroic expectations had not found fulfillment in the new order. Japan's moderation in the 1880's was not very popular, but relatively few concerned themselves with it. (Yet in retrospect it seems successful, peaceful, and "progressive.") By the time the convocation of the Diet approached in 1890, however, waves of antiforeignism were becoming such a problem that government leaders wondered about the desirability of an imperial rescript to discourage the new *jōi* enthusiasm.[71] One reason Itō dissolved the Diet in 1894 was to give Foreign Minister Mutsu freedom from harassment while he carried on the negotiation of treaty reform. The Sino-Japanese War solemnized and focused this enthusiasm, but even then it nearly got out of bounds. So many old samurai dusted off their fathers' swords and asked to be sent to the front that an imperial rescript was issued telling them to get back to work at their jobs.[72] With a popular press, an elective process, and an open forum for debate, superpatriots became an accepted part of the national scene. In a world that seemed to deny Japan its prize through intervention, preventive land grabs on the continent, talk of a yellow peril, and racial discrimination, there were few to call them off. The patriots became useful when national effort was called for and bothersome when the goal had been reached. Reasonable peace treaties became difficult and unpopular. The Progressive Party organ could call for conquest of all China in 1894, and the periodical *Nihon* could denounce Russia as an uncivilized enemy still sunk in barbarism in 1904.[73]

The consequences of this for political modernization were a willingness to forego domestic for external goals and to endure both economic and political setbacks so long as foreign goals received full and vigorous prosecution. "We have no political problems except foreign policy problems," Fukuzawa

[71] Usui, *op.cit.*, pp. 116, 117.   [72] Watanabe, *op.cit.*, p. 197.

[73] Quotes in Oka, "Kokuminteki dokuritsu to kokka risei," pp. 34, 44.

could exclaim in 1897.[74] A generation later Japan had no foreign policy problems that were not political problems. The consciousness of riches waiting only to be claimed, of sacrifices never adequately made good, and of insult that could be wiped out by injury operated as a constant irritant in Japanese politics and society. Foreign policies tended to be discussed in a setting of charge and countercharge, with terms like "positive" and "fundamental" held up in opposition to "weak," "imitative," and "irresolute."

But although the psychological and institutional setting proved congenial to the military primary in twentieth century Japan, it does not follow that modern Japanese diplomacy moved inexorably toward the final holocaust of World War II. Any modern state, whatever its leadership and ideology, would have had to try its hand at the purposes of the Meiji leaders. There had to be a consciousness of national life in a world of competing nation-states. There had to be special machinery developed for the conduct of foreign relations. Japan's borders had to be delineated. Sovereignty within them had to be achieved. And if Japanese tradition and determination guaranteed an effort to join the winners in international society, the leaders of that society set up rules and sanctions that lengthened the process and heightened Japanese determination. Setbacks and checks intensified the sense of competition and disadvantage long after it might have been expected to lose its force and consequently affected the perfection of the Japanese institutional structure within which the future discourse of future politics and diplomacy would be carried on.

In 1941 Admiral Tōgō's pennant once again fluttered from the flagship of a Japanese fleet as it sailed to war. Since both supporters and assailants of that stroke strained to establish continuities in Japan's modern policies, it is necessary to emphasize that there were as many factors external to Japan as there were factors intrinsically Japanese, and as many contingencies as there were inevitabilities in what had come between.

[74] Quoted in Oka, *op.cit.*, p. 35.

Twenty years after Yamagata had set his timetable in 1890, his goals had seemingly been accomplished. Korea, his line of advantage, was Japanese. Japan was a full member of the international and imperialist league, conqueror of and allied with Russia, allied with England, signatory with France. But the kind of absolute security Yamagata had thought possible was no longer tenable. The Japanese themselves had moved beyond national to personal interest. Specialized bureaucracies were doing the jobs they had been trained to do, and a new generation that lacked the broadening experience of weakness the Meiji leaders had known was coming into prominence. Theirs was no longer the only nationalism in East Asia, and the rules they had mastered were no longer acceptable. Yamagata's "independence" had become too static a goal for a world order in rapid change. Perhaps, in fact, it had had meaning only in the agrarian utopia of Tokugawa isolation from which he and his fellows had roused their countrymen.

CHAPTER VI

War and Modernization

NOBUTAKA IKE

JAPAN's surrender in 1945 brought to a close a period of history which had begun with the Meiji Restoration in 1868. It would appear in retrospect that a recurring theme of the epoch was war, either its actual prosecution or preparation for it. In a span of some fifty years the Japanese fought four major wars—the Sino-Japanese War of 1894–1895, the Russo-Japanese War of 1904–1905, the Sino-Japanese War beginning in 1937, and the Pacific war, 1941–1945. Interspersed were other instances of military action, for example the Siberian intervention after the end of World War I. The evidence leads one to the conjecture that war represented an integral part of Japan's modernization process.

The Problem of Military Preparedness

The problem of military preparedness worried the Meiji leadership from the very beginning. There were two reasons for this early concern with military matters: one internal and the other external. To begin with, the Meiji regime had to wage a civil war, albeit a short one, to put an end to Tokugawa resistance. Moreover, even after the elimination of vestiges of Tokugawa rule, there remained antipathy to the new regime in many quarters; and this antipathy found expression in uprisings and rebellions, the largest of which was the Satsuma rebellion in 1877. The new government, therefore, felt impelled to create an army which would be politically loyal to it. Such an army could be used to put down dissident groups which for one reason or another opposed the process of modernization and centralization begun by the Meiji government.

In addition to internal security there was the problem of defense against external foes. The concern for national defense may be explained in part by the nature of the international setting in which Japan developed into a modern nation. Commodore Perry as well as many of his predecessors who had tried to "open" Japan had come in gunboats. The fact that Japan had been forced to abandon her policy of national isolation under duress, so to speak, was still fresh in the memories of the Meiji leadership. Many Japanese were also aware that China had suffered humiliating defeats at the hands of the Western powers. Hence the Meiji leaders, seeing the extension of European colonial rule into Asia and Africa, perceived the international environment as essentially a hostile one. Given this set of perceptions about the outside world, it is understandable that the Meiji elite put a high priority on the creation of a modern military establishment based primarily on European models. In 1870, only two years after the Restoration, the decision was taken to pattern the new army after the French model, and the navy after the British model. In 1872 a French military advisory group, the first of several foreign military missions to be invited, arrived to help organize and train a modern army. In short, the international environment was such that it led the Meiji leaders to believe, rightly or wrongly, that unless their country established adequate defenses, it might be subjected to foreign intervention and exploitation.

A comparison with the Chinese response at about the same time suggests, however, that the international environment was not the only variable. In the latter half of the nineteenth century both China and Japan faced the problem of adjusting their polities and societies to the Western impact. Some far-reaching changes in values, institutions, and social structure were called for if these polities were to survive. Usually adaptive change does not come spontaneously and naturally but requires conscious thought, planning, and a certain amount of coercion of those who do not wish to change—in short what is called for is leadership.

So far as the Chinese leadership was concerned, modernization represented a threat to the very basis of the traditional social order, and so understandably they found it difficult to face up to the challenge. The Japanese leadership, on the other hand, was much more flexible and willing to resort to selective but nevertheless large scale borrowing from the West. It would take us too far afield to get into an extended discussion of the reasons for these differing responses. However, it would appear that for our purposes two reasons ought to be stressed, namely, the recruitment of elite members, and the nature of nationalism.

The Chinese elite was traditionally chosen by means of competitive civil service examinations. In these examinations the applicants were tested for their knowledge of the Confucian classics and the great body of commentaries on the classics which had been built up over the centuries. The nature of the examinations was such that only those who had assiduously studied the classics since early childhood could hope to pass them. The classics stressed the notion that politics were synonymous with ethics and that government by example was the best. According to this view, social stability could be achieved and peace and order made to reign supreme when virtuous leaders governed their subjects by means of moral example. By the same token, social unrest and disorder were taken to mean that the rulers had not set the proper example. Since in such a system elite status was achieved by those who had internalized the dominant values of the Confucian ideology, the members of the elite had naturally a strong intellectual and emotional commitment to that ideology. Just as a leader of a religious order would not be able to retain his position if he adopted a different religion, so the Chinese elite could not abandon the Confucian ideology without jeopardizing their status as leaders.

The situation with respect to the Japanese leadership was somewhat different. In the Tokugawa period the bureaucracy was almost always drawn from the samurai class. It was widely recognized that the samurai formed the dominant class and that their function was to rule. In this sense elite status was something that was achieved primarily through birth since the usual way to become a samurai was to be born into a samurai family. Since certain members of the samurai class provided the leadership for the Restoration movement, the early Meiji government was heavily staffed by men from samurai families. Because unlike their Chinese counterparts the Japanese elite did not achieve their status by virtue of having internalized certain political values, they could be much more flexible in what they believed and professed about political life. After all, their claim to elite status was not based on a commitment to a particular system of political and social values.

As for nationalism, one could scarcely say that the Chinese official class had much of a sense of nationhood. Traditionally the Chinese educated class thought of China as the "Middle Kingdom," which is another way of saying that China represents the center of the universe. According to this view, there were two kinds of people, the Chinese and the "barbarians," who might be thought of as a people who were "not yet" Chinese. Once the "barbarians" adopted the Chinese way of life, they became Chinese for all intents and purposes. Thus Chinese civilization was thought to be universally applicable. Indeed, a twentieth century scholar, K'ang Yu-wei, one of the last of the Confucians, once wrote an essay in which he argued that Confucius had prophesied that eventually there would be one world.[1]

The Japanese leaders, on the other hand, were much more parochial in their outlook, a characteristic to which no doubt both history and geography had contributed. Since Japan was

[1] See Joseph Levenson, *Confucian China and its Modern Fate* (Berkeley, 1958), ch. 5.

an insular country, it had clearly defined boundaries, and this helped to develop among the Japanese a sense of nationhood. Moreover, the Japanese were able to remain for long periods of time in relative isolation from other centers of civilization, a feature which promoted among them a sense of uniqueness.

When Japan was compelled to abandon the traditional policy of national isolation in the middle of the nineteenth century and become a member of the world community, the elite perceived that community as being made up of a hierarchy of unequal nations. Professor Maruyama Masao has argued that the Japanese leadership, which felt that their own society was composed of a hierarchy of unequal classes, interpreted the international community to be similarly hierarchical in structure. "Consequently," he states, "when the premises of the national hierarchy were transferred horizontally into the international sphere, international problems were reduced to a single alternative: conquer or be conquered."[2]

Thus it is not altogether surprising that the Chinese and Japanese elites should have responded differently to the Western impact in the middle of the nineteenth century. The Chinese elite, deeply committed to traditional values with claims to universal applicability, were complaisant because they believed that ultimately China and Chinese values would win out. By contrast, the Japanese elite, with a more parochial outlook, sensed the Western presence as a source of danger to national survival.

Now it is usually the case that elite groups must have cohesion if they are to provide proper leadership in modernization. In the Japanese case cohesion came from several sources. One was common class background. Most of the members of the elite came from the samurai class and hence tended to share common values and prejudices. Second, there was a pronounced regional bias in the composition of the Meiji elite. A great many of the leading officials were drawn from the old

---

[2] Maruyama Masao, *Thought and Behavior in Modern Japanese Politics* (London, 1963), p. 140.

feudal fiefs of Chōshū and Satsuma, and to a lesser extent of Tosa and Hizen. In a country where even today personal and family connections count in interpersonal relations, the fact that many leading officials were born and raised in certain areas added greatly to elite cohesion. Finally, mention must be made of the shared sense of vision and high purpose among the elite. The common vision of Meiji leaders was to assure the independence of their country, and succeeding in that to elevate Japan's status, then relatively low, to that of equality with the great powers of the West. Since great power status in the context of the nineteenth century world was measured in terms of military might, it followed logically that the Japanese elite should place a high priority on this goal.

Thus the desire for a modern military establishment to meet both internal and external needs led to an early decision to create a conscript army to replace the feudal samurai fighting forces. This was not an easy decision to implement since it aroused the antipathy of the proud samurai who looked upon arms-bearing as a social privilege, and of peasant families which were not anxious to see their sons drafted into the armed forces.[3] However, the government, despite resistance and opposition, went forward with its plan, and a new army was created with the help of foreign advisers. As has been mentioned, this army met its first serious test in the Satsuma rebellion of 1877.

The Armed Forces as a Modernizing Agency

There is substantial evidence to show that foreign wars have helped to enhance the sense of patriotism and national unity in Japan. In fact in 1903 Uchimura Kanzō, the Christian socialist and pacifist, wrote that "There is nothing so easy as encouraging present-day Japanese, who have been taught that loyalty to the throne and patriotism must involve fighting with

[3] Oishi Shinsaburo, "Chōhei-sei to ie," *Rekishigaku kenkyū*, No. 194 (April 1956), pp. 1–5.

a foreign country, to launch a war."[4] Indeed, one is not hard put to find examples of national unity in the face of hostilities abroad. For example, prior to the outbreak of the Sino-Japanese War of 1894–1895, the House of Representatives was the scene of intense bickering and acrimony, but once war began, the dissident groups closed ranks and gave full support to the government. A more recent example would be the ideological reorientation of liberals and leftists in the 1930's. So strong was the appeal of nationalism following the invasion of Manchuria in 1931 that even some prominent communists recanted and sought to justify Japanese expansion.[5]

Ultimately, however, the problem of nation-building must necessarily involve the transformation of many individuals from "traditional" man into "modern" man. Whereas traditional man is religious in his outlook and tries to adapt himself to nature, modern man is secular and seeks to control nature. Traditional man, moreover, prefers to solve problems by recourse to time-honored methods, whereas modern man will take a more inventive approach. Finally, traditional man relies very heavily on kin and primary-group relationships, while modern man has the capacity to create large-scale organizations which have specific aims and seek concrete benefits for their members.

Such a modern man, of course, does not automatically come into being, but is a product of a molding process or socialization. In countries undergoing modernization, among the most important agencies for socialization are the armed forces. As Lucian Pye suggests, a soldier is to some extent a modernized man.[6] For example, a peasant youth going into the army

---

[4] Quoted in Ishida Takeshi, *Meiji seiji shisō-shi kenkyū* (Tokyo, 1954), p. 165.

[5] For example, Sano Manabu and Nabeyama Sadachika. See Shisō no Kagaku Kenkyū-kai, *Tenkō*, Jōkan (Tokyo, 1959), pp. 164–200.

[6] Lucian Pye, "Armies in the Process of Political Modernization," in J. J. Johnson, ed., *The Role of the Military in Underdeveloped Countries* (Princeton, 1962), p. 80.

is exposed to a host of new influences. In the early days of conscription in Japan, many of the recruits came from remote mountain communities, and few had gone to elementary school. In the army they learned to read and write and some developed the habit of keeping diaries. In the newly built barracks they saw all kinds of equipment they had never seen before. It is said that on their first exposure to a stove some of them thought it was a religious idol and worshiped it.[7] Hence for many recruits from remote areas, army life represented a unique first-hand experience with aspects of modern civilization and an urbanized social atmosphere. The following contemporary account gives us insight into the socializing process. The author notes that at first the recruits resented their being put into the army, "but once they entered the barracks and mingled with many other soldiers, devoted themselves day and night to military matters, walked around the city streets in the company of others during their off-duty hours, became enamored of the maids working in public baths, became acquainted with the newly established archery booths, developed a taste for *shamo-nabe* [a kind of chicken dish], learned to dance the *kappore,* and day by day learned the ways of the city, their memories of their homes gradually dimmed."[8]

But more important for the question of political modernization was the fact that a recruit's political horizon was likely to be greatly expanded. In the armed forces he rubbed shoulders with recruits from other sections of the country, and he became aware of the world beyond the confines of his native village. The account from which we have just quoted states that "Those who were illiterate when they left their homes learned to read and write while in the service, and not a few read newspapers like the *Chōya* and *Hōchi,* which advocated the peoples' rights, and radical magazines like *Fusō shinshi* and *Kinji hyōron.*"[9]

[7] Shibusawa Keizo, *Meiji Bunka-shi,* xii (Tokyo, 1955), 566.

[8] Tōyama Shōichi, *Minken Benwaku,* reprinted in *Meiji Bunka Zenshū,* v, 228.

[9] *Ibid.*

Not to be overlooked, also, were the more formal influences. In almost any army the recruit is subjected to a good deal of specific training in patriotism and nationalism. For example, in 1882 the Imperial Rescript to Soldiers and Sailors, which provided the basic guidelines for the moral training of men in the armed forces, was issued. The first and most important precept outlined in this document was loyalty. "The soldier and the sailor," it said, "should consider loyalty their essential duty. Remember that, as the protection of the State and the maintenance of its power depend upon the strength of its arms, the growth or decline of this strength must affect the nation's destiny for good or evil."[10]

Thus it was a rare recruit who did not come out of the army a changed man. Moreover, these changes often made an ex-soldier "unfit" for the civilian life which followed. Again we quote from a contemporary document: "When they finish their period of enlistment and return to their homes, their minds are no longer those of the clodhopper they had been a few years ago. They can no longer bear to collect night soil and carry honey buckets on their shoulders. But rice does not descend from heaven, and they cannot avoid collecting night soil, and carrying honey buckets. For this reason, there are few who accept their lot and who are satisfied."[11]

It is little wonder, then, that in many rural communities in Japan returned soldiers (*heitai agari*) were much criticized and resented.[12] What had happened was that the soldier had become more modernized than the environment to which he returned. In this connection it is interesting that a handbook of army regulations admonished the soldier to cultivate social morality and personal integrity while in the service, and "Even after soldiers are discharged and return to their homes, they should, in this spirit, pursue their respective occupations,

[10] As translated in Hillis Lory, *Japan's Military Masters* (New York, 1943), pp. 241–42.

[11] Tōyama, *op.cit.*, p. 228.

[12] Takakura Tetsuichi, ed., *Tanaka Giichi Denki*, Jōkan (Tokyo, 1958), p. 410.

become simple and honest individuals, exert a good influence on their village communities, and thereby elevate the nation."[13]

The Armed Forces as Transmitters of Tradition

Although the armed forces, as suggested above, can act as modernizing agencies in developing nations, it would be a mistake to disregard their concomitant role as preservers of tradition. Morris Janowitz has pointed out that while the military may be technocratic in organization and concerned with modernization, it is also concerned with legitimate authority and with historical and national traditions.[14]

In prewar Japan the armed forces consistently stressed the traditional symbols of social solidarity, namely the emperor, who was to be the object of loyalty and devotion, and the family, which served as a model of interpersonal relations. According to Robert Bellah,[15] the traditional Japanese value system consisted of these components:

1. Value is realized in groups, such as the community, which are thought of as natural groups.

2. These groups possess a sacred quality.

3. There is a divine-human continuity in which the symbolic heads of groups have an especially important place because one of their functions is to relate the group to the divine ancestors and protective deities, for example the family (and its ancestor worship), village (and the local deity), and ultimately the whole country with the emperor and his imperial ancestors at the head.

4. Individuals exist because of the continuous flow of bless-

[13] *Guntai Naimusho*, 1923 ed., pp. 9–10.

[14] Morris Janowitz, *The Military in the Political Development of New Nations* (Chicago, 1964), p. 26.

[15] Robert N. Bellah, "Values and Social Change in Modern Japan," *Asian Cultural Studies*, No. 3 (Oct. 1962), published by International Christian University, pp. 32–33.

ings from the spirits and ancestors through the symbolic heads of groups.

5. All aspects of culture, including ethics, are not ends in themselves, but valued only as they contribute to the group.

6. There is one place where the individual who is merged in this group can be relatively independent and that is in personal expressiveness—art, mysticism, recreation, and skill.

Within this system of values the family occupied a keystone position because it was thought to be the most enduring group to which an individual belonged and because the state was thought of as a large family headed by the emperor, which meant that political loyalty was synonymous with filial piety.

It is worth noting in this connection that in the beginning the conscription system paid deference to the family system by exempting from the draft men who occupied certain positions within the family. Specifically, heads of families, sons and grandsons in line for succession as heads of families, only sons, sons acting as heads of families because their fathers or brothers were incapacitated, and adopted sons (*yōshi*) who would assume the headship of their adopted families. These exemptions provided a handy loophole for countless individuals who wished to avoid service in the army or navy. Particular advantage was taken of the provision for adopted sons, and many second and third sons rushed to be adopted by other families.[16]

There were other exemptions in addition to family considerations. For example, one could buy his way out of the draft by paying 270 *yen*. Actually in 1876 some 82 percent of the men of draft age were exempt for one reason or another.[17] With the passage of years the exemptions were whittled away, and in 1889 the exemptions resting on family status were abolished, despite fears expressed in some quarters that such action would have an adverse effect on the social system.[18]

[16] Oishi, *op.cit.*, pp. 7–8.   [17] *Ibid.*, p. 4.   [18] *Ibid.*, p. 10.

Undoubtedly behind the move to eliminate these exemptions was the need for more manpower, especially in anticipation of a war with China, which came in 1894, and later with Russia in 1904.

On the other hand, within the military establishment itself there was a movement to use consciously the family as a model of social organization. After the Russo-Japanese War particular stress began to be paid to the idea of the army as a large family. As one official document put it, "the barracks are the household of soldiers who share joys and sorrows and life and death."[19] Officers were admonished to treat their men as if they were their own sons, and the enlisted men were told to look upon their superiors as their fathers. Although it is quite true that social cohesion in large-scale organizations depends on personal loyalties and primary-group solidarity developed within, excessive stress on particularistic relationships will create organizational cleavages.[20] If one of the attributes of modernization is the growth of interpersonal relationships based on universal rather than particularistic principles, then it may be said that in important respects the armed forces served to impede modernization.

Undoubtedly there were many reasons for the conscious use of primary-group loyalties, but one of them was probably associated with the marked antiurban bias of the military. For example, about 1910 the army began to encourage the planting of trees and the growing of vegetables in army camps as a part of a program to promote interest in agriculture. This policy was justified in the following manner:

> If soldiers who are in the army, which is made up of a substantial part of the nation, are made to realize through encouragement in agriculture the beauties of nature and that the agricultural way of life, compared to city occupations which are characterized by excessive competition

[19] Fujiwara Akira, *Nihon gendai-shi taikei, gunji-shi* (Tokyo, 1961), p. 112.

[20] Janowitz, *op.cit.*, p. 70.

and evil tendencies, is pure and interesting, they will think of their native districts and come to love the villages of their birth. Accordingly, it will strengthen their desire to revert to agriculture and return to their homes when they complete their military service. There are many people in the advanced civilized countries who abandon farming and go into commerce and industry, giving rise to the evil of the loss of farmers. This evil diminishes the peasantry, which is hardy and hard-working, it weakens the vitality of the state, and in the long run it leads to the decline of the nation. This must give rise to misgivings among intelligent men. Therefore to encourage agriculture within the army not only leads to encouraging the development of agriculture, but it produces favorable effects on the state and on the nature of the army.[21]

Although the foregoing quotation does not touch on it, without doubt recruits from the rural areas made better soldiers than city boys, both with respect to ability to withstand physical hardships and willingness to submit themselves to discipline. Commentators have argued that a substantial portion of the enlisted men in the army were from the farming areas.[22] There appears to be no detailed statistical evidence to support this point of view, but it is a plausible interpretation. If it is true that many of the recruits were from rural areas, then one can see that adjustment to military life was rendered easier if within the army interpersonal relations followed the same patterns that were found in the villages.

It has often been argued that within the officer ranks, too, men of rural origin were found in large numbers. Fragmentary evidence suggests that over the long run officers who came from farming families declined proportionately speaking, while sons of professional soldiers increased in number. Sons of army and navy officers quite often attended military preparatory schools (*yōnen gakkō*), and those who did well

[21] Quoted in Fujiwara, *op.cit.*, p. 118.   [22] See *ibid.*, p. 156.

eventually went on to the academies. In the main, men educated in this fashion were strongly imbued with traditional values, possessed a strong sense of devotion to the emperor, and were uninformed about world affairs. It is noteworthy that of the fifteen leaders of the large-scale army uprising in February 1936, at least eleven were sons of professional soldiers.[23]

So far we have given several examples of traditional influences at work within the armed forces. These influences did not necessarily come to an end when the soldier returned to civilian life. In 1910 the Reservists' Association (*Zaigō Gunjin-kai*) was formed for the purpose of forming the best "link for bringing together the armed forces and the people."[24] Eventually branches of the association were formed in every hamlet in the land, and in the 1920's some branches were established in factories and mines for the purpose of combatting the growth of labor unions.

Perhaps the most notable example of the use of the Reservists' Association for the purpose of intervention in politics occurred in 1935 as a part of the campaign waged by the military and right-wing groups to attack Professor Minobe Tatsukichi and his so-called organ theory of the emperor. For about twenty-five years Professor Minobe, one of the leading authorities on the Japanese constitution, had taught that the emperor was one of the "organs" of the state. What he had tried to do was to find some rationale for reconciling constitutional theory and political practice. He was, however, accused of being subversive by rightists who held to the mystical view that the emperor was the state. In this campaign branches of the Reservists' Association were mobilized to pass resolutions and to send delegations to Tokyo to agitate against Minobe. As a result, "an academic theory accepted as common sense for many years not only by specialist scholars and men of learning but by civil and judicial officials was received by society at large as an improper and even blasphemous way of think-

[23] *Ibid.*, p. 161.   [24] *Ibid.*, p. 122.

ing."[25] In the end irrationalism won the day, and Professor Minobe was forced to resign his seat in the House of Peers and give up his post in the Faculty of Law at Tokyo Imperial University.

Lucian Pye has suggested that modernization involves the problem of creating organizations that are capable of relating means to ends.[26] In terms of the means-ends relationship, it may be said that the ultimate purpose of most military establishments is to fight wars when called upon to do so, and if possible to win them. If this is the case, then the great decisions of war and peace ought to be "rationally" arrived at, that is, the chances of success or failure should be calculated using the best information available and decisions made on the basis of such calculations. The Japanese calculations in connection with the decision to go to war against the United States and its allies were that the chances of victory were high if early in the war the main American fleet sailed into Japanese waters and there occurred a decisive battle or battles between the Japanese and American fleets. But the navy leaders were also certain that such a decisive battle would not occur and that the war would be prolonged. In that event Japan would be in difficulty because of the shortage of materials. To meet this problem, the Japanese planned to occupy Southeast Asia and ship oil and other vital raw materials from that area to Japan. This assumed that Japan would be able to maintain sea communications with Southeast Asia. There were also other assumptions in the calculations. The Japanese leadership counted on a German victory over Britain and war weariness developing in the United States.

Thus at best war with the Allied countries was a risky venture. There were some leaders like Prince Konoe who were reluctant to assume risks. General Tōjō's response to Konoe, which was fairly typical of the outlook of the professional soldier of that period, was that in the course of a man's lifetime he might find it necessary to jump with his eyes closed from

[25] Maruyama, *op.cit.*, p. 62.   [26] Pye, *op.cit.*, pp. 73-74.

the deck of the Kiyomizu Temple in Kyoto into the deep
ravine below.[27] Of a similar vein is a remark attributed to
Admiral Yamamoto Isoroku, who advocated a surprise attack
on Pearl Harbor. The naval general staff was reluctant to
adopt Yamamoto's plan because of the great risks involved.
The admiral is said to have replied that the "only question
that remains is the blessing of heaven. If we have heaven's
blessing, then there will be no doubt of success."[28] Thus although the military was among the first to be modernized, it
continued to retain many premodern features.

War and International Status

We have already mentioned that the Meiji political elite had
as an underlying goal the achievement of equality in the
international community. There is no doubt whatever that
victory in wars against China and Russia helped tremendously
to fulfill these ambitions. As a result of these wars, Japan
became an imperial power and the leading country in the
Far East. As is true with all wars, they took their toll of human life and brought suffering and anguish to families
bereft of fathers, sons, and husbands. Yet these wars appear to
have been supported by the sub-elites and the population at
large. Maruyama Masao explains this phenomenon in terms
of the "transfer of oppression." In his view, the Japanese felt
the pressure of the Great Powers and sought relief from it by
oppressing weaker neighbors. "In this regard," he states, "it is
significant that ever since the Meiji period demands for a
tough foreign policy have come from the common people, that
is, from those who are at the receiving end of oppression at
home."[29]

The Sino-Japanese War and the Russo-Japanese War,

[27] Robert J. C. Butow, *Tojo and the Coming of the War* (Princeton,
(1961), p. 267.
[28] Quoted in Fujiwara, *op.cit.*, p. 276.
[29] Maruyama, *op.cit.*, pp. 18–19.

moreover, were not of long duration. The war against China lasted a little over eight months, while the war against Russia continued about nineteen months. Both wars ended in victory before the nation was bled white economically speaking, and before war weariness set in among the population. One can say with some confidence, therefore, that for the nation as a whole war paid off, for it brought both added prestige and power.

War also served as a stimulus for economic development. In a study of government expenditures and economic growth in Japan, Emi notes that war led to sharp increases in government expenditures and that after the end of the war these expenditures remained on a high plateau. His conclusion is that "war seems to have been the greatest stimulus to the expansion of the economy."[30]

Japan also benefited from World War I. Although a participant, she fought relatively little, and hence suffered only light losses. Furthermore, Japan was in a position to supply much-needed war materials to the Allied cause, and as a result she enjoyed an economic boom. Then at the end of the war she was invited to participate in the peace conference as one of the Great Powers. Thus in a period of about fifty years, Japan had advanced from a backward Asian country into the ranks of the leading nations of the world.

In a sense, therefore, Japan had achieved her goals; yet in another sense she had not. Although she had acquired Great Power status, the Western powers were not willing to admit her as a full-fledged member of the club, so to speak. Indeed, as Japan's status rose, so did tension between her and some of the Great Powers, such as the United States and Great Britain. By 1920 there were predictions, both in and out of military

[30] Koichi Emi, *Government Fiscal Activity and Economic Growth in Japan, 1868–1960* (Tokyo, 1963), p. 33. Not being an economist I am unable to say whether economic expansion would also have occurred if war had not taken place and the resources had been used for peacetime activities.

circles in the United States and in Japan, that war between the two countries would come in a few years.[31]

We would put forward the hypothesis that sometime during the 1920's the goal of equality with the Western powers was tacitly abandoned because of the conviction that such a goal was not really attainable. Stated in another way, the Japanese had previously viewed the world as a single community made up of tiers of unequal nations. Several Western nations were situated at the apex of this pyramidal structure, and Japan's ambition was to win for herself a recognized place within that apex. She felt, however, that the Western powers who had reached the top positions first were unwilling to make room for her and to welcome her, a latecomer, into the select circle.

As a result an alternative goal, discussed intermittently over the years, was explicitly adopted. This goal involved the idea that the world, instead of comprising a single community, would be divided up into several more or less self-contained smaller communities or regional blocs, and within these blocs one country would be dominant. It was assumed that since Japan was the first Asian country to modernize, she would be the natural leader in the East Asian bloc.

Some envisaged an eventual showdown between the Western bloc and the Eastern bloc. Thus Ishihara Kanji, then a colonel, said in a speech to the research section of the Kwantung Army in 1931 that (1) the development of war points to mankind's last great world war; (2) as a result of the last world war, the United States has become the leader of Western civilization; (3) Japan is becoming the leader of Eastern civilization; (4) the trend is for the world in the near future to become one; (5) whether this one world will be centered in Japan or in the United States will be decided in a great world war.[32]

[31] William L. Neumann, *America Encounters Japan* (Baltimore, 1963), pp. 161–62.

[32] Asahi Shimbun-sha, *Taiheiyō sensō e no michi*, Bekkan Shiryō-hen (Tokyo, 1963), p. 96.

The kind of war that Ishihara envisaged, however, was bound to be greatly different from previous wars Japan had fought. From the Japanese point of view, the technological developments in warfare had worked to their disadvantage. World War I had demonstrated at least two things. First, war in the future would be immensely mechanized. The tank had come into its own and the potentialities of aircraft had been suggested. Second, unlike wars in the past which had been won when one side achieved victory in one or two "decisive" battles, the war of the future would be a prolonged affair. Ultimate victory, therefore, would hinge on industrial capacity and the ability to mobilize the total resources of the nation for the prosecution of the war.

For understandable reasons the Japanese military was reluctant to face up to these realities. Compared to the great industrial powers of Europe and to the United States, Japan was weak in terms of industrial potential. Moreover, there was little prospect that in the near future Japan could hope to compete with the Great Powers on equal terms with regard to industrial production. Given these circumstances, the Japanese leaders could have conceded superiority to the Western powers and given up the race. But to have done so would have meant the abandonment of a fundamental reason for having launched on the path of modernization in the Meiji era.

The Japanese response to this predicament took the following form. Increasingly the Japanese military began to deprecate the value of "material" strength and to stress the "spiritual" factors in warfare. The "Japanese spirit" would overcome the material superiority of the West. In essence this meant renewed emphasis on traditional values and symbols. As in the case of sports, the "will to win" is an important element in warfare, but there are definite limits to what "spirit" unreinforced by the more tangible elements of military power can accomplish. It is fortunate for the people of Japan that the war was not prolonged to the point where bamboo spears would have been tested against machine guns and flame throwers.

The other response was to disregard the more recent developments in the nature of warfare. Among the lessons that World War I taught was that in the future wars were likely to require total mobilization. Yet given the fragmented political structure, total mobilization could not be achieved easily in Japan. Accordingly those in charge of military planning in the 1920's and early 1930's for the most part continued to think in terms of past wars, that is, limited wars of short duration which would be won or lost as a result of the confrontation of the main forces of the two sides. Indeed, this kind of mentality appears to have persisted well into World War II.

It has been suggested, moreover, that one of the reasons for the demands put forward by the younger officers in the 1930's for the creation of a Fascist-like structure was the desire to overcome this antiquated approach to warfare and to bring about total mobilization for war purposes.[33] In the late 1930's the Japanese leadership attempted to institute war mobilization and totalitarian controls over the entire population; but compared to the German effort, the Japanese version of totalitarianism was a relatively mild and ineffectual affair.

One of the reasons for this difference was that totalitarian controls in Japan attempted to utilize traditional symbols, the emperor system for instance, as well as traditional forms of social cohesion, namely primary group loyalties. Maruyama writes: "When Japan reached the point of total war, which necessitated a complete reorganization of the nation's life, the negative side of Japanese nationalism became more and more exposed as the slogans grew in number and intensity. One need only recall the deep-rooted psychological resistance that met the shrill demands to enforce conscript labor placement, controlled industrial production and distribution, and forced evacuation plans. The resistance stemmed from none other

[33] Fujiwara, *op.cit.*, ch. 7.

than the family principle, 'agriculture first,' and 'love of the village.' "[34]

Conclusion

It appears that war was not an accidental phenomenon that emerged from some chance factor like the whims of a paranoid leader, but was closely associated with the entire process of political modernization. Modernization usually signifies planned and purposeful change, and almost always change is upsetting and painful and hence likely to be resisted. For this reason modernization, especially rapid modernization, requires the presence of an elite dedicated to leading the nation into the modern era. An elite, to be effective, must possess internal unity and also have a sense of mission. For the Japanese elite the mission was first to assure Japan's independence as a nation, and later to elevate Japan's international status to that of a Great Power in the world community. In articulating these goals, moreover, the national elite struck a responsive chord among the sub-elite. Accordingly, the drive to achieve Great Power status had the function of contributing to nation-building by promoting the growth of a sense of national identity and unity.

Since Japan's drive for Great Power status occurred in the heyday of European expansion, the Japanese very early learned the need for and the value of modern armies and navies. Hence Japan's leaders turned their attention to creating a fighting force patterned mostly after European models. This very fact had the effect of introducing into the Japanese body politic a modernizing agency.

The role of the armed forces as a modernizing agency, however, varied depending on the period. In general, during the Meiji era the armed forces were probably more modern than the rest of the nation in terms of technology and organization. It would appear, however, that by the Taishō period the rest of the nation had caught up with the armed forces as a

[34] Maruyama, *op.cit.*, p. 147.

result of the spread of compulsory education and industrialization.

We have stressed also the fact that the armed forces served
as transmitters of tradition. Of course this was not a phenomenon that was unique to Japan; but the Japanese armed
forces, perhaps more than most others, emphasized primary
relationships in terms of their organization. In this sense it
may be said that the development of the army and navy served
to impede modernization. Another indicator of the persistence of traditional elements in the armed forces was the tendency to engage in "irrational" modes of decision-making.

The wars which the Japanese had fought prior to the Pacific
war paid off. They were of relatively short duration, and each
successive victory enhanced Japan's international stature. In
one sense the goal the Meiji leadership had set for itself was in
the process of being achieved; yet in another sense the goal
was becoming more elusive than ever. Despite Japan's rapid
rise, the Western powers were not ready to accord her full
recognition as a Great Power in the world community. As a
result, the earlier goal was abandoned in favor of another
goal which envisaged a world divided into regional blocs,
with Japan as the leader of the East Asian bloc.

This shift in goals had certain consequences. An anti-
Western mood set in, and intellectual and cultural contacts
with the West decreased. To the extent that modernization
had been spurred by Western knowledge and example as well
as by direct competition with the West, the pace of modernization was slowed.[35] A conscious effort was made to eliminate Western influences and revive traditional ideas and
ideals.

Another fundamental problem was posed by the changes
that occurred in the nature of warfare as a result of World

[35] It is true that in the late 1930's Japanese contacts with Germany
and to a lesser degree with Italy increased, but my impression is that
these contacts worked against modernization. See Bellah's remarks on
Fascism, communism, and modernization in *op.cit.*, p. 24.

War I. Increasingly war became "total" war, necessitating total mobilization. This development was an unfavorable one from the Japanese point of view because Japan was weak in terms of industrial potential and political capacity to mobilize resources, both material and human.

The response which the Japanese leaders made to this problem was to minimize the importance of material factors, such as weapons, military technology, and industrial production, and to stress the importance of "spiritual" factors, such as bravery, devotion to the emperor, and social solidarity. As a result, the Japanese leadership, in calculating the chances of victory in a war against the Allied powers, took a more optimistic view than was warranted by the facts. Thus while war in one sense contributed to modernization, in another sense it led Japan into a historical blind alley. It required the trauma of defeat in World War II to get Japan out of this blind alley. Defeat also sundered the relationship which had existed historically between war and modernization.

CHAPTER VII

Popular Political Participation and Political Development in Japan: The Rural Level

KURT STEINER[1]

A
N ADEQUATE definition of political development should contain psychological as well as institutional components. The concept should involve changes not only in political institutions but also in the political orientations of a society, in what Almond and Verba call its "political culture."[2] In particular developmental cases the local rural community plays a crucial part in this process of modernization.

On the institutional level, for example, nation-building involves subdividing the national territory into units of local government linked, in one way or another, to the national

[1] The writer acknowledges gratefully financial support received from the Committee on East Asian Studies of Stanford University.

[2] Gabriel A. Almond and Sidney Verba, *The Civic Culture: Political Attitudes and Democracy in Five Nations* (Princeton, 1963). The political culture of a nation is defined as "the particular distribution of patterns of orientations to its political objects among the members of the nation." The political objects in question are, first, the "general political system," i.e. the national entity and its overall characteristics; second, the political or "input" process involving the "upward" flow of policy-making; third, the administrative or "output" process, involving the "downward flow of policy enforcement; and finally, the "self" as political actor. In other words, "the political culture becomes the frequency of different kinds of cognitive, effective and evaluative orientations towards the political system in general, its input and output aspects and the self as political actor" (pp. 14-17). The pure types of political culture are the parochial political culture, the subject political culture and the participant political culture. These three pure types and their mixtures form the framework of my inquiry.

government. The traditional village, existing up to now in a "state of nature" so to speak, may itself be designated as such a local governmental unit, or it may for reasons of administrative convenience or for other reasons be combined with others of its kind to form such a unit. Since governmental integration increases as the plans of the national leadership for economic and social development are implemented, national laws will require these administrative villages to take on the performance of new national functions. In doing so the area of the traditional village, as well as its organization, leadership, and decision-making process, may well be subjected to a variety of changes.

Equally important, however, is the role of the local community in reorienting the people's attitudes toward politics. This, too, is part of the process of political modernization. The notion that a community socializes its members in ways which affect the political culture of the larger polity is generally accepted. Thus it is often said that "democracy begins at the grassroots." On the other hand the traditional way of life in the villages has often been praised by conservatives and condemned by progressives as providing a type of socialization which makes the village a bulwark against change and the main support of an essentially nondemocratic political culture.

The manner in which socialization at the community level affects political culture depends on both the character of the local political process and the character of the national political process. If a proper orientation toward participation in the national political process is seen as a goal of socialization at the village level, and participation in the local political process is viewed as a means to that end, then the relationship between the two processes will indicate whether the socialization is fulfilling its desired function. It will be, if the two political processes are congruent; for in this case the lessons learned at the local level can be applied at the national level. For instance, if decisions at the local level are reached in a democratic manner

—including egalitarian participation, articulation of divergent views, and determination of the issue by majority vote—town meetings may indeed be the "primary schools of liberty" about which de Tocqueville wrote. However, in a transitional society the two processes may differ rather sharply from each other. At a time when the modernizing elite may be intent on creating a new national consciousness at the national level, local political processes may be emphasizing subnational and parochial loyalties; or a modernizing elite may be intent on establishing a viable democratic process at the national level while the socialization process at the local level may be completely nondemocratic in nature.

This paper will attempt to probe this problem of the relationship between the types of socialization provided by the local political process and the modernizing aims of the national leadership in the context of rural Japan.[3] For reasons which I hope will become clear, I have focused the investigation on three periods: (1) the period from 1871 to 1888, the time between the abolition of feudalism and the promulgation of the local government codes, with particular emphasis on the decade between 1871 and 1880; (2) the period from 1937 to 1943, a time characterized by a high degree of political centralization based on a Japanese adaptation of totalitarian models; and (3) the period from 1947 to the present, a time when the local governmental system has been based on the notion that grassroot democracy contributes to democracy at the national level. In all three periods the relation between the village as a traditional community and the village as a modern administrative unit emerges as a key element of the analysis.

[3] Because of limitations of space I will not consider the development of popular political participation in urban areas. For the same reason a certain degree of over-generalization has been unavoidable. Japan's leaders were not always in agreement; there may have been greater differences in the types of socialization provided by local governments in certain areas and at certain times than I have been able to indicate.

The Political Culture of Pre-Meiji Villages

The base line for political modernization is normally a parochial political culture: the bulk of the people scarcely relate at all to the political system as a whole; they expect little for themselves from its output; they make few, if any, demands on it; and they have no sense of active political participation.[4] Does the political culture of pre-Meiji Japan fit this description?

As far as orientation toward the "political system as a whole," i.e. toward Japan as a political entity, is concerned, we must recognize that some sense of Japan's national identity was not lost even during the period of feudalism. The ethnic fusion which had occurred by the end of the neolithic period had left no important racial cleavages among the population. Because of the insular position of the country, Japanese society had been able to develop in a relatively homogeneous fashion, eclectically accepting foreign influences while still preserving a certain indigenous quality. During the Tokugawa period, insularity was reinforced by the seclusion policy. One and the same language was written—and, with dialectal variations, spoken—throughout Japan. There were no religious differences which set one region of the country apart from another. All parts of Japan shared a coherent and consistent general system of values, embodied in a Japanese version of Confucianism. Institutions broadly reflecting these values persisted from the seventeenth century to the end of the feudal period. This very persistence of the basic arrangements under which the Japanese people lived contributed to the existence of some sense of identity.[5] Surely the features of

[4] To use Almond and Verba's terms, in a parochial political culture the frequency of orientations toward the four political objects mentioned in note 2 approaches zero (*op.cit.*, p. 17).

[5] See, e.g., G. B. Sansom, *The Western World and Japan* (New York, 1950), pp. 167-69; John W. Hall, "The Nature of Traditional Society," in Robert E. Ward and Dankwart A. Rustow, eds., *Political Modernization in Japan and Turkey* (Princeton, 1964), pp. 16-20;

Tokugawa feudalism which gave it its peculiarly "central-ized" character must have strengthened it. In addition, the emperor was, at least potentially, a symbol of national identity even though he was without power. Indeed, as we look at the difficulties of nation-building in many of the developing countries today, we come to appreciate just how valuable an asset these circumstances were for the creators of a modern state in Japan.

However, it is one thing to recognize the existence of a common racial, religious, linguistic, and cultural identity for a group of people and quite another thing to assert the existence of a political system encompassing this group. In this regard we encounter a somewhat ambiguous situation in pre-Meiji Japan. The theory of a sovereign emperor was maintained, but "the only rulers whom most of the people of Tokugawa Japan knew were the shogun and the daimyo."[6] The daimyo owed loyalty to the Tokugawa shogun as his great vassals, but they ruled their fiefs through their own retainers. The political loyalty of the samurai was confined to the fief lord (whether this was the shogun—as in the case of the direct Tokugawa vassals in the shogun's own domains—or the local daimyo elsewhere). During most of the period there was no perception of allegiance to a political unit called "Japan." When sentiments of national unity and notions of an indi-vidual loyalty transcending the fief arose toward the end of the period, they were considered to be subversive.[7]

Robert A. Scalapino, "Environmental and Foreign Contributions," *ibid.*, p. 67; Marius B. Jansen, "Changing Japanese Attitudes toward Modernization," in the work of the same title, edited by Marius Jansen (Princeton, 1965), pp. 47-48. An important contributing factor, related to linguistic homogeneity and the prevalence of a homogeneous value system, was the extent of school education and of literacy. On this see R. P. Dore, "The Legacy of Tokugawa Education," in Jansen, *op.cit.*, p. 100.

[6] John W. Hall, *op.cit.*, p. 21.

[7] See, e.g., Sansom, *op.cit.*, pp. 209-14, 248-74. As Robert Scalapino points out, however, even the existence of so restricted a system of

When we descend to the level of the lower classes—villagers and townsmen—we step from the world of those who governed to the world of those who were governed. It is somewhat doubtful whether a term such as "political loyalty" can be applied at this level in the same sense as to the samurai class. But there is little doubt that villagers and townsmen identified first and foremost with their own communities. They recognized these communities in their governmental aspects as a constituent part of a fief.[8] However, it is not likely that villagers or townsmen thought of themselves as Japanese subjects or citizens. In general, we can state that in pre-Meiji Japan popular orientation toward Japan as a national political system was minimal.

Tokugawa Japan also had other characteristics of a parochial culture. Expectations regarding the governmental output of the shogunate were low. As far as the samurai class was concerned, the reason for this lies in the feudal character of the system. Their expectations were directed toward their own lord, not toward the shogun. The lower classes did not expect their wants to be satisfied by any government, whether it be the shogunate or the fief government. The village community engaged in a number of tasks, but most of these were not considered to be "governmental."[9] Demands coming from the fief government by way of the district administrator were addressed to the village as a whole.[10] The headman had to see to

political loyalty was a valuable asset in the creation of a modern state. Nevertheless, the Meiji leaders had to "broaden the scope of existing political concepts: to transform the *han* into the nation, and loyalty to the lord into reverence for the emperor." Scalapino, *op.cit.*, p. 70.

[8] There are even examples of villages which, out of allegiance to fief lords transferred by the shogunate, attempted to move to his new domain. See, e.g., Sansom, *op.cit.*, p. 236.

[9] In settling internal disputes, for example, the community fulfilled a governmental demand, but also a demand of morality.

[10] The Tokugawa village came into being as a result of the nationwide cadastral survey begun by Hideyoshi in 1582. It was a legal unit, generally comprising several natural agricultural settlements (see Hall,

it that these demands—typically, but not exclusively, demands
for taxes in kind—were fulfilled. Because he also played a role
in the village in its aspect as a communal living group, pressures were at times exerted on him by his neighbors to protect the community against governmental demands which
seemed overly harsh, thus putting him in a difficult position.
But aside from the negative attitude toward governmental
demands shown in such cases, the general village attitude was
one of passivity. Even the fief government was distant from the
daily life of the villagers; its decrees were generally accepted
and obeyed, but their importance was minimized by such
sayings as "Government laws are but three day laws"
(*Tenka hatto, mikka hatto*).

Similar considerations applied to the villagers' orientations
to the input process, that is to the possibility or desirability of
their making demands on the political system or of participating in political decision-making. The decision-making
process at each level of the hierarchy was considered autonomous, at least so far as the lower levels were concerned.[11] In
regard to the higher levels, Sansom writes: "In the days of
its strength and pride the Yedo government would never
have dreamed of consulting its lieges and followers. It would
have taken its decision boldly and called upon the hereditary vassals and the outside lords to carry out its orders."[12]
Only in its last phase did the shogunate endeavor to ascertain
the opinion of daimyo, court nobles, and some of the feudal
aristocracy. This departure from the normal processes of

---

op.cit., p. 23). However, it also had, or developed, the character of a
community. It is this community which is subsequently referred to as
the "traditional village."

[11] It should be noted that in spite of the autonomy of the decision-
making process at each level, all these processes had basic elements in
common. Thus the village power structure was hierarchical, reflecting
the power structure in the polity. Unanimous decisions were preferred
at all levels. On the village level unanimity was prescribed by written
rule or by unwritten custom.

[12] Sansom, *op.cit.,* p. 282.

decision-making and from the principles on which it was built only accelerated the destruction of a system which had become brittle.

The sharpest break was of course between the samurai class and the rest of the people. Interference by the lower classes in the decision-making prerogatives of the governing class was, in principle, antithetical to an order which made it a demand of morality that everyone "knows his proper place." Channels of upward communication were not entirely lacking, but characteristically such communication had to take the form of petitions, which minimized interference in the decision-making process. Furthermore, the line between the legitimate use of this upward channel and insubordination was a thin one. The "government" was petitioned only in case of unbearable situations or at least serious grievances.[13] Otherwise, the normal passivity in regard to governmental output prevented the rise of any desire for political participation.

To sum up: the political culture of pre-Meiji Japan can be characterized, with some qualifications, as a parochial political culture. In particular as far as the great mass of the inhabitants was concerned, a number of factors combined to strengthen parochial orientations. Most of them were born and lived out their lives within the circle of the village community. Their relations to the community were of tremendous importance. These relations were not only "face to face" relations—with all the diffuseness and affectivity common to such relations—but they were underpinned by a system of mutual economic support and dependence. And the general value system, which stressed collectivity orientation, reinforced the degree of group cohesion and identification which was natural under these circumstances.

Relations between the community and the "government" may have widened the villagers' political horizons to some

[13] Resort to violence—peasant revolts or jacqueries—was the only other method of intermittent participation in the decision-making process.

extent, although the range of governmental actions which impinged on their lives was quite limited. But to the villagers of Tokugawa Japan "government" meant the fief government. And the fief government made it a practice to deal with villages rather than individuals. Whether the object of governmental action was collection of taxes in kind or the maintenance of order and morality, it was the group that was made responsible. The individual's role remained primarily that of obligation to the group. Thus, somewhat paradoxically, the community's political relations with the outside world were such that they also strengthened existing parochial orientations.[14]

Changes in Political Culture during the Early Meiji Period

The efforts of the Meiji leaders to create a modern state involved an attempt to change the existing parochial political culture into a subject political culture.[15] The transformation of the population into "Japanese subjects" involved, among other problems, that of dealing with subnational identifications and loyalties. The most obvious and perhaps the most formidable barrier to identification with Japan as a national political unit was the existence of the fiefs. Aided by the erosion of feudal loyalties toward the end of the Tokugawa period and confident of their military strength, the Meiji leaders abolished the fiefs in 1871 and established in their place new units

[14] When the government imposed on villages the responsibility of seeing to it that the villagers did not leave the community and drift to the cities, this mutual reinforcement between group cohesion and governmental policy became particularly clear.

[15] According to Almond and Verba (*op.cit.*, p. 19), a subject political culture is characterized, first, by "a high frequency of orientations toward a differentiated political system," i.e. an awareness of specialized governmental authority, and, second, by "a high frequency of orientations toward the output aspects of the system." On the other hand, "orientations toward specifically input objects, and toward the self as an active participant, approach zero." The relationship of the subject to the system continues to be essentially a passive one.

of government, the prefectures.[16] The parochial orientations of the mass of the population, living in towns and villages, was yet another problem. They, too, had to be made aware of the existence of a central political regime and imbued with positive feelings toward it and its policies.[17] For the villagers this led to tensions between their loyalties to the local community, which had hitherto been the almost exclusive focus of their identification and commitment, and their feelings toward the new national state and its claims. These tensions first came to the attention of the Meiji leaders on an institutional level as a concomitant of increased governmental integration. Specifically, they arose when land ownership and the obligation to pay taxes were transferred from the community to individuals and when family registration, conscription, and a centralized education system were introduced.

Confronted with this problem the attitude of the Meiji leaders between 1871 and 1878 vacillated between disregard of the traditional village or even animosity toward it, accommodation to its existence outside the institutions of government as a fact of rural life in a transitional period, and, finally, recognition of its potential usefulness to their purposes. On their part, the elite in the villages at various times reciprocated the animosity of the government, demanded recognition for their communities, and, finally, accommodated themselves to the designs of their rulers. This was a period when grandiose

[16] This measure aimed, of course, at concentrating control over the entire country in the hands of the new government. But it must also be seen as an effort to reorient the political loyalty of the samurai toward the nation as a unit.

[17] Thus Kido wrote in a memorial in 1873: "There are now in this country thirty million people who do not yet enjoy the full protection of the government, poor and ignorant persons who have no rights and *do not yet know that the nation exists.*" Quoted in Sansom, *op.cit.*, p. 332 (emphasis added). My emphasis on the local level should not obscure the fact that the main effort toward national integration was made at the national level in the form of the development and propagation of the ideology of the emperor system.

paper plans for local administrative systems were developed and, although imperfectly implemented, were kept on the books until the gap between them and reality became too wide. Then they were replaced by new plans which constituted a compromise between the original intentions of the planners and the demands of reality.[18] These tendencies can be seen in various areas, including that of school administration. Here, however, I shall limit myself to the area of general local administration.

In this field three main periods have to be distinguished. The first of these began with the family registration decree of 1871 and ended with the enactment of the so-called Three New Laws in 1878; the second is the 1878–1888 period during which the Three New Laws were in operation; and the third is the period after the enactment of the City Code and the Town and Village Code, promulgated in 1888.[19]

The conflict between the government and the village community was strongest during the first of these periods, when the government was inclined to see the backwardness of the traditional villages as a handicap to modernization. The governing elite consisted of samurai, who as a class had long looked down upon the peasantry and the townspeople. Early peasant reactions to the new regime and its reforms must have confirmed them in this view. Agrarian revolts, com-

[18] Professor Jansen's comment that the Meiji leaders were "parochial urban types" who knew little of the countryside and thus had to learn by experimentation goes far in explaining this phenomenon.

[19] The main periods in the development of school administration ran roughly parallel: the first period began with the School District System (*gakusei*) of 1872 and ended with the Education Ordinance (*kyōikurei*) of 1879; the second is the period of the Education Ordinance and its successor of 1886, the Primary School Ordinance (*shōgakkōrei*); and the third is the period after the revision of the Primary School Ordinance in 1890. For details see Chiba Masaji, *Gakkuseido no kenkyū: kokka kenryoku to sonraku kyōdōtai* (Tokyo, 1962). Most of the comments on the school system in succeeding footnotes are based on this source. The Three New Laws are identified below in note 25.

223

mon in the late Tokugawa period, increased in frequency between the Meiji Restoration and 1873 when they reached a zenith. While there were usually underlying economic reasons for these revolts, many of them arose, in E. H. Norman's words, from "the instinctive opposition of a conservative-minded peasantry towards the innovations of the new government." Thus tumult and rioting greeted decrees announcing reform of the calendar, the abolition of the queue, the legalization of Christianity, the emancipation of the *eta*, vaccination, the establishment of government schools, conscription, the land survey, numbering of houses, and the like.[20] It is thus understandable that the governing elite felt at first that such measures of modernization had to be imposed on the lower strata of society by the government through its own officials. In institutional terms this meant centralization and the bureaucratization of administration. This issue was clearly posed when the system of family registration was instituted in 1871.

For this purpose new districts, called *ku*, were created in each prefecture. Each district encompassed several villages. Within each district new officials—called variously *kuchō*, *kochō*, and *fukukochō*—were to perform the function of setting up the registers. These officials were appointed by the prefectural governors.[21] The appointment of former village officials to these newly established positions was permitted when this seemed expedient. But this was not meant to be the rule. Sometimes the *kochō* came from a different part of the prefecture or even from another prefecture.

[20] E. Herbert Norman, *Japan's Emergence as a Modern State* (New York, 1940), p. 77, and sources cited there; see also Sansom, *op.cit.*, pp. 392f.

[21] This antagonism to the traditional village leaders is apparent in Ōkubo's comment on the new system, in which he wrote of the elimination of the "old and bad customs of the traditional *shōya*, *nanushi*, *toshiyori*, and so forth." Quoted in Ōshima Tarō, "Koken-ryoku to sonraku kyōdōtai," in a collection of essays entitled *Nihon no nōson* (Tokyo, 1961), p. 24.

At first the traditional village officials were bypassed only so far as the new national task of family registration was concerned. But soon the *kochō* were also engaged in tax collection, conscription, and other national business.[22] What had started as an ad hoc arrangement for a single function became a new system of local administration under which the government ruled the people directly through its own officials rather than indirectly through the traditional community leadership.

But while the *kochō* was engaged in such governmental tasks, the old village community continued to serve a variety of economic, social, and psychological needs of the people. It continued, for example, to own grasslands, forests, irrigation works, and fishery rights, and to manage these in the common interest; it provided for community cooperation and exchange of labor; it maintained the communal shrine and arranged communal festivals. It also retained its headman and continued to meet in the traditional *yoriai* and there decide matters in traditional ways. A wedge was thus driven between the district (*ku*) as a governmental unit and the village as a community of cooperative life (*seikatsu kyōdōtai*). At the same time the government attempted to press the traditional villages into the new administrative mold by amalgamations. The following table shows the results of this amalgamation drive:

[22] Similarly, the School District Ordinance of 1872 established primary school districts (*shōgakku*) as the lowest level of the centralized school system. Originally these districts were separated from the traditional towns and villages and from the *ku* established for family registration purposes. The school district directors (*gakku torishimari*) were appointed by the governor, who was guided only by the general rule that he should select "notables living in the area" and that he might appoint the local *kochō* to the position. The traditional village officials were not mentioned in the ordinance. The primary school district was to maintain its primary school as a corporate group by its own contributions. But before long the *ku* took over the collection of contributions, and more and more *kochō* were appointed simultaneously as school district directors.

TABLE I

Year	Number of towns and villages[a]	Year	Number of towns and villages
1874	78,280	1881	71,781
1875	75,942	1882	71,941
1876	73,287	1883	71,885
1877	72,130	1884	71,888
1878	71,111	1885	71,888
1879	71,664	1886	71,067
1880	71,715		

SOURCE: Kikegawa Hiroshi, *Meiji chihō jichi seido no seiritsu katei* (Tokyo, 1955), pp. 68–69.

[a] At end of year.

Thus the number of towns and villages decreased by 7,213 during this span of thirteen years. These amalgamations did violence to the strong collectivity orientation of the traditional villages and to the feelings of exclusiveness which accompanied it. The resistance of the population accounts for the fluctuations noticeable in the table. Sometimes amalgamated entities were permitted to separate again, and in some years separations outnumbered amalgamations.[23]

[23] On this point, see Kainō Michitaka, *Iriai no kenkyū* (Tokyo, 1943), p. 307, and Tokyo Shisei Chōsakai, *Jichi gojūnenshi* (Tokyo, 1940), p. 266. During the period from 1874 to 1886 relatively few actually new villages, e.g. on reclaimed land, were established. The number of such new villages was insufficient to account for the increase in the number of villages in 1880, 1881 and 1882.

Village antagonisms also created difficulties for the maintenance of primary schools by primary school districts as corporate groups. Many districts were divided and many villages succeeded in establishing their own branch schools. Because school district directors lacked the influence which results from personal relations in a particularistic society, they engaged the assistance of the traditional village leaders. Thus the traditional village community asserted itself also in the area of school administration. Since the communal shrine was a spiritual symbol and basis of the traditional village, it is significant that the government announced, three months after the family registration decree, a policy of establishing one shrine, superior to the communal shrines (*gōsha*), for each *ku*. See Chiba Masaji, "Ichi shichōson ichi-jinja no rinen to sōchinju no sei," in *Shakai to Denshō*, VIII (April 1964), 1-19.

The natural villages, which continued to exist side by side with the new artificial governmental districts, were given some legal recognition, however, in October 1876 when an order of the Council of State regulated the public borrowing of money and grain by *ku* and by towns and villages and the purchase and sale of their common property.[24]

This order was an indication that such complete disregard of the towns and villages was beginning to be seen as unrealistic. In the end this attempt to superimpose completely new administrative units in the form of districts failed because, as Home Minister Ōkubo said, it was "in conflict with popular feelings." This recognition was the reason for the promulgation of the Three New Laws in July 1878.[25] The first of these measures abolished the artificial division of the country into districts and reconstituted towns and villages as basic administrative units.[26] However, the towns and villages which

[24] If a *ku* wanted to borrow money or grain, or to buy or sell property owned in common, the seals of the *kochō* and *fukukochō* as well as those of two representatives of each town and village within the *ku* had to be affixed to the pertinent documents. If the loan, purchase, or sale was to be done by a town or village, the seals of the *kochō* and *fukukochō* as well as those of more than 60 percent of the landowners within the town or village had to be affixed. See Kainō, *op.cit.*, p. 338; S. Shimizu, "Local Government in Japan," in Ōkuma Shigenobu, *Fifty Years of New Japan* (London 1909), p. 328. It will be noted that this order abandoned the traditional system of unanimous decision-making in towns and villages.

[25] See Ōkubo's report to the president of the Council of State, March 11, 1878, reprinted in Tokyo Shisei Chōsakai, *op.cit.*, p. 45. The Three New Laws were the Law for the Reorganization of Counties, Wards, Towns, and Villages; the Rules for Prefectural Assemblies; and the Rules for Local Taxes. A fourth law, the Law regarding Ward, Town, and Village Assemblies, promulgated in 1880, completed the system. The ward (*ku*) was a newly established urban unit.

[26] In 1879 the School District Ordinance was superseded by the Education Ordinance which made towns and villages responsible for establishing and supporting primary schools and entrusted the management of these schools to new officials at the town and village level, the School Affairs Commissioners (*gakumuiin*). By 1885 these offices

227

became the units of local administration under the new system differed from the traditional communities of the same name in a number of ways. First of all, they were the results of mergers of traditional towns and villages which were considered too small in area and too weak in finances and administrative talent to execute the new functions required by the national government. Second, while each of the new towns and villages had, in accordance with the law of 1880, its own assembly (*chōkai* or *sonkai*), this assembly was not an informal gathering of family heads but an elected body which dealt only with matters prescribed by national law. These matters were presented to it by an official, the *kochō,* who not only served as the chief executive of the town or village but also had far-reaching control over the deliberations of its assembly. Third, the jurisdictional area of the *kochō* encompassed a number of new towns and villages.[27] Finally, although the *kochō* was now elected, the prefectural governor had to approve his election.[28]

If the earlier system of districts had disregarded the existing towns and villages altogether, the new system aimed at the gradual establishment of viable units of a centralized administrative system out of these traditional towns and villages by a process of amalgamation, bureaucratization, formalization of their decision-making process, and the delegation of national

---

were merged with that of the *kochō*. Finally, the separation of general local and local educational administration was ended by a revision of the Primary School Ordinance (*shōgakkōrei*) of 1886, which followed in the wake of the adoption of the local government codes.

[27] There was thus a discrepancy between the jurisdictional areas of the village executive and the village assemblies. To overcome this discrepancy federated town and village assemblies (*rengō chōsonkai*) embracing the entire jurisdictional area of a *kochō* were instituted for a while.

[28] After 1884 the town and village assemblies nominated three candidates for the office of *kochō*, of whom the governor appointed one. The offices of the heads of *gun* and *ku* remained throughout subject to appointment by the government.

tasks to them. The gradualism which distinguishes the period of the Three New Laws from the abruptness of the previous period was an indication that the continuing strength of parochial orientations was now accepted as a fact of political life. This is not to say, of course, that village life was now viewed with any esteem by the governmental elite. At the assembly of local governors (*chihōkan kaigi*) in February 1880, which discussed the Law regarding Ward, Town, and Village Assemblies, many speakers ridiculed the traditional village meetings (*yoriai*) as crude, uncivilized, superstitious, boss-ridden, and unfit for serious deliberations. The assembly resolved to delete all references to these meetings from the draft before it. The *yoriai*, Matsuda Michiyuki felt, could continue to deal with matters which had been their primary concern in the past, including the ostracism (*murahachibu*) of morally undesirable persons, the management of village festivals and the collection of money for them, and other such matters beneath governmental concern. The new village assembly, on the other hand, should deal only with governmental affairs and should decide them according to formal rules involving the majority principle. This policy was adopted.[29] Village life thus continued to be bifurcated into an official and an unofficial sphere. In the former sphere the new villages were to act through the new village assemblies (*sonkai*) under bureaucratic supervision exercised by the *kochō*. In the latter sphere the old villages were permitted to act through their traditional leaders and their traditional village meetings (*yoriai*) with a minimum of bureaucratic interference. The decision-making process was to be different in the two spheres: the new village assemblies were to adopt the more modern method of majority decision instead of the traditional method of unanimity.[30]

[29] See Kainō, *op.cit.*, pp. 332ff.

[30] This differentiation began with the above-mentioned order of the Council of State of 1876, continued with the Law regarding Ward, Town, and Village Assemblies of 1880, which standardized the or-

The Town and Village Code of 1888, one of the three codes which long formed the legal basis of local government in pre-war Japan, continued the policy of the Three New Laws in essence. In this context the plea for gradualism contained in Kaneko Kentarō's "Opinion on the Local System" of January 1888 is of interest. He enumerated the problems of merging traditional village units. These were partly of an emotional nature. Villagers who were united by kinship ties and who worshiped at the same ancestral shrine felt that they had little in common with the outside groups with whom they were now to be merged. But economic problems were at least equally important. How was one to amalgamate two villages which had for centuries quarreled about irrigation rights? How was one to merge a rich village, owning forests and grassland or storehouses in common, with a poor village which had always provided rural labor for the former? In particular, how was one to merge them if the poorer village had the greater number of inhabitants and was thus likely to influence decisions regarding the use or sale of this property? How indeed was one to avoid a situation in which, when more and less populous villages were merged, the more populous village would run the affairs of the new unit solely in its own interests? Hasty mergers were likely to aggravate such problems. Kaneko advocated "making allowances for geographical emotional attachments and customs and manners" while gradually "undoing the specific solidarities of towns and villages in order to set up, without the knowledge and consciousness [of the people], the basis for creating one town and village out of several of them."

Kaneko's plea was not heeded. The Town and Village Code expressly permitted amalgamations "regardless of the

---

ganization and operation of the new assemblies, and ended with the local government codes of 1888 and 1890. Considering the preference for unanimous decision-making even in today's village assemblies, we must assume that the differentiation existed more in theory than in practice.

objections of interested parties when a town or village does not possess the capacity of fulfilling the obligations made incumbent upon it by law or when it is necessary for the public interest." A mass amalgamation drive, far more intensive than the earlier one of 1874–1886, followed the adoption of the Code. At the end of 1888, a total of 71,314 towns and villages had been in existence. By the end of 1889 their number was 15,820, a decrease of 55,494.[31]

The towns (*machi*) and villages (*mura*) which were thus created were frequently the equivalents of the areas which had hitherto been under the jurisdiction of a *kochō*. Their chief executives, indirectly elected by the town or village assemblies and confirmed in their offices by the governor, now came to be called town mayor (*chōchō*) or village mayor (*sonchō*).

The local government system of 1888, established with the advice of German experts such as Roesler and Mosse, followed, in general, European models. But it also contained elements of compromise between the governing elite at the national level and the elite at the local level. As a concession to the social and economic parochialism existing in the traditional villages, the Town and Village Code provided that they could retain their "separate property or establishments," such as forests, meadows, wells, net-dyeing vats, shrines, cemetery grounds, and similar communal property. Legally these parts of newly amalgamated towns and villages possessing and administering separate communal property of their own became known as "property wards," but in common parlance they were referred to as "*buraku*." Even under the Town and Village Code, therefore, old village communities retained economic and social importance for their inhabitants, continued their traditional processes, and nurtured the former communal attitudes. On the other hand, the new adminis-

---

[31] Tokyo Shisei Chōsakai, *op.cit.*, pp. 265ff; Kainō, *op.cit.*, p. 308. It appears that there was an increase in the number of towns and villages between 1886 and 1888.

trative units, oriented exclusively outward toward government as they were, were less relevant to the lives of the peasants and failed to capture their emotional attachment. This limited, of course, their effectiveness as agencies of national political socialization, in the attempt to replace political parochial orientations by subject orientations.

Itō Hirobumi seems to have recognized the problem. Reminiscing years later about the creation of the new constitution, he praised the mass of the rural population as "honest, industrious, ready to sacrifice their interest for the sake of their neighbors and especially of their village communities." He continued: "In the past . . . family and quasi-family ties permeated and formed the essence of every social organization . . . and moral tenets laid undue stress on duties of fraternal aid and mutual succor." While granting that "this social peculiarity was not without beneficial influences," he recognized that it also exercised "baneful influences on society, for in a village community, where feelings and emotions hold a higher place than intellect, free discussion is apt to be smothered [and] the attainment and transference of power [is] liable to become a family question of a powerful oligarchy."[32]

Yamagata Aritomo, the architect of the Meiji local government system, also wanted the institutions of local government to foster an affirmative attitude toward the state. They would do so, he felt, if they provided a means for the fulfillment of patriotic obligations, as had his other great achievement, the conscription system.[33] This new patriotic obligation consisted

[32] Hirobumi Itō, "Some Reminiscences of the Granting of the New Constitution," in Ōkuma Shigenobu, *Fifty Years of New Japan* (London, 1909), p. 124.

[33] This point, repeatedly stressed by Yamagata, found expression in the official explanation of the Codes, published in the *Official Gazette* on April 25, 1888: "Bearing responsibility for local affairs will be the duty of the local populace on the same principle as the obligation that young men, as subjects of the emperor, have of serving in the armed forces." (See George O. Totten, *Japanese Municipal Government under*

in rendering assistance to the state by participating in the administration of local affairs. The immediate benefit to the government would be that it would "be spared unnecessary details." Other benefits would lie in the area of political socialization: by participating in the administration of local affairs the people would learn "the difficulties involved in the execution of these affairs." Thus local government would "unite the ideas and hopes of the people and the policies and aims of the officials."[34] In doing so, it would counteract a danger which Yamagata feared above all else: the spread of ideological movements and of party strife into the realm of local government. Local government, he felt, had to be isolated from the currents which were about to engulf government at the national level at a time when a parliament was being created and political parties were already active. Otherwise "[political] influence will extend to the people of the villages, they will hate each other, violence will arise and places which are tranquil, like a spring day's breeze, and which are well suited for the bringing up of one's children and grandchildren, will change to places of noise and struggle."[35] Compared with this danger, parochialism seemed at worst a minor problem. Parochialism could help in preventing the undesirable

---

Meiji and Taisho, 1868-1925, unpublished M.A. thesis, Columbia University, 1949, p. 50; Tokyo Shisei Chōsakai, *op.cit.*, p. 256.) It was consistent with this view of the matter that a person, elected to office, could refuse to serve only for certain reasons enumerated in the law, and that sanctions were provided for an unwarranted refusal to serve.

[34] The quotes are partly from the official explanation of the new local government system and partly from Yamagata's essay on the establishment of the conscription and local government system in Kokka Gakkai, *Meiji kensei keizai shiron* (Tokyo, 1919), p. 379.

[35] Quoted from Yamagata's essay, *op.cit.*, p. 428; see also Ishida Takeshi, *Meiji seiji shisōshi kenkyū* (Tokyo, 1964), p. 110. In his instructions to the conference of prefectural governors on December 25, 1889 (translated in W. W. McLaren, "Japanese Government Documents," *Transactions of the Asiatic Society of Japan*, XLII:1, Tokyo, 1914, p. 419) Yamagata expressed the same ideas.

spread of political ideas to the countryside. It is in keeping with this notion that the Imperial Edict promulgating the City Code and the Town and Village Code declares the "maintenance and strengthening of the traditional customs of neighborly solidarity" to be one of the purposes of the local entities.[36]

It seems clear from the foregoing that Itō felt that communal loyalties below the village level would have to be broken down if the village was to perform its intended political socialization function, while Yamagata denied this. Implicit in Itō's and Yamagata's views were differing strategies of modernization. Yamagata apparently believed that modernization should not engulf all segments of the society— or, at least, that it should not engulf all segments simultaneously. The countryside, which had to play a very important supporting role in industrialization, was to be "held constant."[37] Yamagata's view prevailed in practice. The villagers' life continued to center around the close neighborly relationships of the *buraku* to which he "belonged" and which fulfilled

[36] Quoted by Ishida (*op.cit.*, p. 114) from the *Official Gazette*, No. 143, of April 17, 1888.

[37] Two further points regarding the role of the countryside in the modernization process need to be made: While there are certain advantages in "holding the countryside constant," it is also necessary to "energize" it so that it will support industrialization to the fullest extent possible. In the latter respect the Meiji leaders could build on tendencies existing in pre-Restoration Japan. It appears that in time bureaucratization and routinization tended to blunt these tendencies. Rural initiative, which was quite conspicuous in the early Meiji period, was gradually replaced by an attitude of compliance with and reliance on "those above." See R. P. Dore, "Agricultural Improvement in Japan: 1870-1900," *Economic Development and Cultural Change*, IX:1, pt. II (Oct. 1960), 69-91. Second, "holding the countryside constant" pays diminishing returns as modernization progresses. In time it may actually become dysfunctional. Ultimately the rural population has to be brought into the mainstream of national development rather than being sheltered from it. As will be shown, conservative leaders often fail to recognize this need, especially if they are committed to an ideology of agrarianism.

his economic, social, and psychological needs. Government was perhaps somewhat less distant and its actions at times somewhat more pertinent than in the past, but it was still external to the world of the villagers. The village, as a legal entity, was only an extension of this government. It encompassed in its area people of other *buraku* who were outside the individual family's circle of life. Because *buraku* exclusiveness was the obverse side of *buraku* solidarity, the village was fragmented into separate and often antagonistic areal groups. It became an arena for their competition rather than a focus of a shared identification.

While Yamagata's policy fell short of its purpose of socializing the rural population into a subject political culture, it achieved its other aim of keeping the countryside peaceful and stable. Such changes in the political culture as were effected were due not to socialization through local government but to socialization through national agencies, foremost among them the centralized school system, which established a direct link between the people and the political system personified by the emperor.

The persistence of parochial attitudes was, of course, not the only reason for popular apathy toward local government. The institutions created by Yamagata also handicapped the growth of a civic spirit in regard to the new local entities. It would go beyond the scope of this paper to describe these institutions in detail.[38] We may note here only two points: first, the activities of the local entities were largely confined to the execution of national functions. The development of local initiative was thwarted by national assignments and by the scarcity of financial resources allotted to the local entities. Second, the local assemblies were controlled by the local executive, who, in turn, was controlled by the central government officials at the prefectural and national levels. Participation in local government was thus not a very effective

[38] Regarding these institutions, see ch. 3 of my book *Local Government in Japan* (Stanford, 1965).

or meaningful way to work for the solution of local problems.

Popular participation was also greatly restricted. Only male residents who paid a certain minimum amount of direct taxes were citizens (*kōmin*) and had the franchise. Random reports which are available indicate that usually they constituted less than 5 percent of the population. They were divided into classes according to the amount of taxes they paid and each class, regardless of the number of citizens in it, elected an equal number of assembly members. Needless to say, the citizens were landowners in the village, and the assemblymen, whom they elected from among themselves, tended to be still larger landowners because eligibility for office was linked with an even higher tax payment. It was only this group which was to assist the government and, in Yamagata's view, was to be socialized in the process.

Local Political Culture during the Ultranationalist Period

Space does not permit me to discuss developments during the long span of years between 1888 and 1945 in any detail. Mass amalgamations continued. So did the use of the device of permitting the creation of property wards in order to mollify aroused parochial feelings within the merged units. *Buraku* parochialism and the lack of village autonomy made the frequent exhortations of the government for a greater interest in what was spuriously called "local self-government" rather ineffectual. The tensions between government and society, between village and *buraku*, between the desire for a viable administrative system and the desire to maintain traditional community ways remained unresolved.

This tension came to the surface in 1909 and 1910. At that time more than 41,000 of the existing 76,000 *buraku* owned property, and the acreage of *buraku*-owned property was more than three times that of the property owned by towns and villages. Because towns and villages could not levy rents and fees on *buraku*-owned property, this meant a considerable loss of revenue for them. The national treasury had been depleted by the Russo-Japanese War, and the government wanted the towns and villages to assume a greater share of the financial burden for local administration. It was, therefore, interested in increasing their revenues. In addition, the *buraku* were not always prudent in conserving the resources they owned. For both reasons a policy of adjustment and unification of *buraku*-owned forests and lands, i.e. of transferring them to the villages and towns, was instituted. Some progress was made, but many property wards were permitted to continue their existence.[39]

During the ensuing decades Japan's rapidly increasing industrialization and urbanization resulted inevitably in an erosion of the basis for *buraku* cohesion. The period after World War I witnessed a good deal of agrarian unrest. Frictions between tenants and landlords disrupted the communal solidarity of the *buraku*. There were also some *"mura* unifiers" at work—notably the village office, the village school, and the village shrine—so that over time *mura* unity was increasing at the expense of *buraku* isolation.[40] Yet at the same time the *buraku* was given increasing governmental recognition and new tasks as an adjunct to village government. Thus in each *buraku* or group of *buraku* certain administrative chores, such as tax collection, were performed on behalf of the village by a *buraku* leader who served as liaison with the village office. Government-sponsored societies, such as the Reservists' Association, Women's Patriotic Associ-

[39] See Fujita Takeo, *Nihon chihō zaisei hattenshi* (Tokyo, 1949), pp. 157-67. It should be noted that the transfer policy, as implemented, created hardships for poor *buraku* inhabitants whose livelihood depended to some extent on the communal use of *buraku* property. At the same time the government promoted a policy of amalgamating communal shrines, so that each village—and similarly each town and city—would have one shrine. Failing this, an alternative policy called for the establishment of one main shrine (*sōchinju*) in each locality. I am indebted to Professor Chiba Masaji for this information.

[40] John F. Embree, *Suye Mura, A Japanese Village* (Chicago, 1939), pp. 59, 301 and *passim*.

ation, Young People's Association, while organized on a village basis, all had *buraku* subheads.[41]

In the 1930's governmental integration increased as the country mobilized for its war efforts. On the other hand, the radical right developed an ideology of agrarianism (*nōhon-shugi*) which in its original form emphasized parochial rather than subject orientations. A few examples from the writings of Gondō Seikyō, the ideologist of the Rural Self-Help Movement, may convey the flavor: "Generally speaking, there have been since ancient times two principles in the administration of the state. One is to allow the people a life of autonomy, in which the sovereign hardly goes beyond setting examples, thereby giving the people a good standard. In the other the sovereign takes everything on himself and directs all state affairs. If the former may be termed the principle of autonomy, the latter may be termed *étatisme*. Japan was founded in complete accord with the former principle, and this was the ideal of the ancient sages."

According to Gondō, *étatisme* treats the mass of the people as building material. All organizations are set up solely for administrative convenience, and the rulers control the masses through laws and ordinances. The villages, "the foundation of the country and the source of our habits and customs," have been sacrificed to this centralizing nationalism since Meiji days. The ideal state that Gondō wished to establish was based on the native self-sufficient village community in opposition to what he termed "Prussian nationalism."[42] Some national leaders, especially those who had risen from the military, were not unsympathetic to the sentiments underlying this ideology. But, considering the demands of the time, they could hardly base their policies on them. Premier Tōjō, asked in the Diet in 1943 whether the villages were not endangered by the absorption of their labor power into the armament

[41] *Ibid.*, pp. 23, 166f.
[42] Maruyama Masao, *Thought and Behavior in Modern Japanese Politics* (Ivan Morris, ed., London, 1963), pp. 38f.

industry, replied: "This is a point that truly worries me. On the one hand, I want at all costs to maintain the population of the villages at 40 percent of the total population. I believe that the foundation of Japan lies in giving prime importance to agriculture. On the other hand, it is undeniable that industry is being expanded, chiefly because of the war. . . . A harmony must be created by degrees between the two requirements. But, in creating this harmony, care must be taken to avoid making havoc of the Japanese family system. . . . Although things are not proceeding ideally, I still believe that a method can and will be found to establish a proper harmony in the Japanese manner."[43] As Maruyama notes, this answer reveals "the acute anxiety of the ruling class in the midst of the unprecedented turmoil of total war to preserve the village as a foundation of the Japanese family system."

Total war demanded a more intensive mobilization of the people. Mere obedience to law was no longer sufficient. Passivity was to be replaced by positive "assistance to the imperial rule." To propagate a more activist spirit a movement for national spiritual mobilization was inaugurated in 1937. It is highly significant that the schemes developed in 1940 used the *buraku* (and its somewhat artificial urban counterpart, the *chō*) as their basic organizational unit. The vehicle of the new activism was to be the community, not the individual or the administrative village. These schemes were the creation of the Imperial Rule Assistance Association—which replaced all political parties—and the establishment of a nationwide system of neighborhood associations.

The Imperial Rule Assistance Association was based on the ideas of Prince Konoe's New Order Movement. It was to give a popular foundation to political leadership by organizing the masses, somewhat according to the models of German and Italian totalitarianism. But the association never became a political movement in the same sense as its European prototypes. It denied the notions of individual political commitment, which

[43] *Ibid.*, p. 47.

formed the basis for the European movements; it was organized from the top down without any leeway for popular initiative or spontaneity; and as a consequence it was shot through with bureaucratism. It also had to deny itself the propagandistic advantage of claiming that it embodied the will of the people, because the notion of a government based on the will of the people was contrary to the principles of the emperor system.[44] The point to be stressed here is that the movement failed to separate the individual's political orientations from the diffused solidarities of the village community. The system of neighborhood associations reinforced the traditional community by giving to the *buraku* legal standing as an important echelon of local government.[45] Control from above was rigid. *Burakukai* leaders were normally appointed by the mayor; the days and hours of the regular monthly meetings (*jōkai*) and the agenda were determined by instructions from higher echelons of government. The *burakukai* assumed such administrative tasks as rationing, civil air defense, and fire fighting. But it was also intended to serve a socialization function, defined as "the moral training of people" and the "fostering of their spiritual solidarity." As to the content of this socialization, the statement of purpose in Home Ministry Ordinance No. 17 of September 11, 1940, invokes both "the spirit of neighborly solidarity" and "the principle of assistance of the imperial rule by all subjects," thus reflecting the somewhat conflicting ideological commitments of the national leadership to both parochialism and activism on behalf of national goals.

[44] Maruyama (p. 73) notes that at the outset it was said that the association was designed to "transmit the will of the authorities to the people, and to articulate the will of the people to the authorities." However, this formulation was objected to as being contrary to the national polity (*kokutai*), so that the second half of the statement was changed to "make the conditions of the people known to the authorities." Maruyama quotes a pamphlet of the association as follows: "The important thing is to handle government policy with the speed and harmonious cooperation that prevails in a family."

[45] The governmental unit was called *burakukai*. An echelon below the *burakukai*, the *tonarigumi*, consisted of about ten households.

To sum up: according to the plans of the leaders a partici-patory subject culture was to be created while maintaining parochial orientations. Japanese subjects were to become po-litically active without at the same time developing specifi-cally political attitudes; activism was to be achieved without separation of the individual from the diffuse solidarity nexus of his collectivity; political mobilization was not to lead to political modernization.

Popular Political Participation in Postwar Japan

The postwar Occupation was dedicated to the democrati-zation of Japanese politics. It considered local self-govern-ment—"grassroots democracy"—an important training ground for democratic participation on the national level. At the lowest level the village was to provide such a training ground. The Local Autonomy Law, which replaced the Meiji local government codes in 1947, lessened central controls; made the village mayor, now directly elected by all inhabitants of vot-ing age, accountable to his assembly; increased the assembly's role in local decision making in general; and provided for a degree of direct democracy in the form of a modified system of popular initiatives, including the recall of mayors and assemblymen. Increased possibilities for meaningful partici-pation, it was hoped, would raise the level of civic interest and consciousness. However, civic interest in the village as a unit continued to be weak. The fact that the inhabitants of the vil-lage thought of themselves primarily as members of *buraku* communities handicapped its growth.

Although the *burakukai* were first deprived of their governmental character and then outlawed in 1947, the *buraku* continued its existence as a social unit. Clandestinely it also continued to perform some functions for the village administration. Even today the villagers tend to relate to the village indirectly, the *buraku* serving as intermediary in this relationship. Thus village assembly elections are essen-tially elections of *buraku* delegates to the village assembly. In many cases the informal *buraku* leadership nominates a candidate, and the *buraku* inhabitants vote for him as a block to insure the *buraku*'s representation on the assembly. The voter casts his ballot not as an individual, but as a member of a collectivity; voting in accordance with individual interests arising out of class, occupational, and other differences is looked upon with opprobrium as an interference with the "peace and unity of the *buraku*." Social pressure is applied to ensure the absence of deviance, including abstention. The vote is an expression of communal solidarity, not of civic competence. The development of civic or political consciousness is thus stunted.

Because group solidarity is highly valued, a voter turnout at elections of nearly 100 percent becomes a matter of pride. The nationwide voting rate in village assembly elections is normally above 90 percent, and in some areas it often exceeds 95 percent. But this rate, which is higher than that in any other type of election, indicates the absence rather than the presence of individual political interest.

The assemblymen, thus elected, are naturally conservative (although they usually run as independents). Because they are *buraku* delegates, they see the issues before the assembly from the standpoint of their own *buraku*, not from the standpoint of the village as a whole. The village bylaws—most of them handed down from higher levels of government in the form of model bylaws—are enacted without debate, regardless of the general significance of the policy involved. Only measures affecting one *buraku* or group of *buraku* differently from others arouse interest, debate, and the play of pressures. The question whether a new village schoolhouse should be located in one or the other *buraku*, whether village funds should be expended for the repair of roads in one or the other *buraku,* or whether the village should be merged with a village adjoining one or the other *buraku* are examples of such issues.

Socialized in the environment of the *buraku* and deriving

their positions from it, the assemblymen transfer the norms of decision-making of small functionally diffuse face-to-face groups to the village assembly. Regardless of the provisions of the law in this respect, the typical method of decision-making is that of the *buraku* meeting: recommendation and consensus (*suisen-iginashi*). After a seemingly endless and somewhat indirect discussion, a recommendation, supposedly embodying the consensus of the group, is made and in the absence of objections adopted. The raising of objections would be improper as an indication of a breakdown of group solidarity. Such a system provides little room for the development of the type of responsible individualism which was the basis for de Tocqueville's assumption that town meetings are the grammar schools of liberty and for Bryce's notion that they are "tiny fountainheads of democracy."[46]

Village government thus largely fails to provide the socialization for democratic participation which the Occupation envisioned. It would go beyond the scope of this paper to describe the effect of this failure on the political culture of Japan. But it is important to note that the political process on higher levels of government is strongly influenced by it. The *buraku* is called the "womb of elections"; it constitutes the basic unit of the constituency or *jiban* of conservative politicians who manipulate communal solidarity for political purposes. The resultant deviation from the ideal model of democratic participation is widely felt as a flaw of the political system. Professor Fukutake expresses this point of view when he writes: "The undemocratic character of Japanese politics is linked to that of the *buraku*—or, each depends on the other."[47]

---

[46] Alexis de Tocqueville, *Democracy in America* (New York, Vintage edition, 1954), p. 90; James Bryce, *Modern Democracies* (New York, 1921), I, 131. On *buraku* decision-making see Beardsley, Hall, and Ward, *Village Japan* (Chicago, 1959), p. 354.

[47] Tadashi Fukutake, "Village Community (*buraku*) in Japan and Its Democratization," in Robert J. Smith and Richard K. Beardsley,

The Future of Rural Political Participation

Embree noted in 1939 that the isolation and solidarity of the *buraku* were on the wane. This trend has continued and gathered momentum since then. The total area occupied by *buraku* and the number of those socialized in *buraku* settings are shrinking as industrialization and urbanization increase.[48]

---

eds., *Japanese Culture, Its Development and Characteristics* (Chicago, 1962), p. 87. The linkage has been noted by many writers on this subject. See, e.g., Beardsley, Hall, and Ward, *op.cit.*, chs. 12 and 13; Robert E. Ward, "Urban-Rural Differences and the Process of Political Modernization in Japan: A Case Study," in *Economic Development and Cultural Change*, IX:1, pt. II (Oct. 1960); Kurt Steiner, *Local Government in Japan*, chs. 15, 16, and summary. In Japanese a great number of studies of "political consciousness" (*seiji ishiki*) focus on the linkage.

[48] In this context, two recent governmental programs must be mentioned: Another mass amalgamation movement began with the Law for the Promotion of the Amalgamation of Towns and Villages of 1953 and continued with the Law for the Promotion of New Cities, Towns, and Villages of 1956. By August 1, 1961, the number of villages had been reduced from 7,640 (as of September 30, 1953) to 977. The effect of this movement on the *buraku* is not entirely clear. There is some evidence that it increased the psychological distance between the villagers and the administration of the newly created local units. This may have strengthened the *buraku*, but it may also have strengthened the cohesion of the villages which were amalgamated. In a development paralleling the Meiji amalgamations, they were often permitted to retain their property. They may thus become new intermediary sublegal social units above the *buraku* level. In this case the movement would contribute to the erosion of the *buraku*. Other evidence—e.g. regarding the effect of the role of the *buraku* in elections in the new and larger districts which have come into being— seems to support the latter view. The other program is the promotion of the construction of new industrial cities, which is part of larger plans for economic development. Under it, industrial core cities are being established in hitherto rural areas. As this program is realized, factories and huge apartment complexes, inhabited by newcomers who do not share the communal spirit of the farming population, invade the countryside. The far-reaching sociological changes, which must be expected, will undoubtedly disrupt the pattern of *buraku* life.

The *buraku* becomes less important to the farm family as farming ceases to be the only source of its income. Improved means of communication and transportation bring the outside world closer to the *buraku*; increasing mechanization of agriculture makes the farmer less dependent on the cooperation of his neighbors. The communal forest, once the main source of fuel, is becoming less important as other fuels become available, and as electric cooking and heating appliances find their way to farm houses. Chemical products decrease the importance of the communal grassland as a source of fertilizer. Its importance as a source of feed is lessened as feed becomes a specialized agricultural product and is sold by dealers in towns and villages. The contractor from the nearest town is hired more frequently for road repairs which previously were a community responsibility. The contributions in money and labor which *buraku* members make become rationalized. As Professor Fukutake states, a growing occupational heterogeneity leads to the splitting away of functionally specific groups from the *buraku* community.[49]

The solidarity of the *buraku* in voting is now often justified in terms of interests rather than values: if all *buraku* inhabitants vote together they will get a larger share of the grants which the village receives from the prefecture and from the central government. Thus the orientation toward governmental outputs is increasing, and the *buraku* in setting for itself rational goals becomes a sort of nonassociational interest group for limited, definite, and essentially political objectives. In this process the psychological distance separating it from the village office shrinks. To quote the authors of *Village Japan*:

> *Mura* government as the agent of higher professional bureaucracy has been called on to carry out a growing number of functions having a direct, constant, and highly important bearing on the daily lives and fortunes of its

[49] Fukutake, *op.cit.*, p. 86.

inhabitants. At the same time, the average farmer's legal capacity to participate in and direct the policy and actions of this government has been substantially increased. As a consequence, most persons have a distinctly heightened consciousness of the importance of local government to themselves and their households. They may not yet be strongly resolute in participating meaningfully in the local political process, but they are more interested in this sphere than seems to have been the case before the war. Some of the old mistrust remains, but farmers are no longer so inclined to regard the government of their *mura* as an institution essentially marginal to their wants and welfare.[50]

While the erosion of the *buraku* as a community is viewed with alarm by some conservatives, the belief that agriculture is the base of society is no longer influential in the making of economic policy. Tōjō worried about the absorption of agrarian labor power by industry; former Prime Minister Ikeda, in a move which may involve an agrarian revolution of fundamental significance, specifically planned for the industrialization of the underdeveloped areas of Japan and for a drastic reduction in agrarian labor power. The image of a highly industrialized and urbanized Japan resembling the advanced countries of the West is no longer a nightmare to the leadership. It has become a national aspiration.

The political consequences of this transformation are being taken into account by the leadership. *Buraku* parochialism still permits mobilization of *buraku* inhabitants *en bloc* at election time in favor of conservative candidates. But conservative politicians are beginning to realize that they cannot continue indefinitely to base their future on the lack of political consciousness in rural areas which hitherto assured them solid and automatic support in election after election. The slack resulting from the weakening of traditional be-

[50] *Village Japan*, p. 279.

havior patterns has to be taken up by new types of appeals and by the creation of local party organizations. As the world of the *buraku* shrinks, the possibility of widespread adoption of more positive political attitudes increases. Having passed through the stages of a parochial culture, a parochial subject culture, and a parochial participant culture, Japan may now stand at the threshold of a participant political culture.

CHAPTER VIII

Elections and Political Modernization in Prewar Japan

ROBERT A. SCALAPINO

PERHAPS the most conspicuous symbol of political modernity is that of mass participation elections. Under whatever ideological and institutional rubric, such elections have become the foremost method of seeking legitimization on the part of governments and political elites. Classical democratic theory, of course, held that by means of free and fair elections the citizenry would make their choice among a full range of political alternatives, expressed via competitive political parties and individual candidates. Power would alternate as the governing failed to meet the needs of the governed. Omnipotence would be denied to any single political force or leader. The legitimacy of those in power would constantly be subjected to a testing process. The bonds between ruler and ruled would be frequently renewed through the electoral method.

At least implicit in this theory were several very important assumptions, as political scientists know well. The distance between the major contenders could not be too great if the system were to work. The threat of a sweeping overturn of previous actions could not ensue out of each electoral contest. Moreover, the basic rules of the parliamentary game had to be observed: both sides had to accept the results of an election, and be prepared to honor legitimate requests for another one. The first election could not be the last, and the rights of the minority had to be safeguarded as vigorously as the rights of the majority. Some modicum of fairness had to be maintained, necessarily, if the elections were to be considered valid, although no one in the nineteenth century West assumed that corruption or coercion could be entirely eliminated. The tolerance point, indeed, was considerably higher in the West at an earlier point than can now be recalled, and electoral abuses were omnipresent. The electoral system always rested rather precariously on the edge of legality as far as those who lost were concerned. The movement between ballot and bullet was one often undertaken, and the slow, painful climb toward acceptable procedures and results took many decades.

Until recently, however, whatever the deviations in fact, the theory of elections remained essentially as sketched above. But in recent decades, both the theory and the practice of elections have undergone a certain "broadening." In totalitarian states, mass-participation elections have become an integral part of the pageantry of demonstrating popular consensus behind party or personal dictatorships. The key to totalitarian elections is not choice, but ratification. Techniques to insure overwhelming support have been developed. Voting approaches the nature of an obligation, one of the many duties binding the citizen to the state. To obtain 97% or 99.5% of the vote in such systems is not unusual, nor is a turnout of nearly 100% of the eligible electorate. Indeed, in Communist or Fascist states, percentages short of these marks would now be considered a serious rebuke, with the expected patterns having been so firmly established. It is a striking commentary upon the political span of our age that 51%—even 50.1%—of the vote can often be considered a victory in democratic societies whereas success in a totalitarian state clearly requires over 90% of the vote, however acquired.

The true nature of the electoral process in Communist and Fascist states has not been sufficiently studied, but we are at least aware of the enormous differences that separate that process from the classic democratic model. Selection is not totally absent in the case of totalitarian states, but the element of choice—to the extent that it exists—is likely to be present in the preliminary stages, prior to any general election. In its most critical essentials, the totalitarian electoral process is one of ratification, not decision-making; of consensus, not choice.

Significant variants of this system have developed in many of the new states created in the period since World War II. A number of these states have either one-party or dominant-party systems as is well known, and in many cases the objective is to develop a mass-mobilization party that has organizational roots in every village and district. Once again, the element of selection is generally prominent only at preliminary, intraparty levels. Sometimes functional representation is specified in such a fashion as to limit choice or direct it down certain channels in an effort to obtain "true representation," avoiding a dependence upon the whims of an ill-prepared electorate.

In very basic terms, the new party-election procedures have their ethical and political justification in a concept of tutelage, the necessity of guiding—as well as using—the masses. If the state is to be strong, mass participation is essential. This has become a universal law of modern politics. Mass participation must involve some electoral function, as a part of the mystic of popular sanction for the use of power. It would be unthinkable, however, to allow the masses to *misuse* their ultimate authority, to produce "the wrong result" because of ignorance or through mischief. An avant-garde elite must, therefore, supervise both the political thoughts and the political actions of the society so that the masses will not only participate but participate *properly*.

It is not difficult to develop a moral as well as a political rationale for "guided democracy" in emerging societies. Untended, the people will be immediately corrupted by the electoral process. Not only will their votes be bought, their political judgment will remain narrow and undeveloped. They will respond to purely selfish, strongly local appeals. Free elections will result in competitive parties based upon ethnic, religious, or regional divisions, not policy differences of significance. Thus the divisive tendencies already so deeply implanted in the society will be exacerbated and the nation-building process severely retarded. So runs the argument.

Clearly, "guided democracy," whatever its precise form, places a heavy premium upon the virtue and the wisdom of the ruling elite. If that elite is either purposefully or unconsciously evil, or if it is wrong, few corrective devices exist within the institutional fabric of the polity, and the chances of forceful change vary in proportion to how successfully the prevailing elite has mastered the ingredients of modern power, technical, psychological, and political. There remains, of course, the further question as to whether Lord Acton's maxim concerning the corruption of power does not apply now as in the past. Corruption at the present time, moreover, can have grave international repercussions, especially when it is encased in a totalitarian or authoritarian power structure.

Democratic theory has never been properly based upon a belief in the omniscience of the people. It has rested upon the thesis that *on balance* the people were capable of responding to the broadest issues confronting their society in pleasure-pain terms, and that such a response could be regarded as a legitimate, rational one. Mature democratic theory, however, has never rested upon the argument that each action of the electorate will be rational or "correct," nor, indeed, that man is a totally rational animal. On the contrary, democratic theory at its roots rests upon the thesis that the quotient of irrationality and imperfection in *all* men provides the justification of limiting the powers of *any* man or group, and the need for a constant renewal of the legitimization of political authority under conditions allowing a free response of the governed.

There is no possibility of reconciling the above theories of democracy and the electoral procedures implicit in each. Nor is there any method whereby the substantial paradoxes involved in both major theories (and practices) can be removed, and in any case that is not the purpose of this essay. In the light of great and continuing conflicts over democratic theory and practice, however, it is interesting to explore the way in which elections were utilized in the course of Japanese political modernization. Japan, it will be noted, by virtue of the timing of her modernization process, was forced to accept the classical democratic theory; none other had been operationalized. Moreover, the Japanese avant-garde elite, however different in political views, generally regarded Western-style parliamentarism as the wave of the future and, with varying degrees of reluctance, sought to work within its framework.[1]

We are, therefore, confronted with a series of intriguing questions. How easy was it to adjust the Western model to Japanese needs, and what modifications or supplements were in fact adopted? To what extent did "free elections" and "competitive political parties" reveal or strengthen socioeconomic divisions or regional separations in Japanese society? How was the nation-building process affected? What accounts for the early development and subsequent maintenance of two major parties in Japan rather than the dominant-party pattern so characteristic of most emerging societies today?

To seek answers to these questions, or at least, to pose certain hypotheses concerning them, we must concentrate upon the very precise data pertaining to prewar Japanese

---

[1] It is for this reason that I disagree strongly with the thesis now being advanced by some scholars that it is not appropriate to inquire into the applicability and workability of Western-style political institutions and values in prewar Japan. In my opinion they are confusing two different issues: an ethnocentric, value-laden approach which not only posits Western-style parliamentarism as the best political system but assumes that it can operate in any society, irrespective of conditions; and an analysis as to why borrowed political institutions and values did not, possibly could not operate successfully in a different political milieu, whatever the commitments of the political elite at certain points. The former approach is naturally to be criticized, difficult although it may be to rise above one's cultural and political prejudices. The latter approach is vitally significant, given the central political trends of our times, particularly with respect to emerging societies. For one recent example of the confusion on these issues, see John W. Hall and Richard K. Beardsley, *Twelve Doors to Japan* (1965), particularly ch. 10.

elections available to us. The most complete data available relate to elections for the House of Representatives, and for our purposes, this data should also prove most helpful in approaching the above questions.[2] Election statistics are available on a district by district basis beginning with the second general election of 1892.[3] Thus breakdowns by prefecture are possible for the entire period between 1892 and 1937, a period representing almost the full span of parliamentary politics in prewar Japan. Using election statistics comparatively, we can observe closely the evolving nature of the Japanese party system and, in a broader sense, the unfolding of certain vital aspects of the whole process of Japanese political modernization. This in turn can lead us to ponder the applicability of Japanese modernization—at least in the terms of reference with which we are here concerned— to the emerging societies of today.

The Electoral Record, 1892–1937

Before setting forth any hypotheses, let us turn to a close examination of selected patterns, beginning with the second general election of February 15, 1892. This election, incidentally, was typical in many respects of an early election in an emerging society. First, it was marked by violence and charges (undoubtedly justified in some measure) of governmental repression.[4] Japan had had little experience in the practice

[2] All statistics presented here are taken from Tōyama Shigeki and Adachi Yoshiko, *Kindai Nihon seijishi hikkei* (Tokyo, 1961). A detailed version of the electoral returns for the selected general elections from 1892 to 1937 treated in the following section is set forth separately in the appendix to the present volume.

[3] The first election, held in 1890, was not included in this study because a different system of voting prevailed, making comparison more difficult, and also because statistics on that election are not included in the national survey. The twenty-first election, held in 1942, is of no significance here because it was state-sponsored, with only one party participating.

[4] For the general background of these elections, see my *Democracy and the Party Movement in Prewar Japan* (Berkeley, 1962).

—or idea—of democratic elections. The government was prone to regard the so-called popular parties as dangerous, if not subversive. Such a position was not totally irrational. The possibility of a resort to force still lingered in the minds of certain governmental opponents despite the failure of the Satsuma Rebellion.

In any case, most Japanese officials who made up the top echelons of government deeply distrusted the concept of political parties and were unwilling to identify themselves openly with partisan politics. In the main—and understandably—they held to the concept of a "transcendental" government, a government above "clique" or "faction," with all members serving as representatives of the throne, hence symbols of unity, not diversity. (An adequate substitute perhaps in the eighteenth century for the later concept of a monolithic party representing "the people," but less clearly adequate at the end of the nineteenth century.)

Despite the wishes of the modernizing oligarchy that governed Meiji Japan, the times dictated an acceptance of parliamentarism and free, competitive elections. The challenge was thus to adjust these to the needs and nature of Japanese society. The Meiji leaders used the primary techniques known to them: limitations upon the role of the Diet within the Japanese institutional structure; within the Diet, coequal power between the elected and the appointed Houses. These techniques, it might be noted, differed in type, but not in intent from many of those imposed by emerging societies of today. The Meiji elite, however, had one additional restraint available which is not used today: suffrage limitation. The first electorate was indeed an exclusive one, limited to the some 300,000 males who paid a national tax of 15 *yen* or more, out of a total population of over 30 million.

Whatever their qualms, however, once the Meiji leaders had committed themselves to the classical democratic pattern, despite safeguards and limitations, they would be forced ultimately to play the game in some conformity with the general rules. Thus even in the election of 1892 a progovernment party had been created under the name of the Chūō Club. Moreover, a second party, the Kinki Kokutai, was considered progovernment as were most independents, and government support went to these forces.

In the second general election five parties received a sufficient number of elected candidates to be listed separately. Two of these were the so-called popular parties, the Jiyūtō and the Kaishintō. Two were the progovernment parties noted above, and the fifth was the Dokuritsu Club, most of whose members professed neutrality between the government and popular forces but which was a party sometimes listed with the popular forces. In addition, there were a large number of minor-party and independent candidates.[5]

In technical terms, therefore, Japanese parliamentarism began with a multiparty system, and as we shall note this continued throughout the prewar period. The 1892 election, however, demonstrated clearly that only one party, the Jiyūtō, could be considered a truly national party. The Jiyūtō ran a total of 270 candidates for the House of Representatives in 44 of the 45 *ken* and *to*,[6] electing 94 in 34 of these. (The House at this time contained 300 members.) The second-ranking party, the Chūō Club, ran only 94 candidates in 25 *ken* and *to*, electing 83 in 23 of these, representing approximately one-half of the Japanese prefectures. The second "liberal party,"

[5] The general election statistics make a distinction between those "minor parties" polling a sufficient vote to have some significance on a national scale, and those with purely local or individual relevance. For example, many of the minor parties included in the minor-party–independent category were little more than one-man–one-party types, and there were often scores of these. Moreover, a "candidate" was listed even if he received only a single vote. Thus this final category must not be taken too seriously in terms of number of candidates.

[6] Japan at this time had 42 *ken* (prefectures) and 3 *to* (metropolitan districts), namely Tokyo, Osaka, and Kyoto. Hokkaido and Okinawa were not involved in the early elections. See Appendix for a consolidated list of these election figures.

the Kaishintō, ran 106 candidates in 29 *ken* and *to*, electing 37 in 17. The Dokuritsu Club ran 34 candidates in 17 *ken* and *to*, electing 32 in 15. The Kinki Kokutai, as its name suggests, was essentially a local party confined to the Kinki district running 12 candidates in Osaka and Hyōgo prefecture, and electing all 12.

Thus, while the Jiyūtō had secured only 31% of the elected candidates, it alone among the parties had run a sufficient number of candidates to vie seriously for a Diet majority. Its percentage of victorious candidates to those run was relatively low (35%), reflecting inadequate financing and government interference, no doubt. When Jiyūtō results are observed on a prefectural basis, one notes that the center of Jiyūtō strength lay in northern and central Honshu and Shikoku.[7] In Kantō, the party obtained 52% of the lower House seats, although it did not win a single seat in Tokyo city. It got 40% of the seats in Tōhoku, 38% in Shikoku, and 32% in Chūbu. In southern Honshu and Kyushu the party was comparatively weak: 23% in Chūgoku, 18% in Kyushu, and 14% in Kinki.

The Chūō Club obtained 28% of the elected candidates,

---

[7] Modern Japan can be divided into nine regions, and since we shall use them for analytical and comparative purposes throughout this paper, it would be well to define them here: (1) Hokkaido, the northernmost island; (2) Tōhoku, northeast Honshu, encompassing the prefectures of Aomori, Akita, Yamagata, Iwate, Miyagi, and Fukushima; (3) Kantō, eastern and portions of central Honshu, including Gumma, Tochigi, Ibaraki, Chiba, Tokyo, Kanagawa, and Saitama; (4) Chūbu, central Honshu, including Niigata, Toyama, Ishikawa, Nagano, Yamanashi, Gifu, Shizuoka, and Aichi; (5) Kinki, south central and eastern Honshu, encompassing Shiga, Kyoto, Fukui, Ōsaka, Nara, Wakayama, and Mie; (6) Chūgoku, southern Honshu, including Shimane, Tottori, Hyōgo, Okayama, Hiroshima, and Yamaguchi; (7) Shikoku, including all four prefectures on that island, Kagawa, Tokushima, Kōchi, and Ehime; (8) Kyushu, the entire southern island encompassing its seven prefectures, Fukuoka, Saga, Nagasaki, Ōita, Kumamoto, Miyazaki, and Kagoshima; (9) Okinawa, the main island and the surrounding islands.

scoring a significantly higher percentage of victorious candidates to candidates run (88%). The advantages of government sponsorship were numerous, and this, of course, continued to be true throughout prewar Japanese political history. However, the real stronghold of the government (Chūō Club) was in Kyushu. Nearly one half (31) of its elected candidates came from Kyushu, representing 70% of the seats of that region. The party did reasonably well in Chūgoku (34%), Tōhoku (31%), and Chūbu (29%), but it was extremely weak in Kantō (9%), Kinki (9%), and Shikoku (5%). The Kinki statistic may be somewhat misleading since the government scored via the Kinki Kokutai in that region.

The second "popular" party, the Kaishintō, ran less than half the number of candidates run by the Jiyūtō, and elected only about a third. This represented 12% of the total House membership, with the same ratio of successful to unsuccessful candidates as the Jiyūtō (35%). One third of the successful Kaishintō candidates came from Kantō, although these represented only 20% of the total Kantō Diet members. The Kaishintō also showed strength in Shikoku (33%). In Tōhoku (3%), Kinki (5%), Chūgoku (11%), and Kyushu (2%), however, the party was extremely weak.

The Dokuritsu Club scored a very high ratio of successful candidates to candidates run, electing 32 out of 34, but its elected candidates came essentially from six prefectures: Toyama and Aichi (Chūbu), Nara and Wakayama (Kinki), and Shimane and Tottori (Chūgoku). These six prefectures accounted for 22 of the 32 victorious Dokuritsu Club candidates. Only in one region—Kinki—did this party get a significant percentage of the seats—29%. Its next highest percentage was 13% in Chūbu.

A large number of minor party and independent candidates ran, totaling 271. In many cases, however, these could not be considered serious candidates. Interestingly, "independents" obtained only 42 seats, 14% of the total House, and a ratio of

17% in terms of victorious candidates to candidates running, which we shall henceforth call the win/loss ratio.

The election of 1892 indicated that Japan had only one truly national party at this point, namely the Jiyūtō. Of the other parties, two—the Kinki Kokutai and the Dokuritsu Club— were either wholly or largely sectional and weak in Diet representation (4% and 11% respectively); the Kaishintō while more national in scope was also far behind the Jiyūtō in full national representation and in strength. The Chūō Club, close to the Jiyūtō in elected candidates, had a far greater regional imbalance, obtaining less than 10% of its seats in three of the seven great regions of Japan, and this despite the fact that it enjoyed some government support.

Measured from the perspectives of our times, the extraordinary aspect of this election is that the government had not really exerted itself to establish a major party dominated by it, and then assured the victory of that party. The government, to be sure, had not been unconcerned with the election. Arrests, the surveillance of key opposition candidates, funds dispensed via the Home Minister to "friendly" forces were all used, and no doubt helped to keep the margins of the popular parties, particularly the Jiyūtō, down. Measured against possible actions that could have been taken, however, these techniques were mild and amateurish, primarily because the top Meiji leaders were still essentially ambivalent about the critical question of how they should regard parties and the electoral process, and the relation of these to their own political power. Consequently, the most powerful popular party, the Jiyūtō, operating essentially in the rural areas via its ties with the landowning class, had surrounded the urban citadels of governmental (and industrial) power. Only in Kyushu, where a significant portion of the Meiji oligarchy had strong regional ties, was the Jiyūtō weak.

In many respects the 1892 election demonstrates the fact that Japanese political modernization differed considerably from the modernization efforts of most emerging societies to-day. The Japanese experiment was conducted within the framework of classic democratic assumptions and could be fitted into the broadest Western currents of the time, albeit with "special characteristics" befitting the differences of culture, timing, and immediate problems that marked Japanese society.

Let us now turn to the fifth general election, which was held approximately six years later, on March 15, 1898.[8] The intervening years had been filled with political conflict and instability. Strife between the government and the popular parties had caused repeated dissolutions of the Diet. The national political process, at least as viewed by contemporaries, was working badly. Nevertheless, in contrast to the election of 1892, the fifth general election was devoid of violence and conducted with reasonable fairness. Prime Minister Itō, far less hostile to the concept of political parties than some of his colleagues, had not ordered an all-out campaign of opposition to the popular parties. Indeed, Itō is reported to have promised Itagaki, the Jiyūtō leader, a Cabinet position after the election. Thus, although a new party, the Kokumin Kyōkai, had taken the place of the Chūō Club as a progovernment party, the two popular parties, the Jiyūtō and the Shimpōtō (the old Kaishintō), were unhampered in their campaigns. One additional party, the Yamashita Club, was also in the race, representing a group of businessmen who did not belong to any established party but were generally on the conservative, progovernment side.

In general, the fifth election gave evidence of movement toward a two-party system. The Jiyūtō retained its position as the dominant party in Japan, but by a somewhat narrower margin than in 1892. Running 233 candidates in 42 *ken* and *to*

---

[8] While we have prepared detailed data on each national election, we have chosen to be selective in our presentation prior to 1920, attempting at the same time not to omit any elections that would alter or change the basic themes here presented.

(out of 45), it elected 105 in 35 of these. In percentage of elected candidates, its greatest strength was in Chūbu (41%), Kantō (39%), Kinki (40%), Shikoku (62%), and Chūgoku (33%), indicating a wide distribution of power throughout central and southern Honshu, and in Shikoku. It did not do badly in Kyushu, moreover, obtaining 27% of the elected candidates. Only in Tōhoku where the results of 1892 were decisively reversed did the Jiyūtō run poorly (6%). In both its win/loss ratio and in the percentage of Jiyūtō victors to total Diet membership, the party bettered the record of 1892: 44% to 35% in the former case, 35% to 31% in the latter. The Jiyūtō could now claim to be a party with formidable strength in six of the seven major regions of Japan, and it continued to be the only party posting a sufficient number of candidates to make a command of the lower House of the Diet possible.

In comparison with 1892, however, the gains of the Shimpōtō in the direction of national stature were the more striking. In the 1898 elections, the Shimpōtō ran 174 candidates in 36 *ken* and *to*, electing 103 in 34. It did particularly well in Tōhoku, with 81% of the elected candidates, but it also showed strength in Chūbu (39%), Shikoku (33%), Kantō (32%), and Chūgoku (30%). In all of these regions except Shikoku, where the percentage remained the same, these results represented a substantial advance. Only in Kyushu, where the party obtained 14% of the elected membership, did weakness continue, but that figure must be compared with 2% in 1892. Thus the Shimpōtō could also claim national status at this point, with strength in six of the seven major regions. Its popular vote was still considerably lower than that of the Jiyūtō (164,504 to 191,528), but in its win/loss ratio, it had obtained much better results (59% to 44%), and it was only 1% behind the Jiyūtō in total House of Representatives strength (34% to 35%) after the election.

As of 1898, therefore, Japan had two national parties, not greatly unequal in strength. Popular party gains had been made largely at the expense of the progovernment party. The Kokumin Kyōkai, successor to the Chūō Club, did poorly. It obtained only 10% of the total Diet membership, in comparison to the 28% obtained by the Chūō Club in 1892. Only in Kyushu did it do reasonably well (30%), but the Chūō Club had obtained 70% of the seats there in 1892. In Shikoku, Kinki, Kantō and Tōhoku, it obtained less than 5% of the seats, in Chūbu only 7%, and in Chūgoku, 17%. The 1898 election results must have been a clear indication to government leaders that the old system of giving indirect support to a party of adherents, but eschewing direct participation, would not suffice. Indeed, running only 52 candidates, the Kokumin Kyōkai was not a serious contender for power. Even with this small number, moreover, the party did far less well in its win/loss ratio (55%) than had the Chūō Club in 1892 (88%).

The Yamashita Club did not represent a serious force on the national scene. It ran only 28 candidates scattered among 21 *ken* and *to*, electing 26 members in 20. Thus its win/loss ratio was extremely high, but the victors constituted only 9% of the total House membership. Yamashita Club strength was greatest in the two metropolitan regions, Kinki with 22% of the seats, and Kantō, with 10%, indicating that a business-oriented group could naturally expect its best results in Japan's two most prominent urban centers, and particularly in the Osaka-Hyōgo region which was the heartland of Japanese private enterprise. Without extensive rural support, however, no Japanese political party had any long-range prospects in this era, since Japan was still overwhelmingly agrarian, and suffrage restrictions, based upon national tax payments, further emphasized this fact.

Once again, minor party candidates and independents were relatively numerous, with 118 running in 37 *ken* and *to*. Only 37 were elected, however, representing a mere 12% of total House membership, and a fairly low win/loss ratio (31%).

After less than a decade of parliamentary government, Japan appeared to be moving toward a two-party system, with both parties relatively similar in ideology and policies. Minor parties continued to exist, but the two popular parties had now attained a total of 69% of the Diet seats in the House of Representatives, with the next largest group, the minor party–independents, controlling only 12% of the seats.[9]

Upon what conditions did this evolving two-party system depend? Once again, the Japanese experience is more in line with the historic West than with the contemporary non-West. Similarities in ideology and policies on the part of the two main parties were clearly related in part to the nature of the electorate. The participating citizen still came from the upper socioeconomic brackets. Even with the widening of the suffrage, moreover, at least initially, the government could count upon the common core of values and political principles implanted via universal education and nationalist indoctrination cutting across class lines. Relatively untroubled by deep religious, ethnic, or regional cleavages, Japan would find serious political differences only as a product of "natural" socioeconomic evolution, and the central question would then become whether existing parties could adjust to that evolution or would have to be supplanted by new political forces.

Of equal importance, the evolving two-party system in Japan was dependent upon relatively free and fair elections. In the setting of 1898, as we have noted, the government was serving as a "neutral" force, permitting the operation of the electoral process in a reasonably impartial manner. This enabled diverse factions within the key socioeconomic groups to divide freely between the major contending parties, as well as enabling the expression of differences—never total—between rural and urban interests.

Let us examine the character of Japanese politics during this period more closely. Looking at the regional breakdown, one can assert that there were few "safe" regions for a given

[9] The electoral system in this period was mixed, with the great bulk of the districts being single-seat districts, but with a few districts electing more than one representative.

party at this time. Political affiliations appeared to be fluid. Tōhoku was, of course, a striking example: the Jiyūtō had obtained 40% of the seats in 1892, but only 6% in 1898. This was still a period when shifting personal allegiances were a key to political strength. The personal commitments of prefectural and subprefectural "men of influence" were of critical importance, and these commitments were not immutably fixed, nor were the ties of major national political figures permanent.

In the absence of extensive governmental control over the political process—in lieu of one party highly integrated with state organs and bureaucratically organized to encompass the entire community—a certain natural factional division had occurred, and within each party, far more intricate factional groupings. Japanese politics, moreover, had uniquely personal qualities, allegiances which combined economic interests with the obligations of kinship and assimilated kinship ties.

A few other factors are worthy of note. The Jiyūtō was more solidly rooted in most rural areas than was its rival, the Shimpōtō, and rural Japan still dominated the political scene in numerical terms. Kyushu was the one area not well integrated into the national political scene as yet, and it still represented a conservative stronghold. Otherwise, Japan had developed a fairly uniform pattern of political behavior by 1898, indicating the substantial success which the general nation-building campaign had achieved.

Let us turn next to the tenth general election of May 15, 1908, held one decade after the 1898 election. In these ten years, substantial changes had occurred in the Japanese political landscape. A new party, the Seiyūkai, had been fashioned out of the old Jiyūtō, and this party represented a significant merger of bureaucratic and "pure politician" forces, a potent combination of Japanese interest groups including some of the most influential elements of officialdom, sizeable portions of the rural elite, and some urban business interests. The party was headed by Itō Hirobumi himself, and increasing numbers of officials from both national and local levels were joining it, giving the Seiyūkai access to patronage, organization, and funds. Earlier roots in the rural areas were strengthened by local officials' support, and those segments of industry heavily dependent upon government aid naturally gravitated to this party. In comparison, the second "popular" party, now labeled the Kenseihontō, had much less impressive sources of support. Not having consummated an alliance with any significant element within the bureaucracy, the Kenseihontō was essentially dependent upon its traditional ties with certain district leaders, and particularly its support from elements within the intellectual and business communities whose position was more "liberal," less progovernment, or who had personal ties with Kenseihontō leaders.

The results of the 1908 elections are conclusive evidence of the supremacy of the Seiyūkai. That party, running 246 candidates in all 46 *ken* and *to*[10] elected 188 members to the 379 member Diet, obtaining 50% of the seats and electing 76% of its candidates. It led in six of the eight major regions of Japan and tied in the remaining two. In four regions—Kyushu, Kinki, Chūbu, and Kantō—the Seiyūkai obtained 50% of the Diet seats or more. The party obtained 48% of the seats in Shikoku and 39% in Chūgoku. Only in Hokkaido (33%) and northern Honshu (37%) did the Seiyūkai do less well, sharing honors with other parties.

No other party ran a sufficient number of candidates to offer the Seiyūkai substantial competition. The Kenseihontō put up only 92 candidates in 29 *ken* and *to*, electing 70 in 28 prefectures. While this represented 76% of the candidates running under Kenseihontō banners, it amounted to only 18% of the total Diet membership. In terms of percentage of candidates elected, the Kenseihontō did best in Tōhoku, reflecting the past strength of party ties there (37%), but elsewhere it was uniformly weak, ranging from 0 in Hokkaido and 8%

[10] Beginning with the seventh election, Hokkaido participated.

in Kinki to 15% in Chūgoku and Shikoku, 16% in Kyushu, 18% in Kantō, and 24% in Chūbu.

Two minor conservative parties participated in this election, the Daidō Club and the Yukōkai. The former had been established in December 1906, product of an amalgamation of various small factions; the latter had been organized in December 1907 by Diet members who had previously belonged to the Seikō Club, an independent group. Neither party could claim a major showing in any area except Hokkaido, where the Daidō Club secured 33% of the seats. Elsewhere, the percentage was between 1% and 15% for each party. Running 42 candidates in 22 *ken* and *to*, the Daidō Club scored 29 victories in 16, representing a win/loss ratio of 69%, and a Diet standing of 8% of the seats. The Yukōkai presented a similar picture: running 39 candidates in 21 *ken* and *to*, it obtained 29 seats in 14 for a win/loss ratio of 74% and a Diet representation of 8%.

The number of minor party and independent candidates totaled 102, with 63 being elected in 33 *ken* and *to*, giving them 16% of the total Diet seats and a win/loss ratio of 61%.

Once again, Japan had a dominant party system, with all parties except the Seiyūkai relegated to the status of minor forces. Even the Kenseihontō had run less than one fourth the number of candidates to be elected in the 379 member House of Representatives, and had run no candidates in 17 of the 46 *ken* and *to*. At best, therefore, it represented a weak national party, obtaining over 20% of the House seats in only two of the eight major regions of the nation (Tōhoku and Chūbu) and polling scarcely more than one third the votes of its rival (288,243 to 649,858 for the Seiyūkai). What had produced this situation? Any explanation based upon the nature of the electoral system is faulty. In this period, most electoral districts were still one-member districts, but in some districts up to ten or eleven representatives were chosen on the basis of those with the highest number of votes (no run-off). While the latter districts clearly favored minority parties running a small number of candidates, a close examination of such districts shows no great disparity in results from the single-member districts, although a somewhat lower margin for the Seiyūkai was the general rule. The difference, however, was not substantial, and the Seiyūkai carried most plural-member districts, especially rural districts, with minimal trouble.

One can, of course, associate Seiyūkai victory with the much larger number of candidates run, but this is effect rather than cause. More candidates were run because the party's organization and finances permitted this, and these conditions in turn relate to the coalition of forces now supporting the Seiyūkai. The most basic reasons for Seiyūkai dominance lay in the fact that this party alone had that combination of support critical for any emerging society: the political elite already ensconced in power (in the case of Japan, the key civil officials at both national and district levels), the bulk of the rural elite (including most of the prominent landowning families and village headmen), and significant elements within the urban community (particularly those "political merchants" who needed the patronage of the government).

On the surface, moreover, it appeared likely that the Seiyūkai would remain the dominant political force in Japan for the foreseeable future. The combination of holding the critical heights of political authority at every level of government and organizing support from the most articulate private interest groups in depth seemed to guarantee the Seiyūkai a long, uninterrupted tenure in office. At this point, despite different origins, the Japanese party system appeared to be undergoing a basic change whereby a considerable proportion of the bureaucracy, including the top leaders, would be subsumed under the dominant party, giving that party control of government as well as of the electorate, in a manner not previously possible.

However, the twelfth general election, held on March 15, 1915, toppled the Seiyūkai as the dominant party, with the

Rikken Dōshikai taking its place. To understand why such a change could take place, one must study the details of political developments preceding this election. First, despite the preponderant electoral strength of the Seiyūkai, the *genrō* had shifted the top leadership from Saionji, a Seiyūkai supporter, to a nonparty protégé of Yamagata, Katsura. On January 20, 1913, after heated and prolonged struggles in the Diet, Prime Minister Katsura announced the formation of a new party, the Rikken Dōshikai. Beginning with some 81 Diet members drawn from a variety of sources, the Dōshikai eventually encompassed the great majority of the old Kensei-hontō members. Funds, personal ties, and other inducements were used, along with as much pressure as could be applied. By the time of the twelfth election, moreover, this "second party" had undergone a process of "bureaucratization" similar to that involved in the formation of the Seiyūkai more than a decade earlier. Now it too had a strong "official" wing, and access thereby to district and local officeholders. In sum, a political situation akin to a split in the ruling elite had occurred and had been translated into the emergence of a second party capable of challenging the first party. It is vital to note, moreover, that this development had been made possible because a supra-party force in the form of the *genrō* existed in Japanese politics that could make adjustments in political power irrespective of the status of party strengths or the outcome of elections.

Prior to the 1915 election, Okuma had succeeded Katsura as prime minister. Despite the new prime minister's reputation for liberalism, however, his home minister was widely charged with extensive interference on behalf of the Dōshikai in the course of the 1915 campaign. Indeed, the twelfth general election was often labeled the most corrupt election since 1892. Whether true or not, it is clear that prefectural and local officials for the most part worked on behalf of the government that had, in many cases, appointed them to office. The election results we must now examine in detail.

The Rikken Dōshikai, running 200 candidates in 45 of the 47 *ken* and *to*[11] elected 153 members in 41, thus giving it full national status for the first time in its long history of political operation under various names. Its win/loss ratio was 77%, and it had captured 40% of the seats in the 381-seat House of Representatives, making it the first party by a significant margin. Dōshikai strength was greatest in the north—66% in Hokkaido and 51% in Tōhoku. But it had also done well in central Honshu—49% in Kantō, 44% in Chūbu. It dropped somewhat in southern Honshu, Shikoku, and Kyushu (Kyushu 37%; Chūgoku 37%; Shikoku 26%; Kinki 27%).

The Seiyūkai ran 201 candidates in all 47 *ken* and *to*, electing 108 members in 43. Thus, despite the fact that it lost eighty seats in comparison with the previous election, the Seiyūkai remained a major national party. Its win/loss ratio (54%) and its percentage of Diet members (28%) were comparatively low, but the party had managed to maintain its organization throughout the nation, and in terms of the popular vote it had polled about 85% of the Dōshikai vote (446,934 to 523,228). Its strength in terms of percentage of seats captured had been greatest in Kyushu (45%) if one excepts Okinawa, where it obtained 100% of the seats; it also did reasonably well in Tōhoku (37%), Shikoku (33%), and Chūbu (32%). Its poorest showings were in Chūgoku (9%), Hokkaido (17%), and Kinki (18%), basically areas of traditional Seiyūkai weakness.

In this election, three other parties competed, none of them with great success. The Kokumintō, representing remnants of the Kenseihontō that did not join the Dōshikai, ran 40 candidates in 23 *ken* and *to*, electing 27 members in 14, less than one third of the total. The Kokumintō had a win/loss ratio of 68% and obtained 7% of the Diet seats. Its only significant showing was in Chūgoku, where it obtained 20% of the seats. The Chūseikai, a small liberal party, ran 44 candidates in 22 *ken* and *to*, electing 33 in 18, a win/loss ratio of 75%, and

[11] Beginning with the eleventh election, Okinawa participated.

representing 9% of the total Diet membership. The Chūseikai did best in Kinki (20%), followed by Hokkaido (17%), Shikoku (15%), and Chūgoku (13%). All signs, however, indicated that both of these parties were interim in character and would be quickly swallowed up by some other organization. Finally, a small group campaigned under the label "Count Okuma's Supporters," running separately from the Dōshikai. This group posted 21 candidates in 14 *ken* and *to*, electing 12 in 9, giving it a win/loss ratio of 57% and 3% of the total Diet membership.

Other minor party and independent candidates totalled 109, with 48 being elected, 13% of the total Diet membership. These candidates did best in Shikoku (22%) and Kinki (20%).

After twenty-five years of parliamentary government, Japanese politics appeared to have established again a two-party system as a result of a realignment of the critical political forces in the society. By 1915 the official political elite were more or less equally divided between two parties, the Seiyūkai and the Dōshikai, and this political elite, as represented by the leading civil and military officials on the one hand and the "pure politician" elements on the other, constituted the key to political strength. The latter elements were still strongly reflective of the rural, landowning elite, with urban business represented largely via its connections with the bureaucracy and its financial contributions to party coffers, rather than by means of direct political participation.

The Japanese two-party system as it was now operating, moreover, was abetted by the extra-constitutional system of the *genrō*, as we have noted. Had the political mechanism operated automatically and alone via the party-election system, it is likely that the party in power would have always remained in power. Government patronage shading into multiple forms of corruption would have insured this, and indeed, a party in power had never lost an election in Japan up to this point. But via the instrumentality of the *genrō*, Japanese leadership was changed without the use of elections, and then the new leadership proceeded to ratify its power via the electoral process, thus making possible an alternation of power for the parties, albeit one that was not strictly in accordance with democratic theory.

Meanwhile, smaller clusters of politicians, mainly those of the most liberal stripe who could not be accommodated within the two major parties, formed the system of minor parties. Ordinarily two or three such parties participated in every election, each garnering between 6% and 10% of the vote. Their capacity to be operative was certainly due in part to the multiple-district system, but it also had more basic sociopolitical origins. Japanese political society was not yet so highly integrated that one or two parties could dominate the entire nation. Some of these smaller groups served as subcontractors to the primary political groups or operated at local or regional levels where a political vacuum of power existed in terms of major parties.

The Japanese parties, it must be emphasized, were highly elitist organizations, not mass-based or mass-participating parties. Qualifications for membership included sponsorship, dues paying, and other requirements that made it likely that only those with special personal interests in politics would seek membership. This continued to be true as the suffrage widened. While the Japanese citizens voted in sizeable numbers (usually 65%–75% of the eligible electorate cast ballots), they did not consider themselves party members or, in most cases, closely identify with a given party.

Thus the key to party strength was not mass affiliation but ties with "families of influence" in each particular region, support from local and prefectural office holders, and access to funds. Within each major party, moreover, factional rivalries were often severe. Factional leaders frequently competed with each other, seeking to expand their district or national bases through favors and funds to local leaders. The major parties were thus themselves federations, loosely knit coalitions that were capable of being dissolved and reformed with different alliances being effected.

The very nature of Japanese social organization encouraged political pluralism, and this was further abetted by the fact that top leadership, true to this pattern, was collegiate, not single. Japan, in the course of her political modernization, had no charismatic leader except to the extent that the emperor occupied a portion of that role. This fact strongly militated against the emergence of the strong-man monolithic political organization so characteristic of many of the emerging states of our times.

Nevertheless, had it not been for the *genrō* institution, Japan would probably have had a dominant-party system during this entire period instead of the two-party system under oligarchic tutelage which in reality prevailed. This development, to be sure, hinged upon other conditions as well, some of which were roughly similar to those prevailing in the most successful democracies of the period. Both of the major Japanese parties had a broad similarity in basic philosophy and program. In this connection perhaps it is significant that the Japanese parties were essentially pragmatic, not consciously ideological—characteristic of both the socioeconomic groups that predominated in their structures and the general nature of their society. Important policy differences could and did exist between the two major parties from time to time, but these were nonideological in character—practical problems relating to fiscal policy, agrarian problems, forms of subsidization, and similar matters. At no point did this competition involve a massive ideological confrontation, hence all was retrievable.

How heavily should we weigh the influence of the particular electoral system being applied in Japan? Had a single-member district system been completely in operation, the significance of the minor parties would have been further reduced in all likelihood, and even more importantly, a support for intraparty factionalism would have been removed. There can be no doubt that the multimember district system abetted factionalism within the major parties by making possible the election of several candidates from the same party, and thus encouraging intraparty rivalry. At the same time, however, the full use of the single-member district system would have sharpened the pendulum-like swing involved when a party in office used its full powers to secure a majority, and this in turn would have contributed to a weakening of the permanent organization of both major parties and heightened political instability.

The multimember district system, in short, softened somewhat the impact of the use of power legitimately and illegitimately by the government party. But despite the system, the two major parties between them enjoyed throughout this era control of over two-thirds of the House of Representatives. Since the minor parties and independent members were usually themselves divided, they could not ordinarily constitute a formidable bloc interfering with government policy. It was customary, moreover, in the aftermath of an election for the major parties to seek a strengthening of their position by "buying" as many minor party and independent Diet members as possible. Usually the leading party added between ten and twenty members to its roster in this manner. When all of these factors are surveyed, one cannot assert that the electoral system itself was of primary importance in molding the Japanese party system or the nature of Japanese politics in the prewar era.

The aftermath of World War I saw the ripening of what has been called Taishō Democracy. As is well known to students of modern Japan, vast socioeconomic changes had a progressive impact on politics. The narrow oligarchic power base symbolized by the *genrō* was undermined, and new competitive forces entered the field. The parties moved toward the center of the political stage, and thus the importance of elections was enhanced. Suffrage was greatly expanded, and increasing numbers of citizens participated in the political process.

Consequently, it seems important to examine each election between 1920 and 1937, beginning with the fourteenth general election held on May 10, 1920. It is to be noted that prior to this election the Seiyūkai had been returned to power by the *genrō*. Following an unsuccessful experiment with a non-party government led by General Terauchi, the first commoner to be summoned to the post of Prime Minister, Hara Kei, was appointed on the recommendation of the *genrō*. Initially, Hara had to operate with a Diet which he did not control.

Once again, however, a party already in power used a general election to ratify its position. In the 1920 election, the Seiyūkai reestablished its position as the dominant party in Japan in decisive fashion. Running 418 candidates for the 464-member House of Representatives in all 47 *ken* and *to*, it won 278 seats in all prefectures and districts, obtaining a win/loss ratio of 67% and securing 60% of the total House seats. In only one region, Chūgoku, did it fall below 50% of the seats (45%). Elsewhere its victory was almost unprecedented: Okinawa (80%); Shikoku (75%); Tōhoku (74%); Kyushu (71%); Kantō (58%); Chūbu (58%); Hokkaido (56%); and Kinki (52%). In this election a single party had obtained a clear majority in the lower House for the first time in the history of Japanese parliamentarism.

The Kenseikai (the old Dōshikai) ran 240 candidates in 45 of the 47 *ken* and *to*, and elected 110 in 38. This gave it a win/loss ratio of 46% and a total of 24% of the House seats. The Kenseikai did best in Kantō (32%), Hokkaido (31%), Chūbu (27%), and Chūgoku (27%). It was weakest in Okinawa (0) and Shikoku (11%). In comparison with earlier defeats, Japan's second party managed to maintain somewhat greater strength and a broader base of representation. The statistics clearly reveal, however, that the Seiyūkai was the dominant party again. Blessed with powerful official and rural elite support, and with the full power of its office, that party could not be easily challenged by a party that had a much weaker organizational, interest-group base. A very close look at the election figures of 1920 reveals the fact that the Kenseikai generally had its greatest strength in metropolitan and urban centers, testifying to the growing urban-rural cleavage in Japan.

The Kokumintō slipped in the 1920 elections, running 46 candidates in 21 *ken* and *to*, and electing 29 in 14. This represented a win/loss ratio of 63% and 6% of the total House seats. Minor party and independent candidates also fared badly. Some 135 candidates ran, with 47 being elected, representing 10% of the House seats.

The fifteenth general election was held on May 10, 1924, under the auspices of a "neutral" government. Prime Minister Kiyoura was a veteran official without party affiliation. The Seiyūkai, moreover, had been split into two almost equal factions, one calling itself the Seiyūhontō. The cleavage had developed mainly out of personal and power rivalries, not fundamental policy differences. The repercussions, nevertheless, were serious; the party organization was now openly split in almost every district, with funds and personnel correspondingly divided.

Under these circumstances, the Kenseikai became the leading party, running 265 candidates in 45 of the 47 *ken* and *to* (only in Okayama and Okinawa did the party abstain), and electing 152 in 40 prefectures. This represented a win/loss ratio of 57% and 33% of the total House seats. As usual in its periods of strength, the Kenseikai did best in northern and central Japan, garnering 44% of the seats in Hokkaido, 39% in Tōhoku, 38% in Kantō, and 48% in Chūbu. It did poorly in Okinawa (0), Kyushu (19%), Shikoku (21%), and Kinki (22%). The second party in this election was the Seiyū-hontō, which ran 242 candidates in 45 *ken* and *to*, electing 112 in 35, with a win/loss ratio of 46% and 25% of the total House seats. The Seiyūhontō did best in Okinawa (80%) and Kyushu (49%), poorest in Kantō (11%) and Hokkaido (12%). The Seiyūkai was the third party in the 1924 elections, running

218 candidates in 46 *ken* and *to* (all except Saga), and electing 102 members in 32 prefectures. Its win/loss ratio was thus 47%, and it held 22% of the total House seats. Seiyūkai strength was greatest in Kantō (33%) and Shikoku (32%), weakest in Chūbu (12%) and Kyushu (14%).

The old Kokumintō had been reorganized as the Kakushin Club. This party ran 53 candidates in 25 *ken* and *to*, electing 30 in 15, for a win/loss ratio of 57% and 7% of the House seats. Minor party and independent candidates numbered 194, with 69 being elected, 13% of the total House membership.

Thus the 1924 elections saw three national parties in place of the traditional two. Seiyūhontō-Seiyūkai seats when combined equaled 47% of the total House membership, substantially more than the 33% held by the Kenseikai. Even the weakest of these three parties, the Seiyūkai, moreover, maintained its national organization more or less intact, suggesting that it was far from moribund.

Four years later, on February 20, 1928, the sixteenth general election was held, the first election under the new universal manhood suffrage act. This election was held under a Seiyūkai government. The split in the Seiyūkai had been mended, and General Tanaka, Seiyūkai president, had assumed the prime ministership prior to any national electoral ratification. Once again charges of government pressure in connection with the election were numerous, but the results were still extremely close. The Seiyūkai, running 342 candidates in all 47 *ken* and *to*, elected 217 in 47, obtaining a win/loss ratio of 63% and 46% of the House seats. Seiyūkai strength was greatest in Okinawa (60%), Shikoku (56%), Tōhoku (55%), and Chūgoku (53%); weakest in Kinki (36%) and Kyushu (40%). It will be noted, however, that the party had a fairly uniform strength throughout Japan.

The Minseitō (the old Kenseikai) did equally well. Running 340 candidates in all 47 *ken* and *to*, it elected 216 in 47, obtaining a win/loss ratio of 64% and 46% of the House seats, almost precisely the same results as the Seiyūkai. In popular vote, the Minseitō figure was actually the larger, 4,256,010 to 4,244,384. Minseitō strength was greatest in Kyushu (54%), Kantō (48%), and Kinki (48%), regions encompassing most of the great metropolitan areas of Japan. The party was weakest in Chūgoku (38%) and Okinawa (40%), but once again, the range was a fairly narrow one. For the first time in Japanese political history, the two major parties had both elected candidates in every one of the 47 *ken* and *to,* signifying a heightened degree of political integration, an increasing modernization of Japanese politics. The fact that the Minseitō did so well despite the presence of a Seiyūkai government was another indication of evolution toward successful parliamentarism, whatever the validity of the charges that the Minseitō would have won in a completely fair election. Twenty years earlier, the Seiyūkai margin would undoubtedly have been very large.

Together the two major parties obtained 93% of the House seats, a new record and a further indication of progression toward a two-party system. None of the minor parties obtained a significant vote. A businessman's party dedicated to free enterprise, the Jitsugyō Dōshikai, ran 31 candidates and elected 4, giving it 1% of the House seats. The Kakushintō (formerly the Kakushin Club) ran 15 candidates and elected 3, giving it also 1% of the House seats. More important was the fact that in this election for the first time, the so-called proletarian parties participated. Unfortunately for the socialists, their ranks were badly split, with four separate parties in the field. The national statistics group these four parties together under the label "Musan Seitō." They ran a total of 77 candidates in 31 *ken* and *to,* electing 8 in 5 of these. Their win/loss ratio was thus only 10%, and their members constituted merely 2% of the total House membership. As might have been expected, the successful socialist candidates came from urban or metropolitan districts: Tokyo, Kyoto, Ōsaka, Hyōgo, and Fukuoka.

Two years later, after Tanaka had been forced to resign in the aftermath of the assassination of Chang Tso-lin and a Minseitō Cabinet had been in office for some six months, the new prime minister, Hamaguchi Yūzō, dissolved the Diet and called for new elections. The seventeenth election was held on February 20, 1930. It resulted in a significant victory for the Minseitō. Running 341 candidates in all 47 ken and to, that party elected 273 members to the 466-member House of Representatives from every prefecture and metropolitan area. This represented a win/loss ratio of 80% and 59% of the total House seats. The Minseitō did almost equally well in all nine major regions of Japan, ranging from 80% of the seats in Okinawa, 66% in Kinki, and 61% in Chūbu to lows of 53% in Tōhoku, 54% in Chūgoku, and 54% in Kyushu.

The Seiyūkai, now led by Inukai Tsuyoshi, ran 304 candidates in all 47 ken and to, electing 174 in 47, with a win/loss ratio of 57% and 37% of the total House seats. The party showed particular strength in Tōhoku (47%), Kyushu (45%), and Chūgoku (41%); it was relatively weak in Okinawa (20%) and Kinki (24%). In other areas, however, it maintained a strength in terms of percentage of seats of 36% or higher, indicating continued national strength. In popular vote, the Seiyūkai polled 3,944,493 votes to 5,469,114 for the Minseitō, or 72% of the Minseitō vote.

When combined, the seats of the Minseitō and the Seiyūkai represented 96% of the total Diet seats, indicating the negligible strength of the other parties and the independents. Two conservative-liberal parties again participated as minor groups: the Kokumin Dōshikai and the Kakushintō. The former ran 12 candidates, electing 6; the latter ran 6 candidates and elected 3. This represented a combined total of less than 2% of the House seats. The labor-socialist parties did scarcely better. Running 98 candidates in 34 ken and to (four nationally established parties were involved as well as some district parties), the "proletarian parties" elected only 5 candidates in 4 prefectures and metropolitan districts (Tokyo, Kanagawa, Ōsaka, and

Fukuoka). The win/loss ratio of 5% was extremely poor, and the 5 elected members represented only 1% of the total House seats. Clearly the parties of the left were too badly fragmented, too weak in organization and finances to be considered a major political element at this point. Their total vote, 516,538, was about 4% of the total vote of 12,946,003, somewhat higher than their Diet representation but scarcely denoting major political strength. Minor-party–independent strength had also shrunk to completely negligible proportions. Some 77 candidates were run, only 5 being elected, representing 1% of the total House seats.

The eighteenth general election was held on February 20, 1932, after a series of fateful events climaxed by the Manchurian Incident of September 1931 and the rising militarist tide. These elections were conducted by the government of Seiyūkai President and Prime Minister Inukai, the Wakatsuki government having been forced to resign. They produced a smashing Seiyūkai victory. Running 348 candidates in all 47 *ken* and *to*, that party elected 301 members to the 466-member House, a win/loss percentage of 86%, and 65% of the total House seats. The Seiyūkai ran strong everywhere, ranging from 80% in Okinawa and 73% in Kyushu to 56% in Kinki and 61% in Kantō, the two most metropolitan regions. The Minseitō ran 279 candidates in all 47 *ken* and *to,* electing 146 in 45, a win/loss ratio of 56% and 31% of the total House seats. Minseitō strength was also quite evenly distributed, ranging from 20% in Okinawa and 21% in Kyushu to 37% in Kinki and 35% in Kantō. In the popular vote, the figure for the Seiyūkai was 5,682,647 and for the Minseitō, 3,393,935, or 60% of the former. Taken together, the two major parties again obtained 96% of the total House seats.

The minor parties were even weaker than previously. The Kakushintō ran 3 candidates, electing 2. The "proletarian parties," now represented by two nationally based parties, ran 29 candidates in 12 *ken* and *to*, electing 5 in 3 prefectures and districts: Tokyo, Ōsaka, and Fukuoka. Total proletarian party votes were only 260,122, approximately one half the figure of 1930, although this could be understood in terms of the many fewer candidates run. The win/loss ratio was naturally better (17%) than that of 1930, and the percentage of House seats the same (1%). Minor-party–independent strength was up slightly. Out of 47 candidates, 12 were elected, representing 3% of the total House vote.

The nineteenth general election was not held until February 20, 1936, precisely four years after the 1932 elections. Once again, a national election was held under neutral auspices, since Admiral Okada Keisuke was prime minister, the last party government having been that of Inukai, who had been assassinated on May 15, 1932. The 1936 election provided a victory for the Minseitō, the more moderate and the more liberal of the two conservative parties during this militarist era. Running 298 candidates in all 47 *ken* and *to*, the Minseitō was victorious in 205 cases in 46 prefectures and metropolitan districts. Its win/loss ratio was 69% and it obtained 44% of the total House seats. Minseitō strength was greatest in Kinki (53%), Hokkaido (50%), and Kantō (49%); least in Kyushu (25%) and Tōhoku (39%).

The Seiyūkai, by this time strongly nationalist, ran 340 candidates in all 47 *ken* and *to*, electing 174 in 46. Its win/loss ratio was 51%, and it secured 37% of the total House seats. Its greatest strength was in Tōhoku (49%), Kyushu (46%), and Shikoku (41%); it was weakest in Kinki (26%), Kantō (33%), and Hokkaido (35%). The total Minseitō vote was 4,447,653 while that of the Seiyūkai was 4,191,442, or 94% of the Minseitō vote. Together the two parties obtained 81% of the Diet seats, a considerably lower percentage than in recent elections.

Among the minor parties, the Shakai Taishūtō registered the strongest showing. This party representing the only nationally based labor-socialist party, ran 36 candidates in 17 *ken* and *to*, electing 22 candidates in 12 prefectures and metropolitan districts (Akita, Tokyo, Niigata, Shizuoka, Kyoto, Ōsaka, Hyōgo, Okayama, Kōchi, Fukuoka, and Kagoshima). Six candidates were elected in Tokyo, 4 in Ōsaka, and 2 in Fukuoka. This represented a win/loss ratio of 61%, and 5% of the total House seats.

Two small parties, both with strong nationalist positions, participated in the nineteenth elections. One, the Shōwakai, ran 49 candidates in 29 ken and to, electing 20 in 16, having a win/loss ratio of 41% and 4% of the total House seats. The second, the Kokumin Dōmei, ran 32 candidates in 25 ken and to, electing 15 in 11, representing a win/loss ratio of 47% and 3% of the total House seats. Neither of these parties secured more than 8% of the seats in any region, except in Okinawa where the Kokumin Dōmei, obtaining one seat, scored 20%. The minor-party–independent vote again rose. Of 122 candidates, 30 were elected, representing 7% of the total House seats.

Scarcely one week after the 1936 election, the famous February 26 Incident occurred, and internal friction mounted in Japanese politics. In the aftermath of this attempted coup d'état, the military took commanding positions in the government. A short-lived Hirota government capitulated to most military demands and was followed by a Cabinet headed by General Hayashi Senjūrō. The Hayashi government clashed repeatedly with the Diet, and a few months after it had come into existence dissolved the Diet and called for new elections. Thus only a little more than a year after the 1936 elections the twentieth general election was held, on April 30, 1937. Once again the election was held under relatively neutral auspices, since the military had no party. Although most senior military men probably favored the more nationalist elements within the Seiyūkai and several smaller parties, there was a general antipathy to political parties which was ultimately to result in their being disbanded.

The 1937 election resulted in a draw between the two major parties and a substantial increase for the Shakai Taishūtō, without raising it to the status of a major party. By a narrow margin, the Minseitō remained the leading party. Running 267 candidates in all 47 ken and to, it elected 179, with a win/loss ratio of 67% and 38% of the total House seats. The party was strongest in Hokkaido (50%), Kinki (44%), and Chūbu (44%), weakest in Kyushu (27%) and Chūgoku (34%), but its strength was relatively evenly divided throughout Japan.

The Seiyūkai ran 263 candidates in all 47 ken and to, electing 175. This represented a win/loss ratio of 67% and 38% of the total House seats, precisely the same percentages as achieved by the Minseitō. The Seiyūkai distribution of strength was even more equal than its rival, ranging from 45% in Tōhoku to 30% in Hokkaido. In popular vote, the Minseitō polled 3,677,271, the Seiyūkai 3,585,654, or 98% of the Minseitō vote. It is to be noted that these figures are substantially below the vote of 1936 for the major parties. Taken together, the two leading parties now held 76% of the total Diet seats, indicating a further fall away from their earlier strength.

As noted earlier, the most substantial gains were scored by the moderate socialists, the Shakai Taishūtō. That party, running 66 candidates in 32 ken and to, elected 37 in 19 prefectures and metropolitan districts. The Shakai Taishūtō elected 8 members from Tokyo, 6 from Ōsaka, 4 from Hyōgo, 3 from Fukuoka, 2 from Kanagawa, and 1 each from Akita, Miyagi, Gumma, Tochigi, Saitama, Niigata, Nagano, Gifu, Shizuoka, Kyoto, Okayama, Kagawa, Kōchi, and Kagoshima. Its win/loss ratio was 56%, and it held 8% of the total House seats. Its greatest strength was in Kantō (14%) and Kinki (11%); its weakest position in Okinawa (0), Hokkaido (0), Tōhoku (4%), and Chūbu (5%).

A second, more radical socialist party, the Nihon Musantō, also participated in the 1937 elections, running 7 candidates and electing 3, 1 in Tokyo and 2 in Nagano. The other small parties were again strongly nationalist in character. The Shōwakai ran 36 candidates, electing 19, thereby obtaining 4% of the total

House seats. The Kokumin Dōmei ran 20 candidates and elected 11, 2% of the total House membership. The Tōhōkai also ran 20 candidates and elected 11 for the same percentage. The minor-party–independent candidates totaled 141, of whom 31 were elected, representing 7% of the total House seats, the same percentage as in 1936.

With the twentieth general election, parliamentary elections cast in the liberal mold ended in prewar Japan. The next election, held in the wartime period, was completely dominated by the Imperial Rule Assistance Association, an official government party that presented carefully screened candidates to the electorate. Only a small number of independents successfully competed against the IRAA.

Conclusion

What conclusions can be drawn from a statistical study of Japanese national elections over the half-century between 1892 and 1937? If a working democracy were to be defined in terms of whether an alternation in power took place *via elections*, prewar Japan would qualify only with serious qualifications. As we have noted, a party in power never lost an election during the entire period under consideration. Power did alternate by means of elections, but only when "neutral," non-party governments presided over such elections. True alternation in power between parties took place as a result of the *genrō* system, with the senior Japanese statesmen selecting prime ministers when, in their opinion, conditions necessitated a change. These prime ministers then proceeded to use elections to ratify their power.[12]

[12] To recapitulate the elections under study briefly: in the first two elections, those of 1892 and 1898, the oligarchy was in authority. In 1908 an oligarchic-Seiyūkai government was in power and the Seiyūkai won. But by the time of the 1915 elections, Okuma had been placed in office by the *genrō*, and the party supporting him, the Dōshikai, won. The Seiyūkai under Prime Minister Hara was again in power in 1920 and won easily. The 1924 election was conducted under the "neutral" Kiyoura regime. The 1928 election was an extremely narrow

One may consider the Japanese polity during much of this period as an early type of "guided democracy," with the *genrō*, and later the much weaker Jūshin serving as tutors. This "guided democracy" prevented what would otherwise have probably been the emergence of a dominant-party system. At the outset of the parliamentary experiment, there were indications that the Jiyūtō could easily become the dominant party, particularly if it could unite with some significant portion of the government oligarchy. Such a union took place about a decade later, and the Seiyūkai, its product, had most of the ingredients for long-term power.

The *genrō* themselves, however, continued to stand aloof as a group from this new party, although one of their most prominent members, Itō, led it. Instead, they continued to operate "above parties" in some measure, alternating power throughout the critical two decades that marked the beginning of the twentieth century. Thus Japan developed a curious type of two-party system, one initially dependent upon an external institutional safeguard.

The functioning of this two-party system, of course, was made possible because of other factors as well. We have noted that as early as 1898 Japanese politics had acquired a truly national character. Kyushu, a region still characterized by strong localist, conservative tendencies, was the one area not thoroughly integrated into the national political pattern by the close of the nineteenth century. Even here, however, the election statistics make clear remarkable strides in the

---

victory for the Seiyūkai, then in power; it represents a partial exception to the rule, since the Seiyūkai trailed slightly in popular vote although it obtained 217 seats in the Diet to 216 for the Minseitō. Under the Hamaguchi government, the Minseitō easily won the 1930 elections. The Seiyūkai government of Inukai scored a smashing victory in 1932, and the two final free elections in prewar Japan were conducted under "neutral," nonparty governments. Incidentally, the early elections not presented here (those between 1890 and 1920 omitted from our detailed statistical analysis) do not in any case contradict the basic thesis.

direction of unification with the rest of Japan. In part, a two-party system could emerge in Japan because of the rapid success of the nation-building campaign. If we use national political parties and elections as one primary criteria, we can say that the Japanese nation-building process was largely accomplished three decades after the Meiji Restoration. In thirty years the main outlines of a modern, integrated nation-state had been firmly established.

Further evidence concerning the relatively high level of national integration can be shown in the relatively low percentage of minor-party–independent candidates elected to the House of Representatives, even in the early elections. If we exclude for the moment those "minor partites" receiving a sufficient vote to be listed separately in the national election statistics, the minor-party-independent candidates elected varied between 12% and 16% in the four elections of the 1892–1915 period here presented, and dropped substantially below this after 1920. Beginning in 1928 the independent House member was a negligible factor in Japanese politics, although as parliamentarism came under increasing assault, the minor-party–independents increased slightly in electoral strength. Even in the 1937 election, however, they accounted for only 7% of the successful candidates.

When one adds the more important minor parties which were tabulated separately in the national election statistics, the position of the minor-party–independent forces is somewhat improved. Omitting true "third-party" situations with which we shall deal shortly, the minor-party–independents total about one third of the House members in the early period. By 1920, however, the Japanese two-party system appeared firmly established. Whereas prior to that date the two major parties had garnered about 68% of the vote, beginning with the 1920 election they captured 84% of the vote and reached a high total of 96% in the elections of 1930 and 1932, subsequently declining to 81% in 1936 and 76% in 1937.

It should be noted that on two occasions, in 1892 and in 1924, the elections involved three major parties. In the first instance, the progovernment party, the Chūō Club, was actually the second party, and the Kaishintō was close to the status of a minor party. In 1924, as a result of the split within the Seiyūkai, the totals of the two groups, the Seiyūhontō and the Seiyūkai, were nearly the same, and those of the Kenseikai only slightly higher. In general terms, however, third parties were transitional forces. The two-party system, under the terms we have carefully defined, was the central characteristic of prewar Japanese politics. Such alterations as occurred in the electoral system during the prewar era, moreover, did not affect that basic fact.

If a high level of national integration, achieved at a relatively early point in the thrust toward political modernization abetted the Japanese two-party system along with the particular type of tutelage exercised in that era, the socioeconomic forces underwriting Japanese politics were also a major contributing factor. Japan followed the classic democratic procedure of beginning her parliamentary experiment with a number of "safeguards" against excessive democracy, including a strictly limited suffrage. Suffrage was progressively extended until, thirty-five years after the first session of the Diet had opened, all adult males were eligible to vote. That was a rapid shift. The time involved, however, was sufficient to institutionalize the major parties, establishing their basic structure and mode of operation.

As we have noted, these parties were elitist in character, strongly reflective in their organization of traditional Japanese social patterns. In membership, they combined the most articulate elements of Japanese society: officials, landowners, and industrial elements. This composition made it easier for these parties to be policy-oriented rather than intensely ideological. Policy differences on occasion could be very significant, especially those involving an urban-rural cleavage.[13] No huge

[13] Some data pertaining to the long-range rural-urban cleavage and the relation of the two major parties to this factor can be obtained by

philosophic chasms, however, separated the major contestants for power, and quite frequently even the policy divisions were not major ones. This provided a setting in Japan—as in a few other societies of the world—for a *possible* accommodation within the existing party structure for new socio-economic groups as these began to acquire political consciousness and seek political channels.

A survey of Japanese national elections helps us to see the major stages in the political evolution of this society. The

---

noting the political tendencies of each prefecture throughout this period, using the statistics from each national election. (Robert E. Ward, *Party Government in Japan: Its Development and Electoral Record, 1928-1937,* unpublished doctoral dissertation, University of California, Berkeley, 1948.) Two prefectures, Iwate and Yamaguchi, consistently returned a majority of Seiyūkai candidates to the House of Representatives throughout the entire period between 1892 and 1937. Two other prefectures, Aomori and Yamagata, were almost as consistent, their record "marred" only by ties, or a victory for the Seiyūhontō, the party that had been formed by the split within the Seiyūkai. (It should be noted, of course, that within even these prefectures, district returns varied.)

Another group of prefectures can be defined as pro-Seiyūkai, with that party generally winning a majority of the seats. These prefectures were Miyagi, Ibaraki, Chiba, Saitama, Yamanashi, Shizuoka, Shiga, Wakayama, Okayama, Kagawa, Fukuoka, Ōita, Kumamoto, and Okinawa. These prefectures were among the most rural in Japan, and even among such prefectures as Fukuoka which had an important urban component, Seiyūkai strength was generally based upon its showing in the rural proportion of the prefecture.

The Minseitō and its predecessors had no absolutely "safe districts" at the prefectural level, nor any prefecture where the record was "perfect" except for ties. Those prefectures and metropolitan districts that could be accounted pro-Minseitō in terms of the vote were Gumma, Tochigi, Tokyo, Kanagawa, Niigata, Nagano, Aichi, Kyoto, Ōsaka, Mie, Shimane, Tottori, and Hiroshima. It will be noted that this list includes all of the truly metropolitan areas, and most of the prefectures containing a relatively high level of urbanization. Prefectures not mentioned here can be considered closely divided in political allegiance, with a majority of seats frequently shifting from one party to the other.

first great change occurred between 1890 and 1915. In that period the so-called popular parties shifted in status from being opposition parties to becoming government parties. We can describe this shift as the legitimization of the popular parties, a fundamental alteration in their original position as somewhat subversive challengers to "the system" to becoming a part of the system. That change was symbolized, of course, by the creation of the Seiyūkai and, later, of the Dōshikai. These two parties, while inheriting the content of the old popular parties, differed from them in structure and role. They reflected the very substantial progress made by Japanese society in the modernization process. They represented fusions of professional official power and elitist socioeconomic representation outside governmental circles. We can say that on the one hand the major parties were bureaucratized in some degree, but that on the other the bureaucracy was politicized in similar fashion. With all of the new problems which this produced, it also reflected a new if incomplete fusion between critically important political elements, a higher evolution in the political development of Japan.

A second massive change was signaled as this era came to an end, although its ultimate implications were by no means clear. Japanese political elitism was being challenged from two different sources. On the surface the "rightist," military attack upon parliamentarism was the most obvious challenge, one threatening the very existence of the old parties. Ultimately, this challenge scored a major success when those parties were forced to dissolve and Japan experimented with a one-party system under the authoritarian direction of the state. At the same time, however, another less obvious form of challenge was to be noted, namely the slow rise of the "proletarian" parties. Starting with 2% of the House seats in 1928, the labor-socialist movement had acquired 9% of the seats as a result of the 1937 election. Both the militarist and the labor-socialist movements were reflective of a common phenomenon: the further socioeconomic evolution of Japan and the advent of a mass society. Inevitably the participation of the masses would take one of several directions, and two prominent possibilities were unevenly represented in Japanese politics of the 1930's.

In conclusion, we can perhaps move toward broader speculations that are susceptible to only partial proof from such data as has been advanced here. An electoral profile of prewar Japan sheds at least some light upon three broad aspects of political modernization as they related to Japan. The most natural political expression of emerging societies is undoubtedly a dominant-party system in the initial era, irrespective of the timing of emergence. This has been particularly true, of course, in the most recent period, when the techniques for a mass-mobilization type of party have been so greatly perfected. Japan, however, developed via a type of "guided democracy" that enabled a form of the two-party system to develop, without any complete reliance on elections as a method of change. Any total reliance upon the electoral system in Japan between 1890 and 1930 would almost certainly have produced a dominant-party system, one capable of being altered only under extraordinary circumstances.

When fundamental changes do occur in the political system of an emerging state, they will generally be reflected in three ways insofar as the party movement is concerned: splits and reformations within the major party or parties; the slow rise of new forces (parties) to positions of importance; a revolution or coup d'état that suddenly brings to power a fresh political force which must either have a party already in operation or rapidly create one. Change in prewar Japan was mounted via the first and second of these possibilities, not the third, although the February 26 Incident of 1936 represented an attempt at revolution, Japanese style.

Finally, it is clear that Japan provides a picture of political modernization at a particular time in world history, one when the classical Western model was still the only basic model, and when the full technical and ideological implications of modern mass society could not be realized. Thus in its essentials Japanese political modernization developed in the prewar period within the Western pattern, and this fact distinguishes Japan from many of the emerging societies of today. It would be foolish to attempt any prediction as to what might have happened with respect to Japanese political evolution had the Japanese militarists avoided World War II, or won it. One can only be certain that the present political conditions would not have prevailed. With the militarist era ended, however, Japanese political evolution has hinged upon alternatives well known in the so-called advanced West: Will the established conservative or moderate party(ies) prove sufficiently flexible to adjust to the needs of a majority of the people and hence, irrespective of their socioeconomic position, incorporate them under its banners? Will new, militant political forces gradually be moderated in the course of seeking power by the parliamentary route, so that if and when their advent to power occurs, any massive ideological gap will have been reduced and parliamentarism can survive?

It is with issues such as this that Japan, along with many other "advanced democracies," is involved. The capacity for adjustment to competitive politics on the part of postwar Japan is due in part to the experiences of the prewar era. If Japan had certain "natural" advantages in this respect (the timing of her emergence allowed a somewhat more leisurely experimentation as well as providing only one basic model), free elections and political competition were sustained in the prewar era by certain special institutions and procedures which, as noted, amounted to a form of oligarchic tutelage during the critical opening decades of the modernization thrust.

Will at least some of the forms of "guided democracy" being pursued by various elites throughout the world today lead ultimately to more meaningful mass participation in decision-making actions as the socioeconomic nature of the involved society changes? The Japanese experience does not provide an answer to this question. On the one hand it can be argued that Japanese guided democracy of the Meiji era kept open the channels of political competition and slowly institutionalized procedures and patterns of thought conducive to parliamentarism. One might thus draw the inference that *if* a given form of guided democracy permits some openness in the society and precludes the more rigid forms of totalitarianism while the tasks of nation-building and economic development are being undertaken, various subsequent alternatives in political evolution will have been protected, including those involving free elections and genuine political competition.

On the other hand one must not minimize the enormous distance that separates the era of Japanese emergence from that of today. That distance can only be measured in light years as it relates to techniques of power, pressures of time, and ideological-political alternatives. One must not minimize the fact either that the Japanese experiment in guided democracy did not automatically produce the Japanese polity of today. Parliamentarism *failed* in prewar Japan, and the experiment was reopened in 1945 only as the result of massive external pressure when a new venture in guided democracy commenced. But if Japan does not necessarily provide answers for the political issues of our times, it does represent an enormously interesting early experiment in uniting borrowed political institutions and values with indigenous social proclivities and capacities. Such an experiment still represents the most basic political challenge for all emerging societies, today as in the past.

CHAPTER IX

The Development of Interest Groups and the Pattern of Political Modernization in Japan

TAKESHI ISHIDA

THE Western image of Japan has changed greatly in the last few decades. During World War II and the subsequent Occupation—or at least during the first half of the Occupation—the predominant image of Japan in the West was that of a brutal, semifeudal nation. The present image is that of a non-Western nation which has been exceptionally "successful" in modernizing rapidly. The latter image is found not only in the popular mind but also at more sophisticated levels, as is evidenced by a shift in emphasis in approaches to Japanese studies by Western scholars. During the last war and immediately thereafter, Western scholars were more interested in the Fascist or militarist stage of Japan's development (1930's to 1945), whereas presently they are more interested in the stage of economic development at the point of "takeoff" for modernization, i.e. the Meiji period (1868–1912), or in the rapid economic development in post-war Japan. But even if the Meiji period is chosen as a subject of research, the results would differ according to the focus of interest—for instance, whether the Meiji period is viewed as the point of origin of subsequent militarist regimes or as the takeoff stage for successful modernization in Japan. I personally do not think that the "Meiji oligarchy" or the "Meiji emperor system" inevitably led to a militarist Japan. But neither do I agree that the militarist stage was nothing but an unfortunate and exceptional period in Japanese history and that, since Occupation policy abolished all hindrances for democratic development, Japan can now return to her original way of modernizing and continue to develop further along this path.

The militarist stage was not the sole or inevitable result of modernization in Japan since Meiji times, but we can say that the militarist stage was one of the probable or possible results of Japan's particular path to modernization. What I am seeking here is a statement of the nature of the pattern of modernization in Japan that can explain the whole historical development of Japan, including the Meiji period and the relatively liberal and militarist stages that followed. Another problem that should not be overlooked is the extent to which the overall pattern of modernization has changed between prewar and postwar Japan. Radical changes did take place as a result of Japan's defeat. At the same time, many important characteristics of prewar Japanese society survived or have been revived with modifications.

I am sure that this kind of examination requires a full-length book or even several volumes. Here, however, I will limit my subject to a characterization of the Japanese pattern of modernization through an analysis of the development of interest groups.[1] What does the development of interest groups indicate about the pattern of modernization? In terms of this pattern, what is the significance of the process of development of interest groups, which, emerging during early Meiji, became highly developed about the time of the "Taishō democracy" movement (1912–1924) and were subsequently integrated into

[1] According to the definition by Lasswell and Kaplan, "an interest group is an interest aggregate organized for the satisfaction of the interests." Harold D. Lasswell and Abraham Kaplan, *Power and Society: A Framework for Political Inquiry* (New Haven, 1950), p. 40. In this paper I will consider two factors important when I use this term. One is the purpose, i.e. the satisfaction of the group interest, and another is the means by which the interest is satisfied, i.e. the organization. Therefore, such phenomena as simple personal relationships between a particular businessman and a politician will be outside the scope of my paper, even if the relationship is important in the process of policy-making.

the monistic structure of the Imperial Rule Assistance Association (IRAA) in 1940? Was this the result of strong pressure? The historical facts indicate that many interest groups competed in joining the IRAA in order not to lag behind the others. By order of the Occupation authorities, the IRAA was disbanded. This resulted in the reemergence of many interest groups. How can one compare interest groups of the postwar period with those of the prewar period? Does the process of development indicate that Japan is entering or has already entered upon some other course of modernization?

Before entering into a concrete analysis of these problems, I think it necessary to add some brief comments on my approach. I would like to avoid considering the term "modernization" as a problem of quantitative degrees of such socio-economic conditions as per capita income and exposure to mass media. Instead I should like to emphasize the direction of change in terms of value orientations and social structure. Tentatively, I will define "modernization" as a continuing process of self-sustained growth from relatively particular, diffuse, and ascriptive standards to relatively universal, specific, and achievement-oriented standards.

Next, let me touch briefly on the significance of an analysis of interest groups for the study of modernization in Japan. Above all, the development of interest groups is important as an index of social differentiation. This I believe to be one of the most important factors in the analysis of modernization. The differentiation of functionally specific groups from groups which are diffuse in their value orientation makes it possible for more universalistic values to be pursued within a more delimited field. At the same time achievement according to specified standards can become more important. For instance, if the field of law is specialized, this makes possible the universalization of legal concepts independently of other fields, and, at the same time, lawyers and other persons active in law can acquire achievement orientations within the judicial process much more important than any ascriptive qualification. If business relations become independent of other fields, then particularistic values such as kinship ties become less important, and achievement in terms of economic activities becomes more important. It is worth noting, however, that social differentiation is actually realized in varied forms from culture to culture. Tentatively, let me state the following points.

First, I would like to examine the problem of organizational patterns in the formation of groups for interest articulation. At least in the first stage of modernization, the core group of modernizing elites is structured according to a type of organizational pattern familiar to the culture. The same type of organizational pattern will be found in the case of the emergence of interest groups. Therefore, my basic assumption is that in a particular political culture we can study the overall pattern of modernization through the analysis of organizational patterns of interest groups. For instance, in Western countries, Max Weber has pointed out, religious sects are the prototype of all voluntary associations, including interest groups.[2] In China the core group of modernizing elites was probably first formed as a secret society, while only subsequently did the elites reform the society into a modern political party, such as the Nationalist Party or the Communist Party. In Japan the modernizing elites first organized themselves as cliques within and/or among powerful fiefs (*hanbatsu*). A similar pattern can also be found in Japanese business circles in the organizational type called *zaibatsu* (monopolistic cliques based upon extended family relations).

The process of the institutionalization of interest groups also displays characteristics similar to those encountered in the above-mentioned processes of group formation. For instance, personal relations such as those found in cliques readily became entangled with formal organizational relations. This en-

[2] Max Weber, "Die protestantischen Sekten und der Geist des Kapitalismus," in *Gesammelte Aufsätze zur Religionssoziologie*, 1 (Tübingen, 1922).

tanglement very often caused a "freezing" of the organization involved.[3] The actual development of interest groups in Japan often indicates that once an interest group grows into a full-fledged institution, it loses much of its original function and a new organization for interest articulation becomes necessary. This is partially due to the "governmentalization" of interest groups, a particular type of institutionalization encountered in Japan. In this process the specific purposes of interest groups become fused with governmental purposes and thus accelerate the freezing process. As an example, when the chambers of commerce became the most influential interest groups in business circles, their position was supported and at the same time came to be controlled by the government. Therefore, for purposes of interest articulation on behalf of business circles, a new "voluntary" organization was needed. Thus the Japan Industrial Club (Nihon Kōgyō Kurabu) was established in 1917, but its original function was in turn soon inherited by the Japan Economic League (Nihon Keizai Remmei), founded as early as 1922. Similar phenomena can be found in many spheres. Following the establishment of the IRAA, this association lost many of its original functions in actual

---

[3] I borrowed the term "freezing" from S. N. Eisenstadt, "Modernization: Growth and Diversity" (unpublished paper, 1963). The "freezing" of an organization means a functional paralysis making further development difficult. Probably this tendency toward the freezing of organizations can be found in every country when the institutionalization of organizations takes place. As a phenomenon closely related to the freezing of organizations, we find a common phenomenon in various countries, which I call the "erosion of symbols," i.e. the fact that the specific goals of an organization are subject to erosion and hence that the established symbol, which once indicated specific goals, loses its effectiveness in guiding the organization toward the attainment of that goal. Ishida Takeshi, *Gendai soshiki ron* (Tokyo, 1961), pp. 46-50. In actuality, however, the above phenomena are realized in different degrees and fashions in different countries. In Japan the feeling of the "historically inevitable trend" and the pattern of "social compartmentalization," both of which I will discuss later, marked the specific fashion of realizing the freezing process as well as the erosion of symbols.

operation after its "governmentalization." The frozen IRAA then was augmented through the formation of more popular organizations such as the Adults Imperial Rule Assistance Group (Yokusan Sōnen Dan), established in 1942 as an affiliate of the IRAA.

The second problem I will discuss concerns the interrelationships among interest groups. The types of conflict between interest groups varied from period to period. For instance, in the Meiji period major conflicts occurred between business groups and landowners; since the 1920's labor groups have gained in importance as the competitors of business interest groups. Although the protagonists thus varied from period to period, the pattern of conflict itself has not been very variegated. The continuous conflict has been characterized by a lack of coordination through discussion and by the frequent solution of intergroup disputes by limited measures of intervention on the part of the government. In some cases negotiations between competing groups were carried out without serious discussions on important issues. At any rate, the lack of rational coordination through discussion has been one of the most important common denominators of the relationship between competing groups. Also, "the continuous oscillation between the repressive orientation, on the one hand, and the giving in to the various demands of many groups on the other," has been to a certain extent the case in Japan where relationships between the government and interest groups are concerned.[4] This is especially true where economically powerful groups have been involved. In this case, however, concessions on the part of the government have not been explicit, since in prewar Japan it was difficult for any group to pursue its own specific interest openly without exposing itself to accusations by the public.

The third problem to be dealt with is the position and function of interest groups within the Japanese political system,

[4] S. N. Eisenstadt, "Breakdown of Modernization," *Economic Development and Cultural Change*, XII:iv (July 1964), 362.

particularly the importance of the relationships between interest groups and political parties and between interest groups and the bureaucracy. Interest groups in Japan are generally characterized by a weakness of autonomy but, conditions vary depending on the strength of their financial bases. They tend either to be subsidized by or receive special privileges from the government, e.g. the right to impose membership fees. This was particularly true in the prewar period, but to a degree the situation is the same today, especially among economically weak interest groups. Therefore, those interest groups which are not completely independent of the government naturally make concessions to the governmental bureaucracy, and it is sometimes difficult to know whether to term some of them voluntary associations or semigovernmental organizations.

Since Japanese political parties lack mass organizations,[5] economically strong interest groups that desire to influence the political parties provide them with financial support which more than compensates for the absence of membership fees or contributions from party members.[6] Those interest groups

[5] For example, it is said that in 1958 the Socialist Party, which polled 13 million votes, had only 56,500 party members. This number includes "ghost members." The Socialist Party was also supported by labor unions which had some 1.3 million members. However, not many of the union members were also party members. See Heibonsha, *Sekai daihyakka jiten*, xxii (Tokyo, 1958), 252.

[6] For instance, in 1958 the Liberal-Democratic Party received 882 million *yen* from the Committee for Economic Reconstruction (Keizai Saiken Kondankai), a special organization among business groups contributing money to political parties. This amount indicates only the officially registered amount of money given by this organization. In addition, many firms contributed individually as well to the party or to leaders of important factions within the party. It is difficult to tell exactly how much money was given to the party, because the registered amount shows only a part of it. The above amount includes, besides regular maintenance, funds for the election campaign conducted that year. It is usually said that around that time 20 million *yen* per month was necessary to maintain the ordinary activities of the party organization and that this was also given by the above-mentioned committee.

The ordinary maintenance costs of party organization for the Social-

which lack economic power but have many members are able to supply votes in place of financial support. Such groups can also serve as a source of active campaign workers.

Within the traditional Japanese value system the private interests of any group are not considered legitimate. Therefore, it is relatively difficult for any group to articulate its own interests. At the very least, these groups have to find some way to legitimize their own interests as an aspect of the broader public interest. This tendency to deprecate special interests tends to strengthen the subservience of interest groups to the government bureaucracy, which has often been considered to represent the public interest.

The fourth and the last point which I would like to treat is the importance of the Western impact, which is indicated by the nature and direction of the development of interest groups in Japan. Since 1919, for example, the International Labor Organization has exercised a great influence on the relationships between business groups and labor unions in Japan, and needless to say, during the Occupation period the Western impact again became very strong. Through the analysis of the Western impact upon interest groups in Japan, I hope we can clarify some of the characteristics of modernization in Japan.

Generally speaking, the Western impact has been utilized on their own behalf by economically strong groups that have been closer to the government than the others. This kind of dependence on strong authority outside their own organization is similar to their attitude toward the government. Such dependence, of course, indicates a weakness of organizational discipline within their own groups. At the same time this attitude also reduces the autonomy of organizations of interest groups, because it is easier for them to be dependent on outside authority than to strengthen their own organizational discipline.

---

ists are provided by the Party's members in the Diet. The campaign funds of the party are given by labor unions and by some business firms, but the amount is much less than that for the government party.

The Emergence

As in many other countries, Japanese interest groups first emerged in the business world. Even from the first they were not completely independent of the government. In fact, many merchants in the early Meiji period were called *seishō*, which literally means "political merchants." Thus it may have been difficult for the Japanese of the period to distinguish businessmen from statesmen or bureaucrats. The businessmen's movement for establishment of their own organization drew much of its force from the active encouragement of the government, which had ordered the Bureau of Commercial Development (Kanshō-kyoku) to study the activities of foreign chambers of commerce and to draft a plan for the establishment of a similar organization in Japan. This resulted in the Tokyo Metropolitan Chamber of Commerce (Tokyo Shōhō Kaigisho), the forerunner of today's Chamber of Commerce and Industry (Shōkō Kaigisho), authorized by the governor in 1878.[7] In addition, it became necessary in 1877, when the government started negotiations with foreign governments with a view to amending the existing treaties with foreign countries, to consult the merchants and industrialists of the nation with regard to the problem of customs duties.

The chamber was subsidized by the government, and its office building was supplied by the Tokyo metropolitan government. On the other hand, the chamber's activities were limited to presenting its opinions to the government and playing an advisory role on various issues. At the time of its formation, for example, the Chamber requested governmental authorization of a special committee to arbitrate commercial disputes among the members of the Chamber and between members and nonmembers, a request that was rejected by the government.

[7] For details concerning the beginnings of the Chamber of Commerce and Industry in Japan, see Nagata Masaomi, *Keizai dantai hatten shi* (Tokyo, 1956), pp. 15ff.

When the imperial constitution of Japan was promulgated in 1889 and the policy of the nation became stabilized, interest articulation was also institutionalized. It is important to note the promulgation in 1890 of the Chambers of Commerce Act, which, while conceding a certain measure of autonomy and independence to chambers of commerce, institutionalized them as part of the larger political system.

The same can be said about the draft law on mutual co-operative unions (shin'yō kumiai) that was unsuccessfully introduced in the Diet in 1890. It is also noteworthy that the organization of interest groups in the field of agriculture was first initiated in the form of a bill submitted by the bureaucracy rather than proposed through the initiative of farmers. Although we can find some interest groups in a broad sense in the field of agriculture, most of them were concerned with crops such as raw silk, and tea that were closely related to foreign trade. These groups sometimes ignored the interests of farmers because they were more interested in transactions of such goods than in their production.

There were some common features of the internal organization of interest groups at the time of their emergence. The representatives of interest groups, whether they were appointed or nominally elected, were either former bureaucrats or had close relations with active bureaucrats. Almost all of the important interest groups were approved (in the case of economically strong groups) or established (in the case of weaker groups such as the Imperial Agricultural Association established in 1910) by law. The conduct of their activities was very often governed by a need to help spread and develop the policies of the government, while the original function of interest articulation was more or less suppressed.

Since the national goal of Meiji Japan was "to enrich the country and to strengthen the military," the policy of the government was usually favorable to the rapid industrialization of Japan. On the other hand, Diet members in the Meiji period were mostly landowners, whose interests were sometimes sacrificed in favor of governmental policies in support of rapid industrialization. Therefore during roughly the latter half of the Meiji period conflicts of interest between business circles and the agricultural sector frequently appeared as conflicts between the government and the Diet.

In the late nineteenth century cotton yarn was one of the most important export products of Japan, and the status of textile dealers was very high. Consequently the interests of these cotton textile dealers were reflected in the policies of the National Federation of Chambers of Commerce which maneuvered for and succeeded in having the tariff on raw cotton abolished in 1896. On the other hand, the farmers engaged in the production of cotton were opposed to the abolition of the tariff, and their views were expressed in the Diet through members representing the landowning class. Since the interests of farmers were far less articulated than those of businessmen and dealers, and since the bureaucracy gave priority to the development of modern industry during this period, the abolition of the tariff was carried through despite the resistance of the farmers.

Another activity of the National Federation of Chambers of Commerce causing conflict with the agricultural sector was a demand for the reduction of income taxes after the Sino-Japanese and Russo-Japanese wars. Immediately after the Sino-Japanese War, the National Federation of Chambers of Commerce submitted to the government an advisory opinion with regard to the formulation of postwar policies. The most important point in that opinion was a demand for the reduction of the tax burden. In response to such demands by the business community, the government agreed to suspend tax increases on business and to substitute an increase in the tax rate on land. This policy was, of course, seriously opposed by the landowning class as represented in the Diet. The businessmen representing the chambers of commerce organized a league to work for an increase of the land tax in order to support and reinforce government policy. Although the government bill concerning this policy was amended in many ways in the Diet, the main points demanded by business were incorporated into law.

In 1902 businessmen organized a campaign for the amendment of the act governing the chambers of commerce, which culminated in the enactment of a new Chambers of Commerce Act. According to this, their organizational basis was broadened, and, at the same time, the right of compulsory collection of membership fees was strengthened. This led to an expansion of the organizations and the consolidation of their financial basis, which in turn contributed to the further development of the chambers' activities. The chambers' demand for reduction of the business tax was so strong after the Russo-Japanese War that they were not only opposed by landowners but also by the incumbent Katsura Cabinet. In consequence, the government amended the Chambers of Commerce Act in 1909, depriving the chambers of their right of compulsory collection of membership fees. As this drove some of the weaker Chambers into financial difficulties, the incumbent Ōkuma Cabinet decided in 1916 to return the right of compulsory collection of membership fees with a view to appeasing the business community.

One point which should be added is that the business organizations came to recruit their leaders increasingly on their own volition and quite independently of interference by the government. This trend was emphasized when Shibusawa Eiichi, former vice-minister of finance, was replaced as president of the Tokyo Chamber of Commerce in 1903 by Nakano Buei, who had almost no bureaucratic background. From this time on the leaders of business organizations came to be recruited not from the bureaucracy but from the business community itself, and the functional separation between politicians and businessmen grew wider, while the "political merchant" or businessman with bureaucratic background or connections was replaced more and more by professional businessmen.

"Taishō Democracy"

On the basis of their increased power and relatively specialized autonomy, interest groups in the business community
also became influential within the political arena. Business
interest groups played an important role in the early stages of
the Taishō democracy movement, which started with resistance against *hanbatsu* (fief-clique) autocracy in 1912 and resulted in the passage of the Universal (Manhood) Suffrage
Law in 1925. It is well known that this movement began with
a fireside chat at the Kōjunsha businessmen's club.[8]

The members of the National Federation of Chambers
of Commerce, together with representatives of other business
organizations, undertook various activities in connection with
the Taishō democracy movement. Among other things
they decided to oppose the reelection of those representatives
in the Diet who had opposed the complete abolition of the
business tax. Furthermore, Nakano Buei, president of the
Tokyo Chamber of Commerce, insisted on more active
attempts on the part of businessmen to influence legislation.
As Table I indicates, the number of Diet representatives who
also held posts on the staffs of chambers of commerce approached 10 percent of the total membership of the lower
House by the beginning of the twentieth century. Still, a
more systematic drive to increase this number was undertaken during this period. The creation in 1923 of the Businessmen's Voluntary Association (Jitsugyō Dōshikai) by Mutō
Sanji reflected a tendency among businessmen to form their
own political party. Although this attempt ultimately failed,
the interests of the business community continued to influence
national policy and decision-making by less explicit methods.
It was the small and medium-sized capitalists, such as Mutō
and other textile industrialists, who attempted to become
representatives in the Diet themselves, while the larger capi-

[8] For details see Ishida Takeshi, *Kindai Nihon seijikōzō no kenkyū*
(Tokyo, 1956), ch. 4.

TABLE 1. EXTRA-PARLIAMENTARY CAREERS OF MEMBERS OF THE HOUSE OF REPRESENTATIVES

Election Numbers and Years	Total Number of Seats (Average Age of Members)	Career Categories							Unidentified
		B	E	BE	P	T	A	C	
(1)	300	87	65	33	51				85
	192ᵃ	39	55	16	23				70
	15ᵇ	5	2	0	2				4
1890	(42.2) 93ᶜ	43	8	17	26				11
(2)	300	65	79	33	32				96
	185	30	63	11	17				70
	28	10	6	3	2				8
1892	(44.0) 87	25	10	19	13				18
(3)	300	53	92	21	42				110
	191	18	68	11	13				85
	28	5	8	2	3				11
1894	(43.8) 81	30	16	8	26				14
(4)	300	55	89	26	40				111
	188	21	58	17	15				83
	32	5	14	1	1				11
1894	(43.8) 80	29	17	8	24				17
(5)	300	39	115	20	41				106
	186	14	73	10	18				78
	27	2	13	2	2				9
1898	(44.8) 87	23	29	8	21				19
(6)	300	52	118	14	47				106
	189	14	79	9	21				74
	28	13	14	2	3				8
1898	(44.6) 83	25	25	3	23				24

TABLE I. Extra-parliamentary Careers of Members of the House of Representatives (Cont.)

(7)	376	227	53	15	139	93	15	9	95	32	27	21	18	14	34	25	90	70
1902	(46.1)	41		5		22		2		9		5		3		5		5
		108		33		24		4		54		1		1		4		15
(8)	376	230	42	10	156	106	19	6	92	35	23	19	13	11	29	20	113	87
1903	(47.0)	40		5		17		5		13		2		2		4		10
		106		27		33		8		44		2		0		5		16
(9)	379	228	39	13	159	103	19	3	86	37	21	17	15	14	26	15	119	88
1904	(47.1)	48		4		19		7		13		2		0		7		12
		103		22		37		9		36		2		1		4		19
(10)	379	203	34	9	175	101	19	5	113	36	26	19	10	7	35	21	89	65
1908	(47.1)	47		3		24		2		18		2		1		9		9
		129		22		50		12		59		5		2		5		15
(11)	381	165	25	3	190	86	33	5	111	27	20	12	13	11	37	17	83	55
1912	(49.4)	63		2		39		6		14		5		1		14		10
		153		20		65		22		70		3		1		6		18
(12)	381	161	30	4	198	97	17	2	116	27	27	19	26	18	43	19	76	41
1915	(50.9)	52		3		29		2		16		4		4		10		11
		168		23		72		13		73		4		4		14		24
(13)	381	141	30	4	192	80	20	1	134	29	31	19	23	14	30	8	68	42
1917	(51.1)	69		5		37		4		28		6		4		11		7
		171		21		75		15		77		6		5		11		19

TABLE I. Extra-parliamentary Careers of Members of the House of Representatives (Cont.)

Election Numbers and Years	Total Number of Seats (Average Age of Members)	Career Categories							Unidentified
		B	E	BE	P	T	A	C	
(14)	**463** (50.8)	**39**	**238**	**21**	**143**	**59**	**35**	**38**	**87**
	178	4	105	3	32	36	23	18	53
1920	83	7	41	5	27	13	7	13	12
	202	28	92	13	84	10	5	7	22
(15)	**463** (50.9)	**42**	**228**	**26**	**159**	**56**	**46**	**35**	**82**
	160	2	100	2	29	34	26	11	43
	86	6	49	3	29	13	12	16	10
1924	217	34	79	21	101	9	8	8	29
(16)	**466** (52.8)	**54**	**214**	**21**	**175**	**52**	**35**	**23**	**75**
	147	4	86	11	39	35	26	9	36
	82	7	38	4	24	9	8	8	12
1928	237	43	90	16	112	8	1	6	27
(17)	**466** (52.8)	**51**	**205**	**23**	**191**	**68**	**22**	**26**	**80**
	158	4	89	2	44	49	19	8	37
	80	6	32	4	35	13	3	10	14
1930	228	41	84	17	112	6	0	8	29
(18)	**466** (52.5)	**57**	**192**	**22**	**203**	**94**	**35**	**22**	**66**
	152	4	83	2	44	47	29	11	36
	79	11	31	5	36	40	4	7	6
1932	235	42	78	15	123	7	2	4	24
(19)	**465** (54.2)	**60**	**169**	**18**	**230**	**88**	**48**	**26**	**94**
	168	7	75	1	63	72	41	14	55
	68	10	24	3	35	8	5	5	9
1936	229	43	70	14	132	8	2	7	30
(20)	**465** (53.6)	**56**	**163**	**16**	**213**	**79**	**47**	**21**	**95**
	172	7	80	1	48	59	40	9	50
	73	9	22	2	36	13	5	4	13
1937	220	40	61	13	129	7	2	8	32

NOTES:

Column B lists the number of representatives whose extra-parliamentary career lay in the government bureaucracy.

Column E lists those who served as executives of business firms.

Column BE lists those who belong to both the B and E categories.

Column P lists professionals, such as lawyers, writers, professors, medical doctors, and priests.

Column T lists officers of trade associations (dōgyō kumiai).

Column A lists officers of the Imperial Agricultural Association and its predecessor.

Column C lists officers of the chambers of commerce and industry and their predecessor.

Unidentified lists those whose careers are unidentifiable.

(When a person belongs, for instance, to B and P at the same time, he is included in both categories. Those representatives who belong to other categories than listed above are excluded on account of their relative unimportance for the purpose of this study.)

a For each election the upper row of figures indicates the number of those in that category who have previously served as prefectural assemblymen.

b The middle row of figures indicates the number of those in that category who have previously served as municipal assemblymen, i.e., at the city, town, or village level (excluding those who subsequently served as prefectural assemblymen).

c The bottom row of figures shows the number of those not belonging to either of the above categories.

The blank spaces indicate that no figures are available for the categories concerned, not that there are no members under these categories. The double dividing lines indicate times when the election law was revised.

This table was constructed by Professor Masumi Junnosuke on the basis of materials contained in Shūgiin Jimukyoku, ed., Shūgiin giin ryakureki (Tokyo, 1940).

talists and *zaibatsu* families continued to exercise a powerful influence on political parties through financial assistance kept secret from the public.

At the same time the political activities of business groups led to conflicts with other interest groups. Among these the most important were those between business groups and labor unions, to be discussed below. As a result of campaigns by business groups, the new tax law of 1926 reduced the income tax and increased various indirect taxes. This meant that business's demands were satisfied at the expense of consumers in general, who had no interest groups to represent them.

The Society of Friendship and Love (Yūaikai), formed by Suzuki Bunji and his fourteen friends in 1912, marks the beginning of labor unions in Japan, although the society in its early operations functioned more as a cooperative or social work organization than as a labor union. At the end of World War I, a number of labor disputes occurred throughout the country, many of which were won by the workers. Many of these arose from wage disputes in larger factories, and similar disputes subsequently spread throughout the country. At the same time labor unions expanded and increased their influence.

Immediately after its founding, the Japan Industrial Club in 1918 established a committee to study problems of management-labor relations. It is interesting to note that the first interest of the first completely voluntary and autonomous organization within the business community was the problem of labor unions. It can probably be said that this interest in labor problems was one of the factors which led to the establishment of the club.

In any event the Industrial Club fulfilled the functions of an interest group to a greater extent than had the chambers of commerce. The club had an autonomous position and was not controlled by the government. Funds for the club were raised by members' contributions and membership fees, although it lacked the privilege of compulsory collection. The

Mitsui and Mitsubishi *zaibatsu* contributed 100,000 *yen* each and Dan Takuma, president of the Mitsui Corporation, became president of the club.

It is interesting to note that the committee to study the problems of management-labor relations undertook as its first task the consideration of the impact of external influences thereon. When preparations for the Paris Peace Conference began in 1919, a proposal was put forth by labor unions and socialist groups in Europe and the United States to insert into the treaty a provision bearing on labor, with a view to equalizing the conditions of labor in different countries and thus of reducing competition between the industries of such countries. The Industrial Club sent a dissenting opinion to Makino Nobuaki, Ambassador Plenipotentiary of Japan at the conference.

Labor unions in Japan tried, of course, to make the best possible use of such international opportunities. When the first international conference on labor problems was held in 1919, the Japanese government nominated representatives from the Japanese labor movement, but this step was opposed by many unions, including the Society of Friendship and Love. They urged the representatives appointed by the government to refuse to accept the nomination, and they organized demonstrations. In fact, the Society of Friendship and Love requested the secretariat of the International Labor Conference, through Samuel Gompers of the American Federation of Labor, to refuse to recognize the credentials of the Japanese representatives. Although the conference did accept their credentials, the issue continued to be disputed at each subsequent conference and, as a result, the Japanese government made concessions in 1924, authorizing labor unions to elect their own representatives. The labor union movement had only a limited influence on domestic legislation and other policy decisions of the Japanese government, but the issue of representation at the International Labor Conferences represents one of the most outstanding successes achieved by Japanese labor or, more exactly, by Japanese labor with the help of labor unions in the Western countries.

The businessmen's fear of labor unions was aggravated by such developments. Business groups favored oppression of the labor movement by the police force on the one hand and manipulation of labor through indoctrination on the other. Throughout this period business groups continuously challenged the labor movement. They expressed vehement opposition to the passage of a labor union act in 1925–1926, and again in 1929–1930, with the result that no labor union law was adopted before the end of World War II, despite bureaucratic pressure for its passage. Business groups also strongly opposed a campaign to abolish Article 17 of the Security and Police Act, a clause which enabled the police to suppress labor movements.

An example of the attempts by business groups to manipulate labor was the creation in 1919 of the Management-Labor Collaboration Association (Kyōchōkai), a result of an advisory opinion submitted to the government by the Industrial Club.

Many labor unions were opposed to such instances of oppression and manipulation and at the same time played an important role in the movement for universal suffrage. Some of the more radical groups, however, did not participate in the latter movement because they considered it revisionist. When the first general election under universal manhood suffrage took place in 1928, eight Diet members were elected as representatives of four different working class parties. Conflicts among these working class parties correspondingly stimulated strife among and within labor union groups. The converse was also true and this resulted in more division than unity within the labor movement.

Integration under Governmental Control

After the promulgation of the Peace Preservation Law in 1925 and especially after the outbreak of hostilities in Manchuria in 1931, the suppression of radical trade unions became increasingly severe. Those unions which survived tended to cooperate with the bureaucracy and the military in the hope of avoiding further repression, and they were gradually incorporated into the Association for Service to the State through Industry (Sangyō Hōkokukai) and later into the IRAA. Many unions and working class parties competed with each other, each trying to prove that it was more loyal to the imperial system than the others. Although there was a marked tendency during the 1920's and 1930's to recruit leaders from within the organization itself, the role of intellectuals in this respect remained important, especially with regard to the supplying of doctrinal tenets. In the absence of a firm organizational structure within the unions, some leaders responded to extreme radicalism (often leading to their imprisonment). Others conformed to the official ideology and went over to the national-socialist unions, often in the hope that the latter would be socialistic. They also considered, in the absence of strong working class parties and unions, the only way to realize their demands was to depend on the bureaucracy or on semi-governmental organs such as the Association for Service to the State through Industry. They were thereby prevented from presenting demands to management, and eventually they became part of the IRAA. Some of these leaders, however, succeeded in developing access to the bureaucracy in this way.

A similar process of assimilation into the IRAA can be observed in agricultural interest groups. After the establishment of the Federation of Agricultural Cooperatives (Sangyō Kumiai) was legally authorized in 1909, local organizations of cooperatives developed rapidly. By 1915, 93 percent of the cities, towns, and villages came to have local units of cooperatives.[9] Thereafter, the importance of the cooperatives grew steadily as the influence of the large landowning class, and especially that of absentee owners, gradually decreased in the vil-

[9] Tatsuta Nobuo (penname of Inoue Harumaro), *Nihon sangyō kumiai ron* (Tokyo, 1937), p. 303.

lages. The proportion of Diet members representing the cooperatives gradually increased from the beginning of the twentieth century. For example, in 1933 49 members of the Diet were at the same time officers of cooperatives (11 percent of the total number of Diet members), while officers of cooperatives occupied 39 percent of the seats in the prefectural assemblies.[10] It was not, however, until the agricultural depression which followed the economic crisis of 1929 that there emerged a movement to transform the cooperatives into a strong interest group to safeguard the interests of middle-class farmers against those of large landowners and business. This tendency was underscored by the emergence of youth divisions within the cooperatives after 1927, and the formation of the Cooperatives' Youth League (Sanseiren) at the national level in 1933.

In this situation the Chamber of Commerce and Industry (the Chamber of Commerce was so renamed in 1927) organized an attack on the cooperatives, who retaliated by taking into their own hands transactions in fertilizers, thereby cutting out local merchants. In the ensuing struggle many members of the cooperatives came to believe that they were fighting capitalism, though they themselves were middle-class farmers and their real enemy was small merchants rather than large capitalists. The government, fearing that such anticapitalist sentiments might become popular among young cooperative members, sought to suppress the movement, while at the same time utilizing it to strengthen national integration under government control. It introduced a five year plan for the expansion of the cooperatives. By the time this was completed in 1937, government control over the cooperatives had been greatly strengthened. The farmers' discontent turned in the direction of ultranationalist agrarianism, and the cooperatives and their members were absorbed into the IRAA. This was facilitated by their carte blanche leadership,[11] which was

[10] *Ibid.*, p. 134.

[11] Carte blanche leadership is a type of leadership based on the un-

based on the local solidarity of the hamlet and consequently lacked any firm organizational structure. Unsupported
by the voluntary participation of the rank and file, the co-

---

conditional and unanimous dependence of the rank and file on their
leader, without specifying their demands but with a general expectation
that services will be rendered on their behalf by their leader. In any
organization in any country, once the size of the organization becomes
great, the influence which the rank and file can exert on the organization diminishes, while the leadership comes to exercise greater influence
on the policy-making of the organization. This is what the so-called
iron law of oligarchy explains. Carte blanche leadership shares this
common tendency with oligarchy in that popular control is minimal.
It differs, however, from the general pattern of oligarchy in the following respects. First, under carte blanche leadership the reliance of
the rank and file on their leader is unconditional. In other words, the
rank and file trust him and leave up to his discretion the ways and
means of satisfying their demands, even though these demands are not
usually specifically expressed. To be sure, the leader in this case would
often deem it wise to make efforts to meet these general expectations of
the members in order to secure his leadership position, but even if he
deviates from these expectations of the rank and file there is no way
for them to control him. Their support for the leader being unconditional, there are no limitations on loyalty to him; that is, it is incumbent upon them to give unlimited loyalty to their leader. It is true that
this requirement on the part of the rank and file with respect to their
leader is found only in the most typical of cases of carte blanche
leadership, and that it may not always be fulfilled in practice, but it
should be noted that this kind of requirement exerts a psychological
control over the members.

Second, carte blanche leadership is generally based on the harmonious unanimity, or group conformity, of the rank and file. It is
because of this fact that among the rank and file any minority view
criticizing the leader or demanding that he meet a set of conditions
for leadership is suppressed as injurious to the maintenance of harmony
and to the effectiveness of leadership. It is felt that the general expectations of the rank and file are realized only by strengthening their
identification with the organization or, more specifically, with its
leader. Thus there takes place a displacement of goals, in which the
original goals of the members tend to be slighted and their unanimous
identification with the organization, that is, the maintenance of group
conformity through intense in-group consciousness, becomes the focal
point or goal itself.

operatives had to depend on government aid, and this was followed by government control. Community subleaders active in the cooperatives were satisfied by opportunities to enjoy bureaucratic power as lower-level leaders in the IRAA.

In contrast to the labor movement and agricultural organizations, business groups were conservative rather than ultranationalist. They were also more independent and more confident of their economic power. For instance, they resisted bureaucratic intervention in their internal problems (1940), and prevented the government from taking over control of electric power. They did not, however, oppose the wartime economic system, and when the government's monistic integration of interest groups occurred, many important business groups transformed themselves into associations to control their respective industries (*tōseikai*). Although this meant their suicide as autonomous organizations, the business world was nevertheless able to continue to exert influence because of its economic power.

In spite of the above-mentioned differences among interest groups in different fields, interest groups in prewar Japan as a whole shared certain attributes which were characteristically different from their common features in Western countries. If we examine the prewar developmental process of interest groups, we will notice that social differentiation took place only at the intermediate level. At the top the integrity of the principle of imperial rule (*kokutai*) was strong enough to check extreme differentiation. At the lower levels of the society differentiation was limited by the strong traditional structure of the hamlet (*buraku*) or something similar thereto. Therefore, what I call "differentiated totality"[12] characterized the

[12] The phrase "differentiated totality" means that a relatively developed process of differentiation took place at least at the intermediate level, and at the same time, the monolithic totality of the emperor system was not damaged. This totality was maintained not simply by force but also because of the support afforded by the social structure at the lower levels of the society.

type of social differentiation that took place in prewar Japan. In other words, social differentiation took place within the framework of *kokutai*. In fact, the competition in loyalty to the emperor system among interest groups was one of the reasons why they could not maintain their autonomy; instead they dissolved themselves to join the IRAA. Therefore, interest groups in the prewar period could not be voluntary associations in the strict sense, that is, they could not be associations with complete autonomy from governmental control, free to devote themselves to specified purposes.

Another characteristic which continues to this date can be found in the organizational structure of interest groups. Although various interest groups were already highly developed in prewar Japan and had large and highly bureaucratized structures, they were, and still are, based upon units in which all the members in a certain sphere feel that their sphere is a natural one predetermined by the existing social structure (e.g. the factory in the case of labor unions, and the hamlet among members of agricultural cooperatives). In this sense I have to point out that ever since the prewar period there have been elements which hinder differentiation within any interest group, at least at the lowest level of organization. I will deal with this problem in the following sections.

The Occupation

With the collapse of the emperor system—which in actuality had made the formation of voluntary groups in the strict sense almost impossible—autonomous organizations could, for the first time, articulate their own interests more effectively. Hence the Occupation period (1945–1952) almost marks the beginning of interest groups in Japan in the true sense of the term.

The effect of the Occupation on the growth of interest groups was initially indirect. GHQ disbanded the various government-controlled organizations which had been integrated into a monistic framework since 1941, whereupon a multitude of new groups appeared.[13] GHQ then instituted certain policies which positively encouraged the growth of interest groups. For example, the formation of labor unions was encouraged, and agricultural cooperatives were also organized on a voluntary basis. In some ways, however, the Occupation inhibited the growth of interest groups. For example, it vetoed both the establishment of a central organization of businessmen in 1946 and the proposed labor strike in February 1947, while in 1949 it restricted the right of public employees to strike. More important than such specific interventions, however, was the fact that the whole political system was subordinated to the authority of GHQ. Hence interest articulation was performed not by influencing the decision-making process in a complete and self-regulating political system but by petitioning the Occupation authorities, a process the outcome of which was quite dependent on the will of GHQ. For example, one of the compelling factors in forming the Federation of Economic Organizations (Keidanren) was the need "to unify the channels of contact with GHQ."[14] It is apparent from a review of the first ten years of this federation's history that its activities were largely confined to liaison activities during the period of Occupation.

Under the Occupation, interest groups brought their demands (or, rather, their requests) not primarily to the Diet but to bureaucrats who were close to GHQ, for although the Diet was now legally "the highest organ of state power"[15] and its former competitors (the Privy Council, the House of Peers,

[13] In 1950 the number of groups registered with the authorities had reached 16,729, with a total membership of 10,269,558. See Nihon Seinenkai, ed., *Showa 26 nen kessha soran* (Tokyo, 1951), p. 26. This figure includes every kind of group, not necessarily interest groups. If we contrast the situation immediately before defeat, where there was almost no room for voluntary groups, this figure indicates a remarkable change.

[14] Keizai Dantai Rengōkai, ed., *Keidanren no jūnen* (Tokyo, 1956), p. 21.

[15] The Constitution of Japan, Article 41.

the military, etc.) had been abolished, the functions of political parties were not yet sufficiently developed. GHQ had, therefore, to depend on the bureaucrats to fulfill the parties' functions, and it was mostly to the bureaucrats that the interest groups came. Against GHQ and those bureaucrats who supported its policies, interest groups could accomplish very little. When land reform was undertaken by GHQ and enthusiasts in the Ministry of Agriculture and Forestry,[16] the large landowners were unable to offer effective resistance. Nor could the business community resist the policies of GHQ and certain groups of bureaucrats with regard to the dissolution of the *zaibatsu* and the establishment of labor unions.

The Occupation's attempts to keep interest groups free from outside interference had very important effects on their organizational structure. For example, the right of compulsory collection of membership fees was withdrawn from the Chamber of Commerce and Industry and the right to impose compulsory membership, which bound together the prewar agricultural organizations, was denied to the newly established agricultural cooperatives. In factories employees holding supervisory positions were excluded from membership in labor unions. This contrasted sharply with practice in the state-controlled organizations of the preceding era, which were financially dependent on, and supervised by, the government.

Other important changes resulted from social upheavals such as the purge,[17] the dissolution of the *zaibatsu*, land reform, etc. As a result of changes in social conditions the incumbent leaders of many organizations were deprived of

[16] Some of the bureaucrats of the Ministry of Agriculture and Forestry had had blueprints for this undertaking ever since the war, but they had been isolated as Reds and had not been able to surmount the opposition of landlords.

[17] For details see Hans H. Baerwald, *The Purge of Japanese Leaders under the Occupation* (Berkeley and Los Angeles, 1959).

their positions and replaced by new leaders. The reorganization of the business community was carried out, at least formally, not by the former *zaibatsu* leaders but by newly emerging leaders. This was even truer in the case of labor unions. The majority of top leaders in the labor movement who survived the war had been aligned with the IRAA. They were therefore purged by GHQ. The few who were not purged constituted only a negligible proportion of the number of new leaders who had increased rapidly in numbers after the end of the war.[18] The situation was similar in rural areas. Many officials in farmers' organizations were purged because they had held important positions in ex-servicemen's associations or in branches of the IRAA.

Far more important, however, was the effect of land reform, which took from the landowners the basis of their prestige.[19] It was not they but men with managerial experience and ability (frequently ex-servicemen or lower-ranking bureaucrats repatriated from overseas) who came to occupy important positions in the new agricultural cooperatives. This did not, however, mean a fundamental change in the structure of leadership. By weakening hierarchical relationship, land reform increased the existing strong solidarity of the

[18] According to a survey conducted in 1947, only 9.9 percent of those active in forming labor unions had previously participated in the labor movement, while 81 percent had no prior experience at all. See Tokyo Daigaku Shakai Kagaku Kenyūjo, ed., *Sengo rōdō kumiai no jittai* (Tokyo, 1950), p. 28. Between late 1945 and late 1947 the total number of unions and members had grown from 508 and 370,631 to 2,800 and 6 million, respectively. See Suehiro Izutarō, *Nihon rōdō kumiai undōshi* (Tokyo 1954), pp. 146, 197.

[19] The author's research in Ishikawa Prefecture indicates that among local assemblymen the number of former large landowners is clearly decreasing while there is an increase in the number of those who have important positions in various organizations such as agricultural cooperatives, women's organizations, and labor organizations. See Ishida, *Sengo Nihon no seiji taisei* (Tokyo, 1961), pp. 167-68.

hamlets (*buraku*).[20] The postwar agricultural cooperatives accordingly inherited the prewar tendency of relying not on their consciousness of special interest but on geographic solidarity. Despite the dissolution of the hamlet associations (*burakukai*) by the Occupation, the hamlet remained the natural basic unit of rural life, regulating the entire existence of the farmer.[21] The organizational structure of the new agricultural cooperatives was therefore little different from that of the prewar rural associations, despite the fact that Occupation legislation aimed at making them strictly voluntary.[22] From this fact results the tendency of the members to allow carte blanche leadership, reflecting their apathy, as we shall see later.

The situation was similar in the labor movement, despite its postwar reputation for militancy. As is well known, the basic unit of labor union organization in Japan is the enterprise. Persons working in the same factory belong to the same union irrespective of their trade. Consequently, there is a feeling of solidarity not unlike that in the agricultural cooperatives. Here again this led to apathy on the part of the members and to the growth of carte blanche leadership.

[20] See R. P. Dore, *Land Reform in Japan* (London, 1959), pp. 385, 396.

[21] Remember that even in postwar Japan ostracism in the hamlet (*murahachibu*) sometimes takes place. Once a family is ostracized by the villagers, it cannot continue to live in the village and is often forced to leave. See Ishikawa Satsuki, *Murahachibu no ki* (Tokyo, 1953).

[22] Although the executives of the agricultural cooperatives are formally elected by the members, 69 percent of the interviewed members answered that before the election they had already decided, in the form of "a recommendation of the hamlet" (*buraku suisen*), who the executive should be. See Kokuritsu Yoron Chōsajo, *Nōgyō kyōdō kumiai ni kansuru yoron chōsa* (Tokyo, 1952), p. 35. Usually a recommendation of the hamlet is not decided by voting but by *harmonious* unanimity, in which case minority opinion is psychologically forced to keep silence.

This was accentuated by the circumstances attending the formation of the unions. Initially, the Occupation authorities deliberately encouraged the establishment of labor unions. The organizers were dependent on protection by the authorities. There was also a considerable degree of opportunism[23] and exploitation of the supreme symbol, "democratization." In many cases even the management assisted in the formation of the unions, in order to win favor with the Occupation. Many unions were established largely as the result of the efforts of the firms' subleaders.[24] This naturally produced a close affinity between the respective leadership structures. Even in the more radical unions which resisted Occupation policies, things were much the same—amid the group conformity of the rank and file, a handful of leaders issued instructions.

The situation was, however, somewhat different in employers' organizations. Initially GHQ was opposed to the formation of a powerful central association of business organizations. As a consequence these were built from the bottom up. Unassisted by favorable legislation, their growth was, in comparison with agricultural cooperatives and labor unions, spontaneous. There is little evidence, however, that the function of representation was carried out democratically. As before the war, their influence was exerted not through open pressure activities but by means of surreptitious personal relationships with political leaders. This promoted carte blanche leadership on the part of the more influential individuals.

[23] According to a survey conducted in 1947, 61.4 percent of the organizers of the 234 unions examined answered that their motivation in forming the unions was to adapt themselves to "the trends of the times." See Tokyo Daigaku Shakai Kagaku Kenyūjo, *Sengo rōdō kumiai no jittai*, p. 41.

[24] According to a survey carried out in August 1947, 48.7 percent of those who took a leading part in the formation of labor unions in the metals industry were white-collar workers, of whom the majority were in positions of authority (*kakarichō, shunin*, and above). Of the remaining 51.3 percent, 60 percent were persons with special responsibilities (*yakutsuki kōin*). See *ibid.*, p. 79.

One characteristic common to all these influential interest groups which distinguishes them from those which operated before the war is that they are no longer subordinate, at least legally, to the bureaucracy, although weak interest groups are still under its influence in actuality. The pattern of leadership (which had many characteristics resembling the state bureaucracy) had not, however, undergone any fundamental change. This became apparent when, with the end of the Occupation, the activities of interest groups became more active and overt.

Interest Groups since the Peace Treaty

The termination of the Occupation brought independence to the political system, making it possible for interest articulation to be increasingly concentrated on the Diet. It also released forces suppressed during the Occupation. The activities of ex-servicemen's and former landlords' associations come under this category. It also brought into existence interest groups concerned with foreign policy. There are many organizations working for cooperation with the United States and the "free world." Similarly there are a number of organizations aiming at closer relations and increased trade with China and the Soviet Union. Interest group activities were in part responsible for the restoration of diplomatic relations with the latter in 1956. Among the labor unions, some leaders have visited Communist countries, while others have established links with the International Confederation of Free Trade Unions. The recent agitation for the adoption by Japan of ILO Convention No. 87 (embracing the principles of freedom of association and protection of the right to organize) is very interesting as a continuation of the prewar attempts of labor unions to improve labor conditions in Japan by securing the application of international standards.

What effect did the termination of the Occupation have on the status of interest groups within the political system? By and large it became possible for the more powerful groups to present their demands freely, untrammeled by the restrictions previously imposed by the Occupation. Less powerful groups, however, went to the wall as larger groups coalesced, and thus oligopoly ensued.

The status of interest groups within the political system is defined by their relationship with the bureaucracy and the political parties. As regards the latter, the political instability attending the realignments in the conservative parties following the collapse of the Yoshida Cabinet in 1954 is an important factor. But even after the emergence of the so-called two-party system (1955),[25] the organizational basis of the parties and their ability to formulate independent policies have remained weak. Furthermore, party solidarity continues to be gravely undermined by internal factional conflicts.

While the activities of the large and expanding interest groups attracted increasing attention,[26] the weakness of po-

[25] It is not a two party system in a strict sense; instead, it is one and a half party system. This is not only because the number of Diet members of the opposition party is half that of the government party but also because there is little opportunity for the opposition party to attain power. For details see Ishida Takeshi, *Gendai soshiki ron* (Tokyo, 1961), pp. 80-82.

At the same time, the emergence of a "two party system" or the stabilization of a few major parties is an important prerequisite for the activities of interest groups. For if numerous political parties exist, as was the case in the period immediately after the defeat, the parties were able to promote the particular interests of each small group. In fact in 1946 there were 363 political parties, including "one man parties." See Oka Yoshitake, ed., *Gendai Nihon no seiji katei* (Tokyo, 1958), p. 78.

[26] The intensive pressure group activities connected with the preparation of the 1958 budget and the forthcoming general election attracted particular attention. See Ishida Takeshi, *Sengo Nihon no seiji taisei* (Tokyo, 1961), pp. 115-95. For detailed information concerning important interest groups in 1957, see Tsuji Kiyoaki, "Pressure Groups in Japan," in Henry W. Ehrman, ed., *Interest Groups on Four Continents* (Ann Arbor, 1958), pp. 145-53. For more detailed analysis, see Nihon Seiji Gakkai, ed., *Nihon no atsuryoku dantai* (Tokyo, 1960), a review

litical parties made it possible for the bureaucracy to continue to play an important role in the political system. However, as the mechanism for the allocation of rewards became increasingly stabilized under the quasi-permanent control of successive Liberal-Democratic Party (conservative) governments, there emerged a closer and more stable relationship between the Liberal-Democratic Party, the bureaucracy, and interest groups.[27]

The more powerful groups have by means of financial contributions established close relationships with the party in office, and as a consequence such interests cannot be ignored by the bureaucrats. At the same time they have also managed to maintain good relations with the top bureaucrats by cooperating in putting into effect government policies deemed favorable to them. For example, such influential organizations as the Shipbuilders Association, the Iron and Steel Manufacturers League, and the Automobile Manufacturers Association have had their demands satisfied fairly easily by aligning themselves with the top bureaucrats in the Ministry of Industry and International Trade and the Ministry of Finance, because they contribute large amounts of money to party funds and hence have close relationships with top

---

of which appeared in English in *The Journal of Asian Studies,* XXI (Nov. 1961), 379-80.

[27] One evidence which indicates the close relationship between the government party and the bureaucracy is the fact that more than one fourth of the Liberal-Democrats in the House of Representatives are ex-bureaucrats. See Oka, *Gendai Nihon no seiji katei,* p. 76; Fujiwara Hirotatsu, *Kokkai giin senkyo yōran* (Tokyo, 1959), p. 398. Not a few such ex-bureaucrats won election at least partly because of support by interest groups which had close relationships with the portions of the bureaucracy that these men had formerly represented. This is especially the case in the House of Councilors, which has a national constituency that affords room for occupational representation. In this House, more than one third of the Liberal-Democratic members are ex-bureaucrats (Oka, *Gendai Nihon no seiji katei*).

leaders of the government party. Most legislation subsidizing particular industries, such as the Law for Government Subsidy and Compensation for Financing the Construction of Ocean Liners (1953), has been achieved in this manner. The Japan Federation of Employers Associations (Nikkeiren) has virtually brought under its control the Ministry of Labor, whose favorable response to demands of the federation was apparent in the enactment of a law restricting the right to strike in essential service industries in 1953.[28] Similarly, evasions of the antimonopoly legislation by business organizations were made possible by skillful acts of drafting and interpretation by bureaucrats who through their executive actions covered up violations.

On the other hand, if the situation is such that the interest groups themselves have economic and social power but the government agencies relating to their interests are weak, the former will not consider it very important to have close relationship with the latter and will try to have their demands satisfied even in the face of the opposition of the government agencies. Such was the situation when the Medical Association attempted to enforce its demands in the face of opposition by the Ministry of Welfare. It should be noted, however, that in this instance the opposition of the Medical Association to the ministry was occasioned by the fact that its competitors, the Pharmacists Association and the Health Insurance Federation, were concentrating their lobbying activities on the same ministry to force it to adopt a policy line close to what they had been advocating.[29]

The weaker interest groups have sought to have their demands satisfied by helping the government party members

[28] The Japan Federation of Employers Association is often called jokingly the Ministry of Labor in Marunouchi because of its strong influence on the Ministry of Labor. Marunouchi is the name of the district where the office of the federation is located.

[29] For detail see Taguchi Fukuji and Toshinai Yoshinori, "Atsuryoku dantai to shite no ishikai," *Chūō kōron*, LXXIV (April 1959), 246–68.

retain their majority in the Diet. They try to balance their requests with their offers of personnel for election campaigns or of their influence on the votes they control.[30] Their demands, however, are always whittled down by too great a willingness on the part of their leaders to make concessions to the government party. This is the result of their organizational weakness, particularly of their carte blanche leadership.

The labor unions receive political support only from the Socialists, who hold but one third of the seats in the Diet—equivalent to zero in terms of decision-making power in a country like Japan where the deliberative process has little significance.[31] Since there is little prospect of the Socialists coming to power in the near future, the unions tend to be opposed to the political system itself, as in the past.[32]

[30] For instance, when the bill concerning the mutual benefit association for the employees of agricultural organizations was introduced, a total of 2,000 members of agricultural cooperatives came petitioning to the Diet during a period of five months, and 455,000 people, including the families of these members, signed the petition. See Ishikawa Hideo, "Nōkyō no mittsu no kao," *Chūō kōron*, LXXIII (May 1958), 132-38. It is also said that the number of Diet members elected in 1958 with the support of the agricultural cooperatives came to 18 in the Liberal-Democratic Party, 6 in the Socialist Party, and 2 among the independents. See Nōsei Jānarisuto no Kai, ed., *Kikan nōsei no ugoki*, III (June 1958), 53-54.

[31] The principle of majority rule is often misinterpreted by the government party to mean that the majority party can do anything it likes without taking account of minority opinion. This is mostly due to the one and a half party system and partly to the fact that in traditional Japanese society the most common relationship between persons or groups is either harmony without discussion or tension without possibility of coordination.

[32] This does not mean that labor unions are indifferent to the Diet. In fact in 1959 there were 97 Diet members who had been union leaders and who were elected by the support of unions. Among them 78 were from unions which belonged to the General Council of Japanese Labor Unions (Sōhyō) and the rest from other unions. See Matsushita Keiichi, "Rōdō kumiai no seiji katsudō," Nihon Seiji

The end of the Occupation removed restrictions on the establishment of large organizations and methods of attaining demands appropriate to them. It also opened the way for competition among organizations. Such competition resulted in an emphasis on homogeneity (in the case of the Federation of Economic Organizations, they excluded from membership smaller industries and enterprises in 1952) and in the strengthening of organizational discipline within interest groups. Moreover, since the groups were based on traditional forms of leadership, it became even more difficult for the views of the rank and file to be reflected in action. The structure of the agricultural cooperatives, which are distinctly stratified between a top level which is highly bureaucratized and a lower level where the natural solidarity of the village prevails, is reproduced to a certain degree in practically every interest group in the country.[33]

As time passed after the conclusion of the peace treaty, the Conservative government became increasingly more stabilized and the rewards-allocation mechanism more fixed. Under such circumstances the leadership structure of interest groups gradually adapted itself to the existing patterns of the rewards-

---

Gakkai, ed., *Nihon no atsuryoku dantai* (Tokyo, 1960), p. 99. Because of this and the weakness of the Socialist Party in terms of its organizational basis, the unions' influence on the party is often very strong, although the party has been trying to be independent of labor unions.

[33] Of course the degree of reproduction of this structure is different from group to group. Strictly occupational groups, such as those among professionals (e.g. the Medical Association and the Bar Association) seem to be free from the tendency here described. Indeed, these organizations in Japan have much in common with their counterparts in Western countries. At the same time, however, the all-embracing nature of these organizations allows the presence of an in-group consciousness of a kind among their members which is somehow similar to that among villagers. The reason why I have used many examples drawn from agricultural and labor organizations rather than from groups of professionals is that my major interest lies in finding organizational structures that are relatively peculiar to Japanese interest groups.

allocation mechanism, as exemplified by the replacement of the Socialist president of the Repatriates Federation by a Conservative Party leader.[34] There has been an undeniable tendency on the part of the conservative party to exploit such interest groups as a substitute for an independent party organization, which is extremely difficult to build under the present circumstances. At the same time, from the point of view of the interest groups, especially the weaker ones, it has been considered practically more prudent to depend on the existing rewards-allocation mechanism in order to establish a favorable position in the ongoing interorganizational competition. For example, in 1959 when the amendment of the Social Education Act permitted the government to provide subsidies to various organizations engaged in social education (this practice was prohibited under the Occupation authorities), women's and youths' associations, etc., in order to make certain that they would obtain their shares of these government subsidies, were tempted to exhibit their loyalty to the government even at the expense of their independence as interest groups. This lessened popular control over their internal structures. The same can be said of the Chamber of Agriculture (Nōgyō Kaigisho), which openly asked the government party for increased subsidies in return for the adoption of a resolution pledging their support to the Conservative government on the Security Treaty issue.[35]

Over this period the qualifications for leadership have nevertheless been changing from the traditional emphasis on family ties to an emphasis on organizational and managerial abilities. How is this consistent with the preservation of the old type of leadership discussed above? The answer is that these abilities are judged in terms of success—albeit sometimes short-term superficial success—in dealing with the leaders of the Conservative Party and the government and in se-

[34] For details see Ishida Takeshi, *Gendai soshiki ron* (Tokyo, 1961), p. 99.
[35] *Ibid.*, p. 172.

curing benefits through manipulation and maneuvering on the basis of the carte blanche power delegated by the rank and file. The reason why interest groups, especially the weaker ones, give important executive posts to retired high-ranking bureaucrats is that they have such qualifications by reason of their training and experience.[36] Such leaders may be successful in a short term sense, e.g. in obtaining government subsidies. Even if this is the case, however, whether such subsidies are good for the long-term interests of the organization is another problem. For if the autonomy of the organization is sacrificed for subsidies, the organization cannot continue to achieve its own objectives by itself; instead its objectives may be dictated or at least influenced by the government with its own ends in view.

In addition, in the case of carte blanche leadership, feedback operations cannot be expected because of the lack of popular control. In other words, the tendency toward achievement orientation has been developed to a relatively high degree although the content of the achievement is often not very specific, and at the same time the particularistic relationship between the leader and the rank and file is still strong, as it is between the leader on the one hand and the bureaucrats and party leaders on the other. In this sense the traditional combination between achievement orientation and particularism in Japan that Professor Robert N. Bellah described[37] still has great influence on the pattern of development of Japanese interest groups.

The characteristics of interest groups are, as we have shown,

[36] Many interest groups, either through obtaining government subsidies or establishing other close relationships with the government, have been transformed into a kind of extradepartmental appurtenance of the bureaucracy (*gaikaku dantai*). According to a governmental survey, among 303 such groups, 63 obtain subsidies which amount to 1 billion 240 million *yen* in total; 175 groups have provided retired government officials with executive positions. See Kanryōseido Kenkyū-kai, *Kanryō* (Tokyo, 1959), p. 130.

[37] Robert N. Bellah, *The Tokugawa Religion: The Values of Pre-industrial Japan* (Chicago, 1957).

closely related to those of the bureaucracy and the political parties. Although many changes are taking place in Japan today, it is difficult to predict whether these changes will produce a basic transformation in the pattern of interest groups as described, since the possibility of such a transformation is closely related to changes in the political parties and the bureaucracy, and vice versa.

Conclusion

What light does the development of interest groups as described above throw on the nature of political modernization in Japan? Needless to say, the development of interest groups indicates a tendency toward social differentiation, which, as we have stated, is one of the most important characteristics of modernization. Certain factors were, however, responsible for the type of social differentiation that has resulted in Japan.

In Japan today the loyalty expected of a member toward the organization to which he belongs still assumes the nature of total involvement in the affairs of the organization rather than a partial commitment to the specified objectives for which it was established. To illustrate: relatively differentiated activities such as music, arts, and sports are undertaken by various groups within labor unions and agricultural cooperatives. These organizations encourage this kind of differentiation taking place within them because of its value in maintaining and strengthening members' loyalty to the organizations. This is the reason why organizations tend to avoid overlapping memberships despite the pluralistic nature of present-day society; conflicts of loyalty must be prevented.

Closely related is the tendency for each organization to be all-embracing, to take in all potential members. For example, all villagers usually belong to an agricultural cooperative, and all workers in a factory become, almost automatically, members of the enterprise labor union.[38] Leaders have

[38] The agricultural cooperatives have organized 99.5 percent of all

favored this tendency, which is conducive to the maintenance and development of natural group conformity or in-group consciousness as the basis of solidarity. It was on the basis of just such a concern that they were ready to solicit government intervention in prewar days to achieve compulsory membership in extreme cases such as the agricultural associations.

Total involvement and in-group consciousness which arises from the all-embracing character of an organization enable an interest group to participate in all sorts of activities —ranging from entertainment to election campaigns—which fall outside its original organizational purposes. Therein, however, lie organizational weaknesses; if the activities of an interest group become too broad, its objectives may become vague and diffuse. Moreover, total involvement cannot be attained in the complicated and pluralized social life of today.

These weaknesses produce a more serious problem. If an interest group tries to strengthen in-group consciousness by emphasizing its exclusiveness, as is often the case in Japan, it cannot be an agent for political modernization in the sense used in this paper. For in such a case the interest group will emphasize nonfunctional in-group solidarity at the cost of existing differentiations and thus actually hinder the further development of functional differentiation. Indeed, borrowing Professor S. N. Eisenstadt's term we may call this a "breakdown of modernization" or a tendency toward "demodernization."[39]

To offset such shortcomings of total involvement and the all-embracing character of organization, the leader can and actually

---

farming families. See Nōrin Chūō Kinko Chōsabu, *Nōgyō kyōdō kumiai jūnen no ayumi* (Tokyo, 1957), p. 35. This is, of course, an extreme case among interest groups in Japan. Even in the case of labor unions, the percentage of organized laborers in the entire labor force is around 36 percent. This is lower than in England because many enterprises have no union, but higher than in the United States because almost all workers in an enterprise with a union are union members (Ishida, *Gendai soshiki ron,* p. 89).

[39] See S. N. Eisenstadt, "Breakdown of Modernization," p. 349.

often does tend to depend on carte blanche delegation of power. In such cases, despite the strength of group conformity or in-group consciousness among the members, the leader cannot expect active spontaneous participation by the members in the attainment of specific objectives. All that he can expect is that they should behave in such a way as to maintain group conformity. Therefore, even though all the members seem to be active in doing something to support group conformity, this activity does not indicate spontaneous participation. Instead it is a result of passive obedience to the leader or to the principle of group conformity. In this case, behind the outward appearance of activity, we have to point out the existence of a kind of apathy. Probably we are describing a paradox—the greater the demand for total loyalty, the greater the apathy. This apathy can be accelerated by the vagueness of objectives of the organization due to carte blanche leadership.[40]

Organizations which are dependent on the apathy of members often try to strengthen in-group consciousness instead of spontaneous participation. This in turn increases still further the members' apathy and makes it even more difficult for the organization to be supported by their conscious participation. This kind of vicious circle occurs most frequently when these defects of organization are combined with the difficulties common to present-day interest groups in any country which has huge bureaucratized organizations, e.g. the difficulty in mobilizing rank and file for active participation.

[40] For instance, if one belongs to an interest group like an agricultural cooperative, he is expected to be loyal to the organization without limitation. Members of the cooperative are expected not only to buy cultivators and chemical fertilizers and sell agricultural products through the cooperative, but also to vote for candidates recommended by the cooperative. Of course, the latter expectation cannot be fully satisfied in the actuality of today. In addition, because of difficulty in satisfying the above expectation, members of the organization become apathetic even toward the specific objectives of the organization.

Discontent among the rank and file under the traditional carte blanche leadership can rarely find effective remedy because of the lack of popular control and creative leadership. Minority opinion is considered a hindrance to in-group consciousness and group conformity and is, therefore, rarely respected. Consequently, the discontented members often form a faction within the organization rather than working out their differences with the main group through ordinary organizational procedures. But the leaders of such factions tend in turn to be dependent on the same structure of organization we have described, and hence they have to face the same problems as did the old leaders. It is very difficult for them to change this structure, because it is based upon the leaders' dependence on the total involvement of the members, who in turn are totally dependent on the organization or, often, on its leaders.

When a new faction appears, a serious conflict usually develops between the main group and the new faction, since both seek the total involvement of all members. Such factional conflict is a phenomenon common to almost all organizations in Japan, including political parties. Often the organization splits, in which case the competition to secure all potential members becomes intense.

Struggle among organizations often takes the form of competition for a more general cause than the specific objectives of the organizations concerned. The leaders have to evoke a general cause partly because special interests are rarely considered legitimate in traditional Japanese culture, and partly because the nature of the organizational structure makes the specification of objectives difficult. This is why the IRAA was able fairly readily to integrate many competing organizations.

Another factor to be taken into consideration is the strong impact of the feeling of the "historically inevitable trend." For example, when the IRAA emerged many leaders seemed to feel that the integration of their organizations into the IRAA was inevitable. Therefore, the only question for them was how they could become more influential within the new IRAA than others.

Under present conditions interest groups are unlikely to be integrated into a monistic semigovernmental organization such as the IRAA, because the emperor system, which had integrated the entire society, has ceased to play an important role, either as a political system or as an integrative value system. A phenomenon similar in some respects to the prewar tendency, however, might develop even in postwar Japan, because, first, the basic characteristics of organizational structure have not yet been changed in the sense that I have described, and, second, many people of present-day Japan still tend to consider accumulated or established facts as "inevitable." Even though I used the term "value system" to describe the emperor system in prewar Japan, this value system was not a codified system of normative values. Instead the above-mentioned value system was mostly dependent on accumulated facts including the common attitudes of the people in those days. In this sense a similar tendency continues in Japan even today with some necessary modifications. The extreme importance of the existence of a semipermanent government party, the tendency toward oligopoly among interest groups, and the close relationships between the government party, bureaucracy, and important interest groups are outstanding examples of factors making for this historical continuity. The fixed reward-allocation mechanism as an established fact has made many interest groups consider it prudent or even inevitable to depend upon or adjust themselves to the existing mechanism. Factional conflicts within almost every organization and serious competition and conflicts among various contemporary organizations are also examples of historical continuity.

The existence of many interest groups and the competition among them have, to a certain extent, contributed to political modernization, because this competition has accelerated the tendency toward achievement orientation. More important, however, is the fact that many interest groups, once established, tend to lose their modernizing functions in the structuring process or in the process of institutionalization. Hence they actually become agents of political "demodernization."

Although both the necessity for social differentiation and a certain response to this necessity have existed throughout the history of modern Japan, we should distinguish between conditions in which the response is institutionalized in such a way that functional differentiation can be developed further and conditions where further development is impossible because functional differentiation becomes entangled with the substantial separation of potentially differentiated sectors. I will call the latter case "social compartmentalization" instead of "social differentiation" in the strict sense. This tendency toward social compartmentalization has been pronounced in the structuring process of interest articulation, pointing to one of the most important and interesting characteristics of the pattern of political modernization in Japan.

One may question whether what I have described above represents a Japanese pattern of demodernization rather than of modernization. But in my view there is in every culture a possibility of change from modernization to demodernization. To what extent and in what manner this possibility is realized is, however, different from culture to culture. What I wanted to show in this paper was the characteristic pattern of this change in Japan.

CHAPTER X

Structural and Functional Differentiation in the Political Modernization of Japan

BERNARD S. SILBERMAN

J APAN's experience in political development provides an
exceptionally fine case study for description and analysis
of the evolution of the criteria of specialization and differentiation in political development.[1] Japan's political development is relatively recent and extremely well documented, thus
providing the analyst with a wealth of data for description and
measurement. Furthermore, the process in gross terms is so
well along the way that Japan has, since the 1920's, been
classified as a "developed" rather than as an "undeveloped"
society. The Japanese case is perhaps especially apt because
Japan was the first non-Western society to achieve a level of
economic and political output and complexity approaching
that of the more developed Western societies.

The attempt to isolate the factors which contributed to Japan's rapid transformation has been a major focal point of
study and analysis in a variety of disciplines. Analysis of
specialization and differentiation in Japan's governmental

[1] The term "differentiation" as used in the context of governmental
structure, function, and role is defined as *the formal quantification
and/or definition of the activities of any governmental structure, official, or category of operations hitherto unquantified and/or undefined
by statute.* The term "specialization" as used in the context of governmental structure, function and role is defined as *the formal specification
of the performance of any quantified and/or defined activity of any
governmental structure, official, or category of operations hitherto un-
specified and/or undefined by statute.* The term "quantifications" in
this context is defined as *the specification and/or definition of the
number of governmental structures, officials, or categories of operations.*

structure is one area of examination, however, that has been significantly neglected. This type of analysis may provide not only specific substantive data regarding Japan's political development but may also provide some insight into the various factors and dynamics affecting the rate and "success" of political development in societies which have undergone or are now undergoing an experience similar to Japan's in the last hundred years.

Any attempt to describe, in quantitative and/or qualitative terms, structural, functional, and role differentiation and specialization in the entire Japanese governmental structure would be a project requiring many years and considerable resources and would result in a study of enormous length. This study suggests that the same objective may be achieved by analysis of a more limited area of governmental structure but one which also adequately represents and reflects the entire structure in terms of its role and development.

On the basis of the following considerations the prefectural level of government was chosen as the focus of this analysis: (1) the central ministries were excluded, since they were quite removed from developments taking place at the lowest levels of government and were thus very resistant to demands and pressures emanating from these lower levels; (2) government structure at the *gun* level and below was excluded because of its removal from developments occurring at the central level, that is, the problems faced and dealt with by local government did not adequately reflect the range of problems or the processes developed for dealing with them that emerged at the central level of government; (3) prefectural government before the Occupation reforms, however, was a direct extension of the central government's administrative and, to a certain extent, rule-making and adjudicative machinery, and changes at this level consequently reflected very closely changes at the central level; (4) prefectural structures and functions have tended to be in Japan, and elsewhere as well, a key link between planning at the central national level and implementation at the individual and small-collectivity level of the society. Because of this "linkage" aspect prefectural government has served as a planning, implementing, and adjudicating structure. As a linking structure, prefectural government has tended to be the primary mechanism for introducing innovation and gaining acceptance and support for its implementation. In this multiple role prefectural government was extremely sensitive not only to changes occurring in political function, action, and demands at the central level but also to changes occurring at the lower levels of government. The intermediary or "linking" role of prefectural government makes it, thus, especially important and suitable as an object of analysis in the attempt to understand society-wide political development.

Another major problem with regard to limiting data to manageable proportions is the time span of the analysis. For several reasons the time span for data collection in this chapter was limited to the period 1867–1920. The primary consideration was that by 1920 there had emerged a political structure capable of a remarkably high degree of control, integration, and output. Furthermore, by 1920 Japan had already acquired many of the basic characteristics of an industrialized society or was in a "takeoff" period characteristic of a relatively complex differentiated and specialized economic structure. The same period also saw Japan accepted as a major world power and exerting influences on a worldwide scale. All three of these developments suggest that the early 1920's was the end of the period of greatest innovation and change which had seen Japan emerge as a relatively highly developed modern nation-state. For this reason 1920 was chosen as the terminal date for this analysis.

The attempt to describe and analyze the emergence, development, and characteristics of the two criteria under examination here raises several basic problems. There has long been a general consensus that specialization and differentiation are characteristic of political development.[2] However, no one has yet devised a means of using these two processes to clarify and elucidate the general process of political development. This study attempts to devise a means of isolating some of the major factors affecting specialization and differentiation in governmental structures, functions, and roles and at the same time indicate how the specific nature of the specialization and differentiation processes in Japanese government affected the general course of political development.

The method created, on an experimental basis, to achieve these purposes is based on two generally accepted features of the processes of specialization and differentiation: (1) in societies where there is a tendency to separate the performance of political functions from the performance of other functions such as economic ones, there is proliferation of new political structures, functions, and roles which in turn implies increased specialization in the organization and performance of these new structures, functions, and roles. This is especially the case where, as in Japan, a major goal of government is rapid economic development that forces it to become increasingly involved in a wide range of technical activities demanding functional specialization. (2) In societies where there exists a tendency toward greater structural, functional, and role specialization and differentiation, the magnitude of government decisions and operations also increases. Or, to sum it up quite simply, the tendency toward greater specialization and differentiation is closely associated with increases in the kinds and/or magnitude of services and operations performed.

To the extent that this is true, then, specialization and differentiation may be examined in quantifiable terms by analysis of their apparent correlates—increases and/or decreases in functions and structures. The emergence and development of structural, functional, and role specialization and differenti-

[2] See for example Joseph LaPalombara, *Bureaucracy and Political Development* (Princeton, 1963), pp. 39-44.

ation in Japanese prefectural government can be analyzed then by establishing whether increases in functions actually occurred and whether increases in the number of structural components accompanied such functional increases. Equally important is the determination of the rate at which increases in function and structure took place. Again, if it is true that specialization and differentiation are consequences of increases in function, structure, and roles, then the pinpointing of various stages of development at given points of time will be dependent on and reflected in the pattern of increase. We may call this pattern of increase the *rate configuration*, and the first step of this analysis is the determination of this configuration.

Data on rate configuration may also provide the basis for establishing hypotheses, capable of being tested in other societies, concerning the existence of a general rate configuration in all societies undergoing political development. Wide variations in the speed of political development may obscure the presence of a general configuration or pattern. Thus, for example, regardless of the actual elapsed time involved in reaching a specific level of complexity, there may be in all societies moving from one mode of political operation to another, a pretakeoff period, a takeoff period, a period of high mass consumption of public services, and other, as yet undetermined phases. Ascertaining the presence or absence of such a configuration may be basic for an understanding of the more general problem of determining variables affecting the actual elapsed time necessary to reach various levels of functional, structural, and role differentiation and specialization.

A second area of analysis closely related to the first concerns the problem of ascertaining the political and social structural areas in which functional and structural increases occurred. Determination of the areas in which increases or outputs occurred will indicate in which areas specialization and differentiation occurred most heavily: whether in the political-structural output areas of rule-making, rule-application, or rule-adjudication; or in the social-structural output areas of control, socialization, or role coordination. Analysis of the political and social output increases in terms of time periods should also indicate in what areas specialization and differentiation took place most heavily at various periods of prefectural governmental development. This pattern of increase distribution may be termed *output configuration* and is the second area of focus of this analysis.

In a more general sense analysis of output configuration in prefectural government in Japan may provide the basis for the formulation of hypotheses relating to political output as a factor in the speed of specialization and differentiation in developing societies at large. Thus, for example, it may well be that in a society such as Japan's in mid-nineteenth century where control of the population was well articulated, the process of functional and structural differentiation occurred first and most heavily in the rule-application, role-coordination areas, and the relatively lower economic cost of such structures and functions helped make possible the rapidity of Japan's political and economic development.

The third and final phase of analysis is concerned primarily with the direction or orientation of structural and functional rate-output configurations. If it is correct to assume that increases in functions and structures are accompanied by increasing utilization of the criteria of specialization and differentiation in organizing and performing increased duties, then we should expect to find the emergence of a distinct pattern, closely related to rate and output configurations, of the evolution of these two basic criteria. This pattern we may call an *orientation configuration*. Determination of this configuration may provide insight into why political development proceeds at a more rapid pace in some societies than in others. Ascertainment of the approximate points in time at which various levels of specialization and differentiation emerged in prefectural government may indicate, in conjunction with rate-output configurations, some of the preconditions of rapid political development.

Summing up this rather long introductory statement, we may say first that this analysis of structural and functional differentiation in the political development of Japan is focused on the prefectural level of government, which is viewed as a reflection and indicator of the general process of political development in Japan during its most formative years, 1867–1920. Second, the analysis is conceived as proceeding through three phases: (1) determination of a rate configuration; (2) determination of an output configuration; (3) determination of an orientation configuration. These three steps in the analysis of functional and structural increases should provide both substantive data on political development in Japan and data upon which to develop hypotheses concerning this process in other developing societies.

Methodology

Ascertaining and describing the three configurations outlined above required the use of data sources with certain specifications: (1) the data used in analysis of the three configurations had to be comparable, since the phases of analysis were closely related; (2) the data sources for each phase of examination had to be continuous for the whole period of 54 years, since shifts in the type of data within any one phase could only lead to noncomparability within each step of analysis as well as among the various steps; (3) the data sources had to be generally reliable. The one body of material which seemed to fulfill all of the requirements was the *Collected Statutes* (*Hōrei zensho*). The statutes provided a continuous record of all formal changes in the functions and structure of prefectural government. Furthermore, the statutes provided adequate data for all three phases of analysis. Since the statutes were and are recorded by day, month, and year, they were an excellent source for rate configuration analysis. Statutes, because they define and describe each change carefully, provided probably the best source for determination of output. Comparison of statutes also provided the necessary data for analysis of the orientation configuration. Because the same body of material supplied the data for all three phases of analysis there was no question of noncomparability.[3]

The first step in providing data for all three phases of analysis was the extraction from the *Collected Statutes* of all statutes indicating a change in the function and/or structure of any office, bureau, elected body, or appointed committee or commission at the prefectural level.[4] The total number of such statutes for the years 1867–1920 was 317, ranging from Diet laws and imperial ordinances to ministerial orders. The contents of each statute was coded to provide data for all three phases of analysis. For rate configuration, the month, day, and year of each statute was recorded. For the other two

[3] It may very well be argued that in developing societies there may be a wide gap between formal codes and actual performance and therefore the data source used here is not valid. This objection can be answered by two considerations: (1) contemporary material and later studies indicate that the changes in the formal code were for the greater part carried out in actual performance. See Miyatake Tokotsu, *Fu-han-ken seishi* (Tokyo, 1941); Kuribayashi Teiichi, *Chihō kankai no hensen* (Tokyo, 1930); Kikegawa Hiroshi, *Meiji chihō jichi seido no seiritsu katei* (Tokyo, 1955); Royama Masamichi, *Chihō gyōseiron* (Tokyo, 1937): (2) Even where wide gaps exist between formal code and practice, the formal codes reflect the basic orientation of governmental-administrative practice. The codes will also usually reflect the areas where the greatest difficulties exist with regard to practice, usually through the proliferation of and constant changes in the codes dealing with those areas.

[4] For purposes of this analysis "structural change" is broadly defined as a change involving the creation, elimination, or transfer of any office, bureau, elected body, or appointed committee or commission. "Functional change" is broadly defined as any increase, elimination, or transfer of categories of duties performed by any official, bureau, elective body, or appointed committee or commission. "Categories of duties" are defined as a cluster of operations performed for a formally defined purpose.

phases of analysis the statutes were coded in terms of the following categories:

1. Type of change—functional, structural, both, clarification of function, clarification of structure, specification of criteria for officeholder. (*Both* in the case of the example in 2 below.)

2. Direction of change—increase and/or decrease of structure or function by numbers of changes in terms of political structural and social structural output. That is, each change was recorded in one or more of the following nine categories:[5]

   Rule-making: legislative structures, functions and roles
     control
     socialization
     role coordination
   Rule application: executive-administrative structures, functions and roles
     control
     socialization
     role coordination

---

[5] Each of the political structural outputs is viewed here with regard to the three basic social functions of political systems: (1) *social control*, that is, the control of disruptive behavior such as the illegitimate use of force, institutionally unacceptable innovation, and apathetic behavior with regard to social norms, all seen from the point of view of those who have a monopoly on the legitimate use of force: (2) *socialization*, the control, care, and training of infants, children, and adults; for example, the establishment and maintenance of schools, public health measures, maintenance of religious institutions and rehabilitation institutions; (3) *role coordination*, the planning, allocation, and integration of roles such as planning for the training of needed specialists in government or other areas of the society, the definition of the areas of activity and/or authority of social, economic, and political roles, or behavior or the establishment of mechanisms such as courts and new administrative structures for avoiding or adjudicating conflicts between persons performing various roles.

Rule adjudication: judicial structures, functions and roles
control
socialization
role coordination

As an example we may use the case of the statute establishing the position of *gun* secretary (Home Ministry Regulation 73, November 11, 1878). The statute defines the title of the position, the range of duties ("carry out the administration of the *gun* under the direction of the *gun* chief"), appointment (by the *gun* chief with ratification by the prefectural governor), salary, and annual investigation of performance. As an administrative structural increase the change was coded under rule-application. Since it concerned not only allocation of a category of operations but operations previously performed by the *gun* chief alone, the change was considered as belonging in the area of role coordination, which, as we have seen, also includes role allocation and integration.

3. Ministry for which service was performed (*Home Ministry* in the case of the example in 2).

4. Specific operational area of change, i.e. schools, law enforcement, administration, public relief, public health, agricultural extension, military conscription. A total of forty different such operational areas emerged from examination of the statutes (*administration* in the case of the example in 2).

5. Level of prefectural government at which change occurred —governor's office, central prefectural office, city, *gun* level and below (*gun level and below* in the case of the example in 2).

6. Extent of structural change, i.e. new officer, new bureau, new elective body, new appointed commission, replacement, decrease in officer, decrease of bureau, etc. (*new officer* in the case of the example in 2).

7. Number of increases and/or decreases by categories in 6 above (*one* increase in the case of the example in 2).

8. Specific criteria for new structure or function, i.e. requirements for office explicit and specialized, requirements for office not explicit, operations specifically defined, operations generally defined (*requirements for office not explicit* in the case of example in 2).

9. Existence of internal administrative regulation and control, i.e. increases in structure, function and role require reports, periodic investigation of performance, provide for punishment of nonperformance or ill-performance of duties (in addition to civil service punishment regulations), provide for specific term of office, or passage of a specific level of civil service examination (*periodic investigation of office* in the case of example in 2).

Rate Configuration

A general idea of changes in structure and function may be had from the distribution of the 317 statutes over the fifty-four year period of the analysis. Table 1 shows this distribution in five year steps. The distribution of statutes suggests that the majority of structural and functional changes had

TABLE 1
STATUTE DISTRIBUTION BY FIVE YEAR PERIODS
1867-1920

Year	No.	Percent	
1867-1871	15	4.7	
1872-1876	86	27.1	55.7%
1877-1881	47	14.8	
1882-1886	29	9.1	
1887-1891	40	12.6	
1892-1896	21	6.9	
1897-1901	34	10.6	
1902-1906	11	3.4	44.0%
1907-1911	17	5.3	
1912-1916	12	3.7	
1917-1920	5	1.5	
TOTAL	317	99.7 (100.0)	

occurred by 1886. The concentration of statutes in the five year period 1872–1876 indicates this to be the most crucial period in terms of prefectural and, by inference, national governmental structure, a period of extensive experimentation and change. The sharp decline in the number of statutes after 1901 is an indication of the beginning of a new period of development or a period of stabilization.

Are the inferences suggested by the distribution of statutes supported by the data on rates of structural and functional increase? Table 2 provides data on the distribution of structural increases. The data in Table 2 tends to both support and re-

TABLE 2

STRUCTURAL INCREASES BY FIVE YEAR PERIODS

Year	No. Increases	Percent	Percent Rate of Increase	No. Decreases
1867-1871	31	17.1 ⎫		10
1872-1876	27	14.9 ⎬ 54.6	87.3	1
1877-1881	41	22.6 ⎭	70.7	1
1882-1886	13	7.2	13.1	5
1887-1891	34	18.8	30.3	4
1892-1896	9	5.0	6.1	2
1897-1901	19	10.5	11.6	2
1902-1906	2	1.1	1.1	3
1907-1911	3	1.6	1.7	2
1912-1916	1	.55	.5	0
1917-1920	1	.55	.5	0
TOTAL	181	99.9 (100.0)		30

ject some of the inferences suggested by statute distribution. The distribution of structural increases indicates two distinct periods of development: (1) 1867–1901, in which the rate of structural increase remained above 10% except for 1892-1896, when the rate dipped to 6.1%; (2) 1902-1920, in which the rate of increase remained below 2% and the absolute number of increases did not rise above 3%. Although the statute distribution suggested that over half of the changes and increases occurred by 1886, data in Table 2 shows that in actuality 54.6% of the structural increases had occurred by the end of 1881, only fifteen years after the new government had come into existence. Interestingly enough, while statute distribution indicated that the highest rate of change probably occurred in the period 1872-1876, this was not in fact the case in terms of structural increase or increase and decrease taken together. The period 1872-1876 ranked fourth in the absolute number of increases, although it was highest in rate of increase. The latter was true however only because there was no increase established for the period 1862-1866. The highest absolute increase came in the period 1877-1881, in which 22.6% of all increases occurred. This apparent anomaly between the high number of statutes including structural and/or functional changes which were promulgated in the period 1872-1876, and the relatively small number of structural increases suggests that changes in this period were partly a consequence of the quantification and limitation of prefectural powers rather than of increases in new categories of operations. Changes of the former type would not immediately result in the creation of new structures, since the scope of prefectural powers was being reduced. If this, paradoxically, is true then we should expect to find large increases in function during this period, a consequence of the quantification and definition of prefectural governmental functions.

The number of structural decreases is surprisingly small, only 30 over a fifty-four year period. Some caution must be displayed in the use of this figure, since structural decreases in the first five to seven years of the Restoration were often not explicitly defined. For example, the statute abolishing the fiefs and establishing the prefectural system in 1871 is only a few lines long and does not explicitly eliminate any structure.[6] Some degree of accuracy was achieved by careful comparison of statutes dealing with prefectural changes in im-

[6] *Hōrei zensho*, Imperial Ordinance 353, July 14, 1871, p. 284. (*Hōrei zensho* cited hereafter as *H.Z.*)

mediately preceding and following periods, so that while the figure 30 may not be entirely accurate, it is a close approximation.

Examination of the data on functional increases at the prefectural level exposes a pattern of development similar to that of structural increase. These data are described in Table 3. In-

TABLE 3

Function Increases by Five Year Periods
1867-1920

Year	No. Increase	Percent	Percent Rate of Increase	Decrease
1867-1871	29	6.8 ⎫		1
1872-1876	136	32.0 ⎬ 50.8	469.0	9
1877-1881	51	12.0 ⎭	30.9	1
1882-1886	31	7.3	14.3	10
1887-1891	43	10.1	17.4	1
1892-1896	37	8.7	12.7	3
1897-1901	49	11.3	14.9	1
1902-1906	9	2.1	2.4	1
1907-1911	19	4.5	4.9	0
1912-1916	14	3.3	3.4	1
1917-1920	7	1.7	1.7	0
TOTAL	425	99.9 (100.0)		28

creases in prefectural level operations, as in the case of structure, fall clearly into two broad periods: (1) 1867-1901, characterized by rates of increase above 10% in each five year period, and (2) 1902-1920, in which the rates of increase remained below 5% for any five year period. The years 1867-1881 again emerge as a critical period, one in which over half of the increases in function occurred. The expectation, expressed above, that 1872-1876 would be a period of high function increase is fulfilled. This five year period accounts for almost one third of all increases. This strongly supports the contention that a large proportion of functional increases in this period were due to the redefinition of local power, which brought in its wake apparent but not real increases in function and few increases in structure.

The number of function decreases is very small, only 28 out of 453 changes.[7] Comparison of structural and function decreases for 1867-1871 reveals an interesting surface disparity. In the period 1867-1871 there were ten structural decreases but only one decrease in function. This disparity tends to support the view that the abolition of the *han* structure did not result in widespread changes in the structure of authority at the *ken* level. The small number of statutory decreases may again be an indication that in this period specialization and differentiation in structure and function occurred primarily through quantification and limitation of prefectural powers in general, which, while limiting the scope of power, produced few formal decreases in specific categories of operations.

From this data on the rate of increase in structure and function we may draw some general conclusions. First, it seems evident that there were two distinct periods of prefectural structural and functional increase. The first period from 1867 to 1901 is characterized by relatively high rates of increase or investment in both political structure and function. To use a term current in the literature of economic development, this period might be conceived of as a takeoff period in which the product was an expanding structure of national power and one in which there was considerable experimentation with political "investment." Again using an economic analogy, investment in this period, we may hypothesize, resulted primarily in the creation of the "capital structure" of power; control, socialization, and role planning and coordination. Within this takeoff period we may also conclude that the five years from 1872 to 1876 were the most critical and experimental in generating political change and thus

[7] Again caution must be displayed in use of this figure since elimination of function throughout the whole period under analysis was not always explicitly defined in the statutes. Consequently, some decreases were arrived at by comparison of statutes.

probably the most critical in establishing the direction of change. That this was true on the national as well as the prefectural level is indicated by the fact that the period 1873-1875 was one which saw the emergence of the men of predominantly lower samurai origins as the directors of the national government.[8]

The second period of increase from 1902 to 1920 is characterized by a sharp drop in the rate and number of increases. This would seem to suggest the beginning of a new level of development, one in which investment of resources in expansion of structure and function is replaced by investment in public services, the structures and functions of which had been created in the preceding period. That this conclusion is essentially correct is reflected in the fact that budget allocations for *fu-ken* administration and functions carried out by the *fu-ken* continued to increase after 1902 despite the dramatic decline in structural and functional increases.[9]

These two periods of development are not only descriptively related but also seem dynamically related. For instance, the creation of a structure of universal primary education along with a system of secondary schools and a university system

[8] See Bernard S. Silberman, *Ministers of Modernization; Elite Mobility in the Meiji Restoration: 1868-73* (Tucson, 1964), pp. 52-53, 107.

[9] The following table indicates the growth of *fu-ken* allocations for every fifth year from 1877 to 1920.

1877	5,789,720	1902	8,439,949
1882	4,766,487	1907	9,758,432
1887	7,893,386	1912	9,881,259
1892	5,788,276	[a] 1917	11,494,826
1897	6,263,225	[a] 1920	17,856,856

[a] Preceding year's budget in effect.

The source for these data are the estimated budgets for the years indicated as they appear in the *Hōrei zensho*. These figures include amounts allocated for prefectural offices and officers, shrines, temples, public health, and police. They do not include later additions to the annual estimated budget. (All figures rounded off to the nearest *yen*.)

in the takeoff period certainly tended to generate increasing demands for participation in the entire system in the second period. This did not result in any major changes in structure or function but required the increasing expansion of facilities and resources. In the long run this may have required large-scale changes both in structure and function, but the years immediately following the takeoff period would be ones in which mass consumption of services was brought up to the level of the ability of the existing structures to provide these services. To the extent that this conclusion is essentially correct a study of prefectural government in the period 1920-1940 should reveal a pattern of increase rates and outputs similar to that of the period 1902-1920. One might conclude from this that the extremely high rate of mass consumption of public services characteristic of postwar Japan is merely an expansion and extension of developments which had been in process since the beginning of the century.

Finally, the nature of the rate configuration leads also to the expectation that the process of specialization and differentiation in prefectural structure and function occurred primarily in the period 1872-1902, the years of greatest structural and functional increases. We should also expect to find, accompanying specialization and differentiation in structure and function, the emergence of new criteria for recruitment and advancement within the prefectural administrative structure. The period 1872-1902 should see the emergence of functionally specialized performance as the basis for recruitment, and of achievement in specific duties and examinations as the basis for advancement.

Output Configuration

The second phase of this analysis is concerned with a description and analysis of the rate of prefectural structural-functional increases in terms of political and social structural output. The analysis of structural increases on this basis is indicated in a composite manner in Table 4.

TABLE 4

Political and Social Structural Output of Structural Increases
by Five-Year Periods, 1867-1920

	Areas of Social Output							
	Control		*Socialization*		*Role Coordination*			
Year	*Increase*	*Decrease*	*Increase*	*Decrease*	*Increase*	*Decrease*	*Subtotals*	
							Inc.	*Dec.*
1867-1871								
R.-M.	2	1	–	1	–	1	2	3
R.-Ap.	5	1	9	1	16	2	30	4
R.-Adj.	1	1	–	1	–	1	1	3
Subtotal	8	3	9	3	16	4	33	10
1872-1876								
R.-M.	–	–	1	–	2	–	3	–
R.-Ap.	11	–	12	–	8	1	31	1
R.-Adj.	2	–	2	–	2	–	6	–
Subtotal	13	0	15	0	12	1	40	1
1877-1881								
R.-M.	1	–	2	–	6	–	9	–
R.-Ap.	12	–	7	–	13	1	32	1
R.-Adj.	–	–	–	–	–	–	–	–
Subtotal	13	0	9	0	19	1	41	1
1882-1886								
R.-M.	–	–	–	–	–	–	–	–
R.-Ap.	3	1	2	1	9	2	14	4
R.-Adj.	–	–	–	–	–	–	–	–
Subtotal	3	1	2	1	9	2	14	4
1887-1891								
R.-M.	3	–	1	1	3	–	7	1
R.-Ap.	5	1	3	2	14	2	22	5
R.-Adj.	0	1	0	0	2	1	2	2
Subtotal	8	2	4	3	19	3	31	8
1892-1896								
R.-M.	–	–	–	–	–	–	–	–
R.-Ap.	3	1	7	–	6	1	16	2
R.-Adj.	–	–	–	–	–	–	–	–
Subtotal	3	1	7	0	6	1	16	2
1897-1901								
R.-M.	2	–	–	–	2	–	4	–
R.-Ap.	6	–	4	–	10	2	20	2
R.-Adj.	–	–	–	–	1	–	1	–
Subtotal	8	–	4	0	13	2	25	2

Areas of Social Output

Year	Control		Socialization		Role Coordination		Subtotals	
	Increase	Decrease	Increase	Decrease	Increase	Decrease	Inc.	Dec.
1902-1906								
R.-M.	–	–	–	–	–	–	–	–
R.-Ap.	–	1	2	–	–	2	2	3
R.-Adj.	–	–	–	–	–	–	–	–
Subtotal	0	1	2	–	–	2	2	3
1907-1911								
R.-M.	–	–	–	–	–	–	–	–
R.-Ap.	2	–	1	–	–	2	3	2
R.-Adj.	–	–	–	–	–	–	–	–
Subtotal	2	–	1	–	–	2	3	2
1912-1916								
R.-M.	–	–	–	–	–	–	–	–
R.-Ap.	–	–	–	–	1	–	1	–
R.-Adj.	–	–	–	–	–	–	–	–
Subtotal	–	–	–	–	1	–	1	–
1917-1920								
R.-M.	–	–	–	–	–	–	–	–
R.-Ap.	1	–	1	–	–	–	2	–
R.-Adj.	–	–	–	–	–	–	–	–
Subtotal	1	–	1	–	–	–	2	–
TOTALS	59	8	54	7	95	18	[a]208	[a]33

Rule-Making 25 +; 4 —
Rule-Application 173 +; 24 —
Rule-Adjudication 10 +; 5 —

[a] The differences in increases and decreases between Tables 3 and 4 are accounted for by the fact that some structures were recorded as performing operations in more than one area of political or social output.

As one might expect, the greatest number of structural increases came in the form of additions to the administrative aspect of prefectural government. Rule-application increases accounted for 83.1% of all structural increases. Rule-making and rule-adjudication increases were small in number, amounting to 12.0% and 5.0%, respectively, of the total. In terms of time, 53.7% of rule application increases, 56.0% of rule-making increases, and 70.0% of rule-adjudication increases had occurred by the end of 1881. Since the majority of structural increases were rule-application in character, we should expect the pattern of rate increase to be similar to that of general increase. The data in Table 4 indicates this to be true. There is the maintenance of a steady high rate of increase in rule-application structures from 1867 to 1901. From 1902 there is a sharp decline in increases, pointing again to the conclusion that this marks a new period of development.

The same pattern appears also for the other two areas of structure. Rule-making increases did not occur at all from 1902 to 1920. While no increases occurred at all in 1882-1886 and 1892-1896, the remaining periods contained some increases. Rule-adjudication increases practically disappeared after 1876. The decline of increases in these two areas even before 1902 indicates that the prefectural structure was moving toward greater specialization as an almost purely administrative structure after 1876. Again 1872-1876 appears to be the crucial period in the determination of the direction of political development.

One general conclusion that may be drawn from these data on political structural output is that the period 1867-1901 in addition to being a takeoff period in terms of structural increase was one also of takeoff in terms of specialization and differentiation of prefectural governmental structure taken as a unit. Between 1867 and 1881 the primarily bureaucratic administrative character of prefectural government had emerged. The rule-making and rule-adjudicative aspects of the *ken* predecessor, the *han*, had become differentiated and specialized and largely eliminated from the prefectural structure. Differentiation of prefectural functions was reflected in the increases and decreases of clearly defined rule-making and rule-adjudicative structures appearing by 1881. Thus, for example, of the five rule-adjudicative structural decreases, three occurred after increases had come to an end, indicating the differentiation and transfer of these operations to the Ministry of Justice. Differentiation in this case was accompanied by specialization. The minor adjudicative structures and operations which remained within the prefectural structure were concerned specifically with regulating relations between various administrative divisions in the *ken* and in deciding issues concerned with local taxation.[10] All other adjudicative structures were transferred to the Ministry of Justice by 1876, and at this point prefectural officials, except for members of the prefectural council (*sanjikai*), ceased to perform adjudicative functions.[11]

Much the same is true in the case of rule-making structures. The majority of increases were connected with the establishment of *ken-gun* assemblies, which had jurisdiction only over local financial matters. Rule-making in this case was differentiated from administration, and this too had largely occurred by the end of 1881 and the process was completed by 1901 (see Table 4).

After 1901 the fact that increases came almost exclusively in rule application leads to the conclusion that the role and nature of prefectural government had become stabilized. Furthermore, the small number of such increases tends to support the conclusion arrived at earlier that this represented the beginning of a period of institutional stability in which investment took the form primarily of providing services rather than expansion of structure.

Examination of the data on structural increases in social structural output indicates that almost twice as many increases (45.7%) came in the area of role coordination than in the areas of control (28.3%) and socialization (26.0%). In each of these three categories more than 50% of the increases had occurred by the end of 1881. Between 1867 and 1901 role-coordination increases clearly predominated in every pe-

---

[10] These adjudicative functions were vested in the *fu-ken sanjikai*, or council, which was also an administrative body. *H.Z.*, Diet Law 35, May 17, 1890, pp. 66-84.

[11] Minobe Tatsukichi, *Nippon gyōseihō* (Tokyo, 1936), I, 422-23.

riod with one interesting exception, 1872-1876. In this five year period increases were approximately the same in all three areas of output. After 1901, however, increases in the area of role coordination predominate only slightly.

These data suggest, first, that the primary problems of government in the takeoff period were those concerned with role integration, planning, and allocation. Problems of control and socialization were important but clearly secondary. Only in 1872-1876 were all three categories relatively equal in increases, suggesting that these five years were somehow crucial in determining future political development. After this point investment in role-coordination structures increased and dominated, indicating a trend toward specialization in terms of social output. However, it is important to note that social structural specialization did not proceed to the same level as political structural specialization. Prefectural government continued throughout the whole period to develop structures, primarily administrative in character, in the areas of socialization and control as well as in the area of role coordination. Again the small number of increases after 1901, spread out almost equally among all three categories, points to the emergence of a distinctively new period of development in which role coordination was no longer the primary concern. The decrease of new structures, especially in administrative role coordination, would seem to indicate, in the light of steadily increasing budget allocations, that the primary characteristic of this second period of structural development was the increasing provision of services.

Conclusions reached in the preceding section are strongly supported by analysis of functional increases and decreases in terms of political and social structural output. Analysis of this data is presented in composite form in Table 5.

As Tables 5 and 6 indicate, increases in administrative categories of operations accounted for 87.4%, rule-making categories accounted for 9.3%, and rule-adjudicative categories accounted for 3.5% of the total number of increases.

TABLE 5

POLITICAL AND SOCIAL STRUCTURAL OUTPUT OF FUNCTIONAL INCREASES
BY FIVE YEAR PERIODS, 1867-1920

Year	Control		Socialization		Role Coordination		Totals	
	Increase	Decrease	Increase	Decrease	Increase	Decrease	Increase	Decrease
1867-1871								
R.-M.	4	0	3	0	2	0	9	0
R.-Ap.	7	0	10	0	28	1	45	1
R.-Adj.	5	0	0	0	1	0	6	0
Subtotal	16	0	13	0	31	1	60	1
1872-1876								
R.-M.	4	0	4	0	5	0	13	0
R.-Ap.	26	0	37	0	90	3	153	3
R.-Adj.	1	6	4	0	4	0	9	6
Subtotal	31	6	45	0	99	3	175	9
1877-1881								
R.-M.	5	0	4	0	8	0	17	0
R.-Ap.	29	1	24	0	30	0	83	1
R.-Adj.	0	0	0	0	0	0	0	0
Subtotal	34	1	28	0	38	0	100	1
1882-1886								
R.-M.	0	0	0	0	1	0	1	0
R.-Ap.	8	0	10	1	27	1	45	2
R.-Adj.	0	0	0	0	0	0	0	0
Subtotal	8	0	10	1	28	1	46	2
1887-1891								
R.-M.	5	0	4	0	5	0	14	0
R.-Ap.	13	0	13	1	37	0	63	1
R.-Adj.	1	0	0	0	3	0	4	0
Subtotal	19	0	17	1	45	0	81	1
1892-1896								
R.-M.	0	0	0	0	0	0	0	0
R.-Ap.	11	1	17	0	17	2	45	3
R.-Adj.	0	0	0	0	0	0	0	0
Subtotal	11	1	17	0	17	2	45	3
1897-1901								
R.-M.	3	0	0	0	3	0	6	0
R.-Ap.	15	1	13	0	28	1	56	2
R.-Adj.	0	0	0	0	2	0	2	0
Subtotal	18	1	13	0	33	1	64	2

Year	Control		Socialization		Role Coordination		Totals	
	Increase	Decrease	Increase	Decrease	Increase	Decrease	Increase	Decrease
1902-1906								
R.-M.	0	0	0	0	0	0	0	0
R.-Ap.	6	0	4	0	7	0	17	0
R.-Adj.	0	0	0	0	0	0	0	0
Subtotal	6	0	4	0	7	0	17	0
1907-1911								
R.-M.	0	0	0	0	0	0	0	0
R.-Ap.	12	0	7	0	9	0	28	0
R.-Adj.	0	0	0	0	0	0	0	0
Subtotal	12	0	7	0	9	0	28	0
1912-1916								
R.-M.	0	0	0	0	0	0	0	0
R.-Ap.	6	0	8	0	6	0	20	0
R.-Adj.	0	0	0	0	0	0	0	0
Subtotal	6	0	8	0	6	0	20	0
1917-1920								
R.-M.	0	0	0	0	0	0	0	0
R.-Ap.	4	0	3	0	2	0	9	0
R.-Adj.	0	0	0	0	0	0	0	0
Subtotal	4	0	3	0	2	0	9	0
TOTALS	165	9	165	2	315	8	645	19
							664	

TABLE 6

SOCIAL STRUCTURAL OUTPUT OF FUNCTIONAL
INCREASES BY POLITICAL STRUCTURAL OUTPUT

	Control			Socialization			Role Coordination			Total
	Incr.	Decr.	Total	Incr.	Decr.	Total	Incr.	Decr.	Total	Total
Rule-Making	21	0	21	15	0	15	24	0	24	60
Rule Application	137	3	140	146	2	148	281	8	289	577
Rule Adjudication	7	6	13	4	0	4	10	0	10	27
TOTALS	165	9	174	165	2	167	315	8	323	664

Over 50% of the increases in function for all three political structural categories occurred by the end of 1881. Indeed, functional increases as a whole tend to follow closely the output pattern of structural increases. Increases in rule-application functions dominate throughout the entire period. As in the case of structural increases, functional increases in rule adjudication almost ceased after 1876. In the area of rule-making functions, increases largely ceased after 1891. These data tend to confirm the conclusion that the process of specialization and differentiation in prefectural government reached a critical point in the period roughly between 1867 and 1881. Prefectural government emerged during this period as a predominantly administrative structure with very few nonadministrative structures and functions.

The pattern of functional increases in social structural output closely follows that which appears in the analysis of structural increases. Role-coordination increases equaled 48.8%, control and socialization increases both equaled 25.6% of the total increases. Increases in function were clearly dominated by role-coordination increases in the period 1867-1901 but assumed relative equality with the other categories in the following period. We may conclude from the data that in the period 1867-1901 coordination, planning, and allocation of roles which had developed in both the pre- and post-Restoration period were the primary problems of the political and social structure. Problems of disruptive behavior and apathy, of care, protection, and education apparently were not as pressing as the necessity for regulating already existing and newly emerging roles, integrating roles into nonconflicting collectivities, and planning for the development of new roles to perform necessary functions. Increases in role-coordination functions subsided, and in some cases fell below increases in other categories, after 1901 indicating a resolution of the role-coordination problems of the takeoff period.

Several general conclusions also may be drawn from the data on output of structural and functional increases. As we have seen, the basic direction of prefectural government seems to have been determined by the end of 1881. At this point prefectural government appears to have emerged as a predominantly bureaucratic administrative structure. To the extent that this conclusion is correct and reflects national as well as prefectural developments, it seems safe to say that the direction and character of Japanese governmental development was assured by 1881. The social structural-output configuration also suggests some conclusions with regard to the relatively short span of the takeoff period. The heavy investment in role-coordination activities reflects the fact that problems of control of disruptive behavior, of control of apathy, of public health, of population control, of adequate food supplies, and of value dissemination were not conspicuous problems in the years immediately following the Restoration. Absence of major problems in these areas probably made possible heavier investment in the integration of local and translocal economic and political structures and roles than might have otherwise been possible. This conclusion tends to be supported by the fact that of all structural and functional increases approximately two thirds in each category were concerned with problems of economic and/or political development.[12] The ability to invest heavily in these areas of political-economic role coordination resulted in what appeared to be a highly rapid and "successful" transformation.

The emphasis on economic and political aspects of role coordination also undoubtedly led, in the case of Japan, to the early emergence of a relatively specialized and functionally specific bureaucratic administrative structure. Had the major area of investment or development been control, lower levels of specialization and differentiation probably would have resulted. Control structures tend to require less

[12] Structural increases were divided as follows: economic structures, 32.2%; political structures, 32.2%; control structures (law enforcement, punishment), 19.1%; socialization structures (schools, public health), 17.3%. Functional increases were divided as follows: economic structures, 34.3%; political structures, 33.6%; control structures, 17.4%; socialization structures, 14.7%.

specialization and differentiation since the technology of internal social coercion is considerably less demanding than that of other aspects of political-economic development. Furthermore, if trained manpower and economic resources are relatively scarce, their diversion primarily to control structures and functions hinders the development of role coordinating structures in the areas of political and economic development, political unity, control, and stability. This process is so costly that, in societies where resources are scarce, little is left over for economic development.

Under such conditions a vicious tail-chasing trap develops, out of which the society may not emerge to complete the takeoff period. This is not to say that the Japanese investment in control structures such as police and the armed forces was low or relatively nonexistent. The important point, however, is that structural, functional, role, and economic investment in control structures did not predominate over the investment in the remaining areas of social output. Japan was able to avoid this situation not through the prior existence of an efficient rational administrative bureaucracy but, apparently, because of the existence of widespread accepted values of hierarchical authority disseminated and maintained by strong social structures such as the family. If this is true, then one is led to the conclusion that Japan's rapid political development was in large part dependent on the existence and maintenance after 1868 of certain kinds of "traditional" patterns of behavior in the areas of social control and socialization. We should then expect traditional patterns of behavior to exist alongside nontraditional ones within the prefectural structure where implementation of national laws was effected at the local level. This essentially is the problem to which the final phase of this analysis is directed, the determination of the level of specialization and functional differentiation arrived at in the period 1867-1920.

Orientation Configuration

To this point, analysis has been concerned with ascertaining the magnitude and general character of structural and functional increases at specific intervals over the period 1867-1920. The data in this analysis has suggested that by the end of 1881, as a corollary of the large number of structural and functional increases in the period 1867-1881, specialization and differentiation in structure and role had emerged as basic criteria for the organization and development of prefectural government and therefore of national government as well. The validity of this view may be tested by an examination of the development of one major aspect of prefectural government—prefectural administrative organization. If this view is correct, we should expect to find, in the period 1867-1881, a rapid and major transformation in the nature of prefectural administration. Functional diffusion ˙in role and structure should have been replaced by functional specificity, administrative roles should have increased on the basis of specialization of performance, the hierarchy of responsibility should have emerged clearly and the governor's position transformed from one of considerable autonomous judicial, administrative, and rule-making power to one of restricted administrative power. In short, we should expect to find that by 1882 prefectural administrative organization had taken on characteristics which have been termed "modern."

A general indication of the amount of administrative change which occurred is the large number of major revisions of prefectural administration between 1867 and 1920. In this period there were fourteen major reorganizations or revisions of prefectural administrative structure.[13] In the first reorgani-

13 These revisions are encompassed in the following statutes: H.Z., Dajōkan Ordinance 117, Feb. 5, 1869, pp. 58-62; H.Z., Dajōkan Ordinance 203, Nov. 30, 1875, pp. 769-84; H.Z., Imperial Ordinance 17, July 22, 1878, pp. 11-12; H.Z., Imperial Ordinance 32, July 25, 1878, pp. 143-49; H.Z., Imperial Ordinance 54, July 20, 1886, pp. 284-91; H.Z., Law 1, April 17, 1888, pp. 1-92 (Municipalities Code); H.Z., Imperial Ordinance 225, Oct. 10, 1890, pp. 467-74; H.Z., Imperial Ordinance 162, Oct. 30, 1893, pp. 283-90; H.Z., Imperial Ordinance 253, June 14, 1898, pp. 375-82; H.Z., Imperial Ordinance 34, March 19, 1903,

zation, in 1869, the central structure contained only two permanent positions, governor (*chikenji*) and vice-governor (*hankenji*), above the rank of clerk or administrative assistant, and these positions had no clearly defined area of duties. A hierarchy of responsibility was inferred but nowhere clearly defined. The responsibility of the governor to the central government, for example, was noticeably absent. At the lower levels of prefectural government the *han* system of inspectors (*metsuke*) and village headmen was retained without change, but their responsibility to the central prefectural administration was again only implied. The definition of the scope of prefectural powers was so wide as to indicate that the central government existed almost in name only. These powers included the right to set and collect taxes, to establish laws of administrative procedure, to establish an administrative system, to establish a system of primary education, to encourage industry and commerce and establish taxes for that purpose, and to establish internal boundaries.[14] These wide powers were contained in twelve short and ambiguously worded articles which in effect gave the governor complete control of affairs within the prefecture. Without any prior knowledge of the state of Japanese government in 1869, a reading of this statute would immediately indicate the relatively unspecialized, undifferentiated character of the administrative structure as a whole. The prefecture emerges as an apparently semi-autonomous unit in which the governor had wide undifferentiated powers and governed through an administrative system based primarily on local custom.

The growth of the central government's authority over the next six years coincided with a great increase in prefectural structures and functions (see Tables 2 and 3). The

pp. 34-35; *H.Z.*, Imperial Ordinance 140, April 18, 1905, pp. 163-71; *H.Z.*, Imperial Ordinance 266, July 12, 1907, pp. 349-52; *H.Z.*, Imperial Ordinance 151, June 13, 1913, pp. 194-202; *H.Z.*, Imperial Ordinance 349, July 16, 1919, pp. 350-52.

[14] *H.Z.*, Dajōkan Ordinance 117, Feb. 5, 1869, Articles 1, 2, 4, 8-12.

earlier analysis of increases in output did not specifically indicate whether these increases were a consequence primarily of functions added to already existing prefectural powers or whether they were the result of the quantification and, paradoxically, the narrowing of prefectural activities, although the latter was assumed to be true. Examination of the prefectural administrative reorganization of 1875 indicates that this assumption is correct.[15] Several positions were added, the most important being the *kami* (*rei*) and the *sanji*. Their functions were not clearly defined, but they apparently represented movement toward specialization and differentiation of certain of the governor's functions. The *kami* was the chief executive officer after the governor while the *sanji* was the chief administrative officer directing the various bureaus of the governor's secretariat. It is notable that the bureaus (general affairs, industry and commerce, taxation, police, education, and receipts and disbursements) were still conceived of as part of the governor's office rather than as separate administrative units, although the creation of the *sanji* was a move in this direction. Again, the hierarchy of responsibility was not clearly defined, and nowhere is this lapse more evident than in the repeated failure to define the governor's responsibility to the central government. One concludes from this that while the central government had grown considerably in power, the office of prefectural governor was still a position of considerable autonomy and one which was still functionally diffuse.

This conclusion is supported by the redefinition of the scope of prefectural power and activity which accompanied the structural reorganization. The twelve simple articles which defined prefectural power in 1869 are here expanded to ninety-one articles which reduced the scope of prefectural activities. The ninety-one articles are, in fact, a quantification of the

[15] All revisions discussed below are encompassed in *H.Z.*, Dajōkan Ordinance 203, Nov. 30, 1875, pp. 769-84.

broad ambiguous statement in the earlier statute. The powers were divided into two groups, those completely within the governor's jurisdiction and those derived from the ministries of the central government. The former is more important for those powers which are now specifically omitted from the governor's sole jurisdiction rather than for those which are included. While the governor had the power to reduce taxes at his discretion on specific occasions, he no longer had the power to set the amount of taxes or remit them entirely. Also notably absent is any mention of adjudicative power, which was transferred to a system of courts directly under the Ministry of Justice. Control and regulation of land were also specifically omitted from this list but were included under the list of powers derived from ministries of the central government. This latter list indicated for the first time that the governor's powers at least in part were derived from the central government rather than inherent in the imperial appointment.[16] Included in this list of powers, which now necessitated a ministerial directive, although not prior approval, were several important categories of power and control: land control and regulation (Articles 16, 20, 30-34, 40-41), increasing taxes (Article 15), sale of official property (Articles 11, 16, 26, 27, 42), disbursal of tax monies (Articles 13, 14, 21), auditing of tax receipts (Articles 17-18) and maintenance of the family registers (*koseki*) (Article 1).

One conclusion that may be drawn from this description of the reorganization of 1875 is that increases in structure and function in the period 1872-1876 appear to be primarily a consequence of the quantification and differentiation of existing powers rather than accumulation of totally new areas of activity. This perhaps explains the extremely high rate of structural and functional increases in the area of rule application for a period which was notable for the implementation of only a few widespread social and economic reforms that

[16] Article 2 of this list states, "The governor shall supervise the duties of the various departments."

by themselves would not have resulted in such increases. One other conclusion that might be drawn from this analysis is that quantification, differentiation, and accompanying specialization seems to have been, in this period, a means of undermining the autonomy of local power. The reorganizations of 1869 and 1875 taken together appear to be the reflection of a process whereby the central government, lacking coercive power, sought to undermine local power by gradually transferring or eliminating prefectural powers. Diffuse categories of operation were defined and broken down into differentiated aspects so that they could be gradually eliminated or transferred to the agencies of the central government. The concomitant of this quantification was the multiplication of structure. As differentiation of operations occurred the number of operations increased, requiring more personnel and the emergence of administratively integrating positions such as the *sanji* and *kami*. This, in turn, tended to increase the distance between the governor and the administrative machinery, thus weakening the personal position and power of the governor.

This aspect of the process of differentiation and specialization appears to be confirmed by examination of the prefectural reorganization of 1878.[17] The metamorphosis of the domain into the prefecture was completed by this revision. The governor's functions and his direct responsibility to the central government were made very clear.[18] The hierarchy of

[17] *H.Z.*, Dajōkan Ordinance 32, July 25, 1878, pp. 143-49.

[18] *Article 1.* The city governor and prefectural governor shall exercise full authority over all administrative affairs within his jurisdiction and shall enforce the laws and directives of the government.

Article 2. The governor shall be under the control of the home minister but in matters relating to other ministries he shall carry out the directives of the ministers of the departments concerned.

Article 3. When it is necessary to implement laws or directives of the government, the governor may establish regulations for this purpose and proclaim them in the area of his jurisdiction. In such cases where the governor is authorized to employ his own discretion and establish

responsibility within the prefectural structure was equally clearly defined. Each official was made legally and formally responsible to a given superior. The number of permanent positions at the central administrative level above the rank of administrative assistant or clerk was decreased to two: the governor and secretary (*daishoshikan*). The secretary replaced the *kami* and *sanji* and performed the functions of chief administrative officer and vice-governor. The governor's secretariat was retained and was staffed by the administrative assistants. For the first time police functions were clearly differentiated and placed in the hands of a police division directly responsible to the governor. The predominance of the central government was further reflected in the establishment of definite terms of office and salaries for permanent prefectural officials. The governor's term of office was limited to twelve years with a review of his performance every three years.[19] With this act the governor and his officials became members of the central administrative bureaucracy and liable to removal by the central government, a power not hitherto claimed by the central government.

Implementation of the ordinance creating the district-city-town-village (*gun-ku-cho-son*) system was also provided for by this reorganization.[20] *Gun*, *ku*, and *son* (*mura*) officials, while they continued to be appointed or approved and supervised by the governor, were defined for the first time as officials of the central government.[21] The total result of the

---

regulations and methods for implementation, he must notify the minister of the department concerned.

Article 4. If the methods or regulations employed by the governor are considered contrary to the law or the directives of the government or are considered to be in excess of his powers, the prime minister or the minister of the department concerned may invalidate the governor's orders or regulations.

[19] *H.Z.*, Dajōkan Ordinance 35, Aug. 3, 1878, p. 150.

[20] *H.Z.*, Dajōkan Ordinance 17, July 22, 1878, pp. 11-12.

[21] *H.Z.*, Dajōkan Ordinance 32, July 25, 1878, pp. 143-49. *Article 3.* The *gunchō* shall receive his orders from the governor and shall en-

prefectural reorganization of 1878 was to complete, at least formally, the transformation of the local system of government from a structurally and functionally diffuse, semiautonomous structure to a relatively specialized administrative mechanism of the central government. After 1878 there was no longer a question of the independence of local policy and decision-making; these were now in the hands of the central government. This is perhaps best reflected in the fact that the governor's powers were no longer enumerated. There appeared now only a list of activities for which it was necessary to seek prior approval.[22] The functions of the *gun*, *ku*, and *cho* chief officials (*gun-*, *ku-*, and *kochō*) were also defined, providing also for the first time a relatively clear differentiation between the various levels of prefectural administration and operation.

This brief outline of prefectural changes in 1878 confirms an earlier conclusion that prefectural government had by the end of 1881 taken on its basic form as a primarily administrative role coordinating structure. This conclusion is further corroborated by the nature of the changes in prefectural administration over the next forty years. Throughout this period almost no fundamental changes were made in the nature and function of prefectural administration. The revisions of administration after 1878 were concerned almost totally with providing new positions and bureaus to handle the increasing business occasioned by expansion of duties in those areas left to local government after the revisions of 1875 and 1878.

The Local Government Organization Ordinance of 1886, for example, provided for six new permanent positions (chief tax collector, tax collectors, governor of prisons, chief prison wardens, assistant chief wardens) and expanded the number of secretaries to two. The governor's secretariat was replaced by an administrative system of two divisions, Divisions I and

---

force the laws and directives of the government throughout his jurisdiction and generally administer the affairs of his *gun*.

[22] *Ibid.*, Section III.

II, and two departments, tax and police.[23] The divisional functions and responsibility were more carefully defined than in previous statutes. Finally, a system of insular government was introduced which was similar to the *gun* structure. It is clear that these expansions of structure and personnel were the consequence of increases in number of categories of operations required to implement new systems of taxation, law enforcement, punishment, education, and public health which had been introduced in the period roughly between 1872 and 1886. Very much the same may be said of the changes encompassed in the Local Administration Organization Ordinance of 1890.[24] The major purpose of this ordinance was to create the positions of director of police, councilor, chief and assistant engineers and to establish a governor's secretariat to handle the increased burden of the governor's administrative duties.

The revisions of 1893 and 1899 followed a similar pattern of increasing specialization and differentiation within the administrative organization. The revision of 1893 is characterized by its emphasis on clarification, specialization, and differentiation of duties in the central administrative divisions and governor's secretariat.[25] In the case of the latter, the scope of activities was reduced with the removal of duties relating to foreigners. The number of divisions was increased from two to four with expansion of the police and prison departments. A permanent public health section was added to the internal affairs division (Division I). No new positions were added but the number of officials was expanded. The revisions of 1899 created a separate education section within the internal affairs division, headed by a chief school inspector who supervised the new system of *gun* school inspectors.[26]

[23] *H.Z.*, Imperial Ordinance 54, July 20, 1886, pp. 284-91.

[24] *H.Z.*, Imperial Ordinance 225, Oct. 10, 1890, pp. 467-74.

[25] *H.Z.*, Imperial Ordinance 162, Oct. 30, 1893, pp. 783-90.

[26] *H.Z.*, Imperial Ordinance 253, June 14, 1899, pp. 375-76. The new positions of *ken* and *gun* school inspector were filled on the basis of

After 1900-1901 the revisions of prefectural administration are characterized by gradual increases in specialized personnel, differentiation in duties, and specialization of the administrative structure as a whole. Thus, for example, the revision of 1903 eliminated the prison division, which was transferred to the Ministry of Justice.[27] The reorganization of 1905 added the position of interpreter-translator and changed the secretary to chief administrative officer (*jimukan*), the number of which was now expanded to provide a chief officer for each administrative division. The tax division was now formally eliminated and its duties and officers transferred completely to the Ministry of Finance. This did not reduce the number of divisions (four), since a new division was now created to handle affairs relating to agriculture, commerce, fishing, forestry, and land, functions which had previously been scattered throughout other divisions.[28] The remaining revisions added several new specialized positions (assistant police inspector, internal affairs division chief, bureau chiefs [*rijikan*]), and reduced the number of divisions from four to two (internal affairs and police) but raised the status of division sections in internal affairs to bureaus of which there were now ten.[29] The period after 1901 thus saw a sharp decline in personnel expansion and reorganization of administration. However, the revisions which did take place continued the trend toward increased internal and external specialization and differentiation of structure and role.

Several general conclusions may be drawn from this analysis of prefectural administrative development. First, the

---

specialized performance in teaching or school administration. *H.Z.*, Imperial Ordinance 453, Dec. 5, 1899, p. 769.

[27] *H.Z.*, Imperial Ordinance 34, March 19, 1903, pp. 34-35.

[28] All of these changes are included in *H.Z.*, Imperial Ordinance 140, April 18, 1905, pp. 163-71.

[29] *H.Z.*, Imperial Ordinance 266, July 12, 1907, pp. 349-52; *H.Z.*, Imperial Ordinance 151, June 13, 1913, pp. 194-202; *H.Z.*, Imperial Ordinance 349, July 16, 1919, pp. 350-52.

period between 1867 and 1881 was one in which two forces were at work to provide the impetus toward the emergence of specialization and differentiation as criteria for the organization of prefectural government and administration. On the one hand there was the desire of the central government to remove local government as a competitor for both political and economic resources, and on the other there was the increasing pressure of the necessity to provide new systems of control, socialization, and especially role coordination to replace those of the pre-Restoration period which were no longer viable. By roughly 1881 the operation of these forces had produced a transformation in local government. The prefecture had become primarily an administrative structure whose main purpose was to implement and integrate the innovations of the central government and to integrate the increasing number of exchanges and roles emerging in a society undergoing rapid change.

The period between 1882 and 1901 saw the elimination of one of the pressures toward specialization and differentiation. After roughly 1878 the central government had eliminated the possibility of competition from local power. This, however, did not result in the abandonment of specialization and differentiation as criteria for the organization and performance of local government and administration. On the contrary, the movement toward greater specialization and differentiation was intensified as new systems of taxation, law, law enforcement, punishment, education, and public health were more fully established and implemented.[30] By 1900 the criteria of specialization and differentiation had become accepted as a basic test of administrative organization and operation at the central government and central prefectural level.[31]

---

[30] The decline of increases in structure and function after 1878-1881 followed by a twenty year period of a stable rate of increase is a reflection of these changing pressures.

[31] A corollary of this development was the emergence of the criteria

Insofar as this analysis is correct, then, the period 1867-1901 was not only a takeoff period in terms of magnitude and types of output but was also a takeoff period in terms of the emergence of "modern" criteria for the organization and performance of administrative activity.

A second conclusion concerns the failure of these criteria to penetrate below the central prefectural level. At the district (*gun*) level and below there appears to have been relatively little differentiation and specialization of structure and performance. Absence of differentiation and specialization is reflected in the number of increases in structure and function which occurred at the *gun* level and below as compared with those which occurred at the central prefectural level. Table 7 indicates the level at which structural functional increases occurred.[32]

The central prefectural level received most of the increases in structure (82.0%), indicating that differentiation of structure occurred primarily at this level. Only in 1877-1881 and in 1887-1891 did structural increases at the *gun* level occur in relatively large numbers.[33] Structural increases in all other periods were

---

of achievement or performance as the test of administrative recruitment. This test was formally ratified with establishment of the civil service examinations and the higher and ordinary examination committees in the period 1887-1899. See *H.Z.*, Imperial Ordinance 37, July 23, 1887, pp. 124-29; *H.Z.*, Cabinet Ordinance 20, July 23, 1887, p. 28; *H.Z.*, Cabinet Ordinance 18, July 23, 1887, pp. 25-27; *H.Z.*, Imperial Ordinance 48, March 26, 1890, pp. 60-62; *H.Z.*, Imperial Ordinance 61, March 27, 1899, pp. 68-71; *H.Z.*, Imperial Ordinance 62, March 27, 1899, pp. 71-73.

[32] For purposes of this analysis only two levels were distinguished: (1) the prefectural office level, including the governor's secretariat and the prefectural central administrative offices; (2) the offices below this level beginning with the *gun* offices.

[33] The large increases in 1877-1881 are largely accounted for by reorganization of the prefectural administration from the *gun* level down and the introduction of local assemblies. *H.Z.*, Dajōkan Ordinance 17, July 22, 1878, pp. 1-12. Those in 1887-1891 are accounted for

TABLE 7

STRUCTURAL AND FUNCTIONAL INCREASES BY LEVEL OF
PREFECTURAL OFFICE PERFORMANCE, 1867-1920

Year	Office Level					
	Prefectural		Gun		Total	
	Structure N	Function N	Structure N	Function N	Structure N	Function N
1867-1871	31	29	0	0	31	29
1872-1876	27	36	0	69	27	105
1877-1881	23	51	18	44	41	95
1882-1886	11	31	2	20	13	51
1887-1891	24	43	10	40	34	83
1892-1896	9	37	0	32	9	69
1897-1901	16	49	3	34	19	83
1902-1906	2	9	0	6	2	15
1907-1911	3	19	0	17	3	36
1912-1916	1	14	0	10	1	24
1917-1920	1	7	0	5	1	12
TOTAL	148 (82.0)	425 (60.0)	33 (18.0)	277 (40.0)	181 (100.0)	702[a] (100.0)

[a] There were 277 increases in categories of operations which involved both the central level and *gun* level and below.

few or nonexistent. This would seem to indicate that while the upper levels of prefectural government became increasingly differentiated and specialized the lower levels remained relatively unspecialized.

The same pattern emerges in terms of functional increases. Functional or operational differentiation occurred in much greater quantities at the central prefectural level than at the *gun* level and below. However, the ratio of categories of operation to structure increases is considerably greater at the *gun* level (8:1) than at the central prefectural level (3:1), indicating again a lower degree of specialization occurring at the *gun* level. Apparently there was considerably less role or perform-

largely by the establishment of municipal governments under a distinct municipal code. *H.Z.*, Law 1, April 17, 1888, pp. 1-92.

ance specialization at the lower levels than at the upper levels of prefectural government.

Examination of the development of the *gun* structure supports this conclusion. When the *gun* was established as the chief local administrative division within the prefecture in 1878, there was one permanent rank, that of district supervisor (*gun-chō*).[34]

By 1913 there were only two additions, the *gun* secretary and school inspector, the latter concerned only with school matters.[35] Furthermore, the functions of these officials were not administratively differentiated with the exception of the school inspector. The *gun* supervisor and secretary were responsible at this time for a wide range of operations, including maintaining the local registers (*koseki*), voting lists, epidemic control, regulation of sale of medicines, automobile registration and licensing, copyright application, and many others.[36]

Simultaneously, as we have seen, the central prefectural administration had become increasingly differentiated and specialized in scope and mode of operation. From this evidence one can conclude that officials at the *gun* level and below retained much of the character of the pre-Restoration local official. The prefectural local official emerges as a nonspecialized figure who performed a wide range of functions. The scope of these functions further suggests that the local official, especially the *gun-chō*, was a figure of considerable power and influence. The power to interfere decisively in local economic affairs, public health, education, and other activities must have been a powerful deterrent to the development of independent groups of influence in local areas. Perhaps, then, the relatively

[34] *H.Z.*, Imperial Ordinance 17, July 22, 1878, pp. 11-12.

[35] *H.Z.*, Imperial Ordinance 151, June 13, 1913, pp. 194-202.

[36] See, respectively, *H.Z.*, Diet Law 26, March 30, 1914, pp. 54-90; *H.Z.*, Diet Law 65, March 15, 1898, pp. 214-40; and *H.Z.*, Imperial Ordinance 186, Oct. 3, 1901, pp. 253-58; *H.Z.*, Diet Ordinance 11, March 19, 1907, pp. 9-11; *H.Z.*, Home Ministry Ordinance 16, Aug. 13, 1914, pp. 275-80; *H.Z.*, Home Ministry Ordinance 1, Jan. 11, 1919, pp. 1-5; *H.Z.*, Diet Law 55, April 15, 1910, pp. 209-11.

unspecialized nature of local government contributed to the weakness of local political groups or branches of political parties. Had there been greater specialization and differentiation of operation at the local level, the resultant greater difficulty in coordination of activities would perhaps have opened interstices in which independent influence groups could have developed and operated with greater power and effectiveness.

In a general sense one might say that prefectural government had developed by the imposition of a relatively differentiated and specialized structure on a traditionally oriented and functionally diffuse local base. In this context central prefectural government served as the coordinating link between a "modern" central government and a predominantly "traditional" local political life. The juxtaposition of modern and traditional criteria for the organization of governmental operations suggests that this was a major factor in the rapidity of Japan's political and economic development. The continued existence and maintenance of values conducive to the acceptance of higher authority and the continued strength of such diffuse structures as the family and village which were capable of implementing changes obviated the necessity of bringing about costly, large-scale, conflict-producing changes at the rural local level.

Conclusion

The analysis presented here has attempted to describe certain aspects of the process of differentiation and specialization in the development of prefectural government during the period which saw the emergence of Japan as a powerful nation-state. The analysis suggests that this process occurred in several distinct stages. The first stage covered roughly the years 1867-1881 and would appear to be the most critical. In this period occurred the majority of increases in prefectural structure and function. This period was also one in which there developed an emphasis on investment, in political terms, of resources in rule-application structures and functions and, in social terms, in role-coordination structures and functions. The period was also characterized by a shift to external and internal specialization and differentiation as the basis for administration and organization.

The second stage lasted from approximately 1882 to 1901 and was characterized by lower but still relatively high rates of increase in structure and function. In terms of output this period saw the continuance and intensification of increases in rule application—role-coordination areas. As new systems of taxation, law, law enforcement, education, transportation, communication, and public health introduced in the preceding period came to be implemented, there was a marked shift in the character of prefectural structural and functional specialization and differentiation. The new personnel and structures which emerged in this period were primarily associated with the implementation of these specialized and differentiated systems rather than with the quantification and constriction of early prefectural powers. As a consequence, recruitment for administrative positions in this period came to be based, in part, on a relatively objective test of performance, i.e. civil service examinations and civil service committee screening at various levels of the bureaucracy. The quantification of prefectural power combined with the introduction of new and society-wide systems of control, socialization, and especially integration in the first stage generated further governmental and administrative changes organized on the basis of institutionalized rather than implied patterns of specialization and differentiation in the second stage.

The period between 1902 and 1920 was characterized by extremely low rates of functional and structural increases. Political structural output continued to follow the pattern established in the preceding period but was more evenly distributed over the social structural areas of output. The change of emphasis characteristic of this period was reflected in the decline of the number of increases in personnel and structure in central prefectural administration. It was also reflected in the types of new positions and structures concerned with education (prefectural [*ken*] and district [*gun*] school inspector), police (assistant police inspector), administration (interpreters, bureau chiefs, division and bureau reorganization). The decline in increases, the shift in output emphasis, and the relatively equal number of increases in specialized and differentiated positions and structures in all areas of social output indicate that the third period was the beginning of a new stage of political development.

The two periods 1867-1881 and 1882-1901 taken together may be viewed as a takeoff period, that is, a period in which there not only occurred massive creation of new structures and functions but one in which these increases occurred in a specific configuration of output and institutionalized orientation which made possible rapid economic development and establishment and stability of a new translocal political system. This was a stage, then, which saw the emergence of a relatively specialized and differentiated political system capable of providing a variety of services to the society on a mass scale. The period after 1901 then may be seen as the beginning of a period in which there emerged mass consumption of services. Going somewhat further, one might say that the period approximately from 1902 to 1950 (excepting the period 1935-1945) was one in which the level of mass consumption of public services was slowly brought up to the level of the existing structure's ability to provide those services. The mushrooming of governmental and administrative structures, functions, and roles after 1950 thus might very well represent the beginning of a period in which mass consumption of services finally outgrew the ability of the existing structure to provide those services. In this context, the American Occupation reforms probably played a critical role in creating conditions under which a far greater number of demands could be made for public services than was possible before the reforms. The Occupation-inspired changes thus probably accelerated a process already in existence rather than created a new takeoff period.

This analysis also perhaps throws some light on the question of why the takeoff period was so relatively short and "successful" in laying the foundations for rapid economic and political development. One important factor seems to be the development of a political structure in which emphasis was laid upon administrative role-coordination structures as the means of accomplishing political and economic development. That this particular type of output configuration was associated with successful political and economic development suggests very strongly that it was a factor of major importance. Two specific questions emerge from this conclusion: (1) What made possible the emergence of this output configuration? and (2) What is the nature of the relationship of this configuration to successful economic and political development?

The very nature of the output configuration implies that in the takeoff period problems of control, socialization, and acceptance of superior authority were not major problems. The relatively unspecialized, undifferentiated character of prefectural administration at the *gun* level and below further suggests that control and adherence to the principal of hierarchical authority were assured by the widespread persistence of custom, precedent, and traditional prescriptions on behavior which were enforced and maintained by various elements of the social rather than governmental structure. One consequence of this condition apparently was the emphasis on hierarchical administrative bureaucracy as the major mechanism of political control and social and economic development. The relative absence of divisiveness and of opposition to established authority largely eliminated the possibility of primary dependence on a system of diffuse representative authority such as national and local legislatures.

The same conditions also alleviated the necessity of heavy dependence on control structures, functions, and roles. Since control and coercion were largely assured through the existence and maintenance of traditional values and patterns of belief rooted in the social structure, there was no necessity to

develop disastrously expensive new systems of control, coercion, and political socialization. Major investment could and
did take place in political and economic role-coordinating
structures, precisely the area of development which led to rapid
political and economic development. The relatively low cost
of such structures probably made possible their rapid expansion, specialization, and differentiation. The necessity of invest-
ing resources and manpower predominantly, or even equally,
in control and coercion mechanisms would undoubtedly have
resulted in a much slower rate of development. In societies
where this has been the case, the tendency has been to emphasize expansion, specialization, and differentiation in policing and punishment structures with resultant neglect of the
coordinating structures necessary for the rapid introduction of
innovation and change. Coercive structures, extensive and expensive in character, replace coordinating ones as means of
introducing and integrating change. An almost inescapable
trap is thus created. Resources and manpower for economic
development and for the governmental coordinating structures
such as banking control, taxation, and licensing necessary for
such development are not readily available. This tends to
slow economic and political development, which in turn may
lead to heavier emphasis on coercion to force economic development, leading to a further decline of available resources.
The end result, unless outside economic aid is available, may
be stagnation or complete collapse of economic and political
development.[37]

[37] David Apter has called the system of which this behavior is
characteristic a "mobilizing system." "A mobilization system involves
government in active intervention in technological change and economic development. . . . A manifestation of increasing control is
reliance on coercion to reach objectives that are established for the
system. . . . Such a pattern has a number of effects on economic
development. First, government becomes progressively more enmeshed
in investment and in seeking to control its side-effects in the society.
Furthermore, the costs of coercion result in diverting revenue, hitherto
available for investment into military and police activities and other

Essentially, the widespread existence, in Japan, of specific patterns of values and behavior eliminated the necessity for, or possibility of, the development of expensive systems of diffuse representative authority and equally expensive systems of control and coercion. This in turn allowed the diversion of resources, manpower, and emphasis to the development of a governmental structure dominated by a hierarchically organized administrative bureaucracy whose major sphere of activity was role coordination and integration. The low cost of this type of development allowed concurrently greater investment in economic development, which was itself speeded by the existence of necessary mechanisms of introducing and implementing innovation and change. The early emergence of specialized prefectural bureaus such as education, commerce and industry, agriculture and forestry, land regulation, and public health, and such government sponsored and controlled structures as local land erosion control associations, forest conservation associations, water control and irrigation associations, and business and industrial associations attests to the numerous channels available for introducing and implementing change.

The rapid development of a centralized bureaucratic administrative structure made it extremely difficult for other centers of influence and power, such as political parties, to develop. The all-pervasive character of the prefectural government's activities reduced enormously the areas in which political parties could operate successfully. Nowhere is this bet-

---

punitive institutions. . . . Consequently, the costs of government rise continuously and difficulties in spending investment funds for the expansion of government enterprise are met by raising public revenues and by the intensification of the mobilization process. Simultaneously, an increasing proportion of revenue is diverted to non-productive enterprise, i.e., to system-maintenance rather than to development." David Apter, "System, Process and the Politics of Economic Development," in Bert F. Hoselitz and Wilbert E. Moore, eds., *Industrialization and Society*, UNESCO (1963), pp. 146-47.

ter reflected than at the lower levels of prefectural administration. Here the absence of specialization left an enormous range of legally differentiated and authorized power in the hands of a small number of officials. This lack of specialization but not differentiation of function left very few interstices into which local political parties or groups could insert themselves. Under these conditions the political parties could not serve as intermediaries between a wide range of specialized offices nor could they compete with the family or village in performing services normally thought of as political or governmental. Furthermore, as long as these conditions obtained, political parties could not develop strong local roots and thus had to rely on other sources for income and support. The very extensiveness of the administrative bureaucracy and its activities on the one hand and the persistence of custom and tradition at the local level on the other produced a situation in which political parties found it almost impossible to attract support or to exert influence. The weakness of Japanese political parties in the period prior to World War II was in large part traceable to this juxtaposition of rapid political development at the national and central prefectural levels and continued existence of traditional patterns at the local level.

What was perhaps a major factor in Japan's rapid political and economic development between 1867 and 1920, the persistence of certain traditional patterns at the local level, may have also been a factor in the failure of civil government in the 1930's. The above analysis suggests that traditional customs, values, and prescriptions on behavior served as the basis of a relatively low cost (when compared with other developing societies) coercive system and substituted for more formal governmental mechanisms. Insofar as this is true, then, the very changes introduced by the central government in the takeoff period probably tended to undermine the traditional patterns in the period after 1901. There were at least two forces operating in this direction: (1) provision by the prefectural government of more and more services such as policing, punishment, education, and public health once provided for by other groups; (2) changes in the economic structure which produced far-reaching effects on family, village, and urban life. Both these forces worked toward the destruction of traditional values and patterns of control, coercion, and political socialization. These were replaced by ad hoc administrative control structures and measures in the form of increasing police supervision and censorship laws. The growing number of acts of political terrorism and increasing urban and rural unrest in the early 1930's indicate the failure of the civil bureaucracy's efforts in this regard. The civil government's inability to integrate new social groups and provide adequate systems of control and coercion finally led more and more Japanese to view the army as the only structure capable of exerting sufficient force to end conflict and impose order, and consequently most Japanese probably sighed with relief upon the army's accession to power. Ironically enough, then, some of the factors which contributed in the short run to rapid political and economic development probably also contributed, in the long run, to political instability and a decline in the rate of economic development.

This analysis suggests one general conclusion concerning the nature of political development. A short and "successful" take-off period requires extensive preconditions. Perhaps the most important of these is the existence of a widespread consensus of values and behavior in regard to control, coercion, and a hierarchy of authority. The consensus may be of a traditional type, where control and coercion are effectively maintained through kinship and pseudo-kinship groups and where adherence to a hierarchy of authority takes the form of accepting without question the leadership of a few men who hold their positions by virtue of their social status. The consensus may be of a more "modern" type, where control and coercion are maintained by a consensus embodied in a formal structure of law and where adherence to a hierarchy of authority takes the form of leadership by men who hold their position by virtue of some test of performance. What is important, at least for short term rapid development, is (1) the existence of a formal or informal system of control and coercion to which the majority of the society adhere, and (2) the existence of an overriding principle of hierarchical authority to which a majority of the society subscribes. Thus democratic forms, as we already know, are not necessary for rapid political and economic development.

Unless these preconditions exist, a society bent on political and economic development will in the takeoff period tend to emphasize police and punishment mechanisms with the accompanying consequences of slower or nonexistent political and economic development. For such societies the solution of the problem may be outside economic aid. Aid of this type may allow the development of administrative role-coordinating structures which in turn may speed up the process of acceptance of change and innovation. The danger here, however, is that outside economic aid may be poured into stronger control structures and measures and/or provide the basis for extensive corruption and waste.

The successful transition from the takeoff period to a period of mass consumption of public services seems to be dependent on the level of formal specialized, differentiated, governmental coordination mechanisms available at the urban-rural local level. Failure of these mechanisms to develop during the takeoff period appear to result in loss of information channels on the part of the central government. Changes and increases in demands go unfulfilled and resentment and unrest follow. Unable, or perhaps unwilling, to ascertain these demands, the central administrative bureaucracy, as in the case of Japan in the 1920's and 1930's, may allow the shift to emphasis on control mechanisms as a solution to problems of social unrest. Again, as in the Japanese case, this may lead to a failure in political stability and/or the dictatorship of control and coercive structures. In both cases, the result is deferral of mass consumption of public services and a slower rate of economic development.

Finally, a few words may be said about the method of analysis employed in this study. Although admittedly experimental in nature, establishment of rate, output, and orientation configurations by the methods used here does seem to provide a means of pinpointing, in time, the way in which specialization and differentiation evolve in developing political structures. At the same time if it is true that increases in governmental structures, functions, and roles are closely related to increasing specialization and differentiation, then this type of analysis can be employed as an instrument of periodization indicating various stages of political development on a comparable basis. On a less specific level, employment of this type of quantitative approach, using easily accessible and uniform data, appears to make it possible to speak in other than the most grossly general terms about the whole process of specialization and differentiation of political structures, functions, and roles. The validity of the methods and approach used in this study must, of course, depend eventually on the replication of this study, or one similar, in other developing societies. However, it is offered as one which can be replicated and one which, hopefully, can provide fruitful cross-cultural comparisons of one major aspect of the development process.

CHAPTER XI

Law and Political Modernization in Japan

DAN FENNO HENDERSON

T HIS CHAPTER is concerned with the growth of legal limitations on Japanese governmental power during the past century. In Japan, as elsewhere, the evolution of law-over-power has been dependent on a certain reciprocal support between popular right-consciousness and the apparatus of justiciability: positive-law rights and independent courts, bench and bar. All of these things were largely inspired in Japan by Western models, for as we shall see, there were almost no Tokugawa, positive-law limits on policy or official action—indeed little private adjudication of any kind (as distinguished from the traditional conciliatory techniques for settling civil disputes).

Consequently, our story involves tracing the expansion of Japanese justiciable rights amid considerable tension between these modern Western ideas and the traditional political and legal concepts. But the whole process is emphatically Japanese, with its own Japanese peculiarities, potentials, and limitations. Our inquiry is thus not simply an evaluative search for congenial Japanese analogies to our own Western legalisms, because, of course, the idea of justiciability has been inducted massively into the formal Japanese legal system, and to a degree made politically operative, in two successive stages: first, in the late nineteenth century, drawing largely from German and French code law, then later in the constitutional and other legal revisions after 1945, drawing heavily from Anglo-American jurisprudence. But significantly both of these infusions of Western legal ideas into the Japanese positive law were essentially grants from the top down, leaving critical problems as to whether the Japanese populace could overcome its historical awe for officialdom enough to actually employ justiciability for its intended purposes. Of course, Japanese legal modernization does not imply automatic, correlative social and political modernization. As several Japanese scholars[1] have pointed out, the classical liberal concepts of property and contract underlying the Meiji codes were intertwined in practice with residual, indigenous, and hierarchical power relationships in social practice to preserve much of the old in Japan and to dilute the influence of the new legal theory on prewar Japanese society and politics. We will have more to say later about this broader problem (i.e. the distortion of the legal goals when mirrored in actual social practice) with regard to the narrower concern of this essay: the reciprocity between right consciousness and justiciability.

We should note also that the important system-building and centralizing role of law in the overall modernization process has been largely passed over in this essay as a result of our selective coverage emphasizing judicial development. We should not forget, however, that law was instrumental at every turn in each of the enormous projects of Tokugawa dismantlement and Meiji system-building: for example, in centralizing the administration, abolishing the status hierarchy, structuring the national bureaucracy, creating a modern military establishment and police, revising the feudal fiscal and rice tax system, establishing a court hierarchy separate from the administration, and codifying the Meiji Constitution and codes governing the whole gamut of personal and property relations of the populace—all of this in the context of a cohesive tradition of customary and natural law ideas. These planning, structuring, and channeling functions of modern Japanese law are important parts of the entire story of law and modernization, but they are generally covered in discussions of government and administration, and we will discuss instead the evolution of justiciable rights and the role of the courts.

The relationship between political values and general mod-

[1] E.g., Kawashima Takeyoshi, *Nihon shakai to hō* (Tokyo, 1959), p. ii.

ernization theory also requires preliminary attention because of the special circumstance of the Japanese legal experience and the need to make my own views and usages clear at the outset. The two receptions of Western law mentioned above mark two distinct phases in Japanese legal and political modernization. The primary phase was thoroughly authoritarian in politics and constitutional conception, and the secondary phase has been, to an encouraging degree, democratic to date. Thus considering the way in which events have actually unfolded in Japan during the past century, it would mutilate the story of Japanese modernization to ignore the secondary phase where democratization has been a major built-in goal. Yet in the current global modernization context, it is clear enough that Japan's experience is a special case. Most developing nations are in the primary phase of industrialization, and many nations (notably communist states) do not aspire to liberal democratic goals in any event. Many of the new states of the free world which profess democratic aspirations have also had little success in democratizing the realities of their political practices. Indeed in attempting democratization some have perhaps not only failed in this respect, but have also weakened their basic projects of economic modernization. Thus in my view the most useful concept of modernization in the global context is a value-free one, which treats democratization as a separate goal with its own special problems of prerequisites and timing.

Japanese experience is useful to illustrate how liberal democratic values can be assimilated in the process of this more generalized kind of modernization. This approach avoids the error of complacent, deterministic assumptions that inevitably a pot of democracy lies at the foot of each developmental rainbow however authoritarian it may be at the moment; and second, it helps to emphasize that elite guidance and structuring in the early modernization process is often required to create the prerequisites for effective popular participation in government.

The value-free approach to modernization is not only useful

in that it covers more of the relevant data on the current scene but it also implies an instrumental role for law. For, although admittedly much of the yield of current attempts at industrial modernization is dependent on the past achievements of Western science and technology, the planning, organizing, and directing of the massive human enterprise entailed is an ad hoc matter for indigenous leadership and administration, which may be implemented by different kinds of politics and law in each nation state which seeks such modern minimal material benefits. In broadest terms, then, law, regardless of its quality, has at least an instrumental role in the modernizing process which would enable man better to control his environment to achieve his aspirations. This kind of positive, instrumental, made-law, which has emerged from the early European idea of territorial sovereignty (Hobbes, Austin, Kelsen, etc.), can and has served a variety of programs, "just" or "unjust," and has been employed by either elite or democratic juristic methods. Modern made-law is thus envisaged by some ideal, forged by some kind of politics, publicized by modern media, tinkered with by legal professionals, applied by officials, sanctioned and enforced to a degree at least by state power.

The growth of modern law has been from a multistatus law to a single legal status (subject or citizen). By the same trends, the law has shifted from a local and parochial kind of law to a law of national coverage, and it has thus become progressively more impersonal with an ever widening and deepening range and specificity in the justiciable rules, and with an ever more conscious, flexible, and purposive human use of made-law (as opposed to cosmic natural or social customary law) in positive economic and social planning on a national basis.[2] These characteristics of modern law develop in any

[2] Wolfgang Friedmann, *Law in a Changing Society* (London, 1959), pp. 3-23; Julius Stone, *The Province and Function of Law* (Sydney, 1946), p. 391; Karl Llewellyn, "The Normative, the Legal and the Law Jobs: The Problem of Juristic Methods," *Yale Law Journal*, XLIX (1942), 1355.

modern society without regard to the political character of the regime.

Concern for the social efficacy of national made-law and planning has required a closer adjustment of legal goals with community acceptance. For surely the vision in the statute can only be converted to social action through the psychological transmission belts of individual understanding. Politically, the crux of the matter is, then, that in recent history the necessary community acceptance has as often been engineered by elite guidance and authoritarian indoctrination as by democratic, individual self-assertion. But whichever course is followed will affect the quality and function of the law used to implement the modernization program. Japan has chosen democratic methods, including a set of fundamental human rights during her secondary modernizing phase in the postwar period.

In pursuing our narrower theme of the evolution of Japanese justiciable rights, we require some specific analytical concepts and some historical staging to assist in identifying the major phases of growth. For during a century of Japanese legal evolution we encounter, among other kinds of "law," unlimited official powers, status authority and privilege, family relations, natural law, village custom, customary law, and written law of several sorts: orders, decrees, case reports, statutes, ministerial regulations, and finally even constitutions and comprehensive codes. Like the Japanese *happō bijin* (the pretty girl who smiles in eight directions), this entire mass of diverse Japanese "law" can hardly be true throughout to any single formulation.

In the task of ordering such a variety of legal phenomena into some kind of a useful sequence, the literature on general legal development starting with Maine[3] has a certain relevance,

[3] See Sir Henry J. S. Maine, *Ancient Law* (1st ed., 1861), pp. 7-25. For later classifications and correlations between social and legal types and their development, see Sir Paul Vinogradoff, *Historical Jurisprudence* (London, 1920), I, 148; Roscoe Pound, *Outlines of Lectures on*

but the political aspects of recent Japanese legal evolution require their own specific framework. For in Japan such a basic thing as the political role of law itself, not just its doctrinal form and content, has changed with each of three periods in the past century. For convenience, the legal roles and periods have been set up as follows: (1) rule-of-status (discretionary power of superiors within a multistatus, feudal structure), 1843–1868; (2) rule-by-law (generalized authoritarian law in a de facto, dual-status society, i.e. governors and governed), 1868–1945; and (3) rule-of-law (limited government or modern constitutionalism) in the postwar period, 1945–1967. These ideas, to be explored below, are offered simply as labels for the dominant Japanese uses of law at each stage. But surely a progression of such depth (i.e. from a discretionary exercise of power by status officials to an emphasis on legal regularity and evenhandedness and finally to a rule-of-law or democratic constitutionalism) is an unusual achievement in recent legal history.

The Tokugawa Legacy: Rule-by-Status

The scope of the Japanese modernization problem depends on what from the Tokugawa past had to be changed and what was found to be usable. On both counts a concrete understanding of the actual Tokugawa institutions, especially what we have called the rule-of-status, is essential. But, so far, most Japanese and Western discussions of "Tokugawa influences" in modern Japanese law tend to be prefatory and nominalistic, or descriptions of ghostly remnants of Tokugawa institutions in modern form, for there is little of the heritage existent today which has not been greatly molded to new uses with the passage of time.[4] Also, our 1868 scholarly watershed frequently

---

Jurisprudence (1943), pp. 40-48; Stone, *The Province and Function of Law*, p. 466. For a list of modern schemes see Huntington Cairns, *The Theory of Legal Sciences* (Chapel Hill, 1941), pp. 25-28.

[4] Notable exceptions are Ishii Ryosuke, *Meiji bunkashi; hōseihen* (Tokyo, 1954), and Kobayakawa Kingo, *Meiji hōseishiron* (Tokyo,

causes an overly flat analysis and a consequent tendency to view Japanese legal evolution as sets of analytical antinomies[5] —Anglo-American versus continental European legal influences; modern versus nonmodern Japanese law; Japanese versus non-Japanese; and legal versus nonlegal phenomena— even though the underlying reality is a moving whole which comprehends all of these different facets of Japanese legal modernization. To achieve some flow in the story we need to understand the characteristics of Tokugawa law and litigation of interest to the later political modernization process. Significantly, in the Edo dispute settlement process, we find a few glimmerings of justiciable law—confined largely to judge-made law in the commercial and procedural fields.

SOURCES OF TOKUGAWA LAW

Rule-by-Status, Its Natural Law Concepts. Rule-by-status was the dominant characteristic of Tokugawa law, but its essentials are difficult to grasp without the whole regime in mind.[6] The entirety of Tokugawa legal phenomena was a highly complex accumulation of imperial symbolism; a federalistic, double-decked, feudal order; an elaborate status hierarchy of great constitutional import resting solidly on the rice tax; a base of

---

1940), I, II. They give specific attention to the dismantling of Edo institutions and also to the massive carryover into Meiji practices and even into the law, especially up to 1898, when the Civil Code was enacted. There is a useful translation of Ishii entitled *Japanese Legislation in the Meiji Era*, William Chambliss, tr. (Tokyo, 1958), but for citations to the laws, see the Japanese version.

[5] See, for example, the otherwise excellent articles by seventeen of Japan's leading legal scholars in Arthur von Mehren, ed., *Law in Japan* (1963) which sometimes suffer from an insufficient time dimension.

[6] Ishii, *Nihon hōseishi gaisetsu* (1948), pp. 367-603, contains a brief reliable descriptive survey of Tokugawa legal institutions. For a complete bibliography on Tokugawa law covering 1945 to 1959, see Hōseishi gakkai, ed., *Hōseishi bunken mokuroku* (1962); and see Dan Fenno Henderson, *Conciliation and Japanese Law—Tokugawa and Modern* (Tokyo, Washington, 1965), II for an extensive bibliography on Tokugawa institutions with translated titles.

rural villages regulated intramurally by diverse customary laws covering the whole range of private transactions; and a Confucianistic family system—all made plausible by the isolation policy. As a whole these features may be regarded as a constitution in the English sense, articulated by some key, piecemeal, positive law decrees (e.g. the *buke-shohatto* and the isolation decrees), customary practices, and precedents, all rationalized by the orthodox Tokugawa Confucianistic philosophy (*shushigaku*). Clearly considerable positive law was generated by the shogunate (and daimyo), but before we consider such law it is necessary first to understand the shogunate's own thinking about law itself. Essentially, it was a natural law approach (*ri* as formulated in *shushigaku*). The static legal order was regarded as both natural and just, and positive law decrees were largely declaratory of these laws of nature. Even in the positive law there was little concept of made-law, for the efficacy of human endeavor to shape its environment was at the time low, and the concepts of law reflected that fact.

Perhaps the most significant "natural" principle was that men were unequal and that status-law must treat them unequally. Nor was this originally a whimsical formulation. A profile of a typical late sixteenth century daimyo domain upon which the later Edo regime was based (and which appeared just before the founding of the Tokugawa shogunate) furnishes some inkling of the functional origins of the natural law status divisions. Essentially it was a division of vocations between castle town and rice lands to maximize the production of rice and war, when both were conditions of life and equally necessary to the important centralizing process then in progress. After Hideyoshi's highly constructive legislation including the sword hunt decree (*katana-gari rei*) and for the next three centuries, nothing was as important politically as the ruling warriors' privilege to wear the two swords. The farmers were left alone on the land, but disarmed and relatively helpless. The four vocational statuses—warriors-farmers-artisans-merchants (*shi-nō-kō-shō*)—were later so ranked rather artificially by the Confucianists according to the supposed value of their social role.

Two other aspects of the status law system require mention. First, within the major status groups there was much refinement of rank, title, and status, particularly among the warriors. Even in the rural villages there was a social hierarchy of old and new families and other kinds of people (e.g. serviles, tenants, and so forth), which were often based on unwritten pedigree, custom, and tradition, but sufficiently pronounced to leave no doubt that the village was not egalitarian. Second, the authoritarian Confucian family relations—father and son, husband and wife, older brother and younger brother—constituted a universal status system throughout all strata of society, derived from birth and with profound influence on the law and, as a model, on political concepts as well.

In later years, beginning with Ieyasu's patronage of Fujiwara Seika and Hayashi Razan, the idea of static natural law became the dominant legal philosophy, which conveniently conformed with and rationalized the existent stratified social structure and the ruling status of the warrior therein. Such a comprehensive idea of law was doubtless operative in Tokugawa administration of justice less in the form of abstract theorizing than in the form of unconscious and inarticulate assumptions as to the basic worth of Tokugawa statics as they had developed by say the mid-seventeenth century: the feudal order over which the shogunate presided; its company system of vassals; the rice tax and its paralyzing registries; the social hierarchy; the stratified Confucianistic family and village system, all made plausible by their isolation from outside influences.

In overall concept, *shushigaku* has been likened to Western scholasticism,[7] and today there are, of course, many modern Western adherents of natural law thinking. But the total content of modern natural law thought is essentially a variety of

[7] Maruyama Masao, *Nihon seiji shisōshi kenkyū* (Tokyo, 1952), p. 185, notes the resemblance to Western scholasticism.

political philosophies, and the main stream of modern legal theory[8] generally recognizes this diversity and finds it useful to differentiate between concepts of ultimate justice[9] and man-made law, without overlooking the fact that values (justice) as such do creep into the application of law[10] and without playing down the importance of the problem of "justice" by viewing it as a choice of goals rather than law itself.

Shogunal Positive Law. The shogunate produced considerable positive law in our terms, as distinguished from its own natural law thinking. This law took the form of both decrees issuing

[8] Stone, *Legal Systems and Lawyers' Reasonings* (Stanford, 1964), pp. 1-26, and Friedmann, *Law in a Changing Society* (London, 1959), p. xiii.

[9] We use the term "justice" to refer to the purpose of law, which, especially when the law is vague itself, often means the judge's own values drawn in to interpret the law for a specific case. Sometimes "justice" means a philosopher's own criterion for evaluating the law, which he in turn may hold as an absolute. Or, he may more generously admit of alternatives. Some writers use the term "natural law" in a similar fashion. Hans Kelsen, *General Theory of Law and State* (Cambridge, 1945), p. xiv; Edgar Bodenheimer, *Jurisprudence* (Cambridge, 1962), pp. 126-57. Note that we have used the term "natural law" in a more classical sense to refer specifically to evaluative criteria, such as those of the Tokugawa orthodox Confucianists, who assume that no rule of law can be "law" unless it conforms with their concepts of justice, or more precisely, law and justice are the same and both natural.

[10] There is, of course, an extensive literature on the poverty of juristic method to cover prospectively all of the real eventualities of social activity and how the gaps should be filled by drawing upon officials' and judges' apprehension of legislative intent or community values or the officials' own preferences. See, e.g., Pound, *The Task of the Law* (1944), p. 48. For another approach to the relation between law and justice in the case of "gaps," see Kelsen, *General Theory of Law and State*, p. 145. Modern administrative law as it has developed in the past few decades raises these questions most urgently, for the whole idea of the separation of power is up for reappraisal or circumvention by the process. See Stone, "The Twentieth Century Administrative Explosion and After," *California Law Review*, LII (1964), 513.

from authority and precedents accumulating in the interstices of the dispute settlement process. Politically, the most significant aspects of Tokugawa positive legal phenomena were (1) the administrative "law" (rule-by-status) and (2) a body of justiciable law, which grew out of the numerous diversity cases (*shihai chigai*) spawned by nascent commercialism. These will be treated later, but first it is important to understand the limited scope of shogunal legal competence (jurisdiction), which derived from its position in the entire shogunate-domain (*bakuhan*) system.

The growth of shogunal positive law began with the emergence of the Tokugawa as a source of countrywide authority, filling a power vacuum which had existed for over a century. Still the Edo shogunate was a minimal kind of government at the center of a complex feudal arrangement. The roughly 270 diminutive daimyo feudal orders (each complete and separate in itself) were gathered into the shogunal system by oaths of vassalage between the daimyo themselves and the Tokugawa shogun. The Edo regime was, therefore, not only a double-layered feudal order, but also a federalistic system geographically, comprised of two territorial spheres of shogunal power. The old Tokugawa house organs were enlarged and supplemented to serve this dual territorial capacity, first to administer as a feudal lord the Tokugawa lands, the largest of the feudal domains, and second to preside over all of Japan, including the other hitherto independent feudal domains, as a superlord and shogun, and also to control the imperial courts, foreign relations, communications, anti-Christian registries, currency, and other matters of countrywide importance.

However, the shogunal power of governance outside its own domain was narrowly constricted geographically by its own concepts of feudal jurisdiction. In feudal law, land grants (enfeoffment) and contracts (fealty) between lords and vassals provide the basic security ordinarily obtained from the government, and rights of governance run with the fief. Thus public and private law is said to be coalesced in the feudal legalities

397

of vassalage and enfeoffment. A peculiarity of Tokugawa feudalism, as contrasted with European experience,[11] was the extraordinarily high degree of fidelity with which the shogunate cleaved to this feudal jurisdictional concept that the right to govern and judge ran with the daimyo fief. Except in diversity cases involving two fiefs (*shihai chigai*), the principle that the law of the land flowed with the feudal land law was observed rather completely in administrative and civil law. Even in the criminal law field, the decree of judicial autonomy (*jibun shioki-rei*) promulgated by Tsunayoshi in 1697 confirmed the daimyo's exclusive jurisdiction within his fief to apprehend, convict, sentence, and execute the heaviest penalties, but this criminal power was limited in two ways: (1) to persons registered in the fief and (2) it was to be exercised in conformity to Edo practice. Since there were no defendants' rights to appeal from domain (*han*) decisions, we cannot check the degree of compliance with Edo practice actually achieved, until we have more studies of specific daimyo criminal adjudication.[12]

Throughout the entire Tokugawa period the power of governance remains feudally dispersed in this respect among hundreds of feudatories: daimyo, temple, shrine, *hatamoto,* the

[11] Francois L. Ganshof, *Feudalism* (London, 1952), p. 141, states that fief, jurisdiction, and justice were not necessarily coextensive in French feudalism. Also Marc Bloch, *Feudal Society* (Chicago, 1962), p. 364, for the division between "low" and "high" justice in Germany. In fact, special separate enfeoffments of *justicia* were known in Germany; also see Asakawa Kan-ichi, *Documents of the Iriki* (Tokyo, 1955), p. 78, to the effect that fief and *justicia* did not go together in the Kamakura "dual" feudalism either; but certainly by the Edo period, in general, they did.

[12] See bibliography in Inoue Kazuo, *Shohan no keibatsu 339* (Tokyo, 1965); Hayashi Tōichi, *Owari-han kōhōshi no kenkyū* (Tokyo, 1961), pp. 635-68, gives a detailed study on Owari daimyo's judicial system; also, Takayanagi Shinzō, *Miyagi kenshi* (1961), VII, has considerable detail on the Date domain's judicial system. Hiramatsu Yoshiro, *Kinsei keiji soshōhō no kenkyū* (Tokyo, 1960), pp. 3-244. These recent studies have some detail on daimyo administration of justice, and they emphasize criminal cases.

imperial court, and the shogunate itself. Thus most of the shogunal law of popular concern was effective only over the persons in the Tokugawa domain (about one seventh of the assessed rice-producing capacity of Japan) and on the main highways and certain key cities. It also enforced countrywide regulations on foreign relations, Christianity, currency, and the like. Its feudal law further controlled the top vassals, the daimyo, in a constitutional sense. This meant that throughout the rest of Japan law and justice for the people emanated from the many feudal lords.

This was only half of the story of Tokugawa legal decentralization; the other half concerns the limitation of the law in terms of social depth rather than territorial coverage, and this characteristic was equally true of the daimyo as well as the shogunal law. Although the feudal regulatory law was authoritarian, it was not effectively totalitarian. It did not attempt to penetrate society and displace customary law in the affairs of the people, except where they affected the taxes or basic security. The vast area of private transactions in the towns and villages were governed by custom and sometimes by rules of the village (*muragime*).[13] Also the villages settled their own disputes arising out of village life by conciliatory procedures or village sanctions (e.g. ostracism, *murahachibu*[14]).

[13] Maeda Masaharu, *Nihon kinsei sonpō no kenkyū* (Tokyo, 1952), p. 287. This collection of village law is a valuable supplement to the shogunal law for villages found in Hozumi, *Goningumi hōkishū*, and Nomura, *Goningumichō no kenkyū*. Written rules of the village seldom exceeded 7 articles, whereas the shogunal rules laid down for the village in the preface to the five-man-group registry averaged 47 articles in the 393 collected by Hozumi and 54 in the 86 collected by Nomura: Maeda, *Hōgaku ronsō*, LII (1946), 320, n. 1.

[14] On the limited criminal jurisdiction of the village officials see Maeda Masaharu, "Ryōshuhō jō no keibatsuken to mura seisaiken to no kankei," in Hōseishi gakkai, ed., *Keibatsu to kokka kenryoku* (1960), pp. 101-23; Ōde Yukiko, "Kinsei sompō to ryōshuken," in *Hōsei ronshū* (no. 18), pp. 1-32, and (no. 19), pp. 73, 110 (1962); Fuse Yaheiji, "Murahachibu no soshō," *Nihon hōgaku*, XXIII:iii (1957); Arai Kōjirō, "Seisai," in *Shakai to minzoku* (1962), pp. 173-88. This

RULE OF STATUS AND THE CRIMINAL LAW AUXILIARY

The unifying thread running through the whole Tokugawa governance was the rule-by-status. This was essentially administrative, not legal. From the shogun at the top to the individual person at the bottom, this thread ran by successive delegations of power, unpoliced by justiciable law. We can take the shogunal domain as an example, although presumably the daimyo domains were similarly organized, plus an added vassalage relation with the shogun at the top. The shogun delegated to the senior council (*rōjū*), which delegated to the finance commission (*kanjō bugyō*), which delegated to the deputy (*daikan*), who looked to the village headman (*nanushi*), who looked to the chief of the five man group (*gonin-gumi kashira*), who looked to the househead, who controlled the family members.

We have drawn the foregoing unilinear chain of command so that it penetrates both the feudal (warrior) and nonfeudal (commoner) layers of society. The nexus of feudal and nonfeudal was the headman, for the village was the standard unit of enfeoffment and was under bureaucratic tax control by the lord; intramurally the village was to some degree autonomous. The character and extent of village autonomy is an important and highly controversial matter.[15] But it seems clear enough that the village as a unit had some autonomy, although it was offset by the heavy rice tax and innumerable sumptuary rules to encourage maximum yield, so that the individual villager was surely not free to dispose of much leisure time or excess resources. Our point here is a little different, however,

---

latter book is in the series entitled *Nihon minzokugaku taikei.* Also see Takeuchi Toshimi, "Mura no seisai—shu to shite hōritsuteki no mono ni tsuite," *Shakai keizai shigaku,* VIII (1938), 603-33, 743-72; Maeda, "Mura seisai o tsūjite mitaru wagakuni kinsei sonraku no jishusei," *Hōgaku ronsō,* LII (1946), 318-52.

[15] See the controversial literature on this point cited in Ōde, "Kinsei sompō to ryōshuken," *Hōsei ronshū* (1962) (no. 18), pp. 1-32, and (no. 19), pp. 73-128.

because we are adverting to *how* the intramural autonomy was exercised, not its overall scope vis-à-vis the lord.

The critical fact was that against the authority of any of these superiors (feudal, village, or family) there was almost no right of appeal—no legally justiciable right either before a court or even before the next higher official superior. Indeed, there were no courts separate from the administrative offices, except in a sense the conference chamber (*hyōjōshō*), and all of these offices were proscribed by shogunal law from accepting a petition by a Confucianistic inferior against a superior without his permission. All review and redress was from the top down, even the *ukagai* (sometimes translated "appeal") was simply a query from the lower to the next higher office.[16]

In this respect the authority of the state was analogous to the authority of the feudal master and also of the father, because the feudal state and the family were the same thing on different levels; and the duty of loyal subordination, first to the overlord (*shukun*) and second the househead (*koshu*), combined to become the chief instruments of social discipline. Consistently, the concepts of loyalty to master (*chū*) and family filial piety (*kō*) were considered inseparable. In most of the Tokugawa schools of Confucianism can be found phrases similar to the following by Fujita Tōkō: "Letters and swords are inseparable; loyalty and piety indivisible."[17] Kaibara Ekken's words epitomize the official thought of his time, requiring complete subordination to Confucian superiors: "To

---

[16] See Ishii, *Nihon hōseishi gaisetsu*, p. 480, n. 13, regarding rejection of a *daikan*'s decision (*saikyo kobami*). *Ukagai*, sometimes translated "appeal," was used technically to designate the situation where the lower shogunate official, not the party, requested instruction from a higher official. Kobayakawa, "Futatabi kinsei soshō ni kankatsu oyobi shinkyū ni tsuite," *Hōgaku ronsō*, XXXIII (1935), 635, notes that using a modern term, *shinkyū*, as an equivalent for *ukagai* may have been confusing in his prior article: *Hōgaku ronsō*, XXXII (1935), 110.

[17] See *Kōdōkan-ki* in *Kinnō bunko*, III, 119, and see Kobayakawa, *Hōgaku ronsō*, XXXIX (1938), 534-35, for similar quotations from Yamaga Sokō and Nakae Tōju.

criticize superiors—to criticize the country's administration, that becomes a serious breach of loyalty and piety."[18]

Turning specifically to the attitude of the shogunate toward suits against superiors, the "courts" asserted a strong policy against such actions, backed up by prescribed penalties. That this attitude prevailed at an early date in Tokugawa law covering the commoners as well as the warriors is shown by a section of a regulation circulated throughout Edo in 1655, tenth month, thirteenth day: "In suits between townsmen and their servants, those who submit complaints and go to trial do not understand the proprieties of the master and servant relationship. When the servant is at fault, he will be imprisoned. Furthermore, the complaint is a matter to be entrusted to the master's discretion."[19] In the same regulation, suits between parents and children are discouraged. The family suits to be discouraged were not limited to those between father and son, but also included other suits against family superiors. The wife's incapacity to sue for a divorce, except through the colorful divorce temple (*enkiri-dera*), is another example.[20]

The law thus left settlement of such disputes to the will of the master, father, teacher, or other superiors as a matter of "jurisdiction." Suits were accepted only if the shogunal interest was involved and the superior was found to be seriously at fault,[21] or in cases concerning household or property succession.

Tokugawa law did not stop at simply prohibiting suits against superiors (*shujū soshō*). In the traditional *ritsuryō*

[18] Kaibara Ekken, *Kadōkun* in *Ekken zenshū*, III, 423 (upper).

[19] *Kinreikō zenshū*, v, 292 (bottom; third *hitotsugaki*).

[20] See Hozumi Shigeto, *Rienjō to enkiridera* (Tokyo, 1942), p. 209; Ishii, "Enkiridera—Tōkeiji no baai," *Hōgaku kyokai zasshi*, LXXVI (1959), 401, and LXXVII (1961), 127, 413. Two temples, Mantokuji in Nitta and Tōkeiji in Kamakura, were recognized as asylums for runaway wives, who after three years of life in the temple as a nun were legally regarded as divorced.

[21] This policy is clearly stated in *Tokugawa jidai minji kanreishū, Soshō no bu, Shihō shiryō*, CCXVI (1936), 60, *Meue no mono o aite dori sōrō sojō no koto.*

format, it also supported these prohibitions with harsh criminal penalties in the *Osadamegaki hyakkajō.*[22] Transcendent petitions[23] (*osso, kagoso,* etc.) wherein the inferior petitioned over the head of his superior were severely punished, even by crucifixion if the petition was false. In passing, we should also note that criminal liability to support administrative responsibility was expanded to relatives (*enza*) and to the whole village or group (*renza*) of which the offender was a member.[24] It is well known that torture was an institutionalized part of the conviction procedure. True to its *ritsuryō* conception, the criminal law, as a whole, was primarily an auxiliary of the administration outlined above.[25]

Perhaps the only procedure that might be regarded as an exception to the basic principle of rejecting complaints against authority was Yoshimune's plaint box[26] established in Edo in 1721, but the practice was not to give direct replies to the plaint-box petitioners. Also, the petitions could only be submitted to report a public matter; complaints concerned merely with private or personal mistreatment were not authorized. Even public complaints, if submitted without permission of the petitioner's superior, were out-of-channels (*suji chigai*)[27] and punishable.

We have dwelt upon this lack of redress against authority in Tokugawa administration somewhat at length because in

[22] See *Osadamegaki,* Bk. ii (*Hyakkajo*), Art. 65, which gives some qualifications, too.

[23] Kobayakawa, "Kinsei minji saiban no gainen to tokushitsu," *Hōgaku ronsō,* XLV (1941), 372-402, for the fullest discussion of transcendent petitions: *Osadamegaki,* Bk. ii, Art. 19.

[24] Miura mentions the softening of the use of vicarious liability (*renza* and *enza*) after Yoshimune. Miura Kaneyuki, "Edo jidai no saiban seido," in *Hōseishi no kenkyū* (1925), p. 345.

[25] Hiramatsu, *Kinsei keiji soshōhō no kenkyū* (1960), pp. 3-244, is the standard work on Tokugawa criminal proceedings.

[26] *Osadamegaki,* Bk. i, Arts. 8-12.

[27] *Osadamegaki,* Bk. ii, Art. 4, in *Shiho shiryo bessatsu,* XVII, 29, provides for confinement (*oshikomi*) for a priest or warrior who does not observe channels and handcuffing (*tejō*) for commoners.

this all-pervading feature clearly lies the outstanding political characteristic of the Tokugawa legal order. In general Western jurisprudence, it is a much-mooted question whether unreviewable authority for arbitrary, ad hoc exercises of official power should be included in the concept of basic "lawness" at all, or whether law and arbitrary power (however official) are not opposites. Some scholars feel that the essence of law is its generality of prospective application.[28] Such a distinction between law and discretionary official acts is a useful one, but the unique and highly structured principles of the Tokugawa regime are difficult to classify on such a criterion. Often these hierarchical relationships of man-over-man have been characterized as a rule-of-man,[29] and Confucianistic philosophy also often supports such a term.[30] Hence, the "legal" system has been viewed as a power structure with nothing more than authoritarian duties for subordinates, without any correlative rights; the individual person at the bottom had only status as members of a hierarchical group, but no individual legal status as such.

On the other hand, the Tokugawa interstatus relations (*shi-nō-kō-shō*) and even intrastatus relations were minutely defined, and every daily routine was so ordered by rules of proper procedure and conduct for both inferiors and superiors that paradoxically the society was uncommonly legalistic, although without legal remedies from the bottom up. The concepts of proper status conduct and the downward surveillance of superiors plus the intimacy of village life doubtless

---

[28] Bodenheimer, "Reflections on the Rule of Law," *Utah Law Review*, VIII (1962), 2, criticizes Kelsen and Stammler for considering such official acts "law."

[29] An early use of the term is S. H. Wainwright, "Japan's Transition from a Rule of Man to a Rule of Law," *Transactions of the Asiatic Society of Japan*, XLVIII (1919), 155.

[30] Junshi (Hsün-Tzǔ) Kundōhen (see the phrase "Asamuru no hito ari; osamuru no hō nashi"), in *Kokumin bunko kankōkai*, ed., *Kokuyaku kanbun taisei*, VIII, 32 (separate paging for Chinese), 124 (Japanese).

mitigated the rigors of arbitrary power, especially during the later years. It is, therefore, useful to characterize this phenomenon, which was not without its controls and yet which is not readily comprehended by our legal categories, as a rule-of-status. This way of viewing Tokugawa legalisms takes into account the regime's ideal of governance by moral, wise, and disciplined men, but at the same time it underscores the fact that the discipline was from the top down and that Western and modern Japanese right-oriented juristic method was not available to review aberrant official conduct.

JUSTICIABILITY OF DIVERSITY CASES

As sketched above, the status law with its criminal law supports was the basic core of the Tokugawa legal system and presumably of the daimyo as well. But in some ways the most interesting aspect of Tokugawa law was the positively anti-feudal accretion of judge-made law in the central offices of Edo.[31] It was antifeudal because first the suits which engender this law were mainly money suits (*kanekuji*) arising from the growing commercial activity of lowly merchants, and second because these suits involved parties registered in different fiefs. Therefore, since the lord of neither party had the normal feudal jurisdiction, these antifeudal cases involved diversity of jurisdiction (*shihai chigai*), and the shogunate, as a central super-lord (or government), was pressured into settling them.[32] When we remember that there were hundreds of fiefs, many composed of noncontiguous parts (*tobi-chi*), and that commerce had no respect for such petty boundaries, especially in the Kanto and Osaka/Kyoto complexes, it is easy to understand why, with the rise of commerce, these suits became by far the most numerous kind of litigation in Edo.

[31] Kobayakawa, *Kinsei minji soshō seido, no kenkyū* (Maki Kenji, ed., 1957) contains the most advanced work on Tokugawa civil litigation.

[32] Kobayakawa, "Iwayuru 'shihai chigai ni kakaru deiri' ni tsuite," *Hōgaku ronsō*, XXXIV (1936), 408, 756.

By the early eighteenth century they had become a serious burden on the "courts."[33] The shogunate tried to discourage them by mutual settlement decrees (*aitai sumashi-rei*),[34] which required private settlements; by discard decrees (*kienrei*), which extinguished the debts outright; by dilatory procedures and centralized jurisdiction in Edo; and by stringent requirements of impeccable documentary proof.[35] Still by the mid-eighteenth century a fixed and refined formulary system in hierarchical arrangement was developed as follows: (1) land and water disputes (*ronsho*); (2) main suits (*honkuji*, secured claims without interest); (3) money suits (*kanekuji*, unsecured claims with interest); (4) mutual affairs (*nakamagoto*); "Confucian" suits (*shujū sōshō*, claims against family or feudal superiors).[36] These types of claims were handled by a corresponding hierarchy of procedures of varying adequacy depending on the importance attached by the shogunate to each type of underlying interest. Land suits were important to the tax so they were handled most promptly and adequately; main suits somewhat less adequately; money suits, being unimportant merchant claims, were handled largely by didactic (as opposed to voluntary) conciliatory techniques and toothless judgments, if conciliation failed. Mutual affairs were always rejected summarily; and Confucian suits were not only rejected but ordinarily the petitioner was penalized for complaining against his superior.

[33] See a chart of statistics for Osaka in Haruhara Gentaro, *Osaka no machibugyōsho to saiban* (1962), pp. 12-13, and Takayanagi and Ishii, *Ofuregaki (kanpō) shūsei* (1934), p. 1196, for decrees noticing the problem of numerous *kanekuji* suits in 1702.

[34] Harafuji Hiroshi, "'Aitai sumashi' rei kō," *Kanazawa daigaku hōbungaku ronshū hōkei-hen* (no. 2) (1955), pp. 1-29.

[35] Harafuji, "Kinsei saikenhō ni okeru shōsho no kinō," *Kanazawa hōgaku*, IV:ii (1958), 77; *id.*, V:ii (1959), 47; *id.*, VI:i (1960), 35.

[36] The mature form of the *honkuji-kanekuji* division was fixed in a Conference Decision of the Conference Chamber (*hyōjōsho ichiza hyōketsu*) in 1767. *Tokugawa jidai minji kanreishū, soshō-no-bu* in *Shihō shiryō*, CCXVI (1936), 80.

This hierarchical formulary system[37] for handling *shihai chigai* cases produced the only substantial body of truly national and justiciable law in Tokugawa Japan. All other civil law was a local customary law with much diversity derived from long-established practices of the particular community. And, as noted, the method of applying local law was by local conciliatory techniques, which we have called didactic conciliation because the settlement technique was neither strictly voluntary nor formally judicial, although they may have often approached the standards which students of primitive law have seen as a kind of inchoate adjudication. In addition some local (nondiversity) suits were taken to the shogun's deputies (*daikan*) for a more judicial hearing, but little is known about the actual handling of civil cases at that level.[38]

Dispute Settlement: Personnel and Procedure. The practices in diversity cases carried over massively and directly into the Meiji period, especially up to the Code of Civil Procedure of 1891. Even some of the choices made in drafting the new Meiji codes were influenced by these Edo practices, and modern extensions of the informal conciliatory practices are still with us today in great strength, as well as the statutory progeny of Edo court conciliation (*wakai* and *chōtei*). Yet as a judicial process, it is easy to overrate Edo litigation,[39] and this becomes clear in reviewing its salient characteristics. First, until 1875 Japan had never known an independent court as such. In Edo,

[37] Kobayakawa, "Kinsei minji saiban ni okeru mibunteki seikaku to tōkyusei ni tsuite," *Hōgaku ronsō*, XLVI (1942), 20, 388, sets out this hierarchy of procedure.

[38] Ishii, *Nihon hōseishi gaisetsu,* p. 480, n. 13, says that by rejection of a *daikan*'s decision (*saikyo kobami*), a litigant could get a hearing in Edo, under certain circumstances.

[39] Compare John Henry Wigmore, *Panorama of the World's Legal Systems* (1928), II, ch. 8; and Takayanagi, "A Century of Innovation: The Development of Japanese Law, 1868-1961," in von Mehren, ed., *Law in Japan* (1963), p. 5 at 23.

the Conference Chamber was largely judicial in function, but its "judges" were the members of the three commissions (minus the two *katte-kata kanjō bugyō*). Perhaps the specialization of the judicial officers (*kuji kata*), two of the four finance commissioners, should also be mentioned as quasi judicial. Other "courts" were even more obviously administrative offices with concurrent power to settle disputes. As for the "bench," we should note the legal specialists of the three commissions: the *yoriki*, *tomeyaku*, and *gimmimono shirabeyaku* of the Town, Finance, and Shrine-and-Temple commissions respectively. Although some of these petty underlings were highly skilled in law and trial practice, and presided at most of the trial hearings as examiners, they were not the responsible judges as such and had nothing akin to judicial tenure or independence. Finally, the almost total lack of private practicing lawyers was a striking deficiency which has still not been entirely overcome in modern Japan. The suit innkeepers (*kujiyado*) had an important concurrent role as legal advisors, but these colorful specialists lacked most professional attributes and were not allowed to represent clients.[40]

The trial procedures were equally nonjudicial.[41] Even in diversity cases the Edo procedures never quite broke free from feudal concepts of jurisdiction. For example, the claimant could not sue without the approval of both his village and his feudal lord. Thus suits were still group, not individual matters; they were still not free from a vestigial administrative orientation, which thoroughly smothered the individual even in "private" litigation. Perhaps the most picturesque manifestation of this mode of thinking was the requirement that the

---

[40] See Takigawa Masajiro, *Kujiyado no kenkyū* (1959); and Hiramatsu's review thereof in *Hōseishi kenkyu*, XII (1961), 243. For practices of a Kyoto *kujiyado*, see Takigawa, ed., *Nijoya no kenkyū—kujiyado no kenkyū* (*zoku*) (1962).

[41] For concrete descriptions of several actual trials in Edo, see Nakada Kaoru, "Tokugawa jidai minji saiban jitsuroku," in *Hōseishi ronshū*, III (1943), 753-832, 833-904.

itinerant litigant in Edo (and, of course, at least one party was always an itinerant in diversity cases) obtain his house owner's (innkeeper's) approval, for in Edo all tenants were required to get the approval of their house owner for various "private" transactions. Naturally enough the suit inns (*kujiyado*), which catered to litigants, became experts in Edo litigation, hence their role as legal advisors.

If the civil suit in Edo never quite emerged from the group and administrative trappings of feudal authority, neither did it achieve during trial complete freedom from lapses into criminal procedures. The *deiri suji* was essentially a civil procedure between adversary private parties as opposed to the criminal *gimmi-suji*, but if the party was slow to compromise or otherwise offensive during trial, the officials could proceed to treat the party as a criminal and place him in jail or subject him to torture to bring him into line. This, too, was a habit which Meiji officials were unable to give up until 1879. We have also seen that substantive and procedural law were coalesced in a formulary system in much the same way they were in the forms of action at common law.

Two other features of Tokugawa trials were highly significant to legal evolution: (1) the policy to individualize in deciding cases, and (2) the continual pressure exerted on the parties to compromise their disputes by conciliation even after the suit was accepted. The policy to individualize was encouraged by the fact there were few written rules in the field of civil law, which was governed largely by ancient local custom, called the great law (*taihō*).[42] But in adjudication the *Osadamegaki* and other basic decrees provided that reason (*dōri*) should override the great law as found in custom and precedents.[43] This rule fostered a tendency toward individual-

[42] Nakada, "Kohō zakko," *Hōseishi kenkyū*, 1 (1951), 1-44; and *id.*, "Taihō," *Hōseishi ronshū*, III (1943), 1096.

[43] E.g. Ishii, *Nihon hōseishi gaisetsu* (1960), p. 370, n. 1. Shimada, an Edo town commissioner, had requested permission to make available to his successors compilations of precedents which he had built up

ization in deciding each case, thus creating a basic kind of equity known as Ōoka justice, after the famous judge Ōoka Echizen-no-kami, the father of many trial legends of present-day Japan.[44]

Conciliation was even a stronger feature of Tokugawa justice.[45] As noted earlier, the vast majority of Tokugawa civil disputes were settled by didactic conciliation on the village level, without a suit, or more significantly without a right to sue. But in addition as records of the proceedings show, even in those cases which because of diversity could be brought to Edo, the trials were often little more than a series of hearings given over to pressures by the judge to obtain a compromise settlement. We should not overlook the fact that both the conciliation pressures and the tendency to individualize had the effect of stunting the growth of law through the development of precedent, because neither technique produced decisions that could be publicized and remembered as precedents in future conduct and cases. Furthermore, the coercive character of didactic conciliation resulting from the social differences between the parties and between parties and officials or conciliators, plus the lack of appeals and other alternative remedies, all make us wonder if this conciliation process did not serve well the established authority of the community and tend to perpetuate tradition; conciliation may have been itself traditional and a conduit of other substantive traditions.

---

during his tenure in office. The second shogun, Hidetada (tenure 1605-1622), denied permission on the grounds that such a reliance on precedents would dull the judge's sense of justice.

[44] The strong popular admiration in Japan for this basic equitable type of justice called *Ōoka saiban* after a famous Tokugawa "judge" (*bugyō*), Ōoka Echizen-no-kami (1677-1751), is an important part of the jural tradition illustrative of this point. See *Ōoka seidan* in the series *Kinsei monogatari bungaku*, 1 (1960), which though partly fictional, nevertheless gives the feel for this tradition.

[45] Henderson, *Conciliation and Japanese Law—Tokugawa and Modern* (1965), 1, ch. 6.

CONCLUSION

It remains to consider briefly the meaning of Tokugawa legal experience for modern Japan. Surely the first insight which comes through clearly is that the highest achievements of the Tokugawa was administration and surely not justiciable law. The administration at all levels was efficient, astonishingly well recorded, and above all superlatively authoritarian in concept and implementation. No doubt this remarkable efficacy of administration was based to some degree on the immobility and mutual dependence of rice farmers, all captives of the demands of the rice cycle itself, strapped to the land by the registries, and defenseless in a world of sword-wielding warriors. These administrative elements were later useful: the basic authoritarian family and village, the registries, the ingrained attitudes of a samurai leadership and authority, complemented by "creative obedience" not only in official relations but also built into all tenant, employment, and other contractual relationships and business enterprises. They were cherished and adapted by the Meiji system-builders. There was also the habit of paying an agricultural tax of half the crop, and the established integration of urban and rural communities based on the castle town, plus considerable sophistication in business devices.

But there was no tradition of a separate judiciary or an independent bench and only a beginning of a bar, even to handle private litigation. And, of course, the idea of justiciable law to control the making or execution of official policy is a concept from another world.

This is not to say, however, that Tokugawa "judicial" practice was not influential in later practices. Of course, its influence depended on what part of the post-Restoration period we are discussing. Also, even Western-style reforms before 1890 were influenced by details of Tokugawa practice in that the models were often chosen because they were congenial with the past. Inevitably the Tokugawa practice continued *en masse* in private affairs, with only occasional piecemeal legislative changes, up to the time of the Civil Code (1898), and we know specifically that early civil procedures followed many of the older practices of diversity cases until the Code of Civil Procedure in 1891.⁴⁶ Also, knowing the style of the multihearing Edo trial, one wonders if German procedure was not therefore found convenient. The same can be said for the French *avocat* as a model for the early lawyer's law, and the first procurators had powers like the inspectors (*metsuke*) in the 1870's. The heavy reliance on documentary evidence and the inquisitorial judge are other such examples, where, if the Tokugawa influence is not obvious, its ghost at least causes us to speculate. In the substantive private law as well, many institutions such as the pawnbroker and *sōgo* bank, not to mention the family and employee and tenant relationships, if not identical, are clearly traceable to their Tokugawa ancestors.

But by all odds the most significant influence in dispute settlement from the Tokugawa heritage is the abiding tendency in modern Japan still to avoid the entire apparatus of formal justice and settle out of court. Besides a strong and continuous undercurrent of informal conciliation in modern Japan (*jidan*, etc.), the courts employed a type of conciliation in the early Meiji period (*kankai*), while since the 1920's a new kind of conciliation has become a separate court proceeding called *chōtei*. Throughout the life of the Code of Civil Procedure from 1891 the judges' compromise powers (*wakai*) are also suggestive of the Edo trial. As a negative barometer of Japanese popular right consciousness, this persistent use of conciliation is of great interest throughout modern legal history down to the present day.

Rule-by-Law in Post-Meiji Times, 1868-1945

As is well known, the Japanese, in building the Meiji legal system, became, in the final stages, great admirers of Bis-

---

⁴⁶ Rules for the adjudication of suits involving different prefectures and/or domains (*Fuhanken sōsho junkan kitei*) (Nov. 28, 1870).

marck's Germany—including its civil law system, one of the most fundamental structural principles of which is the pervasive dichotomy between public law and private law. So, regardless of how we judge the validity or utility of such a division,[47] these two basic legal categories necessarily impress a certain order on our subsequent discussion of the development of justiciable rights and the rule-by-law before 1945. In anticipation, we might add that in the private law field, which governs relations between private persons, the requisites of justiciability (procedures, independent courts, bar, bench, and codes) were quite generally achieved in the formal law, and the same can be said for the criminal law (often regarded as a segment of the public law), despite some glaring limitations in both areas. Furthermore, the achievement of justiciability in private law matters should be regarded as a substantial accomplishment and an important part of the rule-by-law. The accomplishments in the public law field were much more modest.

In the first few decades after 1868, the Japanese progress in the field of law generally was fully comparable to their more obvious industrial accomplishments. The positive results included a national administrative structure, a modern military establishment built on conscription, a tax and fiscal system, as well as a new court hierarchy with a system of appeals and relatively independent bench and bar and a set of Western-style codes generally applicable to all subjects alike—all of this systematized under the Meiji constitution by 1900. Nearly all of these projects involved an equally difficult task of dismantling or adjusting long-established pre-Meiji institutions. A review of the flux of forms and series of revisions, the mountains of drafts replete with strange and alien legal ideas which were studied and translated, frequently requiring the invention of

---

[47] Kelsen's early analysis has exposed the theoretical artificialities of the public-private law dichotomy. Kelsen, *General Theory of Law and State*. See also Friedmann, "Public and Private Law Thinking: A Need for Synthesis," *Wayne Law Review*, v (1959), 291.

wholly new legal language—the pressure of diplomacy, the travail and ingenuity apparent in all of this work—can hardly fail to produce a certain compassion for the dedication and efforts of the statesmen who carried this difficult burden forward in the first thirty years after 1868.[48]

The pattern of governance which they created was not liberal or democratic, but measured against their legacy from the past it was surely modern, even visionary, yet realistic enough to escape ineffectual utopianism. As noted, the responsible Japanese used certain facets of their tradition—the whole fabric of legalistic familial and feudal loyalty, the historical elite-leadership capacities and the commoners' "creative obedience," nurtured by centuries of inherited hierarchy and immobility, and embedded in the psychology, language, and manners of the people, not to mention the direct and massive continuity of private law relations until 1898 at least—to provide the guidance and discipline implicit in the bootstrap operation required to elevate Japan to the rank of a militarily strong and industrialized power. Sympathetic as we are with their self-interested yearnings, it is surely arguable whether an attempt to install liberal institutions such as those suggested by Fukuzawa or Okuma, for example, would have produced better results by 1930 at less human cost.

There is little evidence that the makers of the Meiji constitution actually did regard it as merely a phase, yet the Meiji constitution did have some potential for liberal growth. But its illiberal potentialities, more plausible from its structure and implemented by assassinations, won out completely in the 1930's. As Ukai has characterized it in the words of Faust: "Ah, two souls live in my bosom."[49]

[48] The most useful summary is Ishii, *Meiji bunkashi; hōsei-hen* (1954); English: Ishii, *Japanese Legislation in the Meiji Era*, tr. Chambliss (1958).

[49] Ukai, "The Individual and the Rule of Law under the New Japanese Constitution," *Northwestern University Law Review*, LI (1956-1957), 733, 735.

THE FIRST STAGE, 1868-1882: ADMINISTRATION-BUILDING

The abiding political characteristic of the Japanese legal order throughout this long and varied period (1868–1945) was a formal commitment to administration under law, but combined with a complete (and not surprising) lack of legal limitations on policy formation (legislation). This essentially Western arrangement we have labeled, following Takayanagi,[50] the rule-by-law (*hōchishugi*) to distinguish it from the postwar questings for a different but still Western relationship between law and power, the rule-of-law (*hō no shihai*), whereby both official discretion and policy formulation are limited by law in favor of fundamental human rights and the electoral process. Both of these ideas concerning the law–power relationship (rule-by-law and rule-of-law) were, of course, foreign to the pre-Meiji tradition; yet both of them have been implanted rather paternalistically in Japan, in 1889 and 1947 respectively, by visionary reforms which have served as challenges to the Japanese people to develop the right consciousness requisite to their use. We shall have something to say about this social requisite of Japanese legal efficacy at the end of this essay, but first we must consider the implication of what we call here the rule-by-law.

The rule-by-law was derived by the Japanese from the German *Rechsstaat* principle. The "law state" is characterized primarily by the existence of an absolute central authority and a network of general rules guiding the actions of subjects and officials, but not lawmakers. Thus there is a rule-by-law wherever there exists an orderly system of standards which are made known in advance to the subjects, and which are applied equally by courts or officials to all who come within their purview, however illiberal or discriminating they may be. An-

---

[50] These terms (*hōchishugi* and *hō no shihai*) are used by Takayanagi, "A Century of Innovation," in von Mehren, ed., *Law in Japan*, p. 14. Quaere, however, whether *hōchishugi* does not sometimes carry some of the same meaning as *hō no shihai* in postwar usage.

other interesting analogy—besides the nineteenth century German *Rechtsstaat*—is the recent Russian communist theory of law which has moved from a system of expansive discretionary power relationships (law-of-status) to a rule-by-law, more generally referred to as "socialist legality."[51]

Specifically, in Japan the formalistic rule-by-law has meant, as Itō Hirobumi said,[52] legal limits on the administrative exercise of power but no limits on law-making power. We should add that the legal limits on administrative power as practiced in prewar Japan were indeed formalistic and often illusory because of the way the basic public law, private law dichotomy, borrowed from the civil law world, worked in Japan as we shall see later. There was, rather, a de facto dual status, wherein officials remained largely above the justiciable law.

The establishment of a rule-by-law in Meiji Japan involved four major phases. Proceeding in chronological sequence, first, they created a centralized administrative system, plus an auxiliary criminal law and a court hierarchy to support it; second, and by parallel action, the Meiji rulers leveled the old status hierarchy to a single *legal* (but not social) status—the Japanese imperial subject (*shimmin*)—but the status distinctions in Meiji family law are an example of vestigial status-law employed even within the new legal order itself, and, of course, much of the old hierarchical system of employment and landholding was also adapted in the new society. Third, building on these premises, a constitution was provided to codify these prior accomplishments. Fourth, an extensive body of code law was enacted to provide systematic doctrinal rules for the entire private law field.

These four phases in the establishment of a rule-by-law were achieved in two stages: between 1868 and 1882 the administra-

---

[51] Edward Zellweger, "The Principle of Socialist Legality," *Journal of the International Commission of Jurists*, v (1964), 163-202.

[52] Ishii, *Meiji bunkashi: hōsei-hen* (1954), pp. 331-32.

tion-building and status-leveling functions were largely carried through, together with enactment of generalized criminal laws.

All facets of this colossal legal enterprise had their concomitant difficulties: even to build the requisite administrative skeleton the vast federalistic complex of daimyo feudal jurisdictions had to be abolished; to create a judiciary parallel to the new administration was an innovation for which, as noted above, the most advanced Japanese experience furnished only the faintest guidance and almost no professional tradition. The creation of a legally equal imperial subject (as distinguished from a citizen, *kokumin*, with fundamental rights) presupposed the dismantlement of the whole Tokugawa status hierarchy, down to the family. And in order to establish a constitution and codify the doctrinal law, the new government had to study and largely replace the accumulation of several centuries of diverse customary law. This private-law codification project touched the entire property of Japan and the totality of private relations. The enormity of the task can again only be appreciated when we remember that Japan was without a doubt already by 1850 one of the most *socially* organized societies in history, which meant that Japan was a rather modern society already in its degree of social interdependence —even more so in this respect, and also larger in population, than was the United States of the same period. For codification, this meant that the highly refined and diverse customs had to be taken into account—or risk ineffectual legal verbiage.

These major projects meant also the departure, forever apparently, from the mainstream of Chinese traditional institutions which had influenced Japanese law in varying degrees for over a millennium. It meant, too, the outright abolition of several centuries of indigenous feudal law and institutions, most of it developed after the Onin wars (1467), but some dating as far back as the Kamakura period (1185-1333) and even earlier.

Criminal Law as an Auxiliary to Administrative Power, 1868-1882. We will eschew the important Meiji expansion of central power (1868-1882) to replace Tokugawa feudal decentralization and treat the role of the criminal law and then of the Meiji constitution. Parenthetically, we may note, however, that the overall evolution followed what seems to be rather normal patterns of growth: skeletal power and administration preceded the delicacies of codes, courts, and justiciable law; once authority was established, criminal law followed to support it; then a constitutional rule-by-law developed, as a rationalization of power, into the administrative and private law areas in varying incomplete degrees of fidelity to the principle.

Criminal law is always a prime legal tool of an emergent regime, and accordingly the Meiji criminal codes were codified in the early stages of system-building (1868-1882), antedating the civil law codes by twenty years. The first attempts to obtain uniformity in the criminal laws were as early as 1868, when the government ordered that the Tokugawa code (*Osadamegaki*) be applied by all of the domains as well. In the Tokugawa period it had only been officially distributed to a few higher officers of the shogun and was applicable directly only in Tokugawa lands. Soon afterward in the same year, the Provisional Penal Code (*Kari keiritsu*) was issued, followed by the Outlines of the New Criminal Law (*Shinritsu kōryō*) and Amended Criminal Regulations (*Kaitei ritsurei*) in 1870 and 1873, respectively. These criminal laws drew upon Ming (1367-1644) and Ching (1644-1912) Chinese jurisprudence, plus Japanese eighth century *ritsuryō* law patterned after Chinese T'ang dynasty (618-907) law. These Chinese-style criminal laws, including some gradual concessions to Western ideas, were effective until 1882, when they were replaced by the so-called Old Criminal Code and the procedural Code of Criminal Instructions (*Chizaihō*).

Both of these latter codes were initially drafted by Boissanade along French lines. As the first Western-style codes in Japan, they became a great watershed in Japanese law, marking the end of massive Chinese influence in Japanese law, although interestingly enough the T'ang doctrine on concurrent crimes and other vestiges remained.[53] Many features of the French-style code were congenial to Tokugawa practice, but by 1879 all traces of torture as a routine criminal law technique had been abolished from Japanese law. It is interesting to a common lawyer to note that a jury system was included in the drafts until the final stage, when the Cabinet deleted it.

A part of the criminal law of this period which was enormously important to politics was, however, outside of these codes. This body of special laws included the Police Regulations on Public Meetings (1880, revised 1893), the Press (1875, revised 1887 and 1897), Libel (1875), Book Censorship (1869, revised 1887 and 1893), and Peace Preservation (1877). Violations of these controls were criminal offenses. For example, six hundred political figures were banished from Tokyo in the Tokugawa style (*Edo-barai*) on December 26, 1887, under the Peace Preservation Law. This technique of the special police law was a useful vehicle for the authoritarian control of popular or parliamentary agitators throughout the Meiji era, particularly during the period of constitution-making (1881–1890), and it reappeared in all of its virulence in the 1920's.

THE SECOND STAGE, 1882–1898: CODIFICATION

The Constitutional Formulation of the Rule-by-Law. The foregoing brief outline covered the basic system-building during the first fifteen years of the Meiji regime. Enforcement of the new French-style criminal codes (1882) presaged a period of intense codification beginning with the Meiji constitution in 1889. The process of constitution-making with its critical tensions between absolutistic and parliamentary protagonists and their respective foreign models is an important and sepa-

[53] *Id.*, p. 460.

rate story which has been well surveyed and chronicled in Japanese by Inada, Osatake, Kobayakawa, Ishii,[54] and others and in English by Akita, Beckmann, Miller, Siemes, and others.[55] Our interest here is to examine the role of justiciable law in the Meiji legal order as formulated by the new constitution.

Essentially, this formula[56] called for governmental power to be exercised in accordance with law; thus law became the implement of, but not a limitation upon, legislative power. The basic constitutional scheme makes the emperor "the head of

[54] Inada, *Meiji kenpō seiritsushi* (1962), I, II; Osatake Takeshi, *Nihon kenseishi taikō* (1939); Kobayakawa, *Meiji hōseishiron* (1940), I, II; Ishii, *Meiji bunkashi; hōsei-hen* (1954); Kaneko, *Kenpō seitei to ōbeijin no hyōron* (1939); and Suzuki, *Kenpō seitei to Roesureru* (1942).

[55] Akita, *Foundations of Constitutional Government in Modern Japan, 1868-1900* (Cambridge, 1965). Cf. Beckmann, *The Making of the Meiji Constitution* (1957); Frank Miller, *Minobe Tatsukichi* (Berkeley, 1965); and Johannes Siemes, "Hermann Roessler's Commentaries on the Meiji Constitution," *Monumenta Nipponica*, XVII (1962), 1-66; also MacLaren, "Japanese Government Documents," *TASJ*, XLII:i; Itō Hirobumi, *Commentaries on the Constitution of the Empire of Japan* (1906); Itō, "Some Reminiscences of the Grant of the New Constitution," in *Fifty Years of New Japan*, ed. Okuma (1909), p. 122.

We are fortunate also to have Shinichi Fujii, *The Essentials of Japanese Constitutional Law* (1940), and N. Matsunami, *The Constitution of Japan* (1930). Both of the latter English-language treatises are bizarre by democratic standards, but they communicate the tone of the Meiji constitution in its later years. Fujii's work, though written in 1940, has a foreword by K. Kaneko, who traveled in 1889-1890 to Europe at Itō's request for the specific purpose of eliciting comment from constitutional authorities. Kaneko, *Kenpō seitei to ōbeijin no hyōron* (1937), and Fujii S., *Teikoku kenpō to Kaneko-haku* (1942), p. 416. Such men as Dicey, Holmes, and Gneist are said to have approved in general of the Meiji constitution for the time and place. In English, see Takayanagi, "The Development of Japanese Law," in von Mehren, ed., *Law in Japan*, pp. 7-8.

[56] See Pittau, "The Meiji Political System: Different Interpretations," in *Studies in Japanese Culture* (1963), p. 99, for a review of a variety of Japanese theories about the constitution and their overall meaning.

the empire combining in himself the rights of sovereignty" (Article 4), and the emperor was to exercise the law-making power through the Diet (Article 37). Then significantly every right and duty conferred by Chapter II covering "Rights and Duties of Subjects" was to be enjoyed "within the limits of law." This arrangement clearly rejected anything like the French natural right theory or the American social contract theory as limitation on the constitutional policymakers. Rather, as the preamble of the constitution states, these rights were bestowed on the subjects as a benevolent act: "We now declare to respect and protect the security of the rights and of the property of our people, and to secure them the complete enjoyment of the same, within the extent of the provisions of the present constitution and the law."

With this kind of state theory, even the modest goals of administration under law was not to be taken for granted, especially against the historical experience of Japanese law. Nor was its accomplishment in operation ever realized in the field of judicial review except in a token degree. For example, in an early civil code compilation project in 1870, it is said that "certain jurists opposed the coining of the term *minken* (civil right) as an equivalent to the French *droit civil* on the ground that common people were not entitled to any rights"—and here we are discussing only ordinary private rights. In private law, this was consistent with the old idea that suits were heard only as a matter of grace, and in administration, the traditional idea was that a retainer could not appeal against his lord because the retainer owed absolute obedience.

Also, Iwakura included no suggestion for constitutional provisions on rights of subjects in his *General Principles* of 1881, and even in the final stages of constitutional deliberations in the Privy Council, Count Mori Arinori is said[57] to have contended that the title of Chapter II should be changed to read, "The Status of Subjects." "The word 'rights' was inappropri-

[57] Ishii, *Meiji bunkashi; hōsei-hen*, 1954, p. 331.

ate, Mori thought, because in regard to the emperor the Japanese subject had nothing but a definite station in life and obligations." Considering from whence he started (*chu*) and where he arrived (rule-by-law), Itō's defense of the Meiji rights of subjects "within the limits of the law" was rather progressive, if scarcely heroic. Ito's position was sound, of course, that the very determination to grant a constitution once enforced would constrict at least the manner in which imperial power even in the policy-making field would be exercised in the future—that is, by law duly enacted by the Diet (or ordinance later approved by the Diet); such law would, in turn, limit the responsible officials and independent courts in applying it. Even this idea was moving far beyond the Tokugawa natural law theories of downward delegations of discretionary power to status officials who were responsible only to superiors. In this sense, to measure the Meiji formulation by modern democratic standards is rather like criticizing the Oregon Trail because it was an inadequate highway.[58]

But focusing on the potential for constitutional growth after 1890 (i.e. beyond the accomplishment of a rule-by-law) to a popular control of the British parliamentary type over the content of the law, especially concerning "fundamental human rights" of subjects, it is equally clear that the Meiji document and vision was aggressively negative. Iwakura for instance specified in the *General Principles* (1881), which to a remarkable degree shaped the final constitution, that only the government could initiate legislation. Political pressures were able to overcome this restrictive form, but still the Diet was conceived as largely advisory. At first Itō, like George Washington a century earlier, saw no role for parties in the legislature. The Cabinet was to be responsible not to the Diet but the emperor. In sum then, the Meiji constitution-makers sought specifically

[58] See Itō, "Some Reminiscences of the Grant of the New Constitution," in Okuma, ed., *Fifty Years of New Japan* (1909), p. 128, for his appraisal of the effect of the peculiar Japanese milieu, the "vast village community."

to avoid popular parliamentary control over the content of the law; that is, to avoid a rule-of-law of the unique British kind dependent exclusively on the electoral processes. Needless to say, judicial supremacy, an American idea which has proved to be more exportable than the English process, was quite unsuitable to the whole theory and purpose of the constitution. There were but legislative rights, and in understanding the rule-by-law we need only inquire into the character of the Meiji courts both ordinary and administrative and their role in enforcing legislation.

JUDICIAL INDEPENDENCE

The Meiji formula thus included no role for justiciable law to limit the scope of lawmaking. But the theory did, at least, commit the government to keep politics out of administration and adjudication. These functions were to proceed in accordance with law, meaning that each judicial decision and official act was to find its justification in legislation in turn enacted by constitutional organs and procedure. In this section we will discuss not only the prewar courts and the appellate system, but also the bench, bar, and procuracy, since they are all functional essentials of legal professionalism, implied by an independent judicial arm of government. All were important innovations in Japan; none of them had any substantial support in pre-Meiji institutions as we have seen.

Separation of the Courts from Administration. As noted, the Meiji constitution observes the civilian principle (mainly from Germany and Austria) of separating the law into two main categories: public and private law. In adjudication this meant that the constitution provided for separate courts for civil (and criminal, see above) cases as opposed to administrative cases.

This public-private division was established in the Meiji constitution by first providing that "the Judicature shall be exercised by the courts of law, according to law, in the name of the emperor" (Article 57). The phrase authorizing the courts to exercise the judicial power "in the name of the emperor" was chosen, it is said, to indicate that the courts were to exercise the judicial power independently. The other grants of governmental power were phrased so that they were exercised by the emperor *through* the Diet and executive. Then the regular courts are denied jurisdiction over suits which come within the special competence of the Court of Administrative Litigation as established by law (Article 61). In addition, the constitution provided for public trials (Article 59) and for the proper qualification, tenure, and discipline of judges only in accordance with the law (Article 58).

Judicial independence involved three related ideas at that time novel to Japan: (1) separating the judiciary from the administration; (2) noninterference either by their judicial superiors or by the executive branch in the judges' trial of specific cases; and (3) personnel administration calculated to provide professionally qualified and impartial judges. All of these matters were subjects of some evolution in the two decades before the constitution (1889).

The story starts with the designation of the old Tokugawa three commissions (*san bugyō*) as "courts" (*saibansho*) in 1868, although their administrative and judicial functions were still confused. Then by a gradual process, with major steps under Eto Shimpei encouraged by Kido Koin in 1872 and under Oki Takato in 1875, the courts were gradually made separate and relatively independent by February 8, 1890, when a lengthy Law on the Constitution of the Courts (*Saibansho kōseihō*, Law No. 6, February 8, 1890) was enacted following the draft of Otto Rudorff, a German jurist. The new law constituted a dramatic switch from the French models, used in the 1875 law in creating the Great Court of Cassation (*Daishinin*), to the German system of courts. Intermediately, in 1877, the last vestiges of a millennium of fusion of judicial and administrative functions in the same personnel was ended when the local governors were prohibited from acting also as judges. Public trials were authorized in 1875.

Independence of Judges. As a result of the 1890 law, a hierarchy of regular courts was established with both civil and criminal sections.[59] Appellate jurisdiction, which was unknown to Edo practice, was initiated in 1875 and perfected in the *kōso* (law and fact) and *jōkoku* (law only) system of appeals. Judges were selected for legal expertise. Their independence was guaranteed, and in fact observed after the famous test case of Tsuda Sanzō[60] soon after the new courts went into operation. This was a criminal trial of a Japanese policeman who wounded the crown prince of Russia (later Nicholas II) with a sword at Otsu in 1891. The Japanese government, for diplomatic reasons, wanted the death penalty, but the law only provided life imprisonment for attempted murder, unless the victim was a member of the Japanese imperial family. The chief justice, Kojima Iken, refused to accede to political pressures, and the five man section of the court which was trying the case sentenced Tsuda to life imprisonment in accordance with the law. The precedent has become a valuable tradition of the new Japanese judiciary, and, on this level, the independence of the judiciary has been secure since then.

Tenure for life was established in the law (Article 67), though later qualified by specification of a retirement age of sixty-three. Quigley[61] notes that after protests by the judiciary, the judges' salaries were in fact excluded, in deference to their tenure, from a general official salary cut ordered in 1931. Also, dismissal of judges was only possible after criminal conviction or formal disciplinary action as provided by law.

The chief blemish to judicial independence in the prewar period was the executive influence deriving from the fact that the entire court system was under the minister of justice. His

---

[59] The policy to have both civil and criminal cases tried by the same law courts doubtless came from the French. See René David and Henry P. de Vries, *The French Legal System* (Dobbs Ferry, 1958), p. 56.

[60] Osatake, *Konan jiken* (Tokyo, 1951).

[61] Harold Scott Quigley, *Japanese Government and Politics* (New York, 1932), p. 274.

role in selection, promotion, and assignments was doubtless an inhibition to judges, but there is little evidence of interference in specific cases. It is clear, however, that this vestigial remnant of the traditional confusion of administrative and judicial structures gave the courts and judges an undesirable bureaucratic character and outlook.[62]

Administrative Justice. The regular courts were denied jurisdiction over such cases against officials as were reserved by law to the Court of Administrative Litigation (*Gyōsei-saibansho*) (Article 61). The law in turn limited the administrative court jurisdiction to a limited list of enumerated claims.[63] In mechanistic (and unrealistic) theory, the administrative official was not to make policy; he was to apply the law as laid down by statute, and in the prewar system any allegation by a subject or another official to the effect that an officer had misapplied the law was to be heard first by superior officials up to the minister, and then, if a judicial hearing was desired, a suit could be brought, in the enumerated categories of cases, to the Court of Administrative Litigation. These procedures were set out in the *Gyōsei-saibanshohō* of 1890, which was originally drafted by Mosse after an Austrian pattern, and in its fifty odd years of effectiveness, the law was never amended. The Petitions Law (*Soganhō*) fixing the procedures for administrative hearings in the bureaus, which were prerequisites to a later claim in the court, was also enacted in 1890. Significantly, however, a later decision (1937) of the Great Court of Cassation held that it had the power under the Court Organization Law (1890) to review the question of *ultra vires* official orders in an appropriate case.[64]

---

[62] For critical views see Ienaga Saburō, *Shihōken dokuritsu no rekishiteki kōsatsu* (Tokyo, 1962), p. 9, also p. 109; and Sasaki Tetsuzō, *Saibankanron* (Tokyo, 1960), p. 26.

[63] Law No. 6, Feb. 10, 1890; for English translation, see MacLaren, "Japanese Government Documents," *TASJ*, XLII:i (1914), 625.

[64] *Sato v. Japan*, 16 *Daishinin keiji hanreishū* 193 (*Daishinin*, 3d Criminal Dept., Mar. 3, 1937).

Of course, officials, and judges as well, working under the usual modern statute often do, indeed must, make policy. As Llewellyn has put it, this is the molecular theory of law-making; it also happens in any legal system, although the degree of discretion may vary. Nevertheless, the orthodox theory has been that as nearly as possible the law should have the maximum specificity, limiting officials to the application of its prescriptions. In Japan official misapplication was grounds for suit in the special administrative court. But matters left to official discretion were not challengeable, as Nakano has said: "The jurisdiction of the administrative court stops exactly where administrative discretion begins."[65] Since Japanese regulatory statutes, more even than ours in the United States, have generally involved delegations of massive discretion, we can imagine that most of the pressure of government left its imprint on the populace in areas unchallengeable in this prewar court.

Added to the broad area of official discretion was the fact that no administrative court decisions were appealable; conflicts with the regular law courts were not legally determinable,[66] and administrative court procedures were too sketchy, forcing the court to rely on the Code of Civil Procedure, which was inadequate for the purpose. Most serious of all the defects was the fact that the court was one of specified jurisdiction, and the statutory enumeration of cases to be handled (both in the *Gyōsei-saibanshōho* and special statutes) left important gaps. The court itself submitted recommendations in 1931 to institute an appellate system and broaden its jurisdiction, but these were not heeded.[67] The situation was mitigated to some extent by the fact that government action in the pri-

[65] Nakano, *The Ordinance Power of the Japanese Emperor* (1923), p. 230.

[66] The determination of such conflicts was to be by the Privy Council under special rules, which were never issued. Consequently the Privy Council never functioned in such a capacity. Gyōseisho saibansho, *Gyōsei saibansho gojūnenshi* (1941), p. 342.

[67] *Id.* at 337; also see Wada Hideo, "Gyōsei saiban," in Nobushige Ukai *et al., Nihon kindaihō hattatsushi* (Tokyo 1958), III, p. 85 at 163.

vate law field (contracts and torts) could be challenged in the regular law courts as in Germany (*contra* France).

French experience with the law-administrative court dichotomy teaches us that in practice it can be a sound system in a different tradition. But coupled with the all-pervasive attitude of the haughty official (*kanson mimpi*) in prewar Japan, it is fair to say that these factors prevented the realization of a justiciable rule-by-law in the administrative field, except to a token degree. This is borne out by the paucity of litigation in the court; statistics show that, on the average, less than three hundred cases were filed annually between 1890 and 1930.[68]

The Procurator. In prewar criminal justice the procurator had a semijudicial role; he sat on the level of the judge, dressed like the judge, and was housed and trained with the judges.[69] The very great discretion[70] of the procurators in handling criminal complaints (about 30 percent were never prosecuted) together with their role in the preliminary investigations and at the trials are matters which have drawn much persuasive criticism. The bar requested that the procurator be placed on the level of the defense in criminal trials, but this was not accomplished until after World War II. It is interesting to note, too, that until 1874 they were regarded as necessary to supervise the judges at the trials, like the Tokugawa inspectors (*ometsuke*).

The Japanese Bar. The diminutive proportions and limited scope of services of the prewar Japanese bar may fairly be taken as a rough indicator of the dominance of officialdom and the dwarfed rights consciousness of the Japanese subject.

[68] A statistical chart of filings is appended to Gyōsei saibansho, *Gyōsei saibansho gojūnenshi* (1941).

[69] Ishii, *Meiji bunkashi*; *hōsei-hen*, p. 228.

[70] This discretionary power of procurators is analyzed well in Nagashima, "The Accused and Society," in von Mehren, ed., *Law in Japan.*

We have seen the faint glimmerings of a legal expert in the Suit Inn (*Kujiyado*) of Edo. These knowledgeable, if scarcely professional legal draftsmen, negotiators, and litigation guides were employed in Edo only by itinerant parties in *civil* litigation (*deiri mono*). It is highly significant also that although advocates (*daigennin*) similar to the French *avocat* were provided, one per district in 1872, they too acted in civil trials only. These advocates were subjected to further regulations in 1876 and 1880. It was not until the Criminal Code of 1882 that lawyers were specifically provided for in criminal actions. Indeed on May 25, 1876, in response to an inquiry, the Ministry of Justice noted that lawyers were not prohibited in criminal cases, but that they did not appear because of natural custom (*shizen no shūkan*).[71]

Finally, in 1893 the new type of lawyer (*bengoshi*) appeared in a more elaborate law.[72] But his role in prewar Japan was restricted and passive, since he could not question the witnesses directly during the prevailing multiple-hearing type of trial, and in criminal trials he was placed in a rather apologetic position beneath the judge and the procurator. Especially disadvantageous to both client and lawyer was the key fact that during the preliminary hearing before indictment the defendant was detained sometimes for months, without right to counsel and, of course, with no writ of *habeas corpus* available.

After 1890 no changes were made in the Court of Administrative Litigation, and though minor changes were made in the system of ordinary law courts, bench, and procuracy, these institutions retained their essential character fixed by the laws of the early 1890's. The regulations for the bar were substantially changed in 1933. Such was the prewar apparatus for the administration of justiciable law, and on the whole it repre-

---

[71] Ishii, *Meiji bunkashi; hōsei-hen*, p. 232.
[72] Nihon bengoshi rengōkai, *Nihon bengoshi enkakushi* (1959), pp. 2-106, gives a full account of the Meiji lawyer; in English: Hattori, "The Legal Profession in Japan," in von Mehren, ed., *Law in Japan.*

sented a considerable advancement toward modern standards, notwithstanding its many operative shortcomings.

CODIFICATION OF JAPANESE PRIVATE LAW

These bare bones of a centralized state were no sooner established than the Meiji statesmen began to prepare for more thorough codification in the area of private rights, a virgin field for Japanese law of national scope.[73] Among the personalities whose influence helped to develop the national codes, Eto Shimpei (1872, first minister of justice), Ōki Takatō (1873, second minister of justice), and Kido Kōin were prominent in the early period, and, of course, Itō Hirobumi, Itō Myōji, Inoue Kowashi, and Kaneko Kentarō were instrumental in drafting the new constitution. Hozumi Nobushige, Ume Kenjirō, and Tomii Masaaki stood out in the work on the final drafting of the Civil Code, and Okano Keijiro, Ume Kenjiro, and Tabe Kaoru in the redrafting of the Commercial Code.

Western legal advisers[74] were enormously important at all stages of Japanese codification, although the Japanese committees always worked out the final drafts. Bousquet assisted in Eto Shimpei's first Civil Code project in 1872; Boissanade drafted codes for twenty years in Japan beginning in 1873,[75] and he was a central figure throughout the whole process, although over his protests the French drafts were finally abandoned in large part in favor of German-style codes. But the criminal codes adopted earlier (1882) were largely his work. Rudolf von Gneist, Albert Mosse (German), and Lorenz von Stein (Austrian) lectured to Itō in Europe, and later Mosse came to Japan and assisted with the local government laws

[73] See generally N. Hozumi, *The New Japanese Civil Code* (1912); and Ishii, *Meiji bunkashi*; *hōsei-hen*, pp. 507-645.

[74] Kobayakawa, *Meiji kōhō shiron* (1941), II, gives considerable detail on the foreign advisors, and it contains a useful index also listing foreigners at 1394ff.

[75] Wagatsuma, *Gendai Nippon shōshi*, pp. 20-21.

and the Code of Civil Procedures. Roessler (German) was influential in the constitutional drafting process, and also drafted the Commercial Code. The initial drafts of the Code of Civil Procedure were the works of Techow (German), then later Mosse. Otto Rudorff's (German) draft of the Judicial Law was accepted instead of a draft done by Boissanade. Also, Itō mentions Pigott (English) as useful in the constitutional drafting process.[76] Several American lawyers were on the scene, but their influence was largely confined to the teaching field: e.g. Henry Terry and John Henry Wigmore. Another American lawyer who began his Japanese legal career in the Yokohama Consular Courts was Henry Willard Denison, an important Foreign Ministry Adviser on treaty renegotiations and other tasks from 1878 to 1914, and highly esteemed by the Japanese.[77]

From the very beginning the drive for codification was spurred on by a double motivation. The Dutch and English treaties of 1854 and later the treaties with France, Russia, Germany, and the U.S. included provisions for extraterritoriality,[78] so that if a citizen of these foreign powers committed an offense in Japan, he was to be tried by the representative of his own country in Japan.[79] And as soon as Iwakura returned from Europe (1872), it became a constant goal of the government to negotiate new treaties which would return to the Japanese the jurisdiction over foreigners and also over the customs administration.

But parallel to these motivations the Japanese government had been interested in uniform and systematic law for its own

---

[76] Itō Hirobumi, "Some Reminiscences of the Grant of the New Constitution," in Okuma, ed., *Fifty Years of New Japan*, p. 128.

[77] Robert Schwantes brought Denison to my attention.

[78] Gubbins, *The Progress of Japan 1853-71* (1911), gives the text of most of these treaties.

[79] See Francis C. Jones, *Extraterritoriality in Japan* (New Haven, 1931); George H. Scidmore, *United States Courts in Japan* (Tokyo, 1887); Luke T. Lee, *Consular Law and Practice* (New York, 1961), p. 205.

sake. We have already seen the importance attached to a uniform modern criminal code, which was enforced in 1882. But with few exceptions[80] the entire law of family and private transactions, as well as the law of civil procedure, remained until the 1890's Tokugawa customary law in unrecorded form,[81] much of it unsuitable for modern social relations and commerce and in any event highly diverse from place to place. Pressured by diplomacy,[82] the Japanese almost inevitably turned to the Western codes—at first French and later German—for their models. The American and English common laws, as well as Japanese customary law, were not in suffi-

[80] It has been suggested that in the early days before codification these diverse foreign laws entered the Japanese law through the judicial process as an expression of reason (*jōri*), a source of law to be applied by the judges in the 1875 Rules for the Conduct of Judicial Affairs, Art. 3: "Judgments in civil cases shall be governed by custom in the absence of written law; and in the absence of custom, judgment should be based on reason (*jōri*)." N. Hozumi, *The New Japanese Civil Code*, pp. 38-40. Ishii, *Meiji bunkashi; hōsei-hen*, p. 36, treats this interesting point in detail.

[81] Compilations of the customary laws have been printed. See Takimoto, ed., *Minji kanrei ruishū* (1932), 390 pp., originally compiled in 1877; Takimoto, ed., *Shōji kanrei ruishu* (1932), 1130 pp., originally compiled 1883-1884 and also printed, *Nihon keizai taiten*, XLIX, 3-732, and *id.*, L, 735-1130; *Zenkoku minji kanrei ruishū*, originally compiled by the *Shihōshō* in 1880 and printed in *Nihon keizai taiten*, L, 3-390. Perhaps the most useful of the printed versions of these compilations is Y. Kazahaya, ed., *Zenkoku minji kanrei ruishū* (1944), because it is said to combine the better features of both the 1877 and 1880 compilations. John H. Wigmore spent several years after 1936 translating these and other Tokugawa legal materials, but because of World War II only two parts (II and VII) were ever printed. Some of his earlier translations of these same materials may be found in *TASJ*, XX:ii (1893). See Henderson, "Japanese Legal History of the Tokugawa Period: Scholars and Sources," in University of Michigan Center of Japanese Studies, *Occasional Papers*, No. 7 (1957), pp. 100-21, for a description of Wigmore's project.

[82] Sugii, "Paakusu kinan ronsō," *Shirin*, XXXVIII:iv; Nakamura Kikuo, *Kindai Nihon no hōteki keisei* (1956), p. 52. Generally, see Oyama Hironari, "Joyaku kaisei," in *Nihon kindaihō hattatsushi* (Tokyo, 1958), II, 177-231.

ciently coherent form to enable the Japanese to adapt them as solutions to their urgent diplomatic or systematization problems.

In the early years Tsuda Shinichiro had studied (1863) at Leiden under Simon Vissering and upon returning to Japan wrote his *Treatise on the Law of Occidental Countries (Taisei kokuhō ron)*, in which, it is said, he had to invent a word for even such a fundamental term as "right" (*kenri*)[83] itself. Also, he coined the basic word "civil law" (*minpō*) as a translation of the Dutch *bergerlyk regt*. Later, in 1869, Kurimoto Aki-no-kami (*Gaikoku bugyō*) after his trip to France in 1867 praised the Code Napoléon in his *Reminiscences (Gyoso Tsuiroku)*. Mizukuni Rinsho, who was in France in 1867, was commissioned by the new government to translate the various French codes in 1869.

From these early beginnings the process of translating the codes, creating legal terminology, developing law schools (both governmental and private), consulting foreigners, drafting and redrafting, and finally compiling for comparative purposes nationwide compendiums of Japanese customs in the fields of civil, commercial, and procedural law continued feverishly for two full decades. The culmination was a phase extending over another entire decade of the 1890's wherein remarkable, if not perfect, comparative understanding was attained by the Japanese specialists, not only between a variety of possible foreign models but finally between them and the native practices.[84] The finale labeled the "postponement con-

---

[83] Hozumi, *The New Japanese Civil Code* (1912), p. 57.

[84] The erudite and interesting criticisms of the Japanese codemakers by Wigmore and Boissanade regarding their lack of understanding of their own customary law and European law respectively may be unduly harsh. Actually it seems that the Japanese executed the immense codification task rather well under the unrealistic time schedule imposed by the urgencies of diplomacy. See Wigmore, "New Codes and Old Customs," printed in *Japan Mail*, Nov., 1892; and Boissanade, "Les anciennes coutumes du Japon et le nouveau Code Civil," in *Revue française du Japon* (nos. 24, 25, 26) (1894). Cf. Ishii, *Meiji bunkashi*;

troversy" by Hozumi Nobushige[85] was, by any standards, a dramatic episode in the annals of comparative law. For, on the threshold of enforcing the three new codes (Commercial, Civil, and Civil Procedure) a controversy broke out among the Japanese lawyers which extended into the new Diet, resulting in the postponement of the effectiveness of the Civil Code until 1898 and the Commercial Code until 1899.[86]

It is interesting to speculate whether the initial haste in promulgating these codes in 1890 was mainly prompted by desires for treaty revision or in order to avoid the necessity of Diet consideration. In any event, all three of these fundamental codes were promulgated just before the first Diet opened in November 1890. But only the Code of Civil Procedure was allowed to go into effect in 1891, as scheduled; the Civil and Commercial Codes were postponed.[87]

This postponement controversy was an exceedingly complex event, the issues of which can only be judged against the diplomatic and political context of the times, as well as the sociology of the antagonistic legal professionals, and by mastery as a whole of both the new and old drafts against the

---

hōsei-hen, p. 507, for detailed comparison of the old draft codes, supported by Wigmore and Boissanade, with the new codes finally promulgated; especially see Tomii's critique.

[85] Hozumi, *The New Japanese Civil Code*, p. 15.

[86] After Hozumi, a considerable literature has been accumulated, particularly in the last two decades on this problem. E.g. see Hoshino Tōru, *Meiji minpō hensanshi no kenkyū* (1943); *id., Minpoten ronsōshi* (1944), pp. 124-26 for bibliography; and see Nakamura Kikuo, *Kindai Nihon no hōteki keisei* (1956), pp. 297-301, for a list of books and articles. Particularly note the debate in the journals between Nakamura and Hoshino and others over certain aspects of the Civil Code for citations: Nakamura Kikuo, "Minpōten ronsō no keika to mondaiten," *Hōgaku kenkyū*, XXIX (1956), 473-97, 853-75, and also see an analysis of problems prior to the postponement dispute in Mukai and Toshitani, "Meiji zenki ni okeru minpo hensan no keiga to mondaiten," in Hōseishi gakkai, ed., *Hōten hensanshi no kihonteki mondaiten* (1963), p. 215. (For English translation, see *Law in Japan: an Annual*, I (1967), 25-59. Henderson tr.)

[87] Law No. 8 (1892).

background of diverse Tokugawa custom as it had been developed by twenty years of Meiji practice. We have extended contemporary arguments by the antagonistic so-called English (postponement) and French (immediate enactment) schools[88] of Japanese lawyers and also by Boissanade and Wigmore, both generally against postponement.[89] Ishii's recent analysis[90] supporting Tomii's position for postponement seems persuasive on the point that the old draft civil and commercial codes contained important style defects (especially the parts drafted by Boissanade) and internal inconsistencies within each of the codes and between the French-style civil draft and German-style commercial draft. But the whole controversy is surely a subject ripe for careful monographic treatment by a qualified multilingual comparative lawyer with considerable time to devote to it.

In a real sense, then, the requisite law courts, bench and bar, and justiciable criminal and private codes were *formally* established in Japan by 1900. Also a Court of Administrative Litigation and a formal administrative procedure were established in 1890. Although this sphere of the rule-by-law was weak in practice, nonetheless the administration was formally committed to govern according to law. But the Japanese position in this area was different only in degree, if at all, from that of all modern welfare governments, for the problems of subjecting administration to juristic methods, in the context of growing governmental activity and individual dependence thereon, is still a vital and unresolved question in modern jurispru-

---

[88] Hoshino, *Meiji minpō hensanshi no kenkyū*, pp. 349-545, collects many arguments advanced by the two groups during the controversy. E.g. see Hozumi Yatsuka, "Minpō idete chūkō horobu," in *id.*, p. 415. Also, S. Tōyama, "Minpōten ronsō no seijishiteki kōsatsu," *Hōgaku shirin*, XL (1951), 56-87; and J. Matsumoto *et al.*, "Ume Kenjirō hakushi no omoide," *Hōgaku shirin*, XLIX (1951), 88-104. Hoshino, *Minpōten ronsōshi*, pp. 80-83, gives the persons who voted for and against the measure proposing postponement.

[89] See citation n. 84.

[90] Cited n. 84.

dence.[91] What was wholly lacking was the idea that fundamental rights could limit the policy-making power. Policy-
making power was, however, limited by law in the sense that
the policy must be expressed in generalized statutes passed by
the Diet in accordance with the procedures prescribed by the
constitution.

REFINEMENT AND SOCIAL PENETRATION OF THE LAW

The enactment of these Japanese legal formalities, of course,
only expressed the goals of modernization; for, of course, Japanese society with its Tokugawa heritage could only rise to
modern standards envisaged by the Meiji constitution and
codes, when the people began to understand the code provisions and comport themselves accordingly. This populariza-
tion of the new codes had to overcome the usual ignorance
and inertia, besides much positive resistance from tradition,
with the result that the functioning institutions were usually a
blend of old and new. Indeed, as Tomii so eloquently explained,
even the few experts (Boissanade, Roessler, the ministers of
justice, etc.) who drafted the old draft (unrevised) codes were
not properly aware of or apparently concerned with the inconsistencies in and among the codes or with the native practices.
This being the case, surely there were few of the lay populace
who understood the complex codes enough to follow them in
their daily transactions—land, family, and employment relations, sales and contracts, business enterprises, and property
devolution, even dispute settlements—though in practically
every phase of Japanese life change in some degree was *legally*
required by the enactment of the new codes. This observation
simply makes an obvious point that the codes were, in large
part, visionary or expedient, treaty-oriented articulations of
modern Japanese aspirations—an overriding legal system of
nationwide efficacy based on the concept of the "legal individ-

[91] Stone, "The Twentieth Century Administrative Explosion and
After," *California Law Review*, XLII (1964), 513.

ual" as a cluster of justiciable rights.[92] In the sense of the times, the codes were highly legislative in their thrust, and to introduce them into actual Japanese social behavior through the understanding of an ever-increasing number of individuals has been an arduous task, which in no small degree is still in progress. As mentioned earlier, the result up to World War II often perpetuated old power relationships in the name of the codes' contractual, personal, or property rights.

In surveying the legal scene of the decades between 1900 and 1945, the first twenty years to 1920 were dominated by tendencies among Japanese scholars to concentrate on the analysis and exegesis of their new code law. Great effort was required and expended in writing commentaries and annotations, in refining first the Japanese professional understanding of the codes as a system, and then expanding the number of experts in the universities, bureaucracies (official and business), and on the bench and bar who understood the codes in their manifold conceptual interrelationships with each other.

In this vast exegetical work German scholarship of the time proved useful, and Japanese professors leaned heavily upon it. The "aridly logical" Japanese law books that resulted seem immaculate and lifeless to the case-oriented, sure-footed, but not very systematic common lawyer. De Becker's English-language works[93] in the decade after 1910 are useful to show the character of pre-World War I Japanese legal writing. Despite its limitations, this exegesis was a necessary and meaningful second step, after the hasty reception of an alien law; for Japan still had to domesticate its Western borrowings by developing its law language, its legal experts, its detailed legal materials, and education in the law. Only then could massive compliance by the layman be expected.

---

[92] F. S. C. Northrop, "The Comparative Philosophy of Comparative Law," *Cornell Law Quarterly*, XLV (1959-1960), 617, 641-657.

[93] Joseph E. de Becker, "Elements of Japanese Law," *TASJ*, XLIV (1916); and de Becker, *The Principles and Practice of the Civil Code of Japan* (Yokohama, 1921).

In the 1920's the jurisprudence broadened into the fields of (1) freer and more equitable interpretation with less attention to mechanistic concepts, and (2) more concern for social welfare and morally acceptable results. Case studies were emphasized by Suehiro Izutaro and Hozumi Shigeto and their disciples. Legal historians such as Nakada Kaoru and Miura Shuko and their disciples helped the jurists to understand that the popular conduct, if not entirely consistent with the Western spirit of the codes at least was moving in that direction out of a continuity with a past practice which was not instantly or infinitely malleable by fiat. The courts found ways to facilitate the transition and accommodation of old and new through the codes themselves, which made allowance for the living law of society in the form of open-ended references to custom,[94] and above all one must remember that the civil law itself retained the patriarchal, Confucian family and the family register.

The growing legal profession extended the code rules to social behavior—at first in the dispute settlement process. Cases once decided were publicized and their principles learned by laymen, and thus the law began to expand beyond dispute settlement to become a guide for future social conduct. The tendency of lawyers and laymen alike in developed legal orders to undervalue and become impatient with procedures ("adjective law") is because of a failure to recognize procedural primacy in the early stages of the development of justiciable law. As Maine put it,[95] "so great is the ascendancy of the Law of Ac-

---

[94] Law for the Application of Laws (hōrei), Law No. 10, June 21, 1898. Art. 2: "Customs which are not contrary to public policy shall have the same force as law in so far as they are recognized by the provision of a law or an ordinance or relate to matters which are not provided for by laws or ordinances." Commercial Code, Art. 1: "As to a commercial matter, the commercial customary law shall apply if there are no provisions in this Code; and the Civil Code shall apply if there is no such law."

[95] Maine, *Dissertation on Early Law and Custom* (London, 1883), p. 389.

438

tions in the infancy of the Courts of Justice, that substantive law has at first the look of being gradually secreted in the interstices of procedure." If Maine's comment is relevant to the initiation of Japanese behavorial compliance with the new codes, and we suspect it is, then nothing could be more important to further legal growth than efficient judicial administration to produce a body of precedent in concrete cases.

In the 1920's and 1930's, however, a countermovement occurred in the form of more and more reliance on statutory conciliation (*chōtei*). This statutory conciliation, although useful for ad hoc adjustment, was in a sense antilegal, as it was in the Tokugawa period, in that it shunted most of the disputes away from the courts in favor of the traditional compromises. By the 1930's much of the conciliation had become the handmaiden of official discretion, and in the views of some writers a method to avoid the law in favor of enforcing the sense of "justice in the new society," a concept that smacked of Nazi legal theory.[96] We will have more to say later about the persistence of Japanese conciliatory practices and their relation to the Western ideas of the rule-by-law and rule-of-law.

The Japanese Experiment with Rule-of-Law, 1945-1967

THE RULE-OF-LAW IDEA

The Meiji regime was able, through its authoritarian and centralizing Western-style law, to harness certain traditional social skills for industrialization. In this sense the rule-by-law became a bridge to modernity. But the symbiosis of old and

[96] Yasuda Mikita, "Shihō tenka no dankai to shite no chōtei," *Hōgaku kyōkai zasshi*, LI (1933), 1253. Also see *id.*, pp. 1250-51: "Nay, in the settlement of disputes by conciliation, what I am claiming is that there is a fundamental principle which is founded on the sense of justice in the new society which serves to rationalize the requirements of the new society." See also Friedmann, *Legal Theory* (1949), p. 260, for the Nazi law of 1935 which empowered the judge to punish acts which deserve punishment according to the "healthy instincts of the people." In this regard see also Miyazaki Sumio, *Chōteihō no riron to jissai* (1942), pp. 19-30.

new in the Japanese industrialization process does not mean that the old ways are also useful to foster popular government or its legal dimension, a rule-of-law. Instead the old institutions have required extensive postwar changes to accommodate them to the democratic process. It is the legal aspects of this range of problems that demands attention in the limited space remaining.

The rule-of-law is both a philosophy of justice and of positive law in Japan since the constitution of 1947. We need, first, to reconsider briefly the essentials of the rule-of-law (in this sense a concept of justice or an ideal for law), and, second, how the ideal has manifested itself in the Japanese legal order since World War II.[97]

The rule-of-law idea finds its sources in that version of natural law, as old as Aristotle and Cicero and later developed in a liberal direction by Locke and others, concerned with the rights of man, which these men saw as inherent in nature. From these beginnings the idea has expanded and diversified in positive legal orders and become quite complex, with several different institutional forms and emphases within the countries where to some degree it has been achieved. In the postwar period especially, the *idea* of a rule-of-law has also been internationalized by the United Nations, the International Commission of Jurists, the International Association of Legal Science (affiliated with UNESCO), the European Convention for the Protection of Human Rights and Fundamental Freedoms, and other groups and declarations. In Dicey's[98] influential statement of 1885 presaged by Coke in Bonham's case[99] and his tilt with King James I, the rule-of-law was, at first, a highly judicialized concept, with emphasis on independent courts and procedural protections (due process). This

[97] Tanaka Kōtarō, "Democracy and Judicial Administration in Japan," *Journal of the International Commission of Jurists*, ii:ii (1960), 7-20.

[98] A. V. Dicey, *The Law of the Constitution* (6th ed., 1902), pp. 183-84.

[99] 8 Rep. 114 (1610).

emphasis seems somewhat incongruous for an Englishman, for surely in Dicey's England the ultimate protection for rights had become largely electoral and parliamentary. Consequently, in later English theory[100] the rule-of-law has been properly expanded to encompass significant electoral, parliamentary, and administrative law techniques for insuring individual liberties and official responsiveness to popular concerns. In the American experience the idea has become distinctively associated with the written constitutional form and judicial supremacy, and this codified form has generally proved more useful for aspiring foreign borrowers. The recent general literature[101] on the rule-of-law shows all of these facets and more, and they require no further restatement here.

RULE-OF-LAW IN JAPANESE POSTWAR INSTITUTIONS

Institutionally, the Japanese rule-of-law[102] has its own distinctive form in the new constitution, which is a confluence of English and American ideas. The institutional pattern is a kind of "dual supremacy" (Diet and courts). In basic state structure, the constitution follows the English analogy: the emperor becomes a symbol of the state, with a fusion of executive and legislative power in a type of parliamentary government, plus cabinet responsibility. The Diet becomes "the highest organ of state power, and . . . the sole law-making organ of the state" (Article 41). But unlike England, Diet supremacy is accompanied by a judicial supremacy, similar to judicial re-

[100] William Jennings, *The Law and the Constitution* (4th ed., 1952), pp. 53-78.

[101] See e.g. the symposium on "Postwar Thinking About the Rule of Law," *Michigan Law Review*, LIX (1961), 485-613; and International Commission of Jurists, *The Rule of Law in a Free Society* (1959); A. H. Robertson, *Human Rights in Europe* (New York, 1963).

[102] In general, Ukai, "The Individual and the Rule-of-Law under the New Japanese Constitution," *Northwestern University Law Review*, LI, 733 (1956-57); Itō, "The Rule of Law: Constitutional Development," and Hashimoto, "The Rule of Law: Some Aspects of Judicial Review of Administrative Action," both in von Mehren, ed., *Law in Japan* (1963).

view in the United States. But Japanese judicial supremacy is codified as a grant to the judges in the written constitution (Article 81), whereas ours was developed by the judges in the case law, beginning with *Marbury v. Madison*.[103] Further details of judicial supremacy are articulated in Articles 76 to 82 of the new Japanese constitution. The whole judicial power is vested in a Supreme Court (*Saikō saibansho*), and in such inferior courts as are established by law; no extraordinary tribunal may be established; the judges are independent and bound only by the constitution and law (Article 76). Judicial tenure is fully protected (Articles 78 and 79). The Supreme Court is given rule-making power which extends, in pertinent matters of procedure, to attorneys and procurators (Article 77), while the Supreme Court is given the explicit power (Article 81) "to determine the constitutionality of any laws, orders, regulations, or official acts." Article 82 provides for public trials.

Together these provisions accomplish several innovations of great historical meaning in the Japanese context. The courts are freed at last from the supervision of the Ministry of Justice; procurators, though generally subject to the Ministry of Justice,[104] are subject to the rule-making power of the Supreme Court where appropriate, as are attorneys; and attorneys and procurators are of equal status in court. It will be recalled that in 1875 the Great Court of Cassation (*Daishinin*) might have escaped the domination of the Ministry of Justice, if Iwakura had become the chief justice, as some of the drafters had planned. It may be said that Iwakura's refusal relegated the courts to bureaucratic status for seventy-five years, and the

---

[103] 1 Cr. 137 (1803).

[104] Public Procurators Office (*Kansatsushōhō*) Law No. 61 (1947), Art. 14. The Procurators were subjected to the Ministry of Justice to overcome what was regarded as excessive independence; but note the questionable result when, in April 1954, the ministry ordered the Procurator-General not to apply for a warrant to arrest Sato Eisaku (now prime minister) during the investigation of the shipping scandals.

new court's independent power to make rules and administer the courts is of inestimable value against this background. Still, the way in which the new rule-making powers have been narrowly construed probably comes as a surprise or disappointment to the American draftsmen of Occupation days.

Significantly, the constitution (Articles 76 and 81) has been interpreted to place administrative litigation within the jurisdiction of the regular courts; the old, separate, bureaucratic, and atrophied administrative court was abolished in 1946. A system such as Japan's prewar dual courts—ordinary and administrative—can function well, and even afford a valuable division of expertise, as in France, where the late eighteenth century law judges, despised along with other royal officials by the French revolutionaries,[105] brought no special prestige to the courts. But in Japan, with its suffocating tradition of looking-up-to-officials-and-down-on-the-people (*kanson minpi*) and official-omnipotence (*kanken bannō*), and almost no judicial tradition until 1875, a single set of courts applying the same law to officials and citizens alike may facilitate the advent of a new "public servant" concept in Japan and at the same time elevate the status of the judiciary, given time and adequate procedures.

Since 1962 a new and vastly improved Administrative Complaint Investigation Law and also an Administrative Case Litigation Law[106] have been in force but their operative effect cannot be judged yet. A recent case is also significant in re-

---

[105] See generally Charles J. Hamson, *Executive Discretion and Judicial Control: An Aspect of the French Conseil d'État* (London, 1954).

[106] *Gyōsei fufuku shinsahō*, Law No. 160, Sept. 15, 1962, and *Gyōsei jiken soshōhō*, Law No. 139, May 16, 1962; both effective Oct. 1, 1962. It is still too early to ascertain the effect of these important reforms on the actual quantity and quality of litigation thereunder. For a useful discussion of the new law, see Ogawa Ichiro *et al.*, "Gyōsei jiken soshōhō," *Jurisuto*, No. 259 (1962), p. 26; and for further suggestions for future improvement, see Ichikawa Shozakuro, "Rinji gyōsei chōsakai tōshin no kentō," *Jurisuto*, No. 311 (1964), p. 38.

quiring specific reasoning to back official actions.[107] Still in
1962 only 1,190 administrative cases[108] were filed at first instance in all of the district courts and high courts of Japan,
and for a nation of ninety-five million such a figure still represents little use of law to police such an all-pervasive officialdom. No aspect of modern Japan cries more loudly for study
than official behavior, intraprocedures (*naiki*), regulation by
suggestion, and the like. Fortunately much investigation of
both an official and scholarly sort[109] is now under way. The
results of these efforts will be of great interest.

As noted, the entire postwar Japanese institutional embodiment of the rule-of-law, as summarized above, is currently undergoing intensive study in Japan, not only as to implementing
detail but also as to its basic structure. The highly important
Commission on the Constitution (*Kenpō chōsakai*) and the
Special Investigating Commission on the Legal System
(*Rinji shihō seido chōsakai*) headed by Professors Takayanagi Kenzo and Wagatsuma Sakae respectively, as well as the
Special Investigating Commission on Administration (*Rinji
gyōsei chōsakai*) mentioned above, have all made large impressive reports to the government during the past year setting
forth their respective findings based on several years of searching investigation under government auspices by some of Japan's most qualified experts. Significantly, these studies have
raised almost no attacks on the basic worth of the rule-of-law,
although if implemented some of the varied proposals suggested by certain groups would surely weaken it. These recent
reappraisals are far too massive in scope and content to do more
here than note that Japanese legal development is currently
in a highly dynamic phase.

[107] *Udono v. Director of the Tokyo National Tax Bureau* (Tokyo
kokuzeikyokuchō), *Hanrei jihō* No. 337.

[108] *Shihō tōkei nenpō* (*minji-hen*), 1 [1962] (1963), 27, 188.

[109] See Miyazawa Toshiyoshi *et al.*, "Gyōsei kaikaku no hōkō to
mondaiten," *Jurisuto*, No. 310 (1964), pp. 10-52, and Rōyama Masamichi and Satō Atsushi, "Gyōsei kaikaku no arikata to kaikaku no
shuganten," *Jurisuto*, No. 311 (1964), pp. 10-37.

JUDICIAL SUPREMACY

We should now note how Japanese judicial supremacy is organized and the extent to which it has been used to review the constitutionality of legislation. The power of judicial review is explicit, and doubtless the draftsmen had reference to American experience, but the Japanese courts have not yet given this new power its full operative meaning in the Japanese system. One might point out that a half century elapsed before we had our second case (*Dred Scott*)[110] declaring a legislative act unconstitutional, but the tempo and scope of present-day society makes such a comparison somewhat inapt.

One of the chief functions of the court in this arrangement is to enforce the modern bill of rights of the new constitution against both legislative or administrative infringement. The Japanese bill of rights contains the full list of traditional individual rights and liberties supplemented by others consistent with the needs of a twentieth century welfare state. Many are applicable to "every person" (*nani-bito mo*), thus including aliens. Significantly, these rights are not explicitly made subject to such limitations as the statutes may impose, as was the case in the Meiji constitution, though of course the new form and phrasing of these rights have not spared the courts from the usual balancing exercises between public and private needs well known to modern constitutional adjudication everywhere. Indeed such balancing is explicitly required in the Japanese constitution, since Articles 12, 13, 22, and 29 prohibit abuse of rights and require their exercise in a manner consistent with the public welfare.

But these aspects of the postwar Japanese rule-of-law have been discussed enough in English to give a fairly accurate view of its current strengths and weaknesses in the Japanese courts.[111]

[110] *Dred Scott v. Sanford*, 19 How. 404 (1857).
[111] John Maki, *Court and Constitution in Japan* (1964), gives translations of twenty-six key cases; and Itō, "Rule of Law: Constitutional Development," in von Mehren, ed., *Law in Japan*, discusses the major civil liberties litigation.

Significantly, up through 1962 only one statute[112] (Custom Act, Law No. 61, 1954) has been "declared unconstitutional" —to use an Americanism—by a holding of the Supreme Court, in the court's own terms at least. This is because to declare an act "unconstitutional" is procedurally a rather formal matter in Japan.[113] In addition several decisions have been reversed based on the unconstitutionality of acts already repealed, and several judges have considered acts to be unconstitutional in their concurring or dissenting opinions (see below). Some commentators feel that in twenty years the record shows the court to be too timid with its new powers of judicial review under Article 81. A substantive critique of the opinions is beyond our scope here, but instead it is interesting to note how the court has developed its view of this new power to review official acts and statutes. Most obvious is the fact that the judges, largely reared on German scholarship, have had to grope for the meaning of judicial supremacy, and that consequently civil-law ideas have entered the discussion almost as prominently as the American models, of which Article 81 was doubtless regarded by some as a mere codification.

First, the Japanese groped with the question whether the court should not act as a "constitutional court" in the Continental sense (Weimar, West Germany, Italy, and Austria) and decide constitutionality in the abstract; the court held

[112] *Nakamura v. Japan*, 11 *Keishū* (no. 16) 1593 (Sup. Ct., Nov. 28, 1962), critiqued by Kiyomiya Shiro *et al.*, *Jurisuto*, No. 268 (1963), p. 10; B. James George, *Hōgaku kyōkai zasshi*, LXXX (1963), 2.

[113] Note that the Regulations for Disposition of Supreme Court Affairs (*Saikō saibansho jimu shori kisoku* [Sup. Ct. Reg. No. 6, Nov. 11, 1947]) provides as follows regarding judgments of unconstitutionality: Art. 12: "Eight or more judges must agree when a judgment declaring laws, orders, regulations or official acts unconstitutional is rendered." Art. 14: "When a judgment under Art. 12 is rendered, its holding shall be publicly announced in the Official Gazette and the original of the written judgment shall be sent to the Cabinet." If the judgment has held a statute unconstitutional, the original of the written judgment must be sent to the Diet also.

against this view in 1952 (*Suzuki v. Japan*[114]) and in favor of a case-or-controversy doctrine. Second, though it may seem obvious to some, the court had to decide whether inferior courts could exercise the power of Article 81; they can.[115] Third, there was the question whether treaties are reviewable under Article 81; they are by the accepted view (*tsūsetsu*),[116] but there is a surprisingly strong opinion to the contrary. Fourth, the court had to decide whether *judgments of lower courts* could be "declared unconstitutional"; they can.[117] This seems both ambiguous and in a sense obvious to us, but in Japanese theory it is a real question going to the broader question of the effect of a "declaration of unconstitutionality."

On this point of the effect of such a decision, there is no case law, but the scholars are split, some saying the statute is invalidated completely (*ippanteki kōryoku-setsu*),[118] but the more influential view says the decision only decides the invalidity of the law as against the parties in the case.[119] There is ambiguity in applying even our standard in this difficult area.

But by reference to the Supreme Court rules[120] and the court's action thereunder, we can see that in a purely procedural sense it considers that it has only declared one statute unconstitutional in such a way as to presume to have prospective effect and require reporting to the Diet (*Nakamura v. Japan*). It is interesting to note, however, that the decisions in the other customs cases[121] (under the old law) were sent to

---

[114] 6 *Minshū* (no. 9) 783 (Sup. Ct., Oct. 8, 1952) (the case attacking legality of the United States security forces in Japan) followed in *Tomabechi v. Japan*, 7 *Minshū* (no. 4) 305 (Sup. Ct., Apr. 1, 1953).

[115] *Yanagi v. Japan*, 4 *Keishū* (no. 2) 73 (Sup. Ct., Feb. 1, 1950).

[116] Miyazawa, *Chūkai Nipponkoku kenpō* (1956), p. 672.

[117] E.g. *Komatsu v. Japan*, 2 *Keishū* (no. 8) 801 (Sup. Ct., July 8, 1948).

[118] E.g. Kaneko, *Saibanhō* (1959), p. 79, but note that in this view it is only the Supreme Court decisions that have the broader effect. Miyazawa, "Saibansho no hōrei shinsaken," *Hōritsu taimuzu*, 1:iv, p. 11.

[119] E.g. Satō Isao, *Kenpo* (1962), p. 485.

[120] See note 113, *supra*.　　　　[121] See note 122, *infra*.

the Diet *informally*. Thus, although a review of the court's decisions show only one effective statute declared unconstitutional, the court has held unconstitutional several lower court decisions[122] decided under statutes already repealed by the time of these decisions. What retroactive effect such determinations of unconstitutionality might have for similar cases is still unclear. Curiously enough the only civil case in which a lower court decision was declared unconstitutional (i.e. reported to the Cabinet, not the Diet) involved a conciliation statute, of some importance to our final topic—the extent to which the apparatus of justiciability is useful to, or used by, the Japanese.

RIGHT CONSCIOUSNESS AND THE SOCIAL EFFICACY
OF JAPANESE LAW

In 1834 de Tocqueville noted that American legalistic peculiarities were highly political: "If they [Americans] prize freedom much, they generally value legality still more; they are less afraid of Tyranny than arbitrary power."[123] Japan now shares many of our legalisms, but such popular sentiment for justiciable rights is still largely absent. And, if dispute settlement is the context from which much of the growth, social meaning, and political usefulness of justiciable rights derive— and American experience suggests it is—then the traditional tendency of the Japanese to rely on sublegal conciliatory techniques instead of the courts becomes a key obstacle in the path toward the rule-of-law envisaged by the new constitution.

Generally, a survey of the Japanese dispute settlement proc-

---

[122] *Sakagami v. Japan*, 7 *Keishū* 1562 (Sup. Ct., July 22, 1953), involving Order No. 325 of 1950; *Nomura v. Yamaki*, 14 *Minshu* 1657 (Sup. Ct., 1960), involving a compulsory conciliation statute now repealed; *Kunihiro v. Japan*, 16 *Keishū* 1577 (Sup. Ct., Nov. 28, 1962); *Mihara v. Japan*, 16 *Keishū* 1672 (Sup. Ct., Dec. 12, 1962). These last two decisions invalidated government confiscations of a third party's property under the old, pre-1954 customs law.

[123] De Tocqueville, *Democracy in America* (Phillips Bradley, ed., 1951), I, 275.

ess from Tokugawa to modern times leaves little doubt of the continuity and predominance of conciliatory practices down to present-day Japan.[124] In both traditional and modern Japan, conciliation of one sort or another has been and still is effective in settling the vast majority of disputes arising in the gradually changing social context. At the same time Japanese conciliation itself, as might be expected, has become quite diversified in form and practice: informal conciliation (*jidan*), court conciliation (*chōtei*), and court compromise (*wakai*). Especially notable are the changes which have occurred in the relationship between conciliation and adjudication as the positive-law order has evolved and strengthened.

In this respect the recent confrontation in the Supreme Court between prewar compulsory conciliation (*chōtei ni kawaru saiban*) and the new constitutional right of access to the courts (Article 32) has a theoretical significance far beyond the minor legal point actually decided, which was stale since the statute applicable to the case had been repealed before the decision. Also this case (*Nomura v. Yamaki*[125]) was the first civil case where the Supreme Court declared a lower court decision unconstitutional and the first civil case where the court reversed itself on a point of constitutionality. The original suit involved a house evacuation dispute wherein the lower court had first referred the suit to conciliation (*chōtei*), and after conciliation had failed the court then ordered the defendant to vacate. The lower court's compulsory reference of the case to conciliation and the later order disposing of the case were both authorized by a conciliation statute (applicable to this case but already repealed by the time of the Supreme Court appeal) providing for such procedures without further formal trial (*chōtei ni kawaru saiban*).[126] The defendant ap-

[124] Henderson, *Conciliation and Japanese Law—Tokugawa and Modern*, traces the various aspects of the problems. Particularly ch. 9 deals with the problems hereafter discussed.

[125] 14 *Minshū* 1657 (Sup. Ct., 1960).

[126] The legal pattern of the applicable statutes is rather complicated

pealed to the Supreme Court arguing that he had been deprived of his new constitutional right of access to the courts (Article 32) and a public trial (Article 82). The Supreme Court agreed and held nine-to-six that the lower court's judgment applying the compulsory conciliation provision was unconstitutional.

As noted, this was the first case since the war where the Supreme Court reversed its prior position in a civil case; for, four years earlier in an almost identical case,[127] it had held in a disappointing eight-to-seven decision for constitutionality. The reversal was the result of six new judges on the court, although two of the prior judges changed their opinions; Kawamura Matasuke from constitutional to unconstitutional and Shima from unconstitutional to constitutional. But Shima's switch depended on holding to his key point in the prior case, namely that such a lower court judgment was not a bar to a later suit. Since the case was in litigation fourteen years, this

because of the intervening extraordinary wartime statutes (1942), their subsequent partial repeal (1945), the establishment of the new constitution (1947), and the enactment of the new Civil Conciliation Law (1951) repealing the special *chōtei* laws and also the remainder of the wartime laws relating to conciliations. The Wartime Special Civil Law, Art. 19(2) made the Temporary Conciliation Law for Monetary Obligations, Art. 7(1), providing for Substitution of Trial for Conciliation applicable in conciliation cases under the Land-Lease, House-Lease Law, which was the law under which the original *chōtei* was conducted in this case. However, Law 46 (1945) after the war, which repealed the Wartime Special Civil Law, specifically left Art. 19(2) still effective when this case was filed in 1946. In fact said Art. 19(2) was repealed by the Civil Conciliation Law (1951), Supplemental Art. 4, which amended Law 46 by deleting Art. 19 of the Wartime Special Civil Law from the provisions which had been left still applicable by said Law 46 (1945). The Civil Conciliation Law, Supplementary Art. 13, also provided that cases filed before its effective date would be handled by the prior laws. Hence the old provisions for substitution of trial for conciliation were still effective, except for the problem of constitutionality raised by the intervening new constitution, Arts. 32 and 82 (1947).

[127] *Suzuki v. Ishigaki,* 10 *Minshū* 1355 (Sup. Ct., 1956).

argument does not say much for Justice Shima's sense of practicality in the use of constitutional rights. Justice Kawamura Daisuke in a concurring opinion (14 *Minshū* 1669-73) took a more realistic approach and said that to relitigate a case of this kind was so impracticable as to effectively deny access to the courts.

These two cases involved compulsory types of statutory conciliation, as described above, which were repealed in 1951; hence, the cases have little positive-law meaning today, but in constitutional theory they mean that the Supreme Court has worked out a proper political relationship between one kind of compulsory conciliation and adjudication: Conciliation must be voluntary; otherwise it is a violation of the citizen's right of access to the courts as guaranteed in Article 32. On principle this rationale should be extended to other forms of coercion in the current conciliation practices. However, since there were twelve opinions (three concurring, seven dissents besides the two majority opinions) in these two cases, it is difficult to say what they might mean in positive law. *Nomura v. Yamaki* surely would not be binding precedent because the point involved was a type of *chōtei* no longer existent, and besides in Japan precedents are regarded not as law, but more as persuasive analogy. In such a sense, this decision is instructive also.

It is likely that the role of adjudication will increase as the Japanese social practices become gradually rationalized and modernized under centralized codes enforceable in efficient courts; the functions of conciliation might decline accordingly. But the induction of *chōtei* into the legal system, where its voluntary character is protected, amplifies the social value of its normal dispute-settlement role, which will then presumably at some point become balanced with adjudication. For, of course, amicable settlements are valuable, and in fact most disputes can and should be settled by conciliation techniques *without coercion*, and without litigation.

The trend in favor of lawsuits over statutory *chōtei* cases which has continued since 1948 (but at a rather slow rate since 1956) is worth watching in the future. During the 1948–1962 period, the ratio of cases filed for adjudication and conciliation (*chōtei*), including family conciliation, has shifted from roughly 40–60 in 1950 to 60–40 in 1962 in favor of lawsuits.[128] This trend would doubtless increase if the efficiency of the litigation process were improved, not only because the people would file more suits but also because the judges would use less pressure to conciliate as a means of clearing up the backlog on their congested dockets.

The foregoing ratio of filings only shows the conciliatory tendency among Japanese who actually take their disputes to the courts, either for litigation or conciliation. It is much more difficult to quantify the extent to which the traditional, *informal* conciliation is employed in present-day Japanese society outside the cognizance of the courts. But that it is very extensive is fairly indicated by the following kinds of evidence. First, we know that the police settle many cases. For example, in 1958, 21,596 cases were brought to the Tokyo police for conciliation, of which 39 percent were settled, whereas only 6,815 conciliation cases were filed with the Tokyo district court.[129] Second, we know that over 90 percent of all Japanese divorces are divorces by agreement (*kyōgi-rikon*),[130] presumably arranged by go-betweens, relatives, or others. Third, a recent survey[131] in Shimane Prefecture shows that 80

---

[128] 1 *Shihō tōkei nenpō* (1962) p. 2.

[129] See Hironaka Toshio, "Keisatsukan no hatasu hōteki kinō ni tsuite," *Jurisuto*, No. 78 (1955), pp. 31-35; and *id.*, "Shimin no kenri no kakuho to minji saiban," *Hōritsu jihō*, xxxii (1960), 1002-08; and also see Kawashima et al., *Hōritsu jihō*, xxviii (1956), 182-83.

[130] Tanabe Shigeko and Ohama Eiko, "Kyōgi rikon no jittai chōsa," *Hōritsu jihō*, xxx (1958), 337-41; for a lucid, concise explanation of divorce by agreement and some of its social implications, see Kawashima Takeyoshi and Kurt Steiner, "Modernization and Divorce Trends in Japan," *Economic Development and Sociological Change*, ix:i, pt. 2 (1960), 222-25.

[131] Shimane survey only, Sasaki Yoshio, "Minji chōtei ni okeru hōteki

percent of the persons surveyed would consult informal conciliators in case of a dispute. Fourth, we encounter in the Tokyo law practice a marked reluctance to provide for third-party dispute resolution clauses (such as arbitration) in contracts, except among the more sophisticated international trading firms. Fifth, the paucity of lawyers in Japan tends to show negatively that the Japanese do not litigate much. In 1964 there was one Japanese lawyer (total 7,136)[132] for every 13,300 people; in the U.S. there was one lawyer (total practicing 200,586)[133] for every 950. Finally, we find that in 1959–1960 there were fourteen times more suits filed per capita in California, for example, than in Japan,[134] even if we include those cases wherein the Japanese brought their dispute to court for conciliation rather than litigation. The ratio is twenty-three to one if we exclude the Japanese court conciliations. From these indications it is clear enough that the social process of traditional informal conciliation centering around the family and neighborhood dignitaries is still employed today to settle most Japanese disputes that would go to court in a country with a developed sense of justiciable right.

It is worth saying again that this phenomenon does not necessarily push us, so far as its political implications are concerned, to a generally negative evaluation of the Japanese propensity to compromise. Obviously social harmony is desirable and possibly promoted by these ingrained social attitudes. However, our specific concern involves its effect on the growth of a consciousness of political rights which are highly instrumental to the role of the citizenry in popular government. In codifying both the rule-by-law and rule-of-law in the formal legal system of Japan, the role of the populace, at least up

---

handan to jian no kaimei," *Minji sosho zasshi*, No. 7 (1961), pp. 43-176. Also Sasaki Yoshio, "Minji chotei ni okeru 'goi' no kento," *Kanazawa hogaku*, IX:i, ii (Dec. 1963), 1-31.

[132] Supplied by the courtesy of Judge Tao Toji.

[133] *American Bar News*, IX (Apr. 15, 1964), I.

[134] These are my own calculations from the official judicial statistics.

until the recent socialist activity in the courts, has been that of relatively passive political beneficiaries, and only by education and time will a full realization of the value of these grants be achieved. Much of the burden may lie with the courts, for traditionally the tendency to conciliate seems to have sprung from the policy of the Japanese power holders to the effect that "you had better conciliate," because there was no *practicable alternative remedy in court.*

Against such a background the present-day judicial powers to encourage compromise (*wakai*) require close scrutiny. Also, the inefficacy of a lawsuit as an alternative remedy, because of delay, expense, and judicial conciliatory pressures, is probably more of a factor in encouraging this massive conciliation than the popular idea that it is better to be harmonious than right— or that they are the same thing. It may be that the modern Japanese, especially in the cities, would readily agree that voluntary (as opposed to coerced) harmony is most likely to result if people realize that in modern society they must comport themselves according to reasonable and enforceable principles rather than haggling, negotiating, and jockeying about to adjust their personal relationships to fit an ever-shifting power balance among individuals. The most recent work of Sasaki Yoshio[135] seems to confirm that the Japanese share this sentiment to a significant extent and would like to have their disputes handled on such a basis. This is a challenge to Japanese judicial administration, which is, of course, different only in degree, if at all, from similar challenges to modern courts nearly everywhere.[136] Unfortunately, to no small extent cheap-

[135] Sasaki, "Minji chōtei ni okeru 'gōi' no kentō," *Kanazawa hōgaku,* ix:i, ii (Dec. 1963).

[136] See Chief Justice Earl Warren, "Delay and Congestion in the Federal Courts," *J. Am. Jud. Soc'y,* xlii (1958), 9: "These statistics are a record of delay piled upon delay in the federal courts. But, serious as they may be, they are no accurate measure of the extent to which our administrative weaknesses have caused injustice. They do not reflect the hardship and suffering caused to unfortunate victims of such delays, nor the *inadequate settlements which individuals are frequently forced*

er, more efficient, and timely trials in Japan may depend on budgeting support, which has not been easy to elicit from the government, and this policy probably will not change until the people demand it, for the judiciary has never been a very successful lobbyist, especially in Japan. Thus it seems to be a melancholy truth that the people will get no better courts than their democratic efforts elicit.

Conclusion

In summary, since modernization in common parlance is currently a global goal and liberal democracy is not, we have assumed in considering Japanese development that it is most useful to distinguish conceptually between modernization and democratization not because they are always separate, but because democracy, however much we may value it, is not a necessary, deterministic extension of modern trends. Yet in Japan modernization and democratization have become inextricably intertwined in the postwar phases of Japanese legal development as symbolized by the rule-of-law—an admixture of law and liberal politics—which is extending the modernization of Japanese society into secondary phases and in ways rather advanced for present-day Asia. In that sense the experience of Japan with Western law and political values may yield useful insights regarding priorities and timing for aspirant nations. At the same time its peculiarities that have been critical to its success—a refined, traditional social structure,

---

to accept on that account. Neither do these figures include what are probably the worst and most numerous cases of all: those instances in which citizens with causes that cry for justice under law have turned from our court system in despair and have sought ways of working out their problems without resort to the courts at all." (Emphasis added.) See Rinji shihō seido chōsakai ikensho, *Jurisuto*, No. 307 (1964), pp. 62-121, for a thoughtful report of Wagatsuma's committee covering the whole range of judicial administration problems. Some parts of the report have become controversial, and it will be interesting to see whether the legislation and money required to implement all or part of it will be forthcoming.

leadership and followership genius, isolated security, and post-war external guidance—give pause for thought because they do not seem readily reproducible elsewhere.

Regarding timing and priorities, we have seen that the positive, justiciable law of Tokugawa jurisprudence was primitive; but that Tokugawa social "law" and administration (rule-of-status) was remarkably refined, a fact which needs to be fully appreciated to understand the success of Japan's rapid growth after 1868. For, by adapting these traditional skills, Meiji Japan could modernize effectively in the early phase without a very wide range of political participation or a high degree of justiciability. But she could have accomplished little without an effective unified power structure to administer the nationwide programs with minimal disruption by un-institutionalized political competition. This message from Meiji Japan may have utility for those just approaching the ladder of modernity without an effective administration.

As a model for modernizers Japan's postwar democratic phase has many difficulties. First, it is difficult to measure the external (Occupation's) contribution to Japan's successes of the past two decades, and second, there is the difficulty of duplicating such a contribution or finding a substitute for it, or of doing without it, for indubitably the foreign suggestions were quite important to the success of the postwar rule-of-law to date. But simply realizing these facts will underscore the risks of an assumption that liberal democracy will eventuate inevitably from today's widespread authoritarian modernization process. History will doubtless again require some popular assistance to these ends.

CHAPTER XII

Decision-Making in the Japanese Government: A Study of Ringisei

KIYOAKI TSUJI

Ringisei means literally a system of reverential inquiry about a superior's intentions. It is an archaic term that is scarcely comprehensible to many postwar Japanese. Yet it is commonly used in academic and professional circles to describe a method of decision-making that has been extensively employed in Japanese governmental and private agencies since the early days of the Meiji era (1868-1912).[1] Although seldom defined, it is frequently encountered in technical literature.[2] There it is used to refer to a system whereby administrative plans and decisions are made through the circulation of a document called *ringisho*. This is drafted in the first instance by an official of low rank. It is then circulated among other officials in the ministry or agency concerned who

---

[1] Since no brief translation of *ringisei* is possible in English, we will use the Japanese term. Synonyms for *ringi* are *rinshin* and *ukagai*, both of which carry the implication of a subordinate respectfully consulting the opinion of a superior. For studies of the operation of *ringisei* in private enterprises, see Ono Toyoaki, *Nihon-teki keiei to ringiseido* (Tokyo, 1960), or Yamashiro Akira, *Keiei* (Tokyo, 1958). Comparable studies in the field of public administration are Kawanaka Nikō, *Gendai no kanryōsei* (Tokyo, 1962), and Watanabe Yasuo, "Kanryōkikō no kōzōkaikaku," *Chūō Kōron* (Oct. 1961), pp. 315-21. Generally speaking, however, there have been very few studies in this field.

[2] The word *ringi* first appeared as a legal term in Government Ordinance (*Dajōkan fukoku*) No. 106 of Aug. 1, 1876, entitled "Revision of the National Bank Ordinance." See *Hōrei zensho, 1876*, (Tokyo, 1890), p. 83. The first known usage in private enterprise was by the Ōji Seishi Company in 1871.

are required to affix their seals if they agree with the policy proposed. By complex and circuitous paths the document gradually works its way up to higher and higher administrators, and finally reaches the minister or top executive official. When he approves the *ringisho*, the decision is made.

Viewed as a system, this process is called *ringisei*. One should be aware of the fact that it is far more than an administrative technique. *Ringisei* actually is a fundamental characteristic of Japanese administrative behavior, organization, and management. Seen in this light, its most important attributes are:

1. The *ringisho* is initially drafted by a low-ranking official who himself has neither authority nor leadership status.

2. Thereafter the *ringisho* is discussed and examined separately by the officials of all relevant bureaus and divisions. It is not discussed at a joint meeting of the administrators concerned.

3. Although in a technical sense the legal competence to grant or withhold final approval for the *ringisho* lies with the highest executive (e.g. the minister in a ministry or the president of a private business), in actual practice he is expected to approve it without change or modification because of this long process of prior scrutiny—in fact decision-making—by lower administrators.

The process is lengthy and the distance between the person who originates the first draft and the person who makes the final decision is great both in time and space. Because of these characteristics, *ringisei* is sometimes referred to as the "piling-up" or "accumulative" system (*tsumiage hōshiki*). The communications system involved is depicted graphically in Figure 1.[3] Figure 2 provides an actual sample of a *ringisho*, the docu-

---

[3] As shown in the *Report* of the Third Group of the Third Subcommittee of the Temporary Research Commission on Public Administration, p. 11.

ment that must work its way through this communications labyrinth. The particular form involved requests a decision by the Ministry of Agriculture on a projected loan to promote the livestock industry. Forms used in other ministries are practically identical. The relevant officials are required to imprint their seals at the places marked. It is clear that many seals are required on a *ringisho*, a fact that explains the common criticism of Japanese administration as "administration by seal."

Ringisei has some merit in that all administrators concerned with the policy proposed in a *ringisho* are informed of the prospective action and participate in the decision-making process. This makes it impossible for these administrators subsequently to offer open opposition to the policy, and it creates an expectation and a probability that they will cooperate in its execution. However, this kind of decision-making suffers from at least three serious faults.

The first is a lowering of efficiency. It takes a great deal of time to reach a final decision by this method. Much time is consumed because the *ringisho* must be examined separately by each section, division, and bureau. The proper officials may be absent when it arrives, or the *ringisho* may inadvertently be set aside. Sometimes it is intentionally held up by an administrator who disagrees with its recommendations. In Japanese administration it is often difficult for an administrator to express explicit disagreement in the face of pressures from influential figures or interest groups, or in the event that his superior is favorable while he is not. In such cases he may display implicit disagreement by keeping the *ringisho* for a long time.[4] If he were to make his disagreement explicit, there would be friction between him and his colleagues. This must be avoided at all costs, for he has life tenure in his ministry

---

[4] Imai, Kazuo, *Kanryō-sono seitai to uchimaku* (Tokyo, 1953), p. 125. The author, who once held an important position in the Ministry of Finance, points out this fact based on his own experience as a higher civil servant. He calls it "clutching" or "hanging on" (*nigiri-komu*).

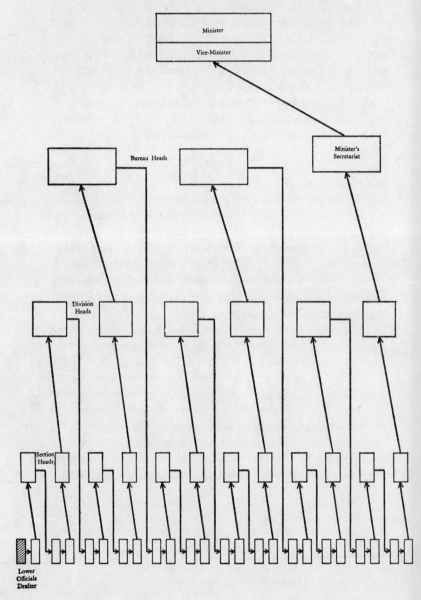

FIGURE I

Model of *Ringisei* Communications System

FIGURE 2
Sample of a *Ringisho*

Date of Final Decision _____

Entry made in Files_____

Referrer's seal_____   Documents Filer's seal_____

Bureau seal_____   Section seal_____

RE: The Establishment of Governmental Measures for Financial Assistance in the Expansion of the Livestock Industry.

Minister   _____

Parliamentary Vice-Minister   _____

Career Vice-Minister   _____

Ministerial Chief Secretary   _____

                                 Chief, Archives Section   _____

                                 Chief, Budget Section   _____

                                 Chief, Local Affairs Section   _____

Chief of the Agricultural
Economics Bureau   _____

Counselor   _____   Chief, General Affairs Section   _____

                                 Chief, Finance Section   _____

Chief of the Livestock Bureau   _____

Counselor   _____   Chief, Livestock Administration
Section   _____

                                 Chief, Economics Section   _____

                                 Chief, Breed Improvement
Section   _____

                                 Chief, Artificial Feeds Section _____

                                 Chief, Natural Feeds Section   _____

                                 Chief, Sanitation Section   _____

                                 Chief, Livestock Management
Section

Drafter _____
                  Name

and expects to remain there until retirement. Face-to-face human relations in the office, therefore, are very important. Another factor adding to delay is that the *ringisho* must start from the beginning again when it becomes necessary to amend the original draft in the course of its circulation.

The second fault is dispersion of responsibility. As we have seen, the chief executive officer is ultimately responsible for the decision. In Japanese public administration, which follows German administrative law, especially its "theory of authority," only the supreme head possesses authority in a legal sense, and he alone, therefore, must decide. Lower-ranking administrators are there to assist the minister in his decision-making. Under *ringisei* all discussions and examinations of a *ringisho* at subministerial levels are regarded as preparatory to decision-making by the minister. While all relevant administrators examine the *ringisho*, they can hardly be expected to have a strong sense of responsibility for the policy involved, because the responsibility is not really theirs.

Moreover, because of the inadequacies of the classification system, the competence and responsibility attaching to each position are not clear, and the relationships between them are very vague. Each position in an organization is described in abstract terms by that organization's constituent law, but its actual content is decided in practice by the conventions obtaining in that office. Each administrator's sense of responsibility is, so to speak, only one of many, because he puts his seal on a *ringisho* as one of many seals, and to him it is apt to mean no more than that.[5] Furthermore, the minister, though legally responsible, may not have either experience or ability to improve the contents of *ringisho* sent to him. Nor does he have a staff who could help him in this respect. The regular "line" administrators are looked upon as his staff, and, since they have already placed their seals on the *ringisho*, it is impossible

[5] *Ibid.*, p. 118. "The bureaucrats leave the results to take care of themselves. It would not be too much to say, it seems to me, that they do not care at all for the results of decision-making."

to expect an independent judgment of them. The result is that the top executive, too, is in no position to exercise effective responsibility for the contents of a *ringisho*. Therefore, except when illegal behavior is involved, those who suffer from this inefficient system of administration cannot put the blame on anyone because it is not possible to determine who is really responsible. This is the reason for which Japanese administration is often called a "system of irresponsibility."

The third fault is lack of leadership. *Ringisei* prevents the minister and higher civil servants from assuming a role of leadership in decision-making. In modern management systems the top managers assign tasks to subordinates who are well qualified by training and experience to perform these tasks. The most important problems with respect to such tasks are settled by the top managers themselves, or by them with the assistance of their staff, and the rest are delegated to subordinates for decision in accordance with standards set by the top managers. In this way both overconcentration of authority and irresponsible diffusion of competence are avoided. Furthermore, in modern management it is clear who is responsible for a particular decision, and thus necessary steps can be taken to narrow the gap between policy formation and its results by matching the former with the latter. In *ringisei*, however, the higher executives cannot assume the role of leaders and decision-makers. A higher civil servant, a friend of mine, once told me that when he thought of a plan or policy that he wanted to effect, he could only send it as a mere proposal or item for future reference to the appropriate low-ranking administrator. Even if this lowest administrator accepted and acted upon it, he still had to wait a long time until the *ringisho* concerning that policy reached him. It seems ridiculous, but is nevertheless true, that this higher civil servant would then have to approve his own plan sent back to him from below.

Should the higher executive ignore the protocol of *ringisei* and try to assume leadership in this decision-making process, he would be certain to antagonize his associates and create disturbances in the office. There are two alternatives for such a higher executive: either accept exclusion from the office, or accept the conventional methods of *ringisei*. The following story is relevant. Before World War II, Kobayashi Ichizō, president of the Hankyū Electric Railways, was appointed minister of international trade and industry. Being a business-man and not a bureaucrat, Kobayashi tried to introduce the methods of business management into the administration of his ministry, but he was confronted with strong resistance on the part of most of its bureaucrats, including the vice-minis-ter, Kishi Nobusuke. He was actually boycotted by his sub-ordinates and was finally compelled to resign his position. More recently, Minister of Construction Kōno Ichirō ordered major reconstructions of Tokyo's streets to be carried out at night to minimize traffic and other problems for the citizenry in general. This new policy shocked the administrators of the Ministry of Construction, who had been accustomed to carry out street construction during the day. The new idea faded away very quickly.

It is apparent, therefore, that *ringisei* makes it difficult for higher executives to assume a role of leadership in decision-making. A by-product of the system is that even an incom-petent higher executive feels that he can remain in his posi-tion, because so many "experts" have already examined and approved the contents of any *ringisho* that comes to him for action. If he has confidence in his subordinate administrators and in the conventional methods of *ringisei*, he can easily ac-cept the *ringisho* as it stands and feel that it contains no seri-ous errors. Many so-called rubber stamps are affixed in this way.[6]

Since the Meiji era most Japanese higher executives have been graduates of faculties of law. Consequently, while they normally have a good deal of knowledge of law and juris-

---

[6] *Ibid.*, p. 127. Imai claims, with some understandable exaggeration, that, when he was a bureau chief, he affixed his seals more than 8,000 times a day.

prudence, they are not usually well informed in other fields. An adequate staff would help them in this regard, but Japanese administrators really have no staff, or only an incompetent one if there is any at all. For this reason, I view *ringisei* as comparable to such premodern systems of authority and decision-making as the feudal lord system (*tonosama hōshiki*) or the patriarchal system (*kachō hōshiki*). In all of these Japanese administrative systems the functions of decision-making are widely dispersed but with technical authority concentrated in a supreme head.

Relationships between Japanese Bureaucracies and Ringisei

Ringisei has been closely linked with Japanese bureaucratic organization and practice in both private industry and government since the Meiji era. A business expert points out that although business and industry in Japan may seem to be modern in form, they have in fact adopted *ringisei*.[7] According to Ono, the development of Japanese business and industry was supported and facilitated by the spirit of the feudal patriarchal system. The family management system of the feudal merchants and the traditional behavior patterns of workers from rural and agricultural areas were adopted along with modern types of organization and technology. This patriarchal element in business and industry makes human relations in the firm similar to those in a feudal family. The interest of the company comes first, not the interest of individuals. The company is thought of as a family, and the positions of workers and managers are determined by age and academic career (a kind of seniority rule). Life tenure for workers is guaranteed by the company, and welfare programs for the workers are considered to be an act of benevolence on the part of the president of the company, i.e. the patriarch. This relationship produces high morale among the workers and prevents them from moving to other companies.

This idea survives today. As is well known, most Japanese

[7] Ono, *op.cit.*, pp. 4-5.

labor unions, which were largely organized after World War II, are not craft unions, but company unions. In such community-like companies the power of the president is very strong, and a deep gulf in status separates white-collar from blue-collar workers. There is no distinction between staff and line. It is *ringisei* that lies at the heart of this patriarchal system of the management of what are in a formal sense modern enterprises in contemporary Japan. Another expert on business management claims that *ringisei* is peculiar to Japanese business and that he cannot find any equivalent to it in other countries.[8]

The characteristics of *ringisei* in private administration have much in common with those in public administration. During the Meiji era the Japanese government changed from the *dajōkan* or conciliar system of top executive organization to a cabinet system, where the emperor stood at the apex of the entire system. This formed a hierarchy in the sense that Max Weber described as one of the characteristics of modern bureaucracy. But in a normal hierarchy the decisions and orders of the supreme head are transmitted to all subordinate positions in the organization without modification. In the case of Japanese administration, however, this flow of "commands" goes in the opposite direction, namely from bottom to top, because of *ringisei*. This reverse flow has been made possible by the fact that each administrative agency is in fact a sort of patriarchal community.

In a discussion of Japanese bureaucracies it should be noted, first, that the close relationship between *ringisei* and the particularism of each ministry is characteristic of Japanese bureaucracy. In each ministry or community internal agreement is obtained by the conventional method of circulating *ringisho*. Once such internal agreement has been obtained, each ministry insists very strongly upon the correctness and interpretations of its own scope and competence, regardless of conflicts with other ministries. To be sure there are factors other than

[8] Yamashiro, *op.cit.*, pp. 173ff.

ringisei that explain this particularism in Japanese administration: the pluralistic nature of political power at the time of the Meiji Restoration; the fact that the Meiji constitution rejected joint responsibility for the Cabinet and made each minister separately responsible to the emperor; the fact that ministers were members of the Cabinet and heads of administrative agencies at the same time; and the establishment of the prerogative of a separate and independent supreme command over the armed forces. Because of such factors a ministry could exert great influence upon decision-making in the Cabinet if that ministry was strongly united internally, resulting in a weakly united Cabinet. Not infrequently cabinets collapsed because of the opposition of single ministries.[9] Thus while particularism cannot be attributed to *ringisei* alone, even today it is one of the most important factors promoting particularism in administration. From the point of view of organizational theory, we can say, therefore, that when the smaller units in a large organization pay too much attention to their own internal communications and their own objectives, the efficiency of the organization as a whole will be seriously qualified.

Second, *ringisei* is calculated to maintain a strict sense of rank among administrators. The word itself, *ringi*, meaning "to ask from below," implies a relationship between master and servant. This in itself may have some psychological influence on administrators. And the resulting sense of separation of higher from lower has been greatly strengthened by the higher civil service examination system (*kōtōbunkan shiken seidō*), which was in effect until the end of World War

[9] In 1901, for example, the fourth Itō Cabinet, ostensibly a strong government headed by a veteran leader of the imperial Restoration, was compelled to resign en masse because of the opposition of a single ministry. When the budget, which had been already decided by the Cabinet, came to be implemented, the minister of finance strongly opposed it and was backed by his subordinates within the ministry. For the reasons for such particularism in the Japanese government, see Tsuji Kiyoaki, *Nihon kanryōsei no kenkyū* (Tokyo, 1952), pp. 67-128.

II. Only those who passed this examination could be promoted to higher positions. Those who were successful were promoted very rapidly, but those who were not spent their lives as lower or middle-ranking administrators until retirement, however able they might be. The discontent felt by these lower administrators was compensated for to some extent because they became more technically experienced and proficient than the higher administrators. It was these permanently low-grade administrators who drafted *ringisho* and who helped the non-expert higher administrators through their experience and practical knowledge. This may have given them some sense of self-satisfaction in their jobs. To use an analogy, their circumstances resembled those of a wife who lives under the despotic control of her husband; she may comfort herself by thinking that she has assisted her husband's career.

On the other hand, the fact that *ringisho* were drafted by these lower administrators on the basis of their own narrow experience tended to insure the narrowness of their perspectives. Since the drafter could refer only to the past experience and precedents of his own office, there was certain to be a built-in lag between the contents of *ringisho* and conditions in the outside world. In other words, *ringisho* tended to be desk plans that were out of touch with reality. Because precedents were considered to be important, their drafters were apt to seek the advice of veteran administrators who also had little hope of promotion. Thus the contents of *ringisho* today tend to be dominated by old precedents, and the conventional knowledge of earlier generations of administrators is transmitted in this way to new generations of lower administrators.

As a result of *ringisei*, higher administrators depend on lower administrators and lower administrators acquire a sense of loyalty to higher administrators. This is the way in which a sense of community is maintained in governmental offices. *Ringisei* contributes to what M. P. Follett called the "final authority system." In other words, the sense of loyalty of the lower to the higher and the overall sense of communal relationships are strengthened by *ringisei,* and this helps to produce the "final authority system."

Third, because of *ringisei* decision-making tends to be influenced by private considerations. Since the drafting of *ringisho* is assigned to lower administrators and the number of relevant administrators involved in the review and approval system are numerous, individuals among them are often in a position to influence the nature of the decision during the circulation of the *ringisho.* In extreme cases, private interests come to dominate public decision-making, especially decisions concerning the issuance of licenses. Lower administrators, like assistants to division heads, are sometimes called barnyard emperors (*hiryō tennō*) because of their capacity to influence the contents of *ringisho.* There have been many cases of corruption in postwar Japan in which lower as well as higher civil servants have been arrested, an indication of the influence of lower civil servants in decision-making in Japanese public administration.

The Reform of Ringisei

Democratization in postwar Japan has been the main factor leading to the reform of *ringisei* in private enterprise. The cartels (*zaibatsu*) were broken up, prewar higher executives were purged, and many new labor unions were organized. Partly as a result of the revision of the Commercial Code and partly for other reasons, decision-making by boards of directors and the role of managers in general became more important in business management. Also American techniques of management were introduced to Japan. In the early stages of these reforms, the main purpose was to increase production and to improve labor management. Job classification, job evaluation, social and job security measures, in-service training programs, wages keyed to positions rather than seniority, and a variety of other innovations were introduced. In this way industrial rationalization and adjustments in human relations within industry were begun. Then came reforms of top management, the comptroller system, and the organization of boards of executive directors, and since about 1955 top leaders in private enterprises have been concerned about planned management and marketing, gradually decentralizing decision-making powers.

The circumstances and needs of postwar business have thus strengthened the role of top management and produced staff organizations whose roles are distinguished from those of line agencies. At the same time a good deal of decision-making power has been assigned to lower levels such as the sales and production divisions. As a result it seems probable that *ringisei* will gradually disappear in the business community.[10]

Criticisms of *ringisei* and the efforts to reform it in private enterprise have also had an impact on public administration, where *ringisei* has been the subject of increasing criticism and of several proposed reforms. The first such reform was proposed in 1949 by the Council for the Reform of Public Administration. It suggested, first, that the Cabinet abandon management from below in order to give more authority to top executives and their assistants, and to enable them to make decisions more promptly, and second, curtail the use of assistants and reassign those that remained to other more appropriate positions. Then, in 1950 the Council for Public Administration recommended that both responsibility and competence be made clear at each level of administration; that a sense of responsibility and will to innovate be cultivated among administrators; and that the handling of business be simplified. It was high time, the proposal of 1950 claimed, to reform *ringisei*, which it criticized as extremely inefficient. Similar reform proposals were presented by the First Public Administration Council in 1953, and by the Fourth Public Administration Council in 1959. The latter, for example, made four proposals for the reform of *ringisei*: (1) the circulation of *ringisho* should be limited to three levels at most, and they should be drafted by the responsible executives or by higher civil serv-

[10] Ono, *op.cit.*, p. 67.

ants; (2) in order to prevent delays in decisions as a result of the circulation of *ringisho*, only a report of the decisions taken rather than a *ringisho* requesting concurrence should be sent to all indirectly affected offices in and outside the ministry concerned; (3) both responsibility for and competence to affix seals should be clarified; and (4) in order to reduce the number of levels involved in decision-making, less important decisions should be made at the division level and more important ones only should be forwarded to higher authorities after formulation by the division head concerned. The Cabinet was impressed by these recommendations and by the force of public opinion and decided that "the number of levels of decision-making should be reduced to as few as possible, and that higher civil servants should participate in drafting *ringisho* wherever possible." This decision by the Cabinet has, however, not actually been carried out in practice.[11]

The Temporary Research Commission for Public Administration presented recommendations for the reform of public administration in September 1964. This commission, which had investigated the problem for two and a half years, strongly recommended the reform of *ringisei*, and suggested the adoption of what they called an "assignment" or "allocation" system (*waritsuke hōshiki*) instead of *ringisei*. Under this system higher civil servants would assign tasks to qualified subordinate administrators and would be responsible for checking their results, thus bringing about a feedback effect in Japanese public administration. As a result of these reforms, the commission said, the following objectives would be realized: leadership by higher executives; a narrowing of the gap between formal competence and actual practice; a speedup in approval

---

[11] In July 1961 a colleague and I interviewed higher civil servants holding positions ranging from division heads to vice-minister in the Ministries of Finance, Agriculture, and Local Autonomy. We asked them about 70 questions. One of these was: "Do you think that there has been any improvement in office management at your agency in the past two or three years?" The answers were: (1) very much—16; (2) some—133; (3) almost none—81; (4) none at all—11.

and licensing procedures; and the prevention of arbitrary administrative decisions. An administrative form exemplifying the recommended procedures is shown in Figure 3.

Actually if a higher civil servant today were required really to assume a role of leadership, it would be a most unsettling experience for him. Should he be required to draft *ringisho,* for example, he would find it practically impossible to do without extensive assistance. In Japanese terms he would be a lonely lord, bereft without his subjects. The situation is not, of course, peculiar to Japan.

The most crucial need in the reform of *ringisei,* however, is for the recognition and provision of staff services. As long as this is not done, all attempts to reform *ringisei* will remain mere paper plans. If higher executives are really to lead, able and experienced staff members to help them are indispensable. The tasks of large organizations are so numerous, complicated, and technical that it is practically impossible to manage them without the help of a staff that plans, advises, suggests, and collects and analyses information for the higher executives. This is true for the individual ministries as well as for the government as a whole.

In Japanese administration, however, staff functions have been little recognized, and staff organization has been very weak. For example, in the case of the Japanese government as a whole, the first attempt at improvement was the establishment of the Planning Agency in 1937, which unfortunately became a refuge for bureaucrats having close relationships with the army and navy rather than becoming a real staff organization. At that time, self-centered and particularistic administration was the rule in all ministries. Consequently the authority of the Planning Agency was largely ignored by the ministries, and each of them continued to operate according to the old precedents and practices to which it was accustomed.

The only exception was the Japanese armed forces. In military organization, the distinction between line and staff had been very clearly defined since shortly after the Restoration.

Pre-Decision Consultation	Post-Decision Disposition
Drafter Chief of the Livestock Management Section	Document No. No._____
Drafting Date _____ / / _____ month day year	Decision Date _____ / / _____ month day year
Endorsements by:	Document examined _____ / / _____ month day year
Chief, Sanitation Section	Document revised _____ / / _____ month day year
Chief, Natural Feeds Section	Decision executed _____ / / _____ month day year
Chief, Artificial Feeds Section	Other matters _____ / / _____ month day year
Chief, Breed Improvement Section	
Chief, Economics Section	
Chief, Livestock Administration Section	
Counselor	
Chief, Agricultural Economics Bureau	Document Filer in charge (name)
Ministerial Chief Secretary	
Parliamentary Vice-Minister	
	File No. No._____

I certify that the following decision has been made: (text of policy decided upon is appended).

_____ ,
(name)   (seal)
Ministry of Agriculture and Forestry

In the army the general staff office became independent as early as in 1878, while in the navy the naval general staff was created in 1886. Both thought highly of the functions and value of staff work. The military ranks of staff members were actually higher than those of line officers. This was so primarily because the emperor's supreme prerogative in military matters was in practice entrusted to and managed by the two general staffs independently of the ministries of the army and navy. This superiority was reinforced when in 1930 Prime Minister Hamaguchi was assassinated after his Cabinet had signed the London Naval Limitation Treaty over the objections of the naval general staff. An additional point that fostered a sense of superiority among staff officers was the wearing of special shoulder straps, distinguishing them from ordinary military officers. One important reason why the functions of the staff are recognized to this extent in military organization is that decisions on military strategy and movements are clearly distinguished from general military administration. These are the vital decisions that can decide the life or death of one's country. They are the keys to victory or defeat.

If the importance of staff organization and services should come to be recognized in public administration as it is in the armed forces, and if additionally it were to become possible to assign responsibility for policy results, the probability that administrative decision-making would become more deliberate and more thoughtful would be greatly enhanced. If military decisions in time of war were made by *ringisei* through the solicitation of opinions from a great variety of private soldiers and higher officers, the battle would be lost every time. Decisions at the front must be expeditiously made and executed, and if the decision is to be a good one, the quality of its preparation is crucial.

Unlike the military, the public does tolerate errors and faults in decision-making without seriously questioning the ability or integrity of public servants or the merits of their system of decision-making. Thus *ringisei* survives in public administra-

474

tion because of the patience and apathy of the public. In fact, because the contemporary system of public administration implicitly assumes that the public will submit to its authority, the very concept of public service has been greatly weakened in the minds of so-called public servants.

The situation is changing, however. The shortcomings of business management in Japan are being criticized because the Japanese economy must face the competition of free trade with other countries. Decision-making in public administration also is now beginning to face an open system, and it should gradually come to adapt itself to this rapidly changing environment. *Ringisei* will shortly face other criticisms even more severe than those of the Temporary Research Commission for Public Administration, which will be leveled against a crucial aspect of Japanese government that has been modernized in form only.

CHAPTER XIII

Reflections on the Allied Occupation and Planned Political Change in Japan

ROBERT E. WARD[1]

I F ONE prescinds from the particularities involved and tries to look at the Allied Occupation of Japan (1945-1952) as a massive experiment in "planned" or "directed" political change, what does one see? What policies, what apparatus, what methods were developed by the Occupying Powers in their attempt to democratize Japan? And, reciprocally, what were the Japanese like in their role as the far-from-inert subject matter of this experiment? Finally, what does an analysis of this sort suggest with respect to the more general problem of the amenability of complex political systems to planned "development" by an external agency such as the Occupation?

These questions provide the major themes for this chapter, but it should be noted that they will be approached in terms that are both partial and somewhat arbitrary. For example, considerations of space will preclude any serious attempt to demonstrate or measure the degree of success that attended upon the Occupation's attempts to "develop"—by which they meant essentially to "democratize"—the Japanese system of government and politics. It is simply assumed that by any realistic standards of evaluation the terms of political competition and decision-making in postwar Japan have altered substantially since the 1932–1945 period, that these changes are democratic in tendency, that they have been stimulated in im-

[1] The author would like to express his gratitude to the Carnegie Corporation of New York for financial assistance in support of the research on which this paper is based.

portant degree by the efforts of SCAP,[2] and that they would not have achieved anything very closely resembling their present status were it not for those efforts. It is freely recognized that this degree of "development" still leaves Japan far short of anything approximating ideal standards of democratic performance—a far from lonely position—and that all of the above may seem debatable propositions to some. Nevertheless, for present purposes they are assumed to be valid.

Basic Characteristics of the Allied Occupation

The basic facts of the Occupation can be briefly recounted. It was brought about by Japan's acceptance on August 14, 1945, of the terms of surrender set forth by the Potsdam Declaration. It began unofficially with the entrance of American naval units into Sagami Bay on August 27, and officially with the formal signature of the terms of surrender aboard the battleship *Missouri* in Tokyo Bay on September 2, 1945. It ended six years and eight months later when, with the effectuation of the Treaty of San Francisco on April 28, 1952, Japan regained her status as a sovereign and independent nation. Between these dates Japan was occupied by foreign troops who, with the exception of a small British Commonwealth force, were exclusively American.

The office of Supreme Commander for the Allied Powers (SCAP) was held by two men, both Americans: General Douglas MacArthur, from the beginning until his abrupt relief on April 11, 1951 (a term of five years and seven months), and General Matthew Ridgway (for the remaining thirteen months). The overwhelming majority of SCAP's staff, both military and civilian, were also American. The same is true of the machinery that determined basic policies for the Occupation. Theoretically two international agencies, the Far Eastern

[2] SCAP stands for Supreme Commander for the Allied Powers. It is used to refer to Generals MacArthur and Ridgway, the two occupants of the position or, in a different context, to denote the entire headquarters staff over which they presided in Tokyo.

Commission and the Allied Council for Japan, were supposed to have important policy-setting and advisory functions, but in practice their roles were negligible in almost all instances. It seems fair to say, therefore, that what was technically an "Allied" Occupation of Japan was in fact almost exclusively an American operation.

The objectives of the Occupation are set forth in somewhat different forms and degrees of specificity in several documents.[3] Since only one of these was prepared specifically and exclusively for the guidance of SCAP—the directive 1380/15 of the U.S. Joint Chiefs of Staff (JCS)—this constitutes the most authoritative and satisfactory source of information about the formal goals of the Occupation. Paragraph 3a of this

---

[3] Japan in the official Declaration of Surrender accepted the Allied terms set forth in the Potsdam Declaration (or Declaration of Berlin) of July 26, 1945. The text of this may be found in SCAP, Government Section, *Political Reorientation of Japan* (Washington, 1949), II, 413. The text of the Instrument of Surrender is given *ibid.*, p. 419. The government of the United States (actually the State-War-Navy Coordinating Committee with the approval of the president) then spelled out its interpretation of the Potsdam terms in much greater detail in a document entitled "United States Initial Post-Surrender Policy for Japan." Although this was informally radioed to General MacArthur on August 29, 1945, just before the Occupation officially got under way, it was not actually approved by the president until September 6, 1945. Its text is given *ibid.*, pp. 423-26. The Joint Chiefs of Staff next took this U.S. Initial Post-Surrender Policy and put it into the form of an even more detailed and specific "Basic Initial Post-Surrender Directive to Supreme Commander for the Allied Powers for the Occupation and Control of Japan." This is technically known as J.C.S. 1380/15 of November 3, 1945. Its text may be found *ibid.*, pp. 429-39. Finally on June 19, 1947, the Far Eastern Commission, acting officially for the eleven powers then members, rewrote with very little substantial change the original "United States Initial Post-Surrender Policy for Japan" under the title "Basic Post-Surrender Policy for Japan (FEC 014/9)." The text of this may be found in Far Eastern Commission, Secretary General, *Activities of the Far Eastern Commission, February 26, 1946– July 10, 1947* (U.S. Department of State, Far Eastern Series 24; Washington, 1947), pp. 49-58.

directive is entitled "Basic Objectives of Military Occupation of Japan." It states these objectives succinctly:

> The ultimate objective of the United Nations with respect to Japan is to foster conditions which will give the greatest possible assurance that Japan will not again become a menace to the peace and security of the world and will permit her eventual admission as a responsible and peaceful member of the family of nations. Certain measures considered to be essential for the achievement of this objective have been set forth in the Potsdam Declaration. These measures include, among others, the carrying out of the Cairo Declaration and the limiting of Japanese sovereignty to the four main islands and such minor islands as the Allied Powers determine; the abolition of militarism and ultra-nationalism in all their forms; the disarmament and demilitarization of Japan, with continuing control over Japan's capacity to make war; the strengthening of democratic tendencies and processes in governmental, economic, and social institutions; and the encouragement and support of liberal political tendencies in Japan. The United States desires that the Japanese Government conform as closely as may be to principles of democratic self-government, but it is not the responsibility of the occupation forces to impose on Japan any form of government not supported by the freely expressed will of the people.

It is frequently claimed that from a domestic political standpoint these goals may be subsumed under two general rubrics: demilitarization and democratization. Such a dichotomy is clearly implicit in the directive, and of the two, for obvious practical reasons, the goal of demilitarization clearly enjoyed an overriding priority during both the planning stage and the opening months of the Occupation. But by the end of 1945 the weight of SCAP's interests and energies was beginning to shift to the far more complicated and difficult goal of democratization.

It is also useful to note that there was an element of planned flexibility built into the policies set forth by this basic directive. Paragraph 3c reads in part: "This directive does not purport finally to formulate long-term policies concerning the treatment of Japan in the postwar world, nor does it seek to prescribe in detail the measures which you are to take throughout the period of your occupation of Japan in the effort to give effect to the surrender and the Potsdam Declaration. These policies and the appropriate measures for their fulfillment will in large measure be determined by developing circumstances in Japan. . . . Supplementary directives will be issued to you through the Joint Chiefs of Staff as may be required."

In practice such supplementary directives were formulated, with considerable frequency, by the State-War-Navy Coordinating Committee (SWNCC) and its successor, the State-Army-Navy-Air Coordinating Committee (SANACC), on a large variety of subjects relating to the Occupation and were duly embodied in JCS directives to SCAP. Thus the question of the definition of specific and instrumental goals and policies for the Occupation was to an important degree left open at the outset so that it could evolve in consonance with developments in Japan and elsewhere.

The basic documents make clear the United States' desire to democratize its erstwhile enemy—primarily for reasons of long-term peace and security in the western Pacific and secondarily because of a sincere and evangelical belief in the superiority of democratic institutions. What they do not clarify is the inordinate complexity of such an undertaking and the strange, but as they turned out favorable, circumstances under which the attempt was to be made. They seek to anticipate and provide guidelines for some of the major and more foreseeable problems involved, but they do so in the necessarily general and abstract terms of the "planner." Brilliantly drawn documents though they were—especially the "Initial" and "Basic Initial Post-Surrender" statements—they can only imply through their statements of goals the vast range of specific problems the Occupation would shortly have to face in its attempts to reorient the Japanese political system along democratic lines. In practice this involved operations ranging from a political purge embracing more than 200,000 individuals to the abolition of Shinto, from the reform of the educational system to land reform, and from drafting a new constitution to checking on the implementation of village ordinances. Scarcely a major sector of Japanese society was left untouched. Almost everything turned out to be related in some way to the problem of democratization. Thus what was initially conceived as primarily political planning for the military administration and political rehabilitation of a defeated enemy soon escalated into something of far greater scope.

The basic documents can only hint also at the extraordinary circumstances in which this massive experiment in democratization was taking place. Some seemed distinctly adverse. On the basis of wartime experience, for example, the Japanese were widely regarded as a people fanatically loyal to their emperor and national tradition, devoted to authoritarian political institutions and practices, xenophobic in the highest degree, and individually and collectively both inscrutable and intractable. From the standpoint of would-be democratizers, these were scarcely auspicious characteristics. Fortunately, the Japanese turned out not to be like this at all, at least under the circumstances of defeat and occupation then obtaining. Consequently other and more extrinsic aspects of the situation became of greater relevance and importance to the success of the democratization program.

There was first the fact of SCAP's complete legal authority in Japan. As General MacArthur's mandate of authority put it: "The authority of the Emperor and the Japanese Government to rule the State is subordinate to you as Supreme Commander for the Allied Powers." There was almost literally nothing that lay beyond the authority of SCAP. MacArthur had plenary power. Second, he did not share this power with foreign collaborators to any appreciable degree. The Occupa-

482

tion of Japan was not like the Occupation of Germany in this sense. There were no "zones" and there were no equal "partners." Third, there was the duration of the Occupation—almost seven years; too long for some and far too short for others, but still a very respectable period of time. If progress was at all possible, one should in this space be able to make appreciable inroads, even against problems as formidable as those confronting the Occupation. Thus a reasonable span of time was allowed for the experiment to be launched and established. Fourth, there was the fact of national isolation. During much of the period concerned, Japan was systematically isolated from the outside world. Japanese citizens, with rare exceptions, were forbidden to travel or live abroad. Foreigners, save for those employed or approved by SCAP, were forbidden to visit or reside in Japan. News and communications both domestic and foreign were subject to censorship. In these ways the subjects of SCAP's experiment were isolated and many, if not all disturbing outside influences were excluded.

This is a rare conjunction of circumstances. If one searches modern history for comparable experiments with externally planned and controlled political change on a national scale, the only examples that readily come to mind are the Communist endeavors in Eastern Europe and a few other locales.[4] Despite obvious differences in goals and immediate consequences, the problems involved are comparable in scale and complexity and so are a number of the methods. Basic in both instances is the desire of a victorious power to convert a defeated enemy to its political beliefs and practices. In a larger sense, therefore, the case of the Occupation of Japan is not

[4] The tutelary and power relationships implicit in the relation of a metropolitan power to its colonies are also similar in some respects—perhaps especially so with respect to such cases as the United States and the Philippine Islands—but the situation also differs in a number of important respects: the relative degrees of modernity or development represented by the principal parties, the origins and bases of the mutual relationship involved, its duration, and the intensity and scale of the dominant party's "reforming" operations.

unique, but it does represent the only instance where this degree of power, control, and initiative has lain with a single *democratic* power. The Occupations of Germany and Austria were multilateral in control, and hence different.

It would be a mistake to overplay the "scientific" qualities of this American "experiment" in Japan. Obviously too many of the prerequisites of scientific status are either lacking or present only in most imperfect degree, e.g. any very precise control over the admixture of active ingredients, the ability to relate particular effects to particular causes with reasonable specificity, and reproducibility. But it would be an equally serious error to underrate the heuristic values implicit within this massive endeavor. It is very seldom that one will encounter so fortuitous a conjunction of unified control over subject matter, isolation from external influence, advance specification of goals, and an at least implicit elaboration of hypotheses about the means by which they might be attained—and all applied on a national scale. Our poverty of experience with respect to the potentialities and limitations of planning endeavors on this sort of scale is too great and our need for such knowledge far too urgent to permit us to neglect on grounds of scientific immaculacy the lessons that may be implicit in such "experiments." This should add then a further dimension of interest and promise to studies of the Occupation of Japan.

Advance Planning

If one views the Occupation, then, as an experiment in controlled or directed political change, it will simplify the problem of exposition to distinguish at the outset two major categories or ways of organizing the data. The first lies along a temporal axis, and the prime break involved falls at September 2, 1945. Decisions taken prior to that date—the formal beginning of the Occupation—were anticipatory, generalized, and of a planning nature. Those taken later, while they were also often of a planning sort, dealt with an established situation and were apt to be somewhat more specific and concrete. The cleavage between the two periods is far from absolute, however, and it is adopted here primarily as an expository device.

The second category relates to the cast of characters in the sense that the Occupation was essentially a dialogue between America and Japan and it therefore becomes important to distinguish the plans, expectations, knowledge, and actions of both participants. The Japanese may have been the subject matter of an experiment, but they were neither inert nor helpless. To the contrary, the positive and assertive role that they played in the Occupation steadily increased with the passage of time. This is one of the less tidy characteristics of this, as of many other, social science "experiments."

The questions to be considered first are then: (1) what decisions did the United States government—as the principal planning agency for the Occupation—adopt prior to September 2, 1945, that may relate to the degree of success subsequently achieved by SCAP in its attempts to democratize Japan? And (2) what, if any, decisions did the Japanese government take during this same period that may subsequently have qualified or otherwise affected these endeavors on SCAP's part?

The most basic of the United States government's presurrender decisions was also the most general. It was the specification in the Initial Post-Surrender Policy of what it called the "ultimate objectives" for a defeated Japan. As noted earlier, these were essentially two—demilitarization and, if possible, democratization. Neither seems very remarkable in its own right. It is worth noting, however, that the policy takes a broad view of "democratization" as an Occupation goal. Obviously its authors had far more than institutional and legal tinkering in mind. The details are left vague, but the statement does not simply order the purge of militarists and ultranationalists, the formation of representative and democratic organizations, and the reform of the judicial, legal, and police systems, but it also treats or implies the necessity of supportive reforms of the educational and economic systems, the encouragement of democratic political parties, and the promotion of new attitudes and desires among the Japanese people. Thus it was recognized from the outset that changes at the institutional level alone were bound to be inadequate. A successful program of democratization required changes ramifying through all major sectors of Japanese society.

This may seem obvious to social scientists in 1967. It was not so in 1945 in this particular context. It was a pioneering move to conceive of the Occupations of both Germany and Japan as opportunities for massive experiments in democratization in this deep and across-the-board sense. In a strictly technical way it was the equivalent in scope and imagination of—and a fitting response to—the Communist designs for the communization of the Eastern European satellite states. The basic planning at least did not underestimate the magnitude or complexity of the task, and it thus provided a suitable foundation and point of departure for the Occupation proper.

Also this basic policy statement served to pose a practically endless series of subordinate questions as to how these goals might best be achieved. It is the decisions taken with respect to these that are of present interest.

The most important related to the control of the Occupation. In theory several general categories of decisions ranging from multilateral to unilateral control were possible. But in practice the general circumstances in which the war had been fought and the peace organized ruled out the possibility of an Occupation exclusively controlled by the United States. In addition, however, the American government seems positively to have desired some form of distinctly limited international participation in the Occupation of Japan.[5] It was the United States that in August 1945 proposed the establishment of a

[5] See, for example, U.S. Department of State, *The Far Eastern Commission: A Study in International Cooperation, 1945 to 1952* (Publication 5138; Washington, 1953), pp. 2-5.

Far Eastern Advisory Commission to make recommendations with respect to the treatment of Japan after surrender, while the U.S. Initial Post-Surrender Policy itself—in Part II, Section I—makes clear that "the occupation shall have the character of an operation in behalf of the principal Allied Powers acting in the interests of the United Nations at war with Japan." It further states that "participation of the forces of other nations that have taken a leading part in the war against Japan will be welcomed and expected."

It was made equally clear, however, that the United States was determined to retain for itself effective control and leadership of the Occupation. And to insure this position vis-à-vis all possible foreign or Japanese challenge, a series of two basic and several subordinate decisions were taken with respect to the control of the Occupation.

First, where the determination of policies for the conduct of the Occupation was concerned, although efforts would be made to satisfy the principal Allied Powers through consultation and the establishment of advisory bodies, the policies of the United States were to prevail in the event of any differences of opinion. This was clearly stated in the U.S. Initial Post-Surrender Policy, and the policy was in fact only slightly qualified when later at Moscow in December 1945 the United States accepted the arrangements for the constitution of the Far Eastern Commission and the Allied Council for Japan. In practice, therefore, other countries were limited to advisory and remonstrative roles.

Second, where the on-the-spot administration of the Occupation was concerned, it was decided that control should be unified in the hands of a single Supreme Commander for the Allied Powers, that an American officer should occupy this post, that he should take his orders directly and only from the United States Joint Chiefs of Staff, and that his authority to rule Japan should be complete. This in an administrative sense subordinated the Occupation to the United States' regular chain of military command. It also had the very important consequence of ruling out any establishment of separate Allied zones of occupation each ultimately responsible to its own government. This had been the pattern followed earlier in Germany with adverse consequences that were already clear, and the United States was determined that this experience should not be repeated in Japan. Any non-American forces accepting the invitation to participate in the Occupation would have to accept an American commander in chief. In the end only the British Commonwealth chose to comply with this condition, though the Chinese might also have done so had it not been for their domestic troubles. Finally, it was made clear by the Joint Chiefs of Staff directive that representatives of civilian agencies of the United States or of other United Nations governments might function in Japan or participate in the Occupation only with the approval of SCAP.

Quite obviously the degree of effective international participation in such an arrangement was minimal. The Allied Powers involved were accorded an institutionalized means of presenting their views and advice with respect to the control of Japan. In a few instances minor changes in American policy were made in response to Allied suggestions or pressures. But as a rule the policies and authority of the United States were enforced in all matters concerning the Occupation of Japan, and Allied participation was more formal than effective.

It might also be noted that this American freedom of decision and action was substantially enhanced by the fact that the Far Eastern Commission and the Allied Council for Japan— although initially authorized by the Moscow Meeting of Foreign Ministers on December 26, 1945—did not actually convene until February 26 and April 3, 1946, respectively. The early months of the Occupation were particularly critical, and during the six months from September 1945 to March 1946 the United States had an almost completely free hand—so far as Allied participation was concerned. A large proportion of the most basic decisions with respect to the policies and programs of the Occupation were made during that period.

The foregoing decisions relate to the control of the Occupation in an international sense, and their purpose was to establish the predominant authority of the United States against possible challenges from any of her Allies. There were also specifically American and Japanese dimensions to this problem of control.

So far as the American dimension is concerned, the basic decision was to create a single Supreme Commander for the Allied Powers and to entrust him with plenary authority. From SCAP the chain of command ran directly to the Joint Chiefs of Staff and through them to the highest levels of the United States government. The authority of SCAP was in this manner carefully protected against foreign incursions. It was also protected with equal care against meddling by other agencies of the United States government and against challenge by the Japanese. Representatives of civilian agencies of the United States government could visit or operate in Japan only with SCAP's approval. In practice also their official communications into and out of Japan could be transmitted only through a signals system controlled and operated by SCAP. This put them at an added disadvantage. Where relations with the Japanese government were concerned, SCAP's instructions from the Joint Chiefs were sweeping: "The authority of the Emperor and the Japanese Government to rule the State is subordinate to you as Supreme Commander for the Allied Powers. You will exercise your authority as you deem proper to carry out your mission. Our relations with Japan *do not rest on a contractual basis, but on an unconditional surrender.* Since your authority is supreme, you will not entertain any question on the part of the Japanese as to its scope."[6]

These were impressive grants of power by any standards. To some extent they were modeled after the authority accorded an American theater commander during the war just finished, but they went even further than that. In substance

[6] *Political Reorientation of Japan*, ii, 427. Emphasis added.

they ruled out the possibility of establishing either civilian or collegial authority of an American or international sort where control of the Occupation was concerned. They opted in favor of a completely unified system of military control and then took pains to protect this against interference from any foreign, American, or Japanese challenge or interference. They left SCAP subject only to control by the Joint Chiefs—a collegial body that often had considerable internal difficulty in reaching agreements—or by the president of the United States —an extremely busy political official with but marginal time and attention to spare for the Occupation of Japan. In practice when one adds to this the reputation, stature, and personality of General MacArthur, who held the office for sixty-seven of the eighty months for which it existed, it is scarcely surprising to find that this grant of authority was utilized to the fullest and that the Supreme Commander himself usually held effective control over the Occupation. It is excessive to attribute sovereign status to General MacArthur, as some of his critics do. He received—from SWNCC via the Joint Chiefs— and carried out a continuous stream of important policy directives with respect to basic Occupation policies, although it is also true that his advice and approval were normally asked before such directives were issued. But he was also a man who believed in the advantages of strong leadership and abundantly supplied it.

The next of the presurrender decisions that seems relevant concerns the matter of basic administrative structure and role. Was the Occupation to be direct or indirect? Was it to resemble the Occupation of Germany in the sense that the Japanese government would officially and actually go out of existence and be replaced by an American or Allied military government that would itself directly administer the affairs of both national and local governments? Or would the Japanese government remain in being and continue to deal with its normal functions subject to control and supervision by SCAP?

Again there were alternatives. There was, first, the prece-

490

dent of the German Occupation and, second, the fact that throughout the war in the Far East there had been a tendency to think of the Occupation of Japan as a progressive operation coinciding with Allied landings and armed invasions that would, in the early stages at least, lead to the control of only those portions of Japanese home territory lying behind our battle lines. The administration of such areas was, therefore, conceived of as a paramilitary and largely local sort of operation. The United States had trained at Charlottesville, Monterey, and other centers a considerable number of military government specialists for use in Japan under such circumstances. But in a planning sense the early surrender of Japan came as a great surprise, and, since it was total, it posed problems of administration on a scale that had not been seriously contemplated for this stage of operations. Still there was an expectation in certain quarters that something resembling the German pattern would be followed and some form of direct military government established.

In fact this was never done. The decision was to administer the Occupation indirectly. The Potsdam Declaration implies and the Initial Post-Surrender Policy makes completely clear the fact that the Japanese governmental machinery and agencies were to continue to function and that SCAP should, save in specified contingencies, exercise his authority through the Japanese government. A by-product of this decision was to reinforce further the unity and solidarity of SCAP's authority. Instead of establishing a separate G-5 staff section, i.e. military government, and importing trainees from the United States to operate what would have been by far the most important function of the Occupation, military government was instead subsumed within the structure of General MacArthur's command without undue disturbance or displacement of existing arrangements. Many of the personnel trained for this purpose were still brought to Japan and used, but not as a separate entity or with separate status. A more important consequence of the decision was that the continuity of the Japanese administrative apparatus and personnel system was never really broken. It was shaken by institutional changes and by the purge, but the effects were not really extensive.

At least two other basic policy decisions were made prior to September 2, 1945. The first related to the ambit of operations of the Occupation in a geographic sense. Was it necessary physically to occupy all of Japan, just strategic parts of it, or perhaps only the immediate Tokyo area? All of these had been discussed as possibilities. The decision was for something approximating a saturation-type Occupation in the early stages (partly to show the flag and bring home to the average Japanese the fact of national defeat), tapering off rather rapidly to an Occupation confined largely to prefectural capitals and other strategic areas. It is not clear that the rapidity with which this shift from a saturation-type to a selective occupation might be achieved was appreciated at the outset, but in fact it did occur very soon. By November 3, 1945, the Joint Chiefs' Basic Directive made such a shift official doctrine.

The second of these basic policy decisions concerned the attitude that was to be officially adopted toward the defeated Japanese government and people. Was it to be vengeful, harsh, lawless? Or was it to emphasize moderation and reconciliation? Stated so baldly, the question seems almost to answer itself, but in fact this was not so. The war had been bitterly and often ruthlessly fought, and both sides had made a good deal of propaganda capital from atrocity stories. Personal feelings about retribution were often very strong, and the racial differences involved might well have exacerbated the situation. Recent history provides plenty of examples of occupations where, deliberately or accidentally, the policies followed toward the occupied people were both harsh and lawless in effect.

An important element of vengeance or retribution—the shading is delicate—was, of course, built into the Japanese surrender terms: the empire was lost and Japan's external assets confiscated; reparations payments were provided for;

"war criminals"—defined in very broad terms—were to be punished; and there was to be a widespread purge of "undesirables" from government office and some private positions. These were not lenient terms. But such aspects of the settlement aside, there was also a marked disposition to deal with Japan in a "constructive" manner. "Constructive" seems usually to have meant "favorable to the ultimate aim of the democratization of Japan." And it was not felt that violence or indiscriminate harshness were conducive to the achievement of this goal. Consequently very serious attempts were made to explain that while the Japanese had only themselves to blame for the harsh aspects of the surrender terms, the Occupation basically wanted to work with them for the creation of a new, happier, and democratic Japan in a prosperous and peaceful world. This is a theme that characterizes the Potsdam Declaration, the United States Initial Post-Surrender Policy for Japan, General MacArthur's Message to the American People concerning the Surrender, and many other early policy statements at the highest levels. Quite a gap separates it from the Morgenthau Plan and other such advocates of a "tough" peace.

It is submitted, therefore, that prior to September 2, 1945, the United States government made at least six decisions of fundamental importance with respect to its policies for the Occupation. These related to:

1. Ultimate objectives
2. The respective roles of the United States and of other Allied Powers with respect to control of the Occupation
3. The structure and extent of SCAP's authority within Japan
4. The question of a direct versus an indirect administration of the Occupation
5. The geographical scope and penetration of the Occupation
6. The basic attitude to be adopted toward the Japanese Government and people

493

From the American and international standpoints, these six decisions determined the authority, basic structure, and broad policy orientations of the Occupation.

They equally set the context within which the Japanese government was to operate for the ensuing eighty months. But even though the Japanese had no choice but to accept and comply with them in an official sense, it is important to examine how they approached this unprecedented experience. The attitude and policy of the Japanese Cabinet toward the impending Occupation could make quite a difference. Had they developed any strategies to cope with this crisis? Or were they planless? What sort of treatment did they anticipate? And what did they propose to do about it? Were they inclined to be cooperative, inert, or positively obstructive? These were all factors capable of affecting at least the initial stages of the Occupation, and we will turn now to a brief examination of them.[7]

One starts with the assumption that there were several aspects of Occupation policy that should have been of vital interest to the Japanese government once the decision to surrender had been taken.[8] There was a period of nineteen days

[7] A fair amount has been written about the inner workings and decisions of the Japanese government during the critical months of July and August 1945. But very few of these studies accord any but incidental treatment to this question of official policy toward the Occupation prior to September 2, 1945. Among the more useful works are: Satō Tatsuo, *Nihonkoku Kempō seiritsushi* (Tokyo, 1962), i; Sumimoto Toshio, *Senryō hiroku* (Tokyo, 1952), i; and a number of accounts scattered throughout the testimony recorded in the forty-nine volumes of Kempō Chōsakai, *Kempō seitei no keika ni kansuru shōiinkai gijiroku* (Tokyo, 1958-1961). Most of the information that follows, however, is based on interviews with members of the Cabinet or governmental officials who were well situated to observe developments at that time. These were conducted by the author in Tokyo during 1963-1964.

[8] Two governments were actually involved—the Suzuki and Higashikuni Cabinets—but since the former was replaced by the latter on August 17, 1945, just three days after the surrender, it is essentially the

between the decision to surrender on August 14 and the beginning of the Occupation on September 2. During this period one might expect that a responsible government imminently confronted with an unprecedented national catastrophe would display keen interest in the probable nature and dimensions of the problems that would soon confront them: What was the probable nature of Allied intentions with respect to the emperor and the imperial system? With respect to war criminals? Would the Japanese government be permitted to remain in existence or might it be superseded by a directly administered occupation? How long was the Occupation apt to last? What sorts of changes were they apt to require in Japan? Was it apt to be harsh or mild in its dealings with the Japanese? Information on these scores would at least permit a more intelligent consideration of particular problems and provide some opportunity to coordinate views and prepare their defenses.

There were several sources from which some advance information of this sort was available, including the Potsdam Declaration, the Zacharias broadcasts, the practices followed earlier in the German Occupation, radio intelligence in general, and the advance surrender delegation sent to Manila by the Japanese government on August 19, 1945. It is somewhat surprising to find how little systematic use was made of such sources and how little constructive consideration seems in fact to have been given these matters by the Cabinet.[9]

Higashikuni government with which we are here concerned. It held office until October 9, 1945.

[9] The following analysis is based primarily upon the author's interviews with Prince Higashikuni Naruhiko, prime minister at the time; Marquis Kido Kōichi, Lord Privy Seal; Yamazaki Iwao, Minister of Internal Affairs; Murase Naokai, Chief of the Cabinet Bureau of Legislation; Okazaki Katsuo, Chief of the Foreign Ministry's Bureau of Research and the chief Foreign Ministry delegate on the Manila Mission; Admiral Takagi Sōkichi, prominent in the presurrender attempts to end the war; and Inaba Masao, then Chief of the Military Affairs Section of the Ministry of the Army and a participant in the

Where observations based upon the practices of the German Occupation are concerned, no one at the highest levels of government seems to have paid much attention. Ambassador Satō in Moscow was sending back some information on this score, and the Japanese embassies in Switzerland and Sweden were doubtless doing likewise. But it does not seem to have been brought to the Cabinet's attention. The situation where the Zacharias broadcasts and radio intelligence in general are concerned is somewhat similar. The Ministry of Foreign Affairs conducted a rather sizable radio monitoring operation throughout the war, and translations or abstracts of such materials were made. But these were officially available only to a very limited number of high officials in the Foreign Ministry and the armed forces and were widely held to be no more than propaganda. Very few others were aware of them. Again, although they may have been utilized within the Army, Navy, and Foreign Ministries, there seems to be no evidence that the Cabinet or the prime minister made serious use of them in connection with this matter of probable Occupation policies.

The case of the Potsdam Declaration is somewhat different. Thanks to pamphlets dropped by Allied planes, its text was widely available throughout Japan and was known to all Cabinet members. It had also been the subject of intensive Cabinet discussion and analysis in late July in connection with the earlier phases of the surrender negotiations. It did, therefore, have some demonstrable impact on the official Japanese conception of the terms involved in the surrender and thus, indirectly, on their notion of what the Occupation would be like. Given the difficulties experienced in the United States and Allied circles in gaining agreement to so obvious a qualification of the "unconditional surrender" formula and the lavish care expended

---

planning sessions for the Manila Mission. Useful accounts of the Manila Mission may also be found in the memoirs of General Kawabe Torashirō, who headed the Japanese delegation: *Ichigayadai kara Ichigayadai e* (Tokyo, 1962), pp. 354; and in Hattori Takushirō's *Daitōa Sensō zenshi* (Tokyo, 1956), VIII, 154ff.

upon finding just the right words and phrases to employ, it is particularly interesting to see how the Potsdam Declaration was interpreted by members of the Japanese Cabinet.

There were at least three schools of thought. The interpretations involved were not necessarily mutually exclusive, but each chose to place prime emphasis on a somewhat different aspect of the declaration. The first, simplest, and, it seems, least widely accepted interpretation took the declaration at face value as an honest statement of what "unconditional surrender of all Japanese armed forces" would in fact mean. The second, which seems to have been in the ascendancy in higher non-military circles, held that its precise specifications made little difference. In fact, Japan would be completely subject to the will of SCAP no matter what the Potsdam Declaration stated. In other words the United States' carefully drawn distinction between the demand for "the unconditional surrender of Japan" at Cairo in 1943 and that for "the unconditional surrender of all Japanese armed forces" at Potsdam in 1945, although recognized, was held by this group to be meaningless, just a play with words intended to gloss over the hard realities of surrender. The third interpretation was prevalent among high military circles. It again focussed on a phrase in the declaration for which its authors had entertained high hopes: "the occupying forces of the Allies shall be withdrawn from Japan as soon as . . . there has been established in accordance with the freely expressed will of the Japanese people a peacefully inclined and responsible government." Instead of taking this as an indirect assurance that the imperial system might be retained should the Japanese people so desire, these military circles chose to regard it as a covert appeal to mob rule and an implicit threat that Japan's future form of government would be demagogically determined. Such was the rather discouraging reception in higher Japanese circles of one of the United States' more carefully calculated endeavors to facilitate the Japanese surrender. There is little evidence that the government as such drew any significant conclusions as to the probable nature of the Occupation from the terms of the Potsdam Declaration.

The case of the Manila Surrender Mission is also interesting. The mission, led by General Kawabe Torashirō, deputy chief of staff, was sent to Manila at the Allies' demand primarily to provide the technical information needed in support of the projected landings of Allied forces in Japan at the end of the month. It was in Manila for only two days, August 19 and 20. In general the relationships between the Japanese and American military men appear to have been stiff and formal. But the two Japanese Foreign Ministry delegates—Messrs. Okazaki Katsuo and Yukawa Morio—both spoke fluent English and had better luck with their after-hours relationships. They talked at length with several well-placed American officers and learned or guessed a good deal. On their return they reported to the Cabinet that the Occupation would be indirectly administered, that there would be no occupation zones of the German sort, and that the higher American officials seemed well-disposed and not harsh in their attitudes toward the Japanese. On the basis of a delightfully indirect and ingenious maneuver, they also concluded that the Allies were intending to make extensive use of the emperor and that it was improbable, therefore, that they would seek either his abdication or an end to the imperial system. The Manila Mission thus produced some information of potential value, but again there is no evidence that it was put to subsequent use by the Cabinet.

So pronounced a lack of activity in the face of crisis may seem strange to some, but there were plausible explanations for it. First, there is the fact that the official and rigorously enforced policy of all Cabinets down to August 14, 1945, was to fight the war to the bitter end. Under such circumstances those few who were in a position to dissent with any effectiveness from this policy concentrated all their energies and resources on a single goal—the discovery of some formula that would permit Japan's surrender. Their struggle was domestic, and they were not particularly concerned about the terms the

United States and its Allies were offering. They held peace to be essential at almost any cost, and all their efforts were directed toward convincing the military of this fact. Thus any concern with the probable nature of an ensuing Occupation seemed either irrelevant or highly secondary prior to August 14.

Second, the same all-absorbing problem—control of the military—continued to dominate the domestic scene right down to September 2, although in a somewhat different guise. The surrender was now a fact but would the armed forces, especially the army, in Japan and overseas accept it or would they choose to go on fighting and attempt to sabotage it? One cannot talk with men in positions of power at the time without emerging with the strongest impression that this problem almost completely dominated the period between August 14 and September 2. The only other subject that is recalled with nearly the force and vividness is their sense of sorrow and shame over the number of their associates, especially in the military, who chose *seppuku* as their last appropriate means of protest. These must have been frantic and harrowing days for the members of the government in particular. There was simply not much time to devote to a matter as vague and perhaps pointless as "antioccupation strategy."

Third, the majority of them seem to have believed that such a concern would be pointless. There was an element of fatalism involved here. They had fought the war as best they could until overwhelmed by the atomic bombings and Russia's entry. They had done what was possible to protect the throne. Now the future lay in the hands of the Americans, and for the time being at least there was nothing that they could do about it. One gets the impression that under these circumstances there was a widespread feeling that the appropriate course of action was to attempt nothing looking to the future, to concentrate on the problems of the moment, and to join their emperor in "enduring the unendurable and suffering what is insufferable."

Finally, the Cabinet members concerned all had serious personal problems to deal with: ill-health, bombed-out houses, family casualties, friends in need, etc. These factors combine to explain their lack of advance attention to the larger issues presented by the imminence of the Allied Occupation.

It should at least be noted in passing, however, that such factors did not preclude a more practical type of advance planning where the allegedly illegal disposition of an estimated one hundred billion *yen* of public property is concerned. A report of December 20, 1947, of the lower House's Special Committee for the Investigation of Concealed and Hoarded Goods (the so-called Katō Committee) claims that the Suzuki Cabinet on August 14, 1945, hurriedly agreed to the widespread distribution to public and private organizations and persons of at least this amount of military stores and supplies other than arms and ammunition. Most of these are said to have found their way into black market channels, and the government is said to have realized little or nothing from the transaction. Since the formal obligations assumed by Japan as of that date involved only "the surrender of arms," it cannot really be said that such an action was illegal. Nor, in ignorance of the type of occupation and policies toward reparations that lay in store for the country, need its motivations necessarily have been discreditable.[10] Still it is interesting that one of the few positive initiatives taken by the Japanese government vis-à-vis the impending Occupation during this August 14–September 2 period should lie in such a field.

It is often claimed that a similar initiative was displayed with respect to Japanese civil and military officials who stood in danger of being charged as war criminals. It is certain that many such persons changed assignments and were sent to distant and inconspicuous posts during this period. There seems to be no evidence, however, that this was due to any deliberate

[10] An English translation of this highly critical report may be found in the *Political Reorientation of Japan*, II, 728-33.

policy or decision by the Cabinet, and it is quite possible that it was conceived and carried out largely at lower levels. As one former member of the Higashikuni Cabinet said: "Only fools and honest men stayed."

All this indicates that the Japanese government did not make any systematic or very significant use of the nineteen day period of grace that intervened between Japan's acceptance of the surrender terms on August 14 and the formal commencement of the Occupation on September 2. They appear to have been too absorbed with other and more urgent matters even to have contemplated the possibility or advantages of concerting in advance attitudes or strategies on issues bound to be presented by the Occupation. They do not even appear to have been seriously interested in obtaining advance information about the probable nature and policies of the Occupation.

To some this may seem strange; but in fact it is more probable that it is deeply characteristic of Japanese political attitudes and practice. From the standpoint of our present interest, however, the important thing is that Japan approached and entered the Occupation period in an uncommitted and potentially plastic posture. The sole official stand taken was in defense of the imperial system. The government had devised no counterstrategies and apparently had not even considered the possibility of any sort of antioccupation conspiracy in high places. The leadership structure remained intact and stood ready, however unhappily, to accept the Occupation and to carry out its orders. This was an enormous advantage from the standpoint of the goals that the United States hoped to achieve in Japan.

Strategy and Conduct of the Occupation

Once the Occupation was under way, the focus of attention tends to shift. While matters of goals and basic structure continue to be of importance—especially in the event of subsequent changes in either—questions of style and method become more important. How did the Occupation actually set about accomplishing its goals? What means did it employ? With what results? And, as in the presurrender phase, what was the role of the Japanese government and people in this process?

These are complicated questions and given the limitations of space and time, perhaps the best that can be done in the way of answering them is to select some of the more critical issues for summary treatment. Let us first attempt to dispose briefly of the questions of changing or evolving goals and of SCAP's organization for their accomplishment.

It will be recalled that the Joint Chiefs' initial directive to SCAP had very sensibly anticipated the possibility of future changes in the basic objectives set for the Occupation. Such changes did occur. Where the two principal objectives of demilitarization and democratization were concerned, those relating to the former were far more dramatic and drastic than those relating to the latter, but both goals underwent some change. Where _de_militarization was concerned, with the initiation of the "cold war" the United States' basic objective after the spring and summer of 1947 gradually shifted to _re_militarization. The question became not how to prevent Japan from again acquiring armament, but how to persuade her to rebuild her armed forces to the point where she could make a more meaningful contribution to the defense of what the United States saw as the causes of stability, security, and democracy in Eastern Asia and in the world. This was not an easy decision for the United States to reach, but the emerging situation in Eastern Asia and the world was such as to make a radically altered policy toward Japan imperative. Thus less than two years after the end of the most bitterly fought war in modern history, the United States was involved in an attempt to make its erstwhile enemy into its principal ally in the Far East.

Naturally, the effects of so fundamental a change in goals could not be confined to the issue of demilitarization versus remilitarization. It also brought about important changes in other spheres. The most important probably was the informal addition of a third basic goal: the economic rehabilitation of Japan. Actually it had never, as is frequently implied, been the policy of SCAP to abstain from either interference in or assistance to the Japanese economy. But it is certainly true that there was at this time a major change in both attitude and in the scale of economic assistance. After roughly January 1948 the reformulated basic objectives of the Occupation may, therefore, be stated as a trilogy: remilitarization, economic rehabilitation, and democratization.

It has frequently been claimed also that this shift in goals marked the abandonment of any serious attempts on the part of SCAP to democratize Japan. In fact this does not appear to be the case. Such judgments seem often to have rested on rather basic differences of opinion within SCAP as to what actually are the characteristics of a democratic society and hence as to what specific types of reforms were appropriate to its achievement in Japan, or they sprang from related disagreements as to the type, degree, and pace of democratic reform programs that it was desirable or realistic for SCAP to sponsor in Japan. It is also true that by early 1947 SCAP had become disenchanted with the left-wing socialists and the Japanese labor movement as instruments of political reform and taken steps to curb what it regarded as their irresponsible and extremist tactics. There is no doubt that the relative emphasis and priority accorded democratization appreciably diminished from late 1947 onward or that this was regarded as a betrayal or serious dilution of earlier objectives by some members of SCAP's staff. But it is also important to take into account that the pace of political reform slowed down because most of the basic new legislation on SCAP's agenda had been written and enforced prior to 1948, that increasing authority was being returned to the Japanese, and that they had begun to whittle away at the foundations of several of the SCAP-enforced changes that they found particularly obnoxious. It is excessive to claim that SCAP had lost interest in the democratization of Japan.

In the sense that there was a shift of emphasis where democratic reforms were concerned, there was some readjustment of both immediate goals and the groups among the Japanese population with which SCAP chose to cooperate. But this seems more a function of the phasing or timing of the Occupation's overall democratization program than it does of any conscious change of view about the desirability or feasibility of democratizing Japan. A study of the overall timing of the Occupation's activities will show that, when possible, it preferred to face its several responsibilities sequentially rather than in across-the-board fashion. At the outset the emphasis was necessarily on demilitarization and the rapid destruction of Japan's armed strength. This was essential to the security of the Occupation itself among other things. The period from September 2 to the end of November 1945 was largely occupied with such primary tasks as the disarmament, demobilization, and repatriation of Japan's armed forces.

The second stage was a preparatory and instrumental one that somewhat overlapped the first but, if one uses the test of dominant activity, it occupied the months of December 1945 and January 1946. This was a period primarily devoted to the establishment of civil and political rights; to the abolition of laws and institutions that restricted freedom of speech, of assembly, of the press, of religion, and of political organization and activity; and to the elaboration of the first purge, a measure intended to clear the way for the free selection and emergence of a new political elite.

There followed from February 1946 a third stage of much greater length and complexity. This was the period of the great political "reforms" and of most of the other major reform legislation as well. Action proceeded rapidly on a variety of fronts, and the periodicities were a bit different depending on the sphere involved: political, economic, social, etc. In the political area, the first part of this third period—down to November 1946—centered about the drafting and adoption of the new constitution, and the second part about the drafting, adoption, and enforcement of a great deal of ancillary legislation, much of it of major importance in its own right. The period as a whole may be said to have ended about November 1947.

Thereafter, between November 1947 and the outbreak of the Korean Incident in June 1950, two things happened: first, the goal of economic rehabilitation—and, incidentally, reform —for Japan intervened and became a major commitment in its own right. In one sense it, rather than political reform, came to occupy the center of the stage. But this period also marked the ascendancy of a new emphasis where political reform was concerned. Actually this had started considerably earlier, but had only become general practice by about the late fall of 1947. This was a period of consolidation and naturalization where the earlier spate of political reforms was concerned. SCAP had now attempted what it considered feasible and desirable in the way of political reform and, if the time had not yet arrived for putting an end to the Occupation, as General MacArthur had urged in March 1947, it was at least a period when it was judged desirable to experiment with a gradual and limited return of power and initiative to the Japanese government. If the SCAP-imposed reforms were to last beyond the Occupation period, it would only be because they had in critical degree gained acceptance by influential circles in Japan. The only way this could be determined was by trial. Accordingly, this was predominantly a time of tentative experimentation marked by increasing initiative on the Japanese side and by tinkering with details, critical observation, occasional positive forays, and the gradual assumption of a supervisory and protective, rather than an innovating role on the part of SCAP.

Then finally from June 1950 to the end of April 1952 one finds a period of rapidly diminishing engagement and authority on the part of SCAP. This is especially pronounced after

505

the relief of General MacArthur in April 1951. During this last stage the Occupation became more or less a formality, and the Japanese government recaptured the bulk of its domestic authority subject only to rather loose and inconsequential controls by a much reduced staff of Occupation officials.

None of the above dates is precise or beyond controversy and none of the five periods is meant to resemble a watertight compartment. There was invariably spillage at both ends, but they do seem to have a general validity and utility in terms of both central tendencies and of our search for an understanding of shifts in goals and methods of operation on SCAP's part. It is not claimed that such a periodicity and strategy were planned from the outset. There was certainly some thought given to it, especially in the initial stages, but the outcome was also to some degree unplanned and induced by circumstances that sometimes lay wholly beyond the control of SCAP. Whatever its precise provenance, however, the schema appears to describe with reasonable accuracy what actually took place, and it does seem relevant to the degree of success that the Occupation ultimately achieved.

Of importance also is the question of the suitability of the organization of SCAP to the accomplishment of the Occupation's goals. This must be considered at two levels: the central or headquarters level and the local level.

It has been noted earlier that General MacArthur chose not to establish a separate G-5 or military government staff section. Instead, after a brief period of experimentation, he settled for the establishment of a series of specialist staff sections that were more or less integrated into the structure of his regular headquarters in Tokyo, i.e. GHQ, SCAP. This headquarters was, incidentally, a command and staff operation and was structurally and physically quite separate from the arrangements for the actual conduct of the military occupation of Japan. The latter was the responsibility of a separate and subordinate command with its headquarters at Yokohama (and a second headquarters at Kyoto as well in the early days).

Within GHQ, SCAP, one found the normal structure of a field command. It was headed by General MacArthur assisted by a chief of staff and four general staff sections. Beneath this and responsible to the chief of staff were the specialist staff sections that actually ran the civilian aspects of the Occupation. By October 1945 there were nine. Later on their number increased to thirteen.

Two of these sections—Government Section and the Economic and Scientific Section—were both larger and generally regarded as being far more important than the others. In both cases the definition of their functions was so broad as to give them practically plenary authority in their respective fields. In some ways this was a distinct advantage; it normally conferred a compass of authority large enough to enable them to deal effectively with the massive problems confronting them without too much concern about trespassing on the preserves of other SCAP sections. Occasionally, however, it brought them into bitter jurisdictional conflict. In both cases also a large majority of their longterm staff members, although in uniform in the early days, were not career military personnel but civilians temporarily in the service. Many were persons of impressive dedication, talent, and ability.

In practice the Government Section enjoyed direct and frequent access to General MacArthur through its longtime chief, General Courtney Whitney. Thus it seems improbable that it was ever seriously impeded by a lack of sympathy or understanding for its plans by the layer of professional military command that theoretically was interposed between it and the commander in chief.

This may seem a somewhat cumbersome form of organization. Whatever the theory, all that can be said is that it usually worked with reasonable efficiency. This may have been due more, however, to its generous grant of authority and the quality of its staff members than to any merit inherent in the particular organizational pattern.

Where the local organization of the Occupation is concerned, it is difficult to see how any degree of individual talent could hope to compete successfully with the organizational shortcomings involved. Local military government teams had no direct or systematic connections with the specialist sections of GHQ. They were subordinate to Eighth Army Headquarters at Yokohama and were a part of its regular chain of command. In theory they also had no direct authority over their Japanese counterparts in the prefectures. They were supposed only to observe Japanese practices, supply informal advice, and complain to GHQ via their chain of command if they found Japanese practice to be not in accord with the directives. The fault would then be remedied by GHQ's transmitting the complaint to the appropriate ministry of the Japanese government and having it issue orders for its correction. It is difficult to conceive a pattern of organization less adequate to its tasks. It is equally interesting to speculate as to the price SCAP may have paid for adhering to it so long and stubbornly.

There remains the question of the method and style of operation used by SCAP to pursue its goals. Here the discussion will be confined to a few illustrations and brief comments drawn from three areas of major political importance: reform of the national bureaucracy, revision of the constitution, and electoral reform. These particular examples are selected because they so well illustrate a spread of SCAP methods and styles ranging from the most rigorous and inflexible sort of dictation, through dictation-cum-negotiation and modest compromise to almost complete laissez-faire. Let us start with the attempt to reform the higher bureaucracy at the national level.

In terms of its timing, the Occupation's attempt to reform the higher Japanese civil service is curious. It is out of phase with most of the other political reform activity. A few early and fairly meaningless gestures aside, it did not really get under way until the arrival of the United States Personnel Advisory Mission to Japan in December 1946. The commission submitted a final report in June 1947, and the first major piece of legislation in the field, the National Public Service

Law, was not enacted until October 21, 1947, the very end of the period of positive political reforms. But actually this was only the beginning of the legislation in this field. The chief of the Civil Service Division of the Government Section was out of Japan at the time the above law was debated in the Diet, extensively amended, and then enacted. He returned determined to repair the damage done through parliamentary amendments, and brought about a basic revision of the law in 1948 and a series of smaller changes in both 1948 and 1949. The Civil Service Division continued to be extremely active in connection with a variety of personnel laws, the establishment of the National Personnel Authority, and the conduct of civil service examinations well into 1950, after other divisions of the Government Section had long since begun to play a more passive and permissive role.

For present purposes, however, the notable thing about these attempts at civil service reform was the highly dogmatic and inflexible style of the SCAP personnel involved. While the Civil Service Division used Japanese informants extensively and thoroughly as sources of technical information, it is widely said to have sought or accepted no advice and to have brooked no protests from the Japanese. When the division's 1948 bill of amendment was sent to the Diet, it was accompanied by verbal orders that not a phrase was to be altered— an episode that rapidly became notorious in Japanese circles. Similarly, where the selection of the first commissioners for the new National Personnel Authority was concerned, the Civil Service Division seems to have picked its own slate and dictated their instalment in office.[11] The degree of arbitrariness involved seems quite remarkable in comparison with most other Government Section undertakings about which information is available.

The question, however, concerns not so much the justifica-

[11] The details of these affairs have been elaborately documented from the Japanese side. See in particular Satō Tatsuo, "Kokka Kōmuinhō seiritsu no keika," *Refuarensu*, nos. 138-39, pp. 1-15, 11-31.

tion for such a technique—a case can doubtless be made—but its consequences. The reform program involved has not failed in its entirety; some aspects remain today and are apt to continue. But it acquired so adverse a reputation in influential Japanese political and bureaucratic circles that it has been constantly on the defensive and vulnerable to attack to a degree that may well have been unnecessary. In practice this hostility has been strong enough to prevent the implementation of most of the features that lay at the heart of the reformed personnel system envisaged by the Civil Service Division: an effective classification plan; standardization of pay and promotion; a strong central personnel agency; and centralized approval for transfers and promotion. The Japanese government and people may well be none the worse off for this failure—the program in retrospect seems both extreme and dated—but some would argue that the cause of civil service reform in general has been unnecessarily and unwisely hampered in Japan by animosities and prejudices deriving from the dictatorial methods employed by the Civil Service Division.

Our second example will be drawn from the highly controversial field of constitutional revision. The principal developments involved are now well known.[12] After deciding that the Japanese government was not itself likely to produce a satisfactorily democratic draft of a revised constitution, the members of the Government Section in early February 1946, under orders from General MacArthur, secretly drafted a

[12] See, for example, Satō Tatsuo, *Nihonkoku Kempō seiritsushi* (Tokyo, 1962, 1965), 2 vols.; Kempō Chōsakai, *Kempō Chōsakai hōkokusho* (Tokyo, 1964) or, more particularly, the voluminous hearings and report of the commission's Subcommittee on the Establishment of the Constitution; Satō Tatsuo, "The Origin and Development of the Draft Constitution of Japan," *Contemporary Japan*, xxiv:iv-vi (1956), 175-89, and xxiv:vii-ix (1956), 371-87; Theodore McNelly, "The Japanese Constitution: Child of the Cold War," *Political Science Quarterly*, lxxiv (June 1959), 176-95; Robert E. Ward, "The Origins of the Present Japanese Constitution," *American Political Science Review*, l (December 1956), 980-1010.

model constitution for Japan. This was presented to representatives of the Japanese Cabinet on February 13, 1946, under circumstances that are not yet entirely clear but which certainly raise the presumption of considerable pressure by SCAP upon the Japanese to adopt this document or something very much like it as their own draft for purposes of constitutional revision. There followed a period of feverish negotiations between the Government Section and the Japanese government marked by a few concessions on SCAP's part but culminating in the acceptance by the Japanese of a document very close in wording and content to the original Government Section draft. At this point what had now become officially the Japanese government's own draft proposal for constitutional revision was published, discussed publicly and privately, revised again on several occasions, and finally introduced to the Diet, debated at length, amended (but always with specific advance consent from the Government Section), and finally adopted in November 1946 as the new constitution of Japan.

The procedure followed may not sound particularly permissive, and in most basic respects it was not. But there was more consultation by SCAP of Japanese sources and sentiments than has generally been recognized.[13] A number of the ideas embodied in the Government Section draft seem to have derived from earlier Japanese suggestions in the press and elsewhere; there was a good deal of discussion by Government Section officers with both Japanese officials and knowledgeable and influential private persons; there was also a strong and systematic attempt made by the Government Section to explain and justify their stands and to convince the Japanese of their merits. While it is quite true that there were definite

---

[13] Enough, for example, to lend some plausibility to the thesis espoused by Professor Takayanagi Kenzō, chairman of the Japanese government's Commission on the Constitution, that the constitution was not really imposed but was the fruit of American-Japanese cooperation. See *Kempō Chōsakai dai 114-kai sōkai gijiroku* (Tokyo, 1963), appendix entitled "Kempō no mondaiten ni tsuite no iken."

and rather exigent limits within which concessions were made, the total impression conveyed to the Japanese was different than in the case of the National Public Service Law. A surprising number of Japanese became convinced of the general desirability of the new constitution, while relatively few were actually aware of the precise nature and strength of the pressures brought to bear by SCAP to secure its enactment. At least the entire transaction, while observing the legally specified forms for constitutional change, did not widely acquire the reputation of arbitrarily and dogmatically imposed legislation to the extent that was true of the civil service "reforms."

The results have been rather startling. Not only the constitution but also practically all of the ancillary legislation involved became law. To be sure, there has subsequently been a fair amount of what SCAP would regard as "backsliding," especially in such areas as police, education, labor, and civil service law and practice. But far more surprising—and important—is the fact that the essentials of the constitutional reform are still in force, and that no revision of the wording of the document has even been seriously attempted in the twenty years since its enforcement. With the submission—in July 1964 after seven years' work—of the final report of the Japanese government's Commission on the Constitution, the issue of the desirability of revising the constitution has at last been publicly and forcefully posed.[14] But even with the dominant Liberal-Democratic Party and an overwhelming majority of the commission favoring some form of revision, the astonishing thing is how strongly entrenched the present constitution has become and how very difficult it promises to be for the government to obtain any form of amendment. This is,

[14] See note 11 above for a citation of the final report. Thirty-one of the thirty-eight members of the commission advocated some form of constitutional amendment. For a detailed account see Robert E. Ward, "The Commission on the Constitution and Prospects for Constitutional Change in Japan," *Journal of Asian Studies*, xxiv (May 1965), 401-29.

among other things, a tribute to the skill with which the Government Section did its work to begin with.

Our final example of SCAP's methods and style of operation is drawn from the field of election law, a basic and highly complex subject in any modern democratic society. Here the policy contrasted strongly with that followed in the two previous examples. SCAP did not lack positive views of importance in the field. In fact as early as October 11, 1945, General MacArthur in his initial interview with the new prime minister, Mr. Shidehara, directly ordered the enfranchisement of women.[15] Some Occupation influence may also have been involved in the reduction of the voting age from twenty-five to twenty, though this is more problematical. The Japanese claim that they were left a quite free hand to determine for themselves the nature and content of their new law governing elections to the lower house of the National Diet, although they were, of course, under orders to reform the existing laws in accordance with more democratic principles.[16]

Again the results are interesting to observe. Left more or less to their own devices, the Japanese first experimented with a large-district, plural-membership, multiple-vote system of limited proportional representation under the Law of December 1945 and—after this pleased no one in authority—reverted in March 1947 to substantially the same system as they had used before the war (medium-sized districts, multiple member constituencies, and single vote) with the addition of

[15] See *Political Reorientation of Japan*, II, 741.

[16] See, for example, Jichi Daigaku, *Sengo jichishi: shūgiin giin senkyohō no kaisei* (Tokyo, 1961), IV, *passim*. The views that follow are also based upon a number of interviews conducted by the author in 1963-1964 in Tokyo with such present or former election officials and specialists as Messrs. Aoki Masashi, Hayashi Keizō, Kobayashi Yosaji, Kōri Yūichi, Matsumura Kiyono, Miura Yoshio, Moji Ryō, Sakurazawa Tōeii, and Shimazaki Zengorō. Due to the controversy over the basic structure of the upper House, SCAP officials played a somewhat more active role with respect to its electoral system.

women suffrage and lower ages for voting and office-holding. This they still have in essence, though the law has been consolidated with other election statutes in the basic Public Offices Election Law of April 15, 1950. Practically all informed sources of all political persuasions will readily admit that the law is both unrepresentative and unsatisfactory in a great many important respects. Yet with the exception of minor tinkerings with the total number of seats and the reapportionment of a few of the most grossly underrepresented election districts such as took place in mid-1964, nothing can be done to improve the situation. The political pressures that have built up about the established system—no matter how poor it may be—are so great and the interests threatened by almost any form of change so critical, and their advocates so influential, that meaningful change has become extraordinarily difficult.

Here then is still another aspect of the changes flowing from SCAP's activities in Japan. The most minimal of guidance and pressure by SCAP resulted in a correspondingly low level of institutional change by the Japanese, if one neglects the short-lived experiment represented by the Law of December 1945. To be sure there have been changes in the field of election administration, but the basic electoral system has changed very little. It has proved in practice to be almost as hard to revise as the constitution.

Finally, in bringing this section to a close a few words must be said about the manner in which the Occupation itself was brought to a close, that is about the termination of this experiment in democratization. The probable duration of the Occupation had been vague from the beginning. Toward the end of the war and during the very early days of the Occupation when the overriding goal for most Americans was the maintenance of future peace and security, it was common to speak in terms of twenty-five years or a generation as a minimal period for the international supervision and control of Japan. Then as political pressures mounted for the return of the troops from overseas and as the cost of conducting the Occupation became clear to more Americans, who—alone with the Japanese—were paying for it, this view lost support rather rapidly. No single policy replaced it, partially because of the impossibility of judging in the early period just when it would be appropriate and feasible to end the operation without undue risk to its ultimate objectives and partially because the problem was complicated by so many international considerations. Practically speaking, the termination of the Occupation involved the negotiation of a treaty of peace with Japan. This could not be done as a result of a unilateral decision on the part of the United States but had to command the broadest possible approval and support among the Allied governments. This was very difficult to obtain.

Under these circumstances several viewpoints developed as to an optimal duration for the Occupation. It will be recalled that General MacArthur at an informal press conference in March 1947 suggested that the time to bring it to an end had already arrived. This came as a shock to many, but the United States government did take up the proposal and attempted in 1947 to obtain general agreement to a peace treaty that would end the Occupation but continue a form of international control over Japanese rearmament. This effort foundered, however, on policy disagreements with Australia, Russia, and China. Nothing further was done at a formal level until Mr. Dulles took the matter in hand in 1950 and obtained the decisions and agreements that led to the signing of the Treaty of San Francisco in September 1951. The Occupation ended formally when the Treaty took effect on April 28, 1952. It had lasted in all for six years and eight months.

It should be noted, however, that in a domestic sense power in most areas had gradually been restored to the Japanese government since the end of 1947 and that positive SCAP intervention in the decisions and workings of the Japanese government was rare after the outbreak of the Korean Incident in June 1950. Thus for many purposes the Occupation may be said to have ceased to play a major role on the Japanese domestic scene some time before it came to a formal conclusion.

It is of some importance also that the end of the Occupation did not mark a clean severance of either the American presence or American influence in Japan. The Security Treaty provided for the retention of American bases and the maintenance of American garrison forces, although these had no Occupation-like functions or authority. More significant probably is the extent and complexity of the economic relationships and ties between the two countries that were established during the Occupation but which have since greatly expanded. Thus out of the Occupation has developed nothing resembling the *status quo ante bellum* but a close, interdependent, and continuing relationship that extends to the political and military as well as the economic fields.

Conclusions

There remains the question posed at the outset. If the foregoing sections are accepted as a rather sketchy summary of principal facts about the Occupation that seem relevant to the degree of success it achieved in the field of "planned" or "directed" political change, what do they add up to? What do they suggest in connection with the general problems attendant upon any attempt by foreigners to control or direct the course of political change in an alien society? While obviously it would be excessive to maintain that the single case of the Japanese Occupation can establish any generally valid proposition with respect to so complex and variable a problem, still the experience gained there is certainly relevant. Although it can prove nothing, it may suggest a good deal. Let us see.

One of the most important factors in determining what degree of success or failure attended upon SCAP's various endeavors was undoubtedly the Japanese themselves. Their attitudes and their contributions and what might be termed their state of national readiness or preparation for the sorts of political change espoused by the Occupation are of critical

516

importance. This is a subject of such complexity, however, that it seems best to confine our treatment to pointing out a few of the most relevant facts.

For example, in all three of the fields and cases outlined above—bureaucratic, constitutional, and electoral reform—Japan's own pre-Occupation experience was rich, deep, and varied. The origins of the modern Japanese bureaucracy go back to at least the end of the seventeenth century, and many of the institutions, attitudes, and practices involved in the establishment and maintenance of an efficient modern civil service appeared in Japan long before the Restoration.[17] Where constitutions are concerned, it is not necessary to go back to Shōtoku Taishi or to the Taika Reform of A.D. 646. The Meiji constitution of 1889–1890 will suffice. It was fully as "modern" as any of its contemporary counterparts and, given its premises and aims, a truly impressive testimony to the political insight and genius of the founders of modern Japan. By 1945 the Japanese people had had at least fifty-five years of experience with constitutional government. In terms of modern electoral systems, Japanese experience also goes back to at least 1890 and thereafter gradually evolves through a series of five basic laws and revisions over a fifty-five year period. The changes made in 1945, while of great political importance, merely added another level to a structure that had long been developing quite independently of the American presence or influence, so that the first point to be made about the Japanese role in these postwar political changes relates to the historical depth and the "maturity" of Japan's own experience with most of the basic institutions concerned. They were in no sense strangers to the mechanics of a democratic political system.

It is equally notable that the Japanese populace was already at the outset of the Occupation a remarkably literate, well-educated, and politically experienced national group. All of

[17] See John Whitney Hall, "The Nature of Traditional Society: Japan," in Robert E. Ward and Dankwart A. Rustow, *Political Modernization in Japan and Turkey* (Princeton, 1964), pp. 27-35.

the mass media and educational apparatus for reaching them, presenting a case, and attempting to influence their views and practices were ready at hand. These media had only to be commandeered and put to use on the Occupation's behalf. The problem was one of manipulating an already modern and well-developed national communications system—not necessarily a simple undertaking, but far easier than creating one from scratch.

It was also the case that there had been sufficient diversity and development within the political experience of most living Japanese to insure that once the initial shock was over the Occupation did not have to face monolithic domestic opposition to their political plans. The years of so-called "liberal parliamentary government (roughly 1924-1932) were not far in the background. At the outset of the Occupation there were still sizable numbers of Japanese with latent intellectual, emotional, or practical preferences for a parliamentary system of government who either honestly disapproved of the recent militarism and ultranationalism or at least deplored its consequences and were seeking some sort of alternative. Thus there was a considerable potentiality for political changes of a democratic sort in Japan. Whether or to what extent this would ultimately have been realized in the Occupation's absence is very difficult to say, but in practice SCAP was able to create an environment that positively encouraged its emergence and development.

This process was, of course, substantially aided by the fact that the Occupation was in a position to make exceedingly difficult or impossible the simultaneous emergence of any large-scale organized opposition movement committed to traditional or nondemocratic principles. SCAP held the field for those who at least professed democratic sentiments and excluded all others. Of course the process of change was also greatly facilitated by widespread popular disillusionment with the merits and efficacy of traditional political institutions due to the experiences of war and defeat and by the absence of an organized and recognized leadership actively pursuing non-democratic goals. In these senses Japan's defeat created a useful ideological vacuum of which SCAP promptly took advantage. Important too was the unity and discipline of both the Japanese people and their leaders. The structure of authority never broke down, the basic loyalty and obedience of the citizenry never faltered.[18] The entire system remained operational and was thus available for immediate takeover and exploitation by the conquerors.

All of these were factors of basic importance that testify to the potentiality for political change present in Japan at the outset of the Occupation. It is very doubtful that the degree of change actually accomplished would have been possible in their absence. Abstractly, however, it is possible to speculate that had the war ended without an Occupation committed to the achievement of far-reaching sociopolitical goals, but perhaps instead just to arms control and the extraction of reparations, this potentiality would in time have developed along lines essentially similar to those that have actually transpired. Except in a very long-term sense, however, the history of the Occupation does not encourage such an interpretation. Too much of what occurred was due wholly or largely to SCAP initiatives and pressures, while the relatively few cases of official Japanese initiative were decidedly modest in terms of the political changes involved. Furthermore, it is seldom clear that they too were not largely responsive to environmental or more specific pressures created by the very existence of SCAP and its known goals.

This in no sense represents an attempt to minimize the important degree of positive assistance and cooperation that SCAP received from a sizable number of individual Japanese, sometimes in highly unlikely positions and circumstances. This was very helpful to the total effort, but the important

[18] One cannot help but wonder if this would still have been the case had Japan, like Germany, actually been invaded and fought over.

point is that it was largely individual rather than systemic in character. The total governmental apparatus involved on the Japanese side in the taking of initiatives of a reforming nature seldom displayed the same courage or inventiveness that some of its individual members did. As a consequence SCAP initiatives were usually essential to impel the Japanese government to action.

One is tempted to note parenthetically the suspicion that SCAP perhaps seriously underestimated this potential for individual or sectoral initiatives and cooperation within the Japanese government. There was, for example, a conviction that seems to have amounted to gospel in Occupation circles that the Ministry of Internal Affairs (Naimushō) was the center of a continual series of conspiracies against the success of cherished reform plans. While there was certainly some justification for this, there are also grounds for feeling that the conviction was arrived at too facilely and without adequate investigation of the chances for a more cooperative relationship. The writer has frequently been surprised by the views expressed—retrospectively it is true, but in contexts that are occasionally checkable—by individuals then holding important posts in that ministry.

The foregoing views are not intended, therefore, to derogate from the essentiality to the Occupation's results of the above-described Japanese potentiality for democratic political change, but they do point up the basically indeterminate nature of such a potentiality. To it had to be added both a catalytic agent and positive direction. These needs were supplied by SCAP. Let us see in general terms how this was done. What factors in the policies, structure, and methods of the Occupation seem to have contributed to or detracted from its results?

SCAP was undoubtedly very fortunate with respect to the quality and decisiveness of the presurrender planning for the Occupation. Both the United States Initial Post-Surrender Policy for Japan and the related directive from the Joint Chiefs of Staff to General MacArthur are remarkably prescient and cogent documents. They provide, admirably in most respects, the sorts of general policy guidelines that a field commander needs in such circumstances. More specifically they were useful to the long-range endeavor in the following ways:

First, they represented a policy-in-being that was operationally feasible. One of the great historic difficulties of nations confronted with the problems of making postwar plans while hostilities are still going on has been an inability to reach timely and practicable decisions either singly or collectively. As a consequence there is apt to be a more or less policyless period of indefinite duration following the end of hostilities while all concerned debate the issues at length and often with acrimony. Since something has to be done with the defeated peoples in the meantime, this interim period is likely to be filled by improvisations determined on the spot or elsewhere. These often turn out to be highly disadvantageous, but they are also often difficult to uproot and change once given a start. At least this was not the situation of the United States where Japan was concerned. The nineteen day period between the armistice and formal surrender proved not to be detrimental, and by September 2, 1945, the United States had a reasonably clear general idea of what it wanted to do with a defeated Japan and how it proposed to go about it. Abstractly viewed, this may seem to be no more than should be expected of any government possessed of a modicum of intelligence and responsibility. Historically viewed, it is rather remarkable.

Second, the policies established prior to the surrender set actionable and reasonable goals. It is of secondary importance from the present standpoint that these later underwent changes. It is more important that during the critical early days—actually for the first two years—there was spelled out for SCAP's guidance an entire range of political, economic, and social goals ranging from the ultimate to the quite specific. And when these did change in the winter of 1947/1948, it is notable that the shift affected primarily the military and

521

economic and not the political dimension of SCAP's mission. Democratization remained a major goal throughout the Occupation.

Third, it seems highly probable that, in this particular context at least, the consolidation of authority first in the hands of a single government and second in the hands of a single individual conferred great administrative advantages. A judgment of this sort cannot be proved and is, furthermore, contingent in the given instance on the quality and policies of the government and the individual concerned. But one can gain some insight in this case into the probable quality of the policy determination or control that might alternatively have been provided by a small and select international body through browsing among the records of the Far Eastern Commission. The experience is not encouraging.

Where the consolidation of authority in the hands of a single individual is concerned, this was largely inevitable in the case of Japan once the initial decision that United States policy was to predominate had been taken. The undertaking was at the outset essentially military and retained an important military dimension for a long time thereafter. It was almost inconceivable that the United States government would entrust its control to other than an individual theater commander. This posed questions, of course, about the suitability of the professional military as agents of democratization, but the implied dilemma seems largely specious. The individuals actually staffing the specialist sections of SCAP were seldom anything but civilians in uniform, while, of course, it was never pretended that a military occupation and full democracy could coexist in Japan. Obviously this was a period of tutelary and limited democracy, so long as the Occupation retained the ultimate controls. Moreover, the Occupation had several goals, of which democratization was only one, and at first not even the primary one.

It was conceivable once the critical early days of the Occupation had passed that the United States government might have elected to replace its military commander by a civilian or perhaps by some form of collegial authority. This was actually discussed, but the stature of General MacArthur and the quality of his performance combined with the domestic and international problems that would have been posed by such an exchange argued against it. As a consequence it is impossible to distinguish between the advantages for the Occupation flowing from the centralization of authority in a single man and the advantages that flowed from the truly impressive personal capacities and accomplishments of General MacArthur. One can only suspect that the organizational device itself confers some positive advantages in this sort of situation.

Fourth, the decision to administer the Occupation indirectly through the Japanese government rather than directly through American military government teams turned out to be very helpful. Of course it can also be said in retrospect that any other decision would probably have led to chaos, but this was not clear at the time. The principal value derived from the system of indirect administration was the fact that it gave to the legally established and generally accepted government of Japan a positive, if limited, stake in supporting the Occupation and its programs, and thus gained for the Occupation the advantages of acting through established, legal channels that were in this case undoubtedly more efficient than any arrangements we might have been able to improvise in their place. It was a device for imposing responsibility upon the Japanese and of making them into more or less reluctant partners in the remaking of their own political system. There is no better nor more ironic example of this than the way in which the Shidehara and Yoshida Cabinets were used by SCAP to sponsor the new constitution.

From the Occupation's standpoint the sanctions and the safeguards for such an arrangement were stronger than may well have been realized at the outset. They were, first, the natural desire of any government to survive as a government, to maintain itself in power; and, second, the Janus-faced fears of the conservative group in control of Japanese politics at the time as to the actions SCAP might take if seriously provoked and as to the unpredictable nature and policies of the government that might succeed them should they resign or be ousted from office. From their standpoint there was a great deal that was precious to be salvaged or protected in Japan, and they regarded themselves as the group best equipped to discharge these responsibilities. By exploiting such factors in some quarters in conjunction with the positive good will and support available in others it was possible for SCAP to elicit a remarkable degree of positive cooperation from the Japanese government. This would probably not have been available in comparable degree under a directly administered occupation, and its absence might well have been critical.

Finally, among these policies adopted prior to the surrender the decision to place a greater emphasis on "constructive" relationships with the Japanese people than on retribution or vengeance was undoubtedly most useful. The retributive elements were, of course, present, but they bore most harshly and directly upon a minority of the Japanese people: in particular on residents or investors in the lost imperial territories overseas and on career military officers and others who could be portrayed as tainted with "war guilt" or war crimes. And since in some degree these same minorities became in Japanese eyes scapegoats for the national failure and defeat, the adverse consequences for the Occupation were of minor degree. Toward the remainder of the population the policy in both official and personal relationships became, after a brief initial period of concern on security grounds, positive and often friendly. The emphasis was on building a better Japan with justice and, eventually, prosperity and happiness for all her citizens. While such claims were doubtless received with skepticism in the beginning, their plausibility was gradually enhanced by the general good conduct of the troops (especially in the critical early days), by the importation at American initiative of food and relief supplies from abroad, and by the manifest interest, good will, and good intentions of most of the personnel staffing SCAP's headquarters. The result was to moderate the natural tendencies among Japanese toward despair for the national future and to afford positive grounds for hope, for constructive effort, and for cooperation. Much of the credit belongs, of course, to the Japanese people themselves, who displayed remarkable resilience, courage, and discipline. But it is also true that Occupation policies were well calculated to foster this result.

The foregoing were all policies designed in Washington in advance of the actual beginning of the Occupation. They all represent instances of intelligent and realistic planning for an Occupation that still lay in the future and have been selected for comment precisely for this reason; they do seem to be positively related to the degree of success that the Occupation subsequently achieved. It is not intended to imply, however, that the presurrender planning documents were in all respects this prescient and practicable. Obviously they were not, as what has already been said about later shifts in their goals should make clear. They also fall considerably short of the mark in such fields as reparations, economic rehabilitation, deconcentration, demilitarization, and domestic insurrection. But on the whole they were soundest in the areas of long-range democratization and the basic structure and authority of the Occupation. In these fields the major goals did not really change and the presurrender planning remained valid and useful.

Where the specific structure and organization of the Occupation is concerned, it is hard to discern features beyond the complete and consolidated nature of its authority that conferred any particular advantages. If anything, one is tempted to conclude that it succeeded in spite rather than because of any merits inherent in its organizational forms or practices.

At the national level, below the level of the Supreme Commander himself, it grafted an awkward array of predominantly civilian specialist sections onto the normal structure of a military general staff, thus creating a sort of built-in antagonism that was more serious in its consequences for some sections than for others. Some provision for intersectional coordination, planning, and clearance was made through the technical subordination of all specialist sections to the office of the chief of staff. But it is not apparent that this was very effective in operation. Staff conferences bringing the heads of the specialist sections together with the Supreme Commander were completely unknown during General MacArthur's regime, that is for almost seven eighths of the total duration of the Occupation. The result seems in practice to have resembled a somewhat lopsided species of bifurcated absolute monarchy with final power consolidated and tightly held at the top but with provisional authority dispersed at lower levels between military and specialist satrapies with at least a technical edge bestowed upon the former. In practice this disadvantage for the specialist sections was probably offset, for some at least, by the direct access their chiefs enjoyed to General MacArthur as well as by the fact that they were in direct control of the Occupation's most important programs and areas of activity and thus possessed the advantages of initiative, specialized knowledge, and continuous liaison with their Japanese counterparts. Despite this, it is hard to discern any positive merit to an organizational pattern of this sort.

One suspects that it worked as well as it did largely because of the quality of many of its critically placed personnel. This is a judgment manifestly true of General MacArthur himself, who, however flamboyant, was an extraordinarily talented and inspiring leader and the sort of person who could pull together and extract the utmost from even a structure such as this. Of equal importance is the fact that he was able to assemble, especially in the early period, a remarkably competent and devoted group of civilians and military to staff the critical posts in the more important specialist sections. Little is known about this group in a collective sense, but judging both from the quality of their results and the impression they made upon their Japanese counterparts, a large share of the credit for the success of the Occupation belongs to this civilian-military group.

The organization of the Occupation at the local level throughout Japan was a much more serious detriment to the achievement of the Occupation's goals than any of the short-comings attributed to the national level. The structure adopted can only be explained as due to an ill-considered preference for subordinating all field operations, whatever their character, to the army's normal chain of field command. While this may have been reasonable in the very early days when there was real concern on security grounds, this justification disappeared within a few months. Thereafter, the explanation seems to lie more in the logistical convenience and general "tidiness" of the arrangement combined with a sensitivity to the claims of military amour-propre rather than in the functional needs of the situation.

In the absence of experience with a more rational system of local organization, it is impossible to determine how high a price the Occupation paid for this shortcoming. It is uncertain, for example, that its local autonomy program could—or, some might add, should—have succeeded under any circumstances. But SCAP probably sacrificed whatever chances the program may have enjoyed through the ineffectuality of the arrangements for its local implementation and supervision. Ironically enough, what success SCAP did enjoy at the local level was quite possibly due in substantial part to the efficacy of Tokyo's centralized controls throughout the country, in other words to precisely the phenomenon that SCAP was seeking to destroy. The result was that the really effective work of the Occupation was done largely in Tokyo. The dangers implicit within such a narrow concentration of impact were, however, appreciably offset by the degree to which the Japanese political and decision-making apparatus was itself centered in Tokyo.

The immediate reasons for the Occupation's successes in bringing about important political changes in Japan lay, however, more in the area of <u>methods</u> than of advance planning or organization. One method in particular was used in connection with a large proportion of the reform programs that have survived the end of the Occupation and thus demonstrated a vitality of their own. This is basically very simple and forthright, yet it is hard to say in retrospect just how explicitly it figured in the minds and planning of the responsible officers of the Government Section at the time the major programs were designed. One suspects that it <u>emerged gradually</u> with experience and at first probably in somewhat more particularistic terms. This is the method that we will call "the creation of new vested interests."

The method requires first of all a <u>clientele</u>. The more positively and actively this clientele is aware of and identifies with the <u>interest</u> concerned, the better the chances of speedy success and durable establishment for the proposed reform program. In practice, however, a rather broad spectrum of possibilities is usually involved. The second stage centers about the <u>activation</u> of this clientele group. If it is already well aware of its own identity and stake in the program concerned and is organized for its <u>accomplishment</u>, the task of the reformer is much simplified. If not, a preparatory campaign to <u>educate</u> and <u>mobilize</u> the group is desirable. The third stage usually involves the enactment of <u>reform legislation</u> and the formal establishment of new rights, institutions, and practices for the clientele involved. In effect rights that have been sought, or at least aspired to, are now accorded legal status and recognition, and in this sense the group concerned is given a <u>new vested</u> interest in their protection and further expansion. This is the essence of the method of reform through the creation of new vested rights. There is nothing mysterious or new about it. Essentially it is very much the manner in which major political changes have always come about. This is simply a somewhat self-conscious and mechanistic way of dissecting the processes involved.

It should also be pointed out, especially in situations where such programs of change are externally imposed, as was the case in Japan, that the method may well also have additional unintended and unwanted stages. A fourth would be, for example, the stage of reaction or of the pendular swing. This occurs when a native leadership group or one hostile to the reform program gains sufficient power to set about its repeal or qualification. If the program was soundly conceived and executed to begin with, it may be surprisingly difficult for such a group to achieve its goals. But quite probably the group can accomplish something along these lines, by administrative subversion if not by explicit legislation. The critical question at this stage, of course, is: "How far back will the pendulum swing?" Incidentally this is an argument for the would-be reformer to set his initial goals somewhat higher and more expansively than he really thinks the situation warrants. If one is fortunate, this tactic may then provide fat rather than flesh and blood to absorb some or most of the subsequent cutting. The judgments involved are subtle and difficult, but there is reason to believe that SCAP sometimes attempted this.

Let us consider briefly the applicability of this method to the three examples of SCAP's methods of operation described earlier: the bureaucratic reform, the revision of the constitution, and electoral reform. It has been pointed out that the Occupation's efforts to reform the higher civil service in Japan were largely a failure in terms of the standards the Civil Service Division set for itself. One suspects that a basic reason for this was the failure to establish and cultivate a clientele group of adequate size and influence. The problem was not completely ignored. They did set up a training and indoctrination program, but it reached essentially only a relatively small number of junior and middle-level bureaucrats who were being groomed specifically for personnel work. The vast bulk and especially the top levels of the higher bureaucracy were left largely untouched. Furthermore, the attitudes and tactics of some at least of the group of American specialists involved were calculated, unintentionally of course, to alienate support and engender active hostility in both Japanese bureaucratic and political circles. As a consequence the number and influence of the "converted," i.e. of the clientele group, was much too small to have more than a peripheral influence on recruitment, promotion, transfer, and pay practices among the higher bureaucracy. The program in most fundamental respects, therefore, never got beyond the generalities of the legislation that the Civil Service Division was able to place on the statute books.

The case of the constitution was quite different. Here there are built-in appeals to the interests of a bewildering array of clientele groups that in one guise or another includes a large majority of the Japanese people. It grants new and enlarged rights of political participation and control to the common people everywhere; it expands greatly the civil rights and protection accorded almost everyone; it makes special appeals to groups as large and diverse as women, youth, scholars, labor, farmers, and the aged. It would take quite a while simply to list the various special and general clientele groups concerned.

The results to date have involved a limited amount of subsequent subversion or evasion of the document's original intent, often by administrative means. But far more remarkable has been the degree to which its provisions have been followed and enforced. The ultimate testimonial has been the difficulties encountered by the politically powerful elements who want to revise the constitution. In at least thirteen years of overt efforts they have not been able to rewrite a single clause nor have they ever felt their position strong enough to sponsor so much as a serious bill of amendment in the Diet. In fact implementing legislation for Article 96, the amendment clause, has never been enacted. Even though they have now obtained from the official Commission on the Constitution—after seven years of study and deliberation—a report that endorses some form of constitutional revision by the overwhelming majority of thirty-one to seven, they are confronted with seemingly insuperable obstacles in acting upon these recommendations. The Government Section architects of the present constitution built their edifice on a foundation of groups and interests that has proved both strong and durable. In fact they might themselves be pleasantly surprised at how difficult it has been to alter their creation.

The case of electoral reform provides a somewhat different *(3)* sort of insight. Here SCAP confined itself to a much more limited role. It may have been responsible, either directly or indirectly, for both women suffrage and the lowering of the voting and eligibility ages as well as for important changes in election administration. Beyond that it seems to have left the revision of the election laws largely to the Japanese. Where both women suffrage and the enfranchisement of the age group from twenty to twenty-five is concerned, the clienteles involved are large and obvious. They were also easy to mobilize in support of their newly vested rights, and at present it would take an unusually courageous or foolhardy politician to seek formally to deprive either of them of their new electoral rights. But it has been far more difficult, or perhaps there has merely been a much greater reluctance to try, to mobilize an adequate clientele to support more sophisticated types of electoral reform. There are few, if any, political changes that are more overdue or more urgently needed in contemporary Japan than a thoroughgoing overhaul of the present laws regarding voting districts, apportionment, balloting, and the relations of political parties to the electoral system. Yet in practice no type of reform has been more difficult to achieve. Adequate clientele groups to press for and support such changes exist in a latent sense, but it is difficult to activate them and, to a degree, unreasonable to expect that a real effort to do so will be made by political figures who are, after all, beneficiaries of the status quo.

This leads one to reflect that one important comment to be made about the Occupation as an experiment in directed political change may well relate to its omissions rather than its actions. Electoral reform is and long has been one of Japan's most urgent needs. At the same time it is a field in which it is peculiarly difficult for Japanese leaders either to sponsor or to effect meaningful changes. In short this would seem to be a field par excellence for foreign-sponsored initiatives and reforms. Yet in practice—beyond the two areas mentioned plus the field of election administration—little seems to have been attempted and almost nothing accomplished. It is hard to understand why this should have been so.

The case is not an isolated one. There are other examples of a similar holding back on the part of SCAP in areas where it does not seem either perfectionist or unrealistic to anticipate interest and activity on their part, e.g. the internal organization and operations of political parties or of labor unions and other major interest associations. One does not know if these represent oversights or deliberate decisions. But the important thing to point out from the standpoint of our present interest is that they have proved to be omissions of major importance. While it remains uncertain, of course, that they were amenable to amelioration by SCAP action, the possibility certainly exists and there are grounds for regret that the endeavor was not made.

In this consideration of factors affecting the success of the Occupation as an experiment in directed political change a word should be said also about the subject of the phasing or timing of SCAP's programs. Earlier we divided the Occupation into five principal periods and noted that practically all of the major political reforms fell into the third of these (February 1946–November 1947). In fact most of them predate May of 1947, which is to say that they were effectuated during the first twenty months of the Occupation—or an even shorter compass of time, about fifteen months, if one discards the September 1945–January 1946 period during which other matters necessarily received priority.

In retrospect it seems to have been wise to crowd SCAP's agenda of basic political reforms into this brief and this early

a period. There are at least two cogent arguments favoring
such a policy. The first is that in an indirectly administered
Occupation there is a strong tendency for the occupied government to reacquire actual power and initiative simply as a
result of the passage of time. It is best to put through the
major reforms before its power of covert opposition and sabotage and its disposition to engage in such tactics becomes too
great. This is a factor that, among others, may have contributed to the failure of the civil service reforms. They simply
started too late. The second reason is that an early start permits time for rectifying errors and for a proper phasing of the
experiment, for a gradual relaxation of Occupation initiative
and control and a concomitant return of authority to the Japanese, with diminishing supervision as warranted by performance. This is important. If the particular reform is not permitted to naturalize itself to some degree—to find its place in
the overall Japanese political system in this case—its chances
of survival are likely to be seriously jeopardized. In general
the Government Section was quite farsighted on this score. It
saw these facts clearly and worked with varying success to
bring about such a phasing where all reforms were concerned.
In the cases of most of the major political reforms, a period
of more than four years was available for testing and for the
gradual phasing out of SCAP control and supervision.

Also related to this question of phasing are the terms under
which the Occupation ended. The degree of stability and capacity for survival conferred on the Occupation's political reforms by the fact that American influence in Japan did not
abruptly end on April 28, 1952, is impossible to assess with
any precision. The present writer doubts that either the Security Treaty or the economic relationships involved have
been in their own right factors of major importance. But it
would be foolish to deny that the continuing involvement
with each other's affairs and policies and the degree of economic interdependence established between Japan and the
United States at least contributed to the creation of an environ-

533

ment generally favorable to the survival of the earlier reforms.

Finally, there is one further matter that seems to have been of major importance to an explanation of results. This is what might be described as an inertial factor. Political changes, once given a fair start and foothold, tend to perpetuate themselves. And perhaps their ability to do so successfully is almost geometrically increased according to the degree to which they are imbedded in a compatible system of changes rather than standing alone.

This is what happened in Japan. The Occupation faced its task in an across-the-board manner. It engendered an entire system of changes that penetrated deeply into most major sectors of Japanese social structure and practice. The system may not have been complete, but it was comprehensive. The political changes involved may be viewed as a major subsystem composed of interconnected and often mutually supportive elements, and the whole imbedded in the framework of a larger and also generally supportive system of new social and economic institutions and practices. No such system is, of course, invulnerable to attack or further change, but it becomes a tougher opponent than would be the case if each of its elements stood alone and unsupported.

In the case of the Japanese political system the overall effect of the several programs of political reform was to bring about a basic and long-range shift in the terms of political competition in Japan. The nation's political leadership groups came to be chosen in new ways; new criteria of selection became operative; new skills and new attitudes had to be cultivated to qualify successfully under these changed conditions; and new political institutions and instruments had to be mastered. Save in the institutional and legal sense, the changes involved were neither massive nor sudden. But there are grounds for believing that slowly and cumulatively the forces set in motion by these institutional and legal changes are producing a quite different form of both political leadership and political competition in Japan. These are not necessarily better than the old

534

in all respects, nor do they necessarily conform to the Occupation's plans or hopes. But in a generic sense they are of the democratic type. Both their merits and their faults are increasingly of a sort made familiar through the earlier history of democratic development in the West.

The combination of the developmental potential present in Japan with this factor of the developmental inertia generated by SCAP's systematic efforts to change the terms of political competition in Japan along more democratic lines may be as basic a reason as can be assigned for the success of the Occupation's experiments. In this light "control" is doubtless too strong a term, but the Occupation certainly can claim to have succeeded in "directing" the general course of political change in postwar Japan.

CHAPTER XIV

The Politics of Japan's Modernization: The Autonomy of Choice

ARDATH W. BURKS

IN AN age when the administrative state in its intrusive and awesome effects is ubiquitous, it is surprising that anyone should seriously question the relative autonomy of political decision-making. In the treatment of modernization generally and of the transformation of Japan specifically, however, it often appears that political factors in the drama of change are the most often overlooked. In an age of reason, complete with models and computer-supplied data, it may be natural to assume that nonpolitical forces (historical, psychological, social, economic, and geographic) determine all outcomes, but it is unfortunate. Too often one set of forces is singled out and identified as the causal factor. Many Japanese writers are well known for assuming the inevitability of history. What happened did happen, and it had to happen. This leaves little room for choice. Others are less certain on this score, however, and their disagreements give rise to a certain amount of confusion.

Nothing quite so well illustrates this sort of confusion as do the attitudes toward the modernization of their own country held by a large number of Japanese observers. In February 1964 at the Japan Socialist Party Congress, for example, an organ of the party submitted for general discussion a paper entitled "The Basic Attitude of the JSP toward Cultural Problems." The document in official translation reads, in part, "After the Meiji Restoration (1868) the dual structure [imported and indigenous] took the forms of modern European culture and Japanese national culture. Before the war there

537

was, on the one hand, modern capitalist culture and on the other backward, pre-modern culture, and this dual structure has survived, though in a changed form. . . . In tackling the problem of reforming Japanese culture, we must size up carefully the dual structure of culture—imported culture and national culture, modern culture and traditional culture—and must, above all, assume the attitude of reforming wholesale the culture of modern monopoly capitalist society."[1]

The assumptions behind such a statement are intriguing. Obviously culture is treated more or less as it is by Mao Tse-tung—as derivative and not basic. Socioeconomic labels are affixed to the specimens: "dual structure," "modern, capitalist culture," "backward, pre-modern culture," "modern monopoly capitalist society." Equally fascinating are the cultural labels: "imported culture," "indigenous culture" and "modern European," "Japanese national," "modern," and "traditional" cultures.

Note that the Socialists imply hereby that Japanese should have a cultural policy. Culture apparently is not for them just a superstructure (made up of beliefs, religions, philosophy, and law), reflecting the class structure of society, which in turn reflects a still more basic substructure (technology, economics, mode of production), to repeat the Marxist schema. The JSP apparently can do something about culture straight off. Its choice of cultures, although limited, nevertheless falls within the limits of political choice.

Countless other examples could be cited. Former Ambassador Edwin O. Reischauer, in his role as professional historian, has written extensively on the problem of Japan's modernization. His views were promptly dismissed by some as "official," the so-called Reischauer line, and defended by others against critics who, it was said, parroted the "Mao Tse-tung line." One Japanese critic in successive breaths even claimed: (1) that Japanese intellectuals (*interi*)—as well as the "masses"—have

[1] "Culture and Socialists: Basic JSP Attitude toward Cultural Problems," *Japan Socialist Review*, LXI (May 1, 1964), 50-52.

been unable to adapt themselves to the modernization process; (2) that Japan's history is one of "abnormal adaptability"; (3) that paternalism prevented the Japanese from assuming a "modern state consciousness" and made them apathetic to politics; and (4) that Japanese have had "an excess of political consciousness."[2] As one Japanese expert put it, most of his colleagues are either "social scientists" attempting to apply their tailor-made theories to history, or "social reformers, leftists, or 'fellow-travelers'" searching for a foundation in history upon which to base their beliefs. Many are historical materialists or affected by this dogma, and almost all strike out at their contemporary political enemies with selected weapons of historical interpretation.[3]

This is not, of course, a representative picture of Japanese scholarship. Nevertheless, solid Japanese scholarship on the subject of modernization has only just begun. It is interesting to note that these studies have recently turned in the direction of leadership analysis, eschewing more generalized concepts of social change. Such a trend emphasizes, of course, the central significance of choice, the vitality of the decision-making process, and the critical influence of decision-makers. The approach is at least open-ended and avoids the baggage of dogma.

The basic issue is simple. Either the Japanese (or any other people, for that matter) had choices in the course of their national development experience, or they did not. And if choice was significant in their history, then the policy process was crucial. Choice and policy are the stuff of political history and also of political science.

[2] Fukuda Tsuneari, "Japan's Modernization: Abnormal Adaptability," *Bungei Shunjū* (Nov. 1963); "The Intellectual Class of Japan," *Bungei Shunjū* (Dec. 1963), summarized in *Trend of Japanese Magazines* (May 1964) (Tokyo: American Embassy, 1964, mimeo.).

[3] Inoue Kiyoshi, "Political History," ch. 2 of Comité Japonais des Sciences Historiques, *La Japon au XIᵉ Congrès International des Sciences Historiques à Stockholm: l'état actuel et les tendances des études historiques au Japon* (Tokyo, 1960), p. 33.

A firm belief that choice is a crucial factor in history does not in itself, however, resolve problems of cultural change and modernization. Indeed it raises all sorts of new problems in a different context. It suggests, for example, inquiry into the complicated fashion in which political culture is related to culture in general. A "traditional" or a "modern" polity is obviously a subsystem of a "traditional" or a "modern" society. At the same time political choices—in modern jargon, the "decision-making process"—can fatefully affect the future shape of society itself. The relationship is complex. If, as is argued here, the essentially political process of *choice* played a central role in the modernization of Japan, then it is necessary to acquire some sense of the *alternative* choices available to the modernizers. *Decisions* were not made in a vacuum but in a particular context of historical and social forces. On one level of conceptualization this context helps explain why certain political acts occurred and why, in the process of choice, certain policies were accepted and certain others were rejected. On another level of conceptualization lie the political acts of leaders, of subleaders, and of followers. To understand them, one must try to explain *motivation*, the vital link between the individual and the wider context of his action.[4] In the view adopted here, a problem-oriented approach (rather than a deterministic one) best illuminates the developmental process.

One other aspect of this problem-oriented approach needs to be clarified. Much of the modern literature on game theory, or on the so-called decision-making approach, overemphasizes the ingredient of rationality. Indeed, rational decision-making is often listed as a key characteristic of the modern polity. Looking closely at policy-making in our own day, however, who is to say that decisions are made rationally? Are they not often made first and then rationalized? Leaders may have made many irrational choices in the course of Japan's modern-

[4] This is the approach adopted in Yoshio Sakata and John Whitney Hall, "The Motivation of Political Leadership in the Meiji Restoration," *Journal of Asian Studies*, xvi (Nov. 1956), 36.

ization in order to win or to maintain power, or to serve what they thought was the national interest. It would be difficult to arrive at a reliable judgment on this score. Consequently, in what follows, the rationality of decisions will not be an issue.

Modernization and Choice

In examining the role of choice in political culture, it is necessary briefly to underline certain assumptions which have to do with current definitions of modernization.

It is difficult not to begin with an *attitude* marked by higher levels of expectation. The essential difference between the traditional and the modern outlook is, in fact, the awareness of choice. Like power over nature, political power is properly described as instrumental rather than causal. Undoubtedly man's increasing control over the forces of nature prepares him for the systematic, purposeful application of his energies to a more rational control of his social environment for the achievement of various human goals. The key concepts are *purposeful application* and *goals*; both suggest political choice.[5]

Despite the existence of alternatives in the modernizing process, the survival of traditional elements in modern societies is remarkable and has been only recently noted. Having equipped themselves with a hopefully universal definition of political modernization, two social scientists in a widely read treatise have to fall back on the concept of "dualism" in political institutions. They find certain kinds of political behavior, usually attributed to "traditional" or even "primitive" stages, embedded in "modern" systems. And these are not marginal, but features which play significant functional roles.

[5] Cyril Black has pointed to man's rapidly increasing control over the forces of nature as a central feature of modernization. Benjamin Schwartz has stated that modernization involves the "systematic, sustained, and purposeful application of human energies to the rational control of man's physical and social environment" for various goals. Charles Frankel has identified a modern attitude as entailing "changes in the concept of social time." See Marius B. Jansen, "On Studying the Modernization of Japan," *Asian Cultural Studies*, III (Oct. 1962), 1-3.

This has led the editor of this volume, Robert E. Ward, to recognize the dilemma inherent in any dichotomy of "traditional" and "modern": "The history of the modernization of Japan challenges the tenability of any such thesis. It demonstrates in many ways not only the ability of 'modern' institutions and practices to coexist with 'traditional' ones for substantial periods of time, but also the manner in which 'traditional' attitudes and practices can be of great positive value to the modernization process."[6]

A Japanese scholar put this in slightly different fashion: in the inheritance from Tokugawa to Meiji Japan, what proved harmful and an obstacle to achieving the goal of an enriched and strong country was abolished as convention; what proved useful was kept as tradition.[7] It may seem to be stating the obvious, and yet it is surprising how often treatments of modernization either imply the elimination of the traditional or, more subtly, assume an evolution in history from the traditional to the modern. In fact, data to support an evolutionary theory in the realm of social change may be harder to come by than experimental data which demonstrate the force of evolution in biology.

Indeed, there are no completely modern societies, even today. All societies may be said to have a mixture of traditional and modern traits. In this context, "tradition" is a word which proves not at all hostile to the contemporaneous; and "modern" becomes a word freighted with temporicentricity (as well as ethnocentricity, when mixed with "Western"). Tradition affects and limits choice.

There is a tendency for modern politics and government to

[6] Robert E. Ward, "Political Modernization and Political Culture in Japan," *World Politics*, xv (July 1963), 579. For the concept of "dualism," see Gabriel A. Almond and James S. Coleman, eds., *The Politics of the Developing Areas* (Princeton, 1960), pp. 20-25.

[7] For his definitions of conventions abolished (*inshū toshite haiki sareta*) and traditions kept (*dentō toshite hozon sareta*), see Sakata Yoshio, "'Nihon no kindaika' kenkyū no tame no oboegaki," *Zinbun Gakuhō*, xv (Jan. 1962), 67-76.

constitute a system, a highly differentiated and functionally specific organization, characterized by vastly expanded demands, functions, services, and obligations. An economist describes this system in balance-sheet fashion: "Political modernization is defined, in part, as a growth in the authoritative (output) functions of government, both their scale and their efficiency in meeting the requirements of modern industrial society. Modernization is also characterized as a growth in political (input) functions in the direction of new modes of integration that widen networks of communication and participation and legitimize the state through its responsiveness to the aspirations of broadening groups and classes."[8]

There is a high degree of integration within this political structure. Of greatest political importance, there is a movement from ascribed to achieved status. The transition, in the classic terms of Sir Henry Maine, is from status to contract; in modern Japan, from *agraria* to *industria*. Both the society and individuals within it—because of heightened geographic, social, and psychic mobility—obtain a wider range of choices.

A highly bureaucratized system of organization (appearing in comprehensive social units, in the economy, in government) means an egalitarian involvement of masses of people, which in turn may mean enjoyment of democratic opportunity or suffering the iron law of oligarchy. Involvement, therefore, does not necessarily mean mass participation in decisions. A transmission belt of loyalty connects popular identification with the tradition, the territory, and the myth of the nation-state. The ethos of a people is transmitted by the most basic devices of acculturation: unstated beliefs, child-rearing, education, and mass inculcation. To the extent that nationalism is supreme, choices are thereby narrowed again.

If we now turn from a descriptive style (listing elements of

[8] William W. Lockwood, "The Political Consequences of Economic Development in Japan," draft prepared for the Seminar on the Political Modernization of Japan and Turkey, Dobbs Ferry, N.Y., Sept. 10-14, 1962 (mimeo.), p. 3.

the modern condition) to a more demanding analytical style (understanding modernization as a moving process), we may well shift our attention from *what* the society is like to *how* political modernization is brought about. On the basis of even a preliminary reevaluation of the political history of the Japanese transformation, one is struck by the rich variety of motivations encountered. These belie simple explanations according to "mode of production," "classes," "the lower samurai," and "traditional versus modern." The study of motivation focuses attention on choices made by specific leaders (modernizers and antimodernizers), by subleaders, and by followers.

Parallel to the increasingly complex political phenomena—indeed, hardly separable at all—is the appearance of economic diversification. For our purposes this term is better than industrialization to characterize modern culture, even though in most cases diversification implies an advanced industrial technology. It is surprising that although modern societies have a wide choice among various simple and complex mixes of occupations, all seem to choose the most diverse. Among Asians, only Gandhi and a few others chose to turn their back on this Pandora's box rather than to rush up and pry it open. In any case, it is a moot point whether the "mode of production" is cause, instrument, or effect of historical change—or all three.

Economic diversification refers to "the application of modern science and technology to achieve a sustained increase in output of goods and services per capita, with the concomitant changes entailed in economic capacities and institutions."[9] Widely interpreted, it means all social change characteristically taking place in the evolution of a modern industrial society, more narrowly the rising importance of manufacturing industries in the structure of income and employment. Here the economist has the advantage of dealing with measurable

[9] William W. Lockwood, "Economic and Political Modernization," in Robert E. Ward and Dankwart A. Rustow, eds., *Political Modernization in Japan and Turkey* (Princeton, 1964), p. 1, n. 1.

data of change. Other social scientists have a more difficult task, that of assigning to the economic factor its proper role among many causes of modernization.

Much the same can be said about another feature of the modernization process. Modern political culture is often identified with a concentration of population in cities, although it remains to be seen just how "modern" this characteristic is. In any case, in our day a rough measure of modernity is provided by the degree of urbanization. In fact, the true role of the city as cause, effect, or instrument of modernization is as yet not clearly understood.

To summarize, choice is first apparent in the political modernization process as a change of attitude. Two political scientists have stated that the process seems to connote "a process of long-range cultural and social change accepted by members of the changing society as beneficial, inevitable, or on balance desirable."[10] Traditional elements coexist with, indeed often make possible, modernization. Modern politics seem to call forth a vastly expanded governmental system, which leads to the involvement of a steadily increasing number of people. All feel the force of the administrative state, but all do not exercise choice in important decisions. Leaders do, but subleaders are also needed to implement decisions and to justify them to followers. Economic diversification is a chosen goal in the modernization process, but it also acts on a society to accelerate the modernizing process, and it interacts with political institutions as well. A modern diversified political and economic system is most often identified with an increasingly urban culture, but whether the city actually opens up or limits choices remains to be explored.

Contributions of the Tokugawa Era

To say that the political culture of Meiji Japan (that is, modern Japanese political behavior), like political behavior anywhere, was rooted in traditional culture is neither to state a

[10] Ward and Rustow, *Political Modernization*, p. 3.

truism nor to engage in contradiction. Within the context of tradition, it is correct to say that Meiji Japan was still colored and affected by a basic and traditional value system that was fully developed during the Tokugawa era.

This system is often summarized as follows. Values are achieved mainly in groups, in the *Gemeinschaft* community (*kyōdōtai*). They are endowed with a sacred quality (they are *Japanese* as compared with, for example, the highly secular view held by Chinese). Symbolic heads of family-style groups within a patriarchal, hierarchical structure have an especially important role. Individual Japanese receive a continuous flow of blessings; in return they are freighted with obligations. There is no universal ethic: philosophy, ethics, education, science, and even politics are of value as they are valuable to the group and not as ends in themselves. In this sense Robert Bellah is partly right and partly wrong when he states, "And consequently I do not think that there was a fundamental tendency towards modernization in Edo Japan."

In practice such a value pattern provided a firm foundation for Japanese modernization. Its emphasis on group loyalty, group coherence, and inherent duties (more than rights) made the rapid transformation possible. In fact, Tokugawa Japan itself cannot be characterized as static. Thus Bellah is quite right when he describes the era as one which prepared the Japanese for choice through "the politicization of Japanese values."[11]

The popular view that the Tokugawa represents an unhappy interlude of stagnation between the first (Japan's "Christian century") and the second (Perry, Harris, *et al.*) encounters with the West has fortunately almost completely disappeared. This assumption does, however, still recur in unspecialized world history textbooks. Pressure from the West was, beyond doubt, an important factor in the transition. It

[11] Robert N. Bellah, "Values and Social Change in Modern Japan," *Asian Cultural Studies*, III (Oct. 1962), 39.

was, however, a catalyst which precipitated a political revolution whose basic motivation sprang from indigenous conditions.

JAPANESE VIEWS

An earlier Japanese view of Tokugawa power as a "refeudalization" of Japanese society has also disappeared from at least the uncommitted literature. This interpretation simply overlooked the evidence of forceful and dynamic growth (even modernization) during the period. Whereas some Japanese scholars, still trapped in a dogma baited by a word, find it hard to credit Japanese "feudalism" with positive contributions to modern Japan, other Japanese and especially Western scholars (Thomas Smith, John W. Hall, and Robert Bellah) have tended to find the roots of Japan's modernization in the institutional foundations of the Tokugawa period.

Similarly, just before and during World War II, the only officially tenable view was the ultranationalist belief that the Restoration consisted of a return to legitimate power of the sacred emperor, coupled with the necessary rooting out of the samurai class. The subversive view, found in scholarship nominally devoted to social and economic history, saw the Restoration either as a transition from a "feudal" to an "absolute" state or as a "bourgeois" transformation. This analysis was not based on concrete political facts.[12]

Indeed, much of earlier Japanese scholarship came out at a point where "absolutism" constituted a "feudal throw-back," or at least involved a large measure of "feudal residue." As a matter of fact, these approaches have lent very little insight

[12] For the official view, see Mombushō Ishin shiryō hensankai, *Ishinshi*, 5 vols. (Tokyo, 1941); as representative of the unorthodox view, see Hani Gorō, *Meiji ishin* (Tokyo, 1935); Osatake Takeshi, *Meiji ishin*, 2 vols. (Tokyo, 1943); *Hattori Yukifusa chōsakushū*, 4 vols. (Tokyo, 1955); Toyama Shigeki, *Meiji ishin* (Tokyo, 1951); Inoue Kiyoshi, *Nihon gendaishi*, 1 (Tokyo, 1951); and Ishii Takashi, *Meiji ishin ni okeru kokusai kankyō* (Tokyo, 1957).

into the process of change. In late Tokugawa and the first half of the Meiji periods, key leaders certainly believed in progress. And to achieve this they made specific and purposeful use of Japanese tradition by, for example, revising Shinto and using the emperor symbol.[13] One must certainly list, among major changes during the Tokugawa era, the achievement of new administrative and bureaucratic controls over large contiguous regions (under leadership of the new lords, the daimyo); the consolidation of a considerable part of Japanese territory under a single authority; and the conversion of the government itself into an increasingly "public" political structure.

Because the Tokugawa era embodied Japanese tradition, it has increasingly drawn the attention of students of modernization. The tendency toward unification implicit in modern nation-states was also found in Japanese centralized feudalism. "Feudal" and "decentralized" may indeed be synonymous, but at the same time they do not necessarily mean "disunited." In Japan, at least, the feudal state was a transitional (that is, more modern) form from the tribal (or better, ancient monarchical) state to a modern civic state. Decentralization meant division of governmental power preliminary to centralization.[14]

The complex Tokugawa bureaucracy operated, it is true, under an appointment system geared to social rank. The right to rule thus was—or appeared to be—ascriptive and, therefore, "feudalistic" in style. From one point of view the shogunate was a dictatorship (which can be, after all, quite modern). From another, this authoritarian government increasingly

[13] Horie Eiichi, for example, emphasized the reactionary character of pre-Restoration *han* reforms as a condition in the formation of anti-shogunate factions: *Hansei kaikaku no kenkyū* (Tokyo, 1955). Historians of the Kyoto school have turned to a careful examination of the significance of the throne as a political symbol and as an instrument of modernization. See Sakata Yoshio, "Tenno-kan no hensen," *Zinbun Gakuho*, VIII (March 1958); and the translation in *PROD Translations*, III (April 1960), 3-12.

[14] Horie Yasuzō, *Meiji ishin to keizai kindaika* (Tokyo, 1963), ch. 2.

sought to channel talent into official duty. Frequently rank was acquired through achievement. One of the last functions of what we would call a modern state to develop was, of necessity, diplomacy.[15]

The administrative system of the Tokugawa headquarters (*bakufu*) has been described by one Japanese scholar as a form of unified rule based on plurality, the functional parts standing in a relation of checks and balances. It was precisely this system in refurbished form which marched directly into the Meiji era. The new central government replaced the shogunate; the prefectures (*fu* and *ken*) replaced the local domains (*han*); and the oligarchy replaced the feudal bureaucracy. Final allegiance was shifted from the *bakufu* to the emperor, who symbolized the nation. The transition was swift and smooth. "Thus the prototype of the Meiji government had already been established in the Edo period."[16]

Modern Political Content in Tokugawa Thought

This remarkable transformation, admittedly seen clearly only after the Meiji Restoration, did not occur automatically. The Edo era also contributed, besides institutions, attitudes that were significant, including a climate conducive to the politics of rational choice. The link between Tokugawa thought and modern thought was Confucianism.

Compared with its parent Chinese strain, Japanese Confucianism was more practical: it paid close attention to the application of principles to politics. We know, for example, that the shogunate established, for the specific purpose of training in what we now call public administration, an institution of

[15] For an identification of an early rational view of Japan's diplomatic alternative, see the author's "A 'Sub-Leader' in the Emergence of the Diplomatic Function: Ikeda Chōhatsu (Chikugo no kami), 1837-1879," in Bernard S. Silberman and H. D. Harootunian, eds., *Modern Japanese Leadership* (Tucson, 1966).

[16] Horie Yasuzō, *Meiji ishin*, p. 23; by the same author, "The Feudal States and the Commercial Society in the Tokugawa Period," *Kyoto University Economic Review*, XXXVIII (Oct. 1958), 3.

higher education (the Shōheikō); while the domains also established schools (*hankō*) for the education of samurai, who were largely responsible for administration. In addition, private and temple schools symbolized the demand for learning among common folk. These schools spread the Confucian emphasis on duty and moral tone throughout the society and made possible the appearance of many leaders at the local level. Their role in modernization was significant in that they served as links between the domain cities and the central government. The fact that there was only a slight difference in language, thought, and education between local societies and the society of the capital was of great importance later for the unification of the nation.[17]

One effect of this sophisticated system of education was to teach that shogun and daimyo alike should be benevolent heads of government. The official doctrine of the Chu Hsi school was extremely logical, starting with the fundamental concept of reason (*ri*, the ultimate cause of creation and change in the universe). The Wang-ming school, protesting the conservative outlook of the classical school, urged the unity of theory and practice. All stressed the value of a positive attitude toward learning—in short, rationalism.

Thus Tokugawa scholarship both encouraged a reversion to classical tradition and at the same time prepared the ground for the reception of Western thought. It is a familiar story how the latter was introduced by the Dutch through Nagasaki. Toward the end of the Tempō era (1830–1843), after news of the Opium War had filtered into Japan, emphasis shifted to the military sciences. But this shift in turn opened up the worlds of mathematics, physics, gunnery, and ship-

[17] Horie Yasuzō, *Meiji ishin*, pp. 40-48; see also his "Confucian Concept of State in Tokugawa Japan," *Kyoto University Economic Review*, XXXII (Oct. 1962), 26. For a clear statement on learning, see R. P. Dore, "The Legacy of Tokugawa Education," in Marius Jansen, ed., *Changing Japanese Attitudes toward Modernization* (Princeton, 1965).

building. All who studied Western learning were, without exception, first schooled in Confucianism.

One of the most interesting features of the Tokugawa governing tradition was an early, rational, and surprisingly modern theory of social organicism. According to some Confucian scholars, lords, retainers, and commoners were to fulfill certain functions according to their status. The objective was to create a wealthy and strong country. Yamagata Bantō (1746–1841), a merchant-scholar of Osaka who mixed his Confucian with Western learning, justified feudalism as "the righteous way to rule over the country." Yamaga Sokō (1622–1685) had earlier supported the Tokugawa system as an ideal structure wherein feudalism and centralism have been ingeniously combined: "In the current system of administration, feudal lords are rightly chosen and they are granted the right of autonomous rule over their respective domains, the remaining land of the country being ruled by *bakufu* officials who are also selected rightly from among the shogun's retainers. . . . With the advantages of combining both the feudal system and the prefectural system, the shogun can easily maintain social order all over Japan."

The relationship, shogun-to-daimyo, was one of whole-to-parts, as Yamaga clearly explained: "Therefore, Heaven has sent to the world a sovereign (*jinkun*), whose duty is to receive the order of Heaven and deliver it to the people, and to be the authority for public cultures and morals. Accordingly, the ruler is made to stand at the height, not for the sake of personal interest, but for the benefit of the people." According to Yamaga, the shogun was the mind, the populace the body, of the state.[18]

Thus when one looks back over Tokugawa achievements in government and political thought, he finds some of the explanations for what appeared to be a sudden outburst of na-

---

[18] The citations, from Yamagata Bantō, *Yume no shiro*; Yamaga Sokō, *Takkyo dōmon*; and *Yamaga gorui*, are contained in Horie Yasuzō, *Meiji ishin*, p. 27.

tionalism in the emergence of Japan as a modern state. It may well be that the Japanese had been conditioned by tradition to think in terms of a nation, but Tokugawa Confucianism provided a rational framework for a new national ideology. In its earlier form, Confucianism aimed at the establishment of a moral state. Gradually the objective became, in the view of Tokugawa scholars, the establishment of a strong and rich country.

The Restoration (actually a transition from the Tokugawa to modern Meiji Japan) has often been referred to as a "collapse" of feudal society. The word "collapse," however, is not an entirely adequate term. The old shogunate did collapse, and the elimination of older class distinctions, already well corroded in the Edo period, did result. Governmental organization was altered in theory more than in practice, however, since it was the same oligarchic type as the *bakufu* had been. The newly established regime was in the hands of modern instead of feudal bureaucrats. Thenceforth Confucianism provided a matrix for loyalty to the emperor and to the state; the individual was vital only as he served the whole social entity.

Add to these points the fact that the new regime was burdened with what we call "the crisis of security," usually a major if not dominant theme in the politics of emergent nations. One has the distinct impression that *bakufu* and Meiji oligarchs always had an eye cocked at menacing foreigners who threatened Japanese traditions, while the Japanese faced fateful choices and made vital decisions.

This is what is meant when it is said that there were both inflexible and flexible factors in the modernization process. Geography, cultural heritage, and the timing of the Western impact were beyond Japan's control. Among the flexible factors, which were subject to choice and political decision, specific items in the general stock of Japanese tradition were very important. Deliberate choices were made to retain an ideology imbedded in Confucianism and state Shinto, the political symbol of the emperor, the ethic of the samurai, and particular forms of hierarchical social organization—all examples of tradition built into modernity.

Leaders, Subleaders, Followers, and Choice

To pay tradition its due and to account for the inheritance by Meiji Japan from Tokugawa Japan is not to imply that tradition alone determined the outcome. This background conditioned attitudes toward alternatives, but leaders still had to make choices. Some leaders escaped into reaction; some boldly sponsored innovation; while most sought a smooth mix of the traditional and the modern. Their specific motivations and decisions may, however, have affected the degree and rate of modernization much more than did comparable motivations and decisions in many Western countries, where societies had a much longer time in which to mature.

A fine example of a new, liberated approach to the study of leadership is provided by the careful work of scholars in the Modernization (*Kindaika*) Seminar of the Institute of Humanistic Studies at Kyoto University. A major premise of their cooperative studies is "that the political history of the Restoration cannot be explained merely by the citation of generalized concepts of social change or by a description of the circumstances which may have influenced the human behavior of the times."[19] They hasten to add, however, that it can be explained in large measure by viewing such circumstances as the context of individual motivations and political actions.

Having surveyed their political history, members of this seminar and other Japanese scholars as well have concluded that the prewar official (as well as the unofficial or subversive)

[19] The author wishes to acknowledge his debt of gratitude to the U.S. Educational Commission in Japan for a Fulbright Research Fellowship in 1958-1959, when he was affiliated with the Kindaika Seminar in Kyoto. As a result of continuing contacts, both in the U.S. and again in Japan in 1962 and 1965, he owes much to his Japanese colleagues for inspiration and data. An excellent preliminary summary of the findings of the Kindaika Seminar may be found in Sakata and Hall, "The Motivation of Political Leadership in the Meiji Restoration."

interpretations had centered entirely too much on "loyalist leaders" (or on "opposition leaders") in early Meiji Japan. Consequently they neglected the older Tokugawa leadership, which in many cases had already made important decisions. In the decade 1830–1840, for example, Tokugawa Nariaki first espoused doctrines of political reform inspired by his reverence for the emperor and strengthened by his desire to keep foreigners out of Japan. Similarly, between 1841 and 1858 Abe Masahiro, Hotta Masayoshi, and Ii Naosuke were influential and set the stage for the complex process of modernization. Japanese scholarship has long tended to push back the time boundaries demarcating "modern" from "traditional" Japan.

During the Tokugawa era samurai became the civilizing class (*kyōka kaikyū*) as well as the ruling class (*chisha kaikyū*). Moreover, the samurai were increasingly conscious of this dual role. Today we may conclude that the Tokugawa bureaucracy, with its emphasis on the leader-follower principle and its failure to stress the role of individual personality, was undemocratic. It did, nevertheless, underwrite discipline, loyalty, and respect for order in social organization.

Incidentally, the identification of the roles played by such Confucian values explains why more leaders of the early Meiji transformation came from the samurai than from any other group. It should also be noted, however, that although they laid down the foundations for a modern state, they played nowhere near as important a role in the truly revolutionary changes which later, after the Restoration, led to the renovation.

Similar care must be exercised in dealing with the precise motivations of those who used the slogan "Reverence the Emperor" ("*Sonnō*"). Often denounced by contemporary Japanese historians as a device which forestalled a truly "bourgeois" uprising and led inexorably to "absolutism," the slogan was nevertheless revolutionary within the context of the stormy period at the end of the Tokugawa age. One Japanese scholar has categorized the motives involved as follows: first, a traditional Confucian sense of moral duty; second, a conviction born of scholarly writings supporting restoration of imperial rule; and third, reverence for the emperor coupled with hatred for foreigners. Thus while from one point of view this slogan sought to turn the sand clock of history upside down, from another (for example, that of Yoshida Shōin) reverence for the emperor aimed directly at the establishment of political order and protection of the national polity (*kokutai*). Much later, at the renovation stage, it also played a key role in implementing the decision to pulverize the old social status system and to make way for a more modern order.[20]

Considerably more research in depth will be necessary before we can fully appreciate the role of leadership in Japan's modernization. It is now apparent that most of the leaders of early Meiji Japan belonged to the samurai class and had been educated according to Confucian standards of learning. Increasingly, however, the new leaders were drawn from a far wider range of intellectuals from throughout the country and added to the Confucian foundation a Western superstructure. The range of choices also was thereby widened.

One other general point about leadership in the modernization process is worth underlining. Japan's experience fully documents the thesis that political change in countries which have been called late modernizers is commonly led by an autocracy or at least by an oligarchy. Meiji Japan represents an accomplishment in modernization; it does not offer an example of democracy.

The precise interrelationship between modernization and democracy should be an open subject of investigation, certainly not an assumed fact. This must be stated clearly because much scholarship in the field of political history—both Japanese and American—continues to measure modernization by

[20] For the various meanings of *Sonnōron*, see Tōyama Shigeki, "Bunkyū 2 nen no seiji jōsei," *Rekishigaku-kenkyū*. no. 114 (1943), cited by Motoyama Yukihiko, "Meiji ishin to sonnōron," *Zinbun Gakuhō*, II (March 1952), 30ff.

means of progress toward democracy. Americans, who are quick to denounce dogmas of the Left, are peculiarly subject to this dogma of their own. It would almost seem that they are saying, with only their own national experience as background, that sooner or later the "internal contradictions" of an authoritarian regime will work for a "liberation" of its subjects. The undemocratic political structure will surely "wither away." Until it does, the state cannot be called "modern."

In the case of Japan, it should also be noted that although the oligarchs-to-be as a group were impressive, it is still true that few stood out as great leaders towering above the others. In this sense even the leaders were a product of the traditional Japanese system of decision-making; they, too, felt most comfortable when choices were made in collegial fashion and were formed out of consensus.

Beyond such preliminary generalizations about Japanese leadership, we can only begin to distinguish the subtle shadings of differences among individual leaders. It is now apparent that social, economic, and political problems generated at least two types of leaders, one marked by a conservative spirit and one by a progressive spirit. Beyond this, generational differences were important. A Japanese scholar has divided leaders identified with the Restoration itself into three groups: those who had been adolescents before the Restoration, the earliest promoters of reform; those who had been adolescents at the time of the Restoration, the men who gained power between 1878 and 1887; and those who had been mere boys at the time of the Restoration, the bureaucrats in power between 1888 and 1897. It is worth noting, too, that it was not until the very end of this last period that some of the new leaders were to be found in the economic sphere.

Finally, it is necessary to make a distinction between the leadership which engineered the imperial Restoration (*Ōsei-fukko*) and that which began the Meiji renovation (*Meiji-ishin*). The former were motivated by a desperate need to balance the power structure and to maintain political unity. Social and economic reorganization was not, at that time, their objective. For them, political choice was on one level. The latter explicitly wanted to create a new society and structure of state. Political choice was on another level.[21]

These top leaders did not pull off the transformation alone. We have recently come to realize the significant role played by officials in the professional bureaucracy. To repeat a somber note, an oligarchy and a bureaucracy, not a democracy, guaranteed the rapid transition. As national life took shape in the Meiji era, however, in both the public and private sectors more and more men climbed the ladders of power, influence, and wealth.

The attention of the Kyoto Seminar was drawn to the "pioneering intellectuals" who gathered around Ōkuma Shigenobu in the Ministry of Finance. (It was estimated that Finance at one point handled 70 percent of all central government affairs.) Their motivation was essentially different from that of the earlier Restoration politicians, and for the first time they set about not only the political but also the social reorganization of the country. In one sense they were indeed "absolutist" in their decision-making: they acted in high-handed fashion particularly toward weak opposition and thus came into conflict with their samurai counterparts who had returned to the local domains. Moving swiftly out of the Restoration stage, the new bureaucrats abolished clans and established prefectures (*haihan-chiken*); bought off most of their samurai opponents by refunding hereditary pension bonds; tackled the critical issue of land tax reform (*chiso-kaisei*); and won final victory against a reactionary minority in the civil war of 1877.[22]

Although the task has begun, further study of what might

[21] Nomura Kanetarō, in *Ishin zengo* (Tokyo, 1941), pp. 10ff., distinguishes between those with "conservative" and with "progressive" spirit. Professor Sakata, " 'Nihon no kindaika' kenkyū," marks off the generational groups.

[22] Sakata Yoshio, "Nihon ni okeru kindai kanryō no hassei," *Zinbun Gakuhō*, III (March 1953), 1; also his "Shoki Meiji seifu no kindaika seisaku," *Zinbun Gakuhō*, IV (Feb. 1954), 1-18.

be called the engineering of consent in the modernizing process is essential. Important in this process was the role of the subleaders. In place of broad generalizations—that modernization was brought off by a "handful of leaders," that initiative was taken by "lower samurai," that smooth transition was made possible because of the "blind obedience of the people"— there must emerge a more vivid description, a detailed analysis of the complex dynamics of Japanese society.

Recent research on the "ministers of modernization" has shown that those who came to dominate the middle-level bureaucracy were united primarily by choice, i.e. their commitment to political and economic change. This "modern" (post-1868) elite was drawn, however, almost entirely from "traditional" (pre-1868) backgrounds. Thus there was a certain continuity of values and leadership. On the other hand, although the elite seems to have been of one stripe, there was in actuality more than one kind of bureaucrat. Subleaders vied for power, and it was not all clear who was to guide Japan until at least 1873.[23]

We know that such subleaders must have stood between the few well-known leaders plus the national bureaucracy in the capital and the people. They formed a strategic stratum of the population, and they already had, as heritage from the Tokugawa period, a relatively high standard of knowledge, a surprising sense of national consciousness, and a vigorous spirit of innovation.[24] Beyond these general characteristics, detailed profiles await painstaking research into the rich data to be derived from local histories.

Below the leaders and the subleaders were the Japanese people, who have been characterized as frugal, disciplined, organized, and equipped with a sense of "creative" rather than "blind" obedience. No prolonged "revolution in popular ex-

[23] Bernard S. Silberman, *Ministers of Modernization: Elite Mobility in the Meiji Restoration, 1868-1873* (Tucson, 1964), pp. 111-12.

[24] See the author's description in "Kindaika," *PROD*, II (May 1959), 3-6.

pectations" arose to plague the Meiji oligarchy and the oligo-
polistic economic system. Popular involvement in the modern society was almost immediate, with integration (through
the nation-state), penetration (from the leaders through the
subleaders to the followers), and, much later if at all, participation (in decision-making).

One can, of course, overemphasize the viability of traditional
Tokugawa political thought; one can also exaggerate the stay-
ing power of administrative practices carried over into the
Meiji era, the factors that relate "traditional" to "modern"
leadership in Japan. In short, one can embrace the revisionist
opinion that little or nothing that was really new happened
between the Tokugawa and the Meiji periods. This view
should, however, be relegated to a place alongside other dogmatic explanations which have thrown so little light on the
important process of political modernization.

The Economic Factor, Master or Handmaiden

The significant background developments during the
Tokugawa era, the critical decisions made during the Meiji
period, and the choices which led to the subsequent renovation
were above all political events. To borrow the words of an
American economist, they were "striking testimony to the autonomy of the political sphere and its capacity to shape the
course of history." This conclusion undercuts the widespread
assumption, made especially in Japanese academic circles, that
the clue to modernization lies in the process of economic development from a "feudal" to a "capitalist" society. A Japanese economist, who is uncommitted to dogma, offers another
reply calculated to put political choice back into proper perspective: "Economic development, however, in my belief cannot take place automatically and independent from other fields
of life, because the master of the economy is the human
being."[25]

[25] Horie Yasuzō, *Kinsei Nihon no keizai to shakai*, translation in
"The Feudal States and the Commercial Society"; the American econo-

This is not to deny that formative influences in the previous Tokugawa era, not the least of which were economic, helped shape the alternatives of choice in the Meiji period. One approach might accept a favorite word among Japanese historians, "contradictions," to describe this Tokugawa background, though perhaps it is wiser to adopt the term "social contradictions," so as to avoid implied dogma.[26] Such social contradictions in Edo society are too familiar to require more than summary treatment in order to assign them proper weights. They included the spread of money through a basically agrarian system, the rise of commerce, the appearance of a merchant class, and what may be called proto-capitalism. There was also a significant shift of about 10 percent of the population into cities (a trend to be examined later).

THE COMMERCIAL SOCIETY

It is well known that agriculture provided the economic base for the Tokugawa feudal lords; they mobilized agriculturalists. And yet increasingly they were forced to seek a standing in trade and commerce as well. Thus they also sought to mobilize merchants and artisans among the townsmen (*chōnin*). The story of how Osaka, for example, turned into "the kitchen of Japan," around which was built the structure of a new national economy, is a familiar one.

Especially after the brilliant Genroku era (1688–1703), official policymakers kept one eye on economic developments. Moreover, the fact that there were economic phenomena and economic laws that transcended moral exhortation began to work itself into the consciousness of scholars and officials alike. Ogyū Sorai is most often quoted as a warning: "As the merchants have increased their influence, the result being that

---

mist is William W. Lockwood, "The Political Consequences of Economic Development."

[26] The phrase is from Sakata Yoshio, "Meiji ishin to Tempō kaikaku," *Zinbun Gakuhō*, II (March 1952), 1-2.

they act as a single body throughout the whole country, and as the commodity prices are balanced and unified from Edo through the remotest regions, it is no wonder that no decrees or statutes by the *bakufu* are powerful enough to curb effectively the rising tendency of commodity prices."

Certainly after the mid-seventeenth century, many Japanese began to grasp the notion that "money is almighty." This inclination was probably a by-product of the rationalism that, as we have seen, had its forerunners in Confucian doctrines but began to appear full force only with the rise of a money economy. In 1721 Tokugawa officials justified the organization of guilds, and at about the same time they authorized the domains to issue paper money. One man, Kaiho Seiryō, even tried to explain contemporary feudal relations in terms of buying and selling.[27]

Gradually a pragmatic spirit, originating among the townsmen, began to permeate all strata of society. This is what is meant by saying, in contemporary terms, that the Tokugawa was a society moving from status to contract, from the stage to the market. According to a Japanese economic historian, the change marked the origin of a "commercial society": "By a commercial society is meant here that all people of a society are linked together on a give-and-take basis: such a society has a tendency to develop into a citizens' society where the relation would come into consciousness and the whole social and political order would be established along this line."[28]

Although the Tokugawa *bakufu* in its economic policies tried to make use of the new commercial society, it also suppressed it. The domains tried desperately to stay abreast of fast-moving developments. Their efforts led to the encouragement of commerce and industry and to the establishment of local monopolies. Eventually the townsmen became almost

---

[27] Ogyū Sorai, in Takimoto Seiichi, ed., *Nihon keizai taiten* (Tokyo, 1928-1930), IX, 6-7; Tokugawa decrees in *Ofuregaki Kempō shūsei*, p. 1019, and Kaiho Seiryō, *Keikodan* (about 1813), all cited in Horie, "The Feudal States."

[28] *Ibid.*, p. 11.

unshakable in their own areas of economic and financial affairs, but they were definitely not the rulers of the country. It should be made quite clear that they were more the objects than the initiators of policy.

As the commercial society became more firmly rooted, unorthodox views began to appear: there was more than a hint of Japan's later mercantilism in the writings of such men as Kanda Kōhei, Honda Toshiaki, Sakuma Zōsan, and Oshima Takatō. Kanda (1828–1898) boldly advocated freedom of economic activity. When a country relies solely on agriculture, he said, it always enjoys economic prosperity.[29] Under increasing pressures emanating from indigenous economic tensions combined with external threats, the Japanese began to weigh the relative merits of alternative economic policies.

JAPANESE VIEWS

Japanese scholarship has properly identified the Tempō era (1830–1843) as a critical turning point at which the so-called social contradictions could no longer be ignored. The extraordinary development of a commodity system was matched by extreme destitution in many domain economies. Tension was exacerbated by *bakufu* despotism. While the daimyo engaged in wild extravagances and the samurai through their more modest demands also supported the commodity system, both groups nevertheless continued to sneer at commercial activities. The famous Tempō reforms were partially successful in stemming the tide. In 1841, for example, Mizuno Tadakuni carried out measures to prohibit extravagant spending on the part of some warriors, and to rescue others from debt and poverty.

This is the period which certain Japanese scholars have identified as "reformist" but heavily marked by a "bourgeois character." While some have pointed to such "bourgeois" developments during the last stages of Tokugawa rule, others have

[29] Kanda Kōhei, *Nō-shō-ben* (1861), cited in Horie, "Confucian Concept of State."

considered this as "the last stage of 'small management'" (as defined by Lenin). Still others, while agreeing with a Marxist approach, concluded that "the formation of absolutism is the last period of the small management stage." This controversy has raged even to the present day. How and why were "modernization" and "democratization" distorted in Japan? The major point of disagreement has to do with the perennial "controversy over Japanese capitalism," with which Japanese scholars have been obsessed. Should the Meiji period be interpreted as a "bourgeois revolution," or as the last stage in "the establishment of absolutism"? The latter view prevailed for a time; of late a refinement has gained ground, namely that the Meiji was an "inconclusive" and "incomplete bourgeois revolution." In all of these views, of course, politics becomes handmaiden to economics.[30]

The Marxist approach (or at least a style of thought influenced by Marx and Weber, on his Marxist side) has thus had a peculiar fascination for Japanese scholars interested in the process of modernization. Even historians uncommitted to dogma have used words which imply economic determinism. In various Japanese versions of the Marxist interpretation of modernization, there is an economic substructure characterized by a "mode of production" that is "feudal" or "capitalist" or "absolutist," with variations. Resting on this substructure is a class system based on some form of relations in production. Then there is the superstructure: cultural elements, religions, philosophy and law, all of which reflect the class structure.

[30] For various representative views of this type, see Naramoto Tatsuya, *Kinsei hōken-shakai-shi ron* (Kyoto, 1948), for research on Chōshū; Horie Eiichi, *Hōken-shakai ni okeru shihon no sonzeikeitai* (Tokyo, 1949), for the "small management" state; Fujita Gorō, *Hōken-shakai no tenkaikatei* (Tokyo, 1952), for "absolutism." For a relatively uncommitted view, see Andō Yoshio, "Social and Economic History: From the Meiji Restoration to the Present," in Comité Japonais, "La Japon," p. 5. Even Andō describes "economic history" in terms of the development of "Japanese capitalism," which should also include the last days of the shogunate (the *bakumatsu*).

Such simplistic views overlook the complex motivation of groups, the vital role played by government in blocking or furthering modernization, the critical place of political decision, and the impact of deliberate choices. Indeed, now that we have more data, the basic implications of the writings of Japanese socioeconomic historians during the 1920's and 1930's are subject to challenge. True, the "social contradictions" which contributed to the decay of the Tokugawa system were significant factors. It is too long a step, however, to leap from this premise to the conclusions imbedded in prewar Japanese Marxist literature, and reinterpreted and widely broadcast in the West. According to this view, "lower class samurai" in coalition with "big city merchants" brought off the Restoration, mainly for economic reasons.[31]

In brief rebuttal, it may be said that despite the rise of a commercial society in the Tokugawa era, the country remained in the hands of the *bakufu*, the various daimyo, and the samurai. Merchants made a choice: to let "money gain money," rather than acting in a fashion suggestive of the entrepreneurial spirit. For a long time—well into the Meiji and modern periods in fact—business was thought to be inseparably linked with the domain or with a family, rather than resting on a class basis or on individual personality. The emerging leadership among the so-called young samurai was anything but "bourgeois," and at no time did the leaders-to-be think of themselves as leading a "middle-class revolution." We now know that while Japan's experience was unique in some ways, on the whole its course of development was not peculiar and was to be found in most "industrial latecomers."[32]

As a matter of fact, there was a period in the earliest stages

[31] See, for example, E. Herbert Norman, *Japan's Emergence as a Modern State: Political and Economic Problems of the Meiji Period* (New York, 1940).

[32] Kazushi Ohkawa and Henry Rosovsky, "A Century of Growth: Major Phases of Japanese Economic Development," draft prepared for the Conference on the State and Economic Enterprise in Modern Japan, Estes Park, Colorado, June 24-29, 1963 (mimeo.), pp. 1-2.

of the Meiji era when political thought and a series of reforms did indeed reflect assumptions of economic determinism. These early assumptions were not, however, Marxist but were closely affiliated with imported doctrines of laissez-faire. There was indeed an "age of translation," when versions of classical economics brightened the hopes of countless Japanese. There was also a widespread belief in liberalism, a faith that in a different sense the economy would be master and politics its handmaiden.

The many policy decisions included: abandonment of the older, monopolistic guilds (1868); freedom of vocational choice, regardless of social status (1871–1872); abolition of fiefs and certification of hereditary pension bonds (1876); and loosening of restrictions on the free planting of fields (1876).

It is now quite clear, however, that it was usually the government which made the critical choices and played the leading role in "entrepreneurship." Those who moved into the forefront were not the younger, frustrated samurai but the "new bureaucrats." Forerunners of the new financial world, men like Shibusawa Eiichi, Godai Tomoatsu, and Gotō Shōjirō, came to occupy the important positions. Ōkuma Shigenobu, Ōkubo Toshimichi, Itō Hirobumi, Inoue Kaoru, and Matsukata Masayoshi were bureaucrats first, with a talent for enterprise second. Later, businessmen with political affiliations began to appear, brokers like the *Mitsui-gumi* and the *Ōno-gumi*, and planners like Morimura Ichizaemon, Ōkura Kihachirō, Nishimura Katsuzō, and Iwasaki Yatarō. A Japanese scholar has characterized them as follows: "In summary, the first modern bureaucrats did not come into existence as a result of being sustained by a bourgeoisie from below, but as a result of efforts to foster a bourgeoisie at the hands of the government from above."[33]

In the transition from late Tokugawa to early Meiji, Japan

[33] Sakata Yoshio, "Nihon ni okeru kindai kanryō no hassei," p. 17; Horie Yasuzō, *Meiji ishin*, pp. 31-32.

was fortunately endowed with "enterprising bureaucrats" and "political businessmen"; they were "samurai-in-spirit and merchants-in-talent"; significant choices were made by "men of Japanese spirit combined with Western knowledge." It is, of course, difficult to choose one representative individual who will adequately symbolize such a complex transition, but if one could be selected, he might be Shibusawa Eiichi.[34]

As a peasant, merchant, politician, banker, industrialist, and moral leader, Shibusawa (1839–1931) offered a blend of the oft-praised samurai virtues with the rationality of new Japanese capitalism. After brief service in the Treasury Ministry in the 1870's, he resigned and from that time until his death he worked unceasingly as a topmost civilian leader of emergent Japan. He was Japan's first powerful businessman, he became an inventive industrialist, he engaged directly and indirectly in diplomacy, and he devoted the rest of his time to the promotion of vocational education, opportunities for women, labor-management relations, and the enrichment of Japanese moral life.

The chief tenets of his business ethic were derived partly from his early exposure to Western commercial techniques. His idea of an entrepreneur (*jitsugyōka*, a word coined about 1890) was that he should work selflessly with dedication and honesty toward furthering national production. In his early development, Shibusawa had gladly embraced the French principle of laissez-faire. In an address titled "Morality of Merchants and Industrialists," he argued that the state consisted of individuals. So long as individuals were allowed to choose their professions, the collective body of individuals would be strengthened naturally. In this earlier view, economic choices were most significant.

Shibusawa also borrowed heavily from Japanese tradition.

[34] In the problems he faced, the personality he brought to bear on them, his ideology and approach, Shibusawa represents the important characteristics of Meiji economic development. See Johannes Hirschmeir, *The Origins of Entrepreneurship in Meiji Japan* (Cambridge, 1954).

After brief service with the ex-shogun, Tokugawa Keiki, he wrote his first treatise on "The *Bushi* Spirit and Merchants." His business ethic was thus also compounded from the way of the warrior (*bushidō*). From Confucius he derived his belief that the accumulation of wealth must always conform to morality, love, and justice. Like his contemporary, Fukuzawa Yukichi, Shibusawa was deeply conscious of his nation. And so, like many Japanese economic thinkers, Shibusawa Eiichi soon returned to the main stream of thought in the process of modernization. By the end of the nineteenth century he swung over to the doctrines of protectionism. As symbolized in the career of Shibusawa, the national flag of the polity was hoisted above the pennant of profit.[35]

Urbanization, Choice, and Political Decision

An interesting variant of the "modernization equals advanced state of economic development" thesis is just beginning to attract the attention of specialists. Most definitions of modernity include the degree of urbanization as a measure of culture change. To put this the other way around, the vast majority of the members of relatively nonmodernized societies live in a rural rather than an urban environment. They are villagers in *agraria* rather than townsmen in *industria*. They are overwhelmingly preoccupied with sedentary forms of agriculture. It is natural, then, that we have come to think of the two ways of life as being at opposite poles. A society is either traditional or modern, which is to say that it is rural or urban.

The ideal type of rural village folk society in Asia is familiar to nonspecialist undergraduate students and even to secondary school teachers in Western countries. Most of the basic field research has concentrated on this level. The benchmark from which change is surveyed is a small, isolated, nonliterate, homogeneous society with a strong sense of group solidarity.

[35] Ardath W. Burks, "The Businessman and Entrepreneurship in the Modernization of Japan," draft prepared for the American Historical Association, Washington, D.C., Dec. 1961 (mimeo.).

Behavior is spontaneous, uncritical, personal, in short "traditional." It stems from what has been called the folk mentality.[36] Kinship, marking off both relationships and institutions, is the type category of experience; the familial group is the unit of action. This way of life is sharply contrasted with a modern, urbanized society. It is natural, then, that we have come to think of the two modes as being at opposite poles: a society is either rural or urban; it is traditional or modern.

An even more significant assumption imbedded in our rather crude comparative sociology of urbanism is that there is a kind of rural-urban continuum. Societies are implicitly viewed as caught in a web leading to the central city, which in turn inevitably effects urbanization of the surrounding countryside. It is easy to slip into the belief that the process of modernization in this sense is predetermined. There is more than a hint of dogma, of what Dr. Sun Yat-sen might have named "social determinism." There is little or no room for choice or decision.

One difficulty in resisting this kind of fatalism is the gloomy observation that the city does indeed seem to be ubiquitous in modern societies. Parallel with the growth of more complex political and economic institutions, alongside the deeper involvement of masses of people with bureaucracy and the market place, there is an almost universal development of urban society. Modernization results in a measurable increase of life expectancy at birth. On the other hand, the individual may find himself living out this increased life span in "the lonely crowd." The result would seem to be that man, who had some room for maneuver before, is caught up in the city and has no choice.

The story of the development of the city in Japan has scarcely been told. When it is related, it will be instructive. Doubtless it will dramatically challenge the easy dichotomy

[36] The outstanding exponent of this approach has been Robert Redfield. See his article "The Folk Society," *American Journal of Sociology*, LII (Jan. 1947).

between "traditional" and "modern." It will become quite clear from study of the long "premodern" history of urban life in Japan that there is actually a difference of degree here, not of kind: urbanization is but one of the factors in the process of integration of communities into a total sociocultural system. And rural society remains a subsystem.

Cities were not, of course, unknown in Japan before the Meiji period. Without going back to the very old metropolitan capitals, it is sufficient to note the evolution of the city under feudalism and, specifically, the remarkable emergence of the castle-town (*jōkamachi*.) There is now little doubt that castle-towns were established with what were primarily military and political motives, reaching full development during the Edo period and later contributing greatly to the realization of unified national government. In the growth of a commercial society, they played a very important economic function. It is necessary, however, to repeat the caution sounded by a Japanese specialist who, in considering the growth of the Japanese city, noted that "the natural economic function is but one element in the formation of the Japanese city, and not always a cause."[37]

Within this same context, the systematic theory of a Western observer, Gideon Sjoberg, is applicable. He has visualized a "non-Western" urban complex, which he calls the "preindustrial city" and describes as having arisen without benefit of stimulus from the "mode of production" associated with the European industrial revolution. The idea has already attracted the attention of specialists on Japan. Countless illustrations of "modern" Japanese city life sketched against the background of the "feudal" scene spring to mind. For example, in Saikaku much of the raw material for reconstructing the "Little Tra-

[37] Yazaki Takeo, *Nihon toshi no hatten katei* (Tokyo, 1962); and his summary-translation, *The Japanese City: A Sociological Analysis* (Rutland and Tokyo, 1962), p. 44. For a review article on this and related material, see Ohshio Shunsuke, "The Urban Phenomenon in Japan," *The Journal of Asian Studies*, xxiv (Nov. 1964).

dition" of the remarkable Genroku urban culture is ready to hand, as are the backdrops for the urban soap operas of Chikamatsu. Grand *kabuki* theater and the marvelous wood-block prints add subtle shadings to the portrait of highly secular urban attitudes. And in fact in 1800 Edo was probably the largest city in the world. This state of affairs has suggested to one distinguished authority that Japan of this period was a "post-feudal" rather than a "pure feudal" society.[38]

Such evidence challenges descriptions of ruralism and urbanism cast in black-and-white, either-or terms. Rather one must recognize both ways of life as subsystems of a changing total sociocultural system.

Unlike the situation in Western Europe, development in Japan saw the implementation of centralized feudalism (as well as later reform, renovation, and economic revolution) carried out from the top. This is why many Japanese decry the fact that the thrust to modernization did not emanate from "among the people," and that "feudalism survives." Bureaucrats, "bred in feudal society as a military class," chose to use the traditional authority of the emperor to introduce legal, political, and economic changes, and to push through "a totalitarian system of centralized authority" from the imperial city, Tokyo, as a core out to the furthest reaches of every Japanese village and town.[39] In this view, at least deliberate choice is plainly identified.

In somewhat more moderate language, political reform after the Restoration resulted in a grand expansion of a bureaucratic system, whereby city-based government organs became integrating agencies throughout the nation. In other

---

[38] E. O. Reischauer, "Japanese Feudalism," in Rushton Coulborn, ed., *Feudalism in History* (Princeton, 1956), pp. 26-48; see also Robert J. Smith, "Pre-industrial Urbanism in Japan," *Economic Development and Cultural Change*, ix:i (July 1961); Gideon Sjoberg, *The Pre-industrial City, Past and Present* (Chicago, 1960).

[39] Yazaki, *The Japanese City*, p. 38.

words, the traditional castle-town at hand was an instrument in the modernization process, put to use after rational political decisions. The Japanese situation is not altogether unique: recent literature on the development of cities in many parts of the world amply illustrates the role of political power, or the political apparatus, as a key independent variable in accounting for the development of cities. This is precisely why Ernest Weismann, in a United Nations study of the modern Japanese city, reports that modernization was performed under the leadership of the government, so that the reasons for the appearance of the modern Japanese city were different from those which account for the rise of the Western city.[40]

To return for just a moment to the assumed rural-urban continuum and to reflect on the characteristics of the "folk community," the contrasted forms of urban life are usually said to include differences in occupational structure, an increasingly complex division of labor, social and psychic mobility, participation in voluntary associations but also personal anonymity in interpersonal contacts, and normative deviation. On the dark side, secularization, mobility, fluidity, ambiguity of norms, and disorganization inherent in the city lead to the erosion of the folk society, the traditional "culture." One is tempted to add slyly that, whereas the actual people involved run breathless and helterskelter toward the throbbing and attractive city and could not care less about what they have left behind, the amateur anthropologist views with alarm the crumbling of the simpler, isolated, better understood "folk society." Perhaps we may safely make one or two tentative observations about this truly remarkable process, of which we know so little.

First, it must always be kept in mind that rural community and city alike, in the process of modernization, are parts of a

[40] Gideon Sjoberg, "The Development of Cities," *Economic Development and Cultural Change,* ix (Oct. 1960), 93; Kagaku Gijutsu-chō Shigenkyoku, *Kokuren ohōsadan oboegaki* (Tokyo, 1963).

larger, changing social organization. Whole regions become metropolitan areas. A new power system forces new alternatives on both the village and the town.

Second, numerous studies have demonstrated that urbanization is not necessarily accompanied by collapse of the social and moral order. The organization man moves to another level of alternatives and to different methods of decision-making. For example, city life in Japan as carried on through the family, school, and workshop has been described as quite stable.[41]

Third, in place of a preliminary conclusion, a question: if man does have a choice; if at various stages of the modernizing process he (or at least his leaders) elects to build more complex political and economic institutions, while trying valiantly to hold on to some familiar tradition; and if he selects the city as a prime instrument for the transition, then how on the average does he fare? The query revives moral issues inherent in choice, issues which were postponed at the very beginning of this analysis.

Modernization and Progress

One of the obvious difficulties with the word "modernization" is that it very often carries the implication that social change does not proceed at random, but specifically in an evolutionary and patterned fashion. Further, "modernization" is often thought to entail an improvement from a "backward" to an "up-to-date" way of life. That is to say, "modernization" is assumed to be progress.

The idea of progress, if it belongs at all in modernization

[41] Suzuki Eitarō, *Toshi shakaigaku genri* (Tokyo, 1957); R. P. Dore, *City Life in Japan: A Study of a Tokyo Ward* (Berkeley, 1958); Ezra F. Vogel, *Japan's New Middle Class: The Salary Man and his Family in a Tokyo Suburb* (Berkeley, 1963). For a recent account of choices in urban life, see David W. Plath, *The After Hours: Modern Japan and the Search for Enjoyment* (Berkeley, 1964).

theory and in the study of politics, belongs to the subdiscipline of political philosophy. In the Western tradition, from the time of the Greeks men have had faith in the gradual evolution of the *polis* toward utopia. This faith deepened into a Hellenistic-Christian-Judaic outlook, but it has also become secularized and separated from its Western roots. We have already noted the historical fact that one of the marked features of the modernization process is an altered attitude, a confidence that environment can be controlled and ordered, an excitement aroused by the prospect of desired change—in short, a belief in progress.

Perhaps the traditional Asian outlook has contained considerably less of a sense of improvability. The pessimistic Buddhist view of life, with its fatalism and asceticism, has often been listed as a barrier to modernization and progress. There are, however, other Asian themes: from the time of Confucius, sages have believed in the moral improvability of man mainly through cultivation and education. Certainly twin features of the powerful Neo-Confucian tradition of Tokugawa Japan were rationalism and the possibility of establishing a moral realm here on earth. Long before the second Western impact, the peculiar early Japanese version of nationalism inspired ideas of building a strong and wealthy country. As Japan's transformation picked up speed, moved into the Restoration stage, and especially entered the renovation process, Japan's leaders demonstrated both a faith in rational choice and a confidence in progress. It has been pointed out that the first three decades (1868-1898) of the Meiji period were dominated by a remarkably coherent attitude of optimism.

So much for the persistent belief on the part of premodern and modern man that he can improve his lot. Whether the transition from primitive through traditional to modern political structures *is* actually progress, however, is another matter. Were the Japanese better off under Meiji modernization than under traditional Tokugawa rule? Did the Japanese enjoy a more favorable position because of the controlled changes under the Occupation after World War II? Are the present Japanese better off, having chosen an urban base for modernization in its second stage and having tasted the bitter-sweet, heady wine of the contemporary durable-consumer-goods boom?

It can certainly be said that if Japanese observers have not always perceived the role of choice in their nation's modernizing process, if they have leaned toward a kind of fatalism in the face of transformation, at least they have been among the most perceptive in describing the psychological results. It has been noted that in the full maturity of the Meiji era, there was a strong comeback of Japanese tradition characterized by the continuity of insularity and self-consciousness. And ironically, in the earliest full bloom of imperial Japan during the first decade of the twentieth century came the intrusion of doubt and pessimism. Representative Japanese thinkers have been singled out to illustrate "the search for meaning in modern Japan." Above all, Japanese novelists have brilliantly illuminated the contradictions and inadequacies of the modern synthesis.[42]

A firm belief in progress would thus seem to be left as an exercise in theology. Hopeful answers to the dilemmas of modernization would seem to rest only on articles of faith.

In any case, with the present state of knowledge about political modernization and choices, it is better for the political scientist to emulate the anthropologist and to escape from bias. Primitive political arrangements are worthy of study for their own sake; traditional structures are revealing; modern polities are intriguing phenomena. Once this objective attitude frees the social scientist to construct a truly universal theory

[42] See, for example, essays in Marius B. Jansen, "Changing Japanese Attitudes toward Modernization": Robert N. Bellah, "Ienaga Saburō and the Search for Meaning in Modern Japan"; and Shūichi Katō, "Japanese Writers and Modernization."

of political modernization, then perhaps the link between modernization and progress can become something other than a monopoly of theology. This step may then lead to an escape from the present preoccupation with behavior in the social sciences, in order to hammer out a viable, normative political theory.

CHAPTER XV

Epilogue

ROBERT E. WARD

Two questions of more general relevance with respect to the present inquiry into the process of political development were posed in the Introduction of this book: "What is meant by political development?" and "What does the particular case of Japan suggest with respect to the process of political development in general?" An attempt was made to deal with the first in the Introduction. Let us now turn to the second.

It might be wise to underscore the verb "suggest" in this query. Obviously, the lone case of Japan does not prove anything with respect to the overall process of political development; it does not even argue a significant degree of probability for any findings that may result from such an inquiry. Comparable findings in a sizable number of cases would be necessary for this. What it does contribute, however, is a small but hopeful beginning on a massive task of historical inquiry and verification. So much of the writing in the field of political modernization has been speculative, episodic, and incompatible. This is useful, and probably inevitable as well, in the early stages of developing a new approach. But the time has come when the most urgent need of the field is for compatible, inductive, and historically oriented investigations calculated to demonstrate how particular political systems have in fact developed over time, and what these particular sequences of development suggest or prove with respect to a general theory of political modernization.

The history of Japan's political development suggests the following very tentative observations:

577

First, it suggests that from the standpoint of the investigator there is a great deal to be said for selecting a mature specimen of political development for historical analysis. It would seem almost self-evident from a methodological standpoint that more is to be learned about the total process of development from the study of mature than of immature cases, from the study of the British, French, American, and Japanese cases, for example, rather than those of Nepal, Chad, or Somalia. Curiously enough, this has not been the procedure usually followed. The overall process of modernization in the current sense of the term, including its political dimension, has been far more frequently and systematically studied in underdeveloped than in developed settings. Such studies are certainly helpful, but they also leave our inventory of essential data lamentably incomplete and unbalanced. After all, at least some of the earlier and more basic stages of modernization almost everywhere have been frequently and legitimately referred to as Westernization. This certainly suggests that we need to know more and in more systematic terms about the developmental process in the West. Compatibly phrased inquiries into the political development of Great Britain, the United States, France, Italy, and Germany would be extraordinarily useful, and might do a great deal to provide us with the beginnings of a viable system of periodizing the development process and identifying stages, sequences, and causal relationships therein.

The case of Japan also suggests several points with respect to the overall timing and periodization of the political development process. First, it stresses the need for further refinements in our use and understanding of such standard periodizations as those that date the beginnings of modern Japan from the Meiji Restoration of 1867–1868. Where such basic traits of a modern political system as functional differentiation of governmental structure, gradual supplantation of ascriptive standards by standards of achievement in the allocation of high bureaucratic positions, or the secularization and impersonalization of the official decision-making process are concerned, the work of such scholars as Professor J. W. Hall demonstrates a most impressive degree of development by the end of the seventeenth century—roughly one hundred and seventy years before the Restoration.

But this dating, too, requires serious qualification. For example, although a higher bureaucracy selected in significant degree in accordance with standards of achievement and a pronounced rationalization of the decision-making system may emerge for the first time in late seventeenth century Japan, a high degree of functional differentiation in governmental organization appears centuries before this in the Kamakura period (twelfth–fourteenth centuries) or perhaps as early as mid-Heian times (eleventh century). On the other hand a commitment to nationalism in the modern sense probably does not appear among a significant segment of the samurai class until at least the early nineteenth century or among the populace in general until the end of that century. Given such a diversity of time ranges for just these four of the eight defining traits of a modern political system, any attempt at an overall periodization of the development process must be approached with considerable caution. My own feeling is that the process does not "go critical" in the Japanese case until the 1860's and 1870's when the final element, an intense sense of nationalism, begins to spread to significant sectors and numbers of the population. At this point only are all the essential elements assembled and only then does the modern political synthesis become operational, a fact that, of course, reaffirms with some qualifications the overall validity and utility of the standard periodization based on the Meiji Restoration.

In a larger sense a finding of this sort with respect to Japan raises the question as to whether the advent of a modern sense of nationalism shared by significant sectors and numbers of a population has played a similarly critical and climactic role in dating the beginnings of political modernity in at least some other societies. My own impression is that it did, for example, in at least the Turkish, Chinese, and a number of colonial cases. If this assumption is in some measure valid, then the advent of nationalism may offer a diagnostic instrument of great value from the standpoint of periodizing the modernization process in this particular class of societies.

The Japanese experience with political modernization also indicates that some aspects of the process at least have deep historical roots in Japanese institutions and culture. While the complete modern political synthesis may date only from the 1860's and 1870's, basic elements of that synthesis such as functional differentiation, achievement orientation, and rationalization have histories that go back from one and a half to five or six centuries beyond that. This substantially alters the traditional time perspective on the political modernization of Japan. It is seen in these terms not as a process that has taken place in the single century that has intervened since the Restoration but as a cumulative product of two and a half to six or seven centuries of gradual preparation, the last century of which was characterized by a greatly increased pace and scope of political change.

In a more general sense this finding suggests two points of interest. First, that perhaps the pace of the developmental process in Japan has in many important respects not been so different from that of the Western European models as has generally been thought. Modern Japan, too, has been the result of several centuries of slow, organic development, rather than a unique and almost miraculous product of the last hundred years. Second, if this is so, then the case of Japan does not lend as much credibility as has been commonly thought to the forced-growth or shortcut types of development plans that are pandemic in the underdeveloped sections of the world today. In the light of Japan's experience it is likely to take far more than a brief series of five or ten year plans to provide the foundations of political modernity.

The Japanese case also suggests a considerable number of propositions that relate to the strategy and tactics of the political modernization process. First among these perhaps we

might consider the choice faced by all modernizing elites between an innovational or a conserving attitude toward their
own political heritage. The early stages of modernization in
particular are often marked by a feeling on the part of the
leadership that what is native is by reason of this very fact also
barbarous, antimodern, and an affront to the dignity and
status of the modernizing society. The other side of this coin
is the matching conviction that what they need most is as
sweeping and rapid a program of political innovation as the
system will tolerate. Japan's leadership felt otherwise in the
critical 1870's. In a number of important instances they opted
for qualified conservation of their heritage rather than
innovation.

Consider, for instance, the transformation of the emperor-
ship from the status of an archaic and neglected symbol of low
popular efficacy to that of symbolic keystone and legitimizer
of the new regime capable of eliciting patriotism, loyalty, discipline, and sacrifice in truly extraordinary measure from practically the entire population. From the standpoint of the needs
of a modernizing leadership this is certainly one of history's
most telling examples of the purposeful and systematic infu-
sion of new content and efficacy into an inherited political institution—in other words of a spectacularly successful instance
of social engineering. Less well known but of comparable importance were such other conserving strategies as the manner
in which the new political leadership treated their predecessors
by making them charter members in a new peerage and provided them with generous pensions; the way in which they
established for themselves a reliable and stable base of political
support in the countryside by maintaining the sociopolitical,
but not in some respects the economic, circumstances of the
individual peasant, the family, and the community in a condition as closely approximating those of Tokugawa times as
was possible (a strategy that I call "holding constant the countryside"); or, to borrow an example from the economic sphere,
the manner in which they systematically preserved and in-

tegrated the traditionally organized small and middle industrial sector into the economy of the state in such a way as to
complement the productivity of the new modern industrial
sector.

These and other similar examples add up to a strategy of
political modernization based on conserving and converting
to modernizing purposes at least a selection of important institutions handed down from a society's past. Of course not all
such institutions are convertible to such purposes, and Japan
may well have been particularly fortunate in this respect. But
the Japanese experience at least argues for the potential utility
of a careful inventory of any society's heritage with this possibility in mind. Presumably the merits of the strategy derive
from the propositions that there is a limit to the amount of
change that any society will tolerate in restricted periods of
time, that some sense of stability and continuity is useful at
such times, and that old familiar symbols and institutions may
have greater popular appeal than new ones. This suggests the
conclusion that, when properly exploited and remolded, a society's premodern heritage may be a powerful supporter of
modernizing change.

Related in part to this is a further point with respect to a
sectoral aspect of the development process. It is normally beyond the economic capacity, and probably the administrative
capacity as well, of most political systems in the early stages of
modernization to engage in development activities on an
across-the-board scale, to press at the same time, for example,
for equal progress in the fields of urbanization and industrialization on the one hand, and agriculture and rural life on the
other. Basically the problem is one of how most effectively to
allocate scarce resources. The Japanese answer to this was complex. It may be of larger relevance.

To begin with, their political leadership had no doubts
about the primary importance of the agricultural sector of the
economy during this early period. The primary industries accounted on the average for approximately two thirds of the

national income until 1882. Major development in the secondary and tertiary sectors would obviously have to be financed in substantial part by surplus funds extractable from the primary sector. This perception led to the adoption of a complex strategy of modernization. Rural tax rates were kept at the same high levels as before the Restoration and in some respects were adjusted to the increased disadvantage of the peasantry. As a result an average of 78 percent of the government's ordinary revenues derived from the land tax until 1881. From these revenues just enough new governmental investment was channeled into agricultural experiment stations and agricultural education to produce fairly steady rises in the productivity of agriculture without at the same time introducing disturbing changes in land tenure, rural class relations, and political behavior. The remainder and substantially larger part of the funds were then devoted to the costs of industrialization, national defense, the creation of a modern communications system, etc.

While the substance of this strategy is largely economic, the basic decisions involved are classically political. In effect the political leadership is making two sorts of decisions, one as to the sources of revenue wherewith to finance the modernization of the country, and a second as to the sectoral allocation of these revenues. In a sense the role of the agricultural sector is prime in both respects: it provides the bulk of the funds and has a high, if limited, priority where their expenditure is concerned. But of greater consequence is the fact that the bulk of the revenues extracted from the peasantry was spent in urban areas to finance nonagricultural aspects of the modernization process. In this sense it is true that the peasantry ultimately financed the modernization of Japan. But then with a population that was upward of 90 percent rural, who else was apt to be able to do so? The analogy with the circumstances of many present-day developing societies seems fairly close. One wonders if they can avoid adopting a similar strategy.

A form of temporal strategy is also implicit in the developmental experience of Japan. It has to do with the timing of the government's campaigns to solve at least two of the most diffi-cult and fundamental political problems confronting it just after the Restoration. Both are very common where develop-ing polities are concerned. The first was the problem of estab-lishing stable national boundaries for Japan, especially in the Kurile, Ryukyu, and Bonin areas; and the second was the problem of recovering full domestic sovereignty by modifying the treaties conferring special judicial and commercial status and rights upon many foreign nationals. The decision was to face these problems sequentially rather than concurrently, and thus to put up with the encumbrances upon Japan's judicial and commercial sovereignty until the more urgent and po-tentially more dangerous territorial problems had been satis-factorily adjusted.

Subsequently the same strategy was eventually successful in dealing with the unequal treaties. The Japanese concentrated first on the somewhat simpler problem of ending extraterri-toriality, and only thereafter on eliminating the conventional tariff and thus regaining full control over commercial trans-actions. Their patience in pursuing this sequential strategy was notable; they did not regain full sovereign power until 1911, fifty-three years after the Harris Treaty of 1858. While it is difficult to conceive of any contemporary developing nation displaying comparable patience when confronted with similar problems, the Japanese strategy of setting priorities and, when possible, attempting to deal with them patiently and in se-quence rather than concurrently may still have a good deal of relevance to present-day circumstances and needs.

The Japanese case also suggests certain reflections concern-ing the psychological aspects of the political modernization process. The first has to do with the development and spread of a sense of identification with the nation on the part of a population. How may this most effectively be accomplished? The answer is not simple. In the Japanese case it was managed partly through explicit programs of nationalist indoctrination in the schools and armed forces and partly through the exploitation of the emperor as a symbol of national glory and unity. But still another and apparently very important part of the formula was fear.

Whether justified or not, the Japanese leadership in the early days of modernization undoubtedly feared both outright intervention and economic exploitation by the Western powers. This fear was communicated to the populace at large where it acted as a catalyst and contributed to the emergence of a full-blown spirit of Japanese nationalism in an astonishingly short space of time. One wonders in the light of this experience whether all nationalisms are not in significant measure defensive and engendered by fear and, if so, whether there is any functional equivalent for the role that fear and a sense of national insecurity have played historically in the production of this basic attribute of the modern political system. Surely this is one principal reason for which the leaders of so many of our contemporary developing societies cherish so desperately the ghosts of their past imperialisms. How else does one unify a fragmented political society?

Fear certainly played such a role in the Japanese case. Not only did it serve to unite the people behind their new political leadership in a sort of defensive reflex to external threats, but it also evoked energy, discipline, and a willingness to sacrifice for the nation's sake that had a great deal to do with Japan's spectacular success. Fear focussed on an external target then served as a stimulus of great positive value in the early stages of the Japanese case. Side by side with it, however, one also finds a quality of essential optimism that in some manifestations seems almost cocky. To the members of the Iwakura mission, for example, Western Europe in 1873 seemed not to be so far ahead of Japan in levels of civilization and general attainment. Professor Soviak quotes their official journal as pointing out that after all Europe's present achievements in these respects are characteristic of only the last fifty to one hundred years. The clear implication is that Japan can readily make up for a gap of this dimension. This combination of psychological attitudes—fear plus optimism—is an interesting one. For Japan at least it was also potent.

Having spoken in this manner of the constructive aspects of nationalist spirit where the political development of Japan is concerned, one should note its counterproductive aspects as well. The case is of unusual interest in the sense that nationalism in Japan was so distinctly a product deliberately created and engineered by the Meiji leadership to serve their contemporary needs and purposes. Ultimately, however, their creation turned out to be a Frankenstein that made captives of its creators, or at least of their successors. But long before the debacle of the 1940's Japanese nationalism had developed characteristics that were counterproductive from the standpoint of political modernization. Perhaps most notable among these were the increasing elements of mysticism and irrationality that it brought to the decision-making system. The general lesson to be drawn from this probably relates to the importance of context, timing, and scale in any endeavor to modernize a political system. Social institutions or forces that are constructive and functional for one set of circumstances, stage of development, or level of input may be destructive and dysfunctional for the modernization process in others. The history of nationalism and of the uses to which the imperial institution was put provide splendid examples of this in the Japanese case. In time they acquired a sort of institutional inertia that was conducive to initially unintended consequences.

Finally, the Japanese experience suggests certain observations with respect to the relationship between forms of government and the process of political development. The Japanese leadership was confronted with quite a spread of options during the twenty-two years between 1868 and 1890 when they were trying to determine just what form of government was most appropriate for their country. The available and practicable models ranged from a continuance of the shogunate under new auspices to arrangements inspired by the then-current institutions of the British monarchy and Parliament. Serious consideration was given to most of these possibilities, and there was appreciable support for many, including some that were surprisingly liberal. In the end they selected a predominantly German model, and it is this that is reflected by the terms of the Meiji constitution of 1890. The question is: "Was this particular selection better adjusted to the needs of a modernizing political system than any of the feasible alternatives?"

History permits only crude and inconclusive findings on questions of this sort that involve the issue of what might have been had not some other arrangement prevailed. But there is a strong temptation to argue in the Japanese case, first, that the predominantly authoritarian and oligarchic system of government established by the Meiji constitution in 1890 was remarkably well adjusted to both the political capacities and needs of a modernizing Japan and, second, that it was probably superior in modernizing efficiency to any practicable alternative at the time. Such an argument would rest upon premises such as the following: that the more traditional alternatives such as a restoration of the shogunate or some form of coalition government dominated by the major fiefs were intrinsically less well suited to the needs of modernization; that the more radical and liberal alternatives proposed by supporters of the *Jiyū Minken Undō* would not in practice have been nearly so liberal as is often claimed and, more important, would have seriously derogated from the unity, stability, and efficiency of political leadership; and finally—when one stops to consider the basic sociopolitical circumstances of Japan in 1890 and the fact that late feudal times lay but twenty-two years in the past—that the Meiji constitution provided a very substantial degree of political innovation and at the same time installed a type of government calculated to maximize national unity, stability, and strong political leadership. These are very impressive accomplishments in the annals of political development that should not be discounted lightly. One can argue quite persuasively that in the case of Japan at least a distinctly authoritarian and oligarchic form of government turned out to be extraordinarily well suited to the needs and strains of the early period of modernization and that there is reason to doubt that more democratic forms would have been equally serviceable.

This is not to claim, of course, that the political forms appropriate to the early stages of modernization are equally suitable to later stages. Actually the original Meiji political system underwent very substantial change and liberalization between 1890 and 1932. It managed this in spite of the seeming rigidity and authoritarianism of its initial arrangements. In fact, a careful study of the political history of this period suggests the hypothesis that in a secular sense liberalizing tendencies are inherent in the modernizing process and that even political systems as authoritarian as Meiji are not in the long run immune to their effect. It is certainly the case that this lengthy prewar experience with gradually liberalizing political institutions provided the foundation upon which the success of the postwar democratization program has been built. In the case of Japan, therefore, the fact that it entered upon the modernizing stage of its history under the control of an authoritarian and oligarchic political system did not foreclose the prospect of a gradual liberalization and democratization of that system, even before the American intervention in postwar times.

This brief account of the democratic aspects of Japan's political development suggests one last observation. If one grants the premise that by any realistic standards of judgment, Japan has today a democratic political system, it becomes particularly important to emphasize the fact that this result cannot be explained solely in terms of developments since 1945 and the Allied Occupation. In a very real and meaningful sense Japan has been preparing for this since at least 1890, i.e. for seventy-seven years at present. The process of preparation has been slow, piecemeal, and usually unspectacular, but the present results are impressive. A developmental experience of this kind leads one to wonder whether a viable democratic society has or can emerge elsewhere in an appreciably shorter period of time or with less extensive preparation. If so, the evidence is not apparent.

To recapitulate, then, the Japanese experience suggests the following propositions with respect to the process of political modernization in general:

1. That we badly need more systematic information about the course of political development in the classic or "mature" Western cases.

2. That standard periodizations of a nation's political history may be only partially or indifferently adjusted to the process of political modernization; they are apt to need further refinement.

3. That the advent of a significant degree of nationalism may distinguish and help to date the beginning of the modern stage of a "nation's" political development.

4. That in a number of important respects the amount of time required for the political modernization of Japan has not been much shorter than that required in the classic Western cases.

5. That Japan's experience does not support the proposition that there are effective shortcuts to political modernization, if one is speaking in terms of less than several generations.

6. That with judicious management elements of a society's traditional political culture may be converted into potent agents of modernization.

7. That in the early stages of modernization firm political

decisions about what sector of the population is going to bear the major share of the costs of development are essential; in many, if not most, cases there is a high probability that this sector will have to be agriculture and the peasantry.

8. That, where possible, there is much to be said in favor of a strategy of development that confronts major political problems in sequence rather than concurrently.

9. That widespread fear of foreign intervention or exploitation can be a powerful stimulus to political modernization.

10. That an added element of basic optimism about the capacity of a nation to attain levels and types of performance equivalent to those in the societies serving as its models is also helpful.

11. That forces and institutions that are supportive of the political modernization process at one time, or on one scale, or in one set of circumstances are capable of being counterproductive in others.

12. That, if the quality of leadership is held constant, authoritarian and oligarchic forms of government may be superior to democratic forms in the earlier stages of political development.

13. That, despite the existence of an authoritarian political system to begin with, significant liberalizing tendencies may be inherent in the modernization process.

14. That the history of the democratization of Japan emphasizes the importance of gradual preparation and prep-

aration in depth for the attainment of a viable democratic political system.

These are all fairly simple and highly generalized propositions. Being based solely on the Japanese experience, they are
also highly suppositious. Given this meagerness of background, however, such limitations are probably unavoidable.
What one can get from an approach of this sort is no more
than a start. But some such start is essential.

To be sure, the really big and meaningful questions are left
unanswered. To what extent were the circumstances of Japan
and the developmental process in Japan unique and hence
without heuristic power elsewhere? To what extent does the
simple passage of time and the difference in international environment that flows therefrom affect the relevance of the Japanese experience to contemporary problems of political development? And to what extent is the process of political development susceptible to planning and direction?

At this stage of inquiry one can only have hunches with
respect to the answers to problems such as these. Two such
hunches suggest themselves. The first is that, when more fully
studied and understood, national developmental experiences
will be seen as rationally distributed along one or several developmental continuums. They probably do not represent
discontinuous or adventitious reactions to unique societal or
temporal circumstances. If this should prove to be the case,
then the first two of the questions posed above—as to the
uniqueness of Japan's circumstances and the effects of a nineteenth rather than a mid-twentieth century international environment upon the process of political development—lose a
great deal of their force. The case of Japan would stand in
some sort of rational and continuous relationship with other
developmental experiences and would thus offer a valid and
useful starting point for inquiry into the total process of political development, even if it ultimately turned out to be an
extreme case or, in more theoretical terms, a limiting case.

I feel somewhat more confident about the second hunch. It is that increased precision, sophistication, and refinement in an inquiry of this type are most apt to flow from the comparison of this sort of particular national developmental experience with the developmental records of a selection of other modern or modernizing political systems. Only from such comparisons can we acquire some more certain feeling for the phasing and periodization of political development, for the nature and causes of different types of developmental sequences, and, hopefully, for the amenability of such processes to some measure of direction or control. For such a quest the experience of Japan can be but a very small beginning, but a beginning that does not, I hope, lack either relevance or interest.

Appendix

Region	Election & Party 2d Election February 10, 1892		Percentage of Seats	Election & Party 5th Election March 15, 1898		Percentage of Seats
Tōhoku	Jiyūtō		40	Jiyūtō		6
	Chūō Club		31	Shimpōtō		81
	Kaishintō		3	Kokumin Kyōkai		4
	Dokuritsu Club		3	Yamashita Club		0
	Kinki Kokutai		0	Independents		9
	Independents		23			
Kantō	Jiyūtō		52	Jiyūtō		39
	Chūō Club		9	Shimpōtō		32
	Kaishintō		20	Kokumin Kyōkai		3
	Dokuritsu Club		6	Yamashita Club		10
	Kinki Kokutai		0	Independents		16
	Independents		13			
Chūbu	Jiyūtō		32	Jiyūtō		41
	Chūō Club		29	Shimpōtō		39
	Kaishintō		15	Kokumin Kyōkai		7
	Dokuritsu Club		13	Yamashita Club		6
	Kinki Kokutai		0	Independents		7
	Independents		11			
Kinki	Jiyūtō		14	Jiyūtō		40
	Chūō Club		9	Shimpōtō		22
	Kaishintō		5	Kokumin Kyōkai		2
	Dokuritsu Club		29	Yamashita Club		22
	Kinki Kokutai		21	Independents		14
	Independents		22			
Chūgoku	Jiyūtō		23	Jiyūtō		33
	Chūō Club		34	Shimpōtō		30
	Kaishintō		11	Kokumin Kyōkai		17
	Dokuritsu Club		14	Yamashita Club		7
	Kinki Kokutai		8	Independents		13
	Independents		10			
Shikoku	Jiyūtō		38	Jiyūtō		62
	Chūō Club		5	Shimpōtō		33
	Kaishintō		33	Kokumin Kyōkai		0
	Dokuritsu Club		5	Yamashita Club		5
	Kinki Kokutai		0	Independents		0
	Independents		19			

Region	Election & Party 2d Election February 10, 1892		Percentage of Seats	Election & Party 5th Election March 15, 1898		Percentage of Seats

Kyushu

Jiyūtō	18	Jiyūtō	27
Chūō Club	70	Shimpōtō	14
Kaishintō	2	Kokumin Kyōkai	30
Dokuritsu Club	2	Yamashita Club	7
Kinki Kokutai	0	Independents	22
Independents	8		

TOTALS

	Number of Candidates	Number Elected	% of Seats		Number of Candidates	Number Elected	% of Seats
Jiyūtō	270	94	31	Jiyūtō	233	105	35
Chūō Club	94	83	28	Shimpōtō	174	103	34
Kaishinto	106	37	12	Kokumin Kyōkai	52	29	10
Dokuritsu Club	34	32	11				
Kinki Kokutai	12	12	4	Yamashita Club	28	26	9
Independents	271	42	14	Independents	118	37	12
	787	300	100		605	300	100

Region	Election & Party 10th Election May 15, 1908	Percentage of Seats	Election & Party 12th Election March 15, 1915	Percentage of Seats
Hokkaido	Seiyūkai	33	Seiyūkai	17
	Kenseihontō	0	Kokumintō	0
	Daidō Club	33	Rikken Dōshikai	66
	Yukōkai	0	Chūseikai	17
	Independents	34	Count Okuma Supp.	0
			Independents	0
Tōhoku	Seiyūkai	37	Seiyūkai	37
	Kenseihontō	37	Kokumintō	4
	Daidō Club	5	Rikken Dōshikai	51
	Yukōkai	9	Chūseikai	2
	Independents	12	Count Okuma Supp.	2
			Independents	4

Region	Election & Party *10th Election* *May 15, 1908*	Percentage *of Seats*	Election & Party *12th Election* *March 15, 1915*	Percentage *of Seats*
Kantō	Seiyūkai	50	Seiyūkai	28
	Kenseihontō	18	Kokumintō	9
	Daidō Club	1	Rikken Dōshikai	49
	Yukōkai	10	Chūseikai	1
	Independents	21	Count Okuma	6
			Independents	7
Chūbu	Seiyūkai	53	Seiyūkai	32
	Kenseihontō	24	Kokumintō	1
	Daidō Club	5	Rikken Dōshikai	44
	Yukōkai	3	Chūseikai	10
	Independents	15	Count Okuma	4
			Independents	9
Kinki	Seiyūkai	58	Seiyūkai	18
	Kenseihontō	8	Kokumintō	13
	Daidō Club	2	Rikken Dōshikai	27
	Yukōkai	10	Chūseikai	20
	Independents	22	Count Okuma	2
			Independents	20
Chūgoku	Seiyūkai	39	Seiyūkai	9
	Kenseihontō	15	Kokumintō	20
	Daidō Club	15	Rikken Dōshikai	37
	Yukōkai	11	Chūseikai	13
	Independents	20	Count Okuma	4
			Independents	17
Shikoku	Seiyūkai	48	Seiyūkai	33
	Kenseihontō	15	Kokumintō	0
	Daidō Club	7	Rikken Dōshikai	26
	Yukōkai	0	Chūseikai	15
	Independents	30	Count Okuma	4
			Independents	22
Kyushu	Seiyūkai	59	Seiyūkai	45
	Kenseihontō	16	Kokumintō	0
	Daidō Club	12	Rikken Dōshikai	37
	Yukōkai	4	Chūseikai	2
	Independents	9	Count Okuma	0
			Independents	16
Okinawa	. . .		Seiyūkai	100%

TOTALS

	Number of Candidates	Number Elected	% of Seats		Number of Candidates	Number Elected	% of Seats
Seiyūkai	246	188	50	Seiyūkai	201	108	28
Kenseihontō	92	70	18	Kokumintō	40	27	7
Daidō Club	42	29	8	Rikken			
Yukōkai	39	29	8	Dōshikai	200	153	40
Independents	102	63	16	Chūseikai	44	33	9
	—	—	—	Count Okuma	21	12	3
	521	379	100%	Independents	109	48	13
					615	381	100%

Region	Election & Party 14th Election May 10, 1920	Percentage of Seats
Hokkaido	Seiyūkai	56
	Kenseikai	31
	Kokumintō	0
	Independents	13
Tōhoku	Seiyūkai	74
	Kenseikai	20
	Kokumintō	4
	Independents	2
Kantō	Seiyūkai	58
	Kenseikai	32
	Kokumintō	5
	Independents	5
Chūbu	Seiyūkai	58
	Kenseikai	27
	Kokumintō	7
	Independents	8
Kinki	Seiyūkai	52
	Kenseikai	16
	Kokumintō	11
	Independents	21
Chūgoku	Seiyūkai	45
	Kenseikai	27
	Kokumintō	15
	Independents	13

Region	Election & Party 14th Election May 10, 1920	Percentage of Seats
Shikoku	Seiyūkai	75
	Kenseikai	11
	Kokumintō	0
	Independents	14
Kyushu	Seiyūkai	71
	Kenseikai	21
	Kokumintō	1
	Independents	7
Okinawa	Seiyūkai	80
	Kenseikai	0
	Kokumintō	0
	Independents	20

TOTALS

	Number of Candidates	Number Elected	% of Seats
Seiyūkai	418	278	60
Kenseikai	240	110	24
Kokumintō	46	29	6
Independents	135	47	10
	839	464	100

Region	Election & Party 15th Election May 10, 1924	Percentage of Seats	Election & Party 16th Election Feb. 20, 1928	Percentage of Seats
Hokkaido	Kenseikai	44	Seiyūkai	50
	Seiyūhontō	12	Minseitō	45
	Seiyūkai	25	Jitsugyō Dōshikai	0
	Kakushin Club	0	Kakushintō	0
	Minor Parties &		Musan Seitō	0
	Independents	19	Minor Parties & Independents	5
Tōhoku	Kenseikai	39	Seiyūkai	55
	Seiyūhontō	20	Minseitō	43
	Seiyūkai	31	Jitsugyō Dōshikai	0
	Kakushin Club	2	Kakushintō	0
	Minor Parties &		Musan Seitō	0
	Independents	8	Minor Parties & Independents	2

Region	Election & Party *15th Election* *May 10, 1924*	*Percentage* *of Seats*	Election & Party *16th Election* *Feb. 20, 1928*	*Percentage* *of Seats*
Kantō	Kenseikai	38	Seiyūkai	48
	Seiyūhontō	11	Minseitō	48
	Seiyūkai	33	Jitsugyō Dōshikai	1
	Kakushin Club	5	Kakushintō	0
	Minor Parties &		Musan Seitō	1
	Independents	13	Minor Parties &	
			Independents	2
Chūbu	Kenseikai	48	Seiyūkai	45
	Seiyūhontō	20	Minseitō	46
	Seiyūkai	12	Jitsugyō Dōshikai	1½
	Kakushin Club	5	Kakushintō	1½
	Minor Parties		Musan Seitō	0
	& Independents	15	Minor Parties	
			& Independents	6
Kinki	Kenseikai	22	Seiyūkai	36
	Seiyūhontō	24	Minseitō	48
	Seiyūkai	24	Jitsugyō Dōshikai	3
	Kakushin Club	11	Kakushintō	2
	Minor Parties &		Musan Seitō	6
	Independents	19	Minor Parties &	
			Independents	5
Chūgoku	Kenseikai	31	Seiyūkai	53
	Seiyūhontō	21	Minseitō	38
	Seiyūkai	15	Jitsugyō Dōshikai	0
	Kakushin Club	16	Kakushintō	2
	Minor Parties &		Musan Seitō	2
	Independents	17	Minor Parties &	
			Independents	5
Shikoku	Kenseikai	21	Seiyūkai	56
	Seiyūhontō	25	Minseitō	44
	Seiyūkai	32	Jitsugyō Dōshikai	0
	Kakushin Club	7	Kakushintō	0
	Minor Parties &		Musan Seitō	0
	Independents	14	Minor Parties &	
			Independents	0
Kyushu	Kenseikai	19	Seiyūkai	40
	Seiyūhontō	49	Minseitō	54
	Seiyūkai	14	Jitsugyō Dōshikai	0
	Kakushin Club	3	Kakushintō	0
	Minor Parties &		Musan Seitō	3
	Independents	15	Minor Parties &	
			Independents	3

Region	Election & Party 15th Election May 10, 1924	Percentage of Seats	Election & Party 16th Election Feb. 20, 1928	Percentage of Seats
Okinawa	Kenseikai	0	Seiyūkai	60
	Seiyūhontō	80	Minseitō	40
	Seiyūkai	20	Jitsugyō Dōshikai	0
	Kakushin Club	0	Kakushintō	0
	Minor Parties &		Musan Seitō	0
	Independents	0	Minor Parties &	
			Independents	0

TOTALS

	Number of Candidates	Number Elected	% of Seats		Number of Candidates	Number Elected	% of Seats
Kenseikai	265	152	33	Seiyūkai	342	217	46
Seiyūhontō	242	112	25	Minseitō	340	216	46
Seiyūkai	218	102	22	Jitsugyō			
Kakushin Club	53	30	7	Dōshikai	31	4	1
Minor Parties &				Kakushintō	15	3	1
Independents	194	69	13	Musan Seitō	77	8	2
	—	—	—	Minor Parties &			
	972	465	100	Independents	159	17	4
					—	—	—
					964	465	100

Region	Election & Party 17th Election Feb. 20, 1930	Percentage of Seats	Election & Party 18th Election Feb. 20, 1932	Percentage of Seats
Hokkaido	Minseitō	55	Seiyūkai	65
	Seiyūkai	40	Minseitō	30
	Kokumin Dōshikai	0	Kakushintō	0
	Kakushintō	0	Musantō	0
	Musantō	0	Minor Parties &	
	Minor Parties &		Independents	5
	Independents	5		
Tōhoku	Minseitō	53	Seiyūkai	68
	Seiyūkai	47	Minseitō	30
	Kokumin Dōshikai	0	Kakushintō	0
	Kakushintō	0	Musantō	0
	Musantō	0	Minor Parties &	
	Minor Parties &		Independents	2
	Independents	0		

Region	Election & Party 17th Election Feb. 20, 1930		Percentage of Seats	Election & Party 18th Election Feb. 20, 1932	Percentage of Seats
Kantō	Minseitō		59	Seiyūkai	61
	Seiyūkai		36	Minseitō	35
	Kokumin Dōshikai		0	Kakushintō	0
	Kakushintō		1	Musantō	2
	Musantō		3	Minor Parties &	
	Minor Parties &			Independents	2
	Independents		1		
Chūbu	Minseitō		61	Seiyūkai	65
	Seiyūkai		36	Minseitō	33
	Kokumin Dōshikai		1	Kakushintō	1
	Kakushintō		1	Musantō	0
	Musantō		0	Minor Parties &	
	Minor Parties &			Independents	1
	Independents		1		
Kinki	Minseitō		66	Seiyūkai	56
	Seiyūkai		24	Minseitō	37
	Kokumin Dōshikai		6	Kakushintō	0
	Kakushintō		0	Musantō	2
	Musantō		2	Minor Parties &	
	Minor Parties &			Independents	5
	Independents		2		
Chūgoku	Minseitō		54	Seiyūkai	62
	Seiyūkai		41	Minseitō	34
	Kokumin Dōshikai		2	Kakushintō	2
	Kakushintō		2	Musantō	0
	Musantō		0	Minor Parties &	
	Minor Parties &			Independents	2
	Independents		1		
Shikoku	Minseitō		63	Seiyūkai	70
	Seiyūkai		37	Minseitō	26
	Kokumin Dōshikai		0	Kakushintō	0
	Kakushintō		0	Musantō	0
	Musantō		0	Minor Parties &	
	Minor Parties &			Independents	4
	Independents		0		
Kyushu	Minseitō		54	Seiyūkai	73
	Seiyūkai		45	Minseitō	21
	Kokumin Dōshikai		0	Kakushintō	0
	Kakushintō		0	Musantō	3
	Musantō		1	Minor Parties &	
	Minor Parties &			Independents	3
	Independents		0		

Region	Election & Party 17th Election Feb. 20, 1930	Percentage of Seats	Election & Party 18th Election Feb. 20, 1932	Percentage of Seats
Okinawa	Minseitō	80	Seiyūkai	80
	Seiyūkai	20	Minseitō	20
	Kokumin Dōshikai	0	Kakushintō	0
	Kakushintō	0	Musantō	0
	Musantō	0	Minor Parties & Independents	0
	Minor Parties & Independents	0		

TOTALS

	Number of Candidates	Number Elected	% of Seats		Number of Candidates	Number Elected	% of Seats
Minseitō	341	273	59	Seiyūkai	348	301	65
Seiyūkai	304	174	37	Minseitō	279	146	31
Kokumin Dōshikai	12	6	1	Kakushintō	3	2	5
Kakushintō	6	3	1	Musantō	29	5	1
Musantō	98	5	1	Minor Parties & Independents	47	12	3
Minor Parties & Independents	77	5	1				
	838	466	100		706	466	100

Region	Election & Party 19th Election Feb. 20, 1936	Percentage of Seats	Election & Party 20th Election April 30, 1937	Percentage of Seats
Hokkaido	Minseitō	50	Minseitō	50
	Seiyūkai	35	Seiyūkai	30
	Shōwakai	5	Shakai Taishūtō	0
	Kokumin Dōmei	0	Shōwakai	5
	Shakai Taishūtō	0	Kokumin Dōmei	0
	Independents	10	Tōhōkai	5
			Nihon Musantō	0
			Independents	10
Tōhoku	Minseitō	39	Minseitō	40
	Seiyūkai	49	Seiyūkai	45
	Shōwakai	6	Shakai Taishūtō	4
	Kokumin Dōmei	2	Shōwakai	4
	Shakai Taishūtō	2	Kokumin Dōmei	3
	Independents	2	Tōhōkai	4
			Nihon Musantō	0
			Independents	0

Region	Election & Party 19th Election Feb. 20, 1936	Percentage of Seats	Election & Party 20th Election April 30, 1937	Percentage of Seats
Kantō	Minseitō	49	Minseitō	37
	Seiyūkai	33	Seiyūkai	37
	Shōwakai	4	Shakai Taishūtō	14
	Kokumin Dōmei	2	Shōwakai	3
	Shakai Taishūtō	9	Kokumin Dōmei	1
	Independents	3	Tōhōkai	0
			Nihon Musantō	1
			Independents	7
Chūbu	Minseitō	45	Minseitō	44
	Seiyūkai	36	Seiyūkai	31
	Shōwakai	1	Shakai Taishūtō	5
	Kokumin Dōmei	4	Shōwakai	1
	Shakai Taishūtō	2	Kokumin Dōmei	4
	Independents	12	Tōhōkai	2
			Nihon Musantō	3
			Independents ·	10
Kinki	Minseitō	53	Minseitō	44
	Seiyūkai	26	Seiyūkai	34
	Shōwakai	3	Shakai Taishūtō	11
	Kokumin Dōmei	2	Shōwakai	3
	Shakai Taishūtō	8	Kokumin Dōmei	0
	Independents	8	Tōhōkai	1
			Nihon Musantō	0
			Independents	7
Chūgoku	Minseitō	46	Minseitō	34
	Seiyūkai	38	Seiyūkai	44
	Shōwakai	8	Shakai Taishūtō	8
	Kokumin Dōmei	3	Shōwakai	11
	Shakai Taishūtō	3	Kokumin Dōmei	1
	Independents	2	Tōhōkai	1
			Nihon Musantō	0
			Independents	1
Shikoku	Minseitō	48	Minseitō	37
	Seiyūkai	41	Seiyūkai	41
	Shōwakai	0	Shakai Taishūtō	7
	Kokumin Dōmei	0	Shōwakai	0
	Shakai Taishūtō	4	Kokumin Dōmei	0
	Independents	7	Tōhōkai	4
			Nihon Musantō	0
			Independents	11

Region	Election & Party *19th Election* *Feb. 20, 1936*	*Percentage* *of Seats*	Election & Party *20th Election* *April 30, 1937*	*Percentage* *of Seats*
Kyushu	Minseitō	25	Minseitō	27
	Seiyūkai	46	Seiyūkai	42
	Shōwakai	7	Shakai Taishūtō	6
	Kokumin Dōmei	8	Shōwakai	6
	Shakai Taishūtō	4	Kokumin Dōmei	6
	Independents	10	Tōhōkai	4
			Nihon Musantō	0
			Independents	9
Okinawa	Minseitō	40	Minseitō	40
	Seiyūkai	40	Seiyūkai	40
	Shōwakai	0	Shakai Taishūtō	0
	Kokumin Dōmei	20	Shōwakai	0
	Shakai Taishūtō	0	Kokumin Dōmei	20
	Independents	0	Tōhōkai	0
			Nihon Musantō	0
			Independents	0

TOTALS

	Number *of* *Candi-* *dates*	*Num-* *ber* *Elected*	*% of* *Seats*		*Number* *of* *Candi-* *dates*	*Num-* *ber* *Elected*	*% of* *Seats*
Minseitō	298	205	44	Minseito	267	179	38
Seiyūkai	340	174	37	Seiyūkai	263	175	38
Shōwakai	49	20	4	S. Taishūtō	66	37	8
Kokumin Dōmei	32	15	3	Shōwakai	36	19	4
Shakai Taishūtō	36	22	5	Kokumin Dōmei	20	11	2
Independents	122	30	7	Tōhōkai	20	11	2
				Nihon Musantō	7	3	1
	877	466	100	Independents	141	31	7
					820	466	100

603

LIST OF CONTRIBUTORS*

ARDATH W. BURKS is Professor of Political Science and Director of International Programs at Rutgers, The State University of New Jersey. He is the author of *The Government of Japan* (1964) and co-author of *Far Eastern Governments and Politics* (1956).

ALBERT M. CRAIG, Professor of History at Harvard University, is the author of *Chōshū in the Meiji Restoration* (1961) and co-author of *East Asia: The Modern Transformation* (1965).

ROGER F. HACKETT is Director of the Center for Japanese Studies as well as Professor of History at the University of Michigan, and author of a forthcoming book on Yamagata Aritomo, and co-author of *A Global History of Man*.

JOHN WHITNEY HALL is Professor of History and Master of Morse College at Yale University. Among his published works are *Government and Local Power in Japan, 500 to 1700* (1966), *Twelve Doors To Japan* (with R. K. Beardsley) (1965), and *Tanuma Okitsugu* (1955). Professor Hall is also chairman of the Conference on Modern Japan.

DAN FENNO HENDERSON, Professor of Law and Director of the Asian Law Program at the University of Washington, is the author of *Conciliation and Japanese Law, Tokugawa and Modern* (1965).

NOBUTAKA IKE is Professor of Political Science at Stanford University and author of *Japan's Decision for War* (1967), *Japanese Politics* (1957), and *The Beginnings of Political Democracy in Japan* (1950).

TAKESHI ISHIDA is Professor of Political Science in the Institute of Social Sciences of Tokyo University. He has published in Japanese *Contemporary Organizations* (1961), *Studies in the Political Structure of Modern Japan* (1956), and *Studies in the History of Meiji Political Thought* (1954).

*This list gives the accomplishments of the contributors only at the time of this book's original publication.

MARIUS B. JANSEN is Professor of History at Princeton University. Among his publications are *Sakamoto Ryōma and thc Meiji Restoration* (1961), and *The Japanese and Sun Yat-sen* (1954).

ROBERT A. SCALAPINO, Professor of Political Science at the University of California (Berkeley), is the author of *The Japanese Communist Movement, 1920-1966* (1967), *The Communist Revolution in Asia* (1965), *Parties and Politics in Contemporary Japan* (with J. Masumi) (1962), and *Democracy and the Party Movement in Prewar Japan* (1953).

BERNARD S. SILBERMAN is Professor of History at Duke University. Among his publications are *Modern Japanese Leadership: Transition and Change* (with H. Harootunian) (1966), *Ministers of Modernization* (1964), and *Japanese Character and Culture: Selected Readings* (1962).

KURT STEINER is Professor of Political Science at Stanford University. He is the author of *Local Government in Japan* (1965) and a contributor to J. M. Maki's *Court and Constitution in Japan: Selected Supreme Court Decisions, 1948-1960* (1964).

KIYOAKI TSUJI, Professor of Political Science at Tokyo University, is one of Japan's leading authorities in the field of public administration and politics. He is editor of the volume on politics in the series *Postwar Materials: a Twenty-Year History* (1966) and author or co-author of *Process and Problems of Democratization in Postwar Japan* (1955), *A Case Study of a General Election* (1955), and *A Study of the Japanese Bureaucracy* (1954).

ROBERT E. WARD is Professor of Political Science and Member of the Staff of the Center for Japanese Studies at the University of Michigan. He is author or co-author of *Japan's Political System* (1967), *Studying Politics Abroad* (1964), *Political Modernization in Japan and Turkey* (1964), *Modern Political Systems: Asia* (1963), and *Village Japan* (1959).

INDEX

Abe Masahire, 43, 554
Acton, John, First Baron, 252
Adachi Yoshiko: cited, 254n
administration, *see* government
Administrative Case Litigation Law (*1962*), 443
Administrative Complaint Investigation Law, 443
Adults Imperial Rule Assistance Group (Yokusan Sōnen Dan), 298
Advertisements from Parnassus (Boccalini), 5
Afghanistan, 176
Africa, 48, 108, 124, 578; colonialism in, 174, 190
agriculture, 173, 209, 197-98; rightist agrarianism, 200-201, 238-39, 246, 262-63, 314-15; village system and, 218n, 234, 244-45, 394, 400, 411, 567; trade and, 245, 303-304, 560-62, 565; cooperatives, 313-16, 317, 318, 319, 320-21, 322, 327n, 328, 331n, 332, 333n; government function in, 346, 372, 382, 543, 581-83, 590. *See also* land; rural areas
Agriculture and Commerce, Ministry of, 72 (table), 176
Agriculture and Forestry, Ministry of, 319, 471n
Aichi, Japan, 257n, 258, 286n
Aizawa Seishisai: quoted, 36n
Aizu, Japan, 69, 74
Akihito, Crown Prince of Japan, 61
Akita, George: cited, 87n, 420
Akita, Japan, 257n, 281, 282
Albert, Prince Consort of England, 154
Alcock, Rutherford: quoted, 101
Allied Council for Japan, 479, 487, 488
Allied Occupation, ix, 50n, 293, 477-535, 588; preservation of the monarchy and, 16, 59-61, 482, 489, 497, 498, 499, 501; Constitution of 1947 and, 16, 441-42, 443, 482,

505, 510-13, 517, 523, 529, 530-31; local government and, 241-43, 338, 482, 527; political purge, 295, 319-20, 323, 469, 482, 485, 493, 500-501, 504, 524; Western values and, 300, 415, 456, 478-79, 481, 574; interest group organization and, 317-23, 469, 528-30, 531; termination of, 323-31, 478, 483, 497, 505, 514-16, 533-35; subsidy prohibitions, 329; mass consumption of government services and, 379, 530, 531, 532, 533-34
Allied Powers, *see* Allied Occupation, *and see specific countries*
Almond, Gabriel A., 4; on political culture, 213, 216n, 221n, 542n
Amaterasu (sun goddess), 26-27, 28
Amended Criminal Regulations (*Kaitei ritsurei*), 418
American Federation of Labor, 311
Andō Shōeki, 35
Andō Yoshio: cited, 563n
Anglo-Japanese Alliance, 89, 93, 178, 184, 188
Aoki Masashi, 513n; quoted, 178
Aomori, Japan, 257n, 286n
apathy, 345n, 361, 362; conformity and, 333-34; decision-making and, 475, 539
Apter, David: quoted, 381n
Arai Hakuseki, 160, 169
Arai Kōjirō: cited, 399n
aristocracy, 23-25, 40, 50, 52. *See also* samurai
Aristotle, 440
arms, 154, 155, 238-39; samurai privilege, 101, 194, 394; postwar rearmament, 500, 502, 515, 519
Army, the, 363, samurai and, 102, 194; Meiji organization of, 155, 173, 176, 178, 181, 189, 190, 194, 209, 585; conscription and, 194, 195-97, 199-200, 222, 224, 225, 232n, 346, 413; rank in, 201-202,